The Possessed
(The Devils)

A Profound Exploration of Politics, Chaos, and Human Nature

A Modern Translation

Adapted for the Contemporary Reader

Fyodor Dostoevsky

Table of Contents

Preface - Message to the Reader

Rebuilding the Greatest Library in Human History

Thousands of years ago, the Library of Alexandria was the heart of global knowledge — a sanctuary where the wisdom of every known civilization was gathered and shared freely.

And then, it was lost.

Now, we're rebuilding it — and you are invited to join us.

At the Library of Alexandria, we've set out to make every book available to *every person on Earth* — not just in print, but in every language, every format, and for every reader.

Here's how we do it:

- **Deluxe Print Editions at True Printing Cost** - Order any book as a high-quality paperback, elegant hardcover, or stunning boxset — and only pay what it costs to print. No markups. No middlemen.
- **Unlimited Access to the Greatest Works** - Enjoy thousands of timeless classics — from Plato to Shakespeare to Tolstoy — in beautiful, modern eBook and audiobook editions. Read and listen without limits — for every reader, everywhere.
- **Modern Translations for Every Language & Dialect** - We're reimagining the classics in clear, accessible language — and translating them into every dialect imaginable. Everyone deserves to understand humanity's greatest ideas.

When you visit **LibraryofAlexandria.com**, you're not just accessing books — you're joining a global movement to restore, preserve, and share the wisdom of civilization.

Join us today at LibraryofAlexandria.com

Together, we'll ensure the light of human wisdom never fades again.

With gratitude,
The Modern Library of Alexandria Team

Visit:

www.libraryofalexandria.com

Or scan the code below:

Introduction

Dostoevsky's Political Inferno: Ideology, Madness, and the Ruin of the Human Soul

Of all the great novels written by Fyodor Dostoevsky, The Possessed—also widely known as The Devils or Demons—is perhaps the most incendiary. Published in 1872 and inspired by a real-life political murder, this sprawling, feverish, and prophetic work is Dostoevsky's most direct confrontation with the ideological forces he believed were dragging Russia—and by extension, the human spirit—toward destruction. A searing exposé of radicalism, nihilism, and political extremism, The Possessed explores what happens when intellectual pride and utopian delusion collide with the messy, sacred, tragic realities of human nature.

At once a political thriller, a philosophical treatise, and a psychological novel of staggering depth, The Possessed was Dostoevsky's response to what he saw as the moral and spiritual crisis of his age. It is an intense, almost apocalyptic novel, driven not by romantic love or personal redemption, but by the breakdown of meaning and the collapse of all moral order. In its pages, we find no Christ-like figure like Prince Myshkin from The Idiot, nor a redemptive arc like Raskolnikov's in Crime and Punishment. What we find instead is a chaotic storm of conflicting ideologies, broken personalities, and demonic fervor that builds toward catastrophe.

The novel takes place in a fictional Russian provincial town, but it is a microcosm for an entire nation—and, in Dostoevsky's view, for all of modern civilization. At the center of the chaos is a small group of radicals, intellectuals, and disaffected youth, all swept up in revolutionary fervor. What begins as idealism quickly descends into terror, conspiracy, and spiritual ruin. The "possessed" of the title are not only the young radicals who fall under the spell of ideology; they are all those whose souls have been emptied of moral and spiritual grounding, leaving them vulnerable to the seductions of power, pride, and nihilism.

This modern translation presents The Possessed in contemporary language that aims to preserve Dostoevsky's complex style, biting irony, and moral urgency, while making the text accessible to today's readers. The novel's original Russian is rich with subtle social cues, religious allusions, and deeply layered characterizations. Our goal in this edition is to retain that richness without sacrificing clarity. The themes Dostoevsky tackles—political violence, ideological extremism, spiritual emptiness, and the seductive appeal of revolution—are as relevant today as they were in his time. In fact, they may be more relevant now than ever.

Reading The Possessed is like watching a slow-motion train crash. We are introduced to characters with intelligence, ambition, and good intentions, only to watch them devolve into madness, despair, and destruction. Yet this is not a nihilistic novel. It is, rather, a desperate moral warning. It is Dostoevsky crying out against the dangers of abstract thinking divorced from human feeling, of ideology divorced from conscience, and of intellect unmoored from humility.

The original Russian title, Besy (Бесы), translates more directly as "Demons," which evokes not only political and psychological possession but spiritual corruption. Dostoevsky, a devout Christian and fierce critic of atheistic materialism, saw the radical movements of his time as a spiritual sickness—a kind of possession in which demonic ideas entered and hollowed out the soul. The result is a novel that is both terrifying and enlightening, filled with moments of dark comedy, prophetic insight, and philosophical reflection.

For modern readers unfamiliar with 19th-century Russian politics, the novel's context may at first seem distant. But the psychological and philosophical dynamics it portrays are timeless. The names may change—today's ideologies may look different on the surface—but the human impulse toward destruction, masked as liberation, remains constant. Dostoevsky foresaw the horror of the 20th century—the gulags, the purges, the genocides—and he laid bare the spiritual forces that make such horrors possible. The Possessed is not merely a historical novel—it is a prophetic one.

4

Revolution and Ruin:
The Collapse of Meaning in a World Without God

At the heart of The Possessed is a war—not between political parties or classes, but between spiritual realities. Dostoevsky saw the revolutionary ideologies of his time—socialism, atheism, utilitarianism—not as misguided politics, but as manifestations of a deeper moral void. In his view, these movements did not emerge from love of justice or compassion for the poor, but from pride, resentment, and the will to power. They were, to use his metaphor, "demons" that entered those who had abandoned the divine order in favor of man-made utopias.

The character of Nikolai Stavrogin is the novel's center of gravity—a brilliant, enigmatic, and dangerously seductive figure who embodies this spiritual crisis. Stavrogin is a man of immense intelligence and charisma, yet he is emotionally hollow and morally indifferent. He plays with the emotions and beliefs of others like a puppet master, yet he himself is possessed by a deep and unnamable torment. In many ways, Stavrogin is the prototype for the modern antihero: detached, brilliant, godless, and fatally alluring. He exerts a magnetic pull on those around him, particularly the young revolutionaries who see in him a symbol of power and rebellion. But Stavrogin himself is empty. He believes in nothing. And this nothingness, Dostoevsky suggests, is more dangerous than any ideology.

Contrasted with Stavrogin is Pyotr Verkhovensky, the ideological puppet master who seeks to incite revolution through chaos and violence. Pyotr is a caricature of the revolutionary agitator—a man who believes that murder, blackmail, and destruction are justified if they serve the cause of revolution. He does not care about justice or truth. He cares only about power. Through Pyotr, Dostoevsky portrays the terrifying logic of ideological extremism: that anything is permissible in the name of the cause.

The young radicals who follow Pyotr and idolize Stavrogin are portrayed with chilling psychological accuracy. They are intelligent, idealistic, and alienated. They seek meaning in a world that has lost its soul. They crave action, not because they understand what they are fighting for, but because they are terrified of being irrelevant. In this, Dostoevsky anticipates the psychology of modern terrorism, political extremism, and mass movements. He shows how young minds, when deprived of moral grounding and filled with abstract ideals, can become instruments of chaos and cruelty.

The moral collapse in The Possessed is not confined to the radicals. The town's social elite—liberals, bureaucrats, landowners—are portrayed as cowardly, hypocritical, and complicit. They are too concerned with appearances and self-preservation to confront the evil growing in their midst. Their cowardice allows the radicals to flourish. Dostoevsky spares no one. He indicts the entire society—not just for its sins, but for its failure to stand against sin when it matters.

Yet amidst this darkness, there are moments of light. Shatov, a former radical who returns to faith and love of country, offers a glimpse of redemption. His spiritual awakening is a quiet resistance to the chaos around him. But even this redemption is short-lived. He is murdered—by the very comrades who once shared his ideals. This tragedy is the moral climax of the novel. It is Dostoevsky's warning that repentance is not enough if the world refuses to follow.

And yet, The Possessed is not a hopeless novel. Its pain is the pain of a prophet crying out for his people. Dostoevsky wrote it not to condemn, but to awaken. He believed in the possibility of redemption—but only through suffering, humility, and the return to God. He believed that the only true revolution is spiritual, not political.

Prophetic Warnings and Contemporary Echoes

When Dostoevsky published The Possessed, many dismissed it as an overreaction—a paranoid critique of fringe movements. But history has proven him right in ways even he could not have imagined. The 20th century bore the fruit of the ideologies he warned against: totalitarian regimes, gulags, genocides, and the mechanization of human life in service of abstract ideals. Stalin, Hitler, Mao—all presided over horrors made possible by the very forces Dostoevsky described: the rejection of God, the worship of ideology, and the dehumanization of the individual in the name of progress.

But The Possessed is not merely a political prophecy—it is a psychological and spiritual diagnosis. It shows how ordinary people can be seduced by radical ideas, how language can be twisted to justify violence, and how conscience can be silenced in the pursuit of "justice." It shows how societies rot from within when they lose the capacity for moral judgment and spiritual reflection.

For modern readers, this novel is both a mirror and a warning. In an age of ideological polarization, social fragmentation, and existential confusion, Dostoevsky's insights feel more urgent than ever. The "devils" of our time may wear different masks—technocratic reductionism, consumer nihilism, digital tribalism—but the underlying forces are the same. When people lose faith in meaning, in the sacred, in the dignity of the human soul, they become vulnerable to possession—not by literal demons, but by ideas that turn them against each other and against themselves.

What Dostoevsky offers is not an escape, but a confrontation. He asks us to face the darkness within ourselves—the pride, the fear, the desire for control—and to resist the seductive simplicity of ideology. He calls us to recover what he saw as the only antidote to chaos: humility, conscience, faith, and love. Not sentimentality, but the hard-won love that sees the brokenness of the world and still chooses to serve it.

This modern edition of The Possessed aims to make Dostoevsky's terrifying and majestic vision accessible to new generations. The characters may seem extreme, the dialogues intense, the events dramatic—but they are all rooted in real human experience. The world Dostoevsky depicts is our world—only stripped of its illusions.

Read carefully. This is not a comfortable novel. It is not meant to be. It is a spiritual and moral battlefield—a place where souls are tested and truths revealed. It is a warning, a challenge, and perhaps, in its darkest moments, a prayer. A prayer that we might see what is coming, and choose, before it is too late, to return to what is good, what is sacred, what is human.

PART 1

Chapter 1

SOME DETAILS OF THE BIOGRAPHY OF THAT HIGHLY RESPECTED GENTLEMAN STEPAN TROFIMOVITCH VERHOVENSKY.

Chapter 1.1

To recount the recent strange events in our town, a place that has until now remained quiet and unnoticed, I feel the need to begin my story with some background on Stepan Trofimovitch Verhovensky, a talented and well-regarded man. My lack of storytelling skill compels me to start this way, as it will at least provide some context before diving into the main events of my narrative.

Stepan Trofimovitch had always played a unique role in our society: he was our "progressive patriot," as he liked to call himself. He was so attached to this identity that it became an essential part of his life. I truly believe he wouldn't have been able to live without it. Now, I don't mean to compare him to a stage actor, as I genuinely respect him. Rather, this was simply a part of his nature, a habit he formed early on, where he imagined himself as a key figure in public life. He enjoyed thinking of himself as a victim of persecution and exile. There was a kind of romantic appeal in these roles that captivated him and lifted him in his own eyes, putting him on a pedestal that satisfied his vanity over the years.

There's a story in an old English satire about Gulliver, who, after returning from the land of Lilliputians—where the people were only a few inches tall—continued to imagine himself as a giant even back in London. He would cry out to passersby to move aside so he wouldn't crush them, still seeing them as tiny Lilliputians. People laughed at him and even lashed out, but it wasn't really his fault; it was simply the power of habit. Stepan Trofimovitch's situation was much the same, though less ridiculous and far more innocent, for he was truly a kind and admirable man.

By the end of his life, it's likely that Stepan Trofimovitch had been forgotten by most. Still, there was a time when his name carried weight. He had once been associated, however briefly, with a group of prominent intellectuals and leaders from the previous generation. For a short while, his name was mentioned alongside figures like Tchaadaev, Byelinsky, Granovsky, and Herzen, who had just begun writing abroad. But Stepan Trofimovitch's moment of influence faded almost as soon as it began, due to what he called "a vortex of combined circumstances." Oddly enough, it later turned out that there was no such "vortex" or even "circumstances" at all.

Recently, I learned, much to my surprise, and from a reliable source, that Stepan Trofimovitch had never actually been an exile in our province, as we'd all believed. He wasn't even under police surveillance. Yet he spent his entire life convinced otherwise. He sincerely believed he was a constant source of concern to the authorities, that every move he made was being closely monitored, and that each of the three governors who served our province over the past twenty years had been specifically warned about him before taking their posts. If someone had shown him undeniable proof that he had nothing to fear, he likely would have been deeply offended.

Despite these delusions, Stepan Trofimovitch was a highly intelligent and gifted man, someone who could have been called a man of science. However, in reality, he didn't accomplish much in the field of science— or, to be honest, anything at all. But that's not unusual for many "men of science" in Russia.

Stepan Trofimovitch returned from abroad and briefly gained fame as a lecturer at the university in the late 1840s. He only managed to deliver a few lectures, which I believe were about the Arabs. He also presented a brilliant thesis on the political and Hanseatic significance of the German town Hanau during the years 1413 to 1428, as well as on the obscure reasons why its potential was never realized. This work was a sharp and skillful critique of the Slavophils of that time, earning him many staunch enemies among them.

Later, after losing his university position, he wrote an essay—almost as a form of revenge—to show what a valuable person they had dismissed. The essay, which was published in a progressive monthly journal that translated Dickens and supported the ideas of George Sand, began as an in-depth investigation into the moral nobility of certain knights during a specific historical period. It upheld a lofty and noble idea. However, the continuation of the essay was reportedly banned, and the journal itself was said to have faced consequences for printing the first part. Whether this is true or not, I cannot say. It's also likely that Stepan Trofimovitch simply didn't finish the essay because he was too lazy to continue it.

His lectures on the Arabs ended abruptly when someone—likely a reactionary enemy—intercepted a letter that supposedly raised questions about him. At the same time, there were rumors of an illegal conspiracy in St. Petersburg involving thirty people, said to have been on the verge of translating Fourier, which created a stir in society. Coincidentally, a poem written by Stepan Trofimovitch six years earlier in Berlin was seized in Moscow around the same time. It had been shared only among a small circle of two poetry enthusiasts and a student. This poem, now lying on my table, was recently sent to me in Stepan Trofimovitch's own handwriting, bound in a luxurious red leather cover and signed by him.

The poem, though strange, has undeniable poetic merit and displays some genuine talent. In those days (more precisely, in the 1830s), it was common to write in such a style. The subject of the poem is hard to describe because I honestly do not fully understand it. It is an allegory in a lyrical-dramatic form, reminiscent of the second part of Faust. The poem begins with a chorus of women, followed by a chorus of men, then a chorus of incorporeal beings, and finally a chorus of unborn spirits eager to come to life. They all sing about vague and abstract ideas, mostly revolving around a curse, but with a touch of higher humor.

Suddenly, the scene changes to a "festival of life," where even insects sing. A tortoise appears, uttering Latin phrases, and a mineral—an inanimate object—joins in the singing. The characters either sing continuously or engage in vague conversations filled with obscure, higher meaning. Eventually, the scene shifts again to a wilderness where a cultured young man wanders among rocks, sucking on herbs. When a fairy asks why he does this, he explains that he seeks to forget himself because he feels overwhelmed by his excess of life. He adds that his deepest desire is to lose his mind entirely.

Next, a stunningly beautiful youth rides in on a black horse, followed by a massive crowd of people from all nations. This youth represents death, whom everyone seems to yearn for. In the final scene, the Tower of Babel appears, and athletes finish building it while singing a song of hope. When they place the final stone at the top, a divine figure (possibly the ruler of Olympus) comically flees, and humanity, realizing its power, takes control and begins a new life with fresh insight.

At the time, this poem was considered dangerous. Last year, I suggested to Stepan Trofimovitch that it could safely be published now, given how harmless it seems today. However, he refused, clearly displeased by my assessment. In fact, he seemed offended by my opinion of its harmlessness, and this caused a coldness between us for two months.

Then, to everyone's surprise, the poem was published abroad in a collection of revolutionary verse without Stepan Trofimovitch's knowledge. At first, he panicked, writing a noble letter of defense to the authorities in St. Petersburg, though he never sent it because he didn't know whom to address. For a whole month, he was in a state of anxiety, expecting a telegram at any moment. Yet, I am certain he was secretly flattered. He even kept the collection hidden under his mattress, wouldn't let anyone touch his bed, and held his head high, despite his worry. When no telegram came, he made peace with me again, which shows the generous and forgiving nature of his gentle heart.

Chapter 1.2

Of course, I don't deny that Stepan Trofimovitch suffered for his beliefs at times, but I'm convinced he could have continued lecturing about the Arabs if he had just provided the necessary explanations. However, he was too proud and quickly convinced himself that his career was ruined forever by some "vortex of circumstance." To be honest, the real reason for his career shift was the delicate offer made by Varvara Petrovna Stavrogin, a wealthy woman and the wife of a lieutenant-general. She proposed that he take on the education and intellectual development of her only son. Along with the position came an impressive salary.

This offer was first made to him while he was in Berlin, shortly after he became a widower. His first wife, a lively girl from our province, had been a youthful, impulsive choice. Although charming, she caused him much trouble due to financial difficulties and other delicate issues. She passed away in Paris after being separated from him for three years, leaving behind a five-year-old son, whom Stepan Trofimovitch once referred to as "the fruit of our first, joyous, and unclouded love." The child had been sent back to Russia from the start, where he was raised by distant relatives in a remote area.

Stepan Trofimovitch declined Varvara Petrovna's offer at the time and married again within a year. His second wife was a quiet Berlin woman, and oddly enough, there was no pressing reason for this marriage. Besides the marriage, there were other reasons for refusing the position. He was drawn to the fame of a renowned professor and hurried to take up the lecturer's chair he had long prepared for, eager to spread his wings. But after his ambitions were dashed, he naturally reconsidered Varvara Petrovna's offer, which had already made him hesitate. The unexpected death of his second wife, who lived less than a year with him, finally pushed him to accept the proposal.

To put it plainly, his decision was largely influenced by the deep and passionate friendship of Varvara Petrovna—a relationship that could even be called "classic" in its elegance. He leaned on this friendship, and his position was secured for over twenty years. When I say he "leaned on her friendship," I mean it in the most morally upright way. Their bond was entirely refined and delicate, uniting these two remarkable individuals for life.

The role of tutor was easier to accept because Stepan Trofimovitch's small estate from his first wife was near Skvoreshniki, the Stavrogins' grand estate on the outskirts of our provincial town. Moreover, in the quiet of his study, far from the overwhelming demands of university life, he believed he could devote himself to science and contribute to Russian literature with scholarly works. These works, however, never materialized. Instead, he spent over twenty years as what some might call a "living reproach" to his country. As a poet once wrote:

"Reproach incarnate thou didst stand

Erect before thy Fatherland,

O Liberal idealist!"

Yet the poet may have been describing someone who truly earned the right to live such a life, despite how dull it must have been. Stepan Trofimovitch, however, was more of an imitator. He grew tired of always "standing tall" and often preferred to rest. To his credit, though, even in repose, he managed to maintain the air of a living reproach, which was more than enough for our province.

You should have seen him at the club during card games. His very posture seemed to declare: "Cards! I, of all people, playing whist with you? Is this consistent with who I am? Who is to blame for this? Who has crushed my spirit and left me to play whist? Ah, Russia, perish!" Then, with great dignity, he would triumphantly lay down a winning card.

To be honest, he loved playing cards, though this fondness often led to tense disagreements with Varvara Petrovna, especially in his later years, as he was always losing. But more on that later. I should point out that he was a man with a tender conscience—at least at times—and this often made him feel depressed. Throughout his twenty years of friendship with Varvara Petrovna, he would regularly fall into what we called "patriotic grief" three or four times a year. However, it was less grief and more of a deep gloom. Still, our esteemed Varvara Petrovna preferred to use the loftier term.

In recent years, this grief had sometimes been mixed with bouts of drinking. Thankfully, Varvara Petrovna's watchful care kept him from giving in to such habits completely. He truly needed someone to watch over him because he could act rather strangely at times. For example, in the middle of his deep sorrow, he might suddenly burst out laughing like an ordinary villager. There were even moments when he started to make jokes about himself. But nothing alarmed Varvara Petrovna more than when he adopted a humorous tone. She was a woman of serious, classical values—a true patron of the arts—who always acted according to the highest principles.

Her influence over her poor friend for those twenty years was incredibly significant. It shaped much of his life. I must describe her in more detail now, which I will proceed to do.

Chapter 1.3

Some friendships are truly strange. These two friends were always on the verge of fighting, often ready to tear into one another, yet they couldn't separate. Parting was simply impossible. The one who initiated a separation would likely fall ill, or worse, if it actually happened. I know for a fact that several times, after an emotional and heartfelt conversation with Varvara Petrovna, Stepan Trofimovitch would jump up from the sofa and punch the wall in frustration. This wasn't an empty gesture—he even chipped off some plaster once.

How do I know such personal details? Well, what if I had seen it myself? Or perhaps Stepan Trofimovitch had, on multiple occasions, cried on my shoulder, pouring out his deepest emotions in vivid detail. He spared nothing during these moments. Yet, after such tearful confessions, he would almost always be overwhelmed with guilt by the next day. He'd either send for me urgently or visit me himself to declare that Varvara Petrovna was "an angel of honor and kindness," while he, in contrast, was utterly unworthy of her.

Sometimes, instead of confiding in me, he would write her long, emotional letters. These letters were nothing short of dramatic confessions. For instance, after an argument, he once wrote to her admitting he had told someone that she only kept him around out of vanity, envied his talents, and secretly hated him but feared expressing it openly because she didn't want him to leave and ruin her reputation. He added that this drove him to self-loathing and thoughts of suicide. He claimed he was waiting for a final word from her to decide his fate. The letter was filled with such over-the-top statements.

I once read one of these letters after a petty argument between them that escalated into something nasty. I was horrified and begged him not to send it.

"I must send it. It's the honorable thing to do. I'll die if I don't confess everything!" he said, almost delirious. And he did send it.

That was the difference between them: Varvara Petrovna would never have sent such a letter. He, however, loved writing and even sent letters to her while they lived in the same house. During particularly emotional times, he might write her two letters a day. I know for a fact that she read every one of them carefully, even if she received two in a single day. She filed them in a special drawer, sorted and labeled, and reflected on them deeply. But she wouldn't respond right away. She would meet him as if nothing had happened, acting as though the previous day's drama didn't exist. Over time, she trained him not to bring up past quarrels. He learned to simply glance at her, searching her eyes for signs of what she thought. She, however, never forgot anything, while he often forgot too quickly. Sometimes, he would laugh and joke with guests over champagne on the very same day as a dramatic letter. She must have looked at him with such disdain in those moments, though he never noticed.

Weeks or even months later, he might suddenly recall something from one of his letters—perhaps a phrase or the entire letter—and be overcome with shame. The memory would upset him so much that he might fall ill with one of his "summer cholera" attacks. These illnesses, often brought on by stress, were a peculiar feature of his constitution.

There's no doubt Varvara Petrovna often felt genuine hatred for him. However, he never truly understood the depth of her feelings. To her, he had become like a son—a creation of hers, even an invention. She cared for him not out of envy for his talents, but because she had made him part of her life. How deeply it must have hurt her when he accused her otherwise! Beneath her anger, jealousy, and contempt, she carried a profound love for him. She would not let the slightest harm come to him, nurtured him for over twenty years, and would have lost sleep if anyone so much as whispered against his reputation as a poet, scholar, or public figure.

She had created him and been the first to believe in her own creation. In a way, he was her dream brought to life. But in return, she demanded a great deal from him—sometimes even servility. Her grudges were legendary; she could hold onto them for incredible lengths of time. I have two stories that illustrate this perfectly.

Chapter 1.4

During the time when rumors of freeing the serfs were spreading across Russia, and the entire country was buzzing with excitement about reform, Varvara Petrovna was visited by a baron from Petersburg. This baron was well-connected and deeply involved in the reforms. For Varvara Petrovna, such visits were rare and highly valued, as her ties to high society had faded after her husband's death. The baron spent an hour drinking tea with her, with only Stepan Trofimovitch present. She had invited Stepan to showcase the kind of people she surrounded herself with, even while living in provincial seclusion.

The baron had heard of Stepan Trofimovitch—or at least pretended to—but didn't pay much attention to him during tea. Stepan, with his refined manners and flawless French, was usually impeccable in such situations. Yet, when the baron confidently confirmed the truth of the rumors about the reform, Stepan couldn't help himself. He shouted "Hurrah!" and made a gesture of excitement. While his reaction was polite and possibly rehearsed in front of a mirror earlier, something about it was off. The baron smiled faintly, though he quickly added a courteous remark about the significance of the event. Shortly after, he left, shaking Stepan's hand with only two fingers—a gesture that stung.

After the baron left, Varvara Petrovna was silent for a few minutes, seemingly searching for something on the table. Then, with a pale face and fiery eyes, she turned to Stepan and whispered sharply, "I shall never forgive you for that!" The next day, she acted as though nothing had happened. But thirteen years later, in a serious moment, she brought it up again, her face turning pale just as it had on that day. Only twice in her life did she utter those words to him: "I shall never forgive you for that." The baron's visit was the second time. The first incident, however, had a much greater impact on Stepan Trofimovitch's life.

The first occasion occurred in May 1855, just after news arrived of Lieutenant-General Stavrogin's death. He had died from a stomach ailment while traveling to Crimea to join the army. Though Varvara Petrovna was now a widow and wore deep mourning, she wasn't deeply grieved by his passing. For the last four years of his life, they had been completely estranged due to irreconcilable differences, and she had been giving him an allowance. The general himself had little beyond his military pay and about 150 serfs. The wealth and estate of Skvoreshniki had always belonged to Varvara Petrovna, the only child of a wealthy contractor. Still, the suddenness of his death shocked her, and she withdrew into solitude, with Stepan Trofimovitch always by her side.

Spring was at its peak, with the evenings filled with beauty and the scent of blooming cherry blossoms. Every evening, the two friends walked in the garden and sat in the arbour, sharing their thoughts and feelings until nightfall. These moments were often poetic. Varvara Petrovna, feeling the shift in her circumstances, spoke more openly than usual, clinging to Stepan Trofimovitch for emotional support. This went on for several evenings.

During this time, Stepan Trofimovitch had an unusual idea. He began to wonder if the grieving widow was expecting him to propose marriage once her mourning period ended. It was a cynical thought, but sometimes the more cultured a man is, the more prone he is to such notions. The idea began to consume him. Her immense fortune was tempting, of course, but Varvara Petrovna was far from beautiful. She was tall, thin, and had a long face that reminded one of a horse. Stepan wrestled with his suspicions, often shedding tears of indecision—he was known to cry easily.

In the evenings, while sitting in the arbour, his expression started to change. Without realizing it, he began to look amused, ironic, even condescending. This subtle shift in his demeanor might have been unintentional, but it didn't go unnoticed. Yet, despite his suspicions, there may have been nothing to them. It's entirely possible that Varvara Petrovna had no such intentions. Changing her last name from Stavrogin

17

to his would have been unthinkable for her, given her pride. Perhaps it was all just the natural expression of femininity, a yearning for connection, which is common in some women. But who can truly understand the depths of a woman's heart?

It seems she quickly understood the meaning behind her friend's strange expression. She was sharp and observant, while he could be quite naive at times. Yet, their evenings continued as before, filled with the same poetic and engaging conversations. Then one night, after a particularly lively and heartfelt discussion, they parted warmly. They pressed each other's hands near the steps of the lodge where Stepan Trofimovitch stayed. Every summer, he moved into this small lodge, which was next to the grand house of Skvoreshniki, almost in the garden.

After saying goodbye, he had just gone inside. Feeling restless, he took out a cigar but didn't light it. Instead, he stood still at the open window, gazing at the soft, feathery clouds drifting around the bright moon. Suddenly, a faint sound behind him made him turn around. To his shock, Varvara Petrovna, whom he had left just minutes earlier, was standing before him again. Her yellowish face looked almost blue, and her lips were tightly pressed together, twitching slightly at the corners.

For a full ten seconds, she stared directly into his eyes, her gaze firm and unyielding. Then, in a rapid whisper, she said, "I shall never forgive you for this!"

Years later, when Stepan Trofimovitch quietly recounted this unsettling story to me, he swore that in that moment, he had been so paralyzed with shock that he hadn't seen or heard how Varvara Petrovna had left. She never mentioned the incident again, and life continued as though nothing unusual had occurred. For the rest of his life, he leaned toward believing it had been an illusion, a symptom of illness—especially since he fell sick that very night and was bedridden for two weeks, which put an end to their conversations in the garden.

Yet, despite his theory of it being a hallucination, he seemed to live in constant anticipation, waiting for the situation to somehow escalate or reach a resolution. He couldn't believe that was the end of it. And if he ever thought about it, he must have looked at his old friend in an unusual way sometimes.

Chapter 1.5

She had personally designed the outfit that he wore for the rest of his life. It was both stylish and unique: a long black frock coat buttoned almost to the top but expertly tailored, a soft hat with a wide brim (or a straw hat in summer), a white batiste cravat tied in a large bow with hanging ends, a cane with a silver knob, and long hair flowing to his shoulders. His hair was dark brown, though it had recently started to turn grey. He was clean-shaven. People said he had been very handsome in his youth, and even in his later years, I thought he still looked striking. Besides, fifty-three isn't old at all.

He didn't try to look younger, but seemed proud of his age, which gave him a certain dignity. Tall and thin, with his flowing hair and elegant outfit, he had a presence that reminded me of a patriarch or, even more, of the poet Kukolnik as depicted in the engraved portrait from the 1830 edition of his works. The resemblance was particularly noticeable when he sat in the garden during summer, under a blooming lilac bush. There, with both hands resting on his cane and an open book beside him, he would gaze at the setting sun in quiet contemplation.

In terms of books, I should note that in later years he began to avoid serious reading, though this only happened toward the end of his life. He still read the newspapers and magazines that Varvara Petrovna ordered in abundance, and he never lost his interest in Russian literature, although he maintained a reserved, dignified attitude about it. At one point, he had been deeply engaged in studying both domestic and international politics but had eventually given up in frustration. It wasn't unusual for him to carry De Tocqueville into the garden while secretly tucking a Paul de Kock novel in his pocket. But such details are hardly significant.

Speaking of Kukolnik's portrait, it's worth mentioning that Varvara Petrovna first came across the engraving when she was a student at an elite boarding school in Moscow. Like many girls her age, she fell in love with it immediately—just as schoolgirls often fall in love with whatever or whoever they come across, especially their teachers, like the drawing or writing instructors. The intriguing part of this story isn't the schoolgirl crush itself, but the fact that even at fifty, Varvara Petrovna still kept the engraving as one of her most treasured possessions. It's possible that this lingering admiration influenced her decision to design Stepan Trofimovitch's outfit in a way that echoed the poet's appearance in the engraving. However, that is a small and unimportant detail.

During the first years—or more accurately, the first half of his time with Varvara Petrovna—Stepan Trofimovitch devoted himself to the idea of writing a book. Every day, he sincerely prepared to work on it. But in his later years, he seemed to have forgotten what he had even intended to write. More and more often, he would say to us, "I feel ready to begin, my materials are all collected, but somehow the work never gets done! Nothing gets finished!"

He would lower his head, looking defeated. This attitude seemed designed to enhance his image as a martyr to science in our eyes, but deep down, he longed for something else. "They've forgotten me! I'm no use to anyone!" he exclaimed more than once. This deep sense of despair became especially pronounced by the late 1850s. Varvara Petrovna eventually realized the seriousness of his state. She couldn't bear the thought of her friend being forgotten and feeling useless. To lift his spirits and restore his reputation, she decided to take him to Moscow, where she had connections in the fashionable literary and scientific circles. However, Moscow didn't provide the satisfaction they were looking for.

It was a strange time, a period of transition. Something new was stirring, unlike the stagnation of earlier years, and this shift was noticeable everywhere, even at Skvoreshniki. Rumors of various kinds reached them. While the facts were often clear enough, it was evident that they were accompanied by an influx of ideas—many ideas—which made things confusing. It was hard to grasp the meaning or direction of these ideas. Varvara Petrovna, driven by her naturally curious and determined nature, felt compelled to uncover their meaning. She began reading newspapers, magazines, forbidden publications from abroad, and even the revolutionary manifestos that were just starting to circulate at the time. She managed to get her hands on all of them, but instead of finding clarity, she became more bewildered. She started writing letters, but the few responses she received only deepened her confusion.

She finally summoned Stepan Trofimovitch and insisted that he explain "these ideas" to her once and for all. However, she was left disappointed by his explanations. Stepan Trofimovitch's view of the growing social and intellectual movement was extremely dismissive. In his opinion, the only real issue was that he had been forgotten and cast aside. Then, unexpectedly, his name began appearing in various publications. At first, it was mentioned in foreign journals as that of an exiled martyr, and shortly after, in Petersburg, he was described as a former luminary in a celebrated intellectual circle. Someone even compared him to Radishchev. Finally, one publication mistakenly announced his death and promised to publish an obituary.

The sudden attention immediately lifted Stepan Trofimovitch's spirits. His scorn for his contemporaries vanished, and he began to dream of joining the movement and demonstrating his talents. Varvara Petrovna, inspired by this renewed interest, was thrown into a whirlwind of excitement. They decided to travel to Petersburg immediately to investigate everything in person, learn about the movement firsthand, and, if possible, immerse themselves fully in it. Varvara Petrovna even declared her intention to establish her own magazine and dedicate her life to it.

Seeing how things were developing, Stepan Trofimovitch became more self-assured and, during the journey, even adopted a somewhat condescending attitude toward Varvara Petrovna. She noticed this immediately and quietly stored it away in her memory as a grievance. However, she had another significant reason for making the trip. She wanted to reestablish her connections with influential people in higher social circles. It was crucial for her to remind the world of her presence— or at least make an attempt to do so. The official purpose of the journey, however, was to visit her only son, who was about to complete his studies at a prestigious Petersburg lyceum.

Chapter 1.6

The two spent nearly the entire winter season in Petersburg, driven by high hopes and grand ambitions. But as Lent approached, their dreams shattered like a delicate soap bubble. The bright optimism that had carried them quickly dissolved into disappointment, leaving everything muddled, even more confusing than before. The connections with influential people in high circles, which Varvara Petrovna had eagerly sought, were either not established at all or achieved only with immense effort and yielded negligible results. This failure deeply wounded her pride and spurred her to throw herself even more fervently into the world of "new ideas."

Determined to make an impact, Varvara Petrovna began hosting evening receptions at her home. She invited a wide range of literary figures, and they arrived in droves. At first, they were brought by acquaintances, but soon they began coming of their own accord, each dragging another along. The people who filled her salon were unlike any she had encountered before. Many of these literary men were incredibly vain, and their self-importance was so brazen that it seemed almost like a performance. Some even arrived visibly drunk, but oddly, this behavior seemed to be worn as a badge of honor, as if it were a new and peculiar virtue. They carried themselves with an air of pride, as though each had stumbled upon some profound secret of the times. They argued heatedly, often insulting one another, yet seemed to take pride in these very disputes.

Their exact contributions to literature were often vague and difficult to pin down, but the group included critics, novelists, playwrights, satirists, and social commentators. Stepan Trofimovitch managed to penetrate their innermost circles, the elite intellectual group that claimed to guide the broader movement. Getting there required incredible effort, as if scaling a lofty peak, but once admitted, he was warmly received—despite the fact that no one seemed to know who he was or what he had accomplished, apart from the vague notion that he "represented an idea." His efforts paid off, and he even succeeded in bringing members of this elite circle to two of Varvara Petrovna's gatherings, despite their Olympian aloofness.

This particular group was different from the others. They were serious, composed, and impeccably polite, but they exuded an air of urgency, as though their time was far too valuable to waste. The other guests clearly feared them, though their presence lent the gatherings a certain weight. Alongside these newcomers, a few former literary greats—figures with whom Varvara Petrovna had long maintained refined correspondence—also attended. To her surprise, however, these older luminaries were subdued, almost servile in their deference to the younger, more radical crowd. Some even shamelessly attached themselves to this rising rabble, cringing before them in ways that shocked Varvara Petrovna.

Initially, Stepan Trofimovitch enjoyed some success in these circles. People took notice of him, and he was invited to participate in public literary events. The first time he stepped onto the stage at a public reading, the audience greeted him with five minutes of rapturous applause. Even nine years later, he would recall this moment with tears in his eyes—though whether from pride or embarrassment remained unclear. As he later confided to me in private, he was convinced that not a single person in that audience actually knew who he was. This candid admission revealed both his self-awareness and his vulnerability. Despite his fleeting success, he signed his name to several collective protests, often without knowing exactly what he was protesting. Varvara Petrovna, too, was persuaded to sign declarations against "disgraceful actions" whose details were never fully explained to her.

Despite opening her doors to the movement's key players, Varvara Petrovna was often met with thinly veiled contempt and sarcasm from many of her guests. Stepan Trofimovitch later hinted to me during moments of bitterness that this period marked the beginning of her jealousy toward him. Though she quickly realized she couldn't truly connect with these people, she still welcomed them with all the frantic enthusiasm her temperament allowed, clinging to the hope of achieving something meaningful. During her gatherings, she spoke little, preferring to listen intently. The conversations ranged from the abolition of censorship to phonetic spelling, from proposals to replace the Russian alphabet with Latin characters to discussions of recent exiles and scandals. They debated ideas like splitting Russia into smaller nations united in a free federation, abolishing the military, restoring Poland's borders to the

Dnieper, reforming the peasantry, and even dismantling traditional family structures, priesthoods, and hereditary privilege. Women's rights and the controversies surrounding Kraevsky's publishing house were also hot topics. The sheer range of subjects discussed was staggering, though it was clear that many of these individuals were impostors. Yet, among the pretenders, there were undoubtedly honest, sincere, and even admirable people. However, it was often impossible to discern who was manipulating whom in this chaotic mix of egos and ideals.

When Varvara Petrovna announced her plan to start a magazine, the influx of visitors grew even larger. But instead of support, she was bombarded with accusations of being a capitalist and exploiting labor, criticisms delivered with shocking bluntness and rudeness. Among her guests was General Ivan Ivanovitch Drozdov, an old friend of her late husband and a man known for his stubbornness and irritability, though he was respected in his own way. At one of her gatherings, the general got into a heated argument with a young man of high standing. The young man insulted him by saying, "You must be a general if you talk like that," implying that "general" was the most contemptible insult he could muster. Ivan Ivanovitch, incensed, responded furiously: "Yes, sir, I am a general, and a lieutenant-general at that! I have served my Tsar, while you, sir, are nothing but a puppy and an infidel!"

This clash epitomized the tensions and contradictions that defined Varvara Petrovna's social experiments that winter. Though her gatherings were lively and full of discussion, they also exposed the vast divide between her aspirations and the chaotic reality of the new intellectual movement.

A scandalous scene unfolded, and by the following day, the entire incident was made public in print. A group began organizing a collective protest, accusing Varvara Petrovna of disgraceful conduct for not immediately expelling General Drozdov from her gathering. To add insult to injury, an illustrated newspaper published a venomous caricature depicting Varvara Petrovna, Stepan Trofimovitch, and General Drozdov as three reactionary allies conspiring together. Accompanying the caricature were satirical verses penned by a popular poet, crafted especially for the occasion. For my part, I must point out the peculiar tendency of many generals to grandiosely proclaim, "I have served my Tsar," as though they alone had a Tsar separate from the rest of us humble subjects, rather than the same ruler we all serve.

Remaining in Petersburg after such public disgrace was, of course, impossible. Matters were made worse by Stepan Trofimovitch's complete and utter failure in his efforts to gain respect among the intellectuals. He could not resist pontificating on the lofty claims of art, but as he continued speaking, the ridicule grew louder and more merciless. At his final lecture, hoping to redeem himself, he attempted to move the audience with patriotic fervor, relying on the authority of his supposed "persecution" to gain their sympathy. He conceded the futility of terms like "fatherland" and admitted to the harmful effects of religion, yet firmly declared that Pushkin was far more important than boots—infinitely more so, in fact. The audience responded with relentless hissing and jeering. Humiliated, Stepan Trofimovitch broke down into tears right there on the platform.

Varvara Petrovna, distressed and protective, took him home, where he babbled incoherently in his misery, muttering phrases like, "On m'a traité comme un vieux bonnet de coton" ("They treated me like an old cotton nightcap"). All night, she cared for him with unwavering attention, administering laurel-drops and repeating over and over, "You will still be of use; you will still make your mark; you will be appreciated... elsewhere, in another place."

The following morning, as if to pile further indignities onto their misfortune, five literary men arrived uninvited at Varvara Petrovna's home. Of these, three were complete strangers she had never seen before. With a tone of self-appointed authority, they announced that they had "carefully considered" the matter of her proposed magazine and had come to deliver their decision. It was an absurd decree: they informed her that she must immediately hand over the magazine—along with all the necessary capital—to their cooperative, which they intended to run as a collective enterprise. She was expected to return to her estate at Skvoreshniki and take Stepan Trofimovitch with her, as he was "out of date" and no longer relevant to the movement. To their credit, they delicately acknowledged her right to property and magnanimously offered to send her one-sixth of the annual profits. What was perhaps most shocking about the situation was that four of the five men seemed entirely sincere and free of self-serving motives. They genuinely believed they were acting in the best interests of the "cause."

Reflecting on the absurdity of it all, Stepan Trofimovitch would later recall with a mix of bewilderment and melancholy, "We left utterly dumbfounded, unable to make sense of what had just happened." During the train ride out of Petersburg, he lapsed into a kind of stupor, mumbling nonsensical fragments to the rhythm of the train:

"Vyek, and vyck, and Lyov Kambek,

Lyov Kambek and vyek, and vyek…"

This surreal refrain accompanied him all the way to Moscow, where, at last, he seemed to snap out of his daze. "It was as though we truly believed we might find something different there," he later admitted.

When recounting these events to us, his voice would sometimes rise with passion as he lamented the fate of his ideals. "Oh, my friends!" he would exclaim. "You cannot imagine the deep anger and sorrow that consume your soul when a great idea—something you've cherished as sacred—is seized by the ignorant, dragged into the streets, and paraded before fools who twist it into something unrecognizable. To see it sullied in the mud, stripped of proportion, robbed of its harmony, and turned into a plaything for simpletons—it is unbearable! No, in our day, things were not like this. This is not what we strove for, not at all. I don't recognize this world we're living in…. But mark my words, our day will return. When it does, all this fragile, tottering nonsense will crumble, and we will once again find the true path. If not… well, what will become of us then?"

Chapter 1.7

As soon as they returned from Petersburg, Varvara Petrovna promptly arranged for Stepan Trofimovitch to travel abroad to "recover his strength." She understood that they needed a temporary separation, a realization that brought her both relief and resolve. Stepan Trofimovitch, on the other hand, was ecstatic at the prospect of leaving.

"At last, I shall be revived!" he declared. "There, I will finally begin my work!" Yet, as was typical of him, his first letter from Berlin struck a very familiar tone of melodrama.

"My heart is shattered!" he wrote to Varvara Petrovna. "I can forget nothing! Everything in Berlin reminds me of my past—my first joys, my earliest sorrows. Where is she? Where are they both? Where are you, my two angels, whom I was never worthy of? Where is my son, my dearest son? And finally, where am I? Where is the man I used to be, strong as steel, firm as a rock, now reduced to this—where some Andreev, a mere shopkeeper, peut briser mon existence en deux." The letter continued in this lamenting strain.

His mention of his son was noteworthy, considering that Stepan Trofimovitch had only seen the boy twice in his life—once at birth and then again during their recent visit to Petersburg. The young man had been raised far away in a distant province by a pair of aunts at Varvara Petrovna's expense. The mention of Andreev, meanwhile, was a peculiar grievance. Andreev was a local merchant, eccentric and self-educated, with a penchant for Russian antiquities. Occasionally, this shopkeeper even dared to compete with Stepan Trofimovitch in intellectual debates, often citing progressive opinions. The more tangible grievance, however, stemmed from a debt of four hundred roubles Andreev owed him for a parcel of timber purchased from his small estate. While Andreev had already paid several installments in advance, allowing Stepan Trofimovitch to cover urgent expenses at the time, the delay in settling the remainder left him despondent. He had counted on that money for unspecified private expenditures and was on the verge of tears when Andreev requested an extension of a month, a request perfectly within his rights.

Varvara Petrovna read this first letter with great interest, pausing to underline the phrase, "Where are they both?" She carefully numbered the letter and placed it in her drawer, recognizing that "they both" referred to his late wives. However, the second letter she received from Berlin had a markedly different tone.

"I am working twelve hours a day!" it declared. "I scour the libraries, collate documents, make notes, and rush from one professor to another. I have also reconnected with the delightful Dundasov family. What a charming creature Lizaveta Nikolaevna remains, even now! She sends her greetings. Her young husband and their nephews are all in Berlin. We stay up until dawn having nearly Athenian evenings—Athenian in their intellectual refinement and sophistication. Everything is conducted in noble style. There is music, discussions of Spanish melodies, dreams of humanity's regeneration, reflections on eternal beauty and the Sistine Madonna, light mingled with shadow. Yet, as they say, even the sun has its spots! My noble friend, my ever-faithful friend! My heart remains with you, always, en tout pays, even in le pays de Makar et de ses veaux. Do you remember, in Petersburg, how we spoke of such things in moments of passionate agitation? Crossing the frontier, I felt a strange and profound sense of safety for the first time in many years."

The letter meandered on in a similar vein, full of overblown sentiment.

"Utter nonsense," muttered Varvara Petrovna as she folded the letter. "If he's staying up until daybreak indulging in these so-called Athenian nights, he cannot possibly be spending twelve hours a day on serious work. Was he drunk when he wrote this? And that Dundasov woman dares to send me her greetings? Let him have his amusements, for now."

The peculiar phrase "dans le pays de Makar et de ses veaux" was Stepan Trofimovitch's awkward, deliberately absurd translation of the Russian idiom "wherever Makar may drive his calves." He had a habit of rendering common sayings into clumsy French, not out of ignorance but because he thought it chic and amusing.

But the amusement did not last long. Stepan Trofimovitch's resolve began to falter, and before four months had passed, he was hurrying back to Skvoreshniki. His final letters from Berlin consisted of little more than effusive declarations of devotion to Varvara Petrovna, overflowing with sentimental affection and often tear-stained. Some people, like lapdogs, are simply too deeply attached to the comforts of home, and Stepan Trofimovitch was one of them.

The reunion between the two friends was filled with emotion. They embraced warmly, and for two days, it seemed as though the separation had never happened. By the end of the second day, however, everything had returned to its usual rhythm—if anything, life felt even duller than before.

One evening, Stepan Trofimovitch confided in me with an air of despair, "My dear friend, I have come to a dreadful realization, something new and profoundly disturbing... je suis un simple dépendant, et rien de plus! Mais r-r-rien de plus." And with that, he sank into a resigned silence, as though the weight of this revelation was too much to bear.

Chapter 1.8

After this, we entered a period of quiet stagnation that lasted for nine long years. Stepan Trofimovitch's periodic hysterical fits and his occasional sobbing confessions on my shoulder did not disrupt the overall peace and prosperity of our lives during this time. Surprisingly, despite the passing years and the indulgences of our provincial life, Stepan Trofimovitch did not grow stout. His nose, perhaps, became slightly redder, and his manner grew even more polished and urbane, but otherwise, he remained much the same. Over time, a small but lively circle of acquaintances formed around him. Although Varvara Petrovna had little direct involvement with our group, her presence loomed large as our unspoken benefactor and patroness.

After the lessons learned from the Petersburg debacle, Varvara Petrovna decided to settle permanently in our provincial town. She divided her time between her estate in the countryside and her spacious town residence. During these years, her social standing reached unprecedented heights. In the seven years leading up to the appointment of our new governor, her influence in provincial society was unparalleled. The previous governor, the mild and unassuming Ivan Ossipovitch, who remained fondly remembered by all of us, was a distant relative of Varvara Petrovna and had, at one time, owed her a significant debt of gratitude. His wife, in particular, seemed to live in constant fear of displeasing her. Provincial society, eager to curry favor, elevated their admiration of her to the level of near-idolatry. This reflected positively on Stepan Trofimovitch as well.

He, too, enjoyed a comfortable existence. As a respected member of the local club, he played cards regularly, losing gracefully and often, and was treated with deference wherever he went. Many people, it is true, saw him merely as a "learned man," but this only added to the mystique surrounding him. As time went on, Varvara Petrovna allowed him to move into a separate house, which increased the sense of freedom in our gatherings. Twice a week, our little circle would meet at his home, where we enjoyed lively conversations and occasional bursts of laughter, particularly when the champagne was flowing freely. The wine, incidentally, came from the shop of Andreev, our eccentric merchant friend. The bills, paid twice a year by Varvara Petrovna, always triggered one of Stepan Trofimovitch's infamous "summer cholera" attacks— perhaps out of shame, guilt, or simply habit.

One of the earliest and most prominent members of our circle was Liputin, an older provincial official and a self-proclaimed liberal, widely known in town for his atheistic views. Liputin had remarried late in life to a young and attractive woman who brought a small dowry into the marriage. He also had three grown daughters from his first marriage. Despite his liberal reputation, he ruled his household with an iron fist, raising his family in the strictest fear of God while maintaining a thrifty and calculating demeanor. Over the years, he had managed to amass a modest fortune and purchase his own home, all on his meager salary. Liputin's reputation in the town, however, was less than stellar. He was known as a meddler and a gossip, and his penchant for scandalous rumors had earned him more than one public humiliation—once at the hands of a military officer and another time from a respected landowner. Despite his unsavory traits, we valued his sharp wit and biting humor, though Varvara Petrovna, for her part, openly disliked him. Liputin, being shrewd, always found ways to ingratiate himself with her, even when her disdain was evident.

Another notable figure in our group was Shatov, who joined us during the later years of this period. Shatov's background was both intriguing and controversial. A former university student, he had been expelled for his involvement in a political disturbance. As a child, he had studied under Stepan Trofimovitch and was, by birth, a serf of Varvara Petrovna, being the son of her former valet, Pavel Fyodoritch. Despite the opportunities afforded to him through Varvara Petrovna's generosity, Shatov's relationship with her was strained. She found his pride and ingratitude unbearable, and she could never forgive him for ignoring the letter she sent after his expulsion. Instead of turning to her for help, he had accepted a humiliating position as a tutor—and, at times, a glorified nurse—for the children of a progressive merchant. This merchant later dismissed Shatov when a young Russian governess in his household, hired primarily for her low wages, was fired for "free-thinking." Shatov followed the governess abroad, and shortly thereafter, in Geneva, he married her. The marriage lasted only three weeks before they parted ways amicably, both recognizing their incompatibility, though poverty likely played a role.

After wandering through Europe, where he reportedly worked as everything from a dockyard laborer to a shoe shiner, Shatov returned to our town a year before this narrative and took up residence with an elderly aunt. When she passed away a month later, Shatov was left to fend for himself. His sister, Dasha, who had also been raised by Varvara Petrovna, remained one of the latter's favorites, though Shatov himself rarely interacted with her. In our group, Shatov was withdrawn and spoke little, though on occasion, when a discussion touched on his deeply held convictions, he would become visibly agitated, his language growing increasingly unrestrained.

"One must tie Shatov down before trying to reason with him," Stepan Trofimovitch would sometimes joke, though he had a genuine fondness for the younger man. Shatov had undergone a dramatic ideological transformation during his time abroad, abandoning his earlier socialist beliefs and embracing an entirely opposite worldview. He was one of those uniquely Russian idealists who, upon encountering an overwhelming idea, would let it consume them completely. This newfound belief weighed on him like a stone, leaving him emotionally and intellectually paralyzed for years. His appearance mirrored his inner turmoil: short and stocky, with disheveled flaxen hair, thick lips, bushy white eyebrows, and a perpetually furrowed brow. His wild, unkempt hair and his hostile, downcast eyes gave him the look of a man burdened by his convictions. At twenty-eight, he seemed older than his years, carrying himself with a heavy, awkward gait that reflected the weight of his thoughts.

"I no longer wonder that his wife ran away from him," Varvara Petrovna remarked one day, her gaze fixed intently on Shatov. Despite his extreme poverty, he always made an effort to dress neatly, as though to maintain a shred of dignity. He avoided asking Varvara Petrovna for assistance, even when times were hardest, and instead eked out a living by taking on odd jobs for local tradespeople. At one point, he worked in a shop; at another, he almost secured a position as an assistant clerk on a freight steamer, but illness struck him just before the ship was due to sail. His capacity to endure the most crushing poverty without so much as a word of complaint was truly remarkable.

After his illness, Varvara Petrovna anonymously sent him a hundred roubles, hoping to provide some relief. Shatov, however, managed to discover the source of the money. After some deliberation, he accepted the sum and even resolved to personally thank her. When he visited her home, she greeted him warmly, clearly pleased with his gesture. Yet, once again, Shatov disappointed her. He stood before her, staring at the floor and smiling awkwardly, unable to muster a single coherent sentence. His silence grew increasingly uncomfortable until, at the worst possible moment, he clumsily rose to leave, bowing awkwardly as he did so. In his confusion, he stumbled into an ornate inlaid work-table, knocking it over and shattering it to pieces. Mortified beyond words, Shatov fled the house, leaving Varvara Petrovna staring after him in stunned silence.

Liputin, always ready with his scathing commentary, criticized Shatov harshly for accepting the money in the first place. He argued that Shatov should have returned it with disdain, given that it came from his former mistress, whom Liputin still referred to as a "despot." Despite such critiques, Shatov continued to live a solitary life on the outskirts of town, refusing to let any of us visit him at home. He would, however, consistently attend the gatherings at Stepan Trofimovitch's house, where he often borrowed newspapers and books.

Another regular attendee at these gatherings was Virginsky, a local clerk and a man who, despite being Shatov's polar opposite in many ways, shared certain similarities with him. Virginsky was a mild-mannered and quiet man in his early thirties, with a modest education that he had largely acquired on his own. He lived a humble life, supporting not only his wife but also her aunt and sister on his meager clerk's salary. His wife, along with the other women in their household, was an ardent advocate for the latest social and political ideas, though their understanding of these ideas often seemed superficial. As Stepan Trofimovitch once quipped, their beliefs were a classic example of "an idea dragged out into the street."

Madame Virginsky, who worked as a midwife in the town, had spent much of her youth in Petersburg and carried with her a certain air of progressive zeal. Virginsky himself was a deeply sincere and idealistic man, and his honesty and dedication to what he called his "bright hopes" were undeniable. "I will never, never abandon these bright hopes," he would often say to me, his eyes shining with quiet conviction. He spoke of these hopes softly, almost in a whisper, as though discussing a sacred secret. Physically, he was a tall, thin, and narrow-shouldered man with lifeless, reddish hair that hung lankly around his pale face.

Though Stepan Trofimovitch often teased Virginsky about his ideas, calling him a "half-hatched chicken" who was still struggling to break free of his shell, he always did so affectionately. "Shatov would give anything to hatch out," Stepan Trofimovitch would add, "but he's half-hatched too." Liputin, of course, could not resist asking how he fit into this metaphor, to which Stepan Trofimovitch dryly replied, "You're the golden mean—you'll find your way anywhere, in your own fashion." Liputin, predictably, took offense.

The story of Virginsky's personal life, however, was well-known and rather tragic. Within a year of his marriage, his wife openly declared that she no longer loved him and had instead given her heart to Lebyadkin, a dubious newcomer to town who falsely claimed to be a retired captain. Lebyadkin, a crude and shameless man, moved into Virginsky's home, eating his food, sleeping under his roof, and even treating Virginsky himself with condescension. It was rumored that when Virginsky's wife announced her feelings for Lebyadkin, Virginsky responded with stoic acceptance, supposedly telling her, "My dear, until now, I have only loved you. Now, I respect you." While this Roman-like renunciation was often

33

repeated, there were those who doubted its authenticity, claiming instead that Virginsky had wept uncontrollably.

The situation reached a breaking point during a picnic to a nearby forest, where the entire household, including Lebyadkin, had gathered for tea. Without any apparent provocation, Virginsky, who had been unusually lively that day, suddenly grabbed the much larger Lebyadkin by the hair while the latter was in the middle of a dance. Dragging him across the ground amid shrieks and shouts, Virginsky seemed overtaken by a feverish rage. Lebyadkin, too shocked to resist, remained silent throughout the ordeal but later demanded retribution. That night, Virginsky spent hours on his knees, begging his wife for forgiveness, but she refused to grant it. She chastised him for his lack of self-control and for the sheer absurdity of kneeling before her.

The captain eventually left town, only to return years later under very different circumstances. During his absence, Virginsky sought solace in the camaraderie of our circle, though he never spoke openly about his domestic troubles. On one rare occasion, while walking home with me after an evening at Stepan Trofimovitch's, he made a vague reference to his situation. Grasping my hand tightly, he said, "It doesn't matter. It's just a personal incident. It has no bearing on the cause—not in the slightest!"

Occasionally, we had other visitors in our circle. Lyamshin, a Jewish musician with a sharp wit, would sometimes join us, as would Captain Kartusov, who had a penchant for loud arguments. There was even an elderly gentleman with an insatiable curiosity who attended regularly for a time, though he eventually passed away. Liputin once brought an exiled Polish priest, Father Slontsevsky, to our gatherings. While we initially welcomed him out of principle, the novelty wore off, and his visits soon stopped. Each of these figures added their own flavor to the dynamic of our little group, but none left as lasting an impression as the regular members.

Chapter 1.9

At one point, rumors began to circulate around the town, claiming that our modest little circle was a hub of nihilism, debauchery, and godlessness. These accusations gained traction despite being absurdly exaggerated. In reality, our gatherings consisted of nothing more than harmless, amiable discussions—the sort of lighthearted, carefree liberal chatter that seemed to flourish in Russia. Ours was a "higher liberalism," characterized by a lack of concrete objectives, a phenomenon uniquely suited to our nation's temperament.

Stepan Trofimovitch, like any man gifted with wit, relished having an audience. It wasn't enough for him to speak; he needed to feel that he was performing a noble duty by spreading his ideas. And, of course, he needed companions to share champagne with—champagne often being the prelude to spirited conversations about Russia, the "Russian spirit," and even the concept of God, particularly the "Russian God." We would frequently revisit the same stories of scandalous Russian affairs, tales everyone already knew and retold endlessly. Town gossip, too, found its way into our conversations, often leading us to deliver severe, lofty moral judgments as though we were the arbiters of righteousness.

We delighted in broad generalizations about humanity and solemn reflections on Europe's future. Many of us spoke with certainty about the impending decline of France, convinced that the rise of Cæsarism would reduce the nation to second-rate status. We were equally assured that the Pope's influence in a unified Italy would dwindle to that of a mere archbishop, a centuries-old debate we dismissed as irrelevant in this modern age of humanitarianism, railways, and industrial progress. Such was the nature of our "higher liberalism"; there was simply no other perspective we could adopt.

Occasionally, Stepan Trofimovitch would speak on the subject of art, his observations always thoughtful, if somewhat abstract. Other times, he reminisced about his youth and the illustrious names of his former friends—figures who had left their mark on Russian intellectual history. He spoke of these individuals with a mix of reverence, nostalgia, and just a hint of envy. When our discussions grew tedious, Lyamshin, the little

Jewish postal clerk and a masterful pianist, would entertain us. Beyond his piano skills, Lyamshin was known for his uncanny imitations, including a pig, a thunderstorm, and even a mother giving birth, complete with the newborn's first cries. His antics, while absurd, were often the highlight of the evening and the primary reason he was invited.

When the wine flowed freely, as it occasionally did, our enthusiasm would overflow as well. On one particularly memorable occasion, we even sang the "Marseillaise" in chorus, with Lyamshin accompanying us on the piano. It's hard to say how well we performed, but the memory of that night lingered for years. The most significant event we celebrated was the nineteenth of February, which we greeted with boundless enthusiasm. For weeks leading up to the day, we toasted it with fervor.

Yet even this joyous occasion carried an undercurrent of anxiety. Before the emancipation of the serfs, Stepan Trofimovitch often muttered to himself lines of verse that hinted at an impending reckoning. "The peasant with his axe is coming, something terrible will happen," he murmured, quoting lines attributed to a liberal landowner of a bygone era. On one occasion, Varvara Petrovna overheard him. "Nonsense! Absolute nonsense!" she snapped before storming out of the room, clearly irritated. Liputin, who was present, seized the moment to remark cynically, "It'll be a pity if the peasants do something nasty to messieurs les landowners to celebrate the day," drawing his finger ominously across his throat.

"Cher ami," Stepan Trofimovitch replied with his characteristic poise, "believe me, that"—he imitated the throat-slitting gesture—"will serve neither the landowners nor anyone else. We Russians will never organize anything, not even without our heads. Our heads, in fact, hinder our understanding more than they help."

Many in our town shared Liputin's grim outlook, expecting unrest to accompany the emancipation. Even Stepan Trofimovitch seemed uneasy, to the point of requesting permission from Varvara Petrovna to go abroad. But the historic day came and went without incident, much to everyone's relief. Soon, Stepan Trofimovitch's condescending smile returned, and he began sharing his reflections on the Russian character and peasantry.

"Like impatient fools, we've rushed to romanticize our peasants," he declared one evening. "For years now, writers have treated them as if they were newly unearthed treasures. We've adorned their lice-ridden heads with laurel wreaths! Do you know what Russian villages have given us in a thousand years? Kamarinsky. That's it." He recounted a famous anecdote in which a Russian poet, overwhelmed after seeing the actress Rachel on stage for the first time, exclaimed, "I wouldn't trade Rachel for a single peasant!" Stepan Trofimovitch went further: "I'd trade all the peasants in Russia for one Rachel. It's time we stopped deluding ourselves with rustic myths and distinguished the stench of pitch from the scent of imperial perfume."

Liputin, ever the opportunist, quickly agreed but added that society demanded hypocrisy. "We have to pretend to praise the peasant," he said, "to appear progressive. Even aristocratic ladies shed tears over sentimental stories like Poor Anton and write letters from Paris instructing their bailiffs to treat the peasants humanely."

As fate would have it, rumors of unrest soon reached our town. A minor disturbance broke out only ten miles from Skvoreshniki, prompting the governor to dispatch a detachment of soldiers. This time, Stepan Trofimovitch's anxiety reached new heights. He burst into the club, demanding reinforcements and urging the governor to telegraph for troops from neighboring provinces. He even offered to send a formal statement to Petersburg, disavowing any involvement in the uprising. His panic proved unnecessary; the unrest subsided quickly, and the situation resolved itself without further incident.

In the years that followed, new ideas like nationalism and "public opinion" began to take root, capturing the imagination of intellectual circles. Stepan Trofimovitch, however, found the entire phenomenon laughable. These shifts, though significant, seemed to him like fleeting distractions, and he treated them with the same bemused detachment he had perfected over the years.

"My friends," Stepan Trofimovitch once declared to us with his characteristic mix of irony and gravitas, "if this so-called nationalism of ours has truly 'dawned,' as the newspapers keep insistently repeating, then let me tell you—it's still in school, hunched over a German book in some dusty Peterschule, reciting lessons dictated by a German teacher. And make no mistake, that same teacher will make it kneel when he feels like it. I do not mean to diminish the German teacher—I respect him—but let us be honest: nothing new has dawned. Nothing has changed. Everything in this vast, holy Russia of ours continues as it has always been, just as ordained by God. Isn't that enough for Russia, for our Sainte Russie?"

He paused for dramatic effect, his words resonating in the room before continuing, "This Slavism, this nationalism, it's not new—it's too ancient to be novel. In fact, nationalism in our land has only ever existed as a kind of diversion for gentlemen's clubs, primarily those in Moscow. And even that was rooted in idleness. Everything in Russia comes from idleness—yes, even the good things. Our noble gentry, with their charming, whimsical leisure, have been the source of whatever progress we've managed to muster. But we, as a nation, have never learned to live by our own labor."

He leaned forward, his voice growing more impassioned. "And now they prattle on about the sudden emergence of public opinion, as though it has dropped from the heavens without any effort. How can they not understand? Before we can claim to have a public opinion, we must first have work—our own work, born of our own initiative and experience. Opinion is the fruit of labor, my friends, and we have yet to plant the seeds. Without labor, without effort, our opinions will always be borrowed, mere shadows of what others—namely, the Germans—have formed for us. For two centuries, they have been our teachers, and still, we lean on them. Do they not see? Russia is too tangled, too vast, for us to unravel without their help—or without hard work of our own."

There was a brief silence, heavy with the weight of his words, as he concluded with a wry smile, "For twenty years, I have sounded the alarm, calling for labor, for action. I gave my life to that appeal, foolishly believing in its power. I no longer believe, but still, I ring the bell. I shall pull the ropes until they toll for my own requiem."

We could do nothing but nod in agreement. His rhetoric was magnetic, even as it cut through our own complacency. We clapped, we praised him, and yet his words left a lingering discomfort.

Amidst these discussions, Stepan Trofimovitch often took the opportunity to clarify his beliefs about God. "I don't understand why people here insist on calling me an infidel," he would remark, almost defensively. "I believe in God, but let's make distinctions, shall we? I believe in Him as a consciousness that exists within me, not as some external being that I must fear or placate with rituals. I can't believe the way my servant Nastasya does, with her unquestioning piety, nor like those country gentlemen who believe 'just to be safe.' Even Shatov's faith is different—his is grounded in principle, almost like a Slavophil dogma."

He would sigh deeply before continuing, "As for Christianity, I have profound respect for it, but I cannot call myself a Christian. No, I'm more of an ancient pagan, like Goethe or the Greeks of old. Christianity, for all its virtues, has failed to understand one crucial thing: woman. George Sand showed this beautifully in one of her novels. And all this bowing, fasting, and other rituals—I see no connection to me in any of it. But don't mistake me; I will not become a Jesuit. I recall Byelinsky, who once wrote that famous letter to Gogol, criticizing him for his belief in God. Imagine Gogol reading those words—the Gogol of that time! It's almost comical to picture."

He chuckled, though his eyes betrayed a trace of sorrow. "But I must say, Byelinsky and those like him—they were men, true men. They knew how to love their people, to suffer for them, to sacrifice for them. Yet they never let themselves become blind to their flaws. They didn't just parrot ideas from the people; they had ideas of their own."

At this point, Shatov, who had been sitting quietly, could contain himself no longer. "They didn't love the people!" he growled, his voice low but trembling with intensity. "They never suffered for the people or sacrificed for them. They merely toyed with the idea, imagining it as some kind of lofty pastime!"

Stepan Trofimovitch's face reddened. "Not love the people? How dare you! They adored Russia!"

"Neither Russia nor its people," Shatov shot back, his eyes blazing.

"How can you love what you don't understand? They had no true conception of the Russian people. All of them—Byelinsky included—looked at the people through a filter of arrogance and disdain. They couldn't see beyond their Parisian ideals. And you, Stepan Trofimovitch, are no different. You've taken an attitude of contempt, ashamed that the Russian people aren't like the French. That's the truth. And let me tell you something—those who lose their connection to their people lose their faith as well. They become atheists, indifferent to everything. That's why you, and all of us now, are nothing but soulless skeptics or reckless fools. Don't take offense, but you're no exception!"

These fiery exchanges were a common occurrence, with Shatov storming out in frustration, convinced he had severed ties with Stepan Trofimovitch for good. Yet, each time, the latter would manage to calm him down, extending a hand with a disarming smile. "Come now, Shatov, must we part ways over such endearments?" he would say, his tone soothing.

Shatov, awkward and visibly torn, would eventually relent. His gruff exterior belied a tender heart, and though he often went too far, he was quick to regret it. He would shuffle back to his chair, muttering under his breath, and the evening would resume, often with wine to toast some figure of historical significance. The tension would dissolve, at least for the moment, but the questions raised lingered long after the wine glasses were emptied.

Chapter 2
Prince Harry. Matchmaking.

Chapter 2.1

There was another person in the world whom Varvara Petrovna cherished as much as she did Stepan Trofimovitch—her only son, Nikolay Vsyevolodovitch Stavrogin. Stepan Trofimovitch had been engaged as the boy's tutor, a task he took up when Nikolay was just eight years old. By then, the boy's father, the frivolous General Stavrogin, had separated from Varvara Petrovna, leaving the child entirely in her care. Despite the strained circumstances, Stepan Trofimovitch proved remarkably adept at winning his young pupil's affection. His secret, it seemed, was his own childlike nature, which allowed him to connect with the boy on a level that transcended their age difference.

At that time, Stepan Trofimovitch lacked close friends and yearned for companionship. Nikolay, though just a child, naturally became the confidant he needed. As their relationship deepened, the boundaries of tutor and student blurred; Stepan Trofimovitch often treated the boy as an equal. It was not uncommon for him to wake his young friend in the middle of the night to share his feelings of hurt or to pour out some family secret, without considering how inappropriate it was to burden a child with such matters. The two would end up in each other's arms, weeping together over shared—or rather, imposed—sorrows. This odd bond had its tender moments, but it left a lasting impression on Nikolay.

While the boy understood that his mother loved him deeply, he seemed not to reciprocate that love with the same intensity. Varvara Petrovna was a commanding figure, and her frequent, silent gazes—intent and searching—seemed to weigh heavily on her son. She rarely spoke to him directly or interfered in his life, but her quiet presence was always felt. Despite her emotional distance, she entrusted Stepan Trofimovitch entirely with Nikolay's education and moral upbringing, putting complete faith in him during those years.

Under Stepan Trofimovitch's tutelage, Nikolay's nerves were perhaps overly stimulated. When the boy left home at sixteen to attend a lyceum, he was pale, delicate-looking, and strikingly introspective. He had a dreamy, quiet demeanor, though this belied the great physical strength he would later develop. During those formative years, it seems likely that the pair continued their nocturnal emotional outbursts, though by then, their tears may have been prompted by less tangible troubles than before. Stepan Trofimovitch had succeeded in awakening in Nikolay a profound sense of yearning—a sacred and eternal longing that some rare souls value even more than its possible fulfillment. For better or worse, this influence shaped Nikolay's character, and while their eventual separation was painful, it was ultimately necessary.

For the first couple of years at the lyceum, Nikolay came home for holidays. During these visits, when his mother and Stepan Trofimovitch were in Petersburg, he occasionally attended the literary evenings hosted by Varvara Petrovna. At these gatherings, he was quiet and reserved, listening attentively but rarely contributing. While his demeanor toward Stepan Trofimovitch remained affectionate, there was now a subtle reserve in his behavior. He no longer engaged in the lofty, emotional discussions of their past, avoiding conversations that touched on sentimental topics or personal memories.

At his mother's insistence, Nikolay joined the military after completing his studies. He received a commission in one of the most prestigious regiments of the Horse Guards, but notably, he did not visit his mother in his uniform—a gesture that deeply pained her. His letters, once frequent, grew sparse, though Varvara Petrovna continued to send him money generously, despite the significant reduction in her estate's income after the emancipation of the serfs. Her financial sacrifices for her son were considerable, as she had to dip into savings accumulated over years of careful management. Yet, she took pride in Nikolay's apparent success in Petersburg's highest social circles. Where she had struggled to maintain connections, Nikolay seemed to thrive, renewing acquaintances and gaining acceptance among people who had once been beyond her reach.

But her joy was short-lived. Whispers soon reached her ears of Nikolay's increasingly erratic behavior. He had reportedly taken to wild, reckless living—not in the form of gambling or excessive drinking, but in displays of savage and dangerous impulsiveness. There were stories of him deliberately running over pedestrians with his horses and of a scandal involving a woman of high social standing whom he first seduced and later humiliated in public. The latter incident was particularly disturbing, marked by a cruel and callous disregard for her dignity. These rumors described a young man who seemed to derive perverse pleasure from causing pain, someone who insulted others seemingly for the sheer thrill of it.

Varvara Petrovna was devastated. Her distress only grew as Stepan Trofimovitch tried to console her, likening Nikolay's behavior to that of

Shakespeare's Prince Harry, who had once caroused with rogues like Falstaff before redeeming himself as King Henry V. Stepan Trofimovitch elaborated on the comparison, weaving an optimistic theory about the stormy passions of a gifted youth that would eventually subside. For once, Varvara Petrovna did not dismiss his words as nonsense. Instead, she latched onto them, even reading Shakespeare herself to find reassurance. Yet, the resemblance did not fully convince her, and she anxiously awaited news from her son.

The letters she received only deepened her despair. The worst of the rumors turned out to be true. Nikolay had been involved in two duels within a short span, both of which he had initiated. One duel ended in the death of his opponent; in the other, he gravely injured his adversary. Facing trial, Nikolay was stripped of his noble status, demoted to the ranks, and reassigned to an infantry line regiment. He narrowly escaped harsher punishment thanks to an intervention that could only be described as an act of mercy.

This turn of events left Varvara Petrovna reeling. Her once-lofty dreams for her son had shattered, replaced by the harsh reality of his self-destructive path. It was a blow not just to her pride, but to her deepest hopes for Nikolay's future.

In 1863, Nikolay Stavrogin managed to distinguish himself in the army, earning a military cross and swiftly advancing to the rank of officer. This brief period of success was accompanied by countless letters from Varvara Petrovna to influential figures in the capital, pleading and petitioning on her son's behalf. Her appeals were often infused with desperation, and in her extreme anxiety, she did not hesitate to humble herself. Her efforts bore fruit, but just as suddenly as his career had taken off, Nikolay resigned his commission. What was even more painful for her was that he did not return to Skvoreshniki or even write to her afterward. For a long time, all news of him came only through whispers and roundabout reports.

It was soon discovered that he was back in Petersburg but living a shadowy existence, entirely removed from his former social circles. He seemed to have retreated into a murky underworld, mingling with dubious characters—impoverished clerks, disgraced soldiers, and even beggars. He frequented filthy tenements and dark alleyways, spending days and nights in the company of drunkards and other outcasts. Astonishingly, it appeared he had embraced this life with an almost deliberate enthusiasm. Despite his descent into this sordid existence, he made no requests for financial support from his mother. Instead, he relied on the modest income from a small estate he had inherited from his father, General Stavrogin. Rumor had it that he had leased this property to a German tenant from Saxony.

Eventually, unable to bear the uncertainty, Varvara Petrovna sent an urgent plea for Nikolay to come to her. To everyone's surprise, "Prince Harry," as Stepan Trofimovitch liked to call him, finally appeared in our town. Like many others, I had never met him before, and I expected to see a wretched, ragged figure ravaged by dissipation. Instead, I was astonished to encounter one of the most elegant and striking men I had ever seen. He was impeccably dressed, exuding refinement and confidence, with a demeanor that spoke of extensive culture and sophistication. The contrast between the rumors and the reality of his appearance was so stark that it left not only me but the entire town bewildered.

Nikolay's arrival caused a sensation. The townspeople, who somehow knew every detail of his scandalous biography, were divided into two sharply opposed camps. One group adored him, captivated by his charm and air of mystery. The other group despised him with an intensity bordering on hatred, though even their animosity seemed laced with a perverse fascination. Women, in particular, were utterly enthralled by him. Some romanticized the idea that he carried a dark and tragic secret, while others seemed thrilled by his reputation as a dangerous man—even a killer.

It quickly became clear that Nikolay was not only handsome but also highly educated and remarkably intelligent. Though our provincial society had modest standards for what constituted "culture," he exceeded them with ease. He spoke with insight on a wide range of topics, offering opinions that were both practical and shrewd. Despite his notoriety, he impressed many with his composed, self-assured demeanor. He was not overly talkative, yet his quiet presence commanded attention. Our local dandies, who had once basked in the limelight, found themselves completely overshadowed by him. Even his physical appearance was captivating. His jet-black hair, strikingly pale complexion, and light-colored, piercing eyes gave him an otherworldly allure. Yet there was something unsettling about his beauty—a sense of artifice or a mask-like quality that made one hesitate to trust him fully.

For six months, Nikolay lived among us, conducting himself with impeccable propriety. He adhered to the strict codes of provincial etiquette, attending social events and fulfilling his familial obligations with flawless precision. His relationship with the governor, a distant relative on his father's side, ensured his acceptance in the highest social circles of the town. Yet beneath this polished exterior, there was an undercurrent of restlessness, as if he were biding his time.

Varvara Petrovna's pride in her son was evident, but so was her unease. She looked at him with a mix of admiration and apprehension, as though she were perpetually on edge, waiting for some calamity to strike. Her maternal devotion, already intense during his Petersburg years, seemed to deepen following his disgrace in the army. It was as though she saw in him a new purpose, a reason to redirect her energies. Yet this devotion came with a price—she appeared almost subservient in his presence, as though she feared some unspoken aspect of his character.

During this time, Varvara Petrovna underwent a transformation. Abandoning her earlier romantic aspirations, such as her plans to start a magazine or her periodic trips to Petersburg, she began focusing entirely on practical matters. She immersed herself in the management of her estate, raising its income to near pre-emancipation levels within just a few years. She also distanced herself from Stepan Trofimovitch, granting his long-standing request to move into separate lodgings. While their relationship remained outwardly amicable, this change marked a subtle shift in their dynamic. Stepan Trofimovitch, always attuned to such nuances, began referring to her as "my prosaic friend," though only in jest and with the utmost caution.

Yet, for all her newfound pragmatism, Varvara Petrovna could not shake the fear that loomed over her whenever she was near her son. She scrutinized him constantly, her gaze filled with questions she dared not voice. And then, just as the townspeople were beginning to believe that the infamous Nikolay Stavrogin had turned over a new leaf, the wild beast within him revealed its claws.

Chapter 2.2

Suddenly and seemingly without any reason, Nikolay Stavrogin committed a series of shocking and senseless acts that defied explanation. These were not ordinary breaches of etiquette or minor mischiefs; they were outrageous, unprecedented, and entirely gratuitous offenses, seemingly performed for no discernible purpose. One particularly scandalous incident took place at the club, where Pyotr Pavlovitch Gaganov, a respected committee member and elderly gentleman of high rank, became the target of one such inexplicable affront. Gaganov, known for frequently exclaiming during debates, "No, you can't lead me by the nose!" had long entertained this habit harmlessly.

But on this occasion, as Gaganov repeated his favorite phrase during a heated discussion among a group of distinguished members, Nikolay suddenly approached him. Without warning, he took Gaganov firmly by the nose with two fingers and, to everyone's astonishment, led him a few steps across the room. The act was so absurd and childish that at first it seemed like a mere prank, albeit a grossly inappropriate one. Yet, those present later recalled how Nikolay appeared strangely detached, almost dreamy, as if acting in a trance. Only afterward did he seem fully aware of the situation, and instead of showing embarrassment or remorse, he smiled in a way that was both cheerful and malicious.

The room erupted in outrage. Members surrounded him, demanding an explanation. Nikolay, however, remained calm and indifferent, looking around at the chaos he had caused with a detached curiosity. Then, as if lost in thought, he frowned slightly, approached the humiliated Gaganov, and muttered a hasty apology: "You must forgive me, of course... I really don't know what came over me... It was foolish." His words, delivered with careless nonchalance, only added insult to injury. The apology, far from soothing tempers, fueled even greater indignation.

The uproar in the club was immediate and overwhelming. Nikolay, unbothered by the commotion, shrugged his shoulders and left. The members, furious and deeply offended, unanimously voted to strike his name from the club's membership rolls. They quickly drafted an appeal to the governor, urging him to use his administrative authority to take action against this "dangerous ruffian" and protect the town's peace. The letter referred to Nikolay as a "dueling bully from the capital" and suggested that even someone of his standing could be brought to justice. The language of the appeal included a deliberate jab at the governor, implying that his connection to Varvara Petrovna might influence his handling of the matter.

Unfortunately for the club, the governor was out of town at the time, attending a christening for the child of a well-known widow. In his absence, the town rallied around the insulted Gaganov, treating him as a hero. People visited him in droves, embracing and congratulating him as if he had achieved something remarkable. There was even talk of hosting a subscription dinner in his honor, though this idea was eventually dropped—perhaps due to the absurdity of celebrating a man who had been publicly humiliated. Despite all the theatrics, a lingering question remained: how could such an incident have happened at all? How could anyone, let alone someone of Nikolay's social standing, stoop to such an outrageous act?

What struck me most was that no one attributed Nikolay's behavior to madness. On the contrary, people seemed almost prepared to expect such bizarre acts from him, as if they were entirely within the bounds of his character. This speaks volumes about the impression he had made on our town. Although he had always been unfailingly polite and courteous—like a gentleman from a fashion plate, as someone once remarked—there was something about him that inspired unease and even hatred. His haughtiness was undeniable, and it seemed to breed resentment among those around him. Even the ladies, who had once adored him, turned on him with astonishing vehemence. Their adoration transformed into scorn overnight, and they began speaking of him with the same hostility as the men.

Varvara Petrovna, however, was devastated. She later confessed to

Stepan Trofimovitch that she had been dreading such an incident for months. "Every day for half a year," she admitted, "I've been waiting for something like this to happen." Her maternal instinct had told her that trouble was brewing, and now her worst fears were being realized. That night, unable to contain her anxiety, she went to Stepan Trofimovitch's lodgings to seek his advice. It was a rare moment of vulnerability for her; she even wept openly, something she had never done in front of anyone before.

The following morning, gathering her courage, Varvara Petrovna approached her son to discuss the incident. Despite her composure, she was visibly trembling. Nikolay, always outwardly respectful to his mother, listened to her without interrupting. But as she spoke, he grew visibly irritated. Without offering any explanation, he abruptly kissed her hand, stood up, and left the room. That very evening, as if deliberately escalating the situation, he caused another scandal. While less egregious than the incident at the club, it further inflamed public opinion against him.

The second incident involved a trivial misunderstanding, but in the charged atmosphere of the town, it became a significant event. Whispers spread like wildfire, fueling the already feverish disdain for Nikolay. People were now convinced that his behavior was not an isolated lapse but part of a calculated campaign to insult and provoke the entire community. Even those who had initially defended him began to distance themselves, and the outcry against him grew louder with each passing day. Varvara Petrovna, who had long held her son as a beacon of hope, found herself grappling with the reality of his enigmatic and increasingly destructive behavior. It was as though a storm had been unleashed, and no one—not even his mother—knew how to contain it.

Liputin, ever the opportunist and eager to ingratiate himself with anyone who could elevate his social standing, wasted no time in extending an invitation to Nikolay Vsyevolodovitch. It was mere hours after the latter's tense exchange with his mother that Liputin turned up at his residence, bearing an earnest request for him to grace a modest gathering that evening in honor of his wife's birthday. Liputin, an ambitious but petty man, rarely entertained, hosting visitors only twice a year, but on these rare occasions, he pulled out all the stops to make an impression.

He knew that Nikolay's recent scandal at the club would be the talk of the town and likely suspected that the young man's presence at his party would add an air of infamy and excitement to the event.

Nikolay, for his part, understood the underlying motives of the invitation. Liputin, a self-proclaimed liberal and admirer of anything that disrupted the established order, likely approved of Nikolay's audacious affront to Gaganov. To him, such actions aligned with the rebellious spirit of their times and were, therefore, something to celebrate. With a knowing smile, Nikolay accepted the invitation.

That evening, the party was well-attended, though the gathering was far from polished. The guests consisted of a colorful mix of small-town personalities, ranging from minor officials and aspiring intellectuals to less reputable characters from the fringes of society. It was a lively and animated crowd, if somewhat lacking in decorum. Liputin spared no expense for the occasion, providing generous refreshments, ample vodka, and even organizing card games at several tables. By the time supper was to be served, the younger guests had begun dancing to the sound of a hastily arranged trio of musicians.

Nikolay made a dramatic entrance, arriving fashionably late but immediately becoming the center of attention. He exuded his characteristic charm, and his polished demeanor stood in sharp contrast to the more provincial air of the attendees. Spotting Madame Liputin, a petite and strikingly pretty woman who seemed overwhelmed by shyness in his presence, he gallantly asked her to dance. She hesitated but eventually accepted, and they took two turns around the room. Nikolay's conversation was light and engaging, and before long, he had drawn laughter from her—a sight that made her even more radiant. Observing her closely, he appeared suddenly captivated by her beauty. Without warning, and to the shock of the entire room, he took her by the waist and kissed her full on the lips, not once but several times, savoring the act with an audacity that left everyone frozen in disbelief.

The effect on the poor woman was immediate. She turned pale and fainted in his arms. Nikolay gently lowered her into a chair, then stood, surveying the stunned onlookers with calm detachment. Turning to

Liputin, who was standing rooted to the spot in a state of paralyzed shock, Nikolay muttered a hurried and almost perfunctory apology: "Don't be angry," and promptly took his leave. Liputin, regaining some composure, ran after his illustrious guest, personally fetching his fur coat and accompanying him to the door. He bowed deeply as Nikolay descended the stairs, his deference unshaken despite the outrageous scene that had just unfolded.

The events of the night were far from over, however. The following morning, a new chapter in the saga unfolded. At ten o'clock, Liputin's servant, Agafya, appeared at Nikolay's house with a message. Agafya, a lively and quick-witted peasant woman, insisted on delivering it directly to Nikolay himself. Despite a pounding headache, he came out to meet her. Varvara Petrovna, ever alert to her son's affairs, happened to be present and listened intently to the exchange.

With the cheerful briskness of someone accustomed to the absurdities of her employer, Agafya relayed the message. "Sergay Vassilyevitch," she began, referring to Liputin by his formal name, "bade me first of all give you his respectful greetings and ask after your health, what sort of night your honor spent after yesterday's doings, and how your honor feels now after yesterday's doings."

Nikolay, amused by her manner and the ridiculous formality of the message, smiled faintly. "Give him my greetings and thank him," he replied, "and tell your master from me, Agafya, that he's the most sensible man in the town."

Without missing a beat, Agafya shot back with a grin, "And he told me to answer that he knows that without your telling him and wishes you the same."

Nikolay raised an eyebrow in mild surprise. "Really? But how could he tell what I would say?"

Agafya's grin widened as she recounted the rest of the tale. "I can't say exactly, but when I had already set off and gone down the street, I heard someone running behind me. There he was, without his cap, shouting, 'I say, Agafya, if by any chance he says to you, "Tell your master he has more sense than all the town," you tell him straight away, "The master himself knows that very well and wishes you the same.'" So, I've done as I was told."

The exchange left Nikolay faintly amused and Varvara Petrovna deeply uneasy. Agafya's message, absurd as it was, captured the peculiar dynamic of the relationships surrounding her son. It was a game of veiled mockery and carefully balanced politeness, a strange dance of provocation and submission that seemed to define his interactions with the world around him. As trivial as the episode may have seemed on the surface, it added another layer of complexity to the growing enigma of Nikolay Stavrogin—a man whose actions were as unpredictable as they were unsettling.

Chapter 2.3

At last, the long-awaited interview between Nikolay Vsyevolodovitch and the governor, Ivan Ossipovitch, took place. The mild-mannered and perpetually cautious Ivan Ossipovitch had only recently returned from his trip and was still reeling from the furious complaints lodged against Nikolay by the club members. It was clear that some sort of action was necessary, but the governor was deeply uneasy. As a relative, he had always treated Nikolay with a degree of leniency, but this latest scandal had pushed even his patience to the brink. Nevertheless, he resolved to handle the matter diplomatically, intending to persuade Nikolay to issue a written apology to the club and the offended party. He even planned to suggest a brief trip abroad—to Italy, perhaps—to improve Nikolay's temperament and help him recover his composure.

This time, however, the meeting was not held in the governor's usual office but in a more modest waiting room, perhaps signaling Ivan Ossipovitch's unease. Present in the room was Alyosha Telyatnikov, a refined and polite young clerk, who was meticulously opening envelopes at a side table. In the adjacent room, a stout, self-absorbed colonel, a former colleague of the governor, sat engrossed in a newspaper, oblivious to the tense proceedings about to unfold nearby.

When Nikolay arrived, it was clear that he was in no mood for familial pleasantries. His usually composed demeanor was overshadowed by a pale, tense expression. He slouched slightly in his chair, his eyes darting around the room, as though he were either suppressing some inner turmoil or simply bored with the entire affair. The governor, for his part, approached the matter with his characteristic delicacy, speaking in a roundabout manner, his voice dropping to a whisper as he edged closer to his young kinsman.

"My dear Nicolas," the governor began hesitantly, "you have always shown yourself to be a young man of exceptional intelligence and culture. You have grown up in the finest circles, and your behavior until now has been a credit to your family. I cannot tell you what a comfort it has been to your mother. But this recent... incident has thrown everything into confusion. I speak to you not only as the governor but as your relative and someone who genuinely cares for you. What has driven you to such reckless acts, so completely out of character? What meaning could such actions possibly have?"

As the old man spoke, Nikolay's face betrayed a flicker of irritation. He listened with half-closed eyes, his fingers drumming lightly on the arm of his chair. Then, with a sudden glint of mischief in his eyes, he leaned forward, beckoning the governor closer. Curious and slightly alarmed, Ivan Ossipovitch inclined his head to listen more closely.

What happened next was so unexpected, so utterly absurd, that it bordered on the surreal. Instead of offering some whispered confession, Nikolay leaned in further and, to the governor's utter shock, bit down on his ear—not savagely, but firmly enough to cause pain. Ivan Ossipovitch froze, unable to process the bizarre assault. His mouth opened soundlessly for a moment before he finally managed to gasp, "Nicolas, this is beyond a joke!"

Neither Alyosha nor the colonel, still engrossed in his newspaper, immediately grasped what was happening. From their vantage point, it seemed as though the two men were simply whispering intently. But as the governor's face grew increasingly pale and his eyes widened in distress, Alyosha and the colonel exchanged uneasy glances, unsure whether to intervene. Meanwhile, Nikolay tightened his grip, his teeth sinking just a fraction deeper.

"Nicolas!" the governor whimpered in a strained voice, his composure breaking entirely. "Please... enough! Let's not carry this joke too far!"

Mercifully, Nikolay released his victim before further damage was done. The governor stumbled back in his chair, trembling and clutching his ear, his face a mask of terror and disbelief. For a full minute, he remained paralyzed, breathing heavily, before succumbing to a minor fit brought on by the shock. Within half an hour, Nikolay was arrested and confined to a special cell in the guardhouse, under strict watch by a personal sentinel.

The decision to detain Nikolay was unprecedented and harsh, especially given his status and connections, but Ivan Ossipovitch, usually so mild and conciliatory, was uncharacteristically firm. He even refused an audience with Varvara Petrovna when she arrived at the governor's residence in a state of near hysteria. The sight of her carriage being turned away at the gates left the town in a state of astonishment.

That night, however, the mystery deepened. At around two in the morning, the previously calm Nikolay suddenly became uncontrollably violent. He began pounding on the walls of his cell, screaming incoherently. With unnatural strength, he tore the iron grating from the door, smashed a window, and badly cut his hands in the process. When the guards rushed in to restrain him, they discovered that he was in the grip of a severe bout of brain fever.

The revelation brought immediate clarity to the situation. The town's doctors unanimously diagnosed him as having been in a delirious state for several days prior to his arrest. This explained not only his erratic behavior but also his seemingly calculated cunning, as it was now clear that his mental faculties had been compromised. The explanation shocked the townspeople, who had been all too eager to view Nikolay's actions as deliberate malice rather than the result of illness. Even Ivan Ossipovitch, deeply embarrassed by his earlier severity, admitted that he had misjudged the young man.

Nikolay remained bedridden for over two months, during which time a renowned doctor was summoned from Moscow to oversee his recovery. The entire town rallied around Varvara Petrovna, who, in her moment of distress, graciously forgave those who had been quick to condemn her son. By the time spring arrived and Nikolay had fully recovered, he agreed to his mother's suggestion that he embark on a tour of Italy to restore his health and reputation.

Before his departure, however, Nikolay surprised everyone by agreeing to pay farewell visits to the town's leading figures, offering apologies where necessary. His meeting with Pyotr Pavlovitch Gaganov, in particular, was described as remarkably tactful, with Gaganov reportedly leaving the encounter feeling satisfied and even reconciled. Nevertheless, there was a palpable sense of relief among the townspeople when Nikolay finally departed. While some remained skeptical of the brain fever diagnosis, suspecting that the entire episode had been an elaborate ruse, most were content to see him leave without further incident.

Even Liputin received a farewell visit, though what passed between the two men remained a mystery. It was clear, however, that Nikolay's departure left a lingering unease in the hearts of those who had crossed paths with him, as though his presence had been a storm cloud finally swept away, but one that might return unexpectedly on another wind.

"Tell me," Nikolay Vsyevolodovitch said, fixing his gaze sharply on Liputin, "how on earth did you manage to guess beforehand what I would say about your 'sense' and prepare Agafya with such an answer?"

Liputin chuckled slyly, leaning back as though savoring the moment. "Ah, it's simple," he said. "I recognised that you're a clever man, and so I anticipated how you'd respond. It wasn't hard to predict your words."

"A remarkable coincidence, nonetheless," Nikolay remarked, his expression unreadable. Then, his eyes narrowed slightly. "But, forgive me, did you honestly consider me a sensible man, and not out of my mind, when you sent Agafya with your little message?"

"For the cleverest and most rational of men," Liputin answered with a grin. "I only pretended to believe that you were insane. And you, being clever yourself, understood my intention at once and sent me a compliment on my wit through Agafya."

"Well, there you're slightly mistaken," Nikolay said, his tone growing cooler. "I truly was … unwell," he added after a pause, his brow furrowing. Then, suddenly, with a burst of energy, he exclaimed, "Bah! Do you seriously think I would attack people like that if I were in my right mind? What possible reason would I have?"

Liputin hesitated, visibly shrinking into himself. His previous smugness dissolved as he struggled to find an adequate response. Nikolay's face seemed to pale—at least, so it appeared to Liputin.

"You have a rather peculiar way of interpreting things," Nikolay continued, his voice laced with both irritation and a faint amusement. "But as for Agafya, I see clearly now that you simply sent her to insult me."

Liputin straightened slightly in his chair, a nervous smile playing on his lips. "Well, I couldn't exactly challenge you to a duel, could I?"

Nikolay raised an eyebrow, his expression sardonic. "Oh no, of course not. And yet, if I'm not mistaken, I've heard you're not particularly fond of duels to begin with?"

"Why borrow such customs from the French?" Liputin retorted, hunching over as if deflecting a blow.

"Ah, I see. You're a nationalist, then?" Nikolay inquired, his voice dripping with mock curiosity.

Liputin shrank further into himself, his posture almost defensive now.

"Bah, bah! What's this I see here?" Nikolay exclaimed suddenly, his eyes lighting upon a conspicuous volume lying on the table. He picked it up and tapped the cover lightly with his finger. "Considérant? You're not trying to tell me you're a Fourierist, are you? Surely not! And yet," he added with a laugh, "isn't this too a case of borrowing from the French?"

Liputin leapt up from his chair, his face flushed with fury. "That is not borrowed from the French!" he cried, his voice quivering with passion.

"That comes from the universal language of humanity! From the language of the future, of the universal social republic, the harmony of all mankind—not simply the French, let me tell you!"

Nikolay burst out laughing. "Foo! Nonsense! There's no such thing as a universal language," he said dismissively, waving his hand as though brushing away an insect.

For a moment, an awkward silence fell over the room. Sometimes, a trivial exchange can stick in one's mind long after it has passed, and so it was with this peculiar interaction. Though much of what occurred during Nikolay's stay in town would later fade into broader narratives, this encounter with Liputin remained vividly etched in his memory.

What stood out to him was not merely the oddity of the interaction but Liputin himself—the unsightly, almost pitiful figure of this provincial bureaucrat. Liputin, a miserly man who hoarded scraps from dinner, was the embodiment of contradictions. A domestic tyrant and jealous despot within his household, he was, at the same time, utterly consumed by fantastical dreams of a future "social harmony." Nikolay could scarcely fathom the absurdity of a man who, in his modest home—bought with years of penny-pinching and secured through a second marriage to a dowried wife—would sit up late into the night poring over visions of utopian phalansteries. Liputin believed fervently in the coming of a universal republic, convinced it would somehow take root even in their isolated province.

And yet, Nikolay reflected with bemusement, for miles around there was not a single soul, including Liputin himself, who seemed remotely capable of embodying such lofty ideals. It was as though Liputin's faith in the future was entirely at odds with his own character and surroundings.

"God only knows how such people even exist," Nikolay mused to himself more than once, recalling the peculiar little Fourierist who, despite his absurdities, had left such a curious impression on him.

Chapter 2.4

Our prince spent over three years traveling abroad, and during that time, he was almost forgotten in our town. Stepan Trofimovitch occasionally shared updates, informing us that Nikolay Vsyevolodovitch had traveled extensively across Europe, ventured into Egypt, and even visited Jerusalem. Remarkably, he had also joined a scientific expedition to Iceland, actually setting foot on that distant land. It was said that he spent one winter attending lectures at a German university. His letters to his mother were rare, arriving only twice a year, if that. Yet, Varvara Petrovna bore no resentment over this infrequency. She accepted, with quiet resignation, the distant and reserved relationship her son had established with her.

She fretted in silence for her "Nicolas," longing for him and dreaming of him constantly, though she kept her worries to herself. She seemed to withdraw even from Stepan Trofimovitch, who had long been her confidant. At the same time, she appeared to grow increasingly thrifty, paying closer attention to her finances and growing visibly irritated by Stepan Trofimovitch's occasional losses at cards. Her demeanor hinted at some secret schemes she was carefully cultivating, though she shared nothing of these plans with others.

In April of this year, a letter arrived from Paris, written by Praskovya Ivanovna Drozdov, the widow of a general and a childhood friend of Varvara Petrovna. The two women had not corresponded for eight years, and the letter came as something of a surprise. Praskovya Ivanovna wrote to inform Varvara Petrovna that Nikolay Vsyevolodovitch had become a close acquaintance of her family and a great friend of her only daughter, Liza. Moreover, he was planning to accompany the Drozdovs to Switzerland, specifically to Verney-Montreux. The letter also mentioned that Nikolay was spending considerable time with the household of Count K., a prominent and influential figure from Petersburg who was then residing in Paris. He had become such a frequent visitor to the count's home that he was treated almost as a member of the family.

The letter, though brief and written in a neutral tone, conveyed an unspoken message that Varvara Petrovna understood immediately. It was clear that her son's connection with the Drozdovs and his apparent intimacy with Liza carried significant implications. Without wasting time on deliberation, she made up her mind at once. Acting swiftly, she began her preparations and, accompanied by her protégée, Dasha (Shatov's sister), set off for Paris in the middle of April. After a brief stay in the French capital, she traveled onward to Switzerland to join the Drozdovs at Verney-Montreux.

By July, Varvara Petrovna had returned alone, leaving Dasha behind to remain with the Drozdovs. Upon her return, she brought the news that the Drozdovs intended to visit our province by the end of August. This announcement created a stir in our little town, as the Drozdovs, though landowners in the region, had never actually visited their estate due to General Ivan Ivanovitch Drozdov's official duties, which had kept him elsewhere. His death the previous year had left the widow inconsolable, and she had traveled abroad with her daughter, partly to distract herself and partly to undergo the grape cure at Verney-Montreux, a treatment they intended to pursue during the latter half of the summer. Their plan upon returning to Russia was to settle permanently in our province.

The Drozdovs were people of considerable means. They owned a large house in the town that had been sitting unused for years, its windows boarded up. Praskovya Ivanovna, like Varvara Petrovna, came from a wealthy family. Her first marriage had been to a retired cavalry captain, Tushin, who was both affluent and capable. When he passed away, he left a substantial inheritance to their only daughter, Liza, who was just seven at the time. Now, at twenty-two, Lizaveta Nikolaevna's private fortune was estimated at 200,000 roubles, not including the family estate, which she would inherit upon her mother's death, as there were no children from Praskovya Ivanovna's second marriage.

Varvara Petrovna returned from her journey visibly satisfied. She seemed pleased with what she described as a successful understanding with Praskovya Ivanovna. Upon her arrival, she was unusually candid with Stepan Trofimovitch, confiding all the details of her trip to him in a burst of uncharacteristic openness. For the first time in years, she appeared effusive in his presence.

"Hurrah!" Stepan Trofimovitch exclaimed, snapping his fingers in delight as though he were sharing in her triumph.

He was utterly enraptured, almost childishly so, as he had spent the entire duration of Varvara Petrovna's absence in a state of profound gloom. When she departed, she had not even properly bid him farewell, nor did she share her plans with "that old woman," as she sometimes called him—likely out of fear that he might chatter about them, betraying her intentions inadvertently. At the time, she was particularly cross with him because of a substantial gambling debt she had discovered unexpectedly. However, before she left Switzerland, she resolved that upon her return, she must make amends for neglecting her old and loyal friend, especially since she had been rather curt with him for an extended period.

Her sudden and mysterious departure had left a deep wound in Stepan Trofimovitch's timid and sensitive heart, and to make matters worse, he was burdened with other personal troubles. A significant financial obligation had been hanging over him for some time—one he had no hope of addressing without Varvara Petrovna's intervention. Adding to his anxiety, the term of office of our gentle and much-loved governor, Ivan Ossipovitch, had come to an end in May of that year under less-than-pleasant circumstances. This marked the arrival of our new governor, Andrey Antonovitch von Lembke, a change that brought an immediate shift in the attitudes of many in our provincial society towards Varvara Petrovna, and by extension, towards Stepan Trofimovitch.

He began noticing subtle but unmistakable signs of social alienation. Certain ladies of standing, who had once been regular visitors to Varvara Petrovna's home, now appeared to distance themselves, their calls growing infrequent or stopping altogether. To make matters worse, he developed a troubling suspicion that he had already been mentioned to the new governor as a potentially dangerous figure—an intellectual "disturber of the peace." Rumors circulated that the governor's wife, who was expected to arrive in the autumn, was an aristocrat of formidable pride. She was said to be "nothing like poor Varvara Petrovna," as one unkind whisper had it. It was widely reported, and taken as fact, that Madame von Lembke and Varvara Petrovna had previously met in society and parted as bitter enemies. The mere mention of Madame von Lembke's name, it was said, caused visible discomfort to Varvara Petrovna.

Yet when Varvara Petrovna returned, her confident and composed demeanor, coupled with her apparent indifference to the gossip of local society, acted as a balm to Stepan Trofimovitch's wounded spirits. Her return revitalized him, lifting the weight of his apprehensions. She seemed utterly unbothered by the shifting social tides, meeting them with the kind of disdainful superiority that had always been her hallmark. This newfound confidence emboldened Stepan Trofimovitch, who now took to describing the new governor's arrival with a peculiar mix of glee and obsequious humor.

"You've no doubt heard, excellente amie," he began with a coquettish drawl, "what is meant by a Russian administrator in general terms, and more specifically, what it means to have a newly-minted, freshly-appointed Russian administrator. Ah, ces interminables mots Russes! But I dare say you've never experienced firsthand what I call administrative ardor."

"Administrative ardor? I've no idea what that is," she replied, narrowing her eyes.

"Well, you see, here in our great land… In short, take the most insignificant functionary, a mere clerk selling railway tickets, and you'll find he immediately adopts the air of a Jupiter Olympian, basking in the glory of his power. 'Now then,' he seems to say, 'I'll show you my authority.' This pompous zeal, this eagerness to flaunt their little shred of power—it's what I mean by administrative ardor. I once read an amusing account of a verger in a Russian church abroad. Imagine this: a distinguished English family, les dames charmantes, were literally driven out of the church before a Lenten service began, simply because the verger deemed them foreigners who shouldn't be loitering. He actually shouted at them, declaring they must wait for the proper time to enter, and sent the poor souls into fainting fits! That verger, I assure you, was a victim of administrative ardor."

"Cut it short if you can, Stepan Trofimovitch," Varvara Petrovna interjected impatiently.

"Well, as I was saying, this Andrey Antonovitch, our new governor, is making a grand tour of the province. A remarkable figure—russified

German, Orthodox by persuasion, and quite a handsome man in his own way, about forty—"

"What nonsense!" she interrupted. "He has eyes like a sheep's."

"Indeed? Yet our local ladies seem to think otherwise," Stepan Trofimovitch replied with mock surrender. "But let's not quibble over aesthetics. What I meant to convey is that he is one of those late-blooming administrators who rise to prominence after forty. Up until now, he's lived in obscurity, stagnating in some insignificant post, until suddenly acquiring a wife or some other desperate means of elevation. He's off touring the province now, but not without first making inquiries about me. I've been informed that certain individuals—ladies among them—have been whispering in his ears that I am a corrupter of youth and the epicenter of provincial atheism."

"Is that so?" she asked, her irritation growing.

"Oh yes," he said with an exaggerated shrug. "And when he was informed, excellente amie, that you were rumored to 'rule the province,' he reportedly said, 'There shall be none of that in the future.' Imagine that!"

"Did he truly say that?" Varvara Petrovna demanded, her tone sharp and cutting.

"Word for word, with all the hauteur one might expect. His wife, Yulia Mihailovna, will be arriving soon—at the end of August, straight from Petersburg."

"From abroad. We met there," she added coolly. "In Paris and in Switzerland. She's related to the Drozdovs."

"Vraiment?" Stepan Trofimovitch exclaimed, clearly taken aback.

His intrigue over this connection with the Drozdovs did not go unnoticed by Varvara Petrovna, though she merely gave a faint, enigmatic smile in response.

"Related! What an extraordinary coincidence! They say she is ambitious and supposedly has great connections," said Stepan Trofimovitch, his tone tinged with intrigue.

"Nonsense! Connections indeed!" Varvara Petrovna snapped. "She was a penniless old maid until she turned forty-five. Now that she's snagged her Von Lembke, her sole objective is to push him forward, to elevate him beyond his means. They're both nothing more than petty intriguers."

"And they say she's two years older than he is?" he asked, eyebrows raised in mild disbelief.

"Five years older, at least. Her mother used to wear out the hems of her skirts begging for invitations to our balls in Moscow when my husband was alive. Can you imagine? And as for this woman—oh, she would sit there all night, planted in some dim corner with her turquoise fly perched on her forehead. Out of sheer pity, I would have to send her a dance partner well past midnight just to save her from humiliation. She was twenty-five at the time but dressed in skirts so short they made her look like a schoolgirl. By the end, it was improper to have them in the house."

"I think I can see that turquoise fly," Stepan Trofimovitch said with a chuckle.

"Mark my words, the moment I arrived, I found myself smack in the middle of an intrigue!" Varvara Petrovna declared, her tone sharp with frustration. "You read Madame Drozdov's letter, didn't you? Could anything be clearer? Yet what did I find when I got there? Praskovya herself—always a fool—looking at me as though to ask why I had even come! Can you imagine my shock? Then there was that Von Lembke woman, flitting about with her schemes, and Drozdov's nephew—an old crony dragged into the drama. It was all so transparent. Of course, I put a stop to all of it in no time, and now Praskovya is back on my side, but what a mess!"

"And as always, you emerged the victor. Bismarck in petticoats!" Stepan Trofimovitch quipped, laughing.

"Bismarck! I hardly need to be Bismarck to cut through stupidity and falseness," she retorted with a derisive snort. "Especially when it's Praskovya's brand of folly! Do you know her legs are swollen now? She's a fool through and through—a simpleton with a good heart, which is the worst kind of fool there is."

"I must respectfully disagree, ma bonne amie. A spiteful fool is far worse," Stepan Trofimovitch replied with exaggerated magnanimity.

"Perhaps you're right," she conceded, her tone softening slightly. "But do you remember Liza?"

"Charmante enfant!" he exclaimed with genuine warmth.

"Not an enfant anymore, but a woman now—a woman of character, no less," Varvara Petrovna continued, her voice carrying a hint of pride. "She's passionate and generous, but what I truly admire is how she stands up to her insipid mother. Why, they nearly came to blows over that ridiculous cousin!"

"Ah, and surely he's no relation of Lizaveta Nikolaevna?" Stepan Trofimovitch ventured.

"None at all!" she confirmed. "He's just some young officer—not talkative, modest even. To be fair, I believe he himself isn't part of the scheming and probably wants no part of it. No, the real villain here is that wretched Von Lembke woman. As for Liza, it's entirely up to her. But I left her on excellent terms with Nicolas, and he promised to join us in November. So, as far as I'm concerned, it's all under control—for now."

"And Praskovya?" Stepan Trofimovitch pressed.

"She's blind to it all! At one point, she even had the nerve to tell me that my suspicions were baseless. I told her outright she was a fool. I'm ready to repeat it before the judgment seat of God. If it weren't for Nicolas pleading with me to let it rest, I wouldn't have left without exposing that Von Lembke woman for the snake she is. She's trying to curry favor with Count K. through Nicolas, to worm her way between mother and son. But Liza is firmly on our side, and Praskovya will follow wherever I lead her."

"And Karmazinov? Is he truly a relation of Madame von Lembke?" Stepan Trofimovitch asked, eyebrows arching with curiosity.

"Yes, distantly," Varvara Petrovna confirmed with a hint of disdain.

"And don't look so surprised. It's not as if he's royalty, despite what he seems to think of himself. That pompous creature is coming here with her. She's already started fawning over him in Paris. Mark my words, she has it in her head to establish some kind of literary society here. Karmazinov, of course, will come to bask in the attention while pretending he's above it all. He's even selling his last bit of property here. I narrowly avoided meeting him in Switzerland and thanked God for it. Though I suppose he'll deign to acknowledge me when he arrives. After all, he used to send me letters in the old days, and he's been a guest in my house."

She paused, her gaze narrowing as she looked him over. "And you—just look at you! You're growing slovenlier by the day. What are you reading now?"

Caught off guard, Stepan Trofimovitch stammered, "I… I…"

"It's the same as ever, isn't it?" she cut in sharply. "Drinking, gossip, the club, cards, and priding yourself on your reputation as an atheist. I've never liked that, Stepan Trofimovitch. It's nothing but empty chatter. It's time someone told you."

"Ma chère…" he began, but she waved him off.

"Listen, I've been thinking a great deal about you during my travels. I've come to a conclusion."

"And what conclusion might that be?" he asked, leaning forward.

"That you and I are not the wisest people in the world," she said flatly, "and that there are people far wiser than us."

"Touché," Stepan Trofimovitch replied, smiling faintly. "If there are wiser people, then there are also those who are more right, and thus we may be mistaken. Is that your point?"

"Precisely. And perhaps it's time you stopped wasting yourself. I expect better from you, especially now that we're dealing with these Von Lembkes and Karmazinovs. My goodness, Stepan Trofimovitch, how you torment me with your idleness!"

Her words stung, and though Stepan Trofimovitch maintained his composure, he withdrew deeply troubled.

Chapter 2.5

Our poor friend had undeniably slipped into a number of bad habits, and these had only worsened of late. It was apparent to all that he was declining both in his demeanor and general comportment. His once-prized elegance had given way to a kind of careless slovenliness. He was drinking more heavily, which had the predictable effect of making him more emotional, more nervous, and far more prone to sudden tears. His artistic sensitivity—once a point of pride—had grown excessive, leaving him vulnerable to even the smallest affront or slightest change in mood. His face, once so dignified, had developed a peculiar ability to shift rapidly from solemn gravitas to the utterly ridiculous. A serious conversation might suddenly veer into something absurd, simply because his expressions could no longer keep pace with the thoughts behind them.

Solitude, once tolerable to him, had become his greatest enemy. He now seemed unable to endure being alone, constantly seeking distraction or company. His thirst for novelty was almost insatiable; every day, someone had to bring him a new story, a fresh piece of gossip, or a juicy local anecdote. Without these small entertainments, he would grow despondent, pacing aimlessly through the rooms of his house like a restless ghost. He would pause at the window, pucker his lips, sigh deeply, and look as though he were about to weep. He was gripped by endless forebodings, haunted by a vague fear of the unexpected, and had developed a troubling timidity. Even his dreams became a source of fixation, as he tried to divine their meaning in search of the doom he was sure was lurking.

That particular day, he was more agitated than usual, a bundle of nerves teetering on the edge of despair. He sent for me, desperate for company, and poured out his thoughts in a torrent of disconnected complaints. Varvara Petrovna had long been aware of how much he confided in me; indeed, he held nothing back. As I sat with him, it became increasingly clear that there was some deeper trouble gnawing at him, something he could not quite articulate even to himself.

Normally, our tête-à-tête conversations would eventually ease into a kind of comfortable rhythm, helped along by the appearance of a bottle of wine. But this time, there was no wine. I could see he was wrestling with himself, resisting the urge to send for it. His agitation simmered, spilling over in childlike complaints, punctuated by dramatic exclamations.

"Why is she always so cross?" he muttered, his voice a mix of petulance and weariness. "Tous les hommes de génie et de progrès en Russie étaient, sont, et seront toujours des gamblers et des drunkards qui boivent in outbreaks.... And yet I am neither! Not truly! I'm not such a gambler, and I'm not such a drunkard! And still, she reproaches me for not writing! Can you imagine? Writing! As though inspiration flows on command! And then—then she demands to know why I lie down! 'You must stand,' she says. 'Stand as an example and reproach.' But, tell me, mon cher, what is a man destined to stand as a 'reproach' supposed to do if not lie down from time to time? Does she think about that?"

He gestured dramatically, his hands trembling slightly, his words teetering between bitterness and self-pity. It was during this conversation that I began to piece together the real source of his turmoil, the particular fear that had been gnawing at him. Several times during our talk, he wandered over to the looking-glass, lingering before it longer than usual. He would study his reflection in silence, the corners of his mouth twitching as though he were fighting some unbearable thought. At last, he turned away from the mirror, his shoulders slumped, and looked at me with a strange expression of despair.

"Mon cher," he said with a faint, almost bitter smile, "je suis un broken-down man."

The words hung in the air, heavy with resignation. Up to that moment, I realized, there had been one belief—one unshakable conviction—that had sustained him through all the changes and challenges of the past twenty years. No matter what shifts occurred in Varvara Petrovna's moods or ideas, no matter how the "new views" swept through society, he had always clung to the comforting notion that he still held some special power over her heart. Not merely as an exiled intellectual, not even as a man of celebrated learning, but as a man. A handsome man.

This belief had been a quiet foundation of his self-esteem, a source of pride and solace. For two decades, it had remained untouched, unchallenged, a soothing constant in a sea of uncertainties. And now, as he stood before the mirror that evening, it seemed that even this fragile belief was beginning to crumble. Was it his appearance that betrayed him? The lines on his face, the slight stoop in his posture? Or was it something more, a deeper awareness that whatever fascination he once held had long since faded?

I could not help but wonder if he sensed, on some unconscious level, the colossal ordeal that awaited him—an ordeal that would soon shatter whatever illusions he still clung to. For now, he clung to the mirror, to his own reflection, as though searching for a vestige of the man he once believed himself to be. But in his eyes, I saw only the flicker of doubt and the weight of inevitable loss.

Chapter 2.6

I will now turn to describing that nearly forgotten incident which serves as the proper beginning of this story.

At the very end of August, the long-anticipated return of the Drozdovs finally took place, causing quite a stir in our small provincial society. Their arrival was just ahead of another noteworthy event—the appearance of our new governor's wife. Both occasions created considerable excitement, but I shall speak of these developments in their due place. For now, it is enough to note that Praskovya Ivanovna brought with her not the clarity and resolution Varvara Petrovna had been so impatiently awaiting, but instead a fresh and deeply perplexing conundrum.

The news was this: Nikolay Vsyevolodovitch had parted ways with the Drozdovs in July, and after encountering Count K. and his family along the Rhine, he had joined their company and set off with them to Petersburg. (It should be noted that the Count had three daughters, all of them of marriageable age.)

"Lizaveta is so proud and obstinate that I could get nothing out of her," Praskovya Ivanovna confessed with an air of frustration. "But I could see for myself that something had happened between her and Nikolay Vsyevolodovitch. I can't tell you precisely what, but it was clear to me that your Darya Pavlovna might know more about it than I do. In my opinion, Liza was offended. And you know what? I'm glad! At least I've done my duty and brought back your favorite—she's your responsibility now. It's a weight off my mind!"

These barbed words were spoken with a tone so sharp and venomous that it seemed she had rehearsed them, savoring in advance the effect they might have on Varvara Petrovna. But the latter, with her usual self-command and disdain for emotional theatrics, was unshaken. She demanded clear and precise explanations.

This challenge, however, quickly overwhelmed Praskovya Ivanovna's defensive stance. Her irritable façade dissolved almost instantly, and she soon found herself retreating into a flood of tears and effusive declarations of friendship. A woman prone to sentimentality, much like Stepan Trofimovitch, she had an endless longing for "true friendship" and often lamented that her daughter, Lizaveta Nikolaevna, failed to be the companion she yearned for.

Yet, despite her tears and explanations, the entire situation remained frustratingly opaque. There had undoubtedly been some quarrel between Nikolay and Liza, but its nature was unclear. It was evident that Praskovya Ivanovna herself didn't fully grasp what had happened. Her earlier insinuations about Darya Pavlovna, too, were hastily withdrawn. She even begged Varvara Petrovna to disregard those accusations, claiming they were spoken in a moment of irritation.

Still, her account left much to be desired. According to her, the quarrel was rooted in Liza's "ironical and headstrong character." Nikolay Vsyevolodovitch, proud as he was, had found Liza's sarcasm intolerable. In retaliation, he had resorted to sarcasm himself, and their disagreements escalated from there. Matters were further complicated by the arrival of a young man—a certain connection of Stepan Trofimovitch.

"Was he the nephew of the 'Professor'?" Praskovya Ivanovna asked vaguely.

"The son, not the nephew," Varvara Petrovna corrected her firmly.

Even in their earlier acquaintanceship, Praskovya Ivanovna had displayed a singular inability to recall Stepan Trofimovitch's name, always referring to him vaguely as "the Professor."

"Well, his son, then—it hardly matters to me," Praskovya continued with a dismissive wave. "A rather ordinary young fellow, lively and free in his manners, but not particularly remarkable. Liza made friends with him, though—clearly with the aim of provoking Nikolay Vsyevolodovitch. Girls are like that; it's natural enough, even charming in a way. But instead of being jealous, Nikolay Vsyevolodovitch made friends with the young man himself, acting as if he didn't notice or didn't care. That drove Liza to distraction.

"After the young man left, she began picking quarrels with Nikolay at every opportunity. She even got worked up over the fact that he occasionally spoke with Dasha. You can imagine what my life was like during all this! The doctors had forbidden me to get agitated, yet I was constantly on edge. And that cursed lake everyone makes such a fuss about—it was unbearable! It gave me toothaches and rheumatism. They even say in the guidebooks that Lake Geneva has that effect on people!"

Praskovya's grievances came in a torrent, but her account of the events at Geneva remained muddled. She claimed that Nikolay received a letter from the Countess and abruptly decided to leave, packing his things in a single day. He parted from the Drozdovs on friendly terms, and Liza, she said, put on a show of cheerfulness and frivolity, laughing and joking as though nothing were wrong. But it was clear that her gaiety was a façade. Once Nikolay was gone, Liza grew pensive and stopped speaking of him altogether, refusing even to let her mother mention his name.

"My advice, dear Varvara Petrovna," Praskovya concluded, "is to say nothing to Liza about Nikolay for the time being. If you keep silent, she might bring it up herself, and then you'll learn more. I believe there's still hope for them—if only Nikolay doesn't delay his return as he promised."

These words were spoken with an air of triumph, as though Praskovya had finally managed to navigate the tangled web of intrigues surrounding her daughter and Nikolay. But Varvara Petrovna, for all her composure, found the entire situation deeply troubling. It was clear that something significant had taken place, and whatever it was, it threatened to unravel the carefully constructed plans she had been nurturing for so long.

"I'll write to him immediately. If that's all there is to it, then the quarrel was trivial nonsense! And as for Darya, I know her too well. It's all nonsense!" declared Varvara Petrovna firmly, though her tone betrayed a hint of residual doubt.

Praskovya Ivanovna was quick to respond. "I regret what I said about Dashenka. It was wrong of me. Their conversations were perfectly ordinary, spoken out loud, with nothing suspicious about them. It's just that everything upset me so much at the time, dear. And I saw for myself that Liza and Dasha were as affectionate with each other again as they had always been."

That very day, Varvara Petrovna penned a letter to Nikolay, urging him to come home at least a month earlier than planned. Yet even as she put her thoughts to paper, a lingering unease crept into her mind. Despite Praskovya's reassurances, Varvara Petrovna felt certain that some piece of the puzzle was missing.

All evening and into the night, she turned the matter over in her mind. Praskovya's perspective struck her as overly innocent, even sentimental—qualities that had marked her since their school days. "Praskovya has always been too naive," Varvara thought with a frown. "Nicolas is not the sort of man to flee from a girl's taunts. There must be another reason behind this, assuming there was truly any breach at all. And then there's that officer—they've brought him back with them, and he's living in their house. And as for Darya, Praskovya backtracked far too quickly in her apology. There's something she's holding back, something she wouldn't tell me outright."

By the next morning, Varvara Petrovna had settled on a bold and unexpected course of action—one that would put to rest at least one source of confusion. The idea was as startling as it was audacious, and it's difficult to say what drove her to it. Her heart, her pride, her sharp intellect—each might have played a part in this curious decision. Yet as a chronicler, I can only record events as they happened, without venturing too far into their motives.

That morning, any lingering suspicion of Darya had vanished from Varvara Petrovna's mind. In truth, such doubts had never fully taken root; she trusted Dasha too deeply. More than that, she couldn't imagine her "Nicolas" being romantically drawn to someone like Darya.

When morning tea was served, Varvara Petrovna observed Dasha with quiet intensity. For perhaps the twentieth time since yesterday, she reassured herself: "It's all nonsense!"

Still, she couldn't help but notice that Dasha seemed more fatigued than usual. Her manner was quieter, more subdued, and tinged with a certain apathy that Varvara had not seen before.

As was their custom, they settled down after tea to work on embroidery. Varvara began asking Dasha about her impressions of the trip abroad—her thoughts on the scenery, the local customs, the architecture, and even the commerce. She seemed intent on hearing about everything Dasha might have observed. Conspicuously, she asked no questions about the Drozdovs or Dasha's interactions with them.

Dasha spoke evenly and monotonously for half an hour, her voice steady yet faint.

"Darya," Varvara Petrovna interrupted abruptly, setting down her embroidery. "Is there nothing special you want to tell me?"

Dasha paused, considering the question. Finally, she replied, "No, nothing." Her light-colored eyes met Varvara's with a calm, almost defiant gaze.

"Nothing weighing on your soul, your heart, or your conscience?"

"Nothing," Dasha repeated, her tone firm but unruffled.

"I knew there wasn't," Varvara Petrovna said, her voice softening. "Believe me, Darya, I shall never doubt you." She leaned back in her chair and fixed her protégée with a searching look. "Now, sit still. Right there, in that chair. I want to see all of you. That's it. Listen to me carefully."

Dasha obeyed without a word, her expression a mixture of curiosity

71

and resignation.

"Tell me, do you want to get married?"

Dasha looked at her with wide, questioning eyes, though she didn't seem especially shocked by the question.

"Wait—don't speak," Varvara Petrovna said sharply. "In the first place, there's a considerable difference in age, but you're a sensible girl, and you understand that such things don't matter. Your life must not be wasted or marred by foolish mistakes. He's still a handsome man, after all. I'm talking, of course, about Stepan Trofimovitch. You've always held him in such respect. Well?"

Dasha's expression grew even more curious, tinged now with something like disbelief. A faint blush crept across her pale cheeks.

"Stop. Don't rush to speak yet," Varvara continued, waving a hand to silence her. "Let me finish. Even though I've ensured you'll have money under my will, you must think about what will become of you when I'm gone. You could be deceived, taken advantage of, robbed blind. But if you marry him, you'll have security. You'll be the wife of a distinguished man."

She paused for a moment, studying Dasha's reaction before pressing on.

"And then, look at him. Even though I've provided for him, what would become of him without me? He's frivolous, self-indulgent, and far too emotional, but he's also helpless, pitiable. He doesn't deserve to be loved in the way a woman loves a man, but he deserves to be cared for because of his helplessness. You must love him for that, do you understand me? For his helplessness!"

Dasha nodded faintly but said nothing.

"Why don't you say something?" Varvara Petrovna demanded irritably. "Well?"

Still, Dasha remained silent, her hands folded neatly in her lap, her head slightly bowed.

"You think I'm handing you off to some scoundrel?" Varvara pressed. "Is that what you think? That I want to be rid of you? You're wrong! I'm

72

asking you to do this because it's the right thing for both of you. He needs you. And whether you know it or not, you need him, too."

Dasha nodded again, her blush deepening. Her quiet, composed demeanor remained unshaken, but there was something in her stillness—something beyond mere obedience—that left Varvara Petrovna momentarily unsettled.

"I knew you would agree. I expected no less of you," Varvara Petrovna exclaimed, her voice rising with a peculiar mix of triumph and irritation. "He will love you, not just because he ought to, but because he simply must. And let me tell you, he will adore you. I know him, Dasha. And another thing—I'll always be here. You can be sure of that. Always. He'll complain about you, of course, whisper things behind your back to whoever will listen, grumble endlessly, and he'll write letters—oh, he'll write you two letters a day from one room to another. But none of that will matter because, in the end, he won't be able to live without you, and that's what truly counts."

Her tone shifted, becoming both exasperated and insistent. "Make him obey you, Dasha. If you can't make him obey, you'll be a fool. And mark my words—he'll threaten to hang himself. He'll moan about it, but don't believe it for a second. It's all nonsense. Still, don't push him too far. Weak people, Dasha—yes, weak people—are the ones who actually do it. That's the first rule of married life: never drive him to an extreme. Remember, too, that he's a poet, and poets are always fragile."

She paused, catching her breath, then leaned closer as if confiding a great secret. "Listen to me, Dasha, there's no greater happiness than self-sacrifice. None. You'll see. And, besides, you'll be giving me immense satisfaction, and if nothing else, that's the most important thing of all. Don't think I'm rambling. I know exactly what I'm saying. I may be selfish, but you must learn to be selfish, too. Of course, I'm not forcing you—it's entirely your choice. As you decide, so it shall be. Well? Why are we sitting here like this? Speak!"

Dasha raised her head and said firmly, "I don't mind, Varvara Petrovna, if I really must be married."

"Must?" Varvara Petrovna's eyes narrowed sharply as she studied the girl's face. "What do you mean by that? What are you hinting at?"

Dasha remained silent, her fingers fiddling with the embroidery canvas in her lap.

"Though you're a clever girl, you're talking nonsense. Yes, I've certainly set my heart on marrying you off, but not because it's necessary. This is about Stepan Trofimovitch—only Stepan Trofimovitch. If it weren't for him, I wouldn't even think of marrying you yet. You're only twenty, after all." She paused, her sharp gaze fixed on Dasha's face. "Well?"

"I'll do as you wish, Varvara Petrovna," Dasha replied quietly but with a firmness that didn't waver.

"Then you consent! But wait—don't rush to agree just yet. I haven't finished. In my will, I've left you fifteen thousand roubles. I'll give it to you immediately, on your wedding day. Of that, you'll hand over eight thousand to him—or rather, to me. It will go toward settling his debt, but he'll need to know it was your money that paid it. The remaining seven thousand will stay with you. Guard it, Dasha. Never let him touch a kopeck of it. Don't even think of paying his debts—if you start, you'll never stop. Understand?"

She straightened in her chair, her tone becoming more commanding. "And don't worry about money. I'll give you twelve hundred roubles a year, with some extras, which will come to fifteen hundred altogether. Plus, board and lodging will remain at my expense, just as it is now. But you'll need to hire your own servants. And listen carefully—his friends may visit once a week. No more than that. If they show up more often, throw them out. Do you hear me?"

Dasha nodded again, her hands still as she listened intently.

"If I die," Varvara continued, "your pension will continue until his death—it's his pension, after all, not yours. And don't forget about the seven thousand you'll have now, which you ought to save carefully. I've also left you another eight thousand in my will. You won't get more than that from me, so you should know where you stand." She paused and leaned forward. "Now, do you consent or not? Say something, will you?"

"I've already told you, Varvara Petrovna," Dasha answered, her tone steady.

"Remember, this is entirely your decision. If you agree, it's because you've chosen it for yourself."

Dasha hesitated, then asked, "Has Stepan Trofimovitch been told about this yet?"

"No, he hasn't. He knows nothing, but he'll speak soon enough." With that, Varvara Petrovna abruptly rose, throwing a black shawl over her shoulders. Dasha blushed faintly, her questioning eyes following Varvara's sudden movements.

Varvara turned back to her, her face flushed with anger. "You're a fool!" she burst out. "An ungrateful fool! What's going on in that head of yours? Do you really think I'd compromise you in any way? Do you think I'd let you suffer for even a moment? Stepan Trofimovitch will crawl on his knees to ask for your hand! He'll be delirious with happiness—it'll be arranged just so. And do you suppose I'd let him marry you just for that eight thousand? What nonsense! You think I'm hurrying off to sell you? Foolish, foolish girl!"

Her voice trembled with exasperation as she grabbed her umbrella. "Give me my things. I'm going now. To him!" And with that, she stormed out, heading down the wet brick pavements and wooden planks toward Stepan Trofimovitch's house, leaving Dasha to sit in stunned silence.

Chapter 2.7

It was true that Varvara Petrovna would never have let Dasha suffer; on the contrary, she truly believed she was acting as the young woman's benefactress. As she wrapped her shawl around her shoulders, preparing to leave, her soul was alight with what she considered righteous indignation. She felt an almost moral compulsion to act decisively, and yet, when her eyes met Dasha's—a gaze filled with hesitance and a glimmer of mistrust—it unsettled her. This girl, her protégée, had been under her care and love since childhood. Praskovya Ivanovna had rightly referred to Dasha as Varvara's favorite. Over the years, she had carefully nurtured the belief that Dasha was unlike her brother, Ivan Shatov, whose nature had always seemed volatile and unpredictable. Instead, Dasha embodied quiet gentleness, the capacity for deep self-sacrifice, and an unusual steadfastness. Most importantly, she was reasonable, modest, and filled with gratitude. Until this moment, Dasha had seemed to fulfill every expectation Varvara had set for her.

"Her life will be without mistakes," Varvara Petrovna had once declared when Dasha was only twelve. True to her character, she had fixated on this dream with fervor, as was her habit when seized by an idea she deemed noble or visionary. Determined to educate Dasha as though she were her own daughter, she had made careful arrangements. She hired a governess, Miss Criggs, who stayed with them until Dasha was sixteen, though she was dismissed under mysterious circumstances. French and piano teachers came and went, including a "real Frenchman," whose departure from the household was abrupt and clouded in secrecy. Yet, Dasha's primary tutor was none other than Stepan Trofimovitch.

In fact, it was Stepan Trofimovitch who had first noticed Dasha's potential. He had begun teaching her before Varvara Petrovna had even formulated her plans. Remarkably, children were drawn to him, perhaps because of his own childlike disposition. Years earlier, he had been the tutor of Lizaveta Nikolaevna Tushin, a charming girl who adored his fanciful lectures on the creation of the world, humanity's history, and ancient peoples. Liza would mimic him at home, often to great comedic effect. Yet when Stepan Trofimovitch discovered this, he was so touched that he wept, moved by her affection. With Liza gone, Dasha became his sole pupil. When other teachers arrived, however, his role in her education diminished, and over time, he barely seemed to notice her.

It wasn't until Dasha turned seventeen that Stepan Trofimovitch took note of her blossoming beauty. One day, at Varvara Petrovna's dinner table, he struck up a conversation with her and was enchanted by her thoughtful answers. This rekindled his interest, and he proposed to give her a comprehensive course on Russian literature. Varvara approved enthusiastically, and Dasha seemed eager to begin. Preparations were made, and the first lesson—covering the most ancient period of Russian literature—was a success. But as soon as Stepan Trofimovitch mentioned the next topic, "The Story of the Expedition of Igor," Varvara Petrovna abruptly announced that the lessons would go no further. Stepan Trofimovitch was visibly wounded but said nothing, while Dasha flushed with embarrassment. The plan was abandoned, and the incident faded into the past—until Varvara's current scheme brought it back to light.

Meanwhile, Stepan Trofimovitch was entirely unprepared for the storm heading his way. He sat alone in his rooms, gazing mournfully out the window as drizzle pattered against the panes. The air was damp and chilly, and he sighed, contemplating whether it was time to have the stove lit. No friends had come to visit, and the loneliness pressed heavily on him. Suddenly, his musings were shattered by the sight of Varvara Petrovna, striding purposefully toward his house. She was on foot, in such weather, and at such an unexpected hour! He was so taken aback that he forgot to put on his coat and greeted her in his shabby pink-wadded dressing gown.

"Ma bonne amie!" he gasped faintly, trying to recover his composure.

She swept into the room with an air of authority, immediately wrinkling her nose at the stale, smoky atmosphere. "You're alone. Good. I can't stand your friends. Heavens, what a mess! You haven't even finished your tea, and it's nearly noon. Disorder! Dirt! It's your idea of bliss, isn't it?"

Her tirade continued as she barked orders to Nastasya, the long-suffering servant. She marched Stepan into the drawing room, criticizing the wallpaper and berating him for neglecting to choose a pattern she had previously sent. Finally, she sat him down with a sharp command: "Listen. I've come on a matter of importance. Sit still and pay attention!"

Stepan Trofimovitch, flustered and confused, hurried to the next room to fetch his coat, reappearing with it draped awkwardly over his dressing gown. Varvara regarded him mockingly but wasted no time. She laid out her plan in clear, emphatic terms: Dasha, the dowry, and the eight thousand roubles. Stepan sat trembling, his eyes widening with every word. He listened, but it was as though he couldn't fully grasp what was happening. When he tried to speak, his voice faltered and broke. Yet one thing was abundantly clear: there would be no protests, no refusals. His fate was sealed. He was, for all intents and purposes, a married man already.

"Mais, ma bonne amie! For the third time, and at my age … and to such a child!" Stepan Trofimovitch managed to stammer at last, his voice trembling with desperation. "Mais, c'est une enfant!"

"A child?" Varvara Petrovna snapped, her tone sharp and unyielding. "She's twenty years old, thank God, and well past being a child. Please, for heaven's sake, don't roll your eyes at me like that. You're not on a stage. Yes, you're clever, you're learned, but you've never understood anything about life. You will always need someone to care for you, someone to keep you from falling to pieces. What will happen to you when I'm gone? She will be that someone—your support, your salvation. She's a modest girl, strong-willed, reasonable. And let me remind you, I'm not planning to die tomorrow. I'll be here to see that everything goes as it should."

Her voice rose with emotion as she pressed her case. "She's an angel of gentleness, and I realized it fully while we were in Switzerland. Do you even comprehend what I'm offering you? Do you understand what it means if I, myself, tell you she's an angel?" Her tone reached a furious crescendo. "Your house is filthy; she will bring order to your chaos. Everything will gleam like a mirror! My God, do you expect me to grovel at your feet, to beg you to accept such a treasure? You should be the one on your knees, thanking me! You—shallow, faint-hearted, ridiculous man!"

"But … I'm an old man," he interjected weakly, trying to reclaim some ground in this overwhelming onslaught.

"Old? Fifty-three is not old! Fifty-three is the prime of life, not the end of it. You are a handsome man, and you know it as well as I do. And you're admired, respected. She looks up to you. She reveres you. What do you think will become of her if I'm gone? But married to you, she'll be safe. She'll have security and direction, and I'll have peace of mind knowing she's cared for. And what's more, you'll do her an honor by making her your wife. You'll give her stability and wisdom. You'll guide her, shape her future, and develop her heart. You'll save her."

Her voice softened slightly, shifting from anger to calculated persuasion. "You'll also save yourself, Stepan Trofimovitch. People lose their way these days because their ideas are all wrong. But you—you have the ability to guide her ideas, to ensure she doesn't fall into the traps others do. And what better time? By then, your book will be finished, and people will be talking about you again."

"My book…" he murmured, distracted by the sudden flattery. "Yes, I've been preparing to return to my Tales from Spanish History."

"Exactly. Everything is falling into place." She seized on his momentary vanity with precision. "But what about her? Have you spoken to her?" he asked nervously, as if still clinging to some faint hope of reprieve.

"You needn't concern yourself with that. Of course, you'll need to ask her formally yourself—you must entreat her to do you the honor of becoming your wife. But don't trouble yourself; leave the rest to me. She respects you, admires you, and, yes, she loves you."

At this, Stepan Trofimovitch felt the ground shift beneath him. The room seemed to sway. There was one thought he could not banish, a terrible thought that left him trembling. "Excellente amie," he said in a voice barely above a whisper, his lips quivering. "I never dreamed that you would give me … to another woman."

Varvara Petrovna's face hardened with a mixture of contempt and exasperation. "You're not a girl, Stepan Trofimovitch," she said icily. "Girls are 'given' in marriage. You are a man. You will take a wife."

"Oui, j'ai pris un mot pour un autre. Mais c'est égal," he muttered, gazing at her with a helpless, despondent expression.

"I see it's all the same to you," she said curtly, barely masking her irritation. "Good heavens, are you about to faint? Nastasya! Water!"

But water wasn't necessary. After a moment, Stepan Trofimovitch pulled himself together, though he was visibly shaken. Varvara Petrovna picked up her umbrella with a flourish, preparing to leave. "There's no point in saying more now," she declared sharply.

"Oui, oui, je suis incapable," he muttered, almost incoherent.

"You'll think it over," she continued, her tone commanding. "By tomorrow, you'll have rested, and you'll see things clearly. Stay home and don't entertain any visitors. If something urgent happens, send word to me immediately, even if it's in the middle of the night. And don't bother writing me letters; I won't read them. I'll come again tomorrow at this time, and I expect a final answer—one I trust will be satisfactory. Oh, and make sure the place isn't such a mess. It's not fit for human eyes." She swept out of the room, barking instructions to Nastasya on her way out.

The next day, Stepan Trofimovitch, of course, gave his consent. What else could he do? There was, however, one circumstance ...

Chapter 2.8

Stepan Trofimovitch's estate, as we often called it (a modest property consisting of fifty souls in the old reckoning and bordering on Skvoreshniki), was not actually his. It had belonged to his first wife, and, upon her passing, it had been inherited by his son, Pyotr Stepanovitch Verhovensky. Stepan Trofimovitch remained only a trustee of the property, a role granted by his son through a formal authorization to manage the estate on his behalf. This arrangement proved advantageous for the younger Verhovensky, who received an annual income of one thousand roubles from the estate—a surprising amount given that, under the new economic realities, it could scarcely yield more than five hundred roubles, and perhaps not even that. How this peculiar financial setup had come about was anyone's guess, but it was clear that the entire sum was sent to Pyotr by Varvara Petrovna, bypassing Stepan Trofimovitch entirely. In the meantime, Stepan Trofimovitch kept all the revenue from the land for himself, a situation that allowed him to live comfortably even as he managed the estate poorly.

In fact, his management had been so negligent that the estate had fallen into a state of disrepair. He had leased it to a dishonest middleman who exploited its resources ruthlessly, and, without Varvara Petrovna's knowledge, he had sold off the estate's timber—the property's most valuable asset. Piece by piece, the woods were sold for a total of five thousand roubles, despite being worth at least eight thousand. Much of this money had been lost to Stepan Trofimovitch's gambling habit, particularly at the club, and he had been too afraid of Varvara Petrovna's wrath to ask her for funds to cover his losses. When she eventually learned of the situation, her fury was palpable, though she managed to contain it.

Matters took a sudden turn when Pyotr announced his intent to return and sell the property outright for whatever he could get. He instructed his father to arrange the sale promptly. This announcement filled Stepan Trofimovitch with a mixture of guilt and dread. As a man of lofty ideals, he was deeply ashamed of how he had handled the estate, especially given that Pyotr was his "dear child" (ce cher enfant), though they hadn't seen each other for nine years, not since Pyotr was a university student in Petersburg. The property, once valued at thirteen or fourteen thousand roubles, was now worth no more than five thousand.

Stepan Trofimovitch, despite his mismanagement, conceived a grand and noble idea: he would somehow gather the maximum sum of fifteen thousand roubles to present to his son upon his return, thus settling their accounts honorably. He imagined an emotional scene in which he would press Pyotr to his heart, tears flowing, and thereby reaffirm their familial bond while demonstrating the magnanimity of his generation in contrast to the crass materialism of the younger one. Stepan Trofimovitch began hinting at this vision to Varvara Petrovna, suggesting that such an act would serve as a poetic culmination of their shared ideals and would elevate their friendship to a new height.

Varvara Petrovna, however, listened in silence. Eventually, she offered her own solution, delivered with an air of finality: she would buy the estate herself and pay what she generously termed its "maximum price," which she estimated at six or seven thousand roubles, even though its fair market value was closer to four thousand. She said nothing about the missing eight thousand lost through the sale of the timber.

This conversation occurred a month before the proposal of Stepan Trofimovitch's marriage to Dasha. Overwhelmed by her decision, he fell into deep reflection. Until then, he had harbored a faint hope that Pyotr might not actually return, though he would have indignantly denied such a hope if confronted. News about Pyotr had always been erratic and unsettling. After completing his university studies six years earlier, Pyotr had lingered in Petersburg without finding work. Rumors soon emerged that he had been involved in distributing a seditious manifesto and was under investigation. He then disappeared abroad, surfacing later in Geneva, presumably having fled Russia to escape prosecution.

"It amazes me," Stepan Trofimovitch confided, visibly distressed, "Petrusha, c'est une si pauvre tête! He's good-hearted, noble even, and terribly sensitive. I admired him when I saw him in Petersburg, especially compared to today's youth. But still, c'est un pauvre sire! All this—this revolutionary nonsense—it comes from their sentimental half-bakedness, their yearning for the poetic side of socialism. It's not realism that draws them in, but the religious, idealistic undertones—the secondhand poetry of it all! And now look at me! I'll be implicated because of him. My enemies here, my enemies there—they'll blame it on me, say it's my influence. Good God, Petrusha a revolutionary? What times we live in!"

Despite his worries, Pyotr's address from Switzerland later confirmed he was not officially an exile; he was free to request money, which was sent as usual. Then, after four years abroad, Pyotr unexpectedly announced his imminent return, writing from southern Russia, where he was said to be engaged in some important private business. His letters, terse and imperious, offered no insight into his activities. These communications had the tone of an old-fashioned landowner issuing instructions to his steward rather than a son writing to his father. Recently, he had sent two letters in quick succession, which was highly unusual.

This new development left Stepan Trofimovitch in a bind. Where would he find the remaining eight thousand roubles to supplement Varvara Petrovna's offer and create the noble tableau he had envisioned? Worse, what if Pyotr uncovered the truth about the estate's condition and chose to pursue legal action? The prospect of such humiliation haunted him. He confided to me his perplexity over what he described as the peculiar duality of socialist fervor and obsessive materialism. "Why is it," he whispered, "that these self-proclaimed socialists, these radicals, are always such misers? The more extreme their ideology, the more they cling to property. Isn't that just another form of sentimentalism?"

Though Stepan Trofimovitch feared the worst, Varvara Petrovna's intervention offered a lifeline. Her willingness to absorb the financial burden left him no choice but to accept her terms. With a heavy heart, and unable to conceive of any alternative, he consented to the arrangement.

As soon as Varvara Petrovna left, Stepan Trofimovitch sent for me and shut himself away for the entire day, refusing to admit anyone else. His emotional state followed a familiar pattern: tears, eloquent and excessive talk, frequent contradictions, and even the creation of a pun, which delighted him immensely. Shortly after, he experienced a mild bout of his usual "summer cholera." In essence, everything unfolded as it always did during moments of personal upheaval. Amid this whirlwind, he unearthed the portrait of his long-deceased German bride, who had passed away twenty years prior, and gazed at it with plaintive reverence, murmuring, "Will you forgive me?" His mood teetered on distraction and melancholy, and before long, we found solace in drink. Inevitably, he succumbed to a gentle, untroubled sleep.

The next morning, Stepan Trofimovitch presented himself with renewed vigor. He tied his cravat with exceptional care, ensuring it sat at just the right angle, and dressed with the meticulous attention of a man who felt the weight of a grand occasion. He visited the mirror repeatedly, scrutinizing his reflection with a mixture of trepidation and satisfaction. A faint trace of scent was sprinkled on his handkerchief—discreet, yet deliberate. However, when he spotted Varvara Petrovna approaching through the window, he hastily swapped it for another handkerchief and hid the perfumed one beneath his pillow.

"Excellent!" Varvara Petrovna declared approvingly when she received his formal consent. "First, you've shown admirable decisiveness, and second, you've finally listened to reason—something you so rarely do in your personal affairs. There's no rush now," she added, her keen eyes examining his tie critically. "For the time being, say nothing. I'll also remain silent. Soon it will be your birthday, and I'll visit you with her. Serve us tea in the evening—nothing more, no wine, no other refreshments. I'll take care of the arrangements myself. Invite your friends, but we'll agree on the guest list together. The day before, if necessary, you may speak with her briefly. At the party, we won't announce or formalize anything, but we'll hint at it subtly, letting people draw their conclusions without any overt ceremony. The wedding can follow two weeks later, and I'll ensure it's simple and free of unnecessary fuss. Perhaps you two could even go away afterward—to Moscow, maybe. I might accompany you as well. The key thing is to remain quiet until then."

Stepan Trofimovitch listened with mounting bewilderment. Stammering slightly, he attempted to object, insisting that he should at least discuss the matter with his prospective bride. But Varvara Petrovna, irritated by his hesitation, cut him off sharply.

"Why? For what purpose? It may not even come to that."

"May not come to that?" he echoed, utterly flabbergasted. "But—but I thought—"

"Yes," she interjected with authority. "I'll see to it. Everything will be handled as I've said. You have no need to meddle. I'll prepare her myself. There's no reason for you to get involved—none at all. What role would you even play in this? Don't write her letters; don't visit her. Leave everything to me. And remember, not a word from you!"

Despite his mounting confusion, she refused to offer any further explanation, brushing aside his faltering protests as she left, clearly irritated. Stepan Trofimovitch was left in a state of utter perplexity. While he had formally agreed to the arrangement, he had yet to fully comprehend his role or the situation as a whole. Instead, a strange air of bravado began to surface—a swaggering confidence tinged with hints of playful defiance.

"I do like this!" he exclaimed later, gesturing expansively as he stood before me. "Did you hear her? She's trying to drive me into a corner, forcing my hand. But I could lose patience too! I could refuse—why shouldn't I? 'Stay out of it,' she says, as though I'm some trivial bystander in my own life! But tell me this: why should I be married simply because she's indulging in one of her whims? I'm a serious man. I can refuse to cater to the idle fantasies of a capricious woman! I have obligations—to my son, to myself! Agreeing to this is a sacrifice, and she ought to acknowledge that. I've agreed, perhaps, because life wearies me and little matters to me anymore. But if she pushes me too far, it will matter! I'll refuse, and rightly so. And then there's the ridicule. What will they say at the club? What will Laputin say? 'Perhaps nothing will come of it,' she says—what an absurd thing to say! It's all too much. I'm being driven into a corner—je suis un forçat!"

Despite his outbursts, a curious levity threaded through his dramatic proclamations. Beneath his complaints, there was a flicker of self-indulgent amusement, as though he relished the absurdity of his predicament. That evening, as often happened during moments of heightened emotion, we drank too much once again.

Chapter 3
The Sins of Others

Chapter 3.1

About a week had passed, and the situation had become even more complicated. I should mention, in passing, that I went through a lot during that miserable week. I hardly left the side of my engaged friend, acting as his closest confidant. What bothered him the most was a deep sense of shame, even though we didn't see anyone that entire week and stayed indoors, just the two of us. But still, he felt embarrassed even in front of me. The more he opened up to me, the more upset he seemed to become about it, as if sharing his thoughts made him feel worse.

He was so nervous and anxious that he was convinced everyone in town already knew what had happened. He imagined that the whole town was talking about it and dreaded being seen, not only at the club but even among his friends. He absolutely refused to go outside for a walk until it was well after dark, when the streets were empty and no one could see him.

A week passed, and he still couldn't figure out whether he was officially engaged or not, no matter how hard he tried. He hadn't seen his supposed bride yet, and he couldn't be sure if she really was going to be his bride at all. In fact, he didn't know if any of it was serious. For some reason, Varvara Petrovna refused to see him. When he wrote her one of his first letters—he wrote a lot of them—she responded quite bluntly, asking him not to contact her for a while. She explained that she was very busy and had many important things to discuss with him, but she needed to wait for the right time. She promised to let him know when he could visit her. She even added that his letters were "pure self-indulgence" and that she would send them back unopened. I remember reading that letter myself—he showed it to me.

Still, all her harshness and vague answers weren't nearly as troubling as his greatest worry. That anxiety tormented him constantly, wearing him down until he was thin and completely miserable. It was something that embarrassed him more than anything else, something he refused to talk about—even to me. On the contrary, he lied about it sometimes and acted awkwardly, like a guilty child. At the same time, he couldn't go two hours without me; he sent for me every single day, as though he needed me as much as air or water.

This behavior hurt my pride a little. Of course, I had already figured out his big secret. I was sure that if this source of his anxiety were revealed, it wouldn't reflect well on him at all. Since I was still young, I was offended by what I saw as his pettiness and the ugliness of his suspicions. In my frustration—and, admittedly, my impatience with always being his confidant—I pushed him to confess, even though I knew it wasn't easy to admit such things. He knew what I was doing; he could tell that I had figured him out, that I was angry with him, and that I wasn't hiding it. In turn, he was angry with me for being angry, for understanding him too well. My irritation may have been childish and foolish, but sometimes being stuck together with a friend for too long can harm even the closest friendships.

In some ways, though, he understood his situation perfectly and could describe it quite sharply when he wasn't keeping secrets.

"Oh, she was so different back then," he would say about Varvara Petrovna. "You wouldn't believe it, but we used to have the best conversations! Back in those days, she actually had ideas—real ideas, and original ones too! But now? Everything is different. She says all of that is just outdated nonsense. She doesn't care about the past anymore. She's become so cold and hard, like some shopkeeper or accountant. And she's always in a bad mood…"

"Why is she cross now if you are carrying out her orders?" I answered.

He looked at me subtly.

"Cher ami; if I had not agreed she would have been dreadfully angry, dread-ful-ly! But yet less than now that I have consented."

He was pleased with this saying of his, and we emptied a bottle between us that evening. But that was only for a moment, next day he was worse and more ill-humoured than ever.

But what I was most vexed with him for was that he could not bring himself to call on the Drozdovs, as he should have done on their arrival, to renew the acquaintance of which, so we heard they were themselves desirous, since they kept asking about him. It was a source of daily distress to him. He talked of Lizaveta Nikolaevna with an ecstasy which I was at a loss to understand. No doubt he remembered in her the child whom he had once loved. But besides that, he imagined for some unknown reason that he would at once find in her company a solace for his present misery, and even the solution of his more serious doubts. He expected to meet in Lizaveta Nikolaevna an extraordinary being. And yet he did not go to see her though he meant to do so every day. The worst of it was that I was desperately anxious to be presented to her and to make her acquaintance, and I could look to no one but Stepan Trofimovitch to effect this. I was frequently meeting her, in the street of course, when she was out riding, wearing a riding-habit and mounted on a fine horse, and accompanied by her cousin, so-called, a handsome officer, the nephew of the late General Drozdov—and these meetings made an extraordinary impression on me at the time. My infatuation lasted only a moment, and I very soon afterwards recognised the impossibility of my dreams myself—but though it was a fleeting impression it was a very real one, and so it may well be imagined how indignant I was at the time with my poor friend for keeping so obstinately secluded.

All the members of our circle had been officially informed from the beginning that Stepan Trofimovitch would see nobody for a time, and begged them to leave him quite alone. He insisted on sending round a circular notice to this effect, though I tried to dissuade him. I went round to every one at his request and told everybody that Varvara Petrovna had given "our old man" (as we all used to call Stepan Trofimovitch among ourselves) a special job, to arrange in order some correspondence lasting over many years; that he had shut himself up to do it and I was helping him. Liputin was the only one I did not have time to visit, and I kept putting it off—to tell the real truth I was afraid to go to him. I knew beforehand that he would not believe one word of my story, that he would certainly imagine that there was some secret at the bottom of it, which they were trying to hide from him alone, and as soon as I left him he would set to work to make inquiries and gossip all over the town. While I was picturing all this to myself I happened to run across him in the street. It turned out that he had heard all about it from our friends, whom I had only just informed. But, strange to say, instead of being inquisitive and asking questions about Stepan Trofimovitch, he interrupted me, when I began apologising for not having come to him before, and at once passed to other subjects. It is true that he had a great deal stored up to tell me. He was in a state of great excitement, and was delighted to have got hold of me for a listener. He began talking of the news of the town, of the arrival of the governor's wife, "with new topics of conversation," of an opposition party already formed in the club, of how they were all in a hubbub over the new ideas, and how charmingly this suited him, and so on. He talked for a quarter of an hour and so amusingly that I could not tear myself away. Though I could not endure him, yet I must admit he had the gift of making one listen to him, especially when he was very angry at something. This man was, in my opinion, a regular spy from his very nature. At every moment he knew the very latest gossip and all the trifling incidents of our town, especially the unpleasant ones, and it was surprising to me how he took things to heart that were sometimes absolutely no concern of his. It always seemed to me that the leading feature of his character was envy. When I told Stepan Trofimovitch the same evening of my meeting Liputin that morning and our conversation, the latter to my amazement became greatly agitated, and asked me the wild question:

"Does Liputin know or not?"

I began trying to prove that there was no possibility of his finding it out so soon, and that there was nobody from whom he could hear it. But Stepan Trofimovitch was not to be shaken. "Well, you may believe it or not," he concluded unexpectedly at last, "but I'm convinced that he not only knows every detail of 'our' position, but that he knows something else besides, something neither you nor I know yet, and perhaps never shall, or shall only know when it's too late, when there's no turning back!…"

I said nothing, but these words suggested a great deal. For five whole days after that we did not say one word about Liputin; it was clear to me that Stepan Trofimovitch greatly regretted having let his tongue run away with him, and having revealed such suspicions before me.

Chapter 3.2

One morning, on the seventh or eighth day after Stepan Trofimovitch had agreed to his "engagement," I set off as usual around eleven o'clock to visit my troubled friend. On my way, however, I had an unexpected encounter.

I ran into Karmazinov, "the great writer," as Liputin mockingly called him. I had known Karmazinov's name since I was a child. His novels and stories were famous among both my generation and the one before. As a boy, I had been enchanted by them; they were part of my youth, filling long hours of wonder and excitement. But over the years, my admiration had faded. I found his later works—those burdened with a "purpose" or message—less engaging. His early writings, which had flowed with natural poetry and imagination, were what I still respected. As for his most recent publications, I couldn't stand them. They seemed hollow, overly polished, and somehow false.

To be honest—and I say this carefully, since one must tread lightly around the reputations of celebrated men—I've noticed that writers like Karmazinov, men who enjoy fleeting fame and are sometimes mistakenly hailed as geniuses during their lifetime, often vanish completely from public memory after their death. What's more, they sometimes fade even during their own lifetime when a younger generation comes along. It's as if someone suddenly flips a stage set, and the spotlight moves elsewhere. This happens with astonishing speed in our country, as though the audience has grown tired and impatient. It's not at all like what happened with the truly great minds—Pushkin, Gogol, Molière, Voltaire—those men who spoke with an original, unmistakable voice, who brought something new to the world.

Writers like Karmazinov, who are merely "talented," don't seem to notice when they start running out of steam. Towards the end of their careers, they often write themselves into irrelevance. It's strange to think of a man who was once praised as deep, profound, and influential eventually revealing himself as shallow and unremarkable in his ideas. When this happens, people forget them without regret, as though it's been a relief to see them disappear. But the writers themselves—particularly the older ones—remain oblivious to this decline. Instead, they grow angrier and cling to their reputations even harder. Their vanity swells to astonishing proportions, as though their years and fading relevance have earned them the right to consider themselves gods—or something close to it.

I'd heard more than once that Karmazinov cared more about his connections to aristocrats and influential people than about his own dignity as a writer. He was known to be charming and utterly captivating when he met someone who might be of use to him, especially if they came recommended. But if a countess or a prince—or anyone he feared—came into the room, he would drop you like you never existed. He would forget you as deliberately as one might swat a fly or sweep away a splinter of wood, even before you had the chance to step aside yourself. People said he considered this "aristocratic behavior" and the hallmark of true refinement.

Despite his fine manners, his impeccable sense of decorum, and the way he always presented himself as an aristocratic gentleman, his vanity was legendary. It had grown so excessive that he couldn't hide it, even in circles that had no real interest in literature. If someone happened to show indifference to him or his work, he would become visibly upset, almost wounded, and then find some way to take his revenge, no matter how petty.

About a year before, I had read one of his essays in a literary journal. It was written with a great deal of pomp and artificial "simplicity," laced with pretentious psychological insights. In it, he described the wreck of a steamer off the coast of England, an incident he had witnessed firsthand. He wrote at length about the storm, the wreckage, the attempts to save the survivors, and the bodies of the dead being brought ashore. Yet the whole piece felt like little more than a performance—an opportunity for him to show off.

As I read, I couldn't help but imagine him whispering between the lines: "Look at me. Pay attention to me. Aren't I fascinating? Forget the drowning people, the dead woman clutching her lifeless child. Don't trouble yourself over those details—I've already described them for you with my great pen. No, what matters here is me. Watch me turn away in horror. Look at how I blinked my eyes and couldn't bear to see it. Isn't that compelling? Aren't I the one who is interesting here?"

When I told Stepan Trofimovitch my opinion of the article, he listened intently. To my satisfaction, he agreed with me completely.

When rumors began to spread that Karmazinov was expected to arrive in the area, I was naturally eager to see him. More than that, I secretly hoped to make his acquaintance, and I was certain I could arrange it through Stepan Trofimovitch. The two had been friends at one time, after all, though I wasn't sure whether that friendship still held. And then, quite unexpectedly, I ran into him at the crossroads. I recognized him instantly. Just two or three days before, someone had pointed him out to me when he rode past in a carriage with the governor's wife.

He was a small, stiff-looking man, though not yet old—perhaps fifty-five at most. His face was red and pinched, and though he had an air of care and composure, his expression wasn't particularly handsome. His thin lips, long and sly-looking, curved a little cruelly, while his nose—rather fleshy—seemed to dominate his face. His small, sharp, and clever eyes had the calculating look of someone always sizing things up. The thick curls of grey hair clustered neatly under the brim of his tall chimney-pot hat, curling precisely around his clean, pink ears.

He was dressed in a somewhat shabby way, wearing a light cape of the kind that might be fashionable in Switzerland or Italy that time of year. Yet in spite of his clothes, there was no mistaking his attention to detail. The little embellishments of his outfit—the studs in his shirt, his perfectly pressed collar, the polished buttons, the tortoise-shell lorgnette dangling on its black ribbon, the well-chosen signet ring—everything about him exuded refined taste and manners, the mark of someone who prided himself on belonging to the best society. I would bet anything that in summer he wore light prunella shoes with tiny mother-of-pearl buttons at the side.

When we met, he was standing still, carefully surveying the street ahead of him, as though checking whether he was on the correct route. Noticing that I was watching him, no doubt with too much curiosity, he turned his sharp little face toward me and spoke in a sugary voice that still carried a shrill edge:

"Allow me to ask, which is my nearest way to Bykovy Street?"

"To Bykovy Street? Oh, it's just here—quite close!" I blurted out, almost stammering in my excitement. "You go straight down this street, then take the second turning on the left."

"Very much obliged to you," he said politely, nodding with a small, knowing smile.

At that very moment, I cursed myself inwardly. I must have looked shy and awkward, maybe even obsequious. I could tell that he noticed it immediately. Worse still, I was certain he had figured out everything about me at once—who he was to me, how I had read his works and revered him as a child, and that I couldn't help feeling flustered by this chance meeting. He nodded once more and began walking in the direction I had pointed out.

I can't explain why, but I turned to look after him—and then, like a complete fool, I ran a few steps alongside him before stopping. I don't know what came over me. He suddenly turned back to me again and called out sharply, "And could you tell me where the nearest cab-stand is?"

That voice! That voice of his was unbearably unpleasant, like an instrument played out of tune.

"A cab-stand? Oh, it's over by the Cathedral," I replied hastily, almost panting. "There are always cabs waiting there." I was so eager to be helpful that I nearly ran off to fetch a cab for him myself. In fact, I think that's exactly what he expected me to do. I only barely managed to stop myself in time and stand still, but he caught the slight movement, and his thin, smug smile returned. He watched me with his sharp, mocking eyes, as though daring me to act like a lackey.

And then came the most humiliating part. He dropped something—a small item he had been holding in his left hand. At first glance, I thought it was a little bag, but on closer look, it was more like a tiny box, or perhaps a wallet or reticule of some sort. In fact, it looked a bit like those dainty old-fashioned purses that ladies sometimes carried. I still don't know exactly what it was, but I do know what I did.

Without thinking, I made a movement as though to pick it up for him. I doubt I actually bent all the way over, but my intention was unmistakable. I froze halfway, realizing how ridiculous I must look, but it was too late. My face turned scarlet.

The sly old man immediately noticed, and he seized on the moment. "Don't trouble yourself, I'll pick it up," he said, in a voice so polite it was positively charming. The worst part was that he spoke after he saw I had checked myself and wasn't going to pick it up. He bent down calmly, as if to outdo me, retrieved the item with practiced nonchalance, nodded yet again, and walked away, leaving me standing there feeling like an absolute fool.

It was as though I had picked it up for him after all, and he had outmaneuvered me completely. For the next five minutes, I burned with shame. I felt like I had humiliated myself irreparably, like this one encounter would disgrace me forever.

But by the time I reached Stepan Trofimovitch's house, the whole incident had struck me as so absurd that I burst out laughing. The meeting was so strange, so ridiculous, that I immediately resolved to tell Stepan

Trofimovitch the entire story. I even planned to act it out for him, imitating Karmazinov's voice and manner. The thought of it cheered me up. I was sure it would amuse my friend as much as it amused me now that the embarrassment had worn off.

Chapter 3.3

This time, to my surprise, I found a dramatic change in him. The moment I entered, he sprang at me with a kind of desperate eagerness. He appeared ready to hang on my every word but listened with such a distracted air that I could tell he wasn't really absorbing what I was saying. However, as soon as I mentioned the name Karmazinov, he erupted into a fit of uncontrollable rage.

"Don't speak of him! Don't you dare say that name!" he shouted, nearly shaking with fury. "Here, look at this! Read it! Read it all!"

He yanked open a drawer and tossed three small sheets of paper onto the table. They were covered in hurried pencil scribbles, all from Varvara Petrovna. The letters were dated across three consecutive days—the day before yesterday, yesterday, and one that had arrived only an hour before my visit. The contents were shockingly trivial, each one fretting over Karmazinov and reflecting Varvara Petrovna's obsessive unease about whether or not he would visit her.

Here is the first letter, dated two days ago (though I couldn't help suspecting there had been even earlier ones, perhaps three or four days prior):

"If he deigns to visit you today, not a word about me, I beg you. Not the faintest hint. Don't speak of me, don't mention me.—V. S."

The second letter, from the previous day, read:

"If he decides to pay you a visit this morning, I think the most dignified thing would be not to receive him. That's my opinion, at least; I don't know what you think.—V. S."

And the third, which had arrived just that morning, was the longest and most absurd of all:

"I feel sure that you're in a complete mess, surrounded by clutter and choking in clouds of tobacco smoke. I'm sending Marya and Fomushka to tidy up. They'll have everything in order within half an hour. Don't interfere; just go and sit in the kitchen while they work. I'm also sending you a Bokhara rug and two china vases. I've been meaning to give them to you for a long time, and I'll send my Teniers painting as well, just for now. You can place the vases in the window and hang the Teniers under Goethe's portrait on the right; it will stand out more there, and it gets good light in the morning.

"If he finally shows up, receive him with the utmost courtesy, but talk only of trivial matters, some intellectual topic perhaps, and behave as though you've seen each other recently. Not a word about me. Perhaps I'll stop by to see you in the evening.—V. S.

"P.S.—If he doesn't come today, he won't come at all."

I read the letters, astonished that such trivialities had thrown him into such an intense state. When I looked up at him, puzzled, I noticed something peculiar: at some point while I was reading, he had changed his usual white tie for a bright red one. His hat and walking stick lay on the table, and his face was pale. His hands trembled slightly as he gestured toward the letters.

"I don't care a bit about her silly anxieties!" he burst out, almost shouting in response to my questioning expression. "Je m'en fiche! She's fretting herself sick over Karmazinov while she refuses to answer my letters! Look—there it is!" He pointed dramatically to an unopened letter lying under a book on the table—Victor Hugo's L'Homme qui rit.

"She sent it back to me yesterday, unopened! Unopened, do you hear? And all this fuss about Karmazinov? Let her wear herself out over Nikolay for all I care! Je m'en fiche, et je proclame ma liberté! To hell with Karmazinov! To hell with Lembke!"

He began pacing furiously from one end of the room to the other, gesticulating wildly.

"I've hidden her vases in the entryway," he continued, "and shoved the Teniers painting into a drawer. And I've demanded—demanded—

95

that she see me immediately. I've sent her a note, a mere scrap of paper, unsealed, written in pencil, and sent by Nastasya. I'm waiting for her answer. I will not endure this any longer! I want Darya Pavlovna to speak to me directly, with her own lips, in the sight of Heaven—or at least in your presence! Vous me seconderez, n'est-ce pas? You'll stand by me as a friend and a witness, won't you? I will not lie. I refuse to live in secrets! No more secrets! Let them confess everything to me, openly, frankly, honorably. And then..." He paused dramatically, his voice trembling. "Then, perhaps I'll astonish everyone with my magnanimity."

He stopped pacing and fixed me with a piercing gaze, his tone suddenly changing to one of accusation. "Tell me, am I a scoundrel or not? What do you think, my dear sir? Am I a scoundrel?"

The intensity of his words and the wildness in his eyes were almost too much to bear. I offered him a glass of water, hoping to calm him down, but he waved it away impatiently. I had never seen him like this before. As he ranted, he moved erratically about the room, but at one point he came to a sudden stop and stood before me in an extraordinary pose, as though bracing himself for judgment.

"Do you think," he began again, his voice trembling with hysterical pride as he scrutinized me from head to toe, "do you think that I, Stepan Verhovensky, lack the moral courage to take up my bag—my beggar's bag—and, placing it on my weary shoulders, walk out the gate and vanish forever when honor and the great principle of independence demand it? Let me tell you, it wouldn't be the first time that Stepan Verhovensky has stood up to despotism with moral strength alone, even when that despotism comes in the form of a madwoman—a despotism that is the most cruel and degrading kind on earth. And yet you, sir, you have the audacity to smile at my words, as if my convictions were a jest!

"Oh, you doubt me, don't you? You can't imagine that I would find within myself the strength to end my life as a tutor in some merchant's household, or even to die alone of hunger in a filthy ditch! Tell me, answer me now—do you believe it, or do you not?" His eyes blazed with intensity as he demanded my response.

But I remained silent on purpose. I deliberately hesitated, feigning a

96

reluctance to wound him with an outright denial but making it clear that I couldn't bring myself to affirm his claim, either. Something in his agitation irritated me—not personally, of course, but in a way I struggled to articulate even to myself. I thought I would explain it later, but for now, I only stared back at him, my silence calculated yet uneasy.

He turned visibly pale, his composure cracking further with each passing second. "Perhaps," he said at last, his voice unnervingly calm, "perhaps you're tired of me, G——v" (he used my surname here), "and you'd rather not visit me anymore. Is that it?"

There was something in his tone, a forced calmness, that made me leap to my feet in alarm. It was the kind of icy restraint that comes just before an emotional explosion. But before either of us could speak again, Nastasya entered the room without a word and handed Stepan Trofimovitch a small piece of paper with something scribbled in pencil. He glanced at it briefly, then threw it toward me as though the sight of it burned him.

I picked it up and read the note. It was written in Varvara Petrovna's distinctive hand and contained only three curt words: "Stay at home."

Without saying anything, Stepan Trofimovitch grabbed his hat and walking stick. His face was set, his movements hurried and precise. Without waiting for any reaction from me, he stormed out of the room. Instinctively, and not knowing why, I followed him.

We hadn't gone far before the sound of quick footsteps and muffled voices echoed down the passage. He froze in place, gripping my arm with such force that I winced. His face had gone deathly pale.

"It's Liputin," he whispered hoarsely, his voice barely audible. "I am finished!"

And at that exact moment, Liputin entered the room.

Chapter 3.4

Why Stepan Trofimovitch felt he would be "lost" because of Liputin, I couldn't begin to understand. His words seemed exaggerated, and I chalked them up to his frayed nerves. Nevertheless, his visible terror was so striking that I resolved to keep a close eye on him.

Liputin entered the room with an air of confidence that suggested he felt he had every right to ignore the standing prohibition on visitors. He wasn't alone. Behind him was a man I had never seen before, evidently a newcomer to the town. Liputin wasted no time in making introductions. Noticing the frozen, almost bewildered stare on Stepan Trofimovitch's face, he immediately announced in a loud, cheerful voice:

"I've brought a guest for you, a very special guest! I hope you'll forgive the intrusion. This is Mr. Kirillov, a distinguished civil engineer. He happens to know your son, the esteemed Pyotr Stepanovitch, very well. In fact, he brings a message from him. He's just arrived!"

The man behind him, Mr. Kirillov, corrected him bluntly, "The message is your own invention. There's no message. But I do know Verhovensky—I left him in the X province, ten days ahead of us."

Stepan Trofimovitch, seemingly in a daze, extended his hand mechanically to Kirillov and gestured for him to sit down. His eyes flitted from me to Liputin and then back again, as if trying to steady himself. After a moment of hesitation, he finally sat down himself, though he still clutched his hat and walking stick, seemingly unaware of it.

"Ah, but it seems you were heading out yourself!" Liputin said with feigned surprise. "I was told you've been completely overwhelmed with work."

"Yes, I'm not well, you see. I thought I'd go for a walk, but…" Stepan Trofimovitch stammered, then abruptly stopped. Realizing the awkwardness of his response, he flung his hat and stick onto the sofa and flushed crimson.

Meanwhile, I had been studying the visitor. Kirillov was a man of about twenty-seven, well-built and neatly dressed. His pale, somewhat sallow complexion gave him a worn look, and his black, dull eyes had an intensity that suggested deep thought, though his manner was restless and distracted. He spoke in short, abrupt sentences, often muddling his words or stumbling over longer phrases, as though unused to expressing himself fluently. Despite his composed exterior, he seemed to radiate an underlying tension, as if something was gnawing at him.

Liputin, fully aware of Stepan Trofimovitch's discomfort, clearly delighted in it. He pulled a wicker chair to the center of the room, positioning himself equidistant from his host and the visitor, who had seated themselves on opposite sofas. His sharp, darting eyes flitted around the room, drinking in every detail with evident satisfaction.

"It's been such a long time since I've seen Petrusha," Stepan Trofimovitch managed to murmur to Kirillov, his voice almost plaintive. "You met him abroad, did you?"

"Yes. Both here and abroad," Kirillov replied curtly.

"Alexey Nilitch has only just returned after spending four years abroad," Liputin interjected smoothly. "He's been traveling to perfect his expertise in civil engineering and has come here in hopes of securing a position on the railway bridge project. He's waiting on a reply. He also knows the Drozdovs and Lizaveta Nikolaevna, through your son, Pyotr Stepanovitch."

Kirillov listened to Liputin's chatter with visible irritation, shifting awkwardly in his seat as though resisting the urge to interrupt. His expression darkened, and he seemed to grow more tense with every word.

"He also knows Nikolay Vsyevolodovitch," Liputin added, throwing in yet another detail with a smirk.

"You know Nikolay Vsyevolodovitch?" Stepan Trofimovitch asked, visibly startled.

"Yes, I know him too," Kirillov said flatly, clearly impatient to move on.

"It's ..., it's been such a long time since I've seen Petrusha," Stepan Trofimovitch repeated, his voice trembling. "And I feel I have so little right to call myself his father—c'est le mot. When I left him in Petersburg, I thought of him as … well, as a nonentity, quelque chose dans ce genre. He was such a nervous, sensitive boy, you know. Very timid. I remember how he used to pray before bed, bowing all the way to the floor and making the sign of the cross on his pillow so that he wouldn't die in the night.… Je m'en souviens."

He paused, as though lost in the memory, then went on, his tone tinged with regret. "There was no sign of anything artistic in him, no deeper feelings, no embryo of an ideal—c'était comme un petit idiot. But I'm afraid I'm rambling incoherently. Excuse me. You've caught me off guard…"

"You're serious when you say he crossed his pillow?" Kirillov asked abruptly, his voice tinged with curiosity.

"Yes, he did," Stepan Trofimovitch replied, taken aback by the question.

"All right. I just wanted to know. Go on," Kirillov said dismissively, waving a hand.

Stepan Trofimovitch turned to Liputin, clearly struggling to regain his composure. "I am grateful for your visit," he said shakily, "but I must confess I'm not in the best condition to receive company right now. May I ask where you are lodging?"

"At Filipov's, on Bogoyavlensky Street," Kirillov replied.

"Ah, that's where Shatov lives," I said, almost involuntarily.

"Exactly," Liputin chimed in with a sly smile. "Same house! Shatov lodges upstairs in the attic, while Kirillov is staying below with Captain Lebyadkin. And Kirillov knows Shatov—and Shatov's wife, too. He was quite close to her abroad."

"Comment!" Stepan Trofimovitch exclaimed, startled and visibly moved. "Do you really know that unhappy woman? That tragic marriage de ce pauvre ami? You're the first person I've met who has known her personally. If only…"

"What nonsense!" Kirillov snapped, his face flushing red. "Why do

100

you add such things, Liputin? I've never even spoken to Shatov's wife. I only saw her once, from a distance, and not at all closely. I know Shatov, yes, but this is ridiculous. Stop exaggerating!"

Liputin grinned but said nothing, clearly enjoying the disarray he had caused. The tension in the room thickened, and I couldn't help but feel that we were hurtling toward something none of us fully understood.

He spun around sharply on the sofa, grabbed his hat as though preparing to leave, then abruptly set it down again, settling back into his seat with visible tension. His black eyes, sharp and angry, fixed on Stepan Trofimovitch in a defiant stare. The suddenness of his movements, coupled with this strange irritability, left me bewildered. What was it about this conversation—or the presence of Liputin—that had put him so on edge?

"Excuse me," Stepan Trofimovitch began, his tone full of calm yet deliberate politeness. "I realize this might be a sensitive subject…"

"There's nothing delicate about it!" Kirillov cut him off abruptly, his voice tight with irritation. "And it's disgraceful! I wasn't shouting at you; I was shouting at Liputin because he keeps adding things. Don't take it personally. I know Shatov, but I don't know his wife at all. I've never known her!" His tone softened slightly, but his irritation still lingered, as though Liputin's earlier comments had struck a nerve.

"I see, I see. My apologies if I pressed too much," Stepan Trofimovitch replied earnestly. "It's only that I've always been fond of our poor friend, notre irascible ami. I've taken a genuine interest in him. His sudden change of views—so abrupt, so extreme—has always puzzled me. He abandoned his youthful but, I dare say, quite sound ideas with such vehemence. And now, to hear him speak of notre Sainte Russie in such exaggerated terms! I've long believed that such an upheaval in his thinking must have been triggered by a deep personal tragedy, perhaps the failure of his marriage. You see, I've spent my life studying our dear Russia, knowing her like the lines on my hand. I can assure you that Shatov's interpretation of the Russian people is—"

"I don't know the Russian people either," Kirillov interrupted, his voice cold and dismissive. "And I don't have time to study them." He shifted sharply on the sofa again, as though the very mention of the subject grated on his nerves. Stepan Trofimovitch froze mid-sentence, startled by the bluntness of the retort.

"He is studying them, though," Liputin interjected with a smirk, clearly relishing the tension. "He's begun a fascinating study on the causes of the rising suicide rates in Russia. It's part of a larger analysis on what influences suicide in society, both its increase and decrease. His conclusions, I must say, are nothing short of extraordinary."

Kirillov's face darkened, and he sat upright with a visible jolt of anger. "You have no right to say that," he snapped, his voice low but seething. "I'm not writing an article. I'm not publishing anything. I spoke to you about it privately, in passing, and you twisted it into something it's not. There is no article. I despise all this nonsense!" His fists clenched as he glared at Liputin, who continued to smile smugly.

"I apologize," Liputin replied, clearly insincere. "Perhaps I misspoke by calling your work an article. He is only collecting observations— scientific ones, of course—and he avoids the moral aspects of the subject entirely. In fact, he rejects morality itself and subscribes to the very latest principle: the necessity of total destruction to achieve eventual good. Alexey Nilitch already demands more than a hundred million heads for the future triumph of reason across Europe—far more than were demanded at the last Peace Congress!"

Kirillov's pale face took on a stony expression as he listened to Liputin's taunts. A thin, contemptuous smile spread across his lips, but he remained silent for a moment. The room grew tense. Even Liputin seemed to pause, as if waiting for a reaction.

At last, Kirillov spoke, his voice calm but firm. "This is nonsense, Liputin. All of it. You take something I said casually—perhaps without precision—and twist it as you like. But you have no right to speak for me. I do not share my thoughts with others, and I have no interest in debating them. If I hold a conviction, it is clear to me, and I do not argue about settled matters. Argument is foolish and tiresome, and I avoid it whenever possible."

"And perhaps that is a sign of your wisdom," Stepan Trofimovitch said gently, attempting to defuse the tension.

"I am not angry," Kirillov replied quickly, speaking faster and with more heat. "Not with you, at least. I simply find Liputin's liberties annoying. I've spent the last four years speaking to almost no one, avoiding people entirely for reasons that concern only myself. Liputin knows this and laughs at it, but I don't mind his laughter. I'm not offended; I am merely... irritated." He paused and looked around the room, his gaze deliberate and resolute. "And if I don't explain my ideas to you, it's not because I fear you might report me to the authorities. Don't imagine such absurdities."

No one responded to this unexpected statement. The words hung in the air, their weight unbroken by a single sound. Even Liputin, always ready with a quip or a smirk, fell silent for once. We exchanged glances, each of us unsure of how to proceed.

Finally, Stepan Trofimovitch broke the silence. Rising from the sofa with an effort, he announced, "Gentlemen, I must apologize, but I'm feeling unwell and upset. Please excuse me."

"Ah, that's our cue to leave," Kirillov said, standing up abruptly and snatching his cap. "Thank you for letting us know. I'm so absent-minded, I wouldn't have noticed." His tone was genuinely apologetic, and he extended his hand toward Stepan Trofimovitch with unexpected warmth.

"I'm sorry for the inconvenience," Kirillov continued. "I shouldn't have come."

Stepan Trofimovitch shook his hand firmly, his composure returning. "I wish you success in your endeavors here," he said, his tone sincere but tinged with subtle irony. "I understand that, having lived so long abroad, cutting yourself off from people and from Russia, you might find us peculiar—just as we, being entirely Russian, might find your perspectives equally strange. Mais cela passera. One thing puzzles me, though: you want to build our railway bridge while simultaneously advocating for universal destruction. Surely they won't let you build the bridge with such principles?"

Kirillov looked startled for a moment, then broke into a sudden, hearty laugh. His face transformed, shedding its usual seriousness, and for a brief moment, he looked almost childlike. The change was so striking that even I, watching silently, couldn't help but feel a touch of warmth toward him. Liputin, meanwhile, rubbed his hands together, clearly delighted by Stepan Trofimovitch's remark.

Yet as I observed the scene, I couldn't shake my curiosity: why had Stepan Trofimovitch been so afraid of Liputin's arrival? What could have made him exclaim, "I am lost," at the sound of his footsteps?

Chapter 3.5

We were all gathered awkwardly in the doorway, the kind of moment when hosts and guests exchange hurried, polite farewells, both parties eager to conclude the visit with a semblance of cordiality. The tension in the air lingered, though, as if unresolved. Liputin, ever the opportunist, took the chance to drop one final comment, spoken with a casualness that only amplified its sting.

"The reason he's in such a foul mood today," Liputin remarked suddenly, just as he was about to leave the room, "is that he had a bit of a scene with Captain Lebyadkin over his sister. That precious sister of his—the mad girl—gets beaten daily with a whip. A real Cossack whip, morning and evening. Alexey Nilitch finally took the lodge just to get away from it. Well, good-bye."

"A sister? An invalid? With a whip?" Stepan Trofimovitch cried out, his voice trembling as though he himself had just felt the lash of the whip Liputin described. "What sister? What Lebyadkin?" His earlier composure evaporated in an instant, replaced by something close to panic.

"Lebyadkin? Oh, that's the retired captain—though he used to call himself a lieutenant."

"What does his rank matter to me?" Stepan Trofimovitch exclaimed, his hands trembling. "What sister? Good heavens… You say Lebyadkin? There used to be a Lebyadkin here, years ago…"

"That's the one," Liputin replied smoothly, as if relishing the moment.

"The same Lebyadkin. You remember him from Virginsky's gatherings, don't you?"

"But he... wasn't he caught forging papers? Surely he couldn't have come back?"

"Well, he did come back. He's been here almost three weeks, under circumstances that are... unusual."

"But... but he's a scoundrel!"

"As though we're short of scoundrels among us," Liputin said with a sly grin, his sharp, mischievous eyes darting toward Stepan Trofimovitch, seeming to pierce right into his thoughts.

"Good heavens!" Stepan Trofimovitch cried, his voice breaking. "I didn't mean that—though I certainly don't disagree with you. But what are you implying? What does this mean? You meant something by this, Liputin. I'm certain of it!"

"Why, it's all quite trivial, really," Liputin said, his voice dripping with feigned indifference. "This captain, it seems, left town years ago—not because of the forgery scandal, mind you, but to track down his sister. She'd run away from him and gone into hiding somewhere. Now he's found her, brought her back here, and that's the whole story."

"Why do you seem frightened, Stepan Trofimovitch?" he added with a smirk. "I only know this from the captain's drunken ramblings. When he's sober, he doesn't mention it at all. He's a hot-tempered man, a bit of an aesthete in his own crude, military way. Lacking in taste, though. And his sister? Lame and mad, poor thing. It seems she was seduced by someone, and for years now, Lebyadkin's been receiving an annual payment from the seducer, supposedly as compensation for the injury to his family's honor—or so he claims when he's drunk. Personally, I think it's all just bragging. These things are usually settled for much less. But it's true he's come into some money recently. Ten days ago, he was walking around barefoot, and now he's carrying wads of cash. His sister has fits every day, and he 'keeps her in line' with the whip. 'You must inspire respect in a woman,' he says. Can you imagine? I don't know how Shatov tolerates living above him. As for Alexey Nilitch, he only moved into the lodge three days ago—just to escape the noise."

"Is this true?" Stepan Trofimovitch asked, turning to Kirillov with a pleading look.

"You do talk a lot, Liputin," Kirillov muttered, his tone sharp and his expression grim.

"Mysteries and secrets! Where do all these mysteries and secrets come from?" Stepan Trofimovitch exclaimed, throwing up his hands in frustration.

Kirillov flushed with annoyance, his face darkening as he shrugged his shoulders and began to leave. "You chatter too much, Liputin," he said curtly. "It's pointless and stupid."

"Wait," Liputin said with a sly smile, "you're being far too modest, Alexey Nilitch. Why hide the noble impulses of your soul? Yes, Alexey Nilitch was the one who grabbed the whip out of the captain's hands, broke it in two, and threw it out the window. That led to quite the quarrel, I assure you."

"Why are you still talking, Liputin?" Kirillov snapped, spinning back around with a glare. "It's foolish. What's the point of all this? Lebyadkin is a worthless idiot, a complete nonentity. He's useless to anyone and does more harm than good. Stop babbling."

"What a pity!" Liputin exclaimed, feigning disappointment. "I was hoping to amuse you with another little story, Stepan Trofimovitch. It's about Varvara Petrovna—perhaps you've already heard it? Oh, it's simply delightful. I came here just to share it, in fact. But if Alexey Nilitch is in such a hurry, I'll save it for another time. Good-bye."

At this, Stepan Trofimovitch seized Liputin by the shoulders, spun him back toward the room, and forced him into a chair with such unexpected force that Liputin looked genuinely startled.

"No, you're not leaving yet," Stepan Trofimovitch said firmly, his voice trembling. "What do you mean by this story about Varvara Petrovna? Out with it!"

Liputin hesitated, glancing warily at Stepan Trofimovitch. "Well," he said at last, his tone measured, "she sent for me the day before yesterday. Quite unexpectedly. And do you know what she asked me? She wanted my 'private opinion'—whether Nikolay Vsyevolodovitch is in his right mind or completely mad. Isn't that astonishing?"

"You're out of your mind," Stepan Trofimovitch muttered, his face pale. Then, as though suddenly overcome by fury, he burst out, "Liputin, you came here on purpose to insult me with this—and to say something worse!"

In that moment, as though struck by lightning, I recalled Stepan Trofimovitch's earlier suspicion—that Liputin not only knew more than we did about our tangled affairs but also possessed some deeper knowledge, something we would never uncover. This thought flashed through my mind like a forewarning, and I could see from Stepan Trofimovitch's face that a similar realization had taken hold of him.

"Upon my word, Stepan Trofimovitch," Liputin mumbled in an unconvincing attempt at contrition, his tone low and hesitant, though his sharp little eyes darted with their usual slyness, "upon my word, I didn't mean…"

"Hold your tongue and begin at once!" Stepan Trofimovitch roared, his voice trembling with a mixture of anger and agitation. "I beg you, Mr. Kirillov, to come back as well and be a witness to all of this. I insist! Sit down, sit down here! And you, Liputin—begin directly. Speak simply, without preamble, without excuses, without any more of your detestable tricks!"

Kirillov, who had already half-turned toward the door, stopped in his tracks and slowly turned back. With a heavy, reluctant step, he re-entered the room and dropped back onto the sofa, his face set in a gloomy scowl as though he were preparing himself to endure something deeply distasteful. He crossed his arms and stared intently at the floor, clearly wishing to be anywhere but there. Liputin, on the other hand, stood for a moment as though enjoying the spectacle. His expression—full of exaggerated concern and a thinly disguised amusement—hovered on the edge of insolence. He shifted his weight from one leg to the other, deliberately dragging out the moment, as though savoring the power he had over his nervous host.

"If I had only known it would upset you this much," he began slowly, with the theatrical air of someone taking great care, though his voice betrayed a hint of mockery, "I wouldn't have mentioned it at all. Really, I wouldn't! And, naturally, I assumed you already knew everything—everything there was to know—straight from Varvara Petrovna herself." He gave a slight shrug, as if washing his hands of the whole matter.

"You didn't think that at all!" Stepan Trofimovitch snapped, his voice ringing with certainty. He was pale and breathing heavily, his hands gripping the arms of his chair as though bracing himself. "You're lying, Liputin. Begin! I tell you to begin!"

Liputin sighed dramatically, as though he were the one being wronged. "Please, Stepan Trofimovitch," he said in a tone of mock placation, "do sit down yourself. How am I supposed to sit here and tell a story when you're pacing the room like a man possessed? It's unsettling! I can't speak clearly or think properly when you're all excitement like this."

At these words, Stepan Trofimovitch paused, drew a deep breath as though physically forcing himself into calmness, and finally sank back into the easy chair with great deliberation. His movements were theatrical and full of wounded dignity, though his trembling hands gave him away. "There. I am sitting down. Now you have no excuse. Speak!"

Liputin shot him a wary glance, though there was still that flicker of malicious satisfaction in his eyes, as if he were taking great pleasure in stretching out the tension for his own amusement. He glanced briefly at Kirillov, who continued to glare at the floor with stoic indifference, and then back at Stepan Trofimovitch. He rubbed his hands together slowly, letting the silence hang in the room just long enough to drive his host further to the edge.

"How am I to begin?" he finally muttered, his voice full of mock despair. "I hardly know where to start... I am quite overwhelmed, really, and so unprepared."

"You are not overwhelmed, and you know perfectly well where to start," Stepan Trofimovitch said sharply, cutting him off. His voice, though quieter now, trembled with restrained rage. "Enough of this! You've had your fun, and now I demand you tell me what you meant, directly, without these detestable tricks of yours. I won't stand for it!"

Liputin smiled faintly, as though Stepan Trofimovitch's righteous indignation had only amused him further. He took a small step toward the chair he'd been pulled into earlier, his gaze darting around the room as though measuring the reactions of everyone present. Then he sank languidly into the chair, his body slumping in exaggerated exhaustion.

"Well, since you insist," he said at last, his voice slow and deliberate, his eyes glinting with a hint of mock humility, "I will tell you what little I know. But truly, it's hardly worth all this fuss, Stepan Trofimovitch. Really, I never imagined..."

"Enough!" Stepan Trofimovitch exploded, cutting him off yet again. His face was crimson now, his voice shaking dangerously. "Stop this nonsense at once! Speak plainly, and stop tormenting us with your insufferable chatter!"

Liputin paused, looking for all the world as though he were offended by this unfair accusation, though his sly little grin betrayed him. He was in his element now, fully aware of the power he held in that moment, and he was clearly relishing it. He drew a long breath, adjusted his position in the chair, and finally began to speak, though his tone remained maddeningly slow, as if he were still taking his time.

"How am I to begin?" he repeated quietly, this time more to himself than anyone else. "Really, I am too overwhelmed..."

I could see Stepan Trofimovitch struggling to keep himself from leaping to his feet again, his knuckles white where they gripped the arms of his chair. Meanwhile, Kirillov sat motionless, his expression dark and unreadable, as though he were carefully tuning all of this out. Liputin, ever the master of provocation, looked at each of us in turn with a faint smile that made my blood boil. He had us exactly where he wanted us, and he knew it.

Chapter 3.6

"The day before yesterday, a servant suddenly arrived at my house," Liputin began, his voice deliberate, as if savoring every detail. "'You are requested to call at twelve o'clock,' the man said. Can you imagine such a thing? I threw down all my work immediately, of course. I didn't dare keep her waiting, and yesterday, precisely at noon, there I was, ringing the bell at her house. I was shown into the drawing room, left to wait for only a moment—and then she came in. You can imagine my astonishment, Stepan Trofimovitch, because you know well how she has always treated me before."

He paused for effect, but Stepan Trofimovitch said nothing. Liputin smirked faintly, clearly enjoying his narrative, and pressed on.

"She walked in and sat down without any fuss, right opposite me. And without so much as an introduction or small talk, she began immediately—straight to the point, you know her way. 'You remember,' she said, 'that four years ago, when Nikolay Vsyevolodovitch was ill, he did certain… strange things. Actions that left the entire town buzzing with gossip until the circumstances were properly explained. One of those actions, if you recall, concerned you personally.'"

Liputin paused again, leaning slightly forward to emphasize his next point. "'When Nikolay Vsyevolodovitch recovered,' she continued, 'he went to see you at my insistence. I know you spoke to him more than once back then. Now, tell me, openly and candidly, what you thought of him. What were your impressions of Nikolay Vsyevolodovitch at that time? What opinion did you form of him—then—and what opinion do you still hold now?'"

Here Liputin stopped dramatically and smiled slyly. "And at this point, Stepan Trofimovitch, she faltered. She paused for nearly a minute, and—you won't believe this—she actually flushed! Yes, flushed! I was stunned. I even grew a little uneasy myself. She began again, though, after composing herself, this time in a tone that I can only describe as impressive. 'I want you,' she said, 'to understand me clearly. I have called for you because I look upon you as an intelligent and discerning man, someone keen-sighted enough to observe accurately.'"

He grinned as though relishing the memory of her compliments. "Can you imagine, Stepan Trofimovitch? Me, Liputin, receiving such praise! She even said that I was impartial—impartial!" He chuckled, then continued more solemnly. "'You see,' she said, 'I am a mother speaking to you now. Nikolay Vsyevolodovitch has suffered many hardships in his life—many changes of fortune. Such experiences,' she said, 'could not help but leave their mark. I'm not speaking of madness, of course—madness is entirely out of the question!'" Here Liputin imitated Varvara Petrovna's tone with an exaggerated haughtiness. "'But,' she said, 'there might be something strange in his way of thinking, some peculiarity of thought, perhaps a certain... restlessness, a disposition toward peculiar impulses. I have noticed this myself,' she admitted, 'and as a mother, it troubles me deeply. But you, as an impartial observer, might have seen things more clearly.'"

Liputin lowered his voice dramatically, leaning closer to Stepan Trofimovitch as though sharing a secret. "'I implore you,' she said—yes, implore was the word she used!—'to tell me the truth without hesitation or concealment. And if you can give me your word to treat this matter with the utmost confidence, I will, in turn, always remain ready to seize any opportunity to show my gratitude.'" He leaned back with a satisfied air. "Well, Stepan Trofimovitch, what do you say to that?"

"You have... so amazed me..." Stepan Trofimovitch stammered, his voice faint and shaky. "That I don't believe you."

Liputin ignored him, his excitement growing as though he hadn't heard. "But think what her request means, Stepan Trofimovitch!" he cried, spreading his hands dramatically. "Consider the agitation, the anxiety, that must have driven a woman of her pride, her grandeur, to condescend to someone like me! And then to implore me, of all people! Clearly, she must have received some troubling news about Nikolay Vsyevolodovitch— some unexpected development, don't you agree?"

"I don't know... I don't know of any news," Stepan Trofimovitch muttered, his confusion evident. He struggled to gather his thoughts. "I haven't seen her for days, but... but if she spoke to you in confidence— how can you now repeat all of this in front of everyone?"

"Exactly in confidence!" Liputin agreed eagerly, his face lit with mock sincerity. "But does that really matter? Are we strangers here? Even Alexey Nilitch, surely, is no stranger."

"I don't share that view," Stepan Trofimovitch replied sharply, clearly struggling to suppress his mounting agitation. "I dare say we three here might keep such a secret, but as for you—I wouldn't trust you with anything."

"Come now, Stepan Trofimovitch!" Liputin protested, throwing up his hands with a wounded expression. "Why should I betray such confidence when I have been promised eternal gratitude! But that's beside the point. There's something even stranger, even more psychological, that happened last night after my meeting with Varvara Petrovna."

He turned toward Kirillov, who had remained silent through this, staring grimly at the floor. "I asked Alexey Nilitch, quite casually, about Nikolay Vsyevolodovitch. After all, he knew him abroad, and even before that in Petersburg. I asked him his opinion of the man—of his intellect, his abilities. Do you know what Alexey Nilitch said?" Liputin paused for effect, glancing around the room. "He said, laconically, that Nikolay Vsyevolodovitch was a man of subtle intellect and sound judgment. But then I pressed further. I repeated Varvara Petrovna's own question. 'Have you ever noticed,' I asked, 'anything peculiar in him? Any strange turn of mind, any peculiar way of looking at things?' And would you believe it? Alexey Nilitch actually grew thoughtful! He frowned, just as he's doing now, and said, 'Yes, sometimes I have thought there was something strange.'"

"Is this true?" Stepan Trofimovitch asked hoarsely, turning to Kirillov.

Kirillov raised his head abruptly, his dark eyes flashing. "I would prefer not to speak of this," he said curtly, his voice firm and cold. "You have no right, Liputin—no right to drag me into this. I gave no full opinion. Yes, I knew Nikolay Stavrogin, but only long ago, in Petersburg. And even though I met him again, I know very little of him now. I beg you to leave me out of this. All of this—it feels like gossip. Scandal."

Liputin threw up his hands again, his face wearing an exaggerated look of innocence. "Scandal? What scandal? I'm merely sharing observations! I repeat, I am only overwhelmed by the situation…"

He trailed off theatrically, looking from one face to another as though seeking sympathy, but this time, no one responded. Stepan Trofimovitch sank back into his chair, pale and visibly shaken, while Kirillov returned to staring fixedly at the floor, his face like stone.

"A scandal-monger! Why not just call me a spy while you're at it?" Liputin flung back, his voice rising sharply with feigned indignation. "It's easy for you to criticize, Alexey Nilitch, when you stand aside from everything and pretend to know nothing. But let me tell you, Stepan Trofimovitch—take Captain Lebyadkin, for example. He's as stupid as they come—stupid beyond words, really; it's embarrassing even to describe how stupid. There's an old Russian saying to convey the depth of that kind of stupidity, though I'll spare you the details. And yet, despite his idiocy, would you believe it? He actually considers himself wronged by Nikolay Vsyevolodovitch! Wronged! At the same time, he's utterly in awe of him. 'I'm amazed,' he said to me yesterday, 'at that man. He's a subtle serpent.' His exact words."

Liputin paused, letting the phrase "subtle serpent" hang in the air with a kind of theatrical weight before continuing. "So then, still under the influence of my earlier conversation—with Varvara Petrovna and later with Alexey Nilitch—I decided to prod him a little. I asked him, 'Well, Captain, what do you think—this subtle serpent of yours, is he mad or isn't he?' Would you believe it? It was as though I'd hit him with a whip from behind! He jumped clean off his seat, completely stunned. 'Yes,' he said—he actually said yes!—'but that,' he added, 'cannot affect…' 'Affect what?' I asked him. But he didn't finish. He just fell silent, and you could see something brooding on his mind. The man grew so pensive, so bitterly thoughtful, that his drunkenness seemed to fall right off him, as though it had never been there. We were sitting, you understand, at Filipov's restaurant. He didn't say another word for half an hour. Then, all of a sudden, he slammed his fist on the table so hard the plates rattled. 'Yes,' he said again, 'maybe he's mad, but that can't affect it.' He said no more after that—just stared ahead like a man trying to untangle something in his mind."

Liputin chuckled spitefully and waved a hand dismissively. "Of course, I'm only giving you a summary, an extract, but you can see the general meaning. You can go ask anyone you like—anyone in town—and they'll tell you the same thing. The idea is in everyone's head now. 'Yes,' they say, 'he's brilliant, a man of exceptional mind, but perhaps he's mad as well.'"

Stepan Trofimovitch sat in silence, staring at Liputin as though struggling to comprehend what he'd just heard. His brow furrowed deeply, and his eyes had a distant, troubled look as he pondered the information. At last, he muttered, almost to himself, "But how does Lebyadkin know? How could he know anything?"

"Why don't you ask Alexey Nilitch?" Liputin retorted, turning abruptly toward the engineer with a sneer. "The man who just accused me of being a spy? I'm a 'spy,' yet somehow I don't know anything, but Alexey Nilitch knows every twist and turn of this affair, and still, he holds his tongue. How strange!"

"I know nothing about it," the engineer snapped back irritably, his voice uncharacteristically sharp. "Or almost nothing. You make Lebyadkin drunk so he'll talk—you extract gossip from him like a parasite. You dragged me here just so you could use me as part of your dirty little games, and then you twist it all around to suit yourself. Yes, you are a spy."

Liputin's face flushed slightly with anger, but his lips curled into a mocking smile. "Not yet," he shot back, almost hissing the words. "I haven't made him drunk yet—he's hardly worth the expense. As for his so-called secrets, they're not valuable enough to me to waste a single ruble. On the contrary, the fool's been throwing money around lately, though only twelve days ago he was begging me for fifteen kopecks to buy bread. And now he's the one treating me to champagne! But you've given me an idea, Alexey Nilitch, you really have. If the opportunity arises, I'll get him drunk, and I'll pull every last thread of your little secrets out of him. Maybe then I'll find out all the things you're so desperate to keep hidden."

Stepan Trofimovitch looked back and forth between the two of them with growing bewilderment, clearly unnerved by the escalating tension. They were both starting to lose their composure, snapping at each other without a hint of restraint. The thought crossed my mind—absurd though it may have seemed at first—that Liputin had orchestrated this entire encounter for his own amusement or purpose. He had likely dragged Alexey Nilitch here just to maneuver him into conversation through a third party, a tactic I'd seen him use before. It was his specialty.

"You see, Stepan Trofimovitch," Liputin went on, his tone sharper now, "Alexey Nilitch knows Nikolay Vsyevolodovitch quite well—much better than any of us, in fact. He just chooses to keep it to himself. And as for your question about Captain Lebyadkin, it's all quite simple: he made his acquaintance six years ago, in Petersburg, during what one might call the obscure epoch of Nikolay Vsyevolodovitch's life—long before he thought to bless our little town with his presence. It was at that time, I suspect, that he also made the acquaintance of this gentleman here." He gestured toward Kirillov with a sardonic nod.

Kirillov's expression darkened further, and he muttered under his breath, "Take care, Liputin. I warn you—Nikolay Vsyevolodovitch will be here soon enough, and he knows perfectly well how to defend himself."

"Warn me?" Liputin sneered, spreading his arms wide in mock innocence. "What is there to warn me about? I've said nothing but the truth. I am the first to proclaim that Nikolay Vsyevolodovitch is a man of rare and refined intellect! In fact, I reassured Varvara Petrovna of that very thing yesterday. 'It's his character,' I told her, 'that I can't vouch for.' And Captain Lebyadkin said the same thing just yesterday. 'A lot of harm has come to me,' he said, 'from his character.'"

Liputin's voice had grown more cutting with each word, and now he turned his gaze squarely on Stepan Trofimovitch. "You shout 'slander!' and call me a spy, but look at yourself, Stepan Trofimovitch. You're sitting there hanging on my every word, wringing it all out of me with the keenest curiosity."

Stepan Trofimovitch opened his mouth to protest, but Liputin cut him off. "Ah, but don't worry! I'm not offended. It's only natural. After all, Varvara Petrovna said it plainly enough herself: I have a personal interest in this business, and I don't deny it. Nikolay Vsyevolodovitch has insulted me publicly—personally—before all decent society, and now, naturally, I'm curious. He's the sort of man who'll shake your hand one

115

day, then slap you in the face the next for no reason at all. And all because he feels like it! As for the women—well, what's to be said? Butterflies and gallant little cupids, the lot of them! If you married, Stepan Trofimovitch, if you took a young, pretty wife—you would be the first to lock your doors and barricade yourself against our prince. Mark my words! And as for Mademoiselle Lebyadkin, who gets whipped by her brother—if she weren't lame and mad, I'd swear she was the cause of Captain Lebyadkin's so-called 'family dishonor.' Why not? Nothing stops him when the mood strikes him."

"The whole town's ringing with it? What's the town ringing with?" Stepan Trofimovitch blurted out, his voice quavering as though he had only just grasped the seriousness of the insinuations.

"That is to say, Captain Lebyadkin is shouting it across the whole town—shouting as though he's standing in the middle of the market square, and isn't that the same as the town ringing with it? How can I be blamed for this? I take an interest in it only among friends—for I do consider myself among friends here," Liputin said smoothly, his innocent air entirely insincere. He swept his eyes across the room, as though challenging anyone to dispute his version of events.

"Something's happened, something rather notable, if you stop to think," he continued, warming to his narrative. "It's said that his excellency sent Captain Lebyadkin three hundred roubles all the way from Switzerland—sent it through a most honorable young lady, a modest orphan, whom I happen to know personally and hold in high esteem. A little later, however, Captain Lebyadkin was informed—again, with the utmost certainty and by a very reliable source, I won't say whom—that it wasn't three hundred roubles sent, but a full thousand! Can you imagine? And now, of course, Lebyadkin is in a rage. He's storming through the town crying out, 'That young lady has pocketed seven hundred roubles of my money!' He's nearly ready to call in the police, or so he says. He makes a racket everywhere he goes, creating an uproar in every corner of the town."

At this, the engineer, who had been sitting rigidly, leapt to his feet as though stung. His face flushed with sudden anger. "This is vile—vile of you!" he shouted, his voice shaking.

Liputin smiled, his composure unshaken. "And yet you are the very 'honorable person,' Alexey Nilitch, who told Captain Lebyadkin that a thousand roubles were sent—not three hundred. You brought him that news from Nikolay Vsyevolodovitch, or so the captain himself declared to me while he was drunk."

"That's… that's an unfortunate misunderstanding," the engineer stammered, visibly agitated. "A mistake—someone's made a mistake. It's nonsense! This is all nonsense, and it's base of you to bring it up like this!"

Liputin's eyes gleamed with malicious amusement as he raised his voice just slightly, drawing out every word. "Ah, but I'm perfectly willing to believe that it's all nonsense," he said silkily. "I'm even distressed to hear such a story circulating. After all, this unfortunate affair drags into the mud a young lady of unimpeachable reputation—first over this alleged sum of seven hundred roubles, and second through her apparent, shall we say, intimacy with Nikolay Vsyevolodovitch."

He paused for effect and gave a theatrical sigh, then added with mock solemnity, "For his excellency, disgracing a girl of good character—or bringing shame upon another man's wife—is a trifle, a diversion. It's like that little incident with me, if you recall. When he comes across a man of goodwill, a generous-hearted soul, he'll force him to cover up for the sins of others, shelter them under his own honorable name. I speak from experience. I've had to endure it myself."

"Be careful, Liputin!" Stepan Trofimovitch interrupted sharply. He had risen from his chair, his face pale as he stared at Liputin with a mixture of anger and apprehension.

"Don't believe it!" the engineer cried, his voice almost desperate. "Don't believe any of it! It's all nonsense—a misunderstanding! Lebyadkin is drunk, that's all—he's drunk! Everything will be explained, you'll see, but I can't—" His words broke off suddenly, his face flushed red, and his movements grew erratic as though he couldn't bear to stay in the room another moment. "I think it's low, vile—I won't listen to any more of this! Enough—enough!"

And without another word, he bolted out of the room, leaving the door swinging behind him.

"What are you doing? Wait—I'm going with you!" Liputin cried, jumping up with a start and chasing after the engineer.

For a moment, the room fell into an eerie silence. Stepan Trofimovitch stood in place, staring at the door with a vacant, bewildered expression. He looked like a man caught in a storm, unable to make sense of what was happening around him. Then, slowly, he turned to me as though he had forgotten I was still there. His lips moved slightly, as if he were about to speak, but instead, he quietly took up his hat and stick and walked toward the door.

I hesitated only for a moment before following him. When we stepped outside the gate, he glanced at me briefly, as though just realizing I was by his side. "Oh yes," he murmured, almost absently. "You may serve as a witness... de l'accident. Vous m'accompagnerez, n'est-ce pas?"

"Stepan Trofimovitch, you aren't going there again, are you?" I asked in alarm. "Think about what might come of it!"

He stopped abruptly and turned to face me. His expression was a strange mix of shame, despair, and something close to ecstasy. His lips trembled as he whispered hoarsely, "I cannot marry to cover 'another man's sins.'"

The words struck me like a blow, though I had been expecting them. This fatal phrase, the one he had kept hidden for so long, was finally spoken aloud. For an entire week, he had danced around it, feigning ignorance, pretending to misunderstand, but now here it was, uttered clearly and unmistakably. I was enraged.

"And you, Stepan Verhovensky," I exclaimed bitterly, "with all your luminous intelligence, your kind heart—you've been harboring such a vile, such a contemptible suspicion all along? And you had it even before Liputin came and fanned the flames!"

He looked at me silently, as though my words had struck him to the core. He said nothing in his defense, merely turned and resumed walking in the same direction. I refused to be left behind. My resolve hardened; I was determined to give Varvara Petrovna my own version of this. I could have forgiven Stepan Trofimovitch if his cowardly, womanish nature had simply made him vulnerable to Liputin's insinuations. But now it was clear—he had thought of this himself, long before Liputin had ever opened his mouth. Varvara Petrovna's domineering behavior, her urgency, her insistence on his involvement—he had twisted all of it into a sordid scheme in his own mind, imagining that she meant to marry him off to cover up the disgrace of her precious "Nicolas." The baseness of it made my blood boil.

"Oh, Dieu, qui est si grand et si bon! Oh, who will comfort me!" Stepan Trofimovitch cried out suddenly, halting again after we had walked a hundred paces.

"Come straight home with me and I'll explain everything," I urged, trying to steer him gently but firmly back toward his house.

At that moment, a fresh, musical voice rang out like a bell behind us. "It's him! It's Stepan Trofimovitch—is it really you?"

We turned to see a lady on horseback, riding toward us with a bright, joyous smile. It was Lizaveta Nikolaevna, radiant and spirited as always, her companion riding dutifully at her side. She pulled her horse up sharply, her face glowing with excitement.

"Come here, come quickly!" she called merrily, beckoning us with her hand. "It's twelve years since I've seen him, and yet I knew him at once, though he... Do you really not recognize me?"

Stepan Trofimovitch stood paralyzed for a moment, staring at her in astonishment. Then, as though awakening from a dream, he approached her reverently, took her extended hand, and kissed it gently. His face had softened into an expression of pure devotion, as though he were gazing upon something miraculous.

"He knows me, and he's glad!" Lizaveta Nikolaevna exclaimed joyfully, turning to her companion. "Mavriky Nikolaevitch, look at him— he's so happy to see me! Why haven't you come to visit us all this time? Auntie said you were ill, that we shouldn't disturb you, but I knew she was lying. I've been furious with you! But I decided you must come to me first—that's why I didn't send for you. Look at him—he hasn't changed at all!"

She leaned down from the saddle, her eyes sparkling with warmth and curiosity as she examined him. "Oh, there are wrinkles now—around your eyes, on your cheeks—and some grey in your hair. But your eyes are still the same. And me? Have I changed? Have I?"

"You…" Stepan Trofimovitch stammered, his voice breaking with emotion. "I… I was just crying out, 'Who will comfort me?' And then I heard your voice. I consider it a miracle—et je commence à croire."

"En Dieu! En Dieu qui est là-haut et qui est si grand et si bon! You see, I still remember all your lectures by heart," she said with a bright laugh, her voice ringing with a mixture of tenderness and playful mischief. "Mavriky Nikolaevitch, you wouldn't believe the faith he used to teach me back then—faith in God, who is so great and so good! Do you remember, Stepan Trofimovitch, your story about how Columbus discovered America? How the sailors cried out, 'Land! Land!' when they saw the shore? My old nurse, Alyona Frolovna, swears I was light-headed that night, and in my fever I kept crying out 'Land! Land!' in my sleep. And do you remember how you told me the story of Prince Hamlet? Or how you described to me those poor emigrants transported from Europe to America? How they sang songs as they sailed, filled with hope for a new life? I found out later, of course, that none of it was true. It wasn't nearly so romantic as you made it sound. But how beautiful your fibs were! They were better than the truth, so much better!"

She threw a teasing glance at Mavriky Nikolaevitch, who sat silently on his horse, watching her with a quiet, steady devotion. "Why are you looking at Mavriky Nikolaevitch like that, dear Stepan Trofimovitch? He's the finest, most honorable man on the face of the earth! And you must love him just as you love me—promise me that! Il fait tout ce que je veux, you see. He's at my command! But enough about him. Tell me, Stepan Trofimovitch, are you unhappy again? You must be, since you're crying out in the street for someone to comfort you. Aren't you unhappy?"

"Now I'm happy," Stepan Trofimovitch murmured, his voice soft and trembling with emotion.

She didn't seem to hear him. "Aunt's been horrid to you again, hasn't she?" she continued, without waiting for a reply. "She's just the same as ever—cross, severe, and unfair. Oh, our precious aunt! And do you remember how you once threw yourself into my arms in the garden when I was just a child, and I comforted you? I cried with you then. Don't be afraid of Mavriky Nikolaevitch," she added, glancing at her silent companion. "He's known everything about you for ages, everything, and he doesn't mind. If you need to cry, you can cry on his shoulder as long as you like. He'll stand there as still as a stone until you're done."

Suddenly her face lit up with an idea. "Take off your hat—lift it up! I want to see your forehead. Come closer, closer! Lift your head, stand on tiptoe! I want to kiss you right here, just as I did the last time we parted. Do you see that young lady watching us from the window over there? Let her admire us. Heavens, how grey you are!"

With a quick, graceful movement, she bent down from her saddle, and before Stepan Trofimovitch could react, she pressed a soft kiss on his forehead.

"Now go straight home!" she commanded, sitting upright again. "I know where you live. I'll come to you myself—give me just a minute. You stubborn man, I'll be there in no time. And after that, you'll spend an entire day with me at home. Go and prepare yourself!"

With that, she spurred her horse and galloped off with Mavriky Nikolaevitch riding close behind her. We returned in silence. Stepan Trofimovitch stumbled into the house, sank onto the sofa, and began to weep.

"Dieu, Dieu," he exclaimed softly, tears streaming down his face. "Enfin une minute de bonheur!"

No more than ten minutes had passed when the sound of hooves returned, and Lizaveta Nikolaevna reappeared, just as she had promised, Mavriky Nikolaevitch close at her side. She burst into the room with her usual brightness, carrying a small nosegay of fresh flowers in her gloved hand.

"Vous et le bonheur, vous arrivez en même temps!" Stepan

Trofimovitch cried, rising from his seat to meet her, his voice almost triumphant.

"Here, this is for you," she said with a flourish, holding out the flowers. "I rode to Madame Chevalier's on the way. She has flowers all year round for name-days, so I bought these just for you. Isn't it lovely? Oh, and here's Mavriky Nikolaevitch—you must be friends now. Shake hands! I wanted to bring you a cake instead of flowers, but Mavriky Nikolaevitch declared that would not be in the proper Russian spirit."

Mavriky Nikolaevitch, a tall and imposing artillery captain, stood with perfect composure. He was a striking man of about thirty-three, with a stern, almost forbidding countenance at first glance. Yet in his quiet reserve, there was an unmistakable kindness, a deep gentleness that became evident the moment you looked at him more closely. He wasn't a man of many words, but there was a solidity to him that inspired trust. Some in the town later dismissed him as "not particularly clever," but I always thought this judgment was hasty and unfair.

As for Lizaveta Nikolaevna, it would be impossible to fully describe her beauty. The entire town was already abuzz with talk of it, though the local ladies and young girls were far from unanimous in their opinions. Some were openly critical, even spiteful, toward her. They resented her pride, her refusal to pay calls, and her habit of riding out on horseback every day—something unheard of for young ladies in our town. The Drozdovs had only just begun to pay visits, and the delay—caused by Praskovya Ivanovna's fragile health—had only added to the gossip.

Yet all this resentment couldn't diminish the impression Lizaveta Nikolaevna made. She was restless, almost unnervingly so. Her energy, her nervous movements, her quick shifts in tone and expression—they all betrayed an underlying unhappiness, though none of us could understand it at the time. Looking back now, I would say that her beauty wasn't conventional; it wasn't the sort of beauty that inspired immediate awe. She was tall, slim, and strong, her figure supple and graceful. Her features were irregular: her eyes were slightly slanted, almost exotic, her cheekbones high, and her complexion pale. Yet there was something magnetic in her—something powerful in the deep, fiery glance of her dark eyes.

She sank onto the sofa and looked around the room with a strange expression, almost wistful. "Why is it that I always feel sad at moments like this?" she asked suddenly. "Explain that mystery to me, you learned man. I've spent my whole life imagining how happy I would be to see you again, to remember everything. And here you are, and yet... I'm not happy at all. Not really. And yet I do love you."

Her eyes suddenly fell on something on the wall, and her face lit up with recognition. "Oh, heavens! You have my portrait! That little miniature—give it here! I remember it. Yes, I remember it!"

It was a small, exquisite watercolor of her at twelve years old, sent years earlier by the Drozdovs from Petersburg. She took it in her hands and stared at it intently, as though seeing it for the first time.

"Was I really such a pretty child?" she asked softly, holding the portrait up to the light. Then she walked over to the mirror, holding the miniature beside her face. "Can that really have been me?"

Suddenly, as if the sight unsettled her, she thrust the portrait back into his hands. "Take it, quickly! I don't want to see it again. Don't hang it up now—wait until I'm gone." She sank back onto the sofa with a sigh. "One life ends, another begins. Then that one ends, too, and a third begins— and so on, endlessly. It's as though every chapter is cut off with scissors. Such a stale thought, isn't it? And yet, how much truth there is in it."

She looked directly at me, her smile bright and curious. It was not the first time she had glanced in my direction, but in his excitement, Stepan Trofimovitch had entirely forgotten his promise to introduce me.

"And why, Stepan Trofimovitch," she asked suddenly, her voice playful yet full of interest, "have you hung my portrait under those daggers? And why on earth do you have so many daggers and sabres on your wall?"

She gestured toward the peculiar display: two crossed daggers and, above them, an ornate, gleaming Circassian sabre, hanging on the wall as though arranged there for effect. The question was directed at Stepan Trofimovitch, but her eyes remained fixed on me so directly that I felt compelled to answer—though I hesitated, unsure of my place in the conversation.

Finally, Stepan Trofimovitch seemed to grasp the situation and, as though startled, said hurriedly, "Ah! Permit me to introduce to you my dear young friend, my confidant and—"

"I know, I know!" she interrupted, brightening immediately as she extended her hand to me with an air of unexpected warmth. "I'm delighted to meet you at last. Mother has told me a great deal about you. Let me introduce you to Mavriky Nikolaevitch as well," she added, turning toward her silent companion. "He's a splendid person, you'll see for yourself."

Mavriky Nikolaevitch gave a polite but brief nod, his expression unchanging, though his eyes regarded me with the same quiet kindness I had already observed in him.

She turned back to me with an almost teasing smile. "You know," she said lightly, "I had already formed an impression of you—quite a funny one, I'll admit. You're Stepan Trofimovitch's confidant, aren't you?"

I felt my face flush red.

"Oh, forgive me! I used the wrong word entirely. Not funny at all. I only meant..." She stopped herself, looking genuinely embarrassed now, and blushed slightly. "But really, why should I be ashamed to say you're probably a splendid person, too? Well, it's time we were going, isn't it, Mavriky Nikolaevitch? Stepan Trofimovitch," she exclaimed, turning back to him suddenly, "you must come to us in half an hour—no later! Mercy, what a lot we'll talk about!" She clapped her hands together joyfully, her entire face alight with anticipation. "Now I'm your confidante, you understand? Everything, you'll tell me everything!"

Stepan Trofimovitch looked immediately alarmed. "Liza, but—"

"Oh, don't worry about him!" she said, nodding toward Mavriky Nikolaevitch. "He already knows everything, so there's no need to be shy."

"What does he know?" Stepan Trofimovitch stammered, his unease growing.

"What do you mean, 'What does he know?'" she repeated, staring at him in genuine astonishment. "Good heavens! You mean it's true that

124

you're all hiding it? I didn't believe it! And Dasha too! Aunt wouldn't let me see her today—told me she had a headache."

"But... but how did you find out?" Stepan Trofimovitch asked, his voice faltering and his face turning crimson.

"Oh, my goodness, just like everyone else!" she said, laughing. "It doesn't take much cunning to learn things here."

"Everyone else knows?"

"Of course! Mother heard it from Alyona Frolovna—my old nurse, you remember her—and she says it was your Nastasya who ran over to tell her. Didn't you tell Nastasya yourself?"

"I... I might have said something once," Stepan Trofimovitch stammered, growing redder still. "But I was nervous... I was ill... and then—"

"And then Nastasya turned up," she finished for him, laughing again. "You didn't have your confidant here to listen, so you settled for Nastasya instead. Naturally, that was enough. Nastasya has plenty of friends to spread the news around. But never mind—it's all for the best. Let them know! Come quickly now, we dine early."

She suddenly stopped, as though struck by a new thought, and sat down again. "Wait! I nearly forgot. What kind of person is Shatov?"

"Shatov?" Stepan Trofimovitch repeated, blinking. "Why... he's Darya Pavlovna's brother."

"I know he's her brother! Really, Stepan Trofimovitch, you're impossible. What I mean is—what sort of man is he? What's he like?"

"C'est un pense-creux d'ici," Stepan Trofimovitch replied, stumbling over the words. "C'est le meilleur et le plus irascible homme du monde."

"I've heard that he's rather eccentric," she said thoughtfully, ignoring the comment. "But that's not what interests me. I've been told he knows three languages, including English, and that he can do literary work. I need someone to help me—right away. Would he take the work, do you think? He's been recommended to me."

"Oh, most certainly, he would! Et vous ferez un bienfait—"

"I'm not doing it as a bienfait," she interrupted sharply. "I simply need his help."

"I know Shatov well," I said suddenly, feeling compelled to speak up. "If you'll trust me with a message, I'll go to him this very minute."

"Perfect! Tell him to come to me tomorrow at noon. Thank you— this is wonderful. Mavriky Nikolaevitch, are you ready now?"

She rose briskly, her energy undiminished, and turned toward the door. Mavriky Nikolaevitch followed her without a word, bowing politely as he passed.

They left. Without wasting a moment, I turned to go straight to Shatov's house, but Stepan Trofimovitch caught up with me on the steps, his face pale and worn. "Mon ami!" he said softly, gripping my arm. "Be sure to come to my lodging at ten—no, at eleven—when I return. I have behaved wrongly toward you... toward everyone. I see that now."

His voice was low, almost trembling with shame, and the weight of his words stayed with me as I hurried off to carry out the errand.

Chapter 3.8

I did not find Shatov at home when I first arrived, nor did I have any better luck when I tried again two hours later. His door remained shut and the house was silent, almost desolate. Finally, at eight o'clock in the evening, I resolved to go once more, prepared this time to leave a note if I didn't find him. Once again, the lodging was locked up, silent as before. Shatov had no servant or anyone else to care for his rooms; he lived entirely alone. Standing in the empty, quiet yard, I briefly considered knocking on Captain Lebyadkin's door downstairs to ask about Shatov's whereabouts. However, the lower part of the house was just as dark and silent as Shatov's rooms. There was neither sound nor light coming from within; it seemed entirely deserted, and the odd stillness only added to my curiosity, especially after all the stories I had heard that day. Feeling frustrated and defeated, I decided to leave the matter for the night and come back early in the morning.

To tell the truth, I didn't put much stock in the effect of a note. Shatov was obstinate, shy, and indifferent to such things; it was entirely possible he would ignore it or refuse to respond. I cursed my own failure, muttering as I turned toward the gate. Just as I was stepping out, I almost stumbled into Mr. Kirillov, who was coming in at that very moment. He recognized me first and, seeing my exasperation, began to question me about what had happened. I explained my unsuccessful attempts to find Shatov and showed him the note I had intended to leave.

"Let's go inside," he said abruptly. "I will take care of it."

I suddenly remembered that Liputin had mentioned earlier that Kirillov had taken the wooden lodge in the yard. It was a small, stand-alone structure with enough space for two or three rooms. It seemed far too large for him alone, but he had not moved in entirely yet. An old deaf woman—some distant relation of the landlord—lived there as well to take care of basic duties. The landlord himself had moved to another street where he now ran a small restaurant, leaving his relative to watch over the empty house.

The lodge was sparsely but tidily furnished, though the wallpaper was faded and peeling in places. In the main room we entered, the furniture seemed to have been collected haphazardly over time: a pair of mismatched card tables, a heavy wooden chest of drawers made from elder, a crude, oversized kitchen table, and a set of chairs along with a stiff, trellis-backed sofa covered in cracked leather. The whole arrangement looked awkward, as though none of the pieces belonged together. In one corner hung an old-fashioned icon with a small lamp burning before it, lit by the old woman before our arrival. Two faded oil portraits hung on the walls: one of Tsar Nicholas I, painted years ago in a somber, imposing style, and the other of a bishop with a stern, bearded face.

Kirillov immediately struck a match, lit a candle, and moved to the trunk that stood unpacked in one corner of the room. From inside, he pulled out an envelope, a stick of sealing wax, and a small glass seal. "Seal your note," he instructed briskly, placing the items on the table.

"It really isn't necessary," I objected, feeling the step a little formal and overdone.

"It's necessary," he said curtly, leaving no room for argument.

I shrugged and quickly addressed the envelope after sealing it, feeling slightly absurd as I did so. When I finished and stood to leave, Kirillov looked up and surprised me by saying, "Stay. You'll have tea. I've bought tea. Will you?"

There was something so unexpectedly hospitable about the offer, so earnest despite its bluntness, that I felt compelled to agree. "Of course, thank you," I replied.

The old woman soon brought in a heavy, chipped teapot full of boiling water, another smaller pot containing concentrated tea, two large earthenware cups decorated with faded flowers, a fancy loaf of bread, and a saucer piled high with coarse, white sugar lumps.

"I love tea at night," Kirillov said simply, as he poured it for us. "I walk a lot in the evening, then drink tea till daybreak. Abroad, it's harder— tea at night is inconvenient there."

"You go to bed at daybreak?" I asked, surprised.

"Always. For a long time now," he replied as though the habit were the most natural thing in the world. "I eat little. I drink tea instead. Liputin is sly, but also impatient."

His sudden comment about Liputin caught me off guard. I decided to seize the opportunity to ask about the morning's unpleasant misunderstandings. "There was a lot of confusion earlier today," I ventured cautiously.

He frowned, his dark eyes narrowing slightly. "Foolishness. Complete nonsense," he said firmly. "All of it started because Lebyadkin is drunk. I explained the nonsense to Liputin—tried to correct him—but he took it wrong. He's impatient. He builds mountains out of nothing. Yesterday, I trusted Liputin."

"And me today?" I asked, half-joking.

Kirillov looked up and considered me for a moment. "You already knew everything this morning. Liputin is weak, or impatient, or malicious—or maybe he's envious."

The last word struck me as peculiar, and I repeated it back. "Envious?"

Kirillov gave a slight, almost dismissive nod. "Yes. Envious. I said a lot of words just now; it would be strange if one of them didn't fit."

"Or perhaps they all fit," I replied.

"Yes. All at once," Kirillov said with a small, humorless smile. "That's what Liputin really is—a chaos." He paused, then added abruptly, "But he wasn't lying this morning when he said I was writing something."

"What are you writing?" I asked, trying not to seem too inquisitive.

Kirillov scowled slightly and stared down at the table. "Why should he lie?" he said, brushing aside my question. I apologized quickly, assuring him that I hadn't meant to pry.

His expression softened, and for the first time, he smiled—a small, childlike smile that seemed entirely at odds with his otherwise serious demeanor. "He invented something about 'heads,'" he said suddenly, his voice almost playful, "out of a book. He told me first and misunderstood it entirely. What I'm writing... I'm only seeking to understand one thing: why men don't dare to kill themselves. That's all. And it doesn't matter."

I blinked, startled by the shift in subject. "Why they don't dare?" I repeated, confused. "Are there so few suicides in the world?"

"Very few," he said calmly.

"Do you really think so?"

Kirillov said nothing. Instead, he rose from his seat and began pacing slowly back and forth across the room, his arms crossed, his gaze fixed intently on the floor as though lost in thought. I watched him in silence, fascinated by the strange intensity that suddenly enveloped him. It was as though he were wrestling with some unspoken truth, something so immense and all-consuming that it left no room for anything else.

"What is it, in your opinion, that restrains people from suicide?" I asked, as he paced back and forth in the dimly lit room. My question seemed to pull him back into the present, as though he had been walking in a fog of his own thoughts. He stopped, looked at me absentmindedly, as if struggling to recall what we had been talking about, and then answered slowly, as though piecing the thought together.

"I ... I don't know much yet," he said softly. "There are only two things that restrain people—two prejudices, two barriers, you might say. One of them is very small, and the other is enormous."

"What is the small thing?" I pressed him.

"Pain."

"Pain?" I repeated, almost incredulously. "Can that really matter so much at such a moment?"

"It matters more than anything," he said with sudden intensity. "There are two kinds of people who kill themselves: some do it suddenly—out of grief, rage, madness, or some other overwhelming feeling—they don't stop to think much about pain. It happens in a single moment. But others—others do it rationally, with deliberation. Those people think about the pain. They think a great deal."

"Do you mean there are people who kill themselves from reason?" I asked, surprised by the suggestion.

"Many," he replied firmly. "Very many. And if it weren't for the big prejudice—if it weren't for superstition—there would be more. Many more. All."

"All?" I echoed, startled.

He didn't answer. He seemed lost in thought again, his eyes fixed on the floor, as though trying to see something invisible beneath the dusty boards.

"But aren't there ways to die without pain?" I asked after a pause, determined to understand his reasoning.

He suddenly turned to face me, his dark eyes sharp and focused. "Imagine," he said, "imagine a stone the size of a house. A massive, solid stone, as big as a great building, hanging above you. Now imagine you are standing underneath it. If it falls, if it crashes down upon you, will it hurt?"

"A stone as big as a house?" I replied, taken aback. "Of course it would be terrifying!"

"I am not speaking of fear," he interrupted, his voice cutting. "I ask you—will it hurt?"

"A stone the size of a mountain, weighing millions of tons?" I paused, trying to follow his strange logic. "No, I suppose it wouldn't hurt at all. It would crush everything in an instant. You wouldn't feel a thing."

"Exactly. But while it hangs there, while you stand beneath it, you will be terrified. You will fear the pain, even though you know it won't hurt. Even the greatest doctor, the wisest scholar, would stand there trembling, afraid of the pain. Everyone would."

I nodded slowly, unsettled by the imagery. "And the second reason? The big one?"

"The other world," he said simply.

"You mean fear of punishment?"

He shrugged. "That's not the point. Just the other world—any idea of it."

"But aren't there atheists who don't believe in the other world at all?" I asked skeptically.

He remained silent, his eyes narrowing slightly as though annoyed by the question.

"Perhaps you judge from yourself," I said carefully.

"Everyone can only judge from themselves," he said suddenly, his voice rising slightly, and a faint flush crept across his face. "There will be full freedom—absolute freedom—when it no longer matters whether one lives or dies. That is the ultimate goal. That is the end for all mankind."

"The goal?" I repeated, trying to make sense of his words. "But if it no longer matters, won't people stop caring about life altogether?"

"No one will care," he replied quietly, with absolute conviction. "No one."

"But man fears death because he loves life," I said, pressing the point further. "That's how I understand it, and that's determined by nature."

131

"That's a deception!" he cried out suddenly, his eyes blazing with unexpected fury. "That is abject! Life is pain; life is terror. And yet man clings to it, embraces it, because he has been tricked into loving pain and terror. That's the deception—they've made life about pain and terror. But man is not what he should be. There will come a time, a new era, when a new man will emerge. A man who is proud, a man who is free. For him, it will not matter whether he lives or dies. He will conquer pain and terror, and he will become a god himself. And that God will cease to be."

"Then this God does exist, according to you?" I asked, startled by his words.

"No," he said firmly, shaking his head. "He does not exist, but He is. He is the fear of death. He is the pain of fear. Conquer that, and you will have no need for God. He who conquers pain and terror will be like a god himself. Everything will be new then—a new man, a new life, a new earth. History will be divided into two parts: from the gorilla to the annihilation of God, and from the annihilation of God to…"

"To the gorilla again?" I interrupted with a touch of irony.

He didn't react to my joke. "To the transformation of man, of the earth, of thoughts, of feelings—of everything. Man will become something new. Do you think man will change physically as well?"

"If it's all the same whether one lives or dies," I said, trying to reason with him, "won't everyone simply kill themselves? Perhaps that is the transformation you're describing?"

"That doesn't matter," he replied softly, his voice calm but filled with something unshakable. "The point is to kill the deception. The ultimate freedom lies in daring to destroy the fear of death. He who dares to kill himself has uncovered the secret of the deception. There is no freedom beyond that. There is nothing beyond. He who kills himself becomes God."

"But there have been millions of suicides," I argued.

"Not one of them did it for that reason," he said flatly. "Not one. They all did it out of terror, despair, or madness—not to overcome fear. He who kills himself to conquer fear alone will become a god at once."

"He wouldn't have time to enjoy it, would he?" I murmured.

"That doesn't matter," he said again, his voice now soft, almost tender, yet laced with pride. "I'm sorry you seem to be laughing," he added quietly after a pause.

"I'm not laughing," I assured him. "It's just strange. You were so irritable this morning, but now you're perfectly calm—even though you speak with such passion."

"This morning?" He smiled faintly. "That was funny. I don't like scolding, and I never laugh," he added with surprising sadness.

"Your nights spent over tea like this—surely they aren't very cheerful," I said, standing up and taking my cap.

"You think not?" He looked at me, almost surprised. "No, I... I don't know. I can't be like others. Others think one thing and then quickly think of something else. I can't do that. I think of one thing my entire life." He paused, then added in a softer voice, as though confessing something. "God has tormented me all my life."

"And one last question," I ventured gently. "Why do you speak Russian so oddly? Surely you haven't forgotten it after five years abroad?"

He blinked and seemed momentarily surprised. "Do I speak it wrongly? I don't know. It's not because of abroad. I've always spoken this way. It doesn't matter to me."

"And another question, a more delicate one," I said carefully. "I can see you don't like talking to people. Why have you spoken so much to me now?"

He looked at me intently, as though weighing his answer, then flushed faintly. "This morning, you sat there quietly. You... I don't know. You reminded me of my brother. You look very much like him—extremely so," he added softly. "He died seven years ago. He was older. Much older."

"Did he influence the way you think?" I asked.

"No," he replied after a pause. "He said very little. He said nothing at all."

"I'll give Shatov your note," he finished quietly.

He took a lantern to light my way to the gate and stood silently as he locked it behind me. "Of course he's mad," I thought to myself as I stepped into the night. And yet, just as I reached the gate, another figure emerged from the darkness, startling me with its sudden appearance.

Chapter 3.9

I had barely lifted my leg over the high wooden barrier at the bottom of the gateway when, without warning, a strong, rough hand grabbed me by the chest.

"Who's this?" boomed a coarse, drunken voice. "A friend or an enemy? Speak up!"

Before I could react, Liputin's voice piped up from somewhere nearby in his usual ingratiating squeal. "He's one of us, one of us! It's Mr. G——v, a young man of classical education, thoroughly connected with the highest society."

"Classical education? High society?" the voice slurred again, this time with some semblance of satisfaction. "Then I love him! I love him for that. Clas-si—that means he's high-ly ed-u-cated," he drawled out each syllable, as though reciting a sacred incantation.

By now, I could see the man clearly in the dim lantern light. It was Captain Lebyadkin—a huge, lumbering man, easily over six feet tall, with a fleshy red face and a tangled mess of curly hair. He was so outrageously drunk that he could scarcely stand upright, swaying before me like a ship in a storm, his lips moving clumsily as he struggled to articulate his thoughts. I had seen him before, though only at a distance.

"The retired Captain Ignat Lebyadkin," he announced, puffing up his chest as though standing on parade. "At the service of the world… and his friends… if they're true ones! If they're true ones," he muttered, his voice dropping to a suspicious growl, "not like those scoundrels!"

He swayed toward me with an exaggerated attempt at grace and then, suddenly catching sight of Kirillov, who still stood quietly nearby with his lantern, Lebyadkin's expression changed. He raised a trembling fist as though preparing for a blow but immediately dropped it, slapping his thigh instead.

"I forgive you for your learning!" he bellowed magnanimously, leaning toward me with his sweaty, flushed face far too close for comfort. "Ignat Lebyadkin—highly ed-u-cated! Listen!" He thrust his finger at me like a poet about to recite his greatest work.

"A bomb of love with stinging smart

Exploded in Ignaty's heart.

In anguish dire I weep again

The arm that at Sevastopol

I lost in bitter pain!"

As he finished, he teetered unsteadily, nearly losing his balance.

"Only… I wasn't ever at Sevastopol, you know," he added suddenly, with absurd seriousness. "And I never lost my arm. But you know what rhyme is!" He grinned stupidly, as though expecting applause.

"He's in a hurry; he's going home!" Liputin interjected quickly, attempting to extricate me. "He'll tell Lizaveta Nikolaevna tomorrow."

"Lizaveta!" Lebyadkin roared, his face lighting up in a grotesque mix of drunken affection and theatrical ardor. "Wait! Stay! I have another—another variation! Listen, listen!"

He staggered forward, grabbing at my coat as though to hold me in place, though I jerked back instinctively.

"Among the Amazons a star,

Upon her steed she flashes by.

And smiles upon me from afar,

The child of aris-to-cra-cy!"

"To a Starry Amazon!" he announced proudly, pointing a shaking finger upward as though revealing the heavens themselves. "You hear that? A hymn, sir, a hymn! But you fools—duffers!—you don't understand!

None of you! Stay, I say!"

I pulled myself away with all my strength, trying not to inhale the strong fumes of alcohol coming off him in waves. "Tell her," he bellowed after me, still clutching the air where my coat had been, "tell her I'm a knight and the soul of honour! And as for that Dasha... I'd pick her up and chuck her out! Just a serf! She dares—"

At this point, he lurched forward so violently that he lost his balance and crashed to the ground with a heavy thud. Seizing the opportunity, I pulled myself free and stumbled into the street. Liputin, however, clung to me like a shadow, breathless and grinning.

"Alexey Nilitch will pick him up," Liputin whispered hurriedly, as if afraid I'd slip away. "Do you know what I just found out from him?" He was practically buzzing with excitement. "Did you hear his verses? He's sealed them—those poems—to the 'Starry Amazon' in an envelope. He's sending them tomorrow to Lizaveta Nikolaevna! Signed with his full name! Can you believe it?"

I turned on him sharply. "I bet you put the idea into his head yourself!"

"You lose your bet!" Liputin said with a sly laugh, his eyes glittering in the faint light. "He's in love, madly in love—like a cat! And do you know how it began? With hatred. He hated Lizaveta Nikolaevna at first— so much that he almost shouted insults at her in the street whenever she rode past on her horse. Imagine that! Just the day before yesterday, he cursed her aloud—thank goodness she didn't hear. And now, look at him: poetry! He's serious, too. Dead serious! He's talking about proposing marriage!"

I stopped abruptly, too angry to go on. "I'm astonished at you, Liputin," I said, glaring at him. "Wherever there's something filthy going on, you're always in the thick of it, egging it on and taking a leading role!"

"Careful, Mr. G——v," Liputin sneered with mock gravity. "Isn't your precious little heart quaking in fear of a rival, perhaps?"

"What?!" I cried, stopping dead in my tracks.

"Well, now you've offended me," Liputin said smugly, crossing his arms. "To punish you, I won't tell you the rest. But wouldn't you like to know? Take this little tidbit and stew over it: that drunken buffoon is no longer just a retired captain—he's now a landowner in our province, and quite a significant one at that. Nikolay Vsyevolodovitch sold him his entire estate just the other day—an estate that once held two hundred serfs!"

I stared at him, stunned.

"And as God's above, I'm not lying," Liputin continued, grinning maliciously. "I only just heard it myself from the most reliable source. Now you can go digging for the details yourself, but I won't say another word. Goodnight."

With that, he turned and hurried off into the shadows, leaving me standing there in the cold, bewildered and disgusted at the sordidness of what I had just witnessed.

Chapter 3.10

Stepan Trofimovitch was waiting for me with what I can only describe as hysterical impatience. He had returned over an hour before, and when I entered his room, his disheveled state startled me. For the first few minutes, I genuinely believed he might have been drinking—his manner was so strange, erratic, and animated, resembling someone intoxicated not with alcohol but with a whirlwind of overwhelming thoughts and emotions. Alas, the visit to the Drozdovs had delivered the final blow to his composure.

"Mon ami!" he cried out, rushing toward me with an air of desperation, his arms flailing slightly as though he didn't quite know what to do with them. "I have completely, completely lost the thread. Lise... oh, I love and respect that angel as before, just as before! But—but I'm convinced they called me there simply to extract something from me, to sift through me like a sieve, and then—then to get rid of me, to dispose of me like rubbish! That's how it is!"

"You ought to be ashamed of yourself for thinking such nonsense!" I couldn't help exclaiming, cutting him short.

"My friend, you don't understand," he continued in the same frantic tone, his pale face flushed in patches. "Now I'm utterly alone. Enfin, c'est ridicule... But listen! Would you believe it? Even there, the place is teeming with secrets, with mysteries—absolutely packed! They pounced on me, all but flew at me, asking questions about ears and noses—no, don't interrupt! I'm serious! Ears and noses! And then, out of nowhere, came Petersburg mysteries too—mysteries, I tell you! Imagine—they had only just now heard about Nicolas' behavior here four years ago! They asked me to my face, 'You were here, you saw it—tell us, is it true he's mad?'"

"Where did they get such an idea?" I asked incredulously.

"That's what I want to know! Why does Praskovya—that spiteful Madame Box—seem so determined that Nicolas must be mad? The woman wants him to be mad, insists upon it! And then Mavriky Nikolaevitch—ce Maurice, brave homme tout de même, but what's his role in all this? And to think Praskovya wrote herself from Paris to cette pauvre amie, and now—now—everything is topsy-turvy! Enfin, this Praskovya is a type, a true Gogolian type! She's Madame Box of immortal memory—but magnified, exaggerated, twisted into something almost monstrous!"

"Madame Box—exaggerated? Then wouldn't that make her a packing-case?" I muttered half-jokingly, trying to inject some calm into his rant.

"Yes, yes! A packing-case if you like!" he shouted, waving a trembling hand. "But don't interrupt me—don't interrupt! I'm all in a whirl, you see! Everything there is in chaos; they're all at each other's throats! Except for Lise—ah, Lise! She keeps up her constant 'Auntie, Auntie!' like a good little girl, but I know there's something sly behind it too. She's hiding something. Secrets everywhere! She's quarreled with her aunt—yes, it's true! Cette pauvre auntie tyrannizes everyone, of course, and on top of that there's the governor's wife, local society's rudeness, Karmazinov's rudeness... and now this ridiculous idea about madness, and ce Liputin—and—and vinegar compresses!"

"What?" I blurted out, bewildered.

"Vinegar compresses!" he repeated, his voice cracking. "They say she's been putting vinegar on her head—her head, mon ami!—and all the while, here am I with my complaints and letters! Oh, how I've tormented her at such a time! Je suis un ingrat! Imagine—I come home and find this—this letter waiting for me. Read it, read it! Look at her kindness! And I—I am nothing but a fool!"

He thrust the letter into my hands. It was from Varvara Petrovna. The tone was calm and composed but firm, with an edge of decision. She invited him to visit her the day after tomorrow—Sunday—at noon, and added that he was welcome to bring a friend. (My name was mentioned in parentheses, which made me raise my eyebrows.) On her end, she promised to invite Shatov, as Darya Pavlovna's brother. The letter concluded with this almost pointed remark: "You can obtain a final answer from her: will that be enough for you? Is this the formality you were so anxious for?"

"Observe the tone of that irritable phrase about 'formality,'" Stepan Trofimovitch murmured, peering over my shoulder as I read. "Oh, pauvre femme! The friend of my whole life... She's so kind, so good, and yet so... so sharp! I confess this sudden finality, this swift resolution, nearly crushed me. It left me breathless. I—I still had hopes, you see. Oui, j'avais des espoirs! But now? Tout est dit. It's all over. All is over! Oh, how I wish that Sunday would never come! I wish time would stop, and everything would stay just as it was before. You would come here to see me, we would talk, and life would go on..."

"You've let all those awful slanders Liputin threw at you poison your mind," I said indignantly.

"My dear, you've pressed your finger on another wound—oh, with such friendliness, such relentless friendliness!" he cried, throwing up his arms in theatrical despair. "You're right—I tried to forget all that this evening, forget all those venomous whispers while I was with Lise. For a moment, I convinced myself I was happy—happy! But now... oh, now I can think only of her, of her kindness, of her patience, her endurance in dealing with me, with my insufferable character! For twenty years, she's been my nurse—no, my mother—and how have I repaid her? With my endless whims, my egoism, my childish demands. And now, at my advanced age, I've sent her letter after letter, pleading for marriage, while her poor head—her poor head!—is wrapped in vinegar compresses! And on Sunday—on Sunday!—I shall be a married man. Oh, quelle horreur! And to think it was I who insisted! I brought this upon myself!"

He collapsed into his chair, trembling and exhausted, his face in his hands.

I seized the opportunity to tell him about my visit to Filipov's house. I described the strange encounter with Kirillov and my suspicion that Lebyadkin's sister—whom I had never seen—might indeed have been victimized in some way by Nicolas during the enigmatic period of his life Liputin had alluded to. I explained how Liputin's insinuations were likely exaggerated or outright misrepresented, and I repeated that Alexey Nilitch himself had assured me there was no truth to the scandal about Darya Pavlovna.

Stepan Trofimovitch, however, listened with the blank, absent air of a man whose mind was elsewhere, as though none of it mattered. "And Kirillov?" he murmured finally, almost as an afterthought.

"Yes, Kirillov," I replied. "He's mad. At least, he seems mad to me."

He said nothing more. He sat slumped in his chair, his hands resting limply on his knees, his tired eyes fixed unseeingly on the floor. For the first time in my life, I pitied him with my whole heart.

"He's not mad, but one of those shallow-minded people," Stepan Trofimovitch muttered listlessly, slumping back in his chair as though the conversation had drained him further. "Ces gens-là suppose nature and human society to be something other than what God has made them and what they really are. They construct their own worlds, their own humanity, and they expect the rest of us to be awed by their cleverness. People try to fawn over them, make up to them, flatter them, but Stepan Verhovensky does not. No, not I." He waved his hand dismissively, his voice gaining a faint note of pride. "I saw their kind back then in Petersburg, avec cette chère amie. Oh, how I used to wound her then, without knowing it! And still, I wasn't afraid of their mockery or even their praise. I'm not afraid now, either. Mais parlons d'autre chose." He suddenly stopped, as though realizing he was rambling, and pressed his fingertips to his temple. "I believe—no, I know—I've done something dreadful. Only fancy, I sent a letter to Darya Pavlovna yesterday, and—oh, how I curse myself for it!"

"What? A letter to Darya Pavlovna? What on earth did you write about?" I asked sharply, feeling a vague apprehension.

"Oh, my dear friend, believe me, I acted only with the most noble of intentions," he said, throwing his arms wide in exaggerated sincerity. "It was all in the spirit of honor. I let her know that I had written to Nicolas five days earlier. Again, I swear, it was noble of me."

I sat up, suddenly understanding his blunder. "Wait! I see now—you linked their names? In writing? What right had you to couple them like that?"

"Mon cher, don't crush me completely," he implored, wilting before my outburst like a man already defeated. "Don't shout at me; I'm already squashed flat, like—like a poor, unfortunate beetle underfoot. And yet, I thought it was all so honorable!" His voice trembled slightly, as though he were about to weep. "Think about it—suppose something really did happen… en Suisse… or was beginning. Wasn't I bound, in my conscience, to question their hearts beforehand? That I might not constrain them, or—how do I put it?—be a stumbling-block in their paths? I wrote purely out of honorable feeling, purely!"

"Oh heavens!" I groaned involuntarily, unable to hide my exasperation. "What an unbelievably stupid thing to do!"

"Yes, yes," he assented with a sudden eagerness, almost as if relieved to hear it spoken aloud. "You have never said anything more just. It was stupid—c'était bête! But what can be done now? Tout est dit! The damage is done. I shall marry her all the same, even if it is to cover 'another's sins.' So there was no point in writing, was there?"

"You're at it again, with that absurd idea!" I snapped.

But he only smiled weakly, a shadow of defiance flickering in his tired eyes. "Oh, you can shout all you like, my friend. It doesn't matter. Before

141

you stands a different Stepan Verhovensky now. The man I once was is buried, il est mort. Enfin, tout est dit. And tell me, why do you cry out so? Is it because you're not the one getting married? Because you won't have to wear the certain… decoration… on your head?" He smirked faintly, teasing but without any real malice. "Ah, my poor friend, you don't understand women at all. And yet I have done nothing but study them all my life. Oh yes, I have studied!"

"What absurdity is this now?" I interjected, but he ignored me and continued, his voice gathering momentum like a fevered monologue.

"'If you want to conquer the world, conquer yourself.' A wise phrase, and the only sensible thing that romantic fool Shatov ever managed to say. I admire that line. It fits my present mood. Here I stand, prepared to conquer myself—and how? By getting married! Marriage, mon ami, is the moral death of every proud soul, of all independence! It will corrupt me, I tell you! It will sap my energy, my spirit, my purpose, my courage in the service of the cause. Children will come too—yes, children! Though mark my words: they won't be mine. Oh no, not mine—certainly not mine! A wise man must not shy away from the truth. And yet what can be done? I have embraced my fate."

"Liputin suggested barricades this morning," he added suddenly, almost to himself. "Imagine that! Barricades to keep Nicolas out. Liputin is a fool. A woman, mon ami, would deceive even the all-seeing eye of God Himself. Le bon Dieu—He must have known what He was doing when He created woman! Or perhaps—no, I'm certain—she meddled in it herself, twisted His plans, insisted on being created this way, with all her attributes and complexities. After all, who would voluntarily create so much trouble for nothing?" He laughed bitterly, but his tone soon softened. "Nastasya might scold me for free-thinking, I know. But… enfin, tout est dit."

He paused, sagging into his chair with the weight of his thoughts. But the gibe he had taken such comfort in only seemed to deepen his despair.

"Oh, if only that Sunday might never come!" he suddenly burst out, his voice trembling with real anguish. "If only this week could pass without a Sunday! If Providence could blot out one single day from the

142

calendar! Would that not be a true miracle? And all to prove His power to the atheists... et que tout soit dit!"

His hands were trembling now as he buried his face in them. "Oh, how I loved her!" he whispered, his voice breaking. "Twenty years! Twenty years! And she has never understood me! Never once! Is it possible that she really believes I'm marrying out of fear, out of desperation, out of poverty? Oh, the shame of it! Auntie, Auntie! I do it for you. Can't she see it? Let her know! She must know—she must understand that she, she, is the only woman I have adored for twenty years. And if she does not... then they will have to drag me to the altar by force, like a condemned man!"

It was the first time I had heard such a confession, uttered with such vigor and sincerity. I won't lie—I nearly laughed at its melodrama. But seeing him in that moment, so crumpled and earnest, I held back. I had been wrong to judge him.

"Oh, but he is the only one left to me now—my one hope!" he exclaimed suddenly, clutching his hands together as though struck by a revelation. "My son—my Petrusha! Only he can save me now! Oh, why does he not come? Why doesn't he come to me? My poor boy—oh, my son! And though I have been unworthy of the name father, though I have been a tiger to him—still..." He broke off, looking suddenly exhausted, his voice trailing into silence.

"Laissez-moi, mon ami," he said faintly, as though all his energy had been drained. "Let me lie down a little, to collect my thoughts. I'm so tired. So tired... And you, you should go to bed too—it's past midnight already. Voyez-vous, it's twelve o'clock..."

He lay back in his chair, his eyes half-closed, his face pale and weary. I felt a pang of pity for him as I quietly rose to leave. The room seemed suffocating with his despair, and yet I knew—despite all his talk—that Sunday would come, just as relentlessly as the next sunrise.

Chapter 4
The Cripple

Chapter 4.1

Shatov, as it turned out, was not obstinate and acted on my note without resistance. At exactly midday, he appeared at the Drozdovs' house. Coincidentally, I arrived at nearly the same time, for this was to be my first formal call as well. When we entered the drawing-room, we found them all—Liza, her mother Praskovya Ivanovna, and Mavriky Nikolaevitch—engaged in an animated, though somewhat comical, argument.

The elder lady, who appeared fatigued and unwell, was insisting that Liza play a particular waltz on the piano, and when Liza had obediently begun, she declared at once that it wasn't the right one. Mavriky Nikolaevitch, with his customary straightforwardness, had taken Liza's part, defending her playing in all sincerity. His attempt at mediation, however, only made matters worse. Praskovya Ivanovna grew so frustrated she began to cry, loudly lamenting that no one ever listened to her anymore. Her frailty was evident—her legs were swollen, and every movement seemed to cause her discomfort. For several days now, she had been prone to outbursts of fractiousness, snapping at everyone in turn, though she still seemed to hold Liza in a certain respectful awe.

When we entered, they appeared pleased to see us, though Liza, as always, stole the moment with her radiant energy. Her cheeks flushed with pleasure, and with a bright "merci!"—clearly intended as a nod to me for arranging Shatov's visit—she went to meet him. She looked at him curiously, her gaze lingering on him with obvious interest, as though she were trying to study every detail of his disheveled appearance.

Shatov, meanwhile, stood stiffly and awkwardly in the doorway, his shoulders hunched and his brow furrowed as though he were already regretting his decision to come. Liza, however, had no patience for his awkwardness. She took his hand gently and led him across the room.

"This is Mr. Shatov, whom I mentioned to you before," she said, presenting him to her mother. "And this is Mr. G——v, a great friend of mine, and also of Stepan Trofimovitch's. Mavriky Nikolaevitch made his acquaintance yesterday, too."

Praskovya Ivanovna squinted up at us, her watery eyes narrowing suspiciously. "And which one of you is the professor?" she asked bluntly, her tone almost accusatory.

"There's no professor here, maman," Liza replied with visible exasperation.

"But there is a professor! You told me there would be one. It's probably this one." She pointed a disdainful finger at Shatov, who shifted uneasily under her glare.

"I never said there would be a professor," Liza corrected patiently. "Mr. G——v is in the service, and Mr. Shatov is a former student."

"A student or professor, it's all the same thing. They all come from the university. You argue too much. But the Swiss one had moustaches and a beard."

Liza laughed lightly. "It's Nicolas you're thinking of, maman. She always calls Stepan Trofimovitch's son 'the professor,'" she explained to Shatov, leading him away to the far end of the drawing-room, where a sofa stood. As they sat down, she bent toward him and whispered: "When her legs swell, she gets like this. She's ill, you understand?" But even as she spoke, she continued to observe Shatov with keen curiosity, her eyes scanning his face, his rough appearance, and particularly his thick, unkempt hair.

Meanwhile, Praskovya Ivanovna turned her attention to me. "Are you an officer?" she demanded abruptly.

"N-no, madam," I stammered, "I'm in the service…"

"Mr. G——v is a great friend of Stepan Trofimovitch's," Liza interjected quickly, attempting to smooth over the moment.

"Oh, so you're in Stepan Trofimovitch's service, are you? And he's a professor too, isn't he?"

"Maman!" Liza cried in irritation. "You must dream of professors all night long!"

"Well, I see too many of them when I'm awake," Praskovya Ivanovna snapped. "You're always contradicting your mother. Tell me—were you here four years ago when Nikolay Vsyevolodovitch was in the neighborhood?"

I replied that I had been.

"And wasn't there some Englishman with you?"

"No, madam, there was no Englishman," I answered, bewildered.

"There you are! All gossip and lies," she muttered bitterly. "Varvara Petrovna and Stepan Trofimovitch are as bad as the rest of them. They all lie."

"Auntie thinks there was an Englishman here because yesterday she overheard us comparing Nikolay Vsyevolodovitch to Prince Harry from Shakespeare's Henry IV," Liza explained with a mischievous smile. "But, naturally, maman took it literally."

"If Harry wasn't here, there was no Englishman!" Praskovya Ivanovna declared triumphantly, as though she had solved a grand mystery. "It was no one but Nikolay Vsyevolodovitch at his usual tricks."

Liza sighed dramatically. "Maman is doing this on purpose, you must know," she whispered conspiratorially to Shatov. "She has heard of Shakespeare. I read her the first act of Othello myself. But today, she's in pain and doesn't mean a word she's saying. Maman, listen—it's striking twelve. It's time for your medicine."

At that moment, the maid entered to announce that the doctor had arrived.

Praskovya Ivanovna rose laboriously to her feet, calling irritably for her dog. "Zemirka! Zemirka, you come with me at least."

The decrepit little creature, however, paid her no heed and crawled under the sofa where Liza sat.

"Fine! If you won't come, I don't want you. Good-bye, my good sir," she said to me suddenly, with an exaggerated politeness. "I don't know

146

your name or your father's."

"Anton Lavrentyevitch…" I began.

"Well, it doesn't matter. It goes in at one ear and out the other with me," she cut me off dismissively. "And don't you dare follow me, Mavriky Nikolaevitch! I was calling Zemirka, not you. I can still walk without anyone's help, thank God. And tomorrow, I shall go for a drive."

With that, she walked—rather angrily—out of the drawing-room.

"Anton Lavrentyevitch," Liza said with a sly smile, "will you talk to Mavriky Nikolaevitch in the meantime? I assure you, you'll both gain from getting to know each other better." She flashed a brilliant smile at Mavriky Nikolaevitch as she spoke, and the stoic artilleryman's face lit up like a boy's, his usually stern demeanor softened into a glowing, almost bashful expression.

There was no escape for me; I resigned myself to conversation with Mavriky Nikolaevitch, while Liza returned to Shatov, still scrutinizing him as though he were some fascinating specimen she had just discovered.

Chapter 4.2

Lizaveta Nikolaevna's purpose in inviting Shatov turned out, to my surprise, to be genuinely focused on literature. I admit that, for some reason, I had assumed there might be a more personal or hidden motive behind her summons. I don't know why I thought so—perhaps because her fiery temperament and impulsiveness always seemed to suggest hidden depths. Yet as she began explaining her idea to Shatov, the seriousness and conviction with which she spoke dispelled my doubts. It was clear that she was genuinely engrossed in her scheme, which, while unusual, had a certain charm to it.

We—Mavriky Nikolaevitch and I—felt no awkwardness in listening to the conversation. After all, Liza and Shatov made no effort to lower their voices or keep their discussion private. Quite the contrary, they spoke with a kind of energetic openness that eventually drew us in. Before long, they even turned to us for our thoughts, inviting our opinions and suggestions.

It turned out that Lizaveta Nikolaevna, spurred by what she had seen and heard during her time abroad, had decided to embark on a project that she believed could benefit society—a book, as she explained it, with a unique purpose. She lacked experience and expertise, so she was looking for someone who could help bring her vision to life. The fervor with which she described her idea surprised me.

"She must be one of the new people," I thought, recalling whispers about her time in Switzerland. "She didn't come back empty-handed, that's for sure."

Shatov, however, remained stoic as ever. He listened intently, his eyes fixed on the floor, his hands clasped in front of him. He showed no trace of the surprise or skepticism that one might expect from a man like him, faced with a spirited young lady in high society proposing such an unusual project.

The scheme itself was curious but not without merit. Liza explained that in Russia, a vast number of newspapers and journals were printed in both the capitals and the provinces. Each day, countless events were reported in them—fires, accidents, speeches, floods, celebrations, and scandals. But when the year was over, what happened to all that information? The newspapers were either stored away in dusty cupboards, torn up and turned into litter, or used as wrapping for parcels. Many facts that had once caught the public's attention were forgotten in time, buried under newer events.

"What a shame," Liza said with warmth. "So much is lost simply because no one has the time or the energy to sift through all that paper."

Her idea was to gather the most significant and characteristic events of the year—events that reflected the moral, spiritual, and personal life of Russia—and condense them into a single book. This would not be a mere collection of reprinted news or official decrees. On the contrary, much of the bureaucratic information, such as laws and local regulations, would be left out. Instead, the focus would be on stories that revealed the character of the people, their struggles and triumphs, their progress and peculiarities.

"Everything of significance would be included—fires, speeches, public subscriptions, acts of charity, crimes, strange incidents, and so on," Liza declared. "Even floods and natural disasters, though only if they speak to something broader about the people or the time. And the book mustn't be dry or dull. It should be clear, interesting, and easy to read— something that everyone would want to have on their table, whether for light reading or as a work of reference."

"In short, you want a picture of Russia for a single year," Shatov said finally, without lifting his gaze. "A reflection of the life of the people, in all its aspects."

"Yes! Exactly!" Liza exclaimed, lighting up with enthusiasm. "It's not about politics or bias. It's about capturing something real—something meaningful. We would be impartial, above all."

Shatov remained silent for a moment, as though absorbing the idea. At last, he murmured: "But impartiality is impossible. If you're selecting events, the very selection itself implies a perspective—a certain tendency."

"No, no!" Liza insisted earnestly. "There will be no political or ideological leanings. It's just a matter of choosing events that are characteristic—that's all."

"A tendency isn't always a bad thing," Shatov replied thoughtfully, his voice gaining energy. "If the purpose is good, even an underlying tendency might serve it. Your idea is ambitious—it's no small task—but there's something compelling about it. It could be done."

"You really think so?" Liza cried, clasping her hands with excitement. "Then it's possible?"

"We would need to think it through carefully," Shatov replied, finally raising his head. His face, usually so stern, had brightened; there was genuine interest in his eyes now. "It's a massive project. It won't come together overnight. It will take time—experience, trial, and error. But it's a good idea, and a useful one."

He seemed almost embarrassed by his own enthusiasm, as though surprised at how easily he had been drawn in. "Was it your idea?" he asked, his voice quieter now, almost deferential.

"I didn't invent it," Liza said with a modest smile. "It came to me on its own—suddenly, out of nowhere. But I liked it, and I felt as though I might actually be able to help bring it to life. I have money, you know—money just sitting there doing nothing. Why shouldn't I use it for something good? I want to work for the common cause. But I knew right away that I couldn't do it alone. I need someone with knowledge, someone who can guide the work and shape it. That's why I thought of you. You would be my co-editor. We'd share everything—half and half. You would provide the plan and the labor. My contribution would be the idea itself, and, of course, the means to publish it. Do you think the book would pay for itself?"

Shatov's eyes flashed again with something like enthusiasm, though his expression quickly grew serious. "If it's done well, with thought and precision, it might succeed. But you must be ready for failure at first. A book like this … it's new. People won't understand it immediately. But that doesn't mean it's not worth doing."

Liza's face lit up, as though his words had given her new hope. "Then you'll help me?"

"We'll talk again," Shatov replied, glancing at her almost shyly. "It's too soon to decide. But the idea—yes, the idea has promise."

Throughout this conversation, Mavriky Nikolaevitch and I sat quietly, exchanging occasional glances. At first, I had expected to be bored, but the passion and earnestness with which Liza spoke—and Shatov's unexpected response to her—held my interest. There was something remarkable about the way these two such different people connected over this peculiar literary project.

Liza, fiery and restless, seemed for the first time in her life genuinely eager to create something of value. And Shatov, who so often scorned and mistrusted society, seemed moved—perhaps even inspired—by her sincerity. It was as though, for one moment, they both believed in the possibility of accomplishing something meaningful together.

for cats and lap-dogs, would not blame the infusoria for its audacity in raising its eyes to the sun. I shall not allow myself the liberty to hope, but shall confine myself to admiration and gratitude. Do not despise my tears; for they are tears of longing and humility, and what is more, of repentance. I am a coarse man, a man of no refinement, no education, and I dare say I don't deserve to be forgiven for the presumption of addressing you. But, alas, it is my fate! Though I'm unlearned and unworthy, even I have been touched by beauty. Even I, crushed beneath the burden of existence, was granted one glance at heavenly radiance, and for that glance I would pay with my life.

Think of me kindly. I will not intrude, but I shall pray for you. If ever you should have occasion to remember me, think of me not as I am now, unworthy and full of foolishness, but as I might have been—your devoted knight, Ignat Lebyadkin, a poor retired captain.

P.S.—This poem was written at night, in a moment of inspiration, and I hope you will forgive the humble expressions of my heart, unpolished as they are."

I finished reading and looked around, not quite sure how to react to the absurd and bizarre letter. Liza, her face flushed, seemed torn between indignation and amusement. She clapped her hands together as though in exasperation and exclaimed:

"Well? What do you say to that, Mr. Shatov? What do you make of such nonsense? Imagine, this is being addressed to me!"

Shatov, who had sat stiffly the whole time, still holding the newspapers on his knees, raised his eyes at last and looked directly at her. His face, pale and almost rigid before, now seemed to darken with a mixture of embarrassment and suppressed anger.

"I don't understand … what you want me to say," he muttered, his voice low and strained.

"I want you to help me understand! Who is this man? What sort of person writes such incredible, ridiculous letters?"

"He's nothing, a fool, a drunkard," Shatov said abruptly, almost spitting the words out. "A petty creature. You ought to ignore him completely."

"I thought so too! But what audacity—sending me such absurd poetry and talking of himself as a knight! And, I hear, he lives beneath you in the same house?"

"Yes," Shatov answered curtly, his lips twitching as though the subject pained him. "It's not my business where he lives, nor does it concern me what nonsense he writes. You should burn such letters without reading them."

"I did think of doing that, but curiosity got the better of me." She turned to me and Mavriky Nikolaevitch with a sharp, nervous laugh. "You can't imagine the ridiculous figure he cuts in the streets. I've seen him shouting verses to himself, like a madman. How can such a man even dream of writing to me?"

"Because he's drunk, because he's ridiculous," Shatov broke in suddenly, almost harshly. "Why waste a thought on him? His drunkenness, his poems—they're nothing, just foolishness. You ought not to think of it at all!"

But Liza did not seem satisfied with this response. Her dark eyes were full of curiosity, and her excitement, which only heightened her beauty, seemed to grow as she spoke.

"There must be something behind it, though—he must have had a reason for writing such a letter! It's not simply drunkenness or foolishness. Who is this sister of his they talk about? What is it they say about her? Does it have anything to do with Nikolay Vsyevolodovitch?"

At this Shatov's face turned red, and he glanced at her quickly, his expression sharp and almost defiant. He opened his mouth to reply but then seemed to reconsider. He lowered his gaze again and said nothing.

"It's not for me to know or to say," he muttered at last. "I don't gossip, and I don't spread rumors. The captain ... is beneath contempt. You should think of him as nothing."

There was something so earnest, so almost pained in the way Shatov said this that Liza seemed for a moment taken aback. She looked at him more closely, her expression softening as though she had suddenly seen something in him that struck her as unexpected.

"I understand," she said at last in a quieter voice. "Forgive me. I don't know why I brought it up." She paused, then added with a trace of hesitation, "You must think I'm just a silly, idle girl who amuses herself with nonsense like this. But I swear to you, I'm not like that. I hate all this idle life! I want to do something real, something useful. That's why I need your help with the book. Won't you help me?"

Shatov was silent for a moment longer. Then, still without lifting his eyes, he said quietly:

"If the idea's real—if you mean it—I'll think about it. But I don't want to waste time on trifles. I ... I can't stand empty things."

"There'll be nothing empty about this," Liza replied at once, her tone passionate again. "I promise you. I'll come to you tomorrow to talk about it. Will you let me?"

Shatov stood up abruptly, holding the bundle of newspapers as though he were clutching a heavy weight. "I'll take these and look at them," he said. "We'll talk later."

Without waiting for more, he turned to go. Lizaveta Nikolaevna watched him as he walked to the door, her face thoughtful.

"What a strange man," she murmured softly when he had gone. "But he's honest. And he'll help me—I'm sure of it."

She looked over at me and Mavriky Nikolaevitch with a smile that was both triumphant and wistful. "You think I'm a silly dreamer too, don't you? But you'll see—you'll see I can make something of this idea!"

There was something so bright, so resolute in her voice that, for the first time, I almost believed her.

"That letter was written by a man in a drunken state, a worthless fellow," I exclaimed indignantly. "I know who he is."

"That letter came yesterday," Liza began to explain, her face flushed and her voice hurried, as though she were eager to get through the subject as quickly as possible. "I saw immediately it was the work of some ridiculous creature, and I haven't shown it to maman yet because I didn't want to upset her even more. But if he keeps this up, I don't know what

153

to do. Mavriky Nikolaevitch suggested going out and giving him a stern warning. But, as I look on you as my colleague,"—she turned suddenly to Shatov—"and as you live in the same house as him, I thought I would ask you so that I could judge what might happen next. I don't know how else to handle this."

"He's a drunkard and a fool," Shatov muttered with a certain reluctance.

"But is he always so absurd?" Liza pressed. "It's hard to believe anyone could write something so silly otherwise."

"No, he's not always like that," Shatov replied slowly, as though forcing himself to speak. "When he's sober, he can be very sharp. He's not stupid at all."

"Ah, so he's clever enough when it suits him!" Liza said thoughtfully, tapping the letter on the table. "It's even clear from this nonsense that he has wit in his own way. What a grotesque character! A man with a brain who chooses to write verses like these."

"Clever enough for his purposes, I suppose," Mavriky Nikolaevitch chimed in unexpectedly, breaking his silence. His tone was calm and almost indifferent, but there was something in the way he spoke that suggested he took a dim view of the whole affair.

"I hear he lives with his sister," Liza continued, undeterred. "Is it true that he's tyrannical toward her? They say he treats her dreadfully."

Shatov looked at her with a sudden scowl, and his expression grew darker. "I don't know," he muttered at last. "What business is it of mine?"

With that, he abruptly turned toward the door, clearly intending to leave.

"Ah, no, wait!" Liza cried out in a flurry of agitation, almost rising from her seat. "Where are you going? We have so much still to talk about...."

"What is there to talk about?" Shatov muttered, half-turning back. "I'll let you know tomorrow."

"But wait—the most important thing is still left! The printing-press!"

154

Liza exclaimed, her voice growing more urgent. "Do you think I'm joking? I'm not. I told you I want to work in earnest! If we decide to publish this book, we need to know where it's going to be printed. That's the key question! It's no use going to Moscow, and the press here in the town is impossible for a publication like this. I've been thinking for a long time of setting up a printing-press of my own—and I thought it might even be in your name. I'm sure maman will allow it if it's in your name."

"How do you know I know anything about printing?" Shatov asked sharply, though he spoke sullenly and without looking up.

"Why, Pyotr Stepanovitch spoke about you in Switzerland!" Liza replied eagerly, almost triumphantly. "He said you knew all about it—that you were familiar with the printing business and would help me set one up. He even meant to give me a note to introduce you, but I forgot to take it."

At the mention of Pyotr Stepanovitch, Shatov's face seemed to stiffen. A shadow passed over his features, and for a moment he stood frozen, staring hard at the floor as if trying to suppress some inner struggle. Then, without another word, he turned and walked out of the room.

Liza stared after him in shock. "What on earth is the matter with him?" she cried, looking at me and Mavriky Nikolaevitch with bewilderment and no small amount of hurt in her voice. "Does he always go out like that? Without a word?"

I shrugged helplessly, unsure of what to say. But before I could reply, Shatov reappeared suddenly in the doorway. He walked straight to the table, placed the bundle of newspapers he had taken earlier back down, and said quietly, almost in a mutter:

"I'm not going to help you. I don't have the time."

"Why not? Why?" Liza cried, genuinely distressed now. "I think you're angry with me!"

The sound of her voice seemed to halt him in his tracks for a moment. He looked at her intently, searching her face with an expression so strange, so full of conflicting emotions, that for a second no one in the room dared to speak. At last, he muttered softly, almost bitterly:

"No matter. I just don't want to."

And with that, he turned and left the room for good.

Liza sank back onto the sofa, clearly overwhelmed. For a moment, she sat motionless, staring at the door through which Shatov had disappeared. Then, turning to us with a mixture of confusion and frustration, she exclaimed:

"What a strange man! How odd he is! You saw it yourselves, didn't you? What can possibly be the matter with him?"

"Wonderfully queer man," Mavriky Nikolaevitch observed aloud, shaking his head slowly, though his tone was more thoughtful than dismissive.

Liza bit her lip, her dark eyes clouded with a mix of curiosity and disappointment. For a moment, she seemed lost in thought, her earlier excitement now subdued. Then she suddenly turned to me, her gaze sharp and probing.

"Do you understand him? What is he like, really? I mean, what kind of man is he?"

I hesitated, unsure how to respond, but before I could answer, Liza looked away again and said softly, almost to herself:

"There's something about him … something I can't quite grasp. He's angry, and bitter, but there's something else too.… I don't know. But I'll find out."

And with that, she fell silent, staring at the floor, clearly deep in her thoughts.

Chapter 4.3

He was certainly a strange man, but something deeper lay behind all this, something I could not grasp. I could not bring myself to believe in the feasibility of this so-called publication; the absurd letter, with its almost brazen insinuations about "documents" and information, suggested something suspicious. Yet no one had mentioned it further; they simply skirted the issue and busied themselves with talk of the printing-press.

156

Shatov's sudden, sullen exit the moment that topic was mentioned only deepened my conviction that something had taken place before my arrival—something unsaid, perhaps deliberately kept from me. I felt as though I had been a witness to something of which I was not meant to be aware. This was not my affair, and I sensed that my presence had become unnecessary, even awkward. I had clearly overstayed my welcome for a first call, so I decided to take my leave. I went up to Lizaveta Nikolaevna to say goodbye.

To my surprise, she seemed almost to have forgotten that I was in the room. She stood by the table, her head bowed as if in deep thought, her gaze fixed intently on some invisible point on the carpet. The intensity of her stillness made me hesitate before speaking.

"Ah, you are going too? Goodbye," she said absently, in a distracted but kind voice. Her tone was friendly and perfunctory, as though she had spoken out of habit rather than full awareness of my departure. "Give my regards to Stepan Trofimovitch, and please persuade him to come and see me soon. Mavriky Nikolaevitch, Anton Lavrentyevitch is leaving. Excuse maman for not coming to say goodbye; she's not well."

I murmured the usual polite farewells and walked out. I had already reached the foot of the stairs and was stepping toward the street when a footman hurried after me and called out:

"My lady requests you to return."

"Which lady?" I asked in confusion. "The mistress, or Lizaveta Nikolaevna?"

"The young lady," he replied respectfully.

Surprised, I turned back and followed him. This time I was shown into the smaller reception room adjacent to the drawing room where we had been earlier. The door leading to the main room had been discreetly shut, leaving Mavriky Nikolaevitch alone. Liza was standing in the middle of the smaller room, pale and visibly agitated. She smiled faintly when I entered, but her nervousness was apparent. She looked as though she were fighting some inner turmoil, struggling with a sudden impulse. For a brief moment, I thought she might change her mind and send me away again. But then, in one swift motion, she took me by the hand and led me to the window, her grip firm and her movements hurried.

"I need to see her at once," she whispered, her voice low and full of a wild urgency that left me dumbfounded. Her dark eyes, ablaze with determination, searched mine for understanding, for acquiescence, as though she could not bear even the hint of opposition. "I must see her with my own eyes, and I beg you to help me."

The fervor in her expression startled me. There was something frantic and almost despairing about her tone, something that would not be denied.

"Who do you mean?" I asked, confused and alarmed. "Who is it you want to see, Lizaveta Nikolaevna?"

"That man's sister—Lebyadkin's sister," she said quickly, almost breathlessly. "That lame girl.... Is it true that she's lame?"

Her words, and the strange intensity with which she uttered them, left me momentarily speechless. I could hardly believe what I was hearing.

"I ... I don't know," I stammered, regaining my composure. "I've never seen her, but I've heard she's lame. I heard it yesterday."

"I must see her—absolutely!" she repeated, her voice almost trembling now, though her resolve did not waver. "Can you arrange it for me today? I trust you, I rely on you. I have no one else."

Her desperation moved me deeply, and I suddenly felt an overwhelming urge to help her in any way I could. "But that's impossible," I began hesitantly. "How could I arrange such a thing? I wouldn't even know where to start."

"If you can't arrange it, I will go myself—alone," she interrupted fiercely, her eyes flashing. "Mavriky Nikolaevitch refuses to help me, so I am asking you. If you don't arrange it by tomorrow, I will go to her, no matter what happens, no matter who finds out. I don't care. I cannot wait any longer."

"Listen, I promise you this," I said after a moment's thought, my voice steady but urgent. "I will go myself today and I will see her—I give you my word of honor. I'll find a way. Let me speak to Shatov, though; I think

I'll need his help."

"Yes, yes, of course, tell him!" she said eagerly, as though relieved to hear his name. "But make sure he knows that I truly want this. Tell him that I wasn't deceiving him earlier. I'm not lying when I say I want to set up a printing press. I do want to do this work, and I do want to help in some way. He may have gone because he is so honest and he thought I was insincere, but I wasn't. Please make him understand."

"He is very honest," I agreed warmly. "He'll understand."

"But if nothing is arranged by tomorrow," she repeated firmly, "I will go alone, and I don't care what happens."

I thought for a moment. "I can't promise to come before three o'clock tomorrow," I said cautiously. "But I'll have news for you then."

"Three o'clock, then," she whispered, relaxing her grip on my hand. For a moment, her expression softened, and she looked at me intently, her eyes filled with a strange, almost wistful warmth. "You know, I thought yesterday at Stepan Trofimovitch's house that you—were rather devoted to me."

She smiled suddenly, though her lips trembled slightly, and before I could reply, she pressed my hand quickly, turned away, and hurried back toward the drawing room, where Mavriky Nikolaevitch was waiting for her.

I was left standing there alone for a moment, feeling a strange mix of exhilaration and unease. What had brought on this sudden frenzy? What did she expect to find when she saw the girl? And why did her eyes, so determined and desperate, haunt me even as I stepped out into the street?

I went out into the street, carrying the full weight of the promise I had made, yet utterly unable to comprehend what had just happened. My mind was in turmoil, as though I had suddenly been thrust into a labyrinth where every turn brought deeper confusion. I had just seen a woman in what could only be described as genuine despair, so tormented by some secret agony that she had not hesitated to compromise herself— entrusting her most intimate and, no doubt, desperate wishes to a man she barely knew. It was as though in her frantic need, she had grasped at me like a drowning person reaches for a branch.

What struck me most, and what lingered like a pang in my chest, was her womanly smile—an involuntary moment of grace and warmth—despite the torment written all over her face. It was not the smile of a coquette but one that seemed to spring from some instinctive sense of trust, fragile yet unshakable. Then there was her half-hinted acknowledgment of what she had observed the day before—that I might harbor some feelings for her. That gentle insinuation, uttered almost absentmindedly at such a critical moment, sent a shiver through me; it was like a subtle blade grazing the surface of my heart. And yet, despite the tenderness of her gesture and the desperate earnestness with which she had appealed to me, I felt no personal triumph, no sense of being singled out by her for special regard. On the contrary, all I felt was a deep and overwhelming pity—pity for her, for her plight, for the hopelessness that seemed to consume her.

Her secrets became sacred to me at once, as though I had been entrusted with something precious and infinitely fragile. I could not bear the thought that someone might try to reveal them to me further. Had anyone, at that moment, offered me an explanation or some key to the mystery of her despair, I would have recoiled in horror, covered my ears, and refused to listen. I did not want to know more than what she had confided. My respect for her anguish was absolute, and yet, despite all my good intentions, I remained utterly bewildered. I could not, for the life of me, see a way to fulfill the promise I had made. What had I agreed to? To arrange an interview, yes, but what sort of interview? Between her and Lebyadkin's sister? For what purpose, and what would come of it? What did she hope to achieve by meeting the girl? The entire request seemed wild, inexplicable, and beyond my comprehension.

Even the prospect of arranging such an encounter seemed fraught with impossibility. How could I bring them together? What would I say to Shatov? He was my only hope, and yet I knew, deep down, that Shatov would never agree to help me with this. He was too proud, too obstinate, and too honest. To him, the entire situation would appear as something sordid or ridiculous; he would refuse outright, and worse, he might despise me for even broaching the subject. But what else could I do? I could not abandon Lizaveta Nikolaevna now, not after she had placed so much faith in me. That thought alone spurred me forward.

With my mind racing and my heart heavy with uncertainty, I quickened my steps in the direction of Shatov's lodgings. The cold air stung my face, but I hardly noticed it as I rehearsed the words I would say to him, knowing all the while how unconvincing and absurd I would sound. For some reason, I felt an irrational hope that, in the course of our conversation, something would emerge—a solution, a way forward, anything. If nothing else, I could at least deliver Lizaveta Nikolaevna's message: that she had been sincere when she spoke of her plans, that her intentions had been genuine, and that she had meant no insult. Perhaps that alone might soften him and make him willing to hear me out.

But as I neared Shatov's house, another thought struck me: What if he refused even to listen? What if he turned me away at the door, refusing to be drawn into what he might consider the schemes of idle society people? That was the sort of man Shatov was—honest to the point of bluntness, and completely intolerant of what he considered insincerity or frivolity. Yet, for all his roughness and obstinacy, I knew there was a deep kindness in him, a capacity for genuine compassion. I had seen it before in his dealings with others, and I could not help but cling to the faint hope that it might be roused now.

As I approached the gate of Filipov's house, I paused for a moment to collect myself. The narrow street was empty, and the house stood in silence, its windows dark. It struck me as strange, almost ominous, that such a tumultuous day should end here, in this quiet and unremarkable place. Taking a deep breath, I opened the gate and made my way to Shatov's door, preparing myself for whatever lay ahead.

Chapter 4.4

"Yes, I was there," Shatov answered curtly, his tone suddenly cold and sharp, as though he had no desire to dwell on the subject. "I spent more than a year in America. I worked as a laborer. And I lived with him— Kirillov. Four months we shared a hut. He is a strange man, you know, utterly strange. But I'm fond of him... or rather, I respect him. Though..."

He stopped abruptly and seemed to lose interest in the explanation. For a moment, his eyes wandered, clouded, and thoughtful, as though he were grappling with memories that had unexpectedly surfaced.

I sat still, waiting for him to continue, though I knew better than to press him with questions. Shatov, as always, spoke in bursts, like someone digging out words with difficulty, but with a peculiar directness and weight. His sudden silences, however, were often far more significant than his words.

"America," he repeated after a moment, as though testing the word. "Yes, that was where we all dreamed of the future, only we didn't know what that future was or what we were dreaming for. Do you know what it's like to live in a place where no one belongs to anything? Where everyone works for themselves, but together they create something soulless—dead? We dreamed about freedom there, we talked about it endlessly, but all I saw was emptiness. A nation without roots—like a man who has forgotten his mother and father."

He broke off again and ran his hand through his thick, unkempt hair. Then, after a pause, he laughed—harshly, bitterly, though without any mirth.

"Kirillov called America 'a country of practical atheists.' He loved it for that at first. He thought it suited him perfectly because no one believed in anything there. But later, he began to say something quite different: that they believed in machines. In machines! Can you imagine? He said that was their religion. He said they had replaced God with levers, gears, and factories. He spoke as though he envied them—'At least they have something,' he would mutter, almost to himself. And then he'd fall silent for hours, lying on the floor, staring at the beams of the roof as though waiting for something. A revelation, perhaps. I don't know."

"What did you work at in America?" I asked, trying to soften the tension that had suddenly fallen between us.

"Anything I could find. I dug ditches. I laid tracks on a railway. I shovelled coal. I broke my back, wore out my hands, and sweated blood under the sun. It was hell, but it was honest work. There's something about that kind of labor—when you feel the ground under your feet and the weight of the tool in your hand. You may have nothing to your name, but you know who you are." He stopped again and gave me a sudden, piercing look. "Do you know why I left Russia? To kill the 'flunkey' in me. I wanted to burn him out, to wipe him from my soul."

"Did you succeed?" I asked softly.

For a moment, I thought he might answer with something impassioned or triumphant, but instead, he gave a weary, almost resigned sigh.

"No. I didn't succeed. I came back. It turns out a man cannot cut away his roots—not if he still has a soul. In America, I realized that Russia is not just my homeland; it's my fate. We are all bound to it—tied to her pain and her madness. And here I am, back among the same people, the same confusion. But I no longer dream. Do you understand me?"

I nodded silently, though in truth, I understood very little. Shatov, as always, was incomprehensible and overwhelming in his declarations. Yet there was a strange grandeur in his words, something that struck deep, even if their full meaning remained elusive.

"And what did you mean about Kirillov? That 'sore' of his you mentioned earlier?" I ventured to ask after a pause.

"Oh, his 'sore'… Well, that's just Kirillov's way of life. He has a sore in his soul, one that he can't heal or cut out. It festers there quietly, and he lets it be. He dreams of killing God—or rather, proving there's no need for Him. But that sore eats away at him while he waits. He waited in America. Now he's waiting here." Shatov's voice sank to a murmur, as though speaking of something too profound or intimate for normal tones.

We both fell silent. Outside, the room grew dimmer as the evening light faded; the faint sound of footsteps and distant voices carried in from the street below. I watched Shatov as he sat hunched in his corner, staring blankly at the floor, the furrow between his brows deepening as though a shadow had passed over his thoughts again.

"I shouldn't have come today," I muttered at last, feeling as though I had intruded on something sacred, some hidden struggle that I had no right to witness.

"No," Shatov said suddenly, lifting his head and giving me a strange, almost kind look. "It's better that you came. Sometimes words are needed, even if they're wasted. Even if they don't save you from yourself."

I left him soon after that, my head swirling with thoughts I could not make sense of, and my heart heavy with the feeling that I had glimpsed something tragic and unspoken—something immense, yet irreparably lost.

Shatov closed the door again and sat down, though this time he did not look at me but kept his gaze fixed on the wall in front of him, as if considering something carefully. There was a long silence in which I did not dare interrupt him. Finally, he spoke, his voice low but clear, as if he had arrived at some conclusion.

"It's not so simple, but I'll arrange it. You will see her tomorrow, in my presence. Only it must be done quietly, without anyone noticing." He paused, and then, as if suddenly struck by a thought, he added, "Why does Lizaveta Nikolaevna want to see her? You must tell me. You owe me that much."

I hesitated, for I myself wasn't entirely certain of Liza's motives. All I knew was that her request was borne out of some deep, irresistible urgency, which I could not explain. Seeing my hesitation, Shatov's expression darkened.

"Do you trust her?" he asked abruptly. "Do you understand her?"

"I trust her completely," I replied with genuine feeling. "As for understanding her—I can't say that I do. I think she's in real torment. She needs to know something, something important, and I think she's acting from her heart."

"Her heart," Shatov repeated, his lips curling into a bitter half-smile. "A heart doesn't always lead one to good places. But no matter—I will help you. Tomorrow, at noon, come to me here. From here, we'll go together to see her."

"And her brother?" I ventured. "What if he interferes?"

"Lebyadkin?" Shatov spat the name out with undisguised contempt.

"That drunken fool won't interfere. He'll be dead asleep by midday if he's been drinking all night, which he probably has. Besides, he knows better than to challenge me. He's a coward at heart. I'll deal with him if necessary."

I was filled with a sudden, almost overwhelming relief. For the first time since I had made my reckless promise to Liza, a path seemed to open before me. Shatov, despite his usual hostility and mistrust, was taking up the task without hesitation. There was something strange in his willingness, something that hinted at a deeper, more personal motive, but I dared not probe too deeply.

"Thank you, Shatov," I said warmly. "I knew I could rely on you."

He looked at me sharply, as though suspicious of my sincerity, but his expression softened slightly. "I'm not doing this for you," he said gruffly. "And not for her either. I'm doing it because … because this must be brought to an end. Do you understand?"

"I don't understand," I admitted.

"You don't need to," he retorted. "Just be here tomorrow. And tell her—tell Lizaveta Nikolaevna—that she'll see what she wants to see. But she must be ready for anything."

"For anything?" I echoed uneasily.

"For anything," he repeated, his tone final and impenetrable. "You'd better go now. It's late."

Realizing he was right, I stood up. Shatov followed me to the door, his gait heavy, his movements abrupt. As I stepped out into the hallway, he stopped me with a hand on my arm.

"One last thing," he said, his voice almost a whisper. "Tell no one about this—no one. Not a word to Liputin, not to that fool Kirillov, and especially not to Varvara Petrovna or anyone connected with the Drozdovs. If anyone gets wind of this, everything will collapse."

"You have my word," I promised earnestly.

Shatov let me go then, and I descended the stairs in silence, my heart still pounding from the tension of our conversation. Outside, the air was sharp and cold, and the street was nearly empty. I stood still for a moment, breathing in the night air and trying to calm my thoughts.

What had I gotten myself into? I wondered. Everything felt unreal, as though I were stepping into the middle of a drama whose plot I could not comprehend. There was Lizaveta Nikolaevna's despair, Shatov's strange willingness to help, and this shadowy figure of Lebyadkin's sister, who seemed at the heart of it all. What truth could possibly come of this meeting? What would Liza find there, and why was she so desperate to see her? The questions whirled in my mind, but no answers came.

At last, I shook myself and started for home. Tomorrow, I told myself, would bring clarity—or perhaps it would bring chaos. Whatever it brought, I knew there was no turning back.

"Laughing at him?" Shatov repeated, almost with surprise, and looking at her closely, as though trying to understand something more in her words.

"Yes, laughing," she replied lightly, but with a serene earnestness that struck me as somehow incongruous with her words. "It's wrong, I know, but sometimes I can't help it. He doesn't understand anything. He always stares, blinks, and then begins shouting, as if he were a general giving orders, and yet he's only a footman, not a general at all. Why should I take him seriously? He doesn't deserve it. I say to him, 'Lebyadkin, you are a fool!' And what do you think he does? He believes it. I tell him he's ridiculous, and he starts crying like a child. I call that funny. Why not laugh?"

"But he beats you," Shatov said in a low, troubled voice.

She glanced at him brightly, as though amused by his seriousness. "He? Lebyadkin? Oh, Shatushka, don't talk nonsense. He's weak and silly, and I don't care. He's nothing at all, like a shadow. Do you know what I say to myself sometimes when he's shouting and stamping about the room? I say: 'This is not happening at all, and he is not real. I will not let it be real.' And then it all stops for me, like a dream that you wake up from. Do you understand that? I turn away from it. And I go on being happy."

"Happy?" I couldn't help asking aloud, startled by her gentle, confident tone.

She turned her soft, grey eyes to me for a moment, and a faint, sad smile passed across her lips. "Yes, I'm happy," she said slowly, as though she were reflecting deeply on the question. "I sit here, I think, I dream. I play my songs, I look in the glass and sometimes I see things in it, beautiful things—better things. And when I'm very tired, I take the cards and try my fortune. I see everything in them: my past, my future, and what is happening far away. You don't believe me, do you? But it's all there."

Shatov sighed heavily, but she did not notice. She seemed utterly absorbed in what she was saying, as though she were lost in her own quiet world, a world that no one else could touch.

"You've got books," I said suddenly, glancing at the battered songbook on the table. "Do you read?"

"Of course I read," she replied with pride. "I learned when I was a girl, and I haven't forgotten. My favorite is poetry. Do you know Pushkin? I love him. I know so many of his poems by heart—so many! Would you like me to recite something?" Without waiting for an answer, she began at once in a soft, measured voice:

"'I loved you once, and still, perhaps, I love...

My love has not yet wholly died away...'"

Her voice trembled slightly, and her pale cheeks flushed faintly. She stopped suddenly and looked down at her hands, which were folded neatly on the table. "I always cry when I read that," she murmured almost apologetically. "I don't know why. It just comes over me."

Shatov bent his head lower, as though hiding his face from her. "And what do you see in the mirror, Marya Timofyevna?" he asked after a pause, his voice quiet, almost tender.

"Things," she said, brightening again. "Strange, wonderful things. Sometimes I see people I don't know—fine people, kind people who smile at me and say things I don't quite hear, but I understand. Sometimes I see a man—always the same man—dressed in fine clothes, with a kind face and bright eyes. He talks to me, he says beautiful things, but I can't hear him. It's like music, though, soft and sweet. Once I thought I heard him say: 'You are not forgotten, Marya. You will live among flowers and light.' And then the glass went dark, and I was alone again."

I shuddered involuntarily. The quiet rapture with which she spoke, combined with the almost childlike simplicity of her words, touched me deeply. It was clear to me now that her happiness was not of this world. She was wrapped up in dreams, fragile and intangible dreams that shielded her from the squalor, cruelty, and misery of her daily life.

"Does he visit you often?" Shatov asked softly.

"Who? Oh, the man in the mirror? Yes, very often. He's always there when I need him. He's my guardian angel, I think."

"And what does your brother say about that?" I couldn't resist asking, though I regretted it at once.

She gave me a look of innocent reproach, as if I had broken something delicate and precious. "Lebyadkin doesn't see him. Lebyadkin doesn't see anything. He only drinks, shouts, and laughs like a fool. He's not worth talking about."

At that moment we heard a noise on the stairs—the heavy, stumbling steps of someone coming up. Shatov and I looked at each other.

"Go," he whispered urgently to me. "He's coming back."

Marya Timofyevna turned her head toward the door, but there was no sign of fear on her face. She merely smiled faintly, as if she were expecting nothing at all.

"Good-bye, Shatushka," she said softly. "Thank you for coming."

We hurried out of the room and into the passage. Shatov paused for a moment, listening to the drunken muttering and cursing outside the door, then closed it quietly behind us.

"She's not mad," he said abruptly as we made our way back upstairs. "But she's not of this world either."

"No," I agreed, shaken. "She's living in her own dream."

"Exactly. And in that dream, she's safe." Shatov sighed deeply, as though he were weighed down by some invisible burden. "But for how long?" he muttered under his breath. I had no answer to that question, and we walked back to his room in silence.

Her voice grew softer and more tremulous as she finished the story, and as she spoke those last words, she seemed to lose herself in thought, staring blankly at the candle flame, her lips trembling slightly. There was no trace of shame or self-consciousness in her words. She seemed to recount her tale with an odd mixture of dreamy pride and sorrow, as though her memories were both her joy and her burden. Her soft, grey eyes, full of a strange clarity and melancholy, now gleamed faintly with unshed tears.

Shatov sat still, his face unusually pale, his rough, thick hands clenched on his knees. It seemed as though he was holding his breath. I, too, was silent, overwhelmed by what I had just heard. The pathos of her words—simple, childlike, yet somehow profound—struck at my heart. It was a confession of a soul that had lived through something unimaginable and yet retained a sense of innocence. This woman, sitting in squalor and poverty, abandoned and abused, had created her own dream-world out of fragments of beauty and pain, and she spoke of it as though she were recalling the most natural occurrences.

"And what happened to the child?" I ventured at last, unable to suppress the question, though I was almost afraid of the answer.

Marya Timofyevna glanced at me for the first time since the conversation began. There was a fleeting look of surprise in her expression, as though she had forgotten my presence entirely, but it quickly melted into her usual serene smile.

"The child?" she said softly, almost under her breath. "I don't know. I don't remember. It seems to me now that I laid him down somewhere … somewhere very safe, in a little hollow in the earth among the flowers. I covered him with the flowers, white ones, and then I kissed him and left him. But when I came back later, I couldn't find him. I searched and searched, but there was nothing there, only the flowers and the earth. Perhaps it was all a dream, Shatushka. Do you think it was a dream?"

Shatov gave a heavy sigh and rubbed his forehead, as though trying to push away the weight of her words. "I don't know, Marya Timofyevna," he muttered thickly, his voice hoarse. "I don't know anything."

"But I do," she said suddenly, with unexpected firmness. "It wasn't a dream. My baby was real, and I shall see him again one day. He is waiting for me. He is somewhere out there, where the light is bright and warm, and where the flowers never fade. I tell myself that every night, Shatushka, and that's how I sleep. That's what I see when I dream."

"And … your brother?" I asked cautiously, though I regretted interrupting the strange calm that had settled over her.

"My brother?" she repeated, blinking as though trying to remember who we were talking about. "Ah, yes—Lebyadkin. He's afraid of me, you know. He thinks I'm mad. That's why he beats me sometimes, to remind himself that he's stronger. But I forgive him. I forgive everything. I think he is mad himself, Shatushka. What do you think? How can a man shout and curse and drink like he does and not be mad? But it's all right. I'm happy. I am happy."

She looked at Shatov with such simple sincerity, her soft voice filled with conviction, that I felt a strange chill go down my spine. Her repeated insistence on happiness, spoken from a place so dark and desolate, felt both tragic and profound, as though she had found a secret key to joy that no one else could comprehend.

"Why do you call him Lebyadkin?" Shatov asked abruptly, as if grasping for some lighter detail to hold on to. "He's your brother. Why not call him by his name?"

"I don't know," she said thoughtfully. "I don't think of him as a brother. I think of him as a footman, or as something else. He's a little creature, like an insect buzzing and making noise. It doesn't matter. I've forgotten what his name even sounds like. But I do know that he's not real. None of this is real, Shatushka. Do you understand? It's all a play, like the ones I used to see when I was a girl, with painted faces and music in the background. I am not real either. I'm just waiting for the real life to begin."

Shatov stood up abruptly, his chair scraping against the floor. "We must go," he said gruffly, as though afraid to hear any more. "It's late, and your brother will be back soon."

"Yes, he will come back," Marya Timofyevna agreed cheerfully. "He will shout, and curse, and make a lot of noise. Perhaps he will beat me again. But I won't mind. I won't feel it. I never feel it. You'll come and see me again, won't you, Shatushka?"

"Yes, I'll come," Shatov muttered, avoiding her gaze. "I'll come soon."

We left quietly, closing the door behind us. As we climbed the stairs, Shatov walked ahead of me in silence, his steps heavy and deliberate. He did not speak until we reached his room. When we entered, he sat down heavily on the edge of his bed and buried his face in his hands.

"What a strange woman," I said softly, breaking the silence. "And yet there's something ... I don't know what ... about her words. As if she's already in another world."

"Yes," Shatov said at last, raising his head. "She's in her own world, but there's truth in it—more truth than in ours. And yet they'll destroy her, just like they destroy everything that's true and fragile."

His voice trailed off, and he sat staring blankly at the floor. Neither of us said another word. The shadow of that room and that woman seemed to linger over us both, as though we had looked into something sacred, tragic, and untouchable.

Shatov was visibly uneasy as he listened to the drunken shouting below, his face tightening as though he were preparing for a blow. I stood awkwardly in his room, unsure of whether to sit down or remain standing. The noise of heavy footsteps stumbling up the stairs made me instinctively glance at the door, as though expecting it to burst open. Shatov, however, seemed to regain his composure and sat down in his usual place, leaning forward with his elbows on his knees.

"That's him," he muttered, as if answering an unspoken question. "Lebyadkin always comes back like this, half-falling, half-crawling, swearing at the gate and at everything else. You'd think it was the gate's fault that he can't walk straight."

As though to confirm his words, the drunken voice roared louder, followed by a series of thuds and the sound of fists pounding on the walls. The muffled cursing grew more intelligible, though it was impossible to make out complete sentences. I heard fragments: something about "villains," "justice," and an accusation of betrayal. Suddenly, there was a scream—short and sharp, followed by laughter. A cruel, mocking laugh echoed in the hallway. I flinched, but Shatov remained unmoving, as if hardened to the chaos below.

"Does he always behave like this?" I asked softly, trying not to sound as disturbed as I felt.

"Every time," Shatov replied with grim finality. "Every evening, as though by clockwork. He stumbles in, shouts, and then either falls asleep where he stands or turns on her. She doesn't mind him as much as you'd think—at least she pretends not to." He paused and glanced up at me. "But I mind. I can't stand it."

I could hear the heavy thud of boots directly below us now, followed by a door slamming violently. Then silence. A heavy, oppressive silence, as though even the walls were holding their breath. It didn't last long. Suddenly, we heard him again, his voice muffled, this time inside his rooms, shouting incoherent threats.

"And she just sits there, quietly?" I asked, astonished.

"Quietly, yes. She doesn't cry or scream, even when he raises his hand. I think she doesn't feel it anymore—or maybe she feels it so deeply that she's learned not to show it. You saw how she looks at him—like he's a buzzing insect, something that barely exists to her. But still, it eats at her—every day, every hour."

At this moment, a shrill crash echoed through the ceiling. Shatov shot a dark glance at the floor, his fists tightening. I could tell he was straining every muscle in his body to keep from running back downstairs. Then he suddenly stood up, walked over to the small window, and flung it open, letting in the cool evening air. He leaned on the sill, staring out into the gathering dusk.

"Why do you go there?" I asked after a moment. "Why do you endure

172

it? She isn't your responsibility."

He turned back to me sharply, his eyes full of an emotion I could not quite identify—something like rage, but softened with pity.

"No, she isn't my responsibility," he said bitterly, "but who else will look out for her? Do you think anyone else cares whether she's alive or dead? She has no one—nothing. Not even herself. I go because I can't stand to see her treated like a dog, beaten for sport."

He sank back into his chair, breathing heavily. His face had paled again, and the furrows on his forehead deepened as he spoke.

"She's the only one of us who isn't afraid," he added quietly, almost as though speaking to himself. "She sits there like a stone, wrapped in her dreams. You saw how she talked about her baby? Maybe she had one, maybe she didn't—what does it matter? She's created a world for herself, one where nothing can touch her. I envy her."

"Envy her?" I repeated, incredulous. "But she's been destroyed, Shatov! A life like hers—how can you envy that?"

"You wouldn't understand," he said abruptly, waving his hand as though brushing away my words. "You're too reasonable, too ordinary. But don't you see? She's already out of reach of all this filth. She has her own truth, however mad it might seem to us. That's more than I can say for myself."

I didn't reply. There was something in Shatov's voice, in the strange mix of bitterness and admiration, that made me hesitate to argue further. He sat staring at the floor again, lost in thought. The sounds from below had quieted for the moment; only the occasional creak of the floorboards reminded us that the captain was still there, lurching about his miserable room.

Finally, Shatov stirred and got up again. "You should go home," he said abruptly. "It's late."

"And what about you?" I asked, though I already knew the answer.

"I'll wait," he said simply. "If I hear him start up again, I'll go back down. He knows what'll happen if I catch him at it." There was something menacing in his voice now, an edge of steel that I hadn't heard before.

I got up and moved toward the door, but before I opened it, I turned back to look at him. He was standing by the window again, staring out into the darkened street, his silhouette sharp against the faint light. For the first time, I noticed how tired he looked—how deeply lined his face had become, how hollow his eyes seemed.

"You're going to wear yourself out like this, Shatov," I said quietly.

He shrugged without turning around. "It doesn't matter. Someone has to keep watch."

I went out into the dark street, feeling a strange heaviness in my chest. The air was cool and damp, but it seemed thick with something unspoken. As I walked away from the house, I could still hear faint echoes of voices—muted, indistinct—coming from somewhere behind me. I quickened my pace, as though trying to leave something behind that refused to be left.

Chapter 4.5

Shatov stood motionless for a moment, his face rigid, as though he were trying to listen for the faintest sound. The house had gone quiet again, and the captain's shouting footsteps had disappeared into a distant, muffled thud, probably indicating that he had collapsed in some drunken heap. Shatov finally turned from the door, shaking his head as if shaking off a cloud of thoughts.

"Do you see now what kind of hell this is?" he muttered to me, as though answering a question I hadn't asked. "And yet, no one cares. She sits there like a shadow, like a ghost, as though she's already gone out of life, and no one even bothers to notice her. That beast comes back every night to bellow and thrash her, but she's forgotten how to be afraid. He gets drunk, he rants and screams—about what, even he doesn't know—yet she just sits there. It's as if she's not really there anymore."

I watched him as he said this, his face marked by both anger and something deeper—something like shame or helplessness. His voice dropped into an exhausted monotone as he sat down at his writing-table, his shoulders slumping.

"Why do you go through it, Shatov?" I asked softly, though I already knew he would only wave my question away. "Why get involved in something like this? It isn't your concern."

He shot me a quick, almost bitter glance. "You wouldn't understand," he muttered, his voice rough and abrupt, though not hostile. "No, you wouldn't understand—because you wouldn't bother. No one does. Everyone else is too busy with their damned lives and their precious principles. The whole world has lost the ability to see what really matters."

I didn't respond immediately, sensing that Shatov wasn't talking to me so much as venting his frustration aloud, as if speaking to himself. Outside, the wind began to pick up, a faint whistling sound sneaking through the old, crooked windowpanes. The thought of the woman upstairs—her strange serenity in such squalor, her dreamy recollections of past griefs and loves—left an inexplicable heaviness in my chest.

"What was that about her brother?" I ventured cautiously after a minute's silence. "What was he threatening to say just now?"

"That doesn't matter," Shatov replied curtly, turning back to the papers on his desk as though to dismiss me and the question altogether. "You heard him—he says a lot, but he says nothing at all. All bluster and noise, as usual. A coward through and through."

"But you seemed to take it seriously," I persisted. "What did he mean by 'documents' the other night, or by that cryptic comment about selling his sister? And why was he so afraid to say more?"

Shatov's face darkened. For a moment, he looked as though he might answer, but he hesitated, struggling with himself. Finally, he muttered, "There's nothing you need to know about that. Don't ask questions where you don't belong."

I understood that I would get no more from him. Still, something gnawed at me—a strange conviction that there were layers to all this chaos, something significant buried under the drunken rants and the cries in the night. What had started as a grotesque, almost farcical scene was beginning to feel like the shadow of something much darker and more real. Shatov's evasiveness only confirmed this.

At last, I rose to go, knowing that lingering further would accomplish nothing. "I'll see you tomorrow," I said quietly, picking up my coat.

"Yes, yes, tomorrow," Shatov replied absentmindedly, as though he hadn't really heard me. He had already turned back to his papers, his shoulders hunched, his face set in the tired frown of someone who had too much on his mind.

Outside, the night had deepened, and the cold wind hit me like a slap as I stepped out of the house and into the dark street. The captain's shouting had ceased completely now; the whole house seemed to have sunk into silence. The faint glow of a candle in the window upstairs was the only sign of life.

I walked home slowly, deep in thought. The events of the day were crowding my mind: Marya Timofyevna's strange, dreamlike stories, Shatov's fury, and Lebyadkin's cryptic drunken ramblings. I felt like I was standing on the edge of some precipice, unable to see clearly what lay below.

Tomorrow would bring answers—or at least I hoped it would. But as I walked through the darkened streets, I couldn't shake the feeling that I was being drawn into something far bigger and far more dangerous than I could yet understand. There was something ominous in the air— something waiting, as though hidden just beyond the edge of sight. And I, despite myself, was being pulled deeper into it.

To begin with, when Stepan Trofimovitch and I arrived at Varvara Petrovna's precisely at twelve o'clock, the very time she had fixed, we were surprised to learn that she was not at home. She had not yet returned from the morning service at the cathedral. My poor friend, already fragile both in body and spirit, was so overwhelmed by this unexpected turn of events that he collapsed into the nearest armchair like a man struck down by fate. It was as if this minor hitch had completely drained him of the composure he had been desperately trying to summon. I suggested that he take a glass of water or, perhaps, lie down for a moment to recover himself. But, despite his trembling hands, pallid complexion, and the nervous flicker of his lips, he refused with dignity, waving his hand as though to banish the suggestion entirely.

He was dressed that day with particular care, almost excessively so. A fine batiste shirt with elaborate embroidery peeped beneath his dark frock coat, a snowy white tie sat perfectly fastened under his chin, and he held in his trembling hand a brand-new hat, alongside an equally new pair of pale yellow gloves. There was even the faintest hint of perfume about him—a final touch to his carefully crafted elegance, as though he were trying to prove something to himself or to the world. I suspected he had spent a good hour at his toilette that morning, or at least pacing his room nervously as he decided what would be "suitable" for the occasion.

We had hardly settled into the awkward silence that followed when the door was opened to admit Shatov, who had evidently been summoned as well. His appearance startled me, though it was in keeping with his usual abrupt manner. He strode into the room, looked from Stepan Trofimovitch to me with a sharp and suspicious glance, and, without uttering a word or acknowledging our presence with so much as a nod, made his way to the farthest corner of the drawing-room. There he dropped heavily onto a chair, crossed his arms over his chest, and stared fixedly at the floor, as though he had come merely to sit and glower. Stepan Trofimovitch cast me a look of sheer dismay, one that seemed to plead for an explanation I couldn't provide. For several minutes, the three of us sat in oppressive silence—each of us looking uncomfortable in his own way—until, at last, Stepan Trofimovitch leaned toward me and began whispering feverishly, though so incoherently and with such agitation that I couldn't catch a single word. Before he could finish, the butler reappeared, ostensibly to rearrange something on the table, though it was perfectly obvious that his real intention was to scrutinize the peculiar trio that had gathered in the drawing-room.

"Alexey Yegorytch," Shatov suddenly broke the silence, his voice loud and harsh, "do you know whether Darya Pavlovna has gone to church with her?"

The butler turned stiffly toward Shatov, clearly displeased by his tone. "Varvara Petrovna was pleased to drive to the cathedral alone, and Darya

Pavlovna was pleased to remain in her room upstairs, being indisposed," he replied in a measured and reproving voice.

This piece of news seemed to strike Stepan Trofimovitch like another blow; he turned even paler and cast another helpless glance in my direction. I shifted uncomfortably in my seat and looked away. Suddenly, we heard the sound of a carriage arriving outside, followed by an unusual commotion that indicated our hostess's return. We all instinctively rose from our chairs, but the noise of hurried footsteps—a brisk, almost frantic pace—suggested something strange. Then, without warning, Varvara Petrovna herself burst into the room with an air of breathless agitation, a most uncharacteristic sight. She looked positively disheveled, and it was clear at once that something extraordinary had occurred.

Before we could gather our wits, another figure followed her—a younger, more energetic presence—none other than Lizaveta Nikolaevna, and in tow, holding tightly to her hand, came a third visitor who took my breath away: Marya Timofyevna Lebyadkin! Yes, it was she—Mlle. Lebyadkin herself, the very woman whom Shatov and I had visited the night before. Her sudden appearance in such a place, at such a moment, was as shocking as it was inconceivable. I might have dismissed it as a hallucination had I not seen the stunned expression on Shatov's face as well.

The entrance of this strange trio was so abrupt, so bewildering, that for a moment none of us spoke. It was as though we had been transported into some surreal scene of a dream. But before I describe what followed, it is necessary to recount how these events unfolded—how Varvara Petrovna, normally composed and severe, came to find herself in this predicament.

The key to the entire matter lay in her experience at church that morning. The cathedral had been unusually crowded; nearly the whole of our town's upper society had gathered there, lured by the prospect of seeing the governor's wife make her first public appearance. The rumors that had already begun circulating about the governor's wife—whispers of her "progressive" ideas and free-thinking ways—had added fuel to the curiosity of our ladies. There had been much speculation about her attire, too, which was expected to be of exceptional splendor, a stark contrast to Varvara Petrovna's own mourning black that she had worn consistently for four years.

It was in the midst of this solemn service that a most peculiar incident occurred. At the height of the sermon—delivered, as usual, by Father Pavel, our well-respected and eloquent preacher—a new arrival made her appearance at the cathedral. A woman, who clearly did not belong to the well-dressed congregation, pulled up in an antiquated hired droshky, the kind in which one had to perch sideways and cling to the driver's sash for stability. Her entrance was hardly dignified, but she leapt from the droshky with an energy that made her appear out of place amid the solemnity of the occasion.

"Isn't it enough, Vanya?" she cried plaintively, handing the driver a paltry sum of four kopecks.

"It's all I've got," she added with a note of untroubled honesty.

The driver, initially inclined to grumble, paused and waved a hand in resignation. "Well, there, bless you. I took you without fixing the price. And it would be a sin to take advantage of you, too," he said, almost philosophically, as though struck by a sudden recognition of her peculiar earnestness.

What followed, though, was nothing short of astonishing. The woman, whom we now know to have been Marya Timofyevna, entered the cathedral—lame, disheveled, and oddly composed—and made her way up the aisle with no hesitation. Heads turned; whispers began to ripple through the crowd. But what happened next, in front of the shocked eyes of the congregation, would send waves through the entire town and bring about the scene I witnessed in Varvara Petrovna's drawing-room.

Then, thrusting his leather purse hastily into his coat, the driver flicked his reins and rattled off, leaving behind a chorus of laughter and jeering remarks from the other drivers loitering at the gates. These jeers, mingled with whispers of curiosity and disbelief, followed the strange lady as she made her way towards the cathedral. The rows of liveried footmen and fine carriages waiting outside for the congregation's departure made her an even more striking and incongruous sight. Indeed, her appearance could hardly fail to astonish anyone: she was painfully thin, with a noticeable limp, and her face, heavily powdered and rouged, seemed to emphasize the hollow lines of her cheeks and the unnatural brightness of her eyes. She wore no shawl or pelisse in spite of the sharp September wind, just an old dark dress ill-suited to the chilly day. Her neck was exposed, long and bare, and her hair, twisted haphazardly into a small knot, was adorned with a single artificial rose—a garish paper flower of the kind typically used to decorate little cherub figurines sold during Palm Week.

This curious accessory brought to my mind the paper wreath of flowers I had noticed in the corner beneath the icons in Marya Timofyevna's room only the night before. But what struck me most was the expression on her face as she walked—eyes downcast with an almost modest demeanor, yet at the same time, a sly, mischievous smile played across her lips, as though she were silently sharing a secret joke with herself. It was as if she knew that her entrance would cause astonishment but did not care, or even relished the effect she produced. If she had lingered another moment in the open space among the carriages, perhaps someone might have stopped her or prevented her from entering. But she succeeded in slipping unnoticed into the crowded cathedral and, with surprising ease, began working her way forward through the dense congregation.

The cathedral was packed to capacity; it was a special day, for not only had the governor's wife chosen to attend for the first time since her arrival, but Father Pavel, our well-respected and eloquent chief priest, was delivering a particularly lengthy sermon. Every face in the congregation reflected a kind of rapt, solemn attention as the preacher's deep, measured voice echoed through the grand hall. And yet, when the strange woman entered, heads began to turn. At first, the glances were furtive, quick, and incredulous, as though people could hardly believe what they were seeing. But when she sank suddenly to her knees in the middle of the crowd, bowed her painted face to the ground, and remained there for a long time, unmistakably sobbing, her strange behavior drew more and more curious stares.

Raising her head at last and rising unsteadily to her feet, she seemed suddenly to recover her composure. Indeed, the tears on her cheeks had hardly dried before her expression turned cheerful, even merry. She began to look around her with an almost childlike sense of wonder and curiosity. Her eyes roved the cathedral, taking in the gilded icons, the high vaulted ceilings, and, most especially, the ladies of society. Every now and then, she would stand on tiptoe to get a better look at someone or something, and once or twice she giggled softly—a strange, stifled sound that rang discordantly in the hushed sanctity of the church.

The sermon was nearing its conclusion. When it finally ended and the ceremonial blessing with the cross began, the governor's wife was the first to approach the altar, as her rank demanded. However, she paused conspicuously two steps short of the cross, making an elaborate gesture of deference to Varvara Petrovna, who was already making her way forward. There was something pointed, almost theatrical, in this gesture— a subtle malice that did not escape the notice of those observing the scene. It was as though the governor's wife wished to declare, in a polite but unmistakable manner, her own sense of superiority and perhaps to undermine Varvara Petrovna's influence in the town. Yet Varvara Petrovna, with her habitual composure and iron dignity, appeared not to notice this slight at all. She proceeded directly to the cross, kissed it with the same stately solemnity as always, and turned to leave the cathedral. A footman in livery moved ahead of her, clearing a path as she passed through the crowd, though people had already begun stepping aside with instinctive respect.

It was just as she reached the porch, where the tightly packed throng momentarily blocked her way, that the extraordinary incident occurred. Out of the crowd, squeezing through with surprising speed and determination, the strange woman with the paper rose appeared. Without a moment's hesitation, she threw herself on her knees before Varvara Petrovna, right in front of the congregation. The crowd gasped audibly; even Varvara Petrovna, who rarely betrayed surprise or discomposure, stiffened and drew back slightly, though her expression remained stern and imperious. She looked down at the kneeling woman with a gaze that was at once commanding and disdainful, clearly demanding an explanation for this bizarre spectacle.

"What is it, my dear? What are you asking?" Varvara Petrovna inquired at last, her voice cold but not unkind, as though she were addressing a particularly eccentric beggar. The kneeling woman's expression was one of utter panic mingled with a sort of pleading reverence. Her lips trembled, and she seemed on the verge of speaking but could not find her voice. At last, faltering and broken, the words came:

"I ... I have come ... I have come only to kiss your hand ..."

Her voice quivered, and then, quite suddenly, she giggled—a strange, nervous sound that seemed both pitiable and absurd. With a childlike impulsiveness, she stretched out her hands, as though to seize Varvara Petrovna's own, but at the last instant, as though overcome by some paralyzing fear, she jerked them back again and clasped them to her chest. Her painted face, with its tears and powder streaking into little muddy rivulets, turned up to Varvara Petrovna with a look so full of yearning, shame, and helplessness that, for all its absurdity, it struck the hearts of those who saw it. The entire scene had unfolded so quickly, so unexpectedly, that it left the congregation frozen in stunned silence, their collective gaze fixed on this strange tableau at the cathedral gates.

Varvara Petrovna, as always, retained her composure. Her imperious gaze swept the crowd, as though demanding an explanation for this strange interruption. None came; the people merely stared, wide-eyed and breathless, as though waiting for her next move. Then, once more, she looked down at the woman kneeling before her.

"You are unhappy? You are in need of help?" she asked again, her tone this time quieter, almost softened.

The woman nodded, though her lips were still quivering. "Yes ... I am in need ..." she whispered. And then, in a voice broken by emotion: "I have come only to kiss your hand..."

At these words, a murmur ran through the crowd, but Varvara Petrovna remained as still as a statue.

"Is that all you have come for?" Varvara Petrovna asked, her tone softening with an unexpected touch of compassion. There was a slight smile on her lips, but her gaze remained steady, her face a picture of controlled curiosity and pity. Without waiting for a reply, she drew out her mother-of-pearl purse, which she carried in her pocket, and with the same deliberate and stately movement, opened it, took out a ten-rouble note, and extended it towards the kneeling woman. The unexpected recipient of this sudden charity clutched the corner of the note with trembling fingers, as though afraid it might be snatched back at any moment. The note fluttered in the draft, but her grip on it tightened, as though it were a lifeline.

"I say, she gave her ten roubles!" a voice whispered from the crowd, and immediately there was a slight stir. The gathering was no longer composed of the usual reverent faces emerging from church; it was a different crowd now—curious, watchful, and more irreverent, eager for a spectacle.

"Let me kiss your hand," the woman murmured in a voice choked with emotion. Her tear-streaked, painted face, for all its grotesqueness, wore such a look of gratitude and humble reverence that it softened the absurdity of her position. She raised her hand toward Varvara Petrovna hesitantly, almost reverently, as though expecting her request to be refused. Varvara Petrovna, frowning slightly, as if the gesture made her uncomfortable, extended her hand nonetheless. The woman seized it eagerly and kissed it fervently, as though performing some sacred rite. Her eyes shone with an almost delirious ecstasy, but she said nothing more.

At this precise moment, the governor's wife appeared, making her stately way through the press of people, surrounded by the usual cluster of society's finest ladies and high-ranking officials. The crowd at the porch had thickened to such a degree that for a moment, even the governor's wife was forced to pause. It was impossible not to see what was happening, and for a fleeting second her imperious gaze fell upon the scene before her—Varvara Petrovna, the kneeling woman, and the growing circle of gawking bystanders.

Varvara Petrovna, as though unaffected by the sudden increase in onlookers, fixed her sharp eyes on the woman and asked, almost abruptly: "Are you trembling? Are you cold?" Her voice was tinged with something akin to reproach, but her manner betrayed a deeper impulse—one of sudden compassion. Without waiting for an answer, she flung off her fur pelisse with a sweeping motion that startled even her own footman, who barely caught it in midair. Underneath, she was wearing a heavy black shawl, an exquisite and costly one, which she now unwound from her own shoulders and, with her own hands, carefully wrapped around the woman's exposed neck.

"Here, take this. But get up, get up from your knees, I beg you!" she said in a firmer tone.

The woman got to her feet with difficulty, as though suddenly realizing her own infirmity. She stood there awkwardly, clutching the shawl about her neck and still holding onto the ten-rouble note as though it were an inseparable treasure.

"Where do you live? Who knows where she lives?" Varvara Petrovna asked aloud, impatiently turning her gaze towards the crowd, as if commanding an immediate answer. But the faces around her were different now. There were no humble parishioners here—only members of the upper class, society people watching with either severe disapproval, sly amusement, or undisguised fascination at this unexpected and unprecedented scene. A few whispered, others stared silently, and some even exchanged subtle, knowing smiles.

At last, someone answered. "I believe her name's Lebyadkin," said a voice from the crowd. It belonged to Nikon Semyonitch Andreev, a highly respectable and well-known merchant, a man in Russian dress with a carefully groomed gray beard and an air of deliberate composure. He held his high-crowned hat in both hands and glanced cautiously at Varvara Petrovna. "They live in Filipov's house, on Bogoyavlensky Street."

"Lebyadkin? Filipov's house? I think I've heard something of this before…" murmured Varvara Petrovna. "Thank you, Nikon Semyonitch." She turned back to the woman. "Your name is Mlle. Lebyadkin?"

"No, my name's not Lebyadkin," the woman said with a faint smile, almost playfully, though her voice was thin and trembling.

"Then perhaps your brother's name is Lebyadkin?" Varvara Petrovna pressed, a hint of impatience in her tone.

"Yes, my brother's name is Lebyadkin."

"This is what I'll do," Varvara Petrovna said resolutely, drawing herself up to her full height. "I'll take you with me now, my dear, and you shall be driven home properly. Would you like that?"

"Oh, I should!" cried the woman in genuine, almost childlike delight, clasping her hands together as though she had been offered a wondrous gift.

"Auntie, auntie, take me with you too!" came an unexpected voice— clear, eager, and full of emotion. It was Lizaveta Nikolaevna, who suddenly broke free from the governor's wife and came running towards Varvara Petrovna. Lizaveta's face was flushed, her movements hurried and impulsive. She threw her arms around Varvara Petrovna, almost pleading.

"My dear, you know I'm always glad to have you," Varvara Petrovna said, startled, though she quickly regained her majestic composure. "But what will your mother say?" She studied Liza with a sharp, penetrating gaze, and seemed to notice for the first time the agitation that was trembling in every line of her face.

"Auntie, please, I must come with you!" Liza whispered, so low and desperately that only Varvara Petrovna could hear. "If you don't take me, I'll run after your carriage, screaming in the street."

The whispered words struck Varvara Petrovna like a blow. She stepped back for a moment, staggered, but her decision was swift. Her sharp gaze softened slightly, and she nodded. "Very well, I'll take you," she said loudly and firmly. Turning to Yulia Mihailovna, she added graciously, "If, of course, you are willing to allow it."

Yulia Mihailovna, the governor's wife, who had been observing everything with the keenest interest, answered with exaggerated sweetness and affability. "Oh, certainly! I wouldn't dream of depriving Liza of such a pleasure," she said with an artful smile, her voice lilting with affected rapture. "Especially as I myself... understand her so well."

There was a general ripple of approval through the crowd, as Varvara Petrovna, with dignified composure, thanked Yulia Mihailovna. The footman assisted Mlle. Lebyadkin into the carriage, and as she climbed in, Varvara Petrovna, with a start, exclaimed:

"What! You're lame?" Her face went pale, and her hand trembled slightly as she steadied herself against the carriage door. The reaction was so startling that those who saw it remembered it, though they could make no sense of it at the time.

The carriage rolled away with its unusual passengers—Varvara Petrovna sitting stiffly silent, as though deep in thought, Liza beside her, flushed and restless, and Marya Timofyevna, who laughed hysterically the entire way. The few minutes' drive to Varvara Petrovna's house passed in eerie contrast—laughter and silence sitting side by side, while an unspoken tension settled over the carriage like a shadow.

Chapter 5
The Subtle Serpent

Chapter 5.1

Varvara Petrovna rang the bell with a decisive, almost imperious air, and sank into an armchair by the window, pulling her shawl tighter around her shoulders. Her lips were set, her expression severe, though there was something deeply troubled and bewildered in her eyes. She surveyed the room quickly, her gaze falling on Marya Timofyevna, who had been placed in a chair by the round table at the center of the room.

"Sit here, my dear," she said, her tone both abrupt and faintly soothing, as if she were speaking to a child or an invalid. Then, turning suddenly to Stepan Trofimovitch, she exclaimed with sharp impatience, "Stepan Trofimovitch! What is the meaning of this? Look—just look at this woman! What on earth is the meaning of it?"

"I … I …" Stepan Trofimovitch faltered miserably, his face growing pale and his hands trembling as he fumbled with his hat. He was utterly at a loss and seemed to shrink under her authoritative gaze.

At that moment, the footman entered the room quietly, but promptly. "A cup of coffee—immediately! And tell them to keep the horses ready!" Varvara Petrovna ordered crisply, as though trying to maintain control of the situation, while her composure was clearly slipping.

"Mais, chère et excellente amie, dans quelle inquiétude ..." Stepan Trofimovitch began weakly, attempting to regain some dignity with his habitual resort to French, but his voice was faint, almost pleading.

"Ah! French! French! Why, this is the highest society, no doubt!" cried Marya Timofyevna suddenly, clapping her hands together with childish delight. Her eyes were bright and laughing as she turned toward Stepan Trofimovitch with a face full of eager anticipation, as though she expected a lively conversation in a language she did not understand. The room fell silent, and Varvara Petrovna, whose expression had shifted from irritation to something like bewilderment, stared at her guest with visible dismay, as if she could not believe what she was seeing.

A profound, almost uncomfortable hush settled over the room. Shatov sat with his head bowed, his face set, staring obstinately at the floor. Stepan Trofimovitch seemed crushed, almost paralyzed by confusion and guilt, though he was innocent of any actual offense. I stole a glance at Liza, who was seated in a corner near Shatov. Her eyes were fixed on Varvara Petrovna and the strange, crippled woman with the same keen intensity as before. Her lips were drawn into a thin smile, but it was not a pleasant one. There was something cruel, mocking even, in the way she watched, and Varvara Petrovna noticed it—her sharp eyes missing nothing.

Meanwhile, Marya Timofyevna remained blissfully unperturbed. She sat perfectly at ease, her gaze wandering around the grand room, taking in every detail with open delight. Her eyes gleamed as they settled on the luxurious furnishings, the intricate patterns of the carpet, the old, faded portraits on the walls, the great bronze crucifix standing solemnly in a corner, and the heavy albums and ornaments on the tables. She seemed entranced, like a child who had wandered into a magical palace.

"And you're here too, Shatushka!" she cried suddenly, her voice full of cheerful recognition. "Why, I saw you earlier, but I thought it couldn't be you! What are you doing here?" She laughed lightly, as though it were all a delightful joke.

"You know this woman?" Varvara Petrovna turned to Shatov abruptly, her voice sharp and demanding.

"I know her," Shatov muttered reluctantly, without lifting his head. He shifted slightly in his chair, but did not move.

"What do you know of her? Speak up—quickly!" Varvara Petrovna pressed.

Shatov hesitated, stammered, then looked up briefly, his face strangely contorted in a mix of stubbornness and discomfort. "She lives in the same house as I do … with her brother … an officer," he said at last, haltingly.

"Well?" Varvara Petrovna demanded impatiently, her gaze drilling into him.

"It's not worth talking about," Shatov muttered, his voice trailing off. He crossed his arms and relapsed into silence, his expression one of dogged determination, as though he had sworn to say no more.

"Of course, I can expect nothing else from you," Varvara Petrovna said sharply, with an air of wounded indignation. Her quick mind had already grasped that something was being deliberately hidden from her. She sensed a conspiracy of silence, as though everyone in the room— Shatov, Stepan Trofimovitch, even Liza—was conspiring to keep something from her.

The footman returned at that moment, carrying a small silver tray with a steaming cup of coffee, exactly as Varvara Petrovna had ordered. At her signal, he moved toward Marya Timofyevna.

"You were cold just now, my dear. Drink this—it will warm you up," Varvara Petrovna said with surprising gentleness.

"Merci!" Marya Timofyevna responded gaily, as though the word were a delightful discovery. But when she caught Varvara Petrovna's reproachful look, she flushed, embarrassed by her own flippancy. She carefully placed the cup back on the table, her hands trembling slightly.

"Auntie, surely you're not angry?" she faltered suddenly, her voice softening into a childish whimper. Her expression was half-playful, half-pleading, as though she were trying to coax forgiveness.

"What did you call me?" Varvara Petrovna demanded sharply, straightening in her chair. Her voice, calm and cutting, struck like a whip. "I am not your aunt. What are you thinking?"

Marya Timofyevna seemed to shrink into herself at the severity of the rebuke. Her face went pale, and her shoulders began to shake slightly in what seemed to be some nervous fit. She sank back into her chair, visibly trembling.

"I … I thought that was the proper way," she stammered plaintively, staring at Varvara Petrovna with wide, bewildered eyes. "Liza called you that just now."

"What Liza?" Varvara Petrovna asked sternly, though there was something wary in her tone now.

"Why, this young lady here," Marya Timofyevna replied, raising her hand and pointing a thin, trembling finger towards Lizaveta Nikolaevna.

"So you're calling her 'Liza' already?" Varvara Petrovna turned a cold, penetrating gaze on Marya Timofyevna.

"You called her that yourself just now," Marya Timofyevna protested timidly, finding a moment of unexpected boldness. Then, with a strange, almost dreamy smile, she added, "And I dreamed of a beauty like that."

Varvara Petrovna's expression softened slightly at these words, and she regarded her guest with a strange, searching look. A faint smile flickered on her lips, as though some private thought or memory had crossed her mind. Seeing this, Marya Timofyevna rose from her chair timidly and limped towards her, clutching the shawl that had been wrapped around her neck.

"Take it," she said softly, holding the shawl out with both hands. "I forgot to give it back. Don't be angry with me—I didn't mean to be rude."

Varvara Petrovna remained silent, staring at her for several seconds before slowly shaking her head. "Keep it," she said at last, her voice quieter, though still firm. "You need it more than I do."

Marya Timofyevna hesitated for a moment, clutching at the black shawl that Varvara Petrovna had draped over her shoulders just minutes before. Then, as though coming to a decision, she began to remove it slowly, holding it out with both hands as if to give it back.

"Put it on again at once, and keep it always," Varvara Petrovna said abruptly, her tone sharp but softened by a touch of unexpected warmth. "Go and sit down, drink your coffee, and don't be afraid of me, my dear. There's no need to worry yourself. I am beginning to understand you."

Her voice, though commanding, had lost some of its earlier edge. She gave Marya Timofyevna a look both searching and perplexed, as though still grappling to comprehend what had just unfolded. Marya Timofyevna blinked, unsure for a moment, but obediently pulled the shawl back around her shoulders. She limped quietly back to her chair, her hands trembling faintly as she picked up the cup of coffee from the table. Her eyes darted nervously around the room, yet there remained a strange cheerfulness in her expression, as though she were trying to make sense of the peculiar scene herself.

"Chère amie…" Stepan Trofimovitch began again, his voice faint and almost imploring. He shifted uneasily in his chair, clearly wishing to be helpful but only contributing to the confusion.

"Ach, Stepan Trofimovitch, it's bewildering enough without you," Varvara Petrovna interrupted sharply, cutting him off mid-sentence. "You might at least spare me your exclamations." Her glance silenced him completely. "Please—do something useful. Ring the bell there, by you, to the maid's room."

Stepan Trofimovitch, almost as though grateful for the distraction, jumped up at once, fumbled for a moment with the bell cord near him, and finally succeeded in ringing. The sound of the bell rang faintly through the house, lingering in the heavy silence that followed. Varvara Petrovna's eyes wandered irritably and somewhat suspiciously over all of us—myself, Liza, Shatov, and Stepan Trofimovitch—pausing on each of our faces for the briefest of moments, as though searching for something hidden, something unsaid.

The door opened, and Agasha, her faithful maid, entered swiftly and noiselessly. She curtsied and stood waiting, her hands folded before her.

"Bring me my check shawl—the one I bought in Geneva," Varvara Petrovna ordered, without looking at her. Her voice had regained its firmness. "And what's Darya Pavlovna doing?"

"She's not very well, madam," Agasha replied softly, with a deferential nod.

"Go to her and ask her to come here. Say that I want her particularly, even if she's not well. I must see her."

"Yes, madam." Agasha curtsied again and left the room.

At that moment, a sudden noise erupted in the next room—a clatter of hurried footsteps, loud voices, and the rustle of skirts. It was the same sound of disturbance as before, only louder and more chaotic. We all turned our heads toward the doorway, waiting in silent anticipation. Then, with theatrical abruptness, Praskovya Ivanovna burst into the room, leaning heavily on the arm of Mavriky Nikolaevitch. She appeared thoroughly flustered and winded, as though she had barely managed to reach the drawing-room in one piece.

"Ach, heavens! I could scarcely drag myself here!" she wailed breathlessly, her voice high-pitched and trembling. She halted in the doorway, panting and clutching at Mavriky Nikolaevitch's arm for support, her face pale and almost distraught. "Liza, you mad girl, how you treat your mother!" she squeaked, directing a look of feeble indignation toward her daughter.

Her voice, though quivering, seemed to carry the full weight of all her accumulated irritation. Weak and irritable people, when pushed to the limit, have a way of distilling all their grievances into one trembling note of complaint, and so it was with Praskovya Ivanovna. She fixed a reproachful stare at Liza, who sat quietly in the corner with a look of calm defiance on her face.

Varvara Petrovna, startled but not entirely unprepared for such an intrusion, turned her sharp gaze on Praskovya Ivanovna. She half-rose from her chair, stiffly and with evident reluctance, as though she were making an effort to preserve her dignity and composure.

"Good morning, Praskovya Ivanovna," she said slowly and with an air of restrained politeness, though her irritation was still evident beneath the surface. "Please be seated. I knew you would come."

Her tone, though courteous, carried the unmistakable chill of suppressed annoyance, as though she were grappling to maintain control of both the situation and her own emotions. The tension in the room, already thick, seemed to deepen as Varvara Petrovna's gaze met Praskovya Ivanovna's, two formidable forces measuring one another in silence.

Praskovya Ivanovna, her indignation somewhat subdued by Varvara Petrovna's cool reception, allowed herself to be led to a chair by Mavriky Nikolaevitch. She sank into it heavily, as though her strength had given out at last. For a moment, she sat there breathing hard, adjusting her shawl and casting nervous glances at everyone in the room.

"And now, perhaps, we may begin to understand what all this means," Varvara Petrovna said quietly, though her voice carried an unmistakable authority. She turned her sharp, penetrating gaze back to Marya Timofyevna, who sat quietly in her chair, still clutching the black shawl around her shoulders and looking both out of place and strangely serene.

We all remained silent, as though waiting for some final revelation to shatter the tension hanging in the air.

Chapter 5.2

Praskovya Ivanovna's entrance into the room was as much a spectacle as it was a declaration of war. There was no mistaking the almost triumphant glint in her eye or the rigid determination in her posture, despite her apparent frailty. She leaned heavily on Mavriky Nikolaevitch's arm as though she were a queen being conducted to her throne, yet her agitated movements betrayed the nervous energy of someone both confident and on edge. Her pale, thin face, flushed slightly with exertion, carried an expression that could only be described as defiant—tinged with grievance and self-righteousness, as though she had arrived not to request her daughter's return, but to claim a moral victory.

Varvara Petrovna, on the other hand, sat like a statue of iron composure, though one could see the spark of something fiery and resentful in her eyes as she watched her old school friend sweep into the room with such theatrical flair. There was no cordiality in the exchange of glances; it was more like two fencers measuring their distance before the first strike.

"There could be nothing surprising to Praskovya Ivanovna in such a reception," I thought to myself, feeling an inexplicable sense of dread in the charged air. Their relationship had long been defined by subtle—and not so subtle—tyranny. Even in their girlhood, Varvara Petrovna had asserted herself as the leader, treating her friend with the same casual but unwavering dominance that she now exhibited. Time, marriage, and age had done little to change this dynamic; it was as though Varvara Petrovna held an unspoken right to the upper hand, and Praskovya Ivanovna had spent decades resenting it, waiting for her moment.

The last few days had deepened the rift between the two households, though no one could quite explain why. Rumors had swirled—some barely intelligible, others hinting at darker, unspoken conflicts—and they had reached Varvara Petrovna in vague and infuriating half-measures. This mysterious fracture had left her not only offended but unsettled, and it was clear she was determined to uncover the truth. She loathed insinuations, despised whispers behind her back, and could not abide the idea that someone—anyone—might presume to adopt a superior stance toward her. Open confrontation suited her better than half-smiles and veiled snubs. And yet, here was Praskovya Ivanovna, standing before her with an expression that seemed to say: Now, you will listen to me.

For her part, Praskovya Ivanovna appeared fueled by a combination of illness, pent-up resentment, and the naïve conviction that she had finally seized some moral high ground over her old friend. This impression was so plain in her demeanor that it was almost comical. It was the air of a weak person who, having swallowed insult after insult for years, suddenly finds the courage—or the provocation—to strike back. And when they do, they strike out with more violence than the situation warrants, as though trying to compensate for all the humiliations they endured in silence.

As for the rest of us, we were little more than witnesses—spectators to a drama that none of us fully understood but which held us in its thrall nonetheless. I glanced nervously at Stepan Trofimovitch, who seemed to be collapsing into himself as the scene unfolded. He had half-fallen into an armchair, his trembling hands clutching the arms for support. His face, pale as parchment, wore an expression of helpless despair as he darted glances at me, as though silently pleading for some reprieve.

Shatov, sitting stiffly in his corner, reacted very differently. At the sound of Praskovya Ivanovna's sharp squeal, he twisted abruptly in his seat, his face darkening. He muttered something under his breath—probably a curse—and for a moment I thought he meant to get up and leave. There was something raw and restless about his movement, as though he were itching to be free of the suffocating tension in the room. Yet he stayed where he was, glowering at the floor, his fists clenched on his knees.

And then there was Liza. She rose from her chair with a startled, almost instinctive movement when her mother's voice cut through the air. But as quickly as she stood, she sank back down again, her eyes drifting into the middle distance. It was clear to me that she had scarcely registered her mother's words. This was not the result of her usual "waywardness" or defiance; no, this was something else entirely. Her expression was abstracted, her face unusually pale, her lips pressed into a thin line. It was as though her mind were elsewhere, utterly consumed by some deep and overwhelming impression, one that had taken complete possession of her senses. She sat there, barely moving, her gaze unfocused—lost to whatever storm was raging in her thoughts.

Curiously, even Marya Timofyevna, who only moments before had been basking in her surroundings with childlike wonder, seemed affected by the growing tension. She stopped giggling and sat very still, clutching Varvara Petrovna's shawl tightly around her as though for protection. Her eyes, wide and searching, flitted from one face to another, though they lingered on Varvara Petrovna with a kind of shy reverence. For a moment, she seemed on the verge of speaking, as though she had something to say that might break the silence, but she thought better of it and lowered her head.

And so we sat, frozen in this tableau of uneasy silence. Varvara Petrovna's gaze, sharp as a blade, remained fixed on Praskovya Ivanovna, who glared back with an air of stubborn indignation. The stillness in the room was unbearable, like the quiet that precedes the first clap of thunder in a summer storm. For my part, I felt like an intruder in a private battle—caught up in forces beyond my understanding, though somehow keenly aware that the events unfolding before me would leave a mark on all of us.

It seemed that nothing short of an explosion could release the tension, and I waited anxiously for the inevitable clash. I was certain that before long, the room would be filled with raised voices and unrestrained accusations—each word sharper than the last, until all the grievances these two proud women had harbored for so many years came spilling out into the open.

Chapter 5.3

The scene unfolded with a crescendo of tension, and each moment seemed to teeter on the edge of chaos. Praskovya Ivanovna, though entering with the determination of a woman wronged, now appeared startled at the effect of her own audacity. Her voice, which had been filled with venom and defiance just moments before, turned suddenly meek and quavering, like that of a child caught in some mischief. She leaned forward in her chair, half-rising with evident strain, her hands wringing anxiously in her lap as she implored forgiveness from her old friend.

Varvara Petrovna, meanwhile, sat utterly still, her face drained of all color. She had sunk back in her chair as though stricken by an invisible blow. Her thin lips, pressed tightly together, quivered imperceptibly; her hands lay motionless on the arms of her chair, though her knuckles were white with the force of her grip. She seemed unable to speak, and for a moment, her dignified composure—the iron control that had always defined her—appeared to falter. It was as though Praskovya Ivanovna's reckless outburst had touched some deep, raw nerve that no one else in the room could understand.

"Varvara Petrovna, dear, forgive me, I didn't mean it!" Praskovya

Ivanovna cried again, her voice rising to a shrill pitch as she looked around in near-panic, no doubt mortified by the sudden shift in atmosphere. Her earlier bravado had completely crumbled, and her features now wore an expression of genuine fear.

Stepan Trofimovitch, as always in moments of crisis, sprang into action with a frantic energy that did little to calm the situation. "Water! She must have water!" he cried in a quavering voice as he darted forward with a kind of helpless fussiness, his arms flailing as though he might conjure a remedy out of thin air. His face was nearly as pale as Varvara Petrovna's, and his panic gave the scene a peculiar absurdity.

"Calm yourself, Stepan Trofimovitch!" I whispered sharply, stepping up beside him. I felt equally unsettled, but there was no denying that someone had to keep their head. "Agasha, bring some water immediately!" I called toward the open door, where the maid had been lingering uncertainly.

The commotion grew as Liza finally rose from her seat and came forward. Her eyes, which had been fixed with such strange abstraction on the carpet moments before, now blazed with renewed intensity. Yet, though she approached, she made no move to comfort her mother or Varvara Petrovna; instead, she stood stiffly, her hands clenched tightly at her sides, her face a mask of suppressed emotion. The atmosphere in the room had grown so oppressive that it seemed to weigh upon all of us, and I noticed even Shatov—who had sat silent and brooding throughout the exchange—glance toward the scene with dark, watchful eyes.

Marya Timofyevna, meanwhile, the unwitting center of all this turmoil, remained obliviously cheerful. With the playful, almost giddy innocence of a child at a fairground, she wiggled gleefully in her chair, her laughter breaking through the heavy silence like a sudden, dissonant note in an already discordant melody. Her reaction was incomprehensible to the rest of us—it seemed that, in her mind, this entire confrontation was nothing more than an amusing spectacle.

"Ach, forgive me, I beg you, Varvara Petrovna!" Praskovya Ivanovna wailed, tears welling up in her eyes as she struggled to hold on to her pride. "I lost my temper, and I don't even know what I'm saying! This cursed tongue of mine runs away with me—Lord have mercy! I only came here for my daughter, and look what I've done...." She fell back into her chair, gasping with exhaustion.

At last, Varvara Petrovna stirred. She seemed to collect herself with visible effort, breathing in deeply and sitting up straighter. Her face remained pale, but the trembling of her lips ceased, and the faintest hint of color returned to her cheeks. She raised her right hand in a slow, almost regal motion, as though commanding silence, and when she spoke, her voice was calm—chillingly so, in contrast to the tumult that had preceded it.

"Praskovya Ivanovna, you have succeeded in outdoing yourself today," she said evenly, though her words carried a weight that made everyone else in the room hold their breath. "You appear to think that you can bring your petty grievances here, into my home, and insult me in the presence of my friends. I am patient, Praskovya Ivanovna—I am more patient than most people think—but I will not tolerate this kind of spectacle. For your own sake, I suggest you compose yourself."

There was a pause—a heavy, ominous silence that settled like a stone over us all. Praskovya Ivanovna seemed to shrink into her chair under Varvara Petrovna's unblinking gaze. She opened her mouth as though to retort, but no sound came. Her earlier confidence had evaporated entirely, leaving her cowed and disarmed.

"Auntie, please, enough!" Liza's voice broke the silence, sharp and anguished. She took a step forward, her face flushed and her eyes blazing. "Maman, you're only making things worse. Can't you see that?" Her voice wavered for a moment, and then she turned to Varvara Petrovna. "And you—what do you expect from all this? To sit in judgment over everyone as though you're above it all? Is that your answer?"

Her words were startling, like the clash of a sword against steel. Varvara Petrovna turned her gaze on Liza with an expression that was at once appraising and cold. "You forget yourself, Lizaveta Nikolaevna," she said softly, but there was a sharpness in her tone that warned against further defiance.

"I forget nothing," Liza shot back. "If there's scandal, it's because you've allowed it to fester, all of you. All you do is talk and whisper, hiding truths until they turn into poison. I don't care anymore—I won't sit here pretending not to see what's in front of me."

We were all stunned into silence. For a moment, it felt as though the very walls of the drawing-room held their breath. Varvara Petrovna narrowed her eyes, and I saw a flicker of something in her face—surprise, perhaps, or recognition.

"Enough," she said at last, rising to her feet with slow, deliberate grace. "Praskovya Ivanovna, Mavriky Nikolaevitch, I believe you came here with a purpose. Perhaps it is time you took your leave."

Praskovya Ivanovna, visibly shaken, struggled to stand, leaning heavily on Mavriky Nikolaevitch's arm. She looked as though she wanted to say something more, but at the last moment she thought better of it. Her face was red with shame and anger as she turned toward the door.

"Come, Mavriky," she muttered hoarsely. "We've had enough of this."

As they departed, the room seemed to exhale a collective sigh of relief, though the air remained heavy with unspoken tensions. I glanced at Stepan Trofimovitch, who sat slumped in his chair, utterly defeated, his head hanging low. Shatov stared grimly at the floor, while Liza stood rooted in place, her arms crossed tightly, as though bracing herself for a storm yet to come.

Varvara Petrovna remained standing, motionless, her gaze fixed on the empty doorway. Whatever battle had just taken place, it was clear that she was already preparing herself for the next one.

Stepan Trofimovitch, who had been standing in a half-dazed stupor by the table, sprang at once to the bell-rope. He moved with an exaggerated eagerness, as though seeking refuge in the simple act of ringing for the footman. The tension in the room was such that even a small sound, like the chime of the bell, seemed unusually loud. Everyone appeared frozen in their positions, as if waiting for the next blow to fall. The drawn faces of the company revealed various shades of emotion—confusion, dread, and unease—all except Darya Pavlovna, whose calm demeanor had returned in full force.

Varvara Petrovna continued to sit rigidly, her gaze sharp and imperious as she surveyed the room. Though her voice remained steady, it was evident to me that beneath the surface, she was struggling to master some deep inner agitation. Her fingers tapped softly against the arm of her chair as though to anchor her focus.

The door opened almost immediately, and Agasha entered with her usual quiet efficiency, glancing discreetly around the room to understand the situation. Varvara Petrovna turned to her sharply.

"Tell Alexey Yegorytch," she said with grave precision, "to send for Captain Lebyadkin at once. I want him here within the hour, without fail. Make it clear that I require his immediate presence."

Agasha gave a slight nod, curtsied, and withdrew, closing the door softly behind her. A new silence followed, heavy and expectant. This sudden summons of Captain Lebyadkin hung over the room like a thundercloud about to break. I noticed that Marya Timofyevna, for all her light-hearted chatter moments before, had become subdued at the mention of her brother. She shrank back into her chair, her smile fading slightly, and clasped her thin, trembling hands together on her lap. Her soft, grey eyes darted nervously from one person to another, as though seeking reassurance.

"I trust this will clarify everything," Varvara Petrovna said at last, addressing Darya Pavlovna directly. Her tone, though softened slightly, retained its steel-edged authority. "I cannot allow such rumors to spread—especially when they touch on my household. If this man is slandering you, we will hear it from his own lips, and he will answer for it. Rest assured, Darya, you have my protection."

Darya Pavlovna inclined her head respectfully. "I am grateful for your understanding, Varvara Petrovna," she said quietly. Her voice was calm, almost deferential, though I detected a subtle firmness beneath her words—as though she were asserting her innocence without needing to plead for it. Her composure in this moment was extraordinary; she sat perfectly still, her hands folded neatly on her lap, her gaze level and unflinching.

"Madam," Praskovya Ivanovna interjected suddenly, though her voice trembled, "surely this scandal has gone far enough. I came here only because of my daughter—out of fear for her good name—but you will admit yourself that appearances have been—" She hesitated, her voice trailing off under Varvara Petrovna's stern glare. "Well, they've been most unfortunate!" she finished weakly.

"Unfortunate?" Varvara Petrovna repeated with a faint, icy smile. "Do you think I don't understand that, Praskovya Ivanovna? I understand everything perfectly. But I also know when it is time to confront appearances rather than hide from them. If someone dares to slander a member of my household, I will deal with it publicly and directly."

Praskovya Ivanovna opened her mouth as though to respond but thought better of it. She slumped back into her chair, defeated, tugging nervously at the shawl draped over her shoulders. Mavriky Nikolaevitch, who had been standing silently behind her like a stone pillar, cleared his throat softly as though to remind everyone of his presence but said nothing.

Meanwhile, Liza, who had sat motionless and silent throughout this entire exchange, finally stirred. She stood up abruptly, her face flushed, and her eyes blazing with some unspoken intensity. "Auntie, you're right to summon him," she said, her voice quivering slightly but resolute. "It's time for everything to come to light. This has gone on long enough."

Varvara Petrovna turned her gaze sharply toward Liza, as though surprised by her sudden intervention. For a moment, they locked eyes, and an almost imperceptible understanding seemed to pass between them—something private, unspoken, and powerful. Then Varvara Petrovna gave a faint nod.

"Sit down, Liza, my dear," she said with unexpected gentleness. "You mustn't upset yourself. This is unpleasant, yes—but it will soon be resolved."

Liza hesitated, as though wanting to say more, but finally sat back down in her chair. Her hands gripped the arms of the chair tightly, her knuckles white.

For my part, I could not help feeling that we were all teetering on the brink of some larger revelation, something that had been building beneath the surface for a long time. Every moment seemed charged with anticipation. Shatov, who had remained silent and sullen in his corner, now shifted restlessly in his chair, his gaze flicking toward the door with an almost anxious impatience. Even Stepan Trofimovitch, who had remained uncharacteristically quiet, seemed unusually absorbed, his brow furrowed and his eyes darting nervously from face to face.

Marya Timofyevna broke the silence suddenly. "Ah, well, let him come," she said softly, with an odd mixture of resignation and cheerfulness. "He's nothing to me. I have my own thoughts—he can't touch them, no matter how much he blusters."

She smiled faintly as though to herself, her gaze distant and dreamy, as if she were recalling something pleasant. The contrast between her serene detachment and the tension in the room only deepened the strangeness of the moment.

Varvara Petrovna turned away, her expression unreadable. The room fell silent again, and we all sat waiting—each of us lost in our own thoughts, yet bound together by the mounting tension that hung in the air like a heavy fog.

Stepan Trofimovitch rang the bell and suddenly stepped forward, his face flushed and full of nervous energy. "If... if..." he began feverishly, stumbling over his words and breaking off, "if I too have heard the most disgusting story—or rather, slander—it was with complete outrage... enfin, he is a lost man, something like an escaped convict..." He trailed off, unable to continue. Varvara Petrovna, narrowing her eyes, looked him up and down carefully.

At that moment, the butler, Alexey Yegorytch, entered. "The carriage," Varvara Petrovna ordered briskly. "And you, Alexey Yegorytch, get ready to escort Miss Lebyadkin home. She will give you the address."

"Mr. Lebyadkin has been waiting downstairs for some time and has been asking to see her," the butler replied.

"That's impossible, Varvara Petrovna!" said Mavriky Nikolaevitch, who had sat silently this whole time. He now stepped forward, clearly alarmed. "If I may say so, he is not a man who can be admitted into society. He… he is completely inappropriate, Varvara Petrovna!"

"Wait a moment," Varvara Petrovna said calmly to Alexey Yegorytch, who immediately left the room.

"He's a dishonest man, and I even think he's something like an escaped convict," Stepan Trofimovitch muttered again, flushing red as he stammered and fell silent.

"Liza, it's time for us to go," Praskovya Ivanovna announced with disdain as she stood up. It seemed she regretted calling herself foolish earlier. She listened to Darya Pavlovna speak, pressing her lips in a mocking way. What struck me most, however, was the look on Lizaveta Nikolaevna's face when Darya Pavlovna had entered. Her eyes burned with hatred, and her expression showed barely concealed contempt.

"Please wait a moment, Praskovya Ivanovna," Varvara Petrovna said firmly. Her tone was polite but carried an undeniable authority. "Sit down again. I need to speak clearly, and you'll need a chair with those bad legs of yours. That's it, thank you. I lost my temper earlier, and I said things I regret. I apologize for behaving foolishly because I value fairness in all things. Now, in your anger, you brought up those anonymous letters. Well, let me say this: any anonymous letter is worthless and despicable just because it is unsigned. If you think otherwise, I am sorry for you. As for me, I refuse to dig into such filthy corners or dirty my hands with nonsense. But you, it seems, have dirtied yours.

"However, since you have brought up the subject yourself, I will tell you this. Six days ago, I too received an absurd anonymous letter. Some fool wrote to me saying that Nikolay Vsyevolodovitch had lost his mind and that I needed to be afraid of some lame woman who, as the letter claimed, was 'destined to play a big role in my life.' I remember the exact phrase. I thought about it and, knowing how many enemies Nikolay Vsyevolodovitch has, I decided to send for a man who lives here—one of his enemies, someone particularly spiteful and contemptible. From my conversation with him, I figured out where this ridiculous letter came from.

"So, my dear Praskovya Ivanovna, if you've been upset by similar letters about me, if people have been bombarding you with such filth, then I am, of course, sorry to be the innocent cause of it. That's all I wanted to explain to you. I'm very sorry to see you so tired and upset. But I've made up my mind about this situation. I plan to see this person that Mavriky Nikolaevitch just said—perhaps a little too strongly—is 'impossible' to receive. Liza, my dear, you don't need to be involved at all. Come here, Liza, let me kiss you."

Liza crossed the room and stood silently in front of Varvara Petrovna. The older woman kissed her, took her hands, and, holding her at arm's length, looked at her with deep feeling. Then she made the sign of the cross over her and kissed her again.

"Well, goodbye, Liza," she said softly, her voice trembling as though she were holding back tears. "Remember that I will always love you, no matter what life has in store for you. God be with you. I have always accepted His Holy Will…"

She seemed ready to say more, but she stopped herself and fell silent. Liza turned and walked slowly back toward her seat. She looked as though she were deep in thought, but halfway there, she stopped suddenly in front of her mother.

"I'm not leaving yet, Mother. I'll stay here a little longer with Auntie," she said in a low voice. The words were quiet, but there was no mistaking the iron will behind them.

"Oh my goodness, what now?" Praskovya Ivanovna cried in despair, throwing up her hands. But Liza didn't respond. She sat down in the same corner and stared off into space again, just as she had before.

Varvara Petrovna's face showed a mix of pride and satisfaction. "Mavriky Nikolaevitch, I need a favor," she said suddenly. "Please go and take a look at that man downstairs. If there's any chance he can be brought up here without causing trouble, bring him in."

Mavriky Nikolaevitch gave a small bow and left the room. A few moments later, he returned, leading Mr. Lebyadkin into the drawing room.

Chapter 5.4

The captain had a rough and unkempt look, but today he appeared surprisingly well-dressed. He was a tall, stocky man in his forties, with curly hair, a bloated, purplish face, and fleshy cheeks that shook when he moved his head. His small, bloodshot eyes had a crafty look at times, and his thick mustache, sideburns, and the beginnings of a double chin made his face appear swollen and unpleasant. What stood out the most, however, was his outfit. He wore a formal black dress coat and clean white linen—an appearance so unusual for him that it felt out of place. As Liputin once said, "Some people just don't look right in clean linen," and this observation seemed to fit the captain perfectly. He was also holding a brand-new black glove in his right hand, while his left, awkwardly stretched into an unbuttoned glove, half-covered his enormous, clumsy fist. In that same hand, he held a shiny, new hat—probably being worn for the first time that very day. This "garb of love," as he had called it while yelling at Shatov the day before, had clearly been real.

It was obvious that the captain hadn't managed this transformation alone. Liputin, I later discovered, had advised him to dress up like this for some mysterious purpose. Someone else had certainly helped him— encouraged him, paid for the clothes, and even arranged his appearance. Without help, the captain would never have managed to clean up, make plans, and dress himself in under an hour, even if he had heard the story about the scene at the cathedral porch right away. He wasn't drunk now, but he still carried the sluggish heaviness of a man who had just woken up after a long binge. It was the kind of dazed state where, if you shook him a couple of times by the shoulders, he'd be drunk again. He rushed into the drawing room but stumbled over a rug near the doorway. Marya Timofyevna burst into laughter, unable to hold back. He shot her a savage glare but ignored her and quickly moved toward Varvara Petrovna.

"I have come, madam..." he bellowed like a trumpet.

"Please sit down over there," Varvara Petrovna said calmly, lifting her head and pointing to a chair near the door. "I will hear you just as well from there, and it will be more convenient for me to see you from here."

The captain stopped abruptly, looking stunned. Then, after a moment of hesitation, he turned and sat where she had told him. His face betrayed a strange mix of arrogance, nervousness, and irritation. It was clear that he was terrified, though his pride seemed deeply wounded, and his vanity made him unpredictable. His awkwardness made him even more uneasy. We all know how some men, when suddenly put into high society, become paralyzed by their own clumsy movements, unable to decide what to do with their hands, their hats, or even where to look. The captain sat stiffly in his chair, clutching his gloves and hat in both hands, while his eyes stared blankly ahead at Varvara Petrovna's stern face. He seemed to want to look around the room more freely, but his fear held him back.

Meanwhile, Marya Timofyevna, finding his appearance hilarious, laughed again. He remained perfectly still, ignoring her. Varvara Petrovna, however, held him in suspense, keeping her eyes fixed on him without mercy. A full minute passed in this unbearable silence before she finally spoke.

"First of all, tell me your name yourself," she said in a slow, measured tone.

"Captain Lebyadkin," he thundered again. "I have come, madam…" He made an awkward motion as if to explain something further.

"One moment, please," Varvara Petrovna interrupted him. "Is this unfortunate woman, who has caught my attention so much, really your sister?"

"My sister, madam. She's gotten away from my care because she's… in a certain condition…"

He suddenly tripped over his words and turned bright red. "Don't misunderstand me, madam," he stammered, clearly embarrassed. "I'm her brother; I wouldn't disgrace her. By 'a certain condition,' I don't mean anything improper. I'm not talking about… about her reputation. It's just that… she's not well…" He faltered again.

"Sir," Varvara Petrovna said sharply, raising her head.

"In her mind, madam!" he burst out at last, tapping the center of his forehead with his finger to make his meaning clear.

A brief silence followed.

"Has she been this way for long?" Varvara Petrovna asked, her tone growing softer, almost curious.

"Madam, I came here to thank you for the kindness you showed her at the cathedral. I wanted to thank you in a Russian, brotherly way."

"Brotherly?"

"I mean—no, not brotherly, exactly—but as her brother, yes, that's what I meant," he stammered, growing red again and tripping over his words. "And let me assure you, madam, I'm not as ignorant as I might seem at first glance in such a fine drawing room. My sister and I are nothing compared to the luxury I see here, but I have enemies who slander us. And when it comes to reputation, madam, I have my pride... I have come to repay you... to show my thanks..."

Suddenly, with a dramatic flourish, he pulled a pocketbook out of his coat and began fumbling through it. He seemed desperate to explain something, though it was unclear exactly what. His hands shook as he flipped through a small stack of banknotes, and his impatience only made his clumsiness worse. His fingers fumbled so badly that he couldn't count the money, which embarrassed him even more. In his flustered state, a green banknote slipped free from the pocketbook and fluttered to the floor in a slow, zigzagging fall, landing on the carpet.

"Twenty roubles, madam," he suddenly shouted, jumping to his feet with the roll of notes in his hand. His face was flushed and shiny with sweat, clearly from his discomfort. He noticed the note that had slipped onto the floor, started to pick it up, but then, as though embarrassed, waved his hand dismissively.

"For your servants, madam. Let the footman who picks it up have it. Let them remember my sister!"

"I cannot allow that," Varvara Petrovna said quickly, her voice almost alarmed.

"In that case..."

He bent down, picked up the note, his face turning a deeper red, and hurried over to Varvara Petrovna. Without hesitation, he held out the stack of notes he had counted.

"What is this?" she cried, startled and genuinely alarmed now, pulling back slightly in her chair.

At this point, Mavriky Nikolaevitch, Stepan Trofimovitch, and I all instinctively stepped forward.

"Don't be frightened, madam. Don't worry—I swear to you I'm not insane. By God, I'm not mad!" the captain assured her in an excited, trembling voice.

"Yes, sir, you are out of your senses," Varvara Petrovna said sharply.

"Madam, you misunderstand me. She—my sister—she is not as you think," he stammered. "I am only an insignificant link in this. Oh, madam, your house is grand and rich, but my sister Marya—Marya Anonyma, as we'll call her for now—lives in poverty, though not forever. No, madam, God will not allow it forever! You gave her ten roubles, and she accepted it because it was from you. Do you hear me, madam? Only from you! From no one else in the world would my sister accept such charity. Her grandfather, the officer who died in the Caucasus in front of Yermolov himself, would turn over in his grave if she did. But you—yes, madam, you—she will accept anything from you. And to show her gratitude, she sends you twenty roubles as a subscription to one of the benevolent committees in Petersburg or Moscow. Committees of which you yourself are a member... You published it, madam, in the Moscow News, saying you would accept subscriptions in this very town and that anyone could donate."

He stopped abruptly, breathing heavily as though he had just completed some enormous task. It was clear that everything he said about the "benevolent society" had been rehearsed, perhaps even written by someone else, likely Liputin. Sweat poured from his face, dripping down his temples. Varvara Petrovna studied him carefully with a sharp, searching gaze.

"The subscription list," she said sternly, "is always kept downstairs by the porter. You can add your contribution there if you wish. And please put your money away; there is no need to wave it around like that. Yes, put it away. I must say, sir, I regret that I misunderstood your sister earlier and treated her like someone in need when, as it turns out, she's quite wealthy. The one thing I still don't understand is why you insisted she can only accept help from me and no one else. You were so determined about it that I must ask you for a full explanation."

"Madam, that is a secret I will take to the grave!" the captain replied dramatically.

"Why?" Varvara Petrovna asked, her voice a little less firm.

"Madam, madam…"

He fell into an awkward silence, his gaze fixed on the floor, his hand clutching at his chest. Varvara Petrovna watched him closely, waiting, her eyes not leaving his face.

"Madam!" he suddenly roared. "Will you allow me to ask you one question? Just one, but I'll ask it honestly, straight from the heart, like a true Russian?"

"Go ahead," she said calmly.

"Have you ever suffered, madam, in your life?"

"You mean to ask if someone has mistreated you or is mistreating you now," Varvara Petrovna replied.

"Madam, madam!" He jumped up again, possibly without realizing it, and struck his chest with his fist. "In this heart, madam, so much has been stored up—so much—that when it's revealed on Judgment Day, even God Himself will be amazed."

"Hm! That's quite the dramatic claim," she remarked dryly.

"Madam, I may be speaking in an irritated tone…"

"Don't worry. I'll let you know when to stop," she said, interrupting him firmly.

"May I ask you one more question, madam?"

"Go ahead," she said without hesitation.

"Do you think it's possible for someone to die purely from the weight of their own feelings—from the generosity of their own heart?"

"I wouldn't know. I've never stopped to ask myself such a question," Varvara Petrovna said, raising her eyebrows slightly.

"You don't know? You've never thought about such a thing?" he repeated, his voice full of ironic disbelief. "Well then, if that's how it is—if that's how it is—"

"Be still, despairing heart!" he suddenly shouted, striking himself hard on the chest again. He was now pacing around the room furiously, his steps heavy and clumsy.

It's typical for people like him to be completely unable to keep their thoughts or desires to themselves. Instead, they have an uncontrollable urge to show them off, no matter how improper they might be, as soon as they come to mind. When someone like that finds himself in a group where he doesn't fit in, he usually starts off timidly—until someone gives him the slightest chance. Then, without warning, he becomes rude and oversteps every boundary. The captain was already visibly excited. He paced back and forth, wildly gesturing with his arms, ignoring questions, and talking only about himself. He spoke so quickly that his words often tumbled over one another, and before finishing one sentence, he would start another. It's likely he wasn't completely sober. On top of that, Lizaveta Nikolaevna was sitting in the room, and though he never looked directly at her, her presence seemed to make him even more agitated. Of course, that's only my guess. There must have been some specific reason why Varvara Petrovna, despite her obvious disgust, decided to listen to him.

Praskovya Ivanovna sat trembling in terror, though I don't think she entirely understood what was going on. Stepan Trofimovitch was shaking as well, but for a different reason—he tended to understand things all too well and make them seem even worse than they were. Mavriky Nikolaevitch stood ready, as though prepared to defend everyone in the room. Liza, on the other hand, sat pale and silent, staring intently at the captain with wide-open eyes. Shatov remained frozen in his seat, just as before. But what was most surprising of all was Marya Timofyevna's reaction. She had stopped laughing altogether and now looked deeply sad. She leaned her elbow on the table and watched her brother with a long, mournful gaze as he rambled on. Only Darya Pavlovna seemed to remain calm.

"All of this is nonsense—nothing but silly allegory," Varvara Petrovna said, finally getting angry. "You still haven't answered my question. Why? I want an answer, and I insist on it."

"I haven't answered why? And you insist on an answer—why?" the captain repeated, winking as if he were sharing a secret joke. "That little word 'why' has echoed through the universe since the very beginning of time. Every minute, nature calls out to its Creator, asking, 'Why?' For seven thousand years, there's been no answer, and yet you demand that Captain Lebyadkin answer? Is that justice, madam?"

"That's pure nonsense and completely irrelevant!" Varvara Petrovna snapped, her patience wearing thin. "And it's impertinent the way you keep talking in this exaggerated, theatrical manner."

"Madam," the captain continued, as if he hadn't heard her, "perhaps I would have liked to be called Ernest, but instead, I'm stuck with the plain name Ignat—why, madam, why? Maybe I would have liked to be Prince de Monbart, but instead, I'm just Lebyadkin, a name that comes from a swan!* And why is that, madam? I am a poet at heart, madam—a true poet. I could be earning a thousand roubles from publishers, but instead, I'm forced to live in a filthy pigsty. Why? Tell me that, madam! To me, Russia is nothing more than a strange mistake of nature."

•   From lebyed, a swan.

"Can you say anything more specific?"

"I can read you my poem, The Cockroach, madam."

"What?"

"Madam, I'm not mad—not yet. I will be, no doubt, but not yet. A friend of mine—an honorable man—wrote a poem in the style of Krylov's fables. It's called The Cockroach. May I read it to you?"

"You want to read me a fable by Krylov?"

"No, madam, it's not a Krylov fable. It's my own, my own creation. But don't take offense, madam—I'm not so ignorant as not to know that Russia already has its great fable writer, Krylov. The Minister of Education even put up a statue for him in the Summer Gardens for the delight of the young. But here's what you need to know, madam—you asked me why? The answer lies at the end of this fable, written in letters of fire!"

"Fine, read your fable," Varvara Petrovna said impatiently.

"Lived a cockroach in the world,

Such was his condition,

In a glass he chanced to fall,

Full of fly-perdition."

"What on earth does that mean?" Varvara Petrovna exclaimed in exasperation.

"That's what happens when flies fall into a glass in summer," the captain explained quickly, clearly annoyed at being interrupted. "It's their doom—any fool can understand that. Don't interrupt me, madam, don't interrupt! You'll see—you'll see!" He waved his arms impatiently.

"But he squeezed against the flies,

They woke up and cursed him,

Raised to Jove their angry cries:

'The glass is full to bursting!'

In the middle of the din

Came along Nikifor,

Fine old man, and looking in—"

"I haven't quite finished the poem yet," the captain admitted suddenly, "but no matter, I'll explain it in my own words." He started talking faster, as if eager to finish. "Nikifor takes the glass and, despite all the shouting and commotion, he empties it—flies, cockroach, and all—right into the pig pail, where they belonged from the start. But notice, madam, the cockroach doesn't complain. And there, madam, is the answer to your question—why?" He turned triumphantly to Varvara Petrovna. "The cockroach doesn't complain! Nikifor, you see, represents nature."

Varvara Petrovna's anger was now plain on her face. "And let me ask you about the money that was supposedly sent to you by Nikolay Vsyevolodovitch but not received. You dared to accuse someone from my household of that?"

"It's a slander!" Lebyadkin roared, throwing up his arm dramatically.

"No, it's not slander."

"Madam, there are times when a man must endure shame within his own family rather than speak the truth. Lebyadkin will not blab, madam!"

At this point, he seemed completely lost in his own thoughts. He was carried away by his self-importance, clearly caught up in some bizarre fantasy. He wanted to insult someone—prove something—just to feel powerful for a moment.

"Ring the bell, please, Stepan Trofimovitch," Varvara Petrovna said coldly.

"Lebyadkin is cunning, madam," he muttered with a twisted smile, winking again. "But even he has his weak spot—those old bottles of hussar wine sung about by Denis Davydov. Yes, madam, in moments like that, Lebyadkin may write a magnificent letter in verse—a letter he later wishes to take back, with tears of regret. But once the bird flies, you can't catch it by the tail. And in those moments, madam, I may have spoken about an honorable young lady—but my slanderers twisted my words against me. Yet Lebyadkin is still cunning, madam! And in the bottom of every bottle, he finds not despair, but Lebyadkin's cunning."

Just then, the porter's bell rang downstairs. Almost at the same moment, Alexey Yegorytch appeared, unusually flustered. "Nikolay Vsyevolodovitch has just arrived and is on his way here," he announced.

At those words, Varvara Petrovna froze. For a moment, she looked pale, but her eyes quickly flashed with determination as she sat upright in her chair. Everyone in the room seemed stunned by the news. Nikolay Vsyevolodovitch's sudden arrival—unexpected for another month—felt like an extraordinary twist of fate, especially at such a moment. Even Lebyadkin stood frozen in the middle of the room, his mouth hanging open in shock as he stared at the door.

From the next room came the sound of hurried footsteps—small, quick steps, as though someone were running. Suddenly, a stranger burst into the room—not Nikolay Vsyevolodovitch, but a young man none of us had ever seen before.

Chapter 5.5

He was a young man of about twenty-seven, a little taller than average, with long, straight, pale blonde hair and a faint, uneven beard and mustache. His clothes were neat and fashionable, though not overly fancy like a dandy. At first glance, he seemed a little awkward and hunched over, but if you looked closely, you'd see he wasn't hunched at all, and his movements were relaxed and natural. He looked like an odd fellow at first, but as time passed, everyone agreed that his manners were pleasant, and he always spoke clearly and to the point.

No one would call him ugly, but few would find his face appealing. His head was long in the back and slightly flattened on the sides, making his face look narrow and pointed. His forehead was tall but narrow, and his features were small: sharp little eyes, a thin nose, and narrow, stretched lips. His face had an unhealthy look about it, as if he'd just recovered from an illness, with deep lines on his cheeks. But this impression was misleading—he was perfectly healthy, strong, and had never been sick.

He moved quickly, almost darting about, but at the same time, he never looked like he was in a hurry to leave. Nothing seemed to throw him off balance. No matter where he was or who he was with, he always stayed exactly the same. He was full of confidence, though he didn't seem to realize it himself.

When he spoke, he did so quickly and with certainty. His words always came out smoothly, and he never hesitated or searched for what to say. Despite his hurried tone, his thoughts were perfectly clear, well-organized, and easy to follow, which made his speaking style especially striking. His pronunciation was sharp and distinct, as though every word was a perfectly polished stone being placed in front of you. At first, this clarity was impressive, but later, it became a little unpleasant, almost unnatural. It made you imagine his tongue as something odd—long, thin, unusually red, and always moving with its sharp little tip.

This was the young man who burst into the drawing room now. To this day, I believe he started talking even before he entered the room and just continued as he walked in. In a flash, he was standing before Varvara Petrovna.

"Just imagine, Varvara Petrovna," he began quickly, his words tumbling out, "I thought I'd find him here already, as he arrived an hour and a half ago. We met at Kirillov's place, and he set off half an hour ago, planning to come straight here. He told me to follow him and come here about fifteen minutes later."

"But who? Who told you to come here?" Varvara Petrovna asked, trying to understand.

"Nikolay Vsyevolodovitch! Surely this isn't the first you're hearing of it? His luggage must have already arrived long ago—how is it no one told you? Then I guess I'm the first to bring you the news. Maybe we should send someone to look for him, though I'm sure he'll be here any moment. As far as I can tell, his timing seems to fit in perfectly with certain plans—some sort of expectations or calculations he's made."

At this, he let his eyes wander around the room until they landed on the captain, and he paused, looking at him closely.

"Ah, Lizaveta Nikolaevna!" he exclaimed, suddenly cheerful. "How lucky I am to meet you here right away—I'm so happy to see you!" He rushed over to Liza, who smiled and offered her hand. He shook it with great enthusiasm. "And I see my dear friend Praskovya Ivanovna hasn't forgotten her 'professor' and isn't mad at me anymore, as she always was in Switzerland. How are your legs, Praskovya Ivanovna? Did the Swiss doctors get it right when they said you needed your native air? What's that? Warm compresses? Well, that should help! Oh, Varvara Petrovna," he spun back toward her without missing a beat, "I was so sorry I didn't get to meet you abroad and pay my respects. I had so much to tell you! I did send word to my old man here, but I imagine he handled things the way he always does…"

"Petrusha!" Stepan Trofimovitch suddenly cried out, jumping to his feet as though waking from a daze. He clasped his hands and rushed toward the young man. "Pierre, my child! Why, I didn't even recognize you!" He wrapped his arms around him, tears streaming down his face.

"Stop it, stop it, no fuss, that's enough!" Petrusha muttered hurriedly, squirming to get free.

"I've done you so much wrong—always!"

"That's enough, I said. We'll talk about that later. I knew you'd make a scene. Just calm down, will you?"

"But it's been ten years since I last saw you!"

"All the more reason not to carry on like this."

"Mon enfant!"

"I believe you care for me, I really do. Now let go of me. You're making a scene and disturbing everyone." He glanced around quickly. "Ah, here's Nikolay Vsyevolodovitch. Please calm yourself."

At that moment, Nikolay Vsyevolodovitch entered the room. He came in quietly, his steps almost soundless. He paused for just a moment in the doorway, taking in the scene with a calm, steady gaze.

I was struck by him the moment I saw him, just as I had been four years earlier when I met him for the first time. I hadn't forgotten him at all. Some faces, I think, always seem to reveal something new every time you see them, no matter how many times you've looked at them before. He appeared to be exactly the same as he had been back then. He was just as elegant and dignified, with the same commanding way of moving. He still looked young, almost unchanged. His faint smile carried the same official kindness and self-assuredness as before. His eyes still held that stern, thoughtful expression, as if he were preoccupied with something important. It felt like we had only parted the day before.

Yet, one thing stood out to me. In the past, even though many had

215

considered him handsome, some sharp-tongued ladies had said his face looked like a mask. But now—now, for reasons I couldn't explain—he struck me as truly and unquestionably beautiful. No one could have said his face looked like a mask anymore. Maybe it was because he seemed a bit paler or thinner than before? Or was it the light in his eyes, as though some new idea had taken hold of him?

"Nikolay Vsyevolodovitch!" Varvara Petrovna cried, sitting straight but not getting up from her chair. "Stop right there!" She raised a hand to halt him with a sharp, commanding motion.

To explain the shocking question that followed—one I would have thought impossible even for someone like Varvara Petrovna—I need to remind the reader of her nature. Despite her strong spirit, sharp common sense, and practical judgment, there were moments when she would completely lose control of herself. She would surrender fully and without any restraint. I ask you to consider that this may have been one of those moments—a moment in which everything, her past, present, and perhaps even her future, felt as if it had been brought together and concentrated into this single point in time.

I must also briefly remind you about the anonymous letter she mentioned earlier to Praskovya Ivanovna. Though she had spoken of it with irritation, it's likely she left out the most important part. That letter may explain why such an unimaginable question came out of her mouth.

"Nikolay Vsyevolodovitch," she said again, her words quick and firm, with a tone like a challenge. "Tell me, right now, from that very spot—don't move. Is it true that this unfortunate cripple"—she pointed to Marya Timofyevna—"is she your lawful wife?"

I remember that moment so clearly. He didn't blink, not even once. He stared straight at his mother, his face calm and unchanging. Then, finally, he smiled—a soft, almost indulgent smile. Without saying a word, he walked quietly toward her, took her hand, and respectfully kissed it. His control over his mother was so strong that she couldn't even pull her hand away. She just stared at him, her whole body tense, as if she couldn't endure the silence for another second.

216

Still, he said nothing. After kissing her hand, he looked around the room, then turned and walked toward Marya Timofyevna. It's hard to describe a person's face at such moments. I remember seeing Marya Timofyevna, frozen with fear as she rose to her feet. She clasped her hands together, almost like she was begging. At the same time, I saw something else—an intense, almost unbearable joy shining on her face, as though she couldn't contain it. It was like her face showed both terror and overwhelming happiness at the same time. I quickly moved toward her, as I thought she might faint.

"You shouldn't be here," Nikolay Vsyevolodovitch said to her softly, in a gentle, musical voice. There was an extraordinary kindness in his eyes. He stood before her with a respect that couldn't be faked, every movement showing how much he honored her. The poor girl stammered in a whisper, almost instinctively.

"But... may I kneel down... to you now?"

"No, you can't do that," he replied with a warm smile.

His smile seemed to brighten the room. She looked up at him and, suddenly, she laughed joyfully too, as if his kindness gave her a sense of safety. In that same soothing voice, he continued, speaking to her like a father would to a child.

"Remember that you are a young woman, and I—though I'm your devoted friend—am still an outsider. I'm not your husband, not your father, and not your fiancé. Give me your arm now, and let's go. I'll take you to the carriage. If you'll allow me, I'll see you safely home."

She listened to him carefully, bowing her head as though considering his words.

"Let's go," she sighed finally, and she held out her hand to him.

But then something happened. She must have moved carelessly, leaning too much on her shorter, lame leg. She lost her balance and fell sideways into the chair. If the chair hadn't been there, she might have fallen to the floor. Nikolay Vsyevolodovitch caught her instantly, supporting her firmly with his arm. Then, holding her carefully, he began to lead her toward the door, moving gently and with obvious sympathy.

She was mortified. Her face turned red, her eyes looked down at the floor, and her whole expression showed how embarrassed she was. She limped painfully, leaning heavily on his arm as though ashamed of her fall. He, however, acted as though nothing had happened, guiding her with patience and care.

I noticed that Liza suddenly jumped up from her chair as they walked out. She stared after them, watching their every step until they passed through the doorway. Then she sat back down, silent again, though there was a strange, nervous twitch in her face—as if she'd just touched something poisonous, something like a snake.

While all this was happening between Nikolay Vsyevolodovitch and Marya Timofyevna, the entire room had fallen completely silent. You could have heard the faintest noise, even a fly buzzing. But as soon as they left, everyone suddenly burst into conversation.

Chapter 5.6

It wasn't much of a conversation, really—mostly just shouts and exclamations. I've lost track of the exact order of things because the whole room fell into chaos. Stepan Trofimovitch let out something in French, clasping his hands together, but Varvara Petrovna completely ignored him. Even Mavriky Nikolaevitch mumbled something hurriedly under his breath. But the most animated of all was Pyotr Stepanovitch. He seemed to be everywhere, wildly gesturing and talking as he tried to convince Varvara Petrovna of something. At first, I couldn't make out what it was. He appealed to Praskovya Ivanovna, then to Lizaveta Nikolaevna, and even threw a loud remark at his father in the middle of it all. He darted around the room like a whirlwind.

Varvara Petrovna, flushed with frustration, suddenly stood up from her chair and shouted to Praskovya Ivanovna, "Did you hear what he said to her just now? Did you hear it?"

But Praskovya Ivanovna was in no state to answer. She could only mutter something incomprehensible and wave her hand dismissively. The poor woman seemed lost in her own troubles. She kept nervously glancing at Liza, watching her with an unexplainable fear, but she didn't dare leave the room until her daughter stood up first. Meanwhile, I noticed that the captain was trying to sneak away quietly. He'd been in a panic ever since Nikolay Vsyevolodovitch arrived, but Pyotr Stepanovitch caught him by the arm and wouldn't let him leave.

"This is necessary—completely necessary," Pyotr Stepanovitch repeated as he stood before Varvara Petrovna. She had sat back down and was now listening to him intently. Somehow, he had managed to grab her attention.

"It's absolutely necessary," he continued, gesturing as he spoke. "You can see for yourself, Varvara Petrovna, that there's been some misunderstanding here. On the surface, everything seems strange, but in reality, it's as clear and simple as daylight. I know I haven't been asked to explain any of this, and maybe I look ridiculous putting myself in the middle. But you see, Nikolay Vsyevolodovitch doesn't see the matter as important at all. And, besides, sometimes there are situations where a man simply can't bring himself to explain everything directly. It's much easier if a third person steps in to clear up the confusion. I promise you, Varvara Petrovna, that Nikolay Vsyevolodovitch isn't to blame for not answering your question fully just now. It's all quite trivial. I've known him since his Petersburg days, and I assure you, the whole story, if anything, only brings honor to him—if I can even use such a word."

"You're saying you witnessed something that led to this misunderstanding?" Varvara Petrovna asked sharply.

"I witnessed it, and I was part of it," Pyotr Stepanovitch quickly declared.

"If you can promise me," Varvara Petrovna said, her tone firm and reserved, "that your explanation won't offend Nikolay Vsyevolodovitch or hurt his feelings toward me—because he never hides anything from me—and if you're sure he would approve of you explaining this…"

"Absolutely, he would approve," Pyotr Stepanovitch assured her confidently. "In fact, I'm certain he would want me to explain it. That's why I see this as a duty, and one I'm happy to fulfill."

The man's eagerness to jump in and tell someone else's story seemed odd—especially since it broke every rule of polite behavior. Still, his insistence struck a nerve with Varvara Petrovna, who was clearly agitated and desperate for answers. I didn't know much about Pyotr Stepanovitch at the time, nor did I understand his motives.

"I'm listening," Varvara Petrovna finally said, though her voice remained careful and guarded. She was clearly aware that she was lowering herself by listening to him, but she couldn't resist.

"It's a short story, really—so short that it's hardly a story at all," Pyotr Stepanovitch said quickly, as if eager to dive in. "Though, of course, a novelist could spin it into a whole book if he wanted to. It's actually a curious little incident, Praskovya Ivanovna. I'm sure Lizaveta Nikolaevna will also find it interesting, because, to be honest, there are parts of it that are both strange and almost unbelievable.

"Five years ago, in Petersburg, Nikolay Vsyevolodovitch met this man here—this very Mr. Lebyadkin who's standing there with his mouth open, no doubt hoping to escape as soon as possible. Excuse me, Varvara Petrovna. You shouldn't try to run away, Captain!" Pyotr Stepanovitch added with a mocking tone. "You were once a clerk in the commissariat department, and I remember you well. Nikolay Vsyevolodovitch and I know exactly what you've been up to here, and don't forget—you'll have to answer for it.

"I'm sorry, Varvara Petrovna," he said quickly, before continuing. "At the time, Nikolay Vsyevolodovitch used to jokingly call this gentleman his 'Falstaff.' That's some kind of old comedic character—someone who lets everyone laugh at him as long as they're paying for the privilege. Nikolay Vsyevolodovitch was living a strange sort of life back then in Petersburg—what you might call a life of mockery. I can't think of a better word for it. He wasn't disillusioned with anything, and he certainly wasn't working at that time. I'm only talking about that period, Varvara Petrovna.

"Now, this man Lebyadkin had a sister—the same woman who was sitting here earlier. The two of them didn't have a home of their own. They moved from one place to another, staying wherever they could find a corner. The captain here used to hang around the arcades of the Gostiny

Dvor, always wearing his old, tattered uniform. He'd stop well-dressed passersby, begging for money, which he would immediately spend on drink. As for his sister, she lived like the birds of the air—doing little jobs for people and finding shelter where she could.

"It was absolute chaos—madness, really. I won't go into detail about that kind of life, one spent borrowing corners to sleep in, but I will say that for some reason, Nikolay Vsyevolodovitch had taken an interest in it."

At that time, it was all just a strange whim. I'm only talking about that period, Varvara Petrovna. As for "whim," that's what he called it. He didn't hide much from me back then. Miss Lebyadkin, who often crossed paths with Nikolay Vsyevolodovitch, was completely taken with him. To her, he was like a diamond sparkling against the grim, dirty backdrop of her life. I'm not good at describing emotions, so I'll skip over them. But once, some of the lowlifes around her started mocking her, and it made her sad. They had always laughed at her, but this time she noticed. Even back then, her mind wasn't quite right, though she was still very different from how she is now. From what I understand, as a child, she had been given some education by a kind, wealthy lady.

Nikolay Vsyevolodovitch had never paid her the slightest attention. He spent most of his time playing cards—preference—with a greasy deck, gambling for tiny stakes with clerks. But one day, when someone was mistreating her, he suddenly grabbed one of the clerks by the collar and tossed him out of a second-floor window—without even asking what had happened. It wasn't some noble gesture of outrage at an innocent girl being hurt. No, the whole thing happened in the middle of loud laughter, and Nikolay Vsyevolodovitch himself laughed the hardest. No one was hurt, and the group soon made up and drank punch together. But Miss Lebyadkin herself didn't forget it.

Of course, this all ended with her completely losing her mind. I said before that I'm not good at describing feelings, but delusion played the biggest role here. And Nikolay Vsyevolodovitch, as if on purpose, made that delusion worse. Instead of laughing at her like everyone else, he suddenly began treating Miss Lebyadkin with a strange respect. Kirillov, who was there at the time—a very unusual man, Varvara Petrovna, quite sharp and direct, though you'll meet him yourself soon since he's here now—well, this Kirillov got upset about it. He told Nikolay Vsyevolodovitch that treating the girl like a noble marquise would only ruin her completely.

Now, I should say that Nikolay Vsyevolodovitch respected Kirillov a great deal. And what do you think he said in response? "You think I'm mocking her, Mr. Kirillov? You're wrong. I truly respect her because she's better than all of us." He said it with such seriousness that no one could argue. Meanwhile, he hadn't spoken more than two sentences to her in two or three months beyond a "good morning" or "goodbye." I remember it well because I was there.

Eventually, she came to believe that he was almost like her fiancé—one who couldn't "elope" with her because of his enemies and family troubles. There was a lot of laughter about this. It ended with Nikolay Vsyevolodovitch arranging for her to receive a yearly allowance when he had to leave for here—three hundred roubles a year, maybe even more. To put it simply, it was nothing but a whim, a fancy of a man who was tired of life. Or, as Kirillov suggested, maybe it was an experiment, a kind of test for a man who was already bored with everything. He wanted to see how far he could push a poor, half-mad cripple who adored him.

But then again, can you really blame a man for the delusions of a crazy woman he barely spoke to? There are things, Varvara Petrovna, that just can't be explained in a sensible way. In fact, it's foolish to even try to talk about them. So let's call it eccentricity—that's as far as it goes. Nothing worse can be said about it. Yet somehow, it's turned into this ugly scandal. I happen to know a little about what's been going on here, Varvara Petrovna."

The speaker suddenly stopped, turning to look at Lebyadkin. But Varvara Petrovna interrupted him. She was clearly agitated, almost overwhelmed.

"Are you done?" she asked sharply.

"Not quite. To finish, I'd need to ask this gentleman a question or two—if you'll allow me. You'll see why in a moment, Varvara Petrovna."

"Enough for now. Leave it for later, I insist. Oh, I was right to let you speak!"

"Just consider this, Varvara Petrovna," Pyotr Stepanovitch said quickly. "Could Nikolay Vsyevolodovitch really have explained all this just now when you asked him so directly? Your question was perhaps a little too sharp."

"Yes, yes, it was."

"And wasn't I right to say that sometimes it's easier for a third person to explain things than for the person involved?"

"Yes… yes… but you've made one mistake. I see with regret that you're still mistaken about something."

"Oh? What's that?"

"You'll see. But won't you sit down, Pyotr Stepanovitch?"

"If you like. I am a bit tired, thank you." He quickly grabbed a chair, placed it where he could face Lebyadkin while keeping Varvara Petrovna on one side and Praskovya Ivanovna on the other, and sat down. He didn't take his eyes off Lebyadkin for a second.

"You are wrong to call it eccentricity…"

"Oh, if that's all…"

"No, no, listen," said Varvara Petrovna passionately, clearly preparing to say much more. Pyotr Stepanovitch immediately became very attentive.

"No, it was something more than eccentricity. I assure you, it was something noble—even sacred! Imagine a proud man who has been humiliated early in life and has now reached this stage of 'mockery,' as you so cleverly called it. A Prince Harry, as Stepan Trofimovitch used to say back then—though to me, he is far more like Hamlet."

"And you're right," Stepan Trofimovitch pronounced solemnly, his voice full of emotion.

"Thank you, Stepan Trofimovitch. Thank you especially for your unwavering faith in Nikolay—your belief in his noble spirit and great destiny. Your faith helped me hold on when I started to lose hope."

"Chère, chère," Stepan Trofimovitch whispered, stepping forward before stopping himself, afraid to interrupt her.

"And if Nikolay had always had someone by his side," Varvara Petrovna nearly shouted, "a kind, humble Horatio—another brilliant expression of yours, Stepan Trofimovitch—he could have been saved long ago from the 'sudden demon of irony' that has tormented him his whole life. That phrase of yours—'demon of irony'—was absolutely perfect! But Nikolay has never had a Horatio. He's never had an Ophelia, either. He had no one but his mother—and what can a mother do alone, especially in such circumstances?

"Now, Pyotr Stepanovitch, I can completely understand how someone like Nikolay could end up in those wretched places you described. I can see so clearly now the kind of life you called 'mockery'— the hunger for contrast, the dark backdrop against which he stood out like a diamond, as you said. And then, there he meets a poor, mistreated girl— crippled, half-insane—who perhaps still carries something noble in her heart."

"Hm… yes, perhaps."

"And yet you still don't understand that he wasn't mocking her like everyone else. Oh, people like you! You can't comprehend his decision to defend her, to treat her with respect—'like a marquise,' as Kirillov put it. That's where the problem began. If that poor girl had been surrounded by different people, maybe she would never have fallen into such a hopeless delusion. Only a woman could understand that, Pyotr Stepanovitch. Only a woman! How I wish you… not that you were a woman, but that you could be one, just for a moment, to see what I mean."

"You mean that the worse a person's life is, the more they cling to hope. I understand, I understand, Varvara Petrovna. It's like religion. The more crushed and poor people feel, the more stubbornly they dream of being rewarded in heaven. And when a hundred thousand priests encourage that dream and take advantage of it, well… I see what you mean, Varvara Petrovna, I promise you."

"That's not exactly what I meant. But tell me this—should Nicolas have laughed at her like the clerks did? Should he have humiliated her just to 'cure' her of her delusions?" (Why Varvara Petrovna chose the word organism at this point, I couldn't say.) "Can you really fail to see the compassion—the deep, noble stirrings of his whole being—when Nicolas told Kirillov, 'I do not laugh at her'? What a sacred, noble answer that was!"

"Sublime," murmured Stepan Trofimovitch.

"And let me tell you, he's not as rich as you think. The money was mine, not his, and he hardly took anything from me back then."

"I understand, I understand all of that, Varvara Petrovna," said Pyotr Stepanovitch, growing a little impatient.

"Oh, it's in my nature! I see myself in Nicolas. I recognize that same impulsive youthfulness, those sudden, passionate actions. If we ever become friends, Pyotr Stepanovitch—and I sincerely hope we do, especially after all I owe you—then maybe you'll understand…"

"Oh, I assure you, I hope for that too," Pyotr Stepanovitch replied quickly.

"Then you'll understand what it feels like to pour your heart into someone completely unworthy of it, someone who doesn't understand you, who takes every chance to hurt you, and yet you lift him up, idealize him, dream about him. You pin all your hopes on him, love him for no reason at all—maybe precisely because he doesn't deserve it. Oh, how I have suffered in my life, Pyotr Stepanovitch!"

Stepan Trofimovitch, his face full of pain, tried to catch my eye, but I turned away just in time.

"And only recently, only just now—I see how unfair I've been to Nicolas! You have no idea, Pyotr Stepanovitch, how they've tormented me—enemies, rascals, even friends. Yes, friends sometimes more than enemies. When I got the first disgusting anonymous letter, you won't believe it, but I didn't have the strength to dismiss it with contempt. I'll never forgive myself for that weakness!"

"I had already heard something about anonymous letters," Pyotr Stepanovitch said with sudden energy. "I'll find out who wrote them, I promise you."

"You wouldn't believe the intrigues they've been spreading here. They've even been harassing poor Praskovya Ivanovna. What reason do they have to bother her? I may have been unfair to you today, my dear Praskovya Ivanovna," she added with a sudden burst of kindness, though her tone still carried a hint of triumph.

"Say no more, my dear," the other woman muttered reluctantly. "I think we've already said far too much." She glanced nervously at Liza, who, however, was still watching Pyotr Stepanovitch intently.

"And I have made up my mind to adopt this poor woman, this unfortunate soul who has lost everything but her heart," Varvara Petrovna suddenly declared. "It is my sacred duty, and I will fulfill it. From now on, she will be under my care and protection."

"And that would be very good in some ways," Pyotr Stepanovitch said eagerly, as though picking up where he had left off. "Excuse me—I wasn't finished earlier. I was about to speak of her care. Would you believe it, Varvara Petrovna, that as soon as Nikolay Vsyevolodovitch left, this gentleman here—yes, Mr. Lebyadkin—decided he had the right to control all the money Nikolay Vsyevolodovitch had provided for his sister. And he did take control of it. I don't know exactly how it had been arranged back then, but a year later, when Nikolay Vsyevolodovitch heard what was happening, he had to change the arrangements. Again, I don't know the details—he'll tell you himself—but I do know that he had the poor woman placed in a quiet convent far away, where she was cared for and watched over.

"But what do you think Mr. Lebyadkin did? He made every effort to find out where she was—his 'source of income,' as he saw her—and as soon as he found her, he took her out of the convent. He dragged her here, claiming he had some kind of right to her. Since then, he hasn't fed her properly, he's beaten her, he bullies her constantly. And every time he gets any money from Nikolay Vsyevolodovitch, he spends it all on drinking. Instead of being grateful, he dares to make demands, to threaten Nikolay Vsyevolodovitch if the money isn't sent directly to him. Can you imagine that? He treats what is really a gift as though it were a tax! Tell me, Mr. Lebyadkin, is what I've said true?"

The captain, who had been staring at the floor silently, took two quick steps forward, his face turning red.

"Pyotr Stepanovitch, you've treated me cruelly," he said abruptly.

"Cruelly? How? We can discuss cruelty or fairness later. Just answer my question now—is what I said true or not? If it's not, then tell us your version of events."

"I... you know yourself, Pyotr Stepanovitch..." the captain muttered, then fell silent again. He stood hunched in front of Pyotr Stepanovitch, who sat lounging in his chair with one leg crossed over the other.

Pyotr Stepanovitch's expression twisted with irritation. "Do you have something to say or not?" he snapped. "Speak up. We're waiting."

"You know yourself, Pyotr Stepanovitch—I can't say anything."

"No, I don't know it. This is the first I've heard. Why can't you speak?"

The captain said nothing, his eyes on the ground.

"Let me leave, Pyotr Stepanovitch," he said firmly.

"Not yet. First, tell me—is everything I said true?"

"It's true," Lebyadkin admitted in a hollow voice. His forehead glistened with sweat.

"Everything?"

"It's all true."

"Nothing to add? Nothing to say for yourself? If we've been unfair to you, speak up. Say it out loud."

"No, I've nothing to say."

"Did you threaten Nikolay Vsyevolodovitch recently?"

"That was... more the drink talking, Pyotr Stepanovitch." He suddenly raised his head. "If a man's family honor and undeserved shame cry out for justice, then—then who can blame him?" he roared, forgetting himself.

"Are you sober now, Mr. Lebyadkin?"

"Yes, I am sober."

"And what did you mean by 'family honor and undeserved shame'?"

"I meant... no one. I meant myself," the captain said weakly, dropping his head again.

"You seem very upset about what I've said. You're easily offended, Mr. Lebyadkin. But let me tell you—I haven't even started talking about your real behavior. Oh, I could go much further."

Lebyadkin flinched, staring at Pyotr Stepanovitch like a frightened animal.

"Pyotr Stepanovitch, I think I'm just waking up now."

"Ah, and it's I who woke you up?"

"Yes, you woke me, Pyotr Stepanovitch. I've been asleep for four years with a storm hanging over me. May I leave now?"

"You may go—unless Varvara Petrovna wishes otherwise..."

But she waved her hand dismissively.

The captain bowed stiffly, took a few steps toward the door, stopped, placed a hand on his chest as if he wanted to say something, thought better of it, and turned to leave.

At the door, he suddenly came face-to-face with Nikolay Vsyevolodovitch. The latter stepped aside, and the captain froze, staring at him with wide eyes, his whole body shrinking as though he'd turned to stone. Nikolay Vsyevolodovitch stood silently for a moment, then waved him aside with a slight motion of his hand and walked calmly into the room.

Chapter 5.7

He looked cheerful and calm. It was as if something good had happened to him, something we didn't yet know about, because he seemed unusually content.

"Nicolas, do you forgive me?" Varvara Petrovna asked quickly, standing up to meet him.

But Nicolas laughed lightly.

"Just as I expected," he said with an amused tone. "I see you already know everything. When I left earlier, I thought on the way that I probably should've told you the story instead of leaving like that. But when I remembered that Pyotr Stepanovitch was still here, I decided not to bother."

As he spoke, he glanced briefly around the room.

"Pyotr Stepanovitch told us an old story from Petersburg about a strange man," Varvara Petrovna said eagerly, "a mad and impulsive man, but someone whose feelings were always noble and chivalrous..."

"Chivalrous? Really? Has it come to that?" Nicolas said with a laugh. "Still, I'm grateful to Pyotr Stepanovitch for being so quick this time." He exchanged a quick look with Pyotr Stepanovitch. "You should know, maman, that Pyotr Stepanovitch is the ultimate peacemaker. That's his role in life—it's his hobby, his weakness. I highly recommend him to you in that regard. I can only imagine the story he's been spinning for you. He's a master at that—he has a whole archive of stories in his head. He's such a realist that he can't lie, you know. He prefers the truth over a good story—except, of course, in those rare cases when the story is more important than the truth." He said this while still looking around the room. "So you see, maman, it's not for you to ask my forgiveness. If there's anything crazy about this whole thing, it's my fault, and I suppose it proves that I really am mad after all. I have to live up to my reputation here..."

He then embraced his mother warmly.

"Anyway, the matter has been discussed enough and is settled," he added, and there was something firm and final in his tone. Varvara Petrovna understood it immediately, though her excitement didn't fade—if anything, it grew stronger.

"I wasn't expecting you for another month, Nicolas!"

"I'll explain everything to you, maman, of course. But right now…"

He moved toward Praskovya Ivanovna.

But she barely turned her head to him, though she had looked overwhelmed when he first appeared. Now, however, she had something else on her mind. The moment the captain had stumbled into Nikolay Vsyevolodovitch at the door, Liza had suddenly begun laughing. At first, it was quiet and broken up, but her laughter quickly grew louder and harder to ignore. Her face flushed red, which was a sharp contrast to how pale and serious she had looked just moments before.

While Nikolay Vsyevolodovitch spoke with Varvara Petrovna, Liza had twice motioned for Mavriky Nikolaevitch to come closer, as if she wanted to whisper something to him. But as soon as the young man bent toward her, she burst into laughter again. It almost seemed like she was laughing at poor Mavriky Nikolaevitch himself. She clearly tried to control herself, pressing a handkerchief to her lips, but couldn't stop. Nikolay Vsyevolodovitch turned to greet her with an open and perfectly innocent expression.

"Please excuse me," she said quickly. "You… you've met Mavriky Nikolaevitch, of course. My goodness, Mavriky Nikolaevitch, you're inexcusably tall!"

She began laughing again. Mavriky Nikolaevitch was tall, but certainly not "inexcusably" so.

"Have… you been here long?" she asked, still trying to hold back her laughter, looking embarrassed though her eyes sparkled.

"More than two hours," Nicolas replied, watching her closely. I should note that he was exceptionally polite and reserved, though his face showed no real interest—he seemed completely detached, even tired.

"And where are you staying?"

"Here."

Varvara Petrovna was also watching Liza closely, but suddenly, a thought struck her.

"Nicolas, where have you been all this time? You said it's been over two hours. The train arrives at ten."

"I first took Pyotr Stepanovitch to Kirillov's. I ran into Pyotr Stepanovitch at Matveyev—three stations away—and we traveled here together."

"I had been waiting at Matveyev since sunrise," Pyotr Stepanovitch added. "The last carriages of our train ran off the tracks during the night, and we almost broke our legs."

"Your legs broken!" Liza exclaimed. "Maman, maman, you and I wanted to go to Matveyev last week—imagine if we'd broken our legs too!"

"Heaven help us!" cried Praskovya Ivanovna, crossing herself.

"Maman, maman, dear maman, don't be so afraid if I break both my legs! It could easily happen to me. You yourself say I ride too recklessly every day. Mavriky Nikolaevitch, will you take care of me if I become lame?" She started laughing again. "If it does happen, I won't let anyone look after me but you—count on it. Well, let's say I only break one leg. Come on, be polite—tell me you'd find it a pleasure."

"A pleasure to be crippled?" Mavriky Nikolaevitch said with a frown.

"But you'd lead me around—just you, and no one else."

"Even then, it would still be you leading me around, Lizaveta Nikolaevna," murmured Mavriky Nikolaevitch seriously.

"What? He's trying to make a joke!" Liza said in mock dismay. "Mavriky Nikolaevitch, don't you dare start doing that! What a selfish man you are! I'm certain you're being unfair to yourself. It would be the other way around—you'd spend all day telling me how much more charming I'd become with only one leg. But there's a problem—you're so incredibly tall, and I'd be so tiny after losing a leg. How would you ever hold me on your arm? We'd look ridiculous together!"

231

She burst into hysterical laughter again. Her jokes were weak and made little sense, but she clearly wasn't thinking about the effect she was having on everyone else.

"Hysterics," Pyotr Stepanovitch whispered to me. "Get a glass of water—quick!"

He was right. Within a minute, everyone was bustling around, and someone brought water. Liza hugged her mother tightly, kissed her warmly, and wept on her shoulder. Then, pulling back to look her mother in the face, she suddenly burst into laughter again. Her mother began to cry softly, too. Varvara Petrovna quickly took them both away to her rooms, leaving through the same door Darya Pavlovna had entered earlier. But they were not gone long, no more than four minutes.

I am trying now to remember every detail of the last moments of that memorable morning. I clearly recall that as soon as the ladies left (with the exception of Darya Pavlovna, who had not moved from her seat), Nikolay Vsyevolodovitch began making the rounds, greeting everyone— except for Shatov, who still sat hunched in his corner, his head bowed even lower than before. Stepan Trofimovitch started saying something witty to Nikolay Vsyevolodovitch, but the latter turned away quickly and headed toward Darya Pavlovna. Before he reached her, though, Pyotr Stepanovitch grabbed him, almost pulling him over to the window. There, he whispered something hurriedly and with great importance, judging by the serious look on his face and the gestures he was making. Nikolay Vsyevolodovitch listened with a distant, distracted expression, wearing his usual polite smile, though he looked impatient, as though he wanted to escape. Just as the ladies returned, he moved away from the window.

Varvara Petrovna sat Liza back in her seat, insisting she rest for another ten minutes. She claimed the fresh air would be too much for Liza's nerves right away. Varvara Petrovna looked after her with great care, sitting down beside her. Pyotr Stepanovitch, now free, immediately came over to them and launched into a fast and cheerful conversation. At that moment, Nikolay Vsyevolodovitch finally walked up to Darya Pavlovna at his usual unhurried pace. Dasha seemed uneasy as he approached, and she quickly stood up, clearly embarrassed, her face flushed bright red.

"I believe congratulations are in order… or is it too soon?" he said with a strange expression.

Dasha replied quietly, but I couldn't hear what she said.

"Forgive me if I'm being intrusive," he continued louder, "but I was specifically informed. Did you know about this?"

"Yes, I know you were specifically informed," she answered.

"Well, I hope I didn't cause any trouble with my congratulations," he said with a smile. "And if Stepan Trofimovitch…"

"What's this congratulations about?" Pyotr Stepanovitch suddenly cut in, popping up next to them. "What are you being congratulated for, Darya Pavlovna? Ah! That's it, isn't it? Your blush gives you away—I've guessed it! What else do people congratulate such lovely, virtuous young ladies for? And what kind of congratulations make them blush like that? Well, let me add mine, then, if I'm right! And don't forget, you owe me. Do you remember our bet in Switzerland? You swore you'd never marry. Oh, wait—Switzerland! That reminds me! That's half the reason I came here, and I almost forgot. Tell me," he said, turning quickly to Stepan Trofimovitch, "when are you going to Switzerland?"

"To Switzerland?" Stepan Trofimovitch repeated, looking confused.

"What? Aren't you going? You wrote to me saying you're getting married!"

"Pierre!" Stepan Trofimovitch cried in shock.

"Why so dramatic, Pierre?" Pyotr Stepanovitch continued cheerfully. "You wanted my opinion right away, so I've rushed here to tell you I'm not against it. You begged me to 'save' you, and I'm here, ready to help. Is it true, Varvara Petrovna?" He turned to her. "I hope I'm not being too nosy, but he wrote that the whole town knows about it and that everyone's congratulating him, so he's only been going out at night to avoid it. I've got his letters here in my pocket. But I have to tell you, Varvara Petrovna, I don't understand any of it. Just answer me, Stepan Trofimovitch: am I supposed to congratulate you, or am I supposed to save you? Your letters are so confusing. In one line you're completely hopeless, and in the next

233

you're full of joy.

"To start with, he begged for my forgiveness—of course, that's typical. Though it's funny, isn't it? He's only met me twice in his life, both times by accident. But suddenly, now that he's getting married for the third time, he's acting like this somehow breaks some 'parental duty' to me! He wrote begging me not to be angry and to give him permission. Please don't be offended, Stepan Trofimovitch—it's very typical of your generation. I take a broad-minded view of it all, and I don't blame you. Really, it's sweet of you, and I respect that. But the problem is, I don't understand what you mean. He writes about 'sins in Switzerland,' and that he's marrying this girl 'for the sins of another,' or something like that—whatever it is, there are definitely 'sins' involved! And the girl, he says, is a pearl and a diamond, and of course, he's 'unworthy' of her. That's just how he talks. But because of these sins or circumstances, he has to marry her, leave everything behind, and flee to Switzerland—to 'save me,' no less! Can anyone here make sense of that?"

He stopped, glancing around the room with a polite smile, as if he were completely innocent. "But judging by your faces," he went on, "I can tell I've made a mess of things again with my clumsy, open way of talking. Nikolay Vsyevolodovitch always says I'm too hasty. I thought we were all friends here—your friends, Stepan Trofimovitch. I'm the outsider, I see that now. You all clearly know something that I don't."

"So Stepan Trofimovitch wrote to you that he was getting married 'for the sins of another committed in Switzerland,' and that you had to rush here 'to save him'? Those exact words?" Varvara Petrovna suddenly asked. Her face looked pale and twisted, and her lips trembled.

"Well, if there's been a misunderstanding, it's not my fault," Pyotr Stepanovitch replied quickly, talking even faster than before. "It's his fault for writing such things. Here's the letter. You know, Varvara Petrovna, his letters are endless—one after another. For the last few months, they've been so constant that, I must admit, sometimes I didn't even read them to the end. Forgive me, Stepan Trofimovitch, for saying that, but you'll admit yourself that you wrote them more for posterity than for me! You can't be offended. We're still friends.

234

"But I did read this letter, Varvara Petrovna. These 'sins'—these so-called 'sins of another'—are probably just some little mistakes of his own. Very innocent ones, no doubt, but he's managed to turn them into a tragic, heroic story for himself. You know what it is? He has a weakness for making things sound dramatic. There's something a little... off about the way he explains it all. And yes, I'll admit, we've had a fondness for cards, haven't we, Stepan Trofimovitch? But I'm talking too much again. Still, Varvara Petrovna, you must understand—he scared me half to death! He made me believe he truly needed saving. I almost thought I'd have to hold a knife to his throat. Am I really such a ruthless creditor? And what's this about a dowry? But tell me, Stepan Trofimovitch—are you really getting married? That would be just like you, saying so much just for the sake of talking. Oh, Varvara Petrovna, I know you're probably blaming me now—just for the way I talk."

"On the contrary, I can see that you are at your wit's end, and you probably have good reason," Varvara Petrovna replied spitefully. She had listened to Pyotr Stepanovitch's "honest outbursts" with a kind of spiteful pleasure. It was obvious he was putting on an act (I didn't yet know what kind, but it was clear and badly overdone).

"On the contrary," she continued, "I'm grateful to you for speaking up; without you, I might not have known any of this. My eyes have been opened for the first time in twenty years. Nikolay Vsyevolodovitch, you said just now that you were specifically informed. Surely Stepan Trofimovitch hasn't written to you in the same style?"

"I did get a very harmless and... and quite generous letter from him..."

"You're hesitating. You're choosing your words carefully. That's enough! Stepan Trofimovitch, I have a request to make of you," she suddenly said, her eyes flashing with anger. "Please leave us immediately, and never set foot in my house again."

I must remind the reader of her earlier state of "exaltation," which hadn't yet passed. It's true that Stepan Trofimovitch was to blame, terribly so! But what surprised me completely was how dignified he looked, even while facing his son's accusations and Varvara Petrovna's harsh words. Where did he find such strength? I later learned that he had been deeply hurt by the way Pyotr Stepanovitch had embraced him earlier. It was a real and genuine pain—at least for his heart and in his own eyes. He also suffered because he realized how shamefully he had acted. He admitted this to me later with total honesty. You know, real grief has a strange effect on people. Even a man who is usually frivolous and unreliable can become strong and calm, at least for a while. Sorrow has a way of making even the most foolish person wise—again, just for a short time. So imagine what sorrow could do for a man like Stepan Trofimovitch! It completely transformed him, though only temporarily, of course.

He bowed to Varvara Petrovna with great dignity and didn't say a word. (To be fair, there was nothing left to say.) He was just about to leave silently when he stopped and turned to Darya Pavlovna. She seemed to sense what he was about to do and began speaking quickly, as though trying to stop him.

"Please, Stepan Trofimovitch, for God's sake, don't say anything," she said in a rush, her voice full of pain. Her hands were outstretched toward him, and her face was flushed with emotion. "Please believe that I still respect you just as much as before... I still think just as highly of you. And... and please think well of me too, Stepan Trofimovitch. That will mean so much to me, more than you know."

Stepan Trofimovitch bowed to her very deeply, almost to the ground.

"It is for you to decide, Darya Pavlovna," Varvara Petrovna said firmly. "You know you are perfectly free in all of this! You always have been, and you always will be."

"Ah! Now I see what's going on!" Pyotr Stepanovitch suddenly cried out, slapping his forehead dramatically. "But—what a position this puts me in! Darya Pavlovna, forgive me, please! And you—what do you call this treatment of me?" he added, turning to his father.

"Pierre, you could speak to me with a little more respect, couldn't you, my boy?" Stepan Trofimovitch said quietly.

"Don't start shouting, please," Pierre replied with a dismissive wave of his hand. "Believe me, this is just your old nerves acting up, and shouting won't help. What you should do instead is explain why you didn't warn me. You must have known I'd speak out at the first opportunity."

Stepan Trofimovitch looked at him closely, as though studying him.

"Pierre, you know so much about everything that happens here. Are you telling me you really knew nothing about all this?"

"What? What is this?" Pyotr Stepanovitch replied sharply. "So, it's not enough for you to act like a child in your old age, you have to act like a spiteful child too! Varvara Petrovna, did you hear what he just said?"

At this point, everyone started talking at once in a loud commotion. But then, something happened—something so unexpected that no one could have seen it coming.

Chapter 5.8

Lizaveta Nikolaevna had been restless for a few minutes. She whispered quickly to her mother and to Mavriky Nikolaevitch, who leaned down to hear her. Her face looked anxious, but it also showed determination. At last, she stood up quickly, clearly in a rush to leave, and tried to hurry her mother along. Mavriky Nikolaevitch began helping her up from her low chair. But it seemed they wouldn't be able to leave before witnessing everything that was about to happen.

Shatov, who had been sitting silently in his corner, forgotten by everyone, suddenly stood up. He had no clear reason to still be there, yet he walked calmly and steadily across the room toward Nikolay Vsyevolodovitch, staring directly at him. Nikolay noticed Shatov approaching and gave him a faint smile, but the smile disappeared as soon as Shatov got close.

When Shatov stood directly in front of him, staring silently into his eyes, the whole room went quiet. Everyone noticed at once. Pyotr Stepanovitch was the last to stop talking. Liza and her mother froze in place in the middle of the room. Five seconds passed in total silence. Nikolay's face went from haughty surprise to clear anger. He frowned deeply.

Suddenly, Shatov swung his long, heavy arm and punched him hard in the face. Nikolay Vsyevolodovitch staggered from the force of the blow.

Shatov hit him in an unusual way, not like a typical slap or fight punch. It wasn't a strike with an open hand but a full punch with his fist, which was big, bony, and covered in red hair and freckles. If the blow had landed on Nikolay's nose, it would have broken it. Instead, it hit his cheek, cutting the left corner of his lip and upper teeth. Blood poured from the wound instantly.

There was a short, sharp scream—perhaps from Varvara Petrovna—but then the room fell into silence again. Everything that happened took no more than ten seconds, but so much occurred in those few moments.

Let me remind you that Nikolay Vsyevolodovitch was not the kind of man who ever felt fear. He was the sort of person who could calmly face an opponent's pistol in a duel and kill without hesitation. If anyone had ever slapped him in the face, I always believed he wouldn't challenge them to a duel—he would simply kill them on the spot. That was his character. He would do it with full awareness, knowing exactly what it meant and what the consequences would be.

Even in moments of extreme anger, Nikolay never lost control of himself. He was not the kind of man to be swept away by blind rage. He always remained cold, calculating, and deliberate. Even knowing he would be sent to prison for it, he would still kill anyone who insulted him, without hesitation.

I've come to understand Nikolay Vsyevolodovitch better over time, and I know now that he shared qualities with certain legendary men of the past. Take the Decembrist L—n, for example: it was said that he actively sought out danger, that he craved the thrill of it. He would challenge people to duels for no reason, fight bears with only a knife, and even wander the forests of Siberia looking for escaped convicts, who were far more dangerous than any bear.

Those legendary men did feel fear, I'm sure of it—otherwise, they wouldn't have chased after danger like that. What excited them was conquering their fear, proving to themselves that nothing could defeat them. L—n, for example, once starved himself rather than take money from his rich father, purely out of stubborn pride. To him, life was a constant battle, whether it was a fight with a bear or the challenge of staying true to his principles.

But Nikolay Vsyevolodovitch was nothing like that. Compared to someone like L——n, he would seem cold and indifferent. He would face a duel or a bear attack not for the thrill, but because it was necessary, and he would do so calmly, without excitement or fear. His anger, though, was something different—darker, colder, and more deliberate than the furious passion of men like L——n. Nikolay's anger was controlled and calculating, which made it all the more terrifying.

So, when Shatov punched Nikolay, what happened next was shocking. Nikolay staggered from the blow, nearly knocked over, and blood immediately began to flow. But instead of striking back, he grabbed Shatov by the shoulders with both hands—then just as quickly pulled his hands away and clasped them tightly behind his back. He didn't say a word. His face turned as white as his shirt.

For a moment, the light in his eyes seemed to go out. Ten seconds later, his eyes were calm—cold, even. But his face remained terribly pale. I don't know what was going on inside his mind; I only saw what happened on the outside. It was as if he had grabbed a red-hot iron bar, held onto it to test his strength, and somehow managed to endure the pain.

Shatov was the first to look away, unable to hold Nikolay's gaze. Slowly, he turned and walked toward the door. His steps were quiet, but his posture was awkward: his shoulders slumped, and his head hung low, as though he were deep in thought. I think he was muttering something under his breath. He carefully avoided bumping into anything, opened the door just a crack, and slipped through sideways. His wild hair sticking up at the back of his head was the last thing I saw.

Then came a terrible scream. Lizaveta Nikolaevna grabbed her mother's shoulder and clutched Mavriky Nikolaevitch's arm, trying desperately to pull them both out of the room. Suddenly, she let out a loud shriek and collapsed to the floor in a faint. I can still hear the sound of her head hitting the carpet to this day.

PART 2

Chapter 1
Night

Chapter 1.1

Eight days had passed. Now that everything is over, and I am writing about it, we know all the details. But at the time, we knew nothing, and many things seemed strange to us. Stepan Trofimovitch and I, at least, stayed locked up for the first part of it, watching events from a distance with a sense of dread. I did, however, go out now and then to gather news, because Stepan Trofimovitch couldn't bear to be without it.

Of course, there were all kinds of rumors spreading through town about the punch Stavrogin received, Lizaveta Nikolaevna's fainting spell, and everything that happened that Sunday. But what surprised us was how quickly and accurately the story had spread. None of the people who had been there had any reason to share what had happened, nor would it benefit them to do so. The servants hadn't witnessed anything.

The only person who might have talked was Lebyadkin, not because he wanted to, but simply because he couldn't keep his mouth shut. However, Lebyadkin and his sister had disappeared the very next day. No one knew where they had gone. There was no trace of them at Filipov's house, and it seemed they had vanished. I tried to ask Shatov about Marya Timofyevna, but he wouldn't even open his door. I believe he locked himself in his room for all eight days and stopped going to work in town. He wouldn't see me at all.

On Tuesday, I went to his apartment and knocked. He didn't answer at first, but I could tell he was home, so I knocked again. Then, from behind the door, I heard him jump up from his bed and shout, "Shatov is not at home!" I had no choice but to leave.

Stepan Trofimovitch and I, though nervous about the idea, eventually came to a conclusion: we decided that the only person who could have spread the rumors was Pyotr Stepanovitch. However, he soon told his father that the story was already on everyone's lips, especially at the club. According to him, even the governor and his wife knew every detail. What was even stranger was that by Monday evening, I met Liputin, and he knew the entire story word for word, as though he'd heard it straight from someone who had been there.

Many of the ladies—especially the more influential ones—were curious about the "mysterious cripple," as they called Marya Timofyevna. Some even wanted to meet her and learn more about her. That's why it was a good thing that someone had quickly hidden the Lebyadkins away. Still, the talk of Lizaveta Nikolaevna fainting stole the spotlight. Everyone was interested in that, particularly because it involved Yulia Mihailovna, who was a relative and patroness of the young woman.

The gossip grew wild, as you might expect. The strange mystery surrounding the events only fueled the rumors. Both houses—Varvara Petrovna's and Praskovya Ivanovna's—remained closed to visitors. People whispered that Lizaveta Nikolaevna was bedridden with brain fever. They said the same of Nikolay Vsyevolodovitch, but with exaggerated details, like a swollen face and a knocked-out tooth. In dark corners, some even claimed that a murder was bound to happen soon, that Stavrogin wouldn't tolerate such an insult and would kill Shatov in secret, like some kind of Corsican revenge. People liked this idea, though the younger crowd scoffed at it with affected indifference.

What stood out the most, however, was the old hostility many people in town felt toward Nikolay Vsyevolodovitch. Even the sensible folks were eager to blame him for something, though they couldn't say exactly what. Whispers began about his ruining Lizaveta Nikolaevna's reputation, hinting at an affair between them in Switzerland. Sensible people tried to stop these rumors, but everyone still listened with interest.

In private conversations—always in hushed tones—stranger rumors began to spread. Some people suggested, without any real proof, that Nikolay Vsyevolodovitch had a secret purpose for being in the province.

241

They said he had important connections in Petersburg through Count K. Some even speculated that he might be involved in some kind of secret government work. Sensible people laughed at the idea, pointing out that a man with a swollen face and so many scandals around him didn't look much like an official. But then someone whispered that he was working in "confidential service," and in those cases, it was necessary to look as little like an official as possible.

That made people pause. After all, everyone knew the government had taken a special interest in the Zemstvo of our province.

Most of these rumors eventually faded, but I must note that some of them came from a retired guards officer named Artemy Pavlovitch Gaganov. He was a large landowner and a man familiar with Petersburg society. He was also the son of the late Pavel Pavlovitch Gaganov, the man who had once had a very public, nasty encounter with Nikolay Vsyevolodovitch, as I mentioned earlier in my story.

People also heard that Yulia Mihailovna made a special visit to Varvara Petrovna's house but was told at the door that "her ladyship was too unwell to see visitors." Two days later, Yulia Mihailovna sent a message asking about Varvara Petrovna's health. After that, she began defending Varvara Petrovna everywhere she went. Of course, she only did so in the loftiest and vaguest terms, but her support silenced much of the open gossip about Sunday's events. People started to believe that Yulia Mihailovna knew the full story, every secret detail, not as an outsider, but as someone directly involved.

At the same time, Yulia Mihailovna was beginning to gain influence in the town, which she had been working hard to achieve. A part of society already admired her for her practical sense and good judgment. But more on that later.

Her growing support partly explained how quickly Pyotr Stepanovitch became popular in town, a success that particularly impressed Stepan Trofimovitch.

We may have exaggerated it a bit. To start with, Pyotr Stepanovitch managed to get to know almost the entire town within just four days of his arrival. He had only come on Sunday, and by Tuesday, I saw him riding in a carriage with Artemy Pavlovitch Gaganov. Gaganov was a proud, irritable man who, despite his good manners, was difficult to get along with. Yet Pyotr Stepanovitch seemed to have won him over.

At the governor's house, too, Pyotr Stepanovitch received a very warm welcome. In no time, he became close to them, like a trusted young friend, treated almost affectionately. He ate dinner with Yulia Mihailovna nearly every day. They had met before in Switzerland, but there was still something odd about how quickly he succeeded in gaining their favor.

There were rumors, true or not, that Pyotr Stepanovitch had once been a revolutionary while abroad. People whispered that he had been involved in secret publications and meetings overseas, something that "can be proven from the newspapers," as Alyosha Telyatnikov spitefully remarked. Alyosha, who had once been treated like a favorite at the former governor's house, was now a retired clerk, so perhaps his bitterness played a part in his gossip.

Still, it was clear: the former revolutionary had not only been allowed back into his beloved Russia but seemed to have been welcomed. Liputin once told me in a low voice that Pyotr Stepanovitch had "repented" for his actions and, upon returning to Russia, had earned forgiveness by mentioning certain names. According to this rumor, he had even promised to serve the government in some way to make up for his past mistakes. I repeated these unkind words to Stepan Trofimovitch, and though he was in no condition for serious thought, he still seemed to consider it deeply.

Later, we found out that Pyotr Stepanovitch had come to town with a very influential letter of recommendation. This letter was addressed to the governor's wife, Yulia Mihailovna, from a very important elderly lady in Petersburg. The lady's husband was one of the highest-ranking officials in the capital, and she was also Yulia Mihailovna's godmother. In the letter, she mentioned that Count K. knew Pyotr Stepanovitch well through Nikolay Vsyevolodovitch, respected him, and thought he was "a fine young man despite his earlier mistakes."

Yulia Mihailovna valued her connections to the upper classes very highly. She had only a few such connections, and they were hard to maintain, so she was probably pleased to receive this letter. Still, there was something strange about the whole thing. She even pushed her husband, Mr. von Lembke, to become friendly with Pyotr Stepanovitch, so much so that Mr. von Lembke began to complain about it—but more on that later.

Even the famous writer in town showed kindness to Pyotr Stepanovitch and invited him to visit right away. This was particularly painful for Stepan Trofimovitch, as the great author's approval stung him more than anything else. However, I saw the situation differently.

By inviting a nihilist like Pyotr Stepanovitch to visit, the great author, Mr. Karmazinov, was likely trying to secure favor with the younger, progressive crowd in Russia's major cities. The truth was, Mr. Karmazinov was deeply nervous about Russia's revolutionary youth. He believed, in his ignorance, that the future belonged to them. Because of this, he tried to win their approval in a pathetic and shameless way, especially since they paid no attention to him at all.

Chapter 1.2

Pyotr Stepanovitch visited his father twice, but unfortunately, I wasn't there either time. He came for the first time on Wednesday, which was four days after their first meeting, and even then, it was strictly for business. The matter of the property was settled quickly and quietly. Varvara Petrovna took care of everything herself, paid all the debts, and took possession of the land. She simply let Stepan Trofimovitch know it was all settled, and that her butler, Alexey Yegorytch, would bring him something to sign. Stepan Trofimovitch signed it in silence, keeping a look of great dignity.

Speaking of his dignity, I hardly recognized him during those days. He behaved completely unlike himself—he hardly spoke at all and didn't even write a single letter to Varvara Petrovna since Sunday, which amazed me. What's more, he was calm, very calm. It seemed like he had fixed on some final and decisive idea that gave him a sense of peace. He had settled on it and was now just sitting still, waiting for something. At first, though, he was unwell, especially on Monday. He had one of his usual attacks of summer cholera.

He couldn't completely go without news, of course, so I brought him updates. But whenever I stopped reporting facts and tried to give my opinion or explain things, he would wave his hand for me to stop. However, both of his meetings with Pyotr Stepanovitch left him upset, though his resolve stayed firm. After each meeting, he spent the entire day lying on the sofa with a vinegar-soaked cloth on his forehead. Still, there was something unshakable about his calmness.

Sometimes, though, I noticed little cracks in this determination. It seemed as though his fixed resolve wavered for a moment and he struggled with new, tempting thoughts. These moments didn't last long, but I couldn't help but note them. I suspected he was tempted to break his silence, to take action, and to make his presence felt once again.

"Cher, I could crush them!" he suddenly blurted out on Thursday evening after his second meeting with Pyotr Stepanovitch. He was lying on the sofa with his head wrapped in a towel.

Up until that moment, he hadn't spoken a single word all day.

"Fils, fils, cher," he muttered. "All those things he says—nonsense, kitchen talk—but fine, let's say it's true. I see it myself. I never gave him food or drink; I sent him as a baby from Berlin to X province by post. And now he says, 'You sent me by post, and now you've robbed me.'"

"But you unhappy boy," I cried to him, "I've carried you in my heart all my life—even if I did send you by post." Il rit—he laughed.

"But I admit it, I admit it. Fine, let's say it was by post," he finished, almost delirious.

"Passons," he said again, after a pause. "I don't understand Turgenev. That Bazarov of his—he's just a made-up character, not real at all. Even the ones who were supposed to represent him disowned him; they said he didn't resemble anyone. Bazarov is some strange mix of Nozdryov and Byron, that's the word. But look at them—look closely. They jump around in excitement, squealing like puppies in the sun. They're happy, they think they've won! What's Byron in them? They're so ordinary. Such

245

petty, irritable vanity. Such a pathetic desire to make noise about their names, without realizing their names mean nothing. It's ridiculous! 'Surely,' I cried to him, 'you don't mean to offer yourself as a substitute for Christ?' Il rit. He laughed. He laughed a lot—too much. He has a strange smile. His mother didn't smile like that. Il rit toujours. He's always laughing."

There was a long silence again.

"They were working together; they planned it on Sunday," he muttered suddenly.

"Oh, no doubt about it," I replied eagerly. "It was so obvious, too obvious, and so badly done."

"I don't mean that," he said sharply. "Don't you see? It was meant to be obvious, so certain people would understand. Do you get that?"

"I don't understand."

"Tant mieux. Passons. I'm very irritable today."

"But why argue with him at all, Stepan Trofimovitch?" I asked.

"Je voulais convertir!" he cried, almost desperately. "You'll laugh, but I wanted to convert him. Would you believe it? I felt like a patriot. I've always felt I was Russian. A real Russian has something blind and foggy inside him. Don't you see?"

"Of course," I said, agreeing.

"My dear boy, the truth always sounds unlikely—do you know that? To make truth sound believable, you have to mix in a little lie. People have always done that. Maybe there's something to it that we just can't understand. What do you think? Could there be something we're missing in that triumphant squeal of theirs? I'd like to think so. I want to think so."

I stayed silent, and so did he. But after a while, he started again, almost feverishly.

"They say French cleverness ... that's a lie, always has been. Why insult the French? It's just Russian laziness—our humiliating inability to create new ideas. We're parasites among nations! Ils sont tout simplement

246

des paresseux! Russians ought to be wiped out for the good of humanity, like pests. We've been striving for something totally different, and now ... I can't understand any of it. 'Do you get,' I told him, 'that if you're so in love with the guillotine, it's only because cutting off heads is easy? What's hard is coming up with an idea. You're lazy! Votre drapeau est un guenille! A rag of impotence. You talk about carts carrying bread being more important than the Sistine Madonna! Do you even understand that suffering is just as necessary to humanity as happiness?' Il rit. He laughed. He said I was just making clever phrases while sitting on a velvet sofa."

We were silent again.

"Cher," he said finally, sitting up, "do you know this is going to end in something?"

"Of course," I answered.

"You don't understand. Passons. Things in our world usually lead to nothing, but this—this will lead to something. It's bound to, it's bound to!"

He got up, paced the room in a fury, and then sank back onto the sofa, exhausted.

On Friday morning, Pyotr Stepanovitch left town and didn't return until Monday. I heard about his trip from Liputin. In the same conversation, Liputin also mentioned that the Lebyadkins, brother and sister, had moved to the riverside district. "I moved them," he added. Then, as if the Lebyadkins no longer mattered, he suddenly told me that Lizaveta Nikolaevna was going to marry Mavriky Nikolaevitch. Though not yet announced, the engagement was already decided.

The next day, I saw Lizaveta Nikolaevna riding with Mavriky Nikolaevitch. It was her first time out since her illness. She smiled and waved at me cheerfully from a distance. I shared all this with Stepan Trofimovitch, but he barely reacted—except for the part about the Lebyadkins.

Now that I've described our confusing and uncertain state during those eight days, I can move on to what happened next. I'll start with the eighth day—Monday evening—because that's when a "new scandal" truly began.

Chapter 1.3

It was seven o'clock in the evening. Nikolay Vsyevolodovitch sat alone in his study—a room he had once been fond of. It was spacious, with rugs on the floor and heavy, old-fashioned furniture. He sat on the sofa in the corner, dressed as though he were going out, though he didn't seem to be planning to. A lamp with a shade lit the table before him, leaving the rest of the room in shadows. His eyes were focused and distant, as though deep in thought. He looked tired, and his face seemed thinner.

He really was unwell. His face was still swollen, though the story about his tooth being knocked out was exaggerated. The tooth had only been loosened, but it had healed, and a small cut on the inside of his upper lip had already closed. The swelling had lingered all week because he refused to see a doctor or have it treated. He wouldn't let anyone near him—not even his mother, except for a brief visit at dusk before the lights came on. He had also refused to see Pyotr Stepanovitch, even though Pyotr had been running back and forth to Varvara Petrovna's house several times a day.

That Monday morning, after being gone for three days, Pyotr Stepanovitch returned to town. He made his rounds, had dinner at Yulia Mihailovna's house, and then finally appeared at Varvara Petrovna's, who had been waiting impatiently for him. The restriction on visiting Nikolay Vsyevolodovitch had been lifted—he was "at home" now. Varvara Petrovna herself led Pyotr to the door of her son's study. She had been looking forward to their meeting and made him promise to tell her everything afterward.

She knocked softly on the door, hesitating before speaking. "Nicolas, may I bring Pyotr Stepanovitch in to see you?" Her voice was careful and low as she tried to see his face behind the lamp.

"You can—of course you can," Pyotr Stepanovitch said loudly and cheerfully, pushing the door open himself and walking in.

Nikolay Vsyevolodovitch hadn't heard the knock. He had been deeply focused on a letter he had just finished reading. He quickly shoved it under a paperweight when he heard Pyotr Stepanovitch's voice, though not quite fast enough. The corner of the letter, along with most of the envelope, was still visible.

"I called out on purpose to give you a moment to prepare," Pyotr said quickly, with exaggerated innocence. He hurried to the table and immediately noticed the corner of the letter peeking out.

"And no doubt you saw how I tried to hide the letter under the paperweight," Nikolay said calmly, without moving.

"A letter? Oh, bless you, what do I care about letters?" Pyotr laughed loudly. Then, in a whisper, he added, tilting his head toward the door, "But ... you know ..."

"She doesn't listen," Nikolay said coldly.

"And what if she did overhear?" Pyotr said loudly, settling into an armchair as though it didn't matter. "I've come to talk to you alone. Finally, I've managed to get to you! First, how are you? You look great. Will you finally show yourself tomorrow?"

"Maybe."

"Good, that will settle everyone down. And me, too!" He waved his hands playfully and smiled. "You wouldn't believe the nonsense I've had to say to calm them down. You probably know most of it, though." He laughed again.

"I don't know everything. I only heard from my mother that you've been ... busy," Nikolay said with a hint of sarcasm.

"Oh, come now, I haven't said anything definite," Pyotr protested immediately, as if defending himself from an attack. "I only stirred up the rumors about your affair in Paris—about Shatov's wife, you know. It was to explain what happened on Sunday. You're not mad, are you?"

"I'm sure you've done your best."

"That's what I was afraid of! What does that mean, 'done your best'? Is that a complaint? You always go straight to the point, don't you?"

"I'm not interested in going straight to anything," Nikolay said irritably, but then he laughed.

"No, no, I didn't mean that!" Pyotr said quickly, waving his hands as if in panic. "Don't misunderstand me. I'm not here to bother you about our business, especially while you're unwell. I just came to sort out what happened on Sunday and plan the next steps. Because honestly, it's impossible to leave things like this. I need to explain everything to you— frankly and honestly. Believe me, I need this explanation more than you do. It's true! It's not about your vanity this time. I want us to be open with each other from now on."

"So, you haven't been open with me before?"

"You know I haven't. I've been sneaky with you more than once." Pyotr smiled, talking faster and faster. "But look, you smiled just now! I was hoping you'd do that. I wanted to provoke that smile. I used the word 'sneaky' on purpose, hoping you'd get mad at me for even thinking I could deceive you. Then, I could explain myself. Do you see? Look how open I'm being now! Well, are you willing to listen?"

Nikolay's face, which had been calm and slightly mocking, now showed a hint of uneasy curiosity. Even though Pyotr Stepanovitch was clearly trying to provoke him with his exaggerated friendliness and deliberate boldness, Nikolay seemed interested, as if wondering where this conversation was going.

"Listen," said Pyotr Stepanovitch, squirming more than ever, "when I came here—meaning this town, of course—ten days ago, I had already decided to play a role. It would've been best to just be myself, don't you think? There's no better trick than acting natural because no one ever believes it. At first, I thought I'd play the fool since it's easier to act stupid than to just be yourself. But being a fool is a bit extreme, and anything extreme makes people curious. So, in the end, I stuck to being myself. And what's my true character? It's the golden middle: not smart, not foolish—just a little clueless, as people here like to say, as though I'd fallen from the moon. Isn't that it?"

"Maybe it is," said Nikolay Vsyevolodovitch with a faint smile.

"Ah, so you agree! I'm glad. I knew that's what you thought already. Don't worry, I'm not offended. I didn't describe myself that way to get a flattering contradiction from you—no need for you to say, 'You're clever.' Ah, you're smiling again! There, I've blundered once more. You wouldn't have said 'you're clever'—I'll let it go. Passons, as my father says. And don't mind if I ramble on too much. I always talk too much, don't I? I use too many words, and I talk too fast, but I never say anything well. And why is that? Because I don't know how to speak properly. People who speak well use fewer words. So that must mean I'm stupid, right? But since stupidity comes naturally to me, why shouldn't I make the best use of it? And I do use it.

"At first, when I got here, I thought it might be best to keep quiet. But silence is a talent, and it doesn't suit me at all. Besides, silence can be risky. So, I decided it's better to talk—and not just talk, but to ramble and ramble, to explain everything in a hurry and then get tangled up in my own explanations. That way, the listener walks away before I finish—either shrugging or, even better, cursing me under their breath. You see, it's perfect! They immediately decide I'm harmless, that I'm boring, and that I'm impossible to understand—all advantages! Do you think anyone would suspect me of having a secret plan after that? Why, they'd be offended if someone even suggested I was plotting anything! And sometimes, I amuse them, which is priceless. Now they forgive me for everything just because they think the clever man who once published manifestos abroad is even stupider than they are. Isn't that so? I can see by your smile that you agree."

But Nikolay Vsyevolodovitch wasn't smiling at all. On the contrary, he was frowning, listening with an irritated expression.

"Eh? What? Did you say 'no matter'?" Pyotr Stepanovitch rattled on, though Nikolay Vsyevolodovitch had said nothing. "Of course, I'm not here to embarrass you or compromise you just by being around you, like claiming to be your comrade or something. But you're being very critical today. I came here lighthearted and open, but you seem to be holding onto every little thing I say. I promise I won't bring up anything unpleasant today—I give you my word. I'll agree to any terms you set ahead of time."

251

Nikolay Vsyevolodovitch remained silent.

"What? Did you say something?" Pyotr Stepanovitch continued. "Oh, I've blundered again. You haven't set any terms, and you're not going to, are you? I get it. I understand. And I'm saying all this out of stupidity— just being stupid again. You're laughing? What is it?"

"Nothing," Nikolay Vsyevolodovitch said finally, laughing faintly. "I just remembered that I did actually call you stupid once, but you weren't there. They must've repeated it to you. Now, can you hurry up and get to the point?"

"I am at the point! I'm talking about Sunday," Pyotr babbled on. "What was I on Sunday? What would you call it? Just plain fussiness, mediocre stupidity. I forced myself into the conversation in the clumsiest way. But they forgave me, first because they've all decided that I've 'fallen from the moon,' and second because I told them a nice little story to get you out of a tight spot. Didn't I, didn't I?"

"So, you told your story in a way that made them think there was some kind of agreement or secret understanding between us, even though there wasn't, and I hadn't asked you to do anything."

"Exactly! That's it!" Pyotr Stepanovitch exclaimed, looking delighted. "That's exactly what I did because I wanted you to think I meant that. I worked hard for your sake—I was trying to trap you and compromise you. Most of all, I wanted to see just how afraid you really are."

"It would be interesting to know why you're being so open now."

"Don't get mad, don't glare at me. Wait, you're not glaring. You're wondering why I'm so open? Well, because everything has changed now. The old way is over, buried in the sand. I've suddenly changed my opinion about you. The old approach is done; if I compromise you now, it'll be in a completely new way."

"You've changed your tactics?"

"There are no tactics anymore. Now it's all up to you. If you want to say yes, say yes. If you want to say no, say no. That's my new approach. I won't say a word about our cause unless you ask me to. You're laughing?

252

Go ahead, laugh. I'm laughing too. But I'm serious this time. I really am serious, though I know someone who's always in a hurry looks stupid, right? Fine, I might be stupid, but I'm serious, I really am."

He was speaking with unusual sincerity and a strange excitement, which made Nikolay Vsyevolodovitch look at him with curiosity.

"You say you've changed your opinion about me?" he asked.

"I changed my mind about you the moment you pulled your hands back after Shatov hit you. That's it, no questions, please. I'm not saying any more about it."

He jumped up, waving his hands like he was swatting away questions. But since no one had asked him anything, and there was no reason for him to leave, he settled back into his chair, looking slightly calmer.

"By the way," he continued, speaking rapidly again, "some people here are saying you'll kill him. They're even making bets about it. Lembke thought about sending the police after you, but Yulia Mihailovna stopped him. Anyway, I just mentioned it so you'd know. Oh, and I moved the Lebyadkins that same day—did you get the note with their new address?"

"I got it," said Nikolay Vsyevolodovitch absently.

"I didn't do that as part of my usual 'stupidity.' I did it sincerely, to help you. If it was foolish, at least it was done in good faith."

"Maybe it was necessary," Nikolay Vsyevolodovitch replied dreamily. "Just don't write me any more letters, I'm asking you."

"Impossible to avoid. It was only one."

"So Liputin knows?"

"Couldn't be helped. But Liputin wouldn't dare—you know that yourself. Oh, by the way, you really should meet 'our group.' Well, not 'ours,' since you don't like that word, but those other guys. Don't worry, not now. It's raining anyway. I'll let them know, and we'll meet in the evening. They're waiting, like baby birds in a nest, mouths open, wanting to see what we'll bring them. They're a fiery bunch. They've started printing leaflets and are already bickering. Virginsky is all about universal brotherhood, Liputin is a Fourierist with a suspicious fondness for police matters—he's useful in one way but needs close watching in others—and finally there's the guy with the long ears, who'll read us his own theory. You know, they're actually upset with me for not taking them seriously enough, but we still need to meet."

"You've made me out to be some kind of leader?" Nikolay Vsyevolodovitch asked, sounding indifferent.

Pyotr Stepanovitch glanced at him quickly.

"By the way," he said suddenly, as though trying to change the subject, "I've been to see her excellency, your mother, a few times, and I had to say quite a lot."

"I figured."

"No, really, don't think anything of it. I just told her you wouldn't kill him, and a few other nice things. And imagine—she found out the next day that I'd moved Marya Timofyevna across the river. Was that you who told her?"

"I never even thought of it."

"I knew it wasn't you. Then who could it have been? Interesting. Liputin, maybe?"

"Of course Liputin."

"N-no, not Liputin," Pyotr Stepanovitch mumbled, frowning. "I'll find out who. It's more like Shatov ... but that's nonsense. Let's drop it. Although it's really important.... Oh, and I thought your mother was going to ask me 'the big question.' At first, she looked so gloomy, but when I visited today, she was beaming! What does that mean?"

"I promised her today that within five days I'd be engaged to Lizaveta Nikolaevna," Nikolay Vsyevolodovitch said calmly, surprising him with his openness.

"Oh! ... Yes, of course," Pyotr Stepanovitch stammered, caught off guard. "There are rumors about her engagement already, you know. It's true, too. But you're right—she'd run straight to you if you called her. You're not mad at me for saying that, are you?"

"No, I'm not angry."

"It's really hard to make you angry today, I've noticed. It's starting to worry me. I'm curious to see what you'll do tomorrow. You must have something planned. You're not mad at me for saying that either, are you?"

Nikolay Vsyevolodovitch didn't answer, which made Pyotr Stepanovitch visibly irritated.

"Wait, did you mean what you said to your mother about Lizaveta Nikolaevna?" he asked.

Nikolay Vsyevolodovitch looked at him coldly.

"Oh, I see, it was just to calm her down."

"And what if I was serious?" Nikolay Vsyevolodovitch replied firmly.

"Well then … God bless you, as people say. It wouldn't get in the way of 'the cause'—you notice I didn't say 'our cause,' since you don't like that. And as for me … well, you know I'm at your service. Always and everywhere, in any situation, no matter what. You know that, right?"

Nikolay Vsyevolodovitch yawned.

"I must have bored you," Pyotr Stepanovitch suddenly cried, jumping up and grabbing his perfectly new round hat like he was about to leave. But he stayed, continuing to talk while standing up. Sometimes, he paced around the room, tapping his knee with his hat whenever he got excited.

"I wanted to entertain you with stories about the Lembkes too," he said cheerfully.

"Later, maybe—not now. How is Yulia Mihailovna?"

"What polite manners you all have! Her health means nothing to you—no more than the grey cat's health—but you ask about it anyway. I like that. She's perfectly fine, by the way. Her respect for you is almost like a superstition now, and her high expectations of you are the same. She doesn't mention what happened on Sunday and believes you'll fix everything just by showing up. I swear, she thinks you're capable of anything. You're even more of an enigmatic, romantic figure now—an incredibly good position to be in. You wouldn't believe how eager everyone is to see you. They were worked up when I left, but now it's even worse. Thanks again for your letter, by the way. They're all afraid of Count K. Did you know they think you're a spy? I keep that rumor going, are you mad about it?"

"It doesn't matter."

"It doesn't matter—it's actually necessary in the long run. They've got their own way of doing things here, and I play into it, of course. Yulia Mihailovna is first on the list, and Gaganov too… Oh, you're laughing? But you know I have my strategy. I ramble on and then, just when they're expecting something clever, I say something that makes them suspicious. They all gather around me, but I keep confusing them again. At this point, they've all given up on me: 'He's got brains but it's like he dropped in from the moon.' Lembke even invited me to join the government service so I could be 'reformed.' I treat him mockingly, though—just enough to embarrass him—and he just stares at me. Yulia Mihailovna encourages it. Oh, and Gaganov is absolutely furious with you. Yesterday, at Duhovo, he said the nastiest things about you. I told him the whole truth—well, not all of it. I spent the entire day at Duhovo. It's a great estate with a fine house."

"So, is he at Duhovo now?" Nikolay Vsyevolodovitch suddenly asked, leaning forward in his chair like he might jump up.

"No, he drove me back this morning. We came together," Pyotr Stepanovitch replied casually, as though not noticing Nikolay's sudden interest. "Oh, what's this? I dropped a book." He bent down and picked up a small volume he'd knocked over. "'The Women of Balzac,' with illustrations." He flipped it open. "I haven't read it. Did you know Lembke writes novels too?"

"Really?" Nikolay asked, showing a bit of interest.

"Yes, secretly, in Russian, of course. Yulia Mihailovna knows about it and allows it. He's henpecked but very proper about it. It's their system. Such discipline, such control! We could use something like that ourselves."

"So you approve of government methods?"

"Of course! It's the only natural and practical approach in Russia. But let's not go there. I'm not talking about that. I won't say a word about any delicate subjects. Good-bye—you look pale, by the way."

"I have a fever."

"I can believe it; you should rest. Oh, one more thing—there are Skoptsi in the area. Strange people... but I'll tell you about them later. Here's another story. There's an infantry regiment stationed nearby. Last Friday evening, I was drinking with the officers—three of them are our friends, you know? They got into a conversation about atheism, and, of course, they quickly dismissed God. They were practically squealing with excitement over it. By the way, Shatov claims that any uprising in Russia would have to start with atheism. Maybe he's right. Anyway, there was this old captain—grizzled and quiet—who didn't say a word the whole time. Suddenly, he stands up, right in the middle of the room, and says, like he's talking to himself, 'If there's no God, how can I be a captain?' Then he grabs his hat, throws up his hands, and walks out."

"That's actually a rather reasonable point," Nikolay said, yawning for the third time.

"Is that so? I didn't quite understand it. I wanted to ask you about it. What else do I have to tell you? Oh, the Shpigulin factory is interesting. You know, they've got five hundred workers there. It's a total breeding ground for cholera—hasn't been cleaned in fifteen years—and the workers are constantly cheated. Meanwhile, the owners are millionaires. I'm telling you, some of those workers have started talking about the Internationale. What? You're smiling? Just give me a little time, you'll see! I already asked you to set a date, and now I'm asking again... Oh wait, I promised not to bring that up. Don't frown, I'll stop.

"Oh!" He suddenly turned back. "I almost forgot the most important thing! I was just told your box arrived from Petersburg."

"You mean..." Nikolay Vsyevolodovitch looked at him, confused.

"Your box! Your things—coats, trousers, shirts. Did it really come?"

"Yes... they mentioned something about it this morning."

"Ah, then can I open it right away?"

"Ask Alexey."

"Tomorrow then, will tomorrow work? My new jacket, dress coat, and three pairs of trousers are in there too—from Sharmer's, on your recommendation, remember?"

"I hear you're trying to look like a gentleman here," Nikolay said with a faint smile. "Is it true you're taking riding lessons?"

Pyotr Stepanovitch's smile turned awkward. "Listen," he said suddenly, speaking quickly, his voice quivering, "Nikolay Vsyevolodovitch, can we drop the personal comments for a while? If you want to despise me, go ahead—if it entertains you—but let's avoid this for now, all right?"

"Fine," Nikolay agreed calmly.

Pyotr Stepanovitch grinned, tapped his knee with his hat, shifted his weight, and seemed to regain his composure.

"Some people here actually think I'm your rival for Lizaveta Nikolaevna. That's why I need to look the part, right?" He laughed. "But where'd you hear that? Hmm. Anyway, it's just eight o'clock, and I have to go. I promised to visit Varvara Petrovna, but I'll probably skip out. You should get to bed—you'll feel better tomorrow. It's dark and raining outside, not the safest place at night. Oh, by the way, there's a runaway convict, Fedka, wandering around town. He's from Siberia. Can you believe it? He used to be one of my family's serfs. My father sent him to the army fifteen years ago and took money for him. He's quite a character."

"You've been talking to him?" Nikolay Vsyevolodovitch asked sharply, studying him closely.

"Yes, he's been in touch. He lets me know where he is. He'll do anything for money—of course—but he's got his own convictions, strange as they are. Oh, speaking of which, if you're serious about that plan—about Lizaveta Nikolaevna—I'm ready to help in any way you want. Anything at all, absolutely at your service...."

"Are you reaching for your stick?" he suddenly blurted out, watching Nikolay closely. "Oh no—imagine that—I thought you were grabbing your stick."

Nikolay Vsyevolodovitch hadn't moved, and he wasn't reaching for anything. He just stood up suddenly, his face hard to read, with a strange look in his eyes.

"If you need help with Gaganov too," Pyotr Stepanovitch added quickly, staring pointedly at the paperweight on the table, "just say the word. I can arrange everything, and honestly, you won't be able to handle it without me."

Without waiting for a reply, he walked out of the room. But he stuck his head back in for one last comment. "I only mention that because Shatov had no right, you know, to risk his life last Sunday when he attacked you. Just something for you to note."

Then, without waiting for a response, he disappeared again.

Chapter 1.4

As Pyotr Stepanovitch left, he might have imagined that Nikolay Vsyevolodovitch would collapse, maybe even pound his fists against the wall in frustration. If so, he was mistaken. Nikolay remained calm. He stood still for a few minutes by the table, deep in thought. Eventually, a cold, tired smile crept onto his face. Slowly, he sat back down in the corner of the sofa and closed his eyes, as if exhausted. The letter still peeked out from under the paperweight, but he didn't bother to cover it.

Before long, he had completely drifted off.

When Pyotr Stepanovitch failed to stop by, as promised, Varvara Petrovna—driven by days of mounting worry—couldn't stop herself any longer. She decided to check on her son, even though it wasn't her usual time to visit. She still hoped he would tell her something final, something conclusive. She knocked gently, just as before, and when there was no reply, she quietly opened the door.

Nikolay was sitting strangely still. He hadn't moved at all. Cautiously, with a pounding heart, she approached the sofa. It was strange how quickly he had fallen asleep, sitting so upright and rigid. He wasn't even breathing noticeably. His face looked pale and stern, almost lifeless, as if frozen. His brow was furrowed into a frown, and his expression was cold and stiff, like a wax figure.

She watched him for three long minutes, holding her breath. Suddenly, a wave of fear gripped her. Quietly, she tiptoed back to the door, quickly made the sign of the cross over him, and left the room with a deeper sense of dread and worry than before.

He slept for more than an hour, still in the same position. His face remained stiff and motionless, his brow furrowed, as though frozen in thought. If Varvara Petrovna had stayed a moment longer, she wouldn't have been able to bear the eerie stillness and might have woken him up. But suddenly, Nikolay opened his eyes. He sat there, unmoving for ten more minutes, staring curiously into the corner of the room as if something there had caught his attention—though there was nothing unusual to see.

The low, deep sound of the clock rang through the room.

He turned his head uneasily to glance at it. Just then, the other door opened, and Alexey Yegorytch, the butler, entered. He held a coat, a scarf, and a hat in one hand, and in the other, a silver tray with a note on it.

"It's half-past nine," the butler said softly, placing the coat and hat on a chair and offering the tray with the note. The note was a small piece of paper, unsealed, with hurried writing in pencil. Nikolay quickly glanced at it, picked up a pencil from the table, scribbled a few words, and placed the note back on the tray.

"Take this back as soon as I've left," he instructed, standing up. "Now, help me get dressed."

Noticing he was wearing a velvet jacket, he paused for a moment and decided to switch to a cloth coat—something more formal. Finally dressed, with his hat on, Nikolay locked the door his mother used to enter earlier. Then he grabbed the letter from under the paperweight and, without another word, left the room. Alexey Yegorytch followed closely behind.

They walked down the narrow stone back stairs into a passage that led straight into the garden. A lantern and a large umbrella were waiting in the corner.

"It's been raining so much the streets are nothing but mud," the butler said softly, almost as if hoping to convince Nikolay to stay in. But without responding, Nikolay opened the umbrella and stepped into the dark, wet garden. The wind howled, shaking the bare trees. The sandy paths were soaked and slippery. Alexey Yegorytch followed behind him, bareheaded in his long coat, holding the lantern to light their way.

"Will anyone notice?" Nikolay suddenly asked.

"Not from the windows," the butler replied calmly. "I've taken care of all that already."

"Has my mother gone to bed?"

"Her Excellency locked herself in at nine, as she's been doing for the past few days. There's no way she'll know anything."

"What time should I expect you back, sir?"

"Around one, maybe half-past. No later than two."

"Yes, sir."

Crossing the garden along the winding paths they both knew so well, they reached the stone wall. In the farthest corner, there was a small door that led to a narrow, empty alley. The door was always kept locked, and Alexey Yegorytch already had the key in his hand.

"Will the door creak?" Nikolay Vsyevolodovitch asked again.

Alexey Yegorytch assured him that it had been oiled yesterday "and again today." By now, the butler was completely soaked. After unlocking the door, he handed the key to Nikolay Vsyevolodovitch.

"If your honor plans on taking a long walk, I must warn you again— I don't trust the people around here, especially in the back alleys and beyond the river," he said firmly.

He was an old servant who had cared for Nikolay as a child, even rocking him in his arms. A serious and solemn man, Alexey Yegorytch loved listening to religious sermons and reading devotional books.

"Don't worry, Alexey Yegorytch."

"May God's blessing rest on you, sir—but only on your righteous deeds."

"What was that?" Nikolay Vsyevolodovitch asked, stopping in the lane.

Alexey Yegorytch repeated his words firmly. He had never dared to speak this way to his master before.

Nikolay Vsyevolodovitch locked the door behind him, put the key in his pocket, and crossed the muddy lane, sinking several inches into the wet ground with every step. Finally, he reached a long, empty street. He knew the town like the back of his hand, but Bogoyavlensky Street was still far away.

It was past ten when he stopped at last in front of the locked gates of Filipov's old house. The ground floor had been empty since the Lebyadkins left, and the windows were boarded up. However, there was a light shining from Shatov's room on the second floor.

There was no bell, so Nikolay Vsyevolodovitch began banging on the gate with his hand.

A window opened, and Shatov looked out into the dark street. It was so pitch black that it was hard to see anything. Shatov squinted into the darkness for almost a minute.

"Is that you?" he called out suddenly.

"Yes," the uninvited guest replied.

Shatov slammed the window shut, went downstairs, and opened the gate. Without a word, Nikolay Vsyevolodovitch stepped over the high threshold, passed Shatov without looking at him, and went straight into Kirillov's lodge.

Chapter 1.5

Everything was unlocked, and all the doors stood open. The hallway and the first two rooms were dark, but there was a light glowing in the last room, where Kirillov lived and drank tea. Strange sounds of laughter and cries could be heard coming from it. Nikolay Vsyevolodovitch walked toward the light but stopped in the doorway without going in.

There was tea on the table. In the middle of the room stood an old woman, a relative of the landlord. She was bareheaded, wearing only a petticoat and a hare-skin jacket, and her bare feet, without stockings, were in slippers. In her arms, she held an eighteen-month-old baby dressed only in a little shirt. Its legs were bare, its cheeks were flushed, and its ruffled white hair made it look as though it had just woken up. The baby seemed to have been crying because there were still tears in its eyes, but at that moment, it was giggling, clapping its hands, and reaching out. It laughed through its sobs the way little children often do.

Kirillov was bouncing a large red rubber ball on the floor in front of the child. The ball shot up toward the ceiling and then came back down again. The baby shrieked, "Baw! Baw!" Kirillov caught the ball and gave it back to the baby. It tried to throw it with its tiny, clumsy hands, and Kirillov rushed to pick it up again.

Finally, the ball rolled under a cupboard. "Baw! Baw!" the child cried. Kirillov lay down on the floor, trying to reach the ball with his hand. At that moment, Nikolay Vsyevolodovitch walked into the room.

The baby noticed him, clung to the old woman, and began crying loudly. The woman immediately carried the baby out of the room.

"Stavrogin?" Kirillov said as he got up from the floor, holding the ball. He showed no surprise at the unexpected visit. "Would you like some tea?"

He stood up straight.

"I'd be glad to have some, if it's hot," Nikolay Vsyevolodovitch replied. "I'm soaked."

"It's hot—almost boiling," Kirillov said cheerfully. "Sit down. You're muddy, but that's all right. I'll clean up the floor later."

Nikolay Vsyevolodovitch sat down and quickly drank the cup of tea Kirillov handed him.

"Would you like some more?" Kirillov asked.

"No, thank you."

Kirillov, who hadn't sat down until then, took a seat across from him and asked, "Why did you come?"

"It's business. Here, read this letter from Gaganov. Do you remember? I told you about him in Petersburg."

Kirillov took the letter, read it, set it on the table, and looked at him, waiting for an explanation.

"As you know, I met Gaganov for the first time about a month ago in Petersburg," Nikolay Vsyevolodovitch began. "We saw each other a few times in company with other people. Even though he didn't speak to me or try to get to know me, he still managed to be very rude to me. I told you about that before. But now I'll tell you something you don't know. Before leaving Petersburg, he sent me a letter—nothing like this one, but still very insulting—and it had no explanation for why he wrote it.

"I responded right away. I wrote to him, honestly saying that he was probably angry with me because of what happened with his father four years ago at the club here. I explained that I was willing to apologize because what I did was unintentional and caused by illness. I asked him to consider my apology and accept it. He left Petersburg without replying.

"Now I've come back here and find him furious. I've been told about several things he's said in public—terrible insults and ridiculous accusations against me. And finally, today, I got this letter, which is probably the rudest thing anyone's ever received. It even says something like 'the punch you got in your ugly face.' I came here hoping you'd agree to be my second."

"You said no one has ever received such a letter before," Kirillov remarked. "People write letters like this when they're angry. It's happened more than once. Even Pushkin wrote one to Hekern. All right, I'll come. Tell me what to do."

Nikolay Vsyevolodovitch explained that he wanted everything settled tomorrow. He would begin by renewing his apology, even offering to send another letter of apology, but only on the condition that Gaganov promised not to send any more letters. He would act as if the letter he just received had never been written.

"That's too much of a concession. He won't agree," Kirillov replied.

"I've come to ask if you'll deliver these terms to him."

"I'll take them. It's your business. But he still won't agree."

"I know he won't. He wants to fight. Decide now how we'll fight."

"The main thing is I want it settled tomorrow. By nine in the morning, you need to go to his house. He'll hear you out but refuse, and then he'll introduce you to his second—let's say by eleven. You'll work out the details with him, and we'll meet at the spot by one or two in the afternoon. Try to arrange that. The weapons will be pistols, of course. I also ask that you set the barriers at ten paces apart. Each of us will start ten paces back from the barriers, and at the signal, we'll walk forward. We must each go right up to the barrier, but we're allowed to fire earlier, while walking. I think that's everything."

"Ten paces is very close," Kirillov remarked.

"All right, twelve paces then, but no more. You know he wants to fight seriously. Do you know how to load a pistol?"

"Yes, I know. I have pistols. I'll give my word that you've never fired them before. His second will give his word about his. There'll be two pairs of pistols, and we'll toss a coin to decide whose we use—his or ours."

"Good."

"Do you want to see the pistols?"

"Sure."

Kirillov squatted down in front of a trunk in the corner. He had never fully unpacked it, though he occasionally took things out when needed. From the bottom, he pulled out a palm-wood box lined with red velvet and opened it, revealing a pair of fine, expensive pistols.

"I have everything—powder, bullets, cartridges. I also have a revolver. Wait a second."

He bent back over the trunk and pulled out an American six-chambered revolver.

"You have plenty of weapons—and good ones, too."

"Yes, very good," Kirillov said proudly.

Though he was poor and almost destitute, it was clear that these weapons meant a lot to him. They must have cost him dearly, but he was proud to show them off.

"Do you still have the same intentions?" Nikolay Vsyevolodovitch asked after a moment, carefully watching him.

"Yes," Kirillov replied shortly. He knew exactly what Nikolay was asking, and he quickly began putting the weapons back in the trunk.

"When?" Nikolay asked cautiously after a pause.

Kirillov had returned the boxes to the trunk and sat back down in his chair.

"That doesn't depend on me, as you know. It will be when they tell me," he muttered. He seemed to dislike the question but was still ready to answer anything else. His dark, dull eyes stayed fixed on Nikolay with calm warmth, almost kindness.

"I understand someone shooting themselves, of course," Nikolay began suddenly, frowning a little after three minutes of thoughtful silence. "I've thought about it myself sometimes. And then an idea comes: if you do something awful—something shameful, even ridiculous—something people would remember for a thousand years and mock for a thousand years, you could just pull the trigger. One shot to the temple, and it would all be over. You wouldn't care anymore that people scorn you for a thousand years, would you?"

"You think that's a new idea?" Kirillov asked after a pause.

"I … I didn't say it was new. But when I thought of it, it felt like a new idea."

"You felt the idea?" Kirillov replied thoughtfully. "That's good. There are lots of ideas that seem like they've always existed, but suddenly they feel new. That's true. I see many things now as though for the first time."

"Imagine you lived on the moon," Nikolay said, interrupting Kirillov and chasing his own thoughts. "Let's say you did all these shameful and ridiculous things there. You know that everyone on the moon will laugh at you and mock you for a thousand years. But now you're here, on Earth, looking at the moon. Do you care at all about what you did there or what people think of you on the moon?"

"I don't know," Kirillov answered. "I've never been on the moon," he added, simply stating a fact without a hint of irony.

"Whose baby was that earlier?" Nikolay asked.

"It's the daughter-in-law's—no, the mother-in-law's... I don't know. She's been here three days. She's sick, and the baby cries all night. Its stomach hurts. The mother sleeps, so the old woman looks after the baby. I play ball with it. The ball is from Hamburg. I bought it there to play catch. It strengthens the spine. It's a girl."

"Do you like children?"

"I do," Kirillov replied, though he sounded indifferent.

"Then you like life?"

"Yes, I like life. What about it?"

"Even though you've decided to shoot yourself."

"What does it matter? Why connect the two? Life is one thing, and death is something else. Life exists, but death doesn't exist at all."

"Do you believe in eternal life now?"

"Not in eternal life after death, but eternal life here and now. Sometimes, you reach a moment where time stops, and that moment becomes eternal."

"You think you'll reach a moment like that?"

"Yes."

"That doesn't seem very likely in our time," Nikolay Vsyevolodovitch said slowly, almost dreamily. They spoke without any irony. "In the Book of Revelation, the angel swears there will be no more time."

"I know. That's true—clear and precise. When all people are happy, there won't be any more time because no one will need it. It's a very true idea."

"What happens to it then?"

"Nowhere. Time isn't a thing; it's just an idea. It will disappear from our minds."

"Those are the same old ideas from philosophy—repeated since the beginning of time," Stavrogin muttered with a kind of pitying scorn.

"Yes, always the same, always the same since the beginning of time, and it will never change," Kirillov said with his eyes shining, almost triumphant at the thought.

"You seem very happy, Kirillov."

"Yes, very happy," he replied as though he were stating something simple and obvious.

"But just recently you were upset, even angry with Liputin."

"Hm… I'm not angry now. Back then, I didn't know I was happy. Have you ever looked at a leaf—a leaf from a tree?"

"Yes."

"I saw one recently, yellow with a bit of green left. The edges were starting to decay. The wind was blowing it around. When I was ten, in the winter, I used to close my eyes on purpose and imagine a bright green leaf, glowing in the sun, with its little veins. I'd open my eyes and not believe them because the thought of it was so nice. Then I'd close them again."

"Is that supposed to be a metaphor?"

"N-no… why would it be? I'm just talking about a leaf. A real leaf. Leaves are good. Everything is good."

"Everything?"

"Everything. People are unhappy because they don't realize they're happy. That's all it is. If someone discovers it, they'll become happy right away. That woman will die, but the baby will live. It's all good. I suddenly realized that."

"And if someone starves to death? Or if someone hurts a little girl? Is that good?"

"Yes! And if someone blows his brains out to save the baby, that's good too. And if someone doesn't, that's still good. It's all good. It's good for those who know it's good. If people knew it was good for them, it would be good for them. But if they don't know, then it's bad for them. That's the whole point—the whole truth."

"When did you discover you were so happy?"

"Last week. Tuesday... no, wait, it was already Wednesday. It was in the middle of the night."

"And how did you figure it out?"

"I don't remember exactly. I was pacing the room. It doesn't matter. I stopped my clock. It was thirty-seven minutes past two."

"As a symbol that time will stop?"

Kirillov didn't say anything.

"They're bad because they don't know they're good. Once they realize it, they'll stop hurting little girls. They'll see they're good and will all become good."

"So, you've realized it—does that mean you've become good too?"

"I am good."

"That, I agree with," Stavrogin said with a frown.

"The one who teaches everyone that they're good will end the world."

"The man who said that was crucified."

"He'll come again, but this time he'll be the man-god."

"The god-man?"

"No, the man-god. That's the difference."

"You didn't light the lamp under the ikon, did you?"

"Yes, I lit it."

"Did you do it because you believe?"

"The old woman likes the lamp lit, and she didn't have time to do it today," Kirillov muttered.

"So, you don't pray yourself?"

"I pray to everything. I look at the spider crawling on the wall, and I thank it for crawling."

His eyes were glowing again. He stared straight at Stavrogin with a firm and steady expression. Stavrogin frowned as he looked back, a little disdainful but without any mockery in his eyes.

"I'll bet that the next time I visit, you'll believe in God," Stavrogin said as he stood up and reached for his hat.

"Why?" Kirillov asked, standing up too.

"If you realize that you believe in God, then you'll believe. But since you don't know it yet, you don't believe," Nikolay laughed.

"That's not quite right," Kirillov said thoughtfully. "You've twisted the idea. That was just a silly joke. But remember, Stavrogin, what you've meant to me in my life."

"Goodbye, Kirillov."

"Come at night. When will you?"

"Did you forget about tomorrow?"

"Ah, I did forget. Don't worry, I won't oversleep. I know how to wake up when I need to. I just tell myself, 'Seven o'clock,' and I wake up at seven. Or 'Ten o'clock,' and I wake up at ten."

"You have quite the talent," Nikolay said, looking at his pale face.

"I'll come open the gate."

"Don't bother. Shatov will open it for me."

"Ah, Shatov. All right then. Goodbye."

Chapter 1.6

The door to the empty house where Shatov was staying was open, but when Stavrogin stepped into the hallway, he found himself in complete darkness. He began feeling his way toward the stairs leading to the upper floor. Suddenly, a door upstairs opened, and a light shone out. Shatov didn't come to meet him but simply opened his door. When Nikolay Vsyevolodovitch reached the doorway of the room, he saw Shatov standing by the table in the corner, waiting for him.

"Are you willing to see me on business?" Stavrogin asked from the doorway.

"Come in and sit down," Shatov replied. "Close the door. No, wait— I'll close it myself."

He locked the door, returned to the table, and sat down facing Nikolay Vsyevolodovitch. Shatov looked thinner than he had a week ago, and now he seemed feverish.

"You've been tormenting me," he said softly, staring at the floor. "Why didn't you come sooner?"

"So you were certain I would come?"

"Yes. Wait, though—I've been delirious... maybe I'm still delirious now... Hold on."

He stood up and grabbed something from the top shelf of his bookcase. It was a revolver.

"One night, in a fever, I imagined you were coming here to kill me. The next morning, I spent my last bit of money to buy this revolver from that scoundrel Lyamshin. I wasn't going to let you do it. Then I came to my senses... There's no powder or bullets in it. It's just been lying on the shelf all this time. Wait."

He went over to the window and started to open it.

"Don't throw it out. What's the point?" Nikolay Vsyevolodovitch stopped him. "It's worth something. Besides, tomorrow people will start saying revolvers are lying under Shatov's window. Put it back—there,

271

that's better. Sit down. Tell me something—why do you seem so regretful about thinking I'd come to kill you? I haven't come here to settle anything between us. I'm here to talk about something important. First, though, let me ask—did you hit me because of my connection with your wife?"

"You know that's not why," Shatov replied, staring down again.

"And not because of the stupid rumors about Darya Pavlovna?"

"No, no, of course not! That's nonsense! My sister told me the truth from the very beginning…" Shatov said harshly, with clear irritation. He even stomped his foot slightly.

"So I guessed right, and you guessed right too," Nikolay Vsyevolodovitch said calmly. "You were right—Marya Timofyevna Lebyadkin is my lawful wife. I married her four and a half years ago in Petersburg. That must be why you hit me, isn't it?"

Shatov, clearly shocked, stared at him in silence.

"I suspected it, but I didn't believe it," he muttered at last, looking at Stavrogin strangely.

"And you still hit me?"

Shatov flushed and began to speak almost incoherently.

"Because of your fall… your lies. I didn't approach you to punish you… I didn't even know, when I walked up to you, that I'd hit you. I hit you because you meant so much to me, once… I…"

"I understand, I understand. Say no more. I can see you're feverish. I've come for a much more urgent matter."

"I've been waiting too long," Shatov said, trembling as he got up from his chair. "Say what you came to say… I'll speak later."

He sat back down.

"What I've come to tell you isn't about any of that," Nikolay Vsyevolodovitch began, watching him closely with curiosity. "For certain reasons, I had to come here tonight to tell you that they might kill you."

Shatov stared at him wildly.

"I know I might be in danger," he said slowly, "but how do you know that?"

"Because I'm part of their group, just like you are. I'm a member of the same society."

"You... you're a member?"

"I can see by your face that you expected anything from me except that," said Nikolay Vsyevolodovitch with a faint smile. "But tell me—did you already know there was a plot against your life?"

"Not at all. And I don't believe it now, even after what you've said... Although... although you never can tell with those fools!" he shouted suddenly, slamming his fist on the table in anger. "I'm not afraid of them! I've broken with them. That idiot has been here four times, warning me it's possible. But..." He turned toward Stavrogin. "What exactly do you know about it?"

"Don't worry—I'm not lying to you," Nikolay Vsyevolodovitch said coldly, like someone fulfilling a duty. "You asked me what I know? I know that two years ago, when the group was still active abroad, you joined it—just before you went to America. I believe it was shortly after our last conversation, the one you wrote to me about in your letter from America. By the way, I owe you an apology for never replying to that letter and instead..."

"To sending the money—wait a moment," Shatov interrupted, quickly pulling out a drawer in the table. He took a colorful banknote from under a pile of papers. "Here, take it. This is the hundred roubles you sent me. If it weren't for you, I would have been done for out there. I wouldn't have been able to pay it back if it hadn't been for your mother. She gave me this note as a gift nine months ago when I was struggling after my illness. But go on, please..."

He was out of breath.

"In America, you changed your views, and when you came back, you wanted to quit the group. They didn't answer you, though. Instead, they told you to hold onto a printing press here in Russia until someone came to take it. I don't know the exact details, but that's roughly the situation.

You agreed, hoping—or on the condition—that this would be the last task they'd ask of you, and then they'd let you go for good. I didn't hear this from them, but by pure chance. Now, here's what I think you don't know: they have no intention of letting you go."

"That's ridiculous!" Shatov shouted. "I told them honestly that I've cut ties with them completely. That's my right—the right to freedom of thought and conscience. I won't stand for it! There's no power on earth that could—"

"Keep your voice down," Nikolay Vsyevolodovitch said firmly, interrupting him. "Verhovensky is the kind of man who could be listening to us right now in your hallway, either himself or through someone else. Even that drunkard Lebyadkin was probably ordered to keep an eye on you, and you on him too, I suppose? Tell me—has Verhovensky accepted your arguments or not?"

"He has. He said it's possible and that I have the right..."

"Well, he's lying to you. I know for a fact that even Kirillov, who barely has anything to do with them, has reported on you to them. They have lots of agents—even people who don't realize they're serving the group. They've been watching you all along. One of Verhovensky's jobs here is to deal with you for good. He's fully authorized to get rid of you as soon as there's an opportunity—because they think you know too much and could betray them. I'm telling you this is certain. On top of that, they're convinced you're a spy, and that if you haven't informed on them yet, you will."

Shatov grimaced in frustration at hearing the accusation stated so plainly.

"If I were a spy, who would I inform?" he said angrily, avoiding a direct answer. "No—leave me alone. Let me go to hell!" he cried suddenly, his anger shifting to a new thought that seemed to torment him even more than the news about his danger. "You—you, Stavrogin! How could you get mixed up in such a shameful, ridiculous, second-rate mess? You, a member of that group? What a humiliating thing for Stavrogin!" he cried in despair.

He clasped his hands together as though this discovery caused him the deepest, most unbearable pain.

"Excuse me," said Nikolay Vsyevolodovitch, surprised. "But you seem to think of me as some kind of hero, while you're just an insect in comparison. I noticed that even from your letter in America."

"You—you know… Oh, forget about me entirely," Shatov broke off suddenly. "Explain something about yourself if you can. Answer my question!" he demanded, his voice feverish.

"Gladly. You asked how I could get involved with something like this? Since I've already told you this much, I owe you some honesty about it. You see, strictly speaking, I don't really belong to the group at all—I never officially joined. I actually have much more right than you to leave them because I never really signed up. From the beginning, I told them I wasn't one of them. If I've helped them at all, it was purely by accident, just because I had nothing else to do. I helped reorganize things for them, but that's all. Now, though, they've decided that letting me go would be too dangerous, and I think I've been sentenced to death too."

"Oh, they're always sentencing people to death, with their silly little sealed documents signed by three people and a half. And you actually think they have real power?"

"You're partly right and partly wrong," Stavrogin replied calmly, almost indifferently. "Sure, there's a lot of nonsense involved, as always with these kinds of groups. A handful of people exaggerating their size and importance. To be honest, I think Pyotr Verhovensky is the only one among them with any real weight, and even he considers himself just an agent. But their main idea isn't completely foolish—no more than other ideas like it. They're connected to the Internationale, they've planted agents in Russia, and they've even come up with a method that's at least original in theory. As for what they plan here, the movements of Russian groups like these are so obscure and unpredictable that they really might try anything. You should also note that Verhovensky is a very stubborn man."

"He's an idiot, a fool, and a clown who doesn't understand a thing about Russia!" Shatov spat out angrily.

"You don't know him very well. It's true that none of them really understand Russia, but not much less than you and I do. And Verhovensky is an enthusiast."

"Verhovensky? An enthusiast?"

"Oh yes. There's a point where he stops being a clown and becomes a madman. Remember what you once said—'Do you know how powerful a single person can be?' Don't laugh about it—he really could pull the trigger. They suspect me of being a spy too. Because they don't know what they're doing, they love accusing others of betrayal."

"But you're not afraid, are you?"

"N-no, not really… But your situation is different. I've warned you so you can keep it in mind. Don't be offended because fools threaten you— danger is still danger, even when it comes from idiots. They've gone after better men than you or me."

He glanced at his watch. "It's already a quarter past eleven," he said, standing up. "I wanted to ask you one completely unrelated question."

"For God's sake!" Shatov exclaimed, jumping up in sudden agitation.

"What?" Nikolay Vsyevolodovitch asked, puzzled.

"Ask your question, for God's sake," Shatov repeated, nearly shaking with excitement. "But only if you let me ask a question too. I beg you…"

Stavrogin paused and then began, "I've heard that you had some influence on Marya Timofyevna, and that she liked listening to you and talking with you. Is that true?"

"Yes… she used to listen," Shatov said, looking embarrassed.

"In the next day or two, I plan to announce our marriage publicly here in town."

"Is that even possible?" Shatov whispered, almost in shock.

"I don't see why not. There are witnesses—Kirillov, Pyotr Verhovensky, and Lebyadkin—who can confirm it. Everything was perfectly legal and proper when it happened in Petersburg. The reason no one knew until now is because the witnesses promised to keep quiet."

"I don't mean that..." Shatov stammered. "You're speaking so calmly... But fine! Tell me—you weren't forced into marrying her, were you?"

"No, no one forced me." Stavrogin smiled faintly at Shatov's anxious urgency.

"And what about this talk she keeps up about her baby?" Shatov asked hurriedly.

"Her baby? I've never heard that before. She never had a baby and couldn't have. Marya Timofyevna is a virgin."

"Ah, I knew it! Listen—"

"What's wrong with you, Shatov?"

Shatov turned away, hiding his face in his hands, before suddenly grabbing Stavrogin by the shoulders.

"Do you even understand why? Do you know why you did all this—and why you're punishing yourself now?"

"You're asking a clever and cruel question," Stavrogin said with surprising calm. "But I'll surprise you—I think I do know why I married her and why I'm doing this now."

"Let's leave that for later!" Shatov shouted. "That's not the main thing—there's something more important!"

Chapter 1.7

"Do you know," Shatov began, his eyes flashing with intensity as he leaned forward in his chair, holding up a finger as if making a point (though he seemed unaware he was doing so), "do you know which people are the only 'god-bearing' nation on earth? The people chosen to renew and save the world in the name of a new God, the ones who hold the keys to life and the future? Do you know who they are and what they're called?"

"Judging by your tone, I'm forced to assume you mean the Russian people," Stavrogin replied calmly.

"And you can laugh at that! Oh, what a people!" Shatov exploded.

"Calm down, please. I'm not laughing. In fact, I expected you to say something like this."

"You expected it? Don't you remember those words yourself?"

"I remember them well. I know exactly what you're getting at. All of this—even the phrase 'god-bearing people'—is just a continuation of our conversation two years ago abroad, right before you left for America. If I recall correctly."

"It's your phrase, not mine! Your own words—not just something that followed from our talk. That conversation wasn't even a conversation. You were like a teacher saying profound things, and I was the student who came back to life. I was that student. You were the teacher."

"But if you remember, right after that conversation, you joined their group. And soon after, you left for America."

"Yes, and I wrote to you about all of that from America. I told you everything. Do you think I could immediately tear my heart away from what I had believed in since childhood? From what I had pinned all my hopes on, what I had loved and hated? It's hard to change gods. I didn't believe you back then because I didn't want to. So, I threw myself into the mud one last time. But your words stayed with me, and the seed grew. Tell me honestly—did you even read my letter from America? Maybe you didn't read it at all?"

"I read three pages—the first two and the last one. I skimmed the middle part. But I always meant—"

"Ah, never mind, forget it! Damn it!" Shatov shouted, waving his hand dismissively. "If you've abandoned those words now, how could you even say them back then? That's what kills me!"

"I wasn't joking with you then," Stavrogin said enigmatically. "Maybe I was more concerned with convincing myself than with convincing you."

"You weren't joking? In America, I spent three months sleeping on

278

straw next to a poor, broken man. It was from him that I learned that at the very moment you were planting ideas of God and the Fatherland in my heart, you were poisoning the heart of that maniac Kirillov with your twisted lies. You filled his mind with dangerous nonsense and pushed him toward madness. Look at him now! He's your creation. You've seen him, haven't you?"

"First of all," Stavrogin replied, "I must point out that Kirillov told me he's happy. He says he's good. And you're almost right about the timing—it did all happen at the same time. But what of it? I told you the truth. I didn't lie to either of you."

"Are you an atheist now? Do you still not believe in God?"

"Yes."

"And back then?"

"The same. I didn't believe then either."

"I didn't ask you to show me respect when I started this conversation," Shatov muttered angrily. "You should have understood that much with your intellect."

"I didn't walk away at your first word," Stavrogin replied quietly. "I didn't shut down the conversation or leave. I've been sitting here patiently, answering your questions and listening to your outbursts. So, I don't think I've been disrespectful yet."

Shatov cut him off, waving his hand.

"Do you remember saying that 'an atheist can't be a Russian,' that 'the moment someone becomes an atheist, they stop being Russian'? Do you remember that?"

"Did I say that?" Stavrogin asked indifferently.

"You're asking me? You don't remember? That was one of the truest things you ever said about the Russian soul! You must remember. Let me remind you of something else: you also said that 'a man who isn't Orthodox can't truly be Russian.'"

"I suppose that's an old Slavophile idea."

"Today's Slavophiles have abandoned it. People think they're smarter now. But you went even further: you said that Roman Catholicism isn't Christianity at all. You claimed that Rome accepted the third temptation of the devil. By insisting that Christ couldn't survive on earth without an earthly kingdom, Catholicism had accepted Antichrist instead. You said that this is what ruined the Western world. France, you said, is suffering now because of Catholicism. She rejected the false God of Rome but hasn't found a new one. That's what you said then! I remember every word of those conversations!"

"If I believed, I would probably say it again now. I wasn't lying when I spoke back then as if I had faith," said Nikolay Vsyevolodovitch seriously. "But I have to tell you, hearing my past ideas repeated like this makes me very uncomfortable. Can't you let it go?"

"If you believed?" Shatov repeated, ignoring his request entirely. "Didn't you once tell me that even if it were mathematically proven that truth didn't include Christ, you would still stick with Christ over the truth? Did you say that or not?"

"But allow me to ask you something," Nikolay Vsyevolodovitch said, raising his voice slightly. "What is the point of this irritated and almost hostile interrogation?"

"This will be the last time. I will never mention it again for all eternity."

"You keep saying that we're outside the limits of time and space."

"Be quiet!" Shatov suddenly shouted. "I might be clumsy and awkward, but let my name be forgotten in shame if it must. I want to repeat your main idea—just the conclusion."

"Fine, go ahead—if it's just the conclusion," Stavrogin said, holding back from checking his watch.

"Not a single nation," Shatov began, his voice steady but intense, "has ever been founded on science or reason. It has never happened, except for a brief moment in some foolishness. Socialism is, by its nature, atheism, because from the very start it declared itself atheistic, claiming it would build society on science and reason alone. But science and reason have always been secondary forces in the lives of nations, and they always will

280

be. Nations are moved by a deeper force, something unknown, something beyond reason—a powerful drive to keep existing and to deny death. It's the force of life itself, what the Scriptures call 'the river of living water,' and the Apocalypse warns that it will one day dry up. Philosophers call it the aesthetic or ethical principle, but I call it simply the search for God.

Every national movement—throughout all history—has been about this search for a god, its own god, who is believed to be the one true god. God is the soul of the people. No nation has ever shared its god with another. When nations start sharing gods, it's a sign they are dying. A strong nation has its own god, separate and unique. There has never been a nation without religion, without some idea of good and evil. Each nation defines its own good and evil. When those definitions start to blur between nations, those nations begin to die. Reason has never been able to define good and evil—it mixes them up instead, creating confusion. Science is even worse. It gives us solutions 'by force.' Half-truths from science have become the greatest plague on humanity, worse than war, famine, or disease.

A half-truth is a tyrant. It has priests, followers, and slaves who worship it blindly. It's something so powerful and destructive that even science bows to it in fear and shame.

Those were your words, Stavrogin—except for the part about half-truths, which I added myself because I know it well. I'm a product of half-knowledge, and I hate it most of all. I haven't changed your ideas or your words—not even a single one."

"I don't agree that you haven't changed them," Stavrogin said cautiously. "You accepted them so passionately that you've twisted them without realizing it. For example, you reduce God to something as simple as a nation's identity."

Stavrogin suddenly looked at Shatov closely, his gaze sharper now, as though he wasn't paying attention to the words so much as to Shatov himself.

"I reduce God to something as small as a nation's identity?" Shatov shouted. "No! I raise the people up to God! The people are God's body!

A people can only survive as long as they believe in their own god and reject all others. They must believe their god alone will conquer and save the world. That's what every great nation has believed since the beginning of time. Every great nation has believed it had the truth.

The Jews lived to await their one true God, and they gave the world that God. The Greeks deified nature and gave us philosophy and art. Rome deified the state and gave us the idea of the state itself. France embodied the Roman idea and developed it through history. If they have now thrown away their Roman god and fallen into atheism—which they call socialism—it's because socialism, at least, is healthier than the dying Roman Catholicism.

If a great people stops believing that it alone has the truth—that it alone can lead and save humanity—then it stops being a great people. A nation without that belief becomes nothing more than a part of history's background, an empty shell. A real nation will never settle for a secondary role in history; it must be first or it will disappear. There is only one truth, and therefore only one nation can carry the true God. That nation is Russia—the Russian people!

Do you think I'm such a fool, Stavrogin," Shatov shouted, suddenly losing control, "that I don't know whether my words are just the same tired old slogans people throw around in Moscow, or something completely new—a final word, a word of rebirth and resurrection? Do you think I care about your smug laughter right now? Do you think I care that you don't understand a single word I'm saying, not one sound? I despise your arrogant smile and the way you're looking at me this very moment!"

He jumped up from his chair, his face twisted with anger, and there was even foam at his lips.

"On the contrary, Shatov, on the contrary," Stavrogin began with unusual calm and seriousness, still sitting in his chair. "Your passionate words brought back some very strong memories for me. In your words, I can hear my own thoughts from two years ago. I won't tell you again that you've exaggerated my ideas. In fact, I believe my thoughts were even stronger and more independent back then. I assure you for the third time

282

that I would gladly confirm every word you've just said—every syllable—but…"

"But you need a hare first?" Shatov interrupted bitterly, sitting down again with a mocking laugh. "That's your own nasty phrase. 'To cook your hare, you first need to catch it.' To believe in God, you need to have a God first. You used to say that in Petersburg, didn't you? Like Nozdryov trying to catch a hare by its hind legs."

"No, what Nozdryov did was boast that he had already caught it. By the way, let me ask you something—I think I've earned the right to ask a question now. Tell me, have you caught your hare?"

"Don't you dare ask me like that! Ask it differently—show some respect," Shatov snapped, trembling all over.

"Fine, I'll ask differently," said Nikolay Vsyevolodovitch, his expression turning colder. "I just want to know—do you believe in God?"

"I believe in Russia… I believe in her Orthodox faith… I believe in the body of Christ… I believe that the new coming will happen in Russia… I believe…" Shatov stammered frantically.

"And in God? Do you believe in God?"

"I… I will believe in God."

Stavrogin's face didn't move a muscle. Shatov stared at him with burning, defiant eyes, as if trying to burn through him with his gaze.

"I haven't told you that I don't believe," Shatov said at last, his voice shaking. "But understand this—I'm just a pitiful, boring book for now, nothing more. So far! So far… But forget me! We're talking about you. I'm nothing, just a man without talent, willing to give my blood—nothing more! But never mind that! I've been waiting here for you for two years. For the last half-hour, I've been standing here in my nakedness before you. You, only you, can raise the flag!"

He stopped speaking and sat down in despair, resting his head in his hands.

"I just find it strange," Stavrogin said suddenly. "Everyone seems to want to give me a flag to raise. Pyotr Verhovensky also believes I could 'raise his flag.' Those were the exact words someone repeated to me. He thinks I could become some kind of Stenka Razin for them. He says I have an 'extraordinary aptitude for crime.' That's what he said."

"What?" Shatov cried. "An 'extraordinary aptitude for crime'?"

"Exactly."

"Hm! And is it true?" Shatov asked with a bitter smile. "Is it true that back in Petersburg you joined some secret group that practiced disgusting depravity? That you could teach lessons to the Marquis de Sade? Is it true you lured and corrupted children? Speak! Don't lie to me. You can't lie to Shatov—the man who struck you in the face. Tell me everything, and if it's true, I'll kill you here on the spot!"

"I did say those things," Stavrogin admitted after a long silence, his face pale and his eyes cold. "But I wasn't the one who harmed children."

"But you said such things," Shatov pressed on fiercely, staring at him. "Didn't you once claim that there was no difference between a disgusting, shameful act and some great heroic deed—like sacrificing yourself for humanity? That both had the same beauty, the same satisfaction? Is that true?"

"I can't answer a question like that... I won't answer," Stavrogin muttered, though he didn't get up or leave.

"I know why you've lost the ability to see the difference between good and evil," Shatov continued, trembling with anger. "Do you know why you made that humiliating, shameful marriage? You did it because the absurdity and disgrace of it reached a level of genius! You don't hesitate—you throw yourself straight into the abyss. You married out of a desire for suffering, for remorse, out of some twisted moral pleasure. It was a sickness of the soul! Defying common sense was just too tempting for you. Stavrogin marrying a crippled, half-witted beggar! Tell me, when you bit the governor's ear, did you feel pleasure? Did you? You empty, arrogant, little snob—did you?"

"You're quite the psychologist," Stavrogin said faintly, turning even paler. "Though you're mistaken about my reasons for the marriage. But tell me—who gave you all this information?" He forced a weak smile.

"Was it Kirillov? No, he couldn't have known."

"You've turned pale."

"What is it you want from me?" Stavrogin suddenly demanded, his voice rising. "I've sat here listening to you rant at me for half an hour, and you haven't told me your reason for it. If you have some actual purpose, you should tell me. Otherwise, let me go."

"An actual purpose?"

"Yes, you owe me that much. I've been waiting to hear it, but all I've gotten is your furious spite. Open the gate for me."

He stood up to leave. Shatov jumped after him, grabbing him by the shoulder.

"Kiss the earth! Water it with your tears! Pray for forgiveness!" he shouted desperately.

"I didn't kill you... that morning..." Stavrogin whispered painfully, looking at the ground. "I stopped my hands..."

"Speak! Tell me why you came to warn me of danger. You let me talk, you're planning to announce your marriage tomorrow. Do you think I don't see it on your face? You're consumed by some new idea—something dark and threatening! Stavrogin, why am I doomed to believe in you forever? Why is it you? Why do I throw away all shame when I speak to you? I should hide myself, but I don't—because it's you! I would kiss your footprints when you leave. I can't tear you out of my heart, Nikolay Stavrogin!"

"I'm sorry, Shatov," Stavrogin replied coldly. "I just don't feel the same way about you."

"I know you don't. I know you're telling me the truth." Shatov's voice shook. "But listen to me—I can fix it. I can 'catch your hare' for you."

Stavrogin said nothing.

"You're an atheist because you're a snob. You've lost touch with the people. But a new generation is coming, born from the people's soul, and you'll know nothing of it—not you, not the Verhovenskys. Not even me, because I'm a snob too. Listen, Stavrogin—work is the answer! Reach God through work!"

"Reach God through work? What kind of work?"

"Work like the peasants. Give up everything you own. Ah, you're laughing—you think it's some trick?"

But Stavrogin wasn't laughing.

"You think you can find God through work, by working like the peasants," he repeated thoughtfully, as if considering something serious. "By the way, you reminded me—I'm not rich at all. I don't have much to give up. I can hardly even provide for Marya Timofyevna's future. I wanted to ask you if you could look after her. You're the only person she listens to."

"All right, all right, we'll talk about Marya Timofyevna later," Shatov said impatiently, holding a candle and waving him towards the door. "Listen—go see Tikhon."

"Tikhon? Who is that?"

"He used to be a bishop. He lives here now, in the monastery. Go see him. Why not? What does it matter to you?"

"This is the first I've heard of him... but thank you, I'll go."

"Come on."

Shatov lit the way down the stairs and opened the gate. "Go on."

"I won't come see you again, Shatov," Stavrogin said quietly as he stepped into the street.

The rain and darkness continued as before.

Chapter 2
Night (Continued)

Chapter 2.1

He walked down Bogoyavlensky Street. The road soon began to slope downward, and his feet slid in the mud. Suddenly, a wide, misty, empty space opened up before him—the river. The houses gave way to shabby little huts, and the street disappeared into a maze of uneven, narrow alleys.

Nikolay Vsyevolodovitch walked along the riverbank for a long time. He moved with confidence, barely thinking about where he was going, as if lost in deep thought. He looked up, surprised, when he suddenly found himself in the middle of a long, wet, floating bridge.

The bridge was completely empty, so it startled him when he suddenly heard a familiar but overly polite voice at his elbow. It was the kind of smooth voice you might hear from an overly formal shopkeeper or a slick young assistant.

"Would you be kind enough, sir, to share your umbrella with me?"

There was indeed someone right beside him, trying to edge under his umbrella. The man was walking close enough to bump his elbow, as soldiers say. Slowing his pace, Nikolay Vsyevolodovitch bent forward to get a better look at the man in the dim light. He was a short fellow, dressed poorly and sloppily, like a worker who had been drinking. A soaked cloth cap, with a torn brim, sat on his curly, matted hair. He looked thin but tough, with dark skin, and his big, hard eyes gleamed with a yellowish tint, like a gypsy's. He appeared to be around forty and, surprisingly, wasn't drunk.

"Do you know me?" asked Nikolay Vsyevolodovitch.

"Mr. Stavrogin, Nikolay Vsyevolodovitch. I saw you at the station last Sunday when the train stopped. You were pointed out to me. I'd already heard plenty about you before that."

"From Pyotr Stepanovitch? Are you... Fedka the convict?"

"I was baptized Fyodor Fyodorovitch. My mother still lives around here—an old woman, more hunched over every day. She spends all her time praying for me, day and night. At least she doesn't waste her last days lying useless on the stove."

"You escaped from prison?"

"My luck changed. I gave up on books, bells, and church because I was serving a life sentence. It was going to take a very long time to finish it."

"What are you doing here?"

"I get by however I can. My uncle just died last week in prison here. He was locked up for making fake coins. To honor his memory, I threw two dozen rocks at some dogs. That's all I've done so far. Also, Pyotr Stepanovitch is giving me hope for a passport—he says maybe even a merchant's one so I can travel all over Russia. I'm waiting for him to be kind enough to follow through. 'My father lost you at cards at the English club,' he told me, 'and I find that inhuman.' Could you spare me three roubles, sir, for a drink to warm myself up?"

"So you've been spying on me? I don't like that. Who told you to do it?"

"Nobody ordered me to do anything. I just know about your generosity—it's well known, after all. Usually, all we get in life is a handful of hay or a kick with a fork. Last Friday I ate so much pie I felt stuffed, like Martin full of soap. But after that, I went a whole day without eating, then fasted the next day, and on the third day—nothing again. I've had my fill of water from the river; it feels like I'm growing fish in my belly. Won't you help me out? I've got a girl waiting for me nearby, but I can't show up to her empty-handed."

"What did Pyotr Stepanovitch promise you I would do for you?"

"He didn't exactly promise anything. He just hinted that I might be useful to you someday if my luck holds out. But he didn't explain how. Pyotr Stepanovitch wants to test me, see if I have the patience of a Cossack. He doesn't trust me very much."

"Why not?"

Pyotr Stepanovitch may know all about God's planets like an astronomer, but even he can be wrong. I stand before you, sir, as though before God, because I've heard so much about you. Pyotr Stepanovitch is one thing, but you, sir, might be something completely different. When he says a man is a scoundrel, that's all he knows about him—that he's a scoundrel. Or if he calls someone a fool, that man has no purpose in his eyes except to be a fool. But I might be a fool on Tuesday and Wednesday and wiser than him on Thursday. He knows I'm desperate to get a passport because, without papers, you can't get anywhere in Russia. So he thinks he's got me trapped. Life is easy for him because he just decides what a man is and treats him that way. Plus, he's stingy—cheap as they come. He thinks I wouldn't dare trouble you without him, but here I am, standing before you on my own. I've been waiting for you here on this bridge for four nights, just to prove I can do it quietly, without his help. "Better to bow to a boot," I thought, "than to a peasant's shoe."

"And who told you I'd be crossing the bridge at night?"

"Well, I'll admit that was mostly by chance. Captain Lebyadkin let something slip—he can't keep his mouth shut about anything. So, three roubles from you, sir, would make up for the three days and nights I've spent here waiting. And my clothes are soaked through. I won't even complain about that."

"I'm going left. You go right. Here's the end of the bridge. Listen, Fyodor: I want you to understand this clearly. I won't give you a single coin. Don't meet me again on the bridge or anywhere else. I don't need you, and I never will. If you don't listen, I'll tie you up and take you to the police. Now go!"

"Eh-heh! At least toss me something for keeping you company. I made your walk a little less lonely."

"Get out of here!"

"But are you sure you know the way? There are so many turns here... I could guide you. This town looks like the devil himself carried it in a basket and dropped it in pieces all over."

"I'll tie you up!" Nikolay Vsyevolodovitch said, turning on him angrily.

"Maybe you'll change your mind. It's easy to push around someone helpless."

"Well, I see you're pretty sure of yourself!"

"No, sir. I'm relying on you more than on myself."

"I've already told you—I don't need you at all."

"But I need you! That's how it is. I'll wait for you on your way back. There's no helping it."

"I give you my word: if I see you again, I'll tie you up."

"Then I'll have a belt ready for you to use. Safe travels, sir. You kept me dry under your umbrella, and for that alone, I'll be grateful until the day I die."

He dropped back, leaving Nikolay Vsyevolodovitch to walk on alone. The encounter had unsettled him. This strange man, appearing out of nowhere, seemed completely convinced that he was essential to him—almost as if he were doing Nikolay a favor. He had been insolent, too, in the way he pushed his services on him. Yet it was possible the tramp hadn't been lying and was acting on his own, without Pyotr Stepanovitch's knowledge. That would be even stranger.

Chapter 2.2

The house Nikolay Vsyevolodovitch arrived at stood alone in a quiet, empty lane, surrounded by fences with vegetable gardens beyond. It was a small wooden house, freshly built and unfinished, with no weatherboarding. One of the windows had an open shutter, and a candle stood on the windowsill, clearly as a signal for the expected late visitor. About thirty paces away, a tall figure could be seen on the doorstep. The man, clearly the owner of the house, was staring impatiently down the road. His voice broke the silence—nervous and eager.

"Is that you? You?"

"Yes," Nikolay Vsyevolodovitch replied as he climbed the steps and folded his umbrella.

"Finally, sir." Captain Lebyadkin—it was indeed him—rushed about fussily. "Let me take your umbrella, please. It's soaking wet. I'll leave it open here on the floor, in the corner. Come in, please, come in."

The passage led straight into a small room, brightly lit by two candles.

"If you hadn't promised you'd come, I would've given up waiting," the captain added, with a mixture of impatience and awkwardness.

"It's already a quarter to one," Nikolay Vsyevolodovitch replied, glancing at his watch as he entered.

"And in this rain! It's such a long way here, and I don't even have a clock... All I see around me are gardens, nothing else. It's easy to lose track of time. Not that I'm complaining—I wouldn't dare complain. It's just that I've been eaten up with impatience all week... waiting for this to finally be settled."

"Settled? How so?"

"To hear my fate, Nikolay Vsyevolodovitch. Please, take a seat."

He bowed politely, gesturing to the chair by the table near the sofa.

Nikolay Vsyevolodovitch looked around the room. It was small and low-ceilinged. The furniture was plain and basic: a few wooden chairs and a simple sofa with no cushions or covering. Two tables were in the room, one near the sofa and the other in the corner, covered with a cloth that had something placed neatly underneath it. Everything looked remarkably clean.

Captain Lebyadkin looked bloated and pale from days of sobriety, with a nervous, puzzled expression in his uneasy eyes. It was clear he didn't know how to act or what tone to take.

"Here," he said, motioning around the room, "I live like a hermit—sobriety, solitude, and poverty, like the knights of old."

"You think knights took such vows?"

"Maybe I'm mistaken. Alas, I'm a man without culture—I've ruined everything. Believe me, Nikolay Vsyevolodovitch, it's here that I've finally

291

overcome my old shameful habits. Not a drop, not even a glass! I have my little home now, and for six days I've had peace of mind. Even the walls here smell of fresh wood and remind me of nature. But what was I before this? What was I?

'At night without a bed I wander,

And my tongue put out by day…'

As the poet says. But you're soaked… Would you like some tea?"

"Don't bother."

"The samovar has been boiling since eight o'clock, but it finally went out—like everything else in this world. Even the sun, they say, will go out someday. But if you'd like, I can light it up again. Agafya isn't asleep yet."

"Tell me, Marya Timofyevna…?"

"She's here, here," Lebyadkin whispered quickly, pointing toward the closed door to the next room.

"She's not asleep?"

"Oh no, not at all. How could she be? She's been expecting you all evening. As soon as she heard you were coming, she started getting herself ready."

He began to smile, almost joking, but immediately stopped himself.

"How is she doing, overall?" Nikolay Vsyevolodovitch asked, frowning.

"Overall? You know yourself, sir." The captain shrugged as if apologizing. "But just now… well, right now she's telling her fortune with cards."

"Very well. We'll get to that later. First, I want to settle things with you."

Nikolay Vsyevolodovitch sat down. Captain Lebyadkin hurried to pull up a chair for himself, sitting close and leaning forward with an eager, trembling expression.

"What's under the tablecloth over there?" Nikolay Vsyevolodovitch asked suddenly, noticing the covered table.

"That?" Lebyadkin turned and looked as well. "That's something I prepared for your housewarming, you might say, after such a long journey in this weather." He gave a nervous little laugh. Carefully, he tiptoed over and lifted the cloth. Underneath was a neatly arranged meal: ham, veal, sardines, cheese, a green glass decanter, and a tall bottle of Bordeaux. Everything was laid out almost daintily.

"Did you do all that yourself?"

"Yes, sir. Since yesterday, I've been doing my best to make everything ready for you. Marya Timofyevna doesn't trouble herself about these things, as you know. Besides, everything here is from your generosity— your provisions, your house—I'm only acting as your agent, so to speak. But even so, Nikolay Vsyevolodovitch, even so, I'm still independent in spirit! Don't take that away from me. It's all I have left!" he finished, almost pleading.

"Hm. Sit back down."

"Grateful, grateful, yet still independent." He sat down again. "Ah, Nikolay Vsyevolodovitch, I've had so much weighing on my heart. I couldn't wait for you to come. You'll decide everything now—my fate, her fate... Then, perhaps, you'll let me pour my heart out to you as I used to, four years ago. You listened to me then. You even read my verses. People might have called me your Falstaff back then, like in Shakespeare, but you meant so much to me! Now, though, I'm full of fear, and I have no one else to turn to. Only you can help me. Pyotr Stepanovitch has been treating me horribly!"

Nikolay Vsyevolodovitch listened closely and studied him carefully. It was clear that although Captain Lebyadkin had stopped drinking, he was far from being in a calm or stable state of mind. Long-term drinkers like Lebyadkin often show signs of confusion, scattered thoughts, or something slightly broken, though they can still lie, trick, and scheme as well as anyone when necessary.

"I see you haven't changed much in these four years, captain," said Nikolay Vsyevolodovitch in a more approachable tone. "It seems like the

293

second half of a man's life is mostly just a repeat of the habits he formed in the first half."

"Such profound words! You've solved the mystery of life!" exclaimed the captain, half-impressed and half sly. He loved hearing clever phrases. "I remember one thing you said in Petersburg above all others. You said, 'It takes a great man to stand up against common sense.'"

"Yes, and it takes a fool too."

"A fool, perhaps, but you've always been full of such wise sayings. Meanwhile, they... Imagine Liputin or Pyotr Stepanovitch saying anything like that! Ah, how cruelly Pyotr Stepanovitch has treated me!"

"And what about you, captain? What can you say about your own behavior?"

"Drunkenness, and too many enemies. But that's all behind me now—I've shed my old skin, like a snake. Did you know, Nikolay Vsyevolodovitch, I'm writing my will? In fact, I've already written it."

"That's interesting. What do you have to leave, and to whom?"

"To my country, to humanity, and to the students. I read about an American in the papers. He left all his fortune to factories and science, gave his skeleton to a medical academy, and had his skin made into a drum so they could beat the national anthem on it day and night. Amazing, isn't it? Such ideas! Meanwhile, we Russians are like children playing in nature's sandbox. If I tried to leave my skin for a drum to be used in the Akmolinsky infantry regiment, where I first served, they'd call it liberalism and reject it. So, I'll settle for leaving my skeleton to the academy. On one condition, though—there must be a label on my forehead that says, 'A repentant free-thinker.' There you go!"

The captain spoke with excitement, genuinely thinking the American will was a brilliant idea. But at the same time, he was being sly, hoping to entertain Nikolay Vsyevolodovitch, as he had done before when playing the fool for him. He also had another purpose, one he was particularly nervous about.

"So you plan to publish your will while you're still alive and collect some praise for it?" Nikolay Vsyevolodovitch asked suspiciously.

"And what if I do, Nikolay Vsyevolodovitch? What if I do?" Lebyadkin replied, watching him carefully. "What sort of luck have I had? I've even given up writing poetry. At one time, even you found my verses amusing. Do you remember how we'd read them over a bottle? But it's all over now. I've only written one last poem—like Gogol's 'Final Tale.' He said it burst from his heart, and it's the same for me. I've sung my last, and now it's done."

"What kind of poem?"

"'In Case She Breaks Her Leg.'"

"What?"

That was what the captain had been waiting for. He admired his own poetry, but there was a kind of sly pleasure in Nikolay Vsyevolodovitch laughing at them, often loudly and uncontrollably. It allowed him to satisfy both his poetic pride and his need to amuse his audience. But this time, he also hoped to defend himself about something he felt deeply guilty about.

"'In Case She Breaks Her Leg.' I'm talking about a lady on horseback—it's a fantasy, a poet's wild idea. One day I saw a woman riding, and I asked myself, 'What would happen if she had an accident?' All her admirers would turn away, all her suitors would disappear. And who would remain? Only the poet—his heart shattered but faithful. Even a lowly creature like a louse can fall in love—it's not against the law! But she was offended by the letter and the poem. I even heard you were angry, Nikolay Vsyevolodovitch. Is that true? I can't believe it. Who could I possibly harm with my imagination? Besides, Liputin encouraged me. He kept saying, 'Send it, send it! Every man has the right to send a letter.' So, I sent it."

"You offered yourself as a suitor, then?"

"Enemies, enemies everywhere!"

"Recite the verses," Nikolay Vsyevolodovitch ordered sternly.

"Madness, just madness."

But he stood up straight, stretched out his hand dramatically, and began:

"With broken limbs my beauteous queen

Is twice as charming as before,

And, deep in love as I have been,

To-day I love her even more."

"That's enough," Nikolay Vsyevolodovitch cut him off with a wave of his hand.

"I dream of Petersburg!" the captain cried suddenly, as if the poetry had never been mentioned. "I dream of a new life, a new beginning. My benefactor, surely you won't refuse me the means to get there? I've been waiting all week for you, like a man waits for the sun!"

"I won't give you anything. I have almost no money left. Why should I give you money?"

Nikolay Vsyevolodovitch's tone suddenly became sharp and angry. In a dry and cold voice, he began listing all of Lebyadkin's faults: his drunkenness, his lies, his wasting of the money meant for Marya Timofyevna, his decision to take her out of the convent, his threats to reveal secrets through letters, and his shameful behavior toward Darya Pavlovna. The captain squirmed, waving his hands and trying to defend himself, but every time he opened his mouth, Nikolay Vsyevolodovitch shut him down with a firm, unyielding word.

"And listen," Stavrogin said at last, "you keep writing about 'family disgrace.' What disgrace is it to you that your sister is the lawful wife of a Stavrogin?"

"But a secret marriage, Nikolay Vsyevolodovitch—a terrible secret! I receive money from you, and then someone asks me, 'What's that money for?' My hands are tied. I can't answer without hurting my sister or ruining the family's reputation."

The captain's voice grew louder. He was eager to bring up this topic, convinced it was his strongest argument. Unfortunately, he had no idea what was coming next.

Calmly, as though discussing the simplest matter, Nikolay Vsyevolodovitch told him that within a few days, perhaps even tomorrow or the day after, he planned to make his marriage public—"to the authorities and to society." That way, the question of family honor would be resolved once and for all, along with the issue of financial support.

The captain's eyes widened in shock. He could hardly understand what he was hearing, and Stavrogin had to explain it again.

"But she's... she's not in her right mind."

"I'll make the necessary arrangements."

"And... your mother? What will she say?"

"Well, she can do as she pleases."

"But will you take your wife to live with you?"

"Maybe. But that's none of your business. It doesn't concern you at all."

"No concern of mine?" the captain cried. "What about me, then?"

"Well, you certainly won't be coming into my house."

"But... but I'm a relation!"

"People try their best to escape from relatives like you. Why would I keep giving you money? Think about it."

"Nikolay Vsyevolodovitch, this can't be happening. You'll change your mind, won't you? You don't want to go through with this. What will people think? What will the world say?"

"I couldn't care less about your 'world.' I married your sister because I felt like it—after a drunken dinner, on a bet. And now I'll make it public because it amuses me."

He spoke with such irritation that the captain began to believe him.

"But what about me? Me! What will happen to me? You're joking, Nikolay Vsyevolodovitch, aren't you?"

"No, I'm not joking."

"Well, then I'll take legal action."

"You're an idiot, captain."

"Maybe I am, but that's all I've got left!" the captain shouted, now panicking completely. "At least back then, we got free room and board for the work she did at the convent. But what happens to me now if you leave me with nothing?"

"You were planning to go to Petersburg to start a new life. By the way, is it true what I've heard—that you're thinking about turning in information to the authorities, hoping to get a pardon by betraying everyone else?"

The captain's jaw dropped, and he stared at Stavrogin, speechless.

"Listen to me, captain," Stavrogin said suddenly, leaning toward the table. Up until now, his tone had been vague and almost mocking, leaving Lebyadkin unsure if Stavrogin was really serious or just toying with him. But now, the stern look on Stavrogin's face sent a chill down the captain's spine.

"Listen carefully, and tell me the truth, Lebyadkin. Have you already betrayed anyone? Have you started anything? Sent any letters in your foolishness?"

"No, I haven't… I haven't done anything," the captain said, his eyes fixed on Stavrogin.

"You're lying. You've thought about it, haven't you? That's why you want to go to Petersburg. If you haven't written anything, have you at least blabbed to someone here? Tell me the truth. I've heard rumors."

"I might have let something slip… when I was drunk. To Liputin. Liputin's a snake. I opened up to him." The captain's voice dropped to a whisper.

"Well, that's just great. You're a fool, captain. If you had a thought like that, you should've kept it to yourself. Smart people keep quiet these days—they don't run their mouths."

"Nikolay Vsyevolodovitch!" the captain stammered, trembling. "You weren't involved in anything, I swear. I didn't…"

"No, you wouldn't dare betray the man who feeds you."

"Think about it, Nikolay Vsyevolodovitch—judge for yourself!" the captain cried out desperately, tears in his voice. Then, overwhelmed, he began recounting his life story over the past four years. It was a confused and pitiful tale of a man who got himself into trouble he barely understood, drunk and reckless, unable to grasp the seriousness of his actions until it was too late.

He explained that, before leaving Petersburg, he had been "dragged into things," simply because of his friendships. "Like a student, though I wasn't one," he said. At first, not realizing what he was doing, he delivered all kinds of pamphlets—leaving them on doorsteps, stuffing them into mail slots, leaving them at theaters, even sneaking them into people's hats and pockets. Later, he admitted he took money for this work, "because how else was I supposed to survive?"

He had distributed all sorts of ridiculous, dangerous materials across two provinces. "Oh, Nikolay Vsyevolodovitch, you can't imagine how disgusting it was! They wrote nonsense, things against civic and patriotic laws. One pamphlet told people to grab pitchforks, promising that anyone who went out poor in the morning could come home rich at night. Can you believe it? It made me shudder, but I still handed it out.

"Or another one—just a few lines, for all of Russia, saying, 'Lock up the churches, destroy God, abolish marriage, end inheritance, take up your knives.' That's it! Who could even understand that? I nearly got caught once, carrying one of those leaflets. The officers in my regiment beat me for it, but thank God, they let me go.

"Last year, I was nearly caught again when I tried to pass off fake French fifty-rouble notes to Korovayev. Luckily, he fell drunk into a pond and drowned, so no one could trace it back to me. I've spoken about communism at Virginsky's, I've handed out papers in June in X district, and now Pyotr Stepanovitch tells me I have no choice but to obey him again. He's been threatening me for months. You have no idea how he treated me last Sunday! Nikolay Vsyevolodovitch, I'm a slave, a worm— nothing more. I am not a god, like Derzhavin wrote. But I have no income, no income at all!"

Nikolay Vsyevolodovitch listened with interest.

"I didn't know half of that," he said. "It seems like anything could have happened to you... Listen, if you want, you can tell them—you know who—that Liputin was lying. Say you were just pretending to offer information to scare me into thinking I was caught up in it too, hoping you could get more money out of me. Do you understand?"

"Nikolay Vsyevolodovitch, is there really such a danger hanging over me? I've been waiting for you to come and tell me."

Nikolay Vsyevolodovitch laughed.

"They wouldn't let you go to Petersburg, even if I gave you money for the trip... But it's time for me to see Marya Timofyevna." He stood up.

"Nikolay Vsyevolodovitch, what about Marya Timofyevna?"

"What about her? I already told you."

"Can this really be true?"

"You still don't believe it?"

"Are you really going to throw me away like an old shoe?"

"We'll see," said Nikolay Vsyevolodovitch with a laugh. "Now, let me go."

"Should I stand outside on the steps... just in case I overhear something by accident? The rooms are small."

"That's a good idea. Go stand outside. Take my umbrella."

"Your umbrella? Am I really worth it?" the captain said in an overly sweet tone.

"Anyone is worth an umbrella."

"With just one sentence, you've defined the minimum of human rights..."

But by now he was mumbling to himself. He was so shaken by what he'd just heard that he couldn't think straight. Yet, as soon as he stepped outside and opened the umbrella, his shallow, scheming mind latched

300

onto a new thought. If they were tricking him, then they were scared of him—and if they were scared, he didn't need to be.

"If they're lying to me, what are they hiding?" the thought gnawed at him. The idea that the marriage would be announced publicly seemed ridiculous. "Then again, with someone like him, anything is possible. He lives to make trouble. But what if he's scared? Maybe since that insult on Sunday, he's afraid like never before. Maybe that's why he's rushing to say he'll announce it himself—so I don't get the chance to do it first. Ah, don't mess this up, Lebyadkin! And why is he sneaking around at night if he really plans to make it public? If he's afraid, then he's afraid right now, for these next few days… Don't make a mistake, Lebyadkin!

"He tries to scare me with Pyotr Stepanovitch. Yes, I'm scared, scared out of my wits! That's the worst part. Why did I have to blab to Liputin? Who knows what these devils are plotting? I never understand any of it. They're stirring things up again, just like five years ago. Who could I even tell, really? 'Have I written to anyone in my foolishness?' Huh! So then, what if I did write something, as if by accident? Is that what he's hinting at? 'You're going to Petersburg on purpose.' Clever devil, reading my mind! It's like he's putting the idea in my head himself. He's playing one of two games: either he's scared because he's gotten himself into trouble, or he's not scared at all and just wants me to snitch on everyone. Ah, this is dangerous, Lebyadkin! You must not mess this up!"

He was so caught up in his thoughts that he forgot to listen at the door. Besides, it wasn't easy to hear anything—the door was thick, and the voices inside were low. He could only make out muffled sounds. Frustrated, he spit on the ground and wandered back outside to whistle idly on the steps.

Chapter 2.3

Marya Timofyevna's room was twice as large as the captain's and furnished in the same plain way. However, the table in front of the sofa was covered with a bright tablecloth, and a lamp burned on it. A handsome carpet lay on the floor. The bed was hidden by a green curtain that stretched across the room, and besides the sofa, there was a large, soft armchair near the table, though Marya Timofyevna never sat in it. In one corner, there was an ikon with a small lamp burning in front of it, just like in her old room. On the table, she had her usual things: a deck of cards, a small mirror, a songbook, and even a loaf of milk bread. There were also two books with colored pictures—one was a popular travel book for children, and the other was a collection of light, uplifting stories, mostly about knights and chivalry, meant for school or Christmas reading. She also had an album full of different photographs.

Of course, Marya Timofyevna had been expecting her visitor because the captain had told her about it. But when Nikolay Vsyevolodovitch entered the room, she was asleep, half-reclining on the sofa with her head resting on a wool cushion. He quietly shut the door behind him and stood still, watching her as she slept.

The captain had been exaggerating when he said she had been dressing herself up. She wore the same dark dress she had on Sunday at Varvara Petrovna's. Her hair was pinned in the same small knot at the back of her head, and her long, thin neck was left bare just as before. The black shawl Varvara Petrovna had given her was folded neatly on the sofa. Her face was still roughly powdered and rouged, just as before. Nikolay Vsyevolodovitch didn't stand there for long. Suddenly, as if sensing his gaze, she woke up. She opened her eyes, sat up quickly, and froze.

Something strange seemed to happen to him too: he stayed where he was, near the door, staring at her with a fixed, intense look. It was as if his expression was too grim or full of dislike, maybe even a cruel satisfaction at seeing her fear—unless that was something left over from her dreams. Her face began to twitch as if she were terrified. She raised her trembling hands and suddenly burst into tears, just like a scared child. It seemed like she was about to scream, but Nikolay Vsyevolodovitch snapped out of it. His face changed in an instant, and he smiled warmly and kindly as he walked toward the table.

"I'm sorry, Marya Timofyevna. I must have scared you by coming in so suddenly while you were asleep," he said, holding out his hand to her.

The sound of his soft, soothing voice calmed her. She stopped crying, though she still stared at him in confusion, as if trying to figure something out. Slowly, she held out her hand, still hesitant. Finally, a shy smile appeared on her lips.

"How do you do, prince?" she whispered, looking at him strangely.

"You must have had a bad dream," he said gently, his voice even warmer.

"But how do you know what I was dreaming about?" she said suddenly, trembling again. She pulled back, raising her hand as if to shield herself, ready to cry again.

"Calm down, that's enough. What are you afraid of? Don't you recognize me?" Nikolay Vsyevolodovitch said, trying to reassure her. But it took a long time to soothe her. She stared at him silently, her face full of confusion and pain, as if she were trying to understand something. Her eyes dropped, then she suddenly glanced at him again in a quick, sharp look. At last, though she was still uneasy, she seemed to make up her mind about something.

"Sit down here, next to me. I want to look at you properly later on," she said, speaking more firmly now, with a clear purpose. "But don't worry. I won't look at you yet. I'll keep my eyes down. You don't look at me either until I tell you to. Sit down," she added impatiently.

Something new was clearly taking hold of her.

Nikolay Vsyevolodovitch sat down and waited. A long silence followed.

"Hm, this all feels so strange to me," she said at last, almost as if she were annoyed. "Of course, I was upset by those bad dreams, but why did I dream about you looking like that?"

"Come on, let's forget about dreams," he said impatiently, turning toward her despite her instructions. Maybe for just a moment, that same cold expression returned to his eyes. He noticed that she wanted to look at him several times but stubbornly forced herself to keep her eyes down.

"Listen, prince," she said suddenly, louder now. "Listen, prince…"

"Why are you turning away? Why won't you look at me? What's the point of this act?" he said sharply, losing his patience.

But she seemed not to hear him.

"Listen, prince," she repeated, her voice resolute, with a strange, fussy expression. "When you told me in the carriage that our marriage was going to be made public, I was scared. I didn't want the mystery to end. Now I don't know. I've been thinking about it, and I realize I'm not cut out for that kind of life. I know how to dress, and maybe I could receive guests. There's not much to asking people to have tea, especially when you have footmen to help. But what will people say? I saw a lot that Sunday morning in that house. That pretty young lady stared at me the whole time, especially after you came in. It was you who came in, wasn't it?

"Her mother is just a silly, snobbish old woman. My Lebyadkin made a fool of himself too. I kept staring at the ceiling to keep from laughing. The ceiling there is beautifully painted. Her mother should be an abbess in a convent. She scares me, even though she gave me that black shawl. They must have come to some strange conclusions about me. I wasn't angry, but I kept thinking, 'What am I to them?' From a countess, you don't expect anything but spiritual qualities; for all the practical stuff, she has her footmen. And of course, a little flirtation helps with foreign visitors. But even so, that Sunday, they thought I was hopeless. Only Dasha is an angel. I'm so afraid they'll say something that will hurt him— something careless about me."

"Don't be scared, and don't worry," said Nikolay Vsyevolodovitch, making a slight grimace.

"Well, it doesn't really matter to me if he's a little ashamed of me. People pity more than they feel shame, although it depends on the person, of course. But he knows that I should be pitying them, not the other way around."

"You seem pretty upset with them, Marya Timofyevna."

"Me? Oh no," she said with a simple, cheerful smile. "Not at all. I watched all of you that day. You were all so angry, all fighting with each other. They meet together, but they don't know how to laugh from their hearts. So much wealth, but no joy at all. It disgusts me. Though, really, I don't care about anyone now except myself."

"I heard that you've had a hard time with your brother since I left."

"Who told you that? That's nonsense. Things are much worse now. Now my dreams are no good—bad dreams, ever since you showed up. Why did you come? What do you want?"

"Would you like to go back to the convent?"

"I knew it! I knew someone would suggest the convent again. What kind of miracle is that supposed to be? Why should I go there? What for? I'm alone now. It's too late for me to start over again—another new life."

"You seem angry about something. Are you afraid I don't love you anymore?"

"I'm not worried about you at all. I'm more afraid that I might stop loving someone else."

She laughed bitterly.

"I must have done something terrible to him," she said suddenly, as if talking to herself. "But I don't know what it is. That's what bothers me the most. Always, always, for the past five years, I've been scared day and night that I hurt him somehow. I prayed and prayed, always thinking about what I did wrong. And now it turns out it was true."

"What turned out?"

"I'm only afraid there's something wrong with him, too," she went on, ignoring his question like she hadn't even heard it. "And besides, he wouldn't be able to live with such awful people. The countess wanted to eat me alive, even though she made me sit next to her in the carriage. They're all in on it together. Could he have betrayed me?" (Her chin and lips started to tremble.) "Tell me, have you read about Grishka Otrepyev, how he was cursed in seven cathedrals?"

Nikolay Vsyevolodovitch didn't say anything.

"But now I'll turn around and look at you," she said suddenly, as if deciding something. "You look at me too—but carefully. I want to make sure one last time."

"I've been looking at you for a long time."

305

"Hm," said Marya Timofyevna, staring at him closely. "You've gotten much fatter."

She seemed about to say something else, but suddenly, for the third time, the same terrified look crossed her face. She shrank back, raising her hand as though to protect herself.

"What's wrong with you?" Nikolay Vsyevolodovitch said angrily.

But the fear passed almost instantly. Her face twitched into a strange, suspicious smile.

"Please, prince, get up and come in," she said firmly.

"Come in? Come in where?"

"I've been imagining for five years how you would come in," she said. "Get up, go out the door, and come back into the room. I'll sit here like I'm not expecting anything, and I'll pick up a book. Then suddenly, you'll come in after traveling for five years. I want to see what it'll be like."

Nikolay Vsyevolodovitch clenched his teeth and muttered something under his breath.

"Enough of this," he said, slapping the table with his hand. "Listen to me, Marya Timofyevna. Pay attention—focus if you can. You're not completely mad, you know!" he added impatiently. "Tomorrow I'm going to announce our marriage to everyone. You'll never live in a palace, so get that idea out of your head. Would you like to live with me for the rest of your life, far away from here? There's a place in the mountains in Switzerland. Don't be afraid—I'll never leave you, and I won't send you to an asylum. I'll have enough money for us to live on without anyone's help. You'll have a servant, and you won't have to work at all. You can pray, go wherever you like, do whatever you want. I won't bother you. I'll stay in the same place with you, and if you want, I won't speak to you for the rest of our lives. Or if you prefer, you can tell me your stories every evening, just like you used to in Petersburg. I'll even read to you if you want. But we'll stay there for the rest of our lives, in one place, and it's a gloomy place. Will you do it? Are you ready? You won't regret it later and torment me with tears and complaints, will you?"

She listened carefully and thought for a long time before speaking.

"It all sounds so strange to me," she said finally, her tone mocking and doubtful. "I might end up living forty years in those mountains," she laughed.

"So what? Then we'll live forty years," said Nikolay Vsyevolodovitch, scowling.

"Hm! I won't go for anything."

"Not even with me?"

"And what are you that I should go with you? I'm supposed to sit on a mountain next to you for forty years? What kind of nonsense is that? Honestly, how patient people have become these days! No, it can't be. A falcon doesn't turn into an owl. My prince isn't like that!" she said proudly, holding her head high, almost triumphantly.

Light seemed to dawn on him.

"Why do you call me a prince? And who do you think I am?" he asked quickly.

"Wait, aren't you the prince?"

"I never was a prince."

"So you're telling me, right to my face, that you're not the prince?"

"I'm telling you I never have been."

"Dear God!" she cried, clasping her hands. "I was prepared for anything from his enemies, but this kind of insolence? Never! Is he alive?" she suddenly screamed, wild with anger, turning on Nikolay Vsyevolodovitch. "Did you kill him? Tell me the truth!"

"Who do you think I am?" he shouted, jumping up from his chair with a twisted expression, but now it was impossible to scare her. She looked victorious.

"Who knows who you really are, or where you came from? My heart knew something was wrong—five years of doubt, and all these dirty schemes. And here I was, sitting here, wondering what kind of blind fool was trying to trick me! No, my friend, you're a terrible actor—worse than Lebyadkin! Give my regards to that countess of yours and tell her to send someone better next time. Did she hire you? Did she give you a job in her kitchen out of pity? I see through all of you. I understand every single one of you."

He grabbed her firmly by the arm, but she just laughed in his face.

"You look like him, I'll give you that. Maybe you're a relative. You're all such sneaky people! But mine—he's a bright falcon, a real prince, and you're just an owl, a shopkeeper! My falcon bows to God if he wants to, and he doesn't if he doesn't. And Shatushka—my sweet, my darling—slapped you across the face. That's what Lebyadkin told me. What were you so scared of when you came in here? Who frightened you then? When I fell down and you picked me up, and I saw your ugly face—it was like a worm crawling into my chest. I knew then: it wasn't him, not my falcon! My falcon would never be ashamed of me in front of some fancy young lady. Oh, my God! These five years, I lived with the thought that he was out there somewhere, beyond the mountains, soaring high, looking at the sun. Tell me, you fraud, how much did they pay you? Did they need to bribe you a lot? I wouldn't have given you a penny! Ha ha ha! Ha ha!"

"Ugh, you idiot!" snarled Nikolay Vsyevolodovitch, still holding her tightly by the arm.

"Go away, you imposter!" she shouted, her voice suddenly firm and commanding. "I'm the wife of my prince, and I'm not afraid of your knife!"

"Knife?"

"Yes, a knife! You've got a knife in your pocket. You thought I was asleep, but I saw you. When you came in, you pulled out your knife!"

"What are you talking about? What kind of dreams are in your head?" he exclaimed, shoving her away hard. Her head and shoulders hit the sofa painfully. He turned to leave, but she leaped up after him, limping and stumbling. Even though Lebyadkin grabbed her, panicked and trying to hold her back, she managed to shout after him into the darkness, shrieking and laughing:

"A curse on you, Grishka Otrepyev!"

Chapter 2.4

"A knife, a knife," he muttered angrily as he walked quickly through the mud and puddles, not bothering to watch his step. At moments, he felt a sudden urge to laugh loudly, almost wildly, but he held himself back for some reason. He didn't recover from his anger until he reached the bridge where Fedka had met him earlier that evening. The tramp was waiting there again. When he saw Nikolay Vsyevolodovitch, he took off his cap, grinned cheerfully, and started talking quickly and happily about something.

At first, Nikolay Vsyevolodovitch ignored him completely and kept walking without stopping. He didn't even listen. Then it suddenly struck him that he had completely forgotten about Fedka. He had forgotten him even while he'd been repeating, "A knife, a knife." In a sudden burst of rage, he grabbed the tramp by the collar and violently shoved him against the bridge railing. For a second, Fedka thought of fighting back, but he quickly realized he was no match for this man who had caught him by surprise. Instead, he crouched down, his arms pinned behind him, and calmly waited for whatever would happen next. He didn't look afraid, and, as it turned out, he had no reason to be.

Nikolay Vsyevolodovitch took off his thick scarf with his left hand, clearly intending to tie up the man's arms, but then, for some reason, he suddenly stopped. He pushed the tramp away instead. Fedka jumped to his feet at once and, in one quick motion, a short, broad knife gleamed in his hand.

"Put that knife away—now!" Nikolay Vsyevolodovitch ordered sharply, waving a hand impatiently. The knife disappeared as quickly as it had appeared.

Without another word or a glance back, Nikolay Vsyevolodovitch kept walking. Fedka didn't leave him this time, though. He followed behind, quietly now, keeping a respectful step away.

They crossed the bridge and turned left, onto a long, empty backstreet that led to the center of town more directly than going through Bogoyavlensky Street.

"Is it true, what people say—that you robbed a church recently?" Nikolay Vsyevolodovitch asked suddenly.

"I went in to pray first," Fedka answered, speaking calmly and respectfully, as though nothing unusual had just happened. He spoke almost with dignity, like a man who had been wronged but was willing to forgive. "But when the Lord led me there," he continued, "I couldn't help but notice the place was full of treasures. It was because of my situation, sir—sometimes a man in my condition needs a little help. But God punished me for it. I got almost nothing for my trouble. Twelve roubles in all, after selling the censer and the deacon's belt. They said the silver chin of Saint Nikolay was just plated, so it went for nothing."

"And you killed the watchman?"

"Well, we cleared out the church together, the watchman and I. But later, by the river the next morning, we fought about who would carry the sack. I admit I made things easier for him."

"So you can just rob and kill again?"

"That's what Pyotr Stepanovitch keeps telling me—he says the same thing, word for word. But he's a hard man, mean, and he doesn't believe in God or anything beyond this world. He thinks everything is just nature, even the animals. He doesn't understand that people like me sometimes need a little help to survive. You can't make it in our kind of life alone."

Fedka paused and then added, "Would you believe it, sir? Back when Captain Lebyadkin lived at Filipov's—before you came—his door was always left wide open at night. He'd be dead drunk, money falling out of his pockets all over the floor. I saw it with my own eyes, sir. But I didn't take it then. Sometimes you have to wait for the right opportunity...."

"So you went into his room at night?"

"Maybe I did, but no one ever knew about it."

"Why didn't you kill him?"

"Well, I thought it through. If I can always get one hundred and fifty roubles whenever I want, why should I settle for that when I could get fifteen hundred by waiting for the right moment? I'll tell you something, sir—when he's drunk, Captain Lebyadkin talks about you everywhere. In every tavern, he brags about his hopes for you. So, hearing this over and over, I started to put my hopes on you too, sir. I'm speaking to you like a brother here, like my own father. Pyotr Stepanovitch doesn't know any of this, and I wouldn't tell another soul. So, won't you spare me three roubles, sir? Set my mind at ease, tell me the truth, because we can't live without a little help."

Nikolay Vsyevolodovitch burst out laughing. He pulled out his wallet, which had about fifty roubles in small notes. First, he threw out one note, then a second, then a third, and finally a fourth. Fedka lunged to catch them in the air as they fell, yelling, "Ech! Ech!" The notes dropped into the mud, and he scrambled to pick them up. Nikolay Vsyevolodovitch didn't stop there; he suddenly flung the entire bundle of money at him and, still laughing, walked off down the street alone.

Fedka fell to his knees in the mud, scrambling to find the notes as they were blown around by the wind and soaked in puddles. For an hour, his cries of "Ech! Ech!" echoed in the darkness as he searched frantically.

Chapter 3
The Duel

Chapter 3.1

The next day, at two o'clock in the afternoon, the duel took place as planned. Things moved quickly because of Gaganov's stubborn determination to fight no matter what. He couldn't understand Stavrogin's behavior and was furious. For a whole month, he had insulted him openly and gotten no reaction, which made him angrier. Gaganov wanted Stavrogin to challenge him to a duel since he had no clear reason to challenge Stavrogin himself. The truth was, Gaganov's deep hatred for Stavrogin came from an old insult to his family four years earlier. But for some reason, he was embarrassed to admit this and thought it wasn't a strong enough reason for a duel, especially since Stavrogin had already offered him two sincere apologies. Gaganov convinced himself that Stavrogin was a coward and couldn't understand why he hadn't fought back after Shatov struck him.

Finally, Gaganov wrote an extremely rude letter to Stavrogin, which pushed him to propose the duel. After sending the letter the day before, Gaganov waited anxiously for Stavrogin's reply. He spent hours going back and forth between hope and doubt, preparing for whatever might happen. He asked Mavriky Nikolaevitch Drozdov, an old school friend whom he respected, to act as his second. When Kirillov arrived the next morning at nine o'clock with the challenge, Gaganov was already prepared.

Stavrogin's generous apologies and unusual willingness to settle things peacefully were rejected immediately. Gaganov refused to hear them and was so angry he could hardly sit still. Mavriky Nikolaevitch, who had only learned about the situation the night before, was shocked by Stavrogin's efforts to make peace. He considered urging reconciliation but decided against it when he saw Gaganov shaking in his chair at the mere thought of giving in. Mavriky stayed only because he felt he should support his old friend during the duel.

Kirillov repeated the challenge. Stavrogin's proposed rules for the duel were accepted without argument, except for one harsh addition: if the first shots failed to decide the outcome, they would fire a second time. If that also failed, there would be a third round. Kirillov frowned and objected to the idea of a third round but, seeing no other option, agreed on the condition that three rounds would be the absolute limit. A fourth was out of the question, and this was accepted.

The duel was set for two o'clock in the afternoon at Brykov, a small wooded area on the outskirts of town between Skvoreshniki and the Shpigulin factory. The rain from the night before had stopped, but the air was damp, gray, and windy. Dark, ragged clouds moved quickly across the cold sky. The tops of the trees creaked and groaned in the wind, making a low, mournful sound. It was a gloomy morning.

Mavriky Nikolaevitch and Gaganov arrived first in a smart char-à-banc pulled by a pair of horses. A groom accompanied them. Shortly after, Nikolay Vsyevolodovitch and Kirillov arrived on horseback, followed by a mounted servant. Kirillov, who had never ridden a horse before, sat upright and firm in the saddle, gripping a heavy box of pistols in his right hand. He refused to let the servant carry it. Because he was inexperienced, he kept pulling the reins with his left hand, causing the horse to toss its head and threaten to rear. Kirillov, however, seemed unbothered by this.

Gaganov, who was already suspicious of everything, took their arrival on horseback as another insult. To him, it showed that they were so confident they didn't even think they might need a carriage in case they were wounded. He climbed out of the char-à-banc, his face pale with anger, and whispered to Mavriky Nikolaevitch that his hands were shaking. When Nikolay Vsyevolodovitch bowed politely to him, Gaganov turned away without responding.

The seconds cast lots to decide which pair of pistols would be used. Kirillov's pistols were chosen. The ground was measured, and the barrier was marked out. The carriages and horses were moved back three hundred paces. The weapons were loaded and handed to the duelists.

I must apologize for telling this part of the story so quickly and without much detail. But I can't help making a few comments. Mavriky Nikolaevitch was quiet and distracted, lost in thought. Kirillov, on the other hand, was perfectly calm. He carried out his duties carefully and precisely, without showing the slightest sign of nervousness or curiosity about the duel's outcome. Nikolay Vsyevolodovitch was paler than usual. He wore a light overcoat and a white beaver hat. He looked tired, frowned occasionally, and didn't bother to hide his bad mood.

However, the most interesting person in that moment was Gaganov. It's impossible not to say something about him.

Chapter 3.2

I haven't yet described what Gaganov looked like. He was a tall man, thirty-three years old, and rather well-fed—some would even say fat. He had straight, light-colored hair, and his features were what most people would call handsome. He had retired from the military as a colonel, but if he had stayed and risen to the rank of general, he probably would have looked even more impressive and might have become an excellent combat leader.

It's worth mentioning that the main reason he left the army was the lingering shame and disgrace he felt over an insult Nikolay Stavrogin had delivered to his father at a club four years ago. Gaganov believed it was dishonorable to remain in the military after such an event and convinced himself that his mere presence brought shame to his regiment and fellow officers, even though none of them knew about it.

Interestingly, Gaganov had already considered leaving the army years before the insult to his father, but for a very different reason. When the serfs were emancipated on February 19th, he had taken it as a personal insult. This made little sense because Gaganov was one of the wealthiest landowners in the region, and he lost almost nothing financially. He was even intelligent enough to understand the moral value and economic benefits of the reform. But his reaction was emotional, not logical, and because it was unconscious, it felt even stronger.

He held off on resigning until after his father's death. By then, Gaganov had gained a reputation among high-ranking circles in St. Petersburg for his "gentlemanly" values and his desire to maintain connections with people of influence. He was a very private, self-contained man, and he belonged to a strange group of Russian nobles who took their ancient lineage very seriously. They were obsessed with their "pure blood" and the honor of their family name. At the same time, Gaganov couldn't stand Russian history and despised many Russian traditions, which he found crude and uncivilized.

Even as a child in his elite military school—a school reserved for the sons of the wealthiest and most distinguished families—Gaganov had been a dreamer. He loved the romance of castles, knights, and chivalry. He was deeply ashamed of the old days when Russian tsars were allowed to beat noble boyars with their own hands. This stiff, severe man, who was very knowledgeable about military science and had always done his duty perfectly, had always had a poetic side.

Some people said Gaganov was a good public speaker, that he could make powerful speeches at meetings, but the truth was that in all his thirty-three years, he had never spoken publicly. Even in the social circles of St. Petersburg, where he had recently spent time, he acted with extreme pride and arrogance.

When Gaganov first met Nikolay Stavrogin in St. Petersburg—just after Stavrogin had returned from abroad—it nearly drove him mad with rage. Now, as he stood at the barrier, waiting for the duel to begin, he was extremely tense. He kept imagining that something would go wrong and that the duel wouldn't happen. Any small delay made him tremble. His face showed the torment he was feeling when Kirillov, instead of immediately giving the signal to fire, started speaking instead.

"Just for the sake of formalities," Kirillov said loudly, "now that the pistols are in your hands and I must give the signal, I'll ask you one last time: will you not be reconciled? It's my duty as a second to ask."

As if to irritate Gaganov even more, Mavriky Nikolaevitch, who had been silent until now, suddenly jumped in. He had spent the entire day blaming himself for agreeing to be part of the duel.

"I agree with Mr. Kirillov," Mavriky said with obvious emotion. "This idea that reconciliation is impossible once you're standing at the barrier—that's just a silly tradition. It's only suitable for the French! Besides," he added nervously, "I don't even see what the offense is here. I've wanted to say this for a long time… since every apology has already been offered, hasn't it?"

His face turned red. He rarely spoke so much, let alone with so much feeling.

"I repeat my offer to apologize as much as possible," Nikolay Stavrogin said quickly.

"This is impossible!" Gaganov shouted, furious. He turned to Mavriky Nikolaevitch, his face livid, and stomped his foot in rage. "Explain to him!" He pointed his pistol at Stavrogin. "If you're my second and not my enemy, Mavriky Nikolaevitch, tell him that these so-called apologies only make the insult worse! He's acting as if being insulted by me is beneath him. He thinks it's no disgrace to walk away from me at the barrier! What do you think of that? What does he take me for?"

He stomped his foot again, foam gathering at the corners of his mouth.

"You're just making me angrier so I'll miss on purpose!" he shouted at Mavriky Nikolaevitch.

"Negotiations are over! Listen to the signal!" Kirillov shouted, raising his voice. "One! Two! Three!"

At the count of three, both men raised their pistols and aimed. Gaganov immediately fired on the fifth or sixth step. He froze for a moment and, realizing that he had missed, walked forward to the barrier. Nikolay Stavrogin also walked forward. He raised his pistol but held it unusually high and fired almost carelessly, barely aiming.

After he fired, Stavrogin pulled out a handkerchief and wrapped it around the little finger of his right hand. It was then that everyone saw Gaganov hadn't missed him completely after all. The bullet had grazed the flesh of Stavrogin's finger, leaving a small scratch, but it hadn't touched the bone.

Kirillov immediately announced that the duel would continue unless both sides were satisfied.

"I swear," Gaganov said hoarsely, his throat dry, as he turned to Mavriky Nikolaevitch, "that this man"—he pointed again at Stavrogin—"shot into the air on purpose... deliberately. That's an insult too. He's trying to make the duel pointless!"

"I have the right to shoot how I want as long as I follow the rules," Nikolay Stavrogin said firmly.

"No, he doesn't! Explain it to him! Tell him!" Gaganov yelled.

"I completely agree with Nikolay Vsyevolodovitch," Kirillov said calmly.

"Why is he sparing me?" Gaganov shouted, unable to hear anyone. "I despise his mercy... I spit on it... I..."

"I swear I didn't mean to insult you," Nikolay said impatiently. "I shot high because I don't want to kill anyone—not you or anyone else. It's not about you personally. It's true that I don't feel insulted, and I'm sorry that bothers you. But I won't let anyone take away my rights."

"If he's so scared of bloodshed, then why did he challenge me?"

Gaganov screamed, still speaking to Mavriky Nikolaevitch.

"How could he not challenge you?" Kirillov cut in. "You refused to listen to reason. How else could he get rid of you?"

"I'll say just one thing," Mavriky Nikolaevitch added, clearly struggling to find his words. "If someone says ahead of time that they're going to shoot into the air, then the duel can't continue... for obvious and... well, delicate reasons."

"I never said I would fire into the air every time," Stavrogin interrupted sharply, his patience running out. "You don't know what's in my mind or what I'll do next. I haven't broken the rules of the duel."

"In that case, the duel can continue," Mavriky Nikolaevitch said to Gaganov.

"Gentlemen, take your places," Kirillov ordered.

They faced off again. Gaganov fired and missed once more, while Stavrogin shot high into the air again. This time, it looked less obvious that he'd missed on purpose. He didn't aim at the sky or the trees, but shot a little above Gaganov's head, almost as though he had aimed at him. The second shot was lower than the first, making it look even less deliberate. Gaganov was beyond reason now—nothing would convince him otherwise.

"Again!" Gaganov muttered through clenched teeth. "It doesn't matter! I've been challenged, and I'll use my right to fire a third time, no matter what happens."

"You have every right," Kirillov said quickly. Mavriky Nikolaevitch said nothing.

The two men took their places for the third time, and the signal was given. Gaganov walked right up to the barrier and, standing just twelve paces away, started aiming. His hand was shaking too much for him to aim well. Stavrogin, however, stood still with his pistol lowered, waiting calmly for Gaganov to fire.

"You're taking too long! Fire! Fire!" Kirillov shouted impatiently.

Finally, the shot rang out. This time, Stavrogin's white hat flew off.

317

Gaganov's aim had been close—too close. The bullet pierced the crown of the hat just a fraction of an inch from his head. If it had been a little lower, the duel would have ended very differently.

Kirillov picked up the hat and handed it back to Nikolay.

"Fire! Don't keep your opponent waiting!" Mavriky Nikolaevitch said nervously, seeing that Stavrogin wasn't firing but was instead looking at the hole in his hat with Kirillov.

Stavrogin flinched, as though realizing he had forgotten something. He looked briefly at Gaganov, then turned away and fired his shot carelessly into the nearby trees, ignoring all the formalities of the duel.

The duel was over. Gaganov stood frozen, as though in shock. Mavriky Nikolaevitch walked over to him and began speaking, but Gaganov didn't seem to hear or understand anything.

Kirillov removed his hat, nodded to Mavriky Nikolaevitch, and walked away. Stavrogin, however, didn't bother with such politeness this time. After firing into the woods, he didn't even glance toward the barrier. He handed his pistol back to Kirillov and walked quickly to the horses, his face cold and angry. He said nothing.

Kirillov didn't speak either. They mounted their horses and galloped away.

Chapter 3.3

"Why aren't you saying anything?" Stavrogin called impatiently to Kirillov as they neared home.

"What do you want?" Kirillov replied, nearly sliding off his horse as it reared up.

Stavrogin controlled his irritation.

"I didn't mean to insult that... idiot, and yet I've done it again," he said quietly.

"Yes, you insulted him again," Kirillov said curtly, "and besides, he's not an idiot."

"I've done everything I could, haven't I?"

"No."

"What was I supposed to do then?"

"You shouldn't have challenged him."

"Take another slap in the face?"

"Yes, take another one."

"I don't understand anything anymore," Stavrogin said angrily. "Why does everyone expect things from me that they wouldn't expect from anyone else? Why am I supposed to endure what no one else would, and carry burdens that no one else can bear?"

"I thought you were looking for a burden."

"I'm looking for a burden?"

"Yes."

"You've... noticed that?"

"Yes."

"It's that obvious?"

"Yes."

They rode in silence for a moment. Stavrogin looked deep in thought, his face troubled. He seemed almost shaken.

"I didn't aim because I didn't want to kill him. That's all it was, I swear," he said quickly, sounding almost defensive.

"You shouldn't have insulted him."

"What else was I supposed to do?"

"You should have killed him."

"Are you upset that I didn't kill him?"

"I'm not upset about anything. I just thought you were going to kill him. You don't know what you're looking for."

"I'm looking for a burden," Stavrogin said with a bitter laugh.

"If you didn't want blood, why did you give him the chance to kill you?"

"If I hadn't challenged him, he would have killed me anyway—without a duel."

"That's not your concern. Maybe he wouldn't have killed you."

"So he would've just beaten me?"

"That's not your business. Carry your burden. Otherwise, there's no value in it."

"Forget your 'value.' I'm not looking for anyone's approval."

"I thought you were," Kirillov said calmly, without a trace of emotion.

They rode into the courtyard of the house.

"Do you want to come inside?" Stavrogin asked.

"No, I'm going home. Goodbye."

Kirillov got off his horse and tucked the box of pistols under his arm.

"You're not mad at me, are you?" Stavrogin said, holding out his hand.

"Not at all," Kirillov replied, turning around to shake his hand. "If my burden is light, it's because that's my nature. Maybe your burden is heavier because that's yours. There's no need to be too ashamed—just a little."

"I know I'm no good, and I don't claim to be strong," Stavrogin said.

"Better not claim it, because you're not. Come have some tea."

Nikolay Stavrogin went into the house, deeply troubled.

Chapter 3.4

The moment Alexey Yegorytch entered, he told Nikolay Vsyevolodovitch that Varvara Petrovna was happy to hear he had gone out for a ride—his first time leaving the house after being sick for eight days. She had ordered the carriage and gone for a drive on her own, "like she used to in the past, since she had forgotten what fresh air felt like."

"Alone, or with Darya Pavlovna?" Nikolay Vsyevolodovitch

interrupted sharply. He frowned when Alexey replied that Darya Pavlovna "had stayed in her room, saying she wasn't feeling well."

"Listen to me," he said suddenly, as though making up his mind. "Keep an eye on her today. If you see her trying to come see me, stop her. Tell her I can't see her for a few days, at least. Tell her it's my decision, and I'll let her know when I'm ready. Do you understand?"

"I'll tell her, sir," Alexey said with a worried tone, lowering his eyes.

"But only if she comes on her own."

"Don't worry, sir. I won't make a mistake. All your meetings have always gone through me. You've trusted me for help before."

"I know. But only if she comes by herself. Now bring me some tea right away."

The old man had barely left when the door suddenly opened again. Darya Pavlovna stood in the doorway. Her face was pale, but her eyes were calm.

"Where did you come from?" Stavrogin asked in surprise.

"I was waiting for him to leave so I could come in," she said. "I heard the instructions you gave him. When he walked out, I hid around the corner so he wouldn't see me."

"I've been meaning to break things off with you, Dasha... for now... for a while. I couldn't see you last night, even after your note. I wanted to write to you myself, but I don't know how to put it into words," he added with frustration, almost disgust.

"I thought we should stop seeing each other too. Varvara Petrovna is too suspicious of us."

"Let her be suspicious."

"She doesn't need the worry. So now we'll part until the end."

"You're still waiting for that 'end'?"

"Yes, I'm sure it will come."

"But nothing in the world ever truly ends."

"This will end. Then call for me. I'll come. Now, goodbye."

"And what kind of end will it be?" Stavrogin asked with a faint smile.

"You weren't hurt, and… you didn't spill blood?" she asked, avoiding his question.

"It was stupid. I didn't kill anyone. Don't worry. You'll hear all about it soon enough. I'm not feeling well."

"I'm going. The marriage won't be announced today?" she asked hesitantly.

"It won't be today, and it won't be tomorrow. I don't know about the day after that. Maybe we'll all be dead by then, and that might be better. Now leave me alone, please."

"You're not going to ruin that other poor girl, are you?"

"I'm not going to ruin either of those crazy women. It's the sane people I seem to ruin. I'm so vile, Dasha, that I might really call for you at the 'end,' as you say. And despite how sane you are, you'll still come. Why do you insist on destroying yourself?"

"I know that in the end, I'll be the only one left for you… and I'm waiting for that."

"And what if I don't call for you after all? What if I run away instead?"

"You won't. You will call for me."

"There's a lot of contempt for me in that."

"You know there's more than just contempt."

"So, there is contempt, then?"

"I chose the wrong word. God knows, I wish with all my heart that you'll never need me."

"One phrase is as good as another. I wish I hadn't ruined you."

"You could never ruin me, and you know that better than anyone."

Pavlovna spoke quickly and firmly. "If I don't come to you, I'll become a nurse, a sister of mercy. I'll care for the sick or sell the gospel on the streets. I've decided that. I can't be anyone's wife. I can't live in a house like this either. That's not the life I want... You already know that."

"No, I never really understood what you want," he replied. "It seems like you're interested in me the way some old nurses get attached to one patient more than the others. Or maybe like those pious old women who go to funerals and think one corpse is more interesting than the others. Why are you looking at me so strangely?"

"Are you very ill?" she asked softly, looking at him in a peculiar way. "My God! And you think you can live without me?"

"Listen, Dasha, I keep seeing phantoms now. Yesterday on the bridge, some devil came to me and offered to murder Lebyadkin and Marya Timofyevna, to solve this marriage problem and cover everything up. He wanted me to pay him three roubles up front but hinted the whole thing wouldn't cost less than fifteen hundred. Can you imagine? What a calculating little devil! Like a shopkeeper. Ha ha!"

"But you're sure it was just a hallucination?"

"Oh no, not a hallucination at all! It was Fedka the convict, the robber who escaped from prison. But that's not the point. Do you know what I did? I gave him everything I had, all the money in my purse, and now he thinks I've already paid him the advance!"

"You met him at night, and he suggested that? Don't you see that you're being trapped, surrounded on all sides?"

"Well, let them trap me. But I can tell you have a question on the tip of your tongue. I can see it in your eyes," he added with a resentful and irritated smile.

Dasha looked frightened. "I don't have any question, and I don't doubt anything! Just stop talking!" she cried desperately, as if trying to push his words away.

"Then you're sure I won't go to Fedka's little shop?"

"Oh, God!" she said, clasping her hands. "Why are you tormenting me like this?"

"Forgive me for that stupid joke. I'm picking up bad habits from them.

323

You know, since last night, I've felt like laughing—nonstop, forever. It's like I need to burst out laughing. It's like a sickness... Oh, my mother's here. I can always tell by the sound of the carriage stopping outside."

Dasha grabbed his hand. "God save you from your demon, and... call me, call me quickly!"

"Oh, it's not much of a demon. It's just a pathetic little imp, sick and sniffling, one of the failures," he said with a twisted smile. "But you still have something you're afraid to say, don't you, Dasha?"

She looked at him with pain and sorrow in her eyes, then turned toward the door.

"Wait," he called after her with a bitter, mocking smile. "If... yes, if... just imagine, even if I did go to that little shop and did something terrible... and I called for you after that—would you still come?"

She walked out without answering, covering her face with her hands.

"She'll still come, even after the shop," he whispered to himself, thinking for a moment. A look of scorn and bitterness crossed his face. "A nurse! Hmm... maybe that's exactly what I need."

Chapter 4
All In Expectation

Chapter 4.1

The news of the duel spread quickly through town and caused quite a stir. What stood out the most was how suddenly everyone began to defend Nikolay Vsyevolodovitch. Even his former enemies started calling themselves his friends. This sudden change of heart came largely because of one person who hadn't spoken about the matter before but now said a few words that caught everyone's attention.

This happened the day after the duel. The whole town had gathered at the Marshal of Nobility's house to celebrate his wife's name day. Yulia Mihailovna was there, of course, and she seemed to be in charge of the evening. She was accompanied by Lizaveta Nikolaevna, who looked stunning and unusually cheerful. Many of the ladies noticed this right away and found it suspicious, considering the timing. By this point, Lizaveta's engagement to Mavriky Nikolaevitch was already well-known. When a retired general, who was quite an important figure, jokingly asked her about it, Lizaveta replied openly that she was indeed engaged. But oddly enough, not a single one of the ladies believed her. Instead, they insisted there must be some secret romance, some family drama, or something mysterious that had happened in Switzerland. For some reason, they also suspected that Yulia Mihailovna had something to do with it.

The moment Yulia entered the room, everyone turned to look at her, their eyes full of curiosity and expectation. People were eager to talk about the duel but were cautious since the situation was still fresh, and it wasn't clear yet what the authorities might say about it. Neither of the men involved had been questioned by the police, as far as anyone knew. Gaganov had already left for his home early that morning without any trouble.

Still, people were desperate for someone to break the silence and bring up the duel out loud. Everyone looked toward the general mentioned earlier, a landowner who wasn't very wealthy but had a strong presence in the community. He was known for being outspoken and for loudly saying what others were whispering quietly. It was almost his role at events like this. He had a particular way of speaking—slow and deliberate, with a smooth, drawn-out tone—something he had probably picked up from the wealthy landowners of the past who had been hit hardest by the emancipation of the serfs. It was often said that the more ruined a landowner was, the more delicately he spoke.

This general was a distant relative of Gaganov, though they didn't get along and were even fighting a court case against each other. Years ago, the general had fought two duels himself and had even been demoted and sent to the Caucasus for one of them. That gave his opinion extra weight in matters like this.

Somebody brought up the fact that Varvara Petrovna had finally gone out for a carriage ride after being indoors "sick" for several days. However, the real topic of conversation wasn't her health but the beautiful four grey horses she had driven, which came from the Stavrogins' own stables. At that moment, the general announced that he had seen "young Stavrogin" earlier that day riding on horseback.

The room immediately fell silent. The general smacked his lips, played with the golden snuff-box in his hands, and finally spoke. "It's a pity I wasn't here a few years ago," he began, dragging out his words. "At the time, I was at Carlsbad. I remember hearing a lot of rumors about that young man back then. Someone even told me he had lost his mind. Another said he had been insulted by some student in front of his cousins and crawled under the table to get away. And yesterday, I hear from Stepan Vysotsky that he fought a duel with Gaganov—just to let the poor man shoot at him and get it over with. Hm! Quite like the officers in the guards back in the 1820s. Tell me, does he visit anyone's house here?"

The general paused, clearly waiting for an answer. His words had opened the door for the conversation everyone was dying to have.

"What's so surprising about it?" said Yulia Mihailovna, raising her voice sharply. She was irritated because everyone had turned to stare at her as if on command. "Is it really so strange that Stavrogin fought Gaganov but ignored the student? He couldn't challenge someone who used to be his serf!"

The remark was simple and clear, yet no one had thought of it before. It changed everything. All the gossip, rumors, and idle chatter faded into the background. People suddenly saw the event in a new light, and a new side of Stavrogin's character was revealed—one that was almost noble in its severity. Insulted by a student, a man no longer a serf, he had ignored the offense because his attacker had once been his serf. Society had criticized him, looked down on him, mocked him for being slapped in the face. But Stavrogin had shown he didn't care about a public opinion that failed to live up to higher ideals, even while it endlessly talked about them.

"And here we are, Ivan Alexandrovitch, sitting around discussing the proper standards," an older club member said warmly to his friend, almost with a hint of guilt.

"Yes, Pyotr Mihailovitch, that's exactly it!" the other replied with enthusiasm. "And then people talk about the younger generation!"

"It's not about the younger generation," a third man chimed in thoughtfully. "No, it has nothing to do with them. Stavrogin is a star, not one of those younger men. That's how you need to see it."

"And that's exactly what we need—men like him. They're rare," another added.

The key point, of course, was that this "new man" wasn't just a nobleman; he was also the wealthiest landowner in the province. That meant he could be a leader and someone who could help others. The landowners, who had been uncertain before, suddenly grew enthusiastic.

"He didn't just ignore the student's attack. He put his hands behind his back, remember that, your excellency," someone pointed out.

"And he didn't drag the student to court either," another added.

"Even though he could have gotten fifteen roubles in damages for being insulted as a nobleman! Ha ha ha!"

"No, I'll tell you the truth about these new courts," a third person suddenly shouted in excitement. "If someone's caught stealing or cheating, all they have to do is rush home, kill their own mother, and—boom!— they'll be found innocent! Ladies will even wave their handkerchiefs for them from the courtroom!"

"It's true! It's absolutely true!" another voice chimed in.

Then the stories began to flow. People started talking about Stavrogin's connection with Count K., a man well known for his stern independence and his strong stance on reforms, even if his influence had faded a bit in recent years. Suddenly, everyone was convinced that Nikolay Vsyevolodovitch was engaged to one of the count's daughters, though no one had any real evidence for this. As for the rumors about Lizaveta Nikolaevna and her supposed adventures in Switzerland, even the ladies stopped talking about it. The Drozdovs, meanwhile, had finally managed to pay all the visits they had missed when they first arrived in town.

Now, everyone agreed that Lizaveta Nikolaevna was just an ordinary girl, a little overly sensitive perhaps, but nothing more. Her fainting spell on the day Stavrogin arrived was blamed on the shock of the student's outrageous behavior. People even went out of their way to strip the situation of any romantic mystery they had tried to attach to it before. As for the lame woman who had been the center of so much gossip earlier, she was completely forgotten. No one wanted to mention her anymore.

"And even if there had been a hundred lame girls—well, we were all young once!" someone said with a laugh.

People also began to talk about Stavrogin's good qualities. His respect for his mother was praised, and suddenly all sorts of virtues were discovered in him. They talked approvingly of the education he had received during his four years at German universities. Gaganov, on the other hand, was harshly criticized. People said his behavior had been tactless, that he didn't know how to tell friend from foe.

Yulia Mihailovna's sharp insight was quickly recognized and accepted.

So, when Nikolay Vsyevolodovitch finally appeared in public again, he was welcomed with serious attention. Everyone watched him eagerly, full of anticipation. Nikolay Vsyevolodovitch, however, chose to wrap himself in a stern silence, which oddly enough pleased people even more than if he had spoken for hours. In short, he was a success—he was fashionable. Once someone stands out in provincial society, there's no way to fade back into the background. Nikolay Vsyevolodovitch began carrying out all his social obligations in the province just as he had done before. People didn't find him very cheerful company, but this only added to his appeal: "A man who has suffered," they said. "A man who isn't like others—he has something to be sad about." Even the pride and aloofness that had made him so disliked four years earlier was now admired and respected.

Varvara Petrovna was triumphant. It's hard to say how much she mourned her broken dreams about Lizaveta Nikolaevna. Her family pride probably made it easier to bear. Strangely, though, Varvara Petrovna had convinced herself that Nikolay Vsyevolodovitch had "made his choice" at Count K.'s household. The oddest part was that this idea came from rumors spread by others, not any direct information. She was too afraid to ask Nikolay Vsyevolodovitch herself. A few times, though, she couldn't resist teasing him good-naturedly for keeping secrets from her. Nikolay Vsyevolodovitch just smiled and said nothing. His silence was taken as agreement. Still, Varvara Petrovna couldn't get the crippled woman out of her mind. The thought of her weighed heavily on her heart, haunting her with worries and strange suspicions, even as she dreamed of Count K.'s daughters. We'll come back to this later.

Meanwhile, Varvara Petrovna began receiving more respect and deference from society again. But she didn't take much advantage of it and rarely went out. However, she did pay a formal visit to the governor's wife. Of course, no one had been more pleased by Yulia Mihailovna's words at the marshal's party than Varvara Petrovna. Those words had lifted a huge weight off her heart and relieved much of the worry she had been carrying since that awful Sunday.

"I misjudged that woman," she declared. True to her nature, she told Yulia Mihailovna directly that she had come to thank her. Yulia Mihailovna was flattered but remained dignified. Around this time, she had started to become a little too aware of her own importance. For instance, during the conversation, she announced that she had never heard of Stepan Trofimovitch as being a notable figure or scholar.

"I know young Verhovensky, of course, and I value him greatly. He's a bit reckless, but he's young. He's very well-informed, though—not an outdated, old-fashioned critic like the others."

Varvara Petrovna quickly defended Stepan Trofimovitch. She said he had never been a critic, had lived in her house all his life, and was famous because of events early in his career, "known far too well to the whole world." Recently, he had been working on Spanish history and now planned to write about modern German universities. He was also considering a study on the Dresden Madonna. In short, Varvara Petrovna was not about to let Yulia Mihailovna dismiss Stepan Trofimovitch so easily.

"The Dresden Madonna? You mean the Sistine Madonna?" Yulia Mihailovna corrected her. "Dear Varvara Petrovna, I sat for two hours looking at that painting and came away completely disappointed. I didn't understand it at all and was amazed. Karmazinov says the same—no one sees anything special in it anymore, not the Russians or even the English. All its fame comes from the last generation."

"So fashions have changed, then?" Varvara Petrovna asked dryly.

"What I believe," Yulia Mihailovna continued, "is that we shouldn't be too hard on the younger generation. Yes, they talk about communism, but we need to understand them. I read everything now—newspapers, communism, science—because we need to know what's happening around us and who we're dealing with. We can't spend our whole lives up on some imaginary pedestal. I've come to a decision that kindness is the best way to keep young people on the right path. Believe me, Varvara Petrovna, only people like us, people from good society, can use our warmth and influence to keep them from falling into disaster.

"Oh, it's good to hear about Stepan Trofimovitch. You've given me an idea—he might be helpful at our literary matinée. I'm organizing a whole day of events—a fundraiser for the poor governesses of our province. There are six governesses here, and many more scattered around the country. We also have two girls working at the telegraph office, and two others in training at the academy, but the rest don't have the money to study. The fate of Russian women is so tragic, Varvara Petrovna! That's why there's so much talk now about university education for women—it's even been discussed in the Imperial Council.

"In Russia, everything is so chaotic. It's only through the kindness and leadership of people like us that we can guide these issues in the right direction. There are so few noble people left among us! Some exist, but they're scattered and isolated. We need to come together to be stronger. So, here's my plan: we'll have a literary matinée first, then a light luncheon, a short break, and finally, in the evening, a ball. We were going to start the evening with living pictures, but it's too expensive. Instead, we'll have one or two quadrilles in masks and costumes, representing well-known literary schools. It's a humorous idea Karmazinov came up with, and he's been a big help.

"Do you know, he's going to read us his last work? No one has seen it yet. He's giving up writing for good, and this essay is his farewell to the public. It's called Merci. The title is French, which makes it more amusing and refined. I even suggested the name myself! I think Stepan Trofimovitch could read something too—something short and not too serious. I believe Pyotr Stepanovitch and someone else might read something as well. I'll send Pyotr Stepanovitch over to tell you the full program. Or better yet, I'll bring it to you myself!"

"Let me add my name to your subscription list too. I'll speak to Stepan Trofimovitch and ask him to agree."

Varvara Petrovna returned home completely charmed. She was ready to defend Yulia Mihailovna through anything, and for some reason was already annoyed with Stepan Trofimovitch, while the poor man sat at home completely unaware.

"I'm in love with her. I don't understand how I could have been so wrong about that woman," she said to Nikolay Vsyevolodovitch and Pyotr Stepanovitch when they stopped by that evening.

"But you really should make up with the old man," Pyotr Stepanovitch suggested. "He's miserable. You've completely cut him off. Yesterday, he bowed when he passed your carriage, and you turned away. We'll need him, you know. I have plans for him, and he could still be useful."

"Oh, he'll read something at the event."

"I don't just mean that. I was going to stop by and see him today anyway. Shall I tell him?"

"If you like. Though I don't know how you'll manage it," she said hesitantly. "I was planning to talk to him myself and set a time and place."

She frowned.

"Oh, there's no need to set a time. I'll just pass along the message."

"Fine, go ahead. But make sure to tell him I'll definitely arrange a time to see him soon. Be sure to say that."

Pyotr Stepanovitch ran off, grinning. To be honest, as far as I can remember, he had been especially spiteful during this period and was unusually short-tempered with almost everyone. Oddly enough, people seemed to forgive him for it. It was as though everyone had agreed that he wasn't to be judged like an ordinary person.

I should note that he was particularly irritated about Nikolay Vsyevolodovitch's duel. It had completely caught him off guard. When he heard about it, he turned pale with anger. Maybe his pride was hurt because he had only found out the day after, when everyone else already knew.

"You had no right to fight, you know," he whispered to Stavrogin five days later when they happened to meet at the club. It was strange that they hadn't seen each other once during those five days, even though Pyotr Stepanovitch had been dropping by Varvara Petrovna's almost every day.

Nikolay Vsyevolodovitch looked at him silently, with a distant, distracted expression, as though he didn't understand what was going on, and then kept walking. He was crossing the main hall of the club, heading toward the refreshment room.

"You've been to see Shatov too… You plan to make your marriage to Marya Timofyevna public," Pyotr Stepanovitch muttered, hurrying after him. Without thinking, he grabbed Stavrogin's shoulder.

Nikolay Vsyevolodovitch shook his hand off sharply and turned around to him with a dark, threatening scowl. Pyotr Stepanovitch stared at him with a strange, drawn-out smile. It all lasted only a moment. Nikolay Vsyevolodovitch turned back and walked away.

Chapter 4.2

He went straight to "the old man" from Varvara Petrovna's house, rushing there out of spite, wanting to get back at him for an insult that I didn't yet know about. The fact was that during their last meeting the previous Thursday, Stepan Trofimovitch, though he had started the argument himself, had ended it by kicking Pyotr Stepanovitch out with his cane. At the time, he didn't tell me what had happened. But now, as soon as Pyotr Stepanovitch strolled in with his usual smug grin and his nosy, searching eyes, Stepan Trofimovitch quickly signaled to me not to leave the room. This was how I came to witness their conversation and see their real relationship for the first time.

Stepan Trofimovitch was stretched out on a lounge. He looked thinner and more pale since that Thursday. Pyotr Stepanovitch sat down beside him without any hesitation, tucking his legs up under him in a way that took up far more space than he should have. Stepan Trofimovitch quietly moved aside, maintaining his dignity.

On the table lay an open book. It was the novel What's to Be Done? I must admit that my friend had one strange weakness: he had this growing fantasy that he needed to emerge from his solitude and fight one last battle. I suspected he was reading that book only so he could learn the "shriekers'" methods and arguments directly from their own guidebook. That way, when the inevitable fight came, he could defeat them all, triumphantly, in front of her. Oh, how that book tortured him! Sometimes he'd throw it aside in frustration, leap up, and pace the room like a madman.

"I admit that the author's main idea is true," he told me, speaking feverishly, "but that makes it even worse. It's our idea—ours! We planted the seeds, prepared the ground for it. What could they possibly say that's new after us? But, heavens, look how it's expressed! It's twisted, mutilated, butchered!" He tapped the book with his fingers angrily. "Is this what we were striving for? Who could even understand the original idea in this mess?"

"Reading up on new ideas, are you?" Pyotr Stepanovitch sneered, picking up the book and reading the title. "About time. I'll bring you better books, if you want."

Stepan Trofimovitch said nothing, still holding on to his dignity. I was sitting on the sofa in the corner, watching.

Pyotr Stepanovitch quickly explained why he had come. Stepan Trofimovitch was stunned, listening with a mix of alarm and growing anger.

"And she sent me this message through you?" he asked, his face pale.

"Well, you see, she wants to set a time and place for a talk—a little leftover from your sentimental back-and-forth. You've been flirting with her for twenty years and got her used to all kinds of silly habits. But don't worry, things are different now. She says herself that she's only just now

333

starting to 'open her eyes.' I told her straight out that this so-called friendship of yours was nothing but sentimental nonsense. She told me all kinds of things, my friend. Ha! What a pathetic role you've been playing all this time. Honestly, I was embarrassed for you."

"I've been playing a pathetic role?" cried Stepan Trofimovitch, unable to hold back.

"Worse than that—you've been a parasite. A willing servant, too lazy to work but happy to take her money. She's figured all that out now. You wouldn't believe the things she said about you. I had a good laugh over the letters you wrote her—shameful, pathetic stuff. But you're all like that. Charity always has something rotten about it, and you're a perfect example of that!"

"She showed you my letters?"

"All of them—though, of course, no one could read them all. My goodness, you've filled up so much paper! I think there are over two thousand letters here. You know, old man, I think there was even a moment when she might have married you. You missed your chance in the dumbest way. I'm saying this from your point of view, of course. Even that would have been better than now, when you've nearly been married off just to 'cover up another man's sins'—like some clown, for a joke, for money."

"For money? She said it was for money?" wailed Stepan Trofimovitch in agony.

"What else? But don't worry, I defended you. That's the only excuse you've got, you know. She sees for herself that, like everyone else, you needed money, so maybe it made sense from your point of view. I explained to her, as clear as two plus two equals four, that it was just a business arrangement. She was the rich one, and you were her sentimental little servant. She's not even mad about the money—you took plenty of it, like milking a goat. No, she's furious that she trusted you for twenty years, that you tricked her with all your so-called noble feelings and made her lie for so long. She'll never admit that the lies were her own choice, so you'll pay for it even more. I just don't understand how you didn't realize there'd be a reckoning one day. I mean, you're not totally stupid. Yesterday, I suggested she put you in a care home. A nice one, don't worry—nothing humiliating. I think that's what she'll do. Do you remember the last letter you sent me, three weeks ago?"

"You didn't show her that, did you?" Stepan Trofimovitch cried, leaping up in horror.

"Of course, I did! That was the first thing I showed her. The one where you said she was using you, that she was jealous of your talent. Oh, and where you talked about 'covering other men's sins.' You've got quite an ego, haven't you? I laughed so hard at that one. Normally your letters are unbearable—horribly written. Half the time I don't even read them. I've got one lying around that's still unopened. I'll send it back to you tomorrow. But that last letter—that one was a masterpiece. Oh, how I laughed!"

"Monster! You monster!" wailed Stepan Trofimovitch.

"Oh, come on now, don't start whining. You're getting all huffy again, just like last Thursday."

Stepan Trofimovitch stood tall, trembling with anger. "How dare you speak to me like this?"

"What do you mean? I'm speaking clearly and simply."

"Tell me, you monster, are you my son or not?"

"You'd know that better than I would. After all, fathers like to turn a blind eye to these things."

"Silence! Be quiet!" shouted Stepan Trofimovitch, shaking all over.

"You're screaming at me again, just like last Thursday. You even tried to hit me with your stick, remember? But you know, I found that letter. I spent all night rummaging through my trunk, out of curiosity. It's not very clear, so you can take some comfort in that. It's just a letter from my mother to that Polish guy. But judging by her character..."

"One more word and I'll slap your face."

"What a family!" Pyotr Stepanovitch said suddenly, turning to me.

"You see? This is how we've been ever since Thursday. I'm glad you're here this time, though—you can judge for yourself. Let's start with a fact: he's mad at me for what I said about my mother. But didn't he start it? Didn't he wake me up twice in the middle of the night back in Petersburg when I was a teenager? He hugged me, cried like a woman, and what do you think he talked about? The same ridiculous stories about my mother! I heard them first from him!"

"I meant it in a higher sense! You didn't understand! You didn't understand anything!" cried Stepan Trofimovitch in despair.

"But even so, what you did was worse than what I'm doing—admit that. I don't care about this stuff, but I'm looking at it from your point of view. Don't worry about mine. I don't blame my mother. If it's you, then fine. If it's the Polish guy, then fine. Makes no difference to me. It's not my fault that you and she made a mess of things in Berlin. Like you would have handled it any better! Aren't you all ridiculous? And does it even matter to you whether I'm your son or not? Look," he said, turning to me again, "he never spent a penny on me. Until I was sixteen, he didn't even know I existed. Later, he just used me and took whatever money he could. Now he cries that he's loved me his whole life. He acts like he's performing on a stage. I'm not Varvara Petrovna, you know."

He stood up and grabbed his hat.

"I curse you forever!" Stepan Trofimovitch said, as pale as a ghost, stretching out his hand like a curse.

"What nonsense a man can sink to!" said Pyotr Stepanovitch, genuinely surprised. "Well, goodbye, old man. I won't come see you again. Send me that article in advance, don't forget. And keep it free of nonsense this time. Facts, facts, facts—and make it short. Goodbye."

Chapter 4.3

Outside influences had also played a role in this situation. Pyotr Stepanovitch definitely had some plans regarding his father. It seemed like he wanted to push the old man to despair, hoping he would cause some sort of public scandal. This, in turn, would help Pyotr achieve another, more distant goal of his own, something I'll explain later. At the time, his mind was overflowing with all kinds of schemes and ideas, most of them far-fetched or unrealistic. But Stepan Trofimovitch wasn't his only target. As it turned out later, he had quite a few people in his sights, but one of his main victims was Andrey Antonovitch von Lembke.

Lembke belonged to that group of people in Russia who were perfectly ordinary and numerous but seemed to share an unspoken understanding among themselves. This wasn't something planned or agreed upon—it happened naturally. They all seemed bound to help each other wherever they were, under any circumstances. Lembke had been fortunate enough to attend one of Russia's elite schools, which only accepted boys from wealthy or well-connected families. After graduating, most of these students quickly secured important positions in government offices. Lembke himself had an uncle who was a colonel in the army and another who was a baker, but somehow he managed to get into this prestigious school. There, he met many other young men in situations similar to his own.

Lembke wasn't particularly bright in school, but he was cheerful and well-liked. While some of his classmates—especially the Russian ones—were already having deep discussions about the great questions of the day and imagining themselves fixing the problems of the world after graduation, Lembke was still absorbed in silly schoolboy things. He liked to entertain others with his childish pranks, which were never clever but often crude. For example, he would blow his nose loudly just as a professor asked him a question, making everyone laugh, including the professor. Or, in the dormitory, he would perform some silly or inappropriate skit to amuse his friends. He could also play the overture to Fra Diavolo with his nose quite skillfully. He even took pride in being intentionally messy, as though that was funny.

In his final year at school, Lembke started writing poetry in Russian, even though he only knew his native language poorly, like many of his countrymen living in Russia. This interest in poetry led him to befriend a gloomy classmate who was the son of a poor Russian general. The other boy was considered a future star of literature and acted as a kind of mentor to Lembke. But three years after finishing school, that same boy, who had quit his government job to pursue a literary career, was now wandering the streets in torn boots and shivering from the cold in a thin summer coat. One day, on the Anitchin Bridge, he bumped into Lembke but didn't recognize him at first. Standing before him was a well-dressed young man with neat reddish whiskers, stylish pince-nez glasses, shiny leather boots, and perfectly clean gloves. Lembke wore an expensive coat from Sharmer's and carried a portfolio under his arm.

Lembke greeted his old classmate warmly and gave him his address, inviting him to visit. Now, however, he was no longer "Lembka," but "Von Lembke." The classmate decided to visit him, probably out of spite or curiosity. On the staircase, covered in red felt but neither elegant nor grand, the porter stopped him and asked questions. A loud bell rang upstairs. But instead of finding wealth, the visitor was led to a small, dark side room, divided by an old green curtain. The room was poorly lit, with worn but comfortable furniture, and narrow windows covered with dark green blinds. Lembke lived in the house of a distant relative, a general who was also his benefactor.

Lembke welcomed his visitor politely, speaking seriously and behaving with perfect manners. They talked about literature, though they kept the conversation very formal. A servant wearing a white tie brought them weak tea and small, dry biscuits. Out of spite, the classmate asked for seltzer water. It was brought, but only after a slight delay, which embarrassed Lembke, as he had to call the servant again. Despite this, Lembke offered supper, though it was clear he hoped the visitor would decline. When the guest refused and left, Lembke seemed relieved.

It was clear that Lembke was carefully building his career and living under the protection of his influential relative.

At that time, he had been infatuated with the general's fifth daughter, and he thought she felt the same way about him. But Amalia was soon married to an older factory owner, a German man who had been a friend of the general's. Andrey Antonovitch didn't grieve for long. Instead, he built a paper theater. The curtain would lift, actors would come out and wave their arms, and there were tiny spectators in the boxes. The orchestra played, with mechanical fiddlers moving their bows, and the conductor waved his baton. In the stalls, little officers and gentlemen clapped their hands. It was all made of cardboard, entirely designed and built by Lembke himself. He worked on it for six months. The general held a friendly gathering just to show it off. All five daughters attended, including Amalia with her new husband, along with many other families. Everyone admired the little theater, and then they danced. Lembke was very pleased with the praise and quickly got over Amalia.

Years went by, and his career steadily advanced. He always earned good positions, typically working under superiors who came from the same background as him. Eventually, he rose to a respectable place for a man his age. For some time, he had been wanting to marry and was carefully looking for a wife. Without telling his superiors, he even tried sending a novel to a magazine, but it was rejected. Not discouraged, he crafted a working toy train instead. Passengers stood on the platform with bags, children, and even dogs. The guards moved aside, the bell rang, the signal was given, and the train rolled off. He spent a year building this clever little invention.

Despite his hobbies, he still needed to get married. He had many acquaintances, mostly among people from his own background, though his job brought him into contact with Russians as well. Finally, when he turned thirty-nine, he inherited a legacy. His uncle, the baker, passed away and left him thirteen thousand roubles. All he needed now was a comfortable post and a wife. For a man like him, a small, independent government position—something with perks like access to free timber— would have been enough to make him happy for life. But instead of the simple girl he had hoped for, like a Minna or an Ernestine, Yulia Mihailovna appeared.

Yulia had a fortune equivalent to two hundred serfs, as people used to measure in the past, and she had powerful connections. Lembke, on the other hand, was handsome, and Yulia was already over forty. Surprisingly, he genuinely fell in love with her as they spent more time together. On the morning of their wedding, he even sent her a poem. She was thrilled by all of this, even the poem—it's no small thing to be forty. Soon after their marriage, his career took a major leap. He received a promotion, earned a medal of distinction, and was appointed governor of our province.

Before they arrived, Yulia Mihailovna worked hard to shape her husband into what she thought he could become. She believed he had potential. He could make an impressive entrance, listen with deep seriousness, and even deliver a decent speech. He had picked up a touch of modern liberalism, which was useful, but he wasn't very quick to adopt new ideas. After years of grinding away at his career, he clearly wanted to settle down and relax. Yulia, however, tried to light a fire under him and inspire ambition. Instead, he built a toy church. In his little creation, the pastor came out to give a sermon, the congregation sat with their hands folded, one lady wiped her tears, and an old man blew his nose. The organ played, all operated by a mechanism. It was custom-made in Switzerland, regardless of the cost. Yulia was so alarmed by this childish project that she packed it up immediately and locked it in a box in her room. To keep him occupied, she let him write a novel, but only on the condition that no one would know about it. After that, Yulia began to rely entirely on herself.

Unfortunately, there was something shallow and poorly thought-out in Yulia's efforts. Fate had kept her unmarried for too long, and now her mind was overflowing with ideas. She dreamed of ruling the province, becoming the center of an important social circle, and even playing a political role. She had all kinds of ambitious plans. Von Lembke was a bit unsettled by her energy, but his experience as an official told him not to worry too much about the actual running of the province. The first few months in their new role went smoothly. But then Pyotr Stepanovitch arrived, and everything began to change.

From the very start, young Verkhovensky showed no respect for Andrey Antonovitch. He acted as though he had the right to boss him around. What made things worse was that Yulia Mihailovna, who had always been so careful about her husband's dignity, completely ignored Pyotr Stepanovitch's rudeness or brushed it off as unimportant. Soon, the young man became a regular in their house, eating, drinking, and practically living there.

Von Lembke tried to push back. He called Pyotr "young man" in public and patted him on the shoulder like a superior, but none of it worked. Pyotr always seemed to be laughing at him, even when he spoke to him seriously. He would say outrageous things to Von Lembke in front of guests without the slightest hesitation. One day, when Lembke came home, he found Pyotr asleep on the sofa in his study, uninvited. When questioned, Pyotr casually explained that he'd come by, found no one home, and decided to take a nap.

Von Lembke was offended again and complained to his wife. Laughing at his irritation, she sharply told him that he clearly didn't know how to maintain his dignity. She added that "the boy" had never dared to overstep any boundaries with her. "He's naïve and a bit unconventional, but not rude," she said. Von Lembke sulked. This time, she stepped in to make peace. Pyotr Stepanovitch didn't exactly apologize, but he made a crude joke. Normally, this would have been taken as another insult, but on this occasion, it was accepted as a kind of apology.

The real problem for Andrey Antonovitch was that he had made a mistake early on. He had revealed the secret of his novel to Pyotr Stepanovitch. Believing the young man to be an eager, poetic soul and desperate to share his writing with someone, he had read two chapters aloud to him. Pyotr Stepanovitch had listened with obvious boredom, yawned rudely, and said nothing positive. But as he was leaving, he asked for the manuscript so he could take a closer look at it later. Andrey Antonovitch handed it over. Since then, Pyotr Stepanovitch had not returned it, though he visited every day. When asked about it, he always brushed it off with a laugh. Eventually, he claimed he had lost it in the street. When Yulia Mihailovna heard about this, she was furious with her husband.

"Did you tell him about the church too?" she asked almost in shock.

The situation began to weigh on Von Lembke. Brooding was not good for him, as the doctors had warned. Beyond the problems in his personal life, there were troubling signs of unrest in the province, which made things worse. But his heart was wounded too. When he got married, he never imagined there would be disagreements or conflict. That didn't fit with the dreams he had carried all his life—dreams of a calm and peaceful marriage, just like the stories he had always pictured about his

Minna or Ernestine. He didn't think he could handle arguments at home. Finally, Yulia Mihailovna had a serious talk with him.

"You can't be upset about this," she said. "After all, you're just as smart as he is and far more important socially. The boy still has traces of his old rebellious habits. I think he's just trying to stir things up for fun. You can't change everything overnight. We need to treat young people kindly and keep them from going too far."

"But he says such terrible things," Von Lembke argued. "How am I supposed to stay calm when he says—right in front of other people—that the government gives the people vodka on purpose to make them stupid and keep them from revolting? How am I supposed to respond to that?"

As he spoke, Von Lembke remembered a recent conversation he'd had with Pyotr Stepanovitch. Trying to show off his "liberal" side, he had brought out his private collection of manifestos—pamphlets and documents, both Russian and foreign—that he had been collecting since 1859. He wasn't just collecting them for fun; he felt it was important to study these ideas. Pyotr Stepanovitch had looked through the collection and said there was more truth in one line of some of the manifestos than in an entire government department—"maybe even yours," he added.

Von Lembke winced.

"This kind of thing is premature here," he said, almost pleadingly, as he pointed to the papers.

"No, it's not premature. If you're afraid, then that means it's not too early."

"But look here," Von Lembke said, pointing at one paper, "this one calls for burning down churches!"

"And why not?" Pyotr replied bluntly. "You're an intelligent man; you don't believe in that nonsense yourself. You know religion only exists to keep the people ignorant and under control. Telling the truth is better than telling lies."

"I agree with you, I do," Von Lembke stammered. "But it's too soon for this here. It's premature—premature for our country!"

342

"How can you serve the government then? You agree with burning down churches and leading an armed revolt on Petersburg, and for you, it's just a question of timing?"

Pyotr's blunt response caught him off guard. Von Lembke grew flustered.

"That's not true! Not at all!" he cried, growing more upset and defensive. "You're young and don't understand our goals. You're completely wrong about us. Listen, my dear Pyotr Stepanovitch, you call us government officials, don't you? But what do you think we are really doing? The responsibility is ours, yes, but in the end, we work for progress just like you do. The difference is that we hold everything together while you are trying to tear it apart. Without us, everything would collapse into chaos. We're not your enemies. Not at all! We say, go ahead and push for progress, even shake things up where needed. But we're here to keep everything within reasonable limits. Without us, you would destroy Russia and strip her of any dignity. Our job is to preserve that dignity. Don't you see? We need each other. In England, the Whigs and Tories balance each other out. You're the Whigs, and we're the Tories. That's how I see it."

Andrey Antonovitch became unusually passionate as he spoke. He had always enjoyed talking about liberal and intellectual ideas, even back in Petersburg, but now he had the freedom to do so without worrying about spies listening.

Pyotr Stepanovitch said nothing and kept an unusually serious look on his face. This made the governor even more excited as he spoke.

"Do you realize," he said, pacing around the room, "that I, as the 'person responsible for this province,' have so many duties that I can't actually do any of them? And at the same time, there's nothing for me to do at all! The whole secret lies in the government's attitude. Suppose one day the government decided to form a republic—whether to calm public unrest or for political reasons—while also strengthening the power of the governors. Then we governors would swallow up that republic in no time. And not just the republic—anything at all! I, for one, am ready for anything. If the government sent me a telegram saying 'unlimited action,' I'd give them exactly that—unlimited action! I've already told people here

343

to their faces: 'Gentlemen, to keep the balance and develop all the provincial institutions, we must strengthen the governor's power.'

"You see, these institutions—like the local zemstvos and courts—need to exist, yes, but at the same time, they shouldn't. It all depends on the government's wishes. If tomorrow the government decides these institutions are necessary, I'll have them up and running in no time. If the need for them passes, they'll quietly disappear under my management. That's what I call 'unlimited action.' But you can't achieve that without giving the governor more power. We're speaking in confidence, you and I. You know, I've even requested from Petersburg the need for a special guard to stand in front of my house. I'm still waiting for their answer."

"You should have two guards," Pyotr Stepanovitch said.

"Two?" Andrey Antonovitch stopped walking and stared at him.

"One isn't enough to command respect. Two guards would be better," Pyotr said with a straight face.

Andrey Antonovitch frowned. "You… you take far too many liberties, Pyotr Stepanovitch. You take advantage of my good nature. You make sharp remarks and act like some kind of 'gruff but kind' friend."

"Well, that's your opinion," Pyotr muttered. "Either way, you're paving the way for us and helping us succeed."

"What do you mean, 'us'? What success are you talking about?" Andrey Antonovitch asked, confused. But Pyotr gave no answer.

When Yulia Mihailovna heard about this conversation, she was very displeased.

"But I can't use my authority against your 'favorite,'" Andrey Antonovitch said defensively. "Especially when we're speaking privately… sometimes I say too much because of my soft heart."

"Too much kindness of heart! I didn't even know you had a collection of manifestos. Show them to me," she demanded.

"But… he only asked to borrow them for one day."

"And you let him take them again?" Yulia Mihailovna exclaimed angrily. "How careless of you!"

"I'll send someone to collect them immediately," Andrey Antonovitch promised, his face turning red.

"He won't give them back," she said firmly.

"I'll demand it!" Andrey Antonovitch shouted, jumping to his feet. "Who does he think he is that we should be afraid of him? And who am I, if I can't stand up for myself?"

"Sit down and calm yourself," Yulia Mihailovna said sharply. "I'll answer your question. He came to me with excellent recommendations. He's talented, and sometimes he says very clever things. Even Karmazinov told me that he has connections everywhere and incredible influence over young people in Petersburg and Moscow. If I can use him to attract those young people and bring them under my influence, I'll be saving them from disaster. I'll guide their ambition in a better direction. He's devoted to me completely and listens to me in everything."

"But while you're spoiling him, who knows what trouble he might cause? Of course, it's an idea…" Andrey Antonovitch muttered, still trying to defend himself. "But… I've heard that they found some manifestos in the X district."

"There were rumors about that in the summer—manifestos, counterfeit money, and all kinds of things—but nothing has been proven. Who told you this?"

"Von Blum mentioned it to me."

"Don't talk to me about that man! Never bring him up again!" Yulia Mihailovna snapped. She was so angry she couldn't speak for a moment. Von Blum, a clerk in the governor's office, was someone she particularly disliked.

"Please stop worrying about Verhovensky," she concluded. "If he were involved in anything dangerous, he wouldn't talk so openly to you and everyone else. People who talk like that aren't dangerous. In fact, if something did happen, I'd be the first to hear about it from him. He's completely loyal to me."

Looking back, it was clear that Yulia Mihailovna's stubbornness and pride were largely to blame for what happened later. If not for her refusal to see the truth, much of the chaos these people caused could have been avoided. She was responsible for a great deal.

Chapter 5
On The Eve of The Fete

Chapter 5.1

The date for the event Yulia Mihailovna was organizing to benefit the governesses of the province had been set and postponed several times. She was constantly surrounded by Pyotr Stepanovitch and a small clerk named Lyamshin. Lyamshin, who used to visit Stepan Trofimovitch, had suddenly become a favorite in the governor's house because of his piano playing, and now he was useful for running errands. Liputin was also a regular presence, and Yulia Mihailovna planned for him to be the editor of a new, independent provincial newspaper. Several women, both married and single, were involved, along with Karmazinov. Although he didn't "bustle" like the others, Karmazinov proudly announced that he would amaze everyone during the literary quadrille.

An impressive number of donors and subscribers had come forward—members of the town's upper society. Even people from lower classes were allowed to participate, as long as they paid the entry fee. Yulia Mihailovna insisted that it was sometimes a duty to mix the classes because, as she put it, "Who else will enlighten them?"

A private committee was formed to plan the event, and they decided that it should have a "democratic" feel. The long list of donations encouraged them to dream big and plan something grand, which is why the event kept getting postponed. They couldn't decide whether to hold the ball in the large house of the marshal's wife, which she offered for the day, or at Varvara Petrovna's mansion in Skvoreshniki. Although Skvoreshniki was farther away, some members of the committee thought it would feel "freer" there. Varvara Petrovna herself hoped to host the event at her home. Oddly, this proud woman seemed to be trying to win over Yulia Mihailovna. Perhaps it pleased her that Yulia Mihailovna appeared to favor Nikolay Vsyevolodovitch and was more gracious to him than to anyone else.

Pyotr Stepanovitch was constantly whispering in the governor's house, reinforcing an idea he had planted earlier—that Nikolay Vsyevolodovitch had mysterious connections with secret, powerful groups and that he had arrived with some special mission.

People seemed to be in a strange mood during this time, especially the women. There was an unusual sense of frivolity and carelessness in the air, and it seemed to appear out of nowhere. Ideas that would have seemed shocking before were suddenly being treated lightly. The atmosphere was lively, but not always in a pleasant way. People later blamed Yulia Mihailovna and her circle for encouraging this attitude, but at first, everyone praised her for bringing the community together and adding excitement to the town.

Several scandalous incidents occurred, though Yulia Mihailovna wasn't directly responsible for them. At the time, people were amused rather than alarmed. A large group of people—young men and women—gathered around Yulia Mihailovna, almost naturally, as if drawn to her. In this group, especially among the younger members, it became acceptable to act out and play pranks, sometimes going too far. It seemed to become a kind of principle among them.

Some of the young people in this circle organized outings, rode around town in carriages and on horseback, and sought out adventures. Sometimes, they even created trouble just for the sake of having a good story to tell. They treated the town as if it were a stage for their jokes. People began calling them the "jeerers" because they mocked everything and everyone.

One shocking incident involved the young wife of a local lieutenant. She was a small brunette, still young, but clearly worn down by her husband's mistreatment. At a party, hoping to win enough money to buy herself a new mantle, she played whist for high stakes. Instead of winning, she lost fifteen roubles. Afraid of her husband and desperate, she secretly asked for a loan from the mayor's son, a nasty, spoiled young man. Not only did he refuse, but he went laughing straight to her husband to tell him what had happened.

The lieutenant, who was poor and lived on his salary alone, took his wife home and punished her brutally, ignoring her cries and pleas for forgiveness. The story spread across the town and, shockingly, caused nothing but laughter.

One of the women from the "cavalcade"—a bold, adventurous character—heard about the situation. She knew the lieutenant's wife and decided to intervene. She went to the house, took the young woman away, and brought her home. Once there, the woman was surrounded by the lively group. They showered her with gifts, made her feel welcome, and kept her for four days without letting her return to her husband.

During this time, the lieutenant's wife joined the group in all their escapades. She went on rides, danced at their gatherings, and joined in their carefree fun. The group encouraged her to take her husband to court and promised to support her. They even offered to testify on her behalf.

The lieutenant stayed quiet, too afraid to oppose the group. Eventually, though, the young wife realized she had gotten herself into a hopeless situation. Terrified, she snuck away one evening and returned to her husband. No one knows exactly what happened between them, but for two weeks after, the shutters of their small house remained closed.

When Yulia Mihailovna heard about the incident, she was furious with the group. She especially disapproved of the woman who had taken the lieutenant's wife away, even though that same woman had formally introduced the young wife to her. However, like most things, the story was soon forgotten.

One time, a petty clerk—a respectable family man—married his daughter, a beautiful seventeen-year-old known by everyone in town, to another young clerk from a different district. The next day, it came out that the young husband had been cruel to his wife on their wedding night, punishing her for what he considered a stain on his honor. Lyamshin, who had stayed the night at the wedding after getting drunk, quickly spread the story as soon as the sun rose.

Within no time, a group of about a dozen people had gathered. They rode around on horseback, with some on rented Cossack horses—Pyotr Stepanovitch and Liputin included. Despite his gray hair, Liputin took part in almost every scandalous adventure of these reckless young people. When the newlywed couple set out the next morning in a carriage to make their formal calls—something expected in our town the day after a wedding—the entire group surrounded their carriage. They followed the couple around town, laughing and joking all morning. While they didn't directly insult the bride and groom, they still caused a scene. The entire town was talking about it. Everyone laughed, of course, but Von Lembke was furious and had another heated argument with Yulia Mihailovna about the matter.

Yulia Mihailovna, too, was angry. She even planned to turn the troublemakers out of her house. But by the next day, after some smooth talking from Pyotr Stepanovitch and a few joking comments from Karmazinov, she forgave them. Karmazinov had said, "It fits the traditions of this town. It's bold and amusing. Everyone's laughing; you're the only one upset."

Still, there were other pranks that went beyond what anyone could tolerate.

For example, a respectable woman from the artisan class came into town to sell gospels. People began talking about her because newspapers in Petersburg had recently published interesting articles about such women. Lyamshin, along with a theology student on break while waiting for a teaching position, decided to play a cruel trick on her. Pretending to buy books, they slipped a bundle of indecent photographs into her bag. These photos had been provided—shockingly—by a well-known, older gentleman with a medal on his chest who claimed to "enjoy a healthy laugh and a good joke."

When the poor woman opened her bag to sell her gospels in the marketplace, the photos fell out and scattered everywhere. The crowd roared with laughter but soon grew angry. People began shouting at her, and things might have turned violent if the police hadn't arrived in time. The woman was taken to the police station, but later that evening, thanks to Mavriky Nikolaevitch, who was disgusted by the whole affair, she was released and escorted safely out of town.

Yulia Mihailovna was so angry she was ready to ban Lyamshin from her house. But that same evening, the group brought him to her with news that he had composed a new piano piece, persuading her to at least listen to it. The piece turned out to be genuinely clever and funny, titled "The Franco-Prussian War."

The piece began with the grand and ominous tones of the "Marseillaise"—the French anthem. The music captured all the pride and excitement of expected victories. But soon, from somewhere in the background, came the silly and cheerful strains of the German song "Mein lieber Augustin." The two melodies clashed as if unaware of each other.

The "Marseillaise" became louder and prouder, reaching a glorious peak, but "Augustin" refused to go away. Slowly, the German tune grew stronger and more persistent. The "Marseillaise," like someone irritated by a buzzing fly, tried to push "Augustin" aside, but "Augustin" only became more confident and obnoxious. Finally, the French anthem faltered. Its triumphant melody began to mix awkwardly with the carefree waltz, losing all its grandeur. The music became a pathetic cry of defeat, as though Jules Favre himself were weeping on Bismarck's chest and surrendering everything.

But the German tune didn't stop there. It grew wilder and louder, turning into a drunken, triumphant roar—a mix of beer-soaked self-celebration and greedy demands for wealth, cigars, and champagne. The "Franco-Prussian War" was over.

The audience erupted into applause. Even Yulia Mihailovna smiled and said, "Now, how can I throw him out?" Peace was restored. Lyamshin, for all his faults, really did have talent.

Stepan Trofimovitch once told me that great artistic talent can sometimes exist in the most despicable people, and one doesn't cancel out the other. Later, there were rumors that Lyamshin had stolen the piano piece from a quiet, talented young man who preferred to remain anonymous. But by then, it didn't matter.

Lyamshin became a fixture in Yulia Mihailovna's circle. This same man, who used to hang around Stepan Trofimovitch's house and entertain guests by mocking everything—imitating peasants, mimicking old women making confessions, even staging ridiculous scenes—now performed at Yulia Mihailovna's gatherings. Once, he even parodied Stepan Trofimovitch himself under the title "A Liberal of the Forties," and everyone laughed so hard that it became impossible to banish him. He had become too entertaining, too necessary.

Besides, Lyamshin shamelessly flattered Pyotr Stepanovitch and acted like his loyal follower. By this time, Pyotr Stepanovitch had gained a strange and surprising influence over Yulia Mihailovna, which no one could quite explain.

There was another disturbing story—one that I cannot leave out. Even though it's believed Lyamshin played a part in it, his exact role is still debated.

One morning, the entire town was buzzing with news of a shocking and disgraceful act. At the entrance to our large marketplace stood the old church of Our Lady's Nativity, one of the oldest and most important landmarks in the area. Just outside the church gates, there was an icon of the Mother of God, placed behind glass and protected by a metal grate. That night, the icon had been vandalized. The glass was smashed, the grate broken, and several stones and pearls—though not necessarily valuable—had been stolen from the crown and the decoration.

What made the crime even more disgusting was the senseless insult added to it. Behind the broken glass, a live mouse was found in the morning. Months later, it was confirmed that the convict Fedka was the main culprit, but rumors spread that Lyamshin had been involved, too. People said it was Lyamshin who put the mouse there. At the time, no one suspected him, but now, everyone seemed sure of it.

I remember the officials were shaken by the news. A crowd gathered near the scene early in the morning. It wasn't enormous, but about a hundred people constantly came and went. As they approached, people crossed themselves, bowed to the icon, and left small offerings. Soon, a collection dish appeared, along with a monk to oversee it. It wasn't until

351

about three in the afternoon that the authorities finally thought to tell the crowd to move along after praying.

The incident left a deep impression on Von Lembke. It was said that Yulia Mihailovna later noticed a strange sadness in her husband from that very day. This depression, she claimed, lingered until he left the province two months later due to illness. Even now, in Switzerland, where he is recovering, it seems to haunt him.

I remember walking across the marketplace at around one in the afternoon. The crowd was quiet, and everyone looked solemn. A fat, pale merchant rode up in a carriage, got out, bowed deeply to the ground, kissed the icon, and dropped a rouble into the dish. Sighing, he climbed back into his carriage and drove off.

Shortly after, another carriage arrived carrying two ladies and two young men, both known troublemakers. The two men, one of whom wasn't so young anymore, stepped out of the carriage and carelessly pushed their way through the crowd. They didn't remove their hats, and one of them even pulled out his pince-nez and put it on his nose. A murmur ran through the crowd, low and unfriendly. The man with the pince-nez reached into his wallet, stuffed full of banknotes, pulled out a single copper coin, and tossed it into the dish. Both of the men laughed loudly, chatting as they strolled back to their carriage.

At that very moment, Lizaveta Nikolaevna galloped up on her horse, with Mavriky Nikolaevitch following closely behind. She leaped off her horse, handed the reins to him, and instructed him to stay on his horse. She approached the icon just as the coin had been tossed. Her face turned red with anger. She took off her hat and gloves, knelt on the muddy ground, and bowed deeply three times before the icon.

Then she reached into her purse, but she only had a few small coins. Without hesitation, she removed her diamond earrings and placed them in the collection dish.

"May I? Can they be used to decorate the icon?" she asked the monk.

"It is permitted," the monk replied calmly. "Every gift is welcome."

The crowd watched in silence, showing neither approval nor

352

disagreement.

Liza got back on her horse, her riding clothes now muddy, and rode off quickly with Mavriky Nikolaevitch still behind her.

Chapter 5.2

Two days after the incident I described, I saw her again among a group of people heading out on an outing. They were traveling in three carriages, with others riding alongside on horseback. She waved at me, stopped her carriage, and insisted that I join them. I was given a seat in one of the carriages, and she introduced me with cheerful laughter to her companions—several well-dressed ladies. She explained that they were going on a very "interesting" trip. She was laughing and seemed almost too happy. Recently, her mood had been unusually lively, even playful.

The outing itself was strange. They were all headed across the river to visit the merchant Sevastyanov's estate. In a lodge on his property lived a man known as Semyon Yakovlevitch, a supposed saint and prophet who was famous not just in our town, but also in nearby provinces and even in Petersburg and Moscow. He had been living there quietly for ten years, enjoying a comfortable and peaceful life. Visitors came to see him regularly, hoping to hear some strange prophecy, leaving offerings at his feet. Some of these donations were significant. If Semyon Yakovlevitch didn't direct the money elsewhere, it usually ended up at the monastery of Our Lady. A monk from the monastery was always nearby to help with these matters.

The group was excited about the visit. No one had met Semyon Yakovlevitch before, except Lyamshin, who claimed that the prophet had once ordered him to be swept out with a broom and had thrown two baked potatoes at him. Among those on horseback, I noticed Pyotr Stepanovitch again, sitting awkwardly on a rented Cossack horse, and Nikolay Vsyevolodovitch, who also joined the party on horseback. Although he usually avoided such outings, when he did participate, he always seemed cheerful. Still, as always, he spoke little.

When we crossed the bridge and approached the town's hotel,

someone announced that a traveler had been found in one of the rooms after shooting himself. The police were on their way. Immediately, someone suggested we stop and take a look at the scene. The idea was eagerly accepted—none of the ladies had ever seen a suicide before. I remember one of them even said out loud, "Everything is so boring lately. You can't be picky about entertainment as long as it's interesting."

Most of the group went inside, though a few stayed back. To my surprise, I saw Lizaveta Nikolaevna among those who entered the building. The door to the room was open, and no one stopped us from looking inside.

The young man who had killed himself couldn't have been more than nineteen. He was handsome, with thick blond hair, a fine oval face, and a smooth forehead. The body was already stiff, and his pale, peaceful face looked like marble. A note lay on the table, written in his own hand. It said that no one was to blame for his death, that he had killed himself because he had "squandered" four hundred roubles. The word "squandered" was actually used, and in the short note, there were three spelling mistakes.

A plump country gentleman, clearly distressed, explained that the young man had been sent to town by his family—a widowed mother, sisters, and aunts. They had saved up the four hundred roubles for ten years and entrusted him to buy clothing and items for his eldest sister's wedding trousseau. With much worry and prayer, they had sent him off, blessing him with signs of the cross. Until now, he had been a trustworthy and well-behaved boy.

But when he arrived in town three days before, he did not go to his relatives. Instead, he checked into the hotel and went straight to the club, hoping to find a gambling game. That night, there was no card game or "travelling banker," so he returned to the hotel at midnight and ordered champagne, Havana cigars, and a large supper. However, the champagne got him drunk, and the cigar made him sick. He left the food untouched and passed out.

The next morning, fresh as ever, he immediately went to the gypsy camp outside town, where he stayed for two days. Finally, at five o'clock on the afternoon before, he returned to the hotel, clearly drunk, went to bed, and slept until ten at night. When he woke up, he ordered a cutlet, a bottle of Château d'Yquem, grapes, and some paper and ink. He also asked for the bill. He seemed calm and polite, and no one noticed anything unusual about him.

He must have shot himself around midnight, though it was strange that no one heard the gunshot. The alarm wasn't raised until midday, when staff broke down the door after knocking repeatedly. The bottle of Château d'Yquem was half-empty, and there were some grapes left on the plate. The small revolver had fallen to the carpet after he fired a shot straight into his heart. There was very little blood. The boy's body was slumped in the corner of the sofa. Death must have come instantly because his face looked peaceful, almost happy, as though nothing had ever troubled him.

Everyone in our group stared at the body with eager curiosity. There is something about witnessing tragedy that always draws people in, as though someone else's misfortune somehow lightens our own burdens. The ladies were silent, but the men began cracking jokes and making casual remarks. One said that the boy had found the best way out of his troubles, that there was nothing smarter he could have done. Another added that at least he had enjoyed himself, even if only for a moment.

A third suddenly asked aloud why people had started killing themselves so often lately, as though everyone had lost their footing, like the ground was falling out from under their feet. No one liked his comment, and they looked at him coldly.

Then Lyamshin, who always tried to act like a fool for laughs, grabbed a bunch of grapes from the plate. Another man, laughing, took some too. A third reached for the wine, but the police captain arrived just in time to stop him. The captain ordered everyone to leave. Since they had already seen enough, the group walked out without arguing, though Lyamshin stayed back to bother the captain about something.

The group's mood was twice as cheerful on the way back. There was laughter, jokes, and playful chatter as though nothing had happened.

We arrived at Semyon Yakovlevitch's place exactly at one o'clock. The gate of the large house was open, and the path leading to the lodge was clear. We were told right away that Semyon Yakovlevitch was having lunch but was receiving visitors. The entire group of us went inside.

The room where the saint dined and welcomed guests had three windows and was quite large. It was divided into two equal parts by a wooden partition about three or four feet high. Regular visitors stayed on one side of the partition, but lucky ones, invited by Semyon Yakovlevitch himself, were allowed through the small gate to sit with him. If he was in the mood, he would let them sit on the old leather chairs or on the worn-out sofa. He himself always sat in an old, shabby Voltaire armchair.

Semyon Yakovlevitch was a large, bloated man, about fifty-five years old, with a yellowish face. He was bald, with thin, light-colored hair. He had no beard, and his right cheek was swollen, making his mouth look slightly crooked. A big wart sat on the left side of his nose. His eyes were narrow, and his expression was calm, sleepy, and dull. He wore a black European-style coat but no waistcoat or tie. Underneath, a plain white shirt peeked out. Something was wrong with his feet, so he wore slippers. People said he used to be a clerk and had even earned a small rank in the service.

He had just finished a bowl of fish soup and was starting on his second dish—boiled potatoes with salt, which was the only food he ate. However, he drank a lot of tea, which he loved. Three servants, provided by the merchant who owned the house, were busy serving him. One wore a swallow-tail coat, another looked like a workman, and the third resembled a church verger. A lively boy of about sixteen also ran about helping. There was also an older, grey-haired monk holding a jug, though he was noticeably plump.

On one table, a large samovar boiled with tea, surrounded by nearly two dozen glasses. On another table nearby, offerings had been laid out—loaves of bread, a couple of pounds of sugar, two pounds of tea, embroidered slippers, a silk handkerchief, cloth, linen, and other items. Money donations went straight into the jug held by the monk.

The room was crowded with at least a dozen visitors. Two of them

356

were sitting with Semyon Yakovlevitch on the other side of the partition—a grey-haired peasant pilgrim and a small, dried-up monk sitting quietly with his eyes lowered. The other visitors stood on the far side of the partition. Most of them were peasants, except for one poor older woman, a landowner, and a stout merchant from a nearby town. The merchant, dressed in traditional Russian clothing, was said to be worth a hundred thousand roubles.

No one dared speak to Semyon Yakovlevitch. Four visitors were kneeling, but the one who drew the most attention was the landowner, a heavy man of about forty-five. He knelt directly against the partition, clearly determined to get a word or a glance from the saint. He had been there for an hour, but Semyon Yakovlevitch ignored him.

Our ladies pushed their way to the front, chattering and laughing softly. They didn't hesitate to push aside the other visitors, even the ones kneeling, though they didn't disturb the stubborn landowner clinging to the partition. They stared at the saint eagerly, their faces full of curiosity, using lorgnettes, pince-nez, and even opera glasses. Lyamshin, for instance, peered through an opera glass.

Semyon Yakovlevitch slowly scanned the group with his small eyes. Then he suddenly said, in a rough, staccato voice, "Milovzors! Milovzors!"

Our group burst into laughter. "What does 'Milovzors' mean?" they asked each other. But Semyon Yakovlevitch said nothing else and calmly finished eating his potatoes. When he was done, they handed him some tea.

Normally, he didn't drink tea alone. He poured glasses for visitors he chose, though his choices were often surprising. He would sometimes ignore the wealthy and important people and instead pour tea for a poor peasant or an old woman. Other times, he would pass over the beggars and serve a wealthy merchant. He also served the tea differently—some glasses had sugar, while others didn't. Some visitors were given sugar separately, and others received none at all.

This time, the monk sitting beside him received tea with sugar, while the old pilgrim got his tea without any sugar. The fat monk holding the jug received nothing, though he usually had a glass every day.

"Semyon Yakovlevitch, please say something to me. I've wanted to meet you for so long," called one of the well-dressed ladies from our group. She squinted her eyes and smiled as she spoke. This was the same woman who had said earlier that one shouldn't be too picky about amusements as long as they were interesting.

Semyon Yakovlevitch didn't even glance at her. The kneeling landowner let out a deep, loud sigh, sounding like a pair of large bellows.

"With sugar in it!" said Semyon Yakovlevitch suddenly, pointing to the wealthy merchant. The merchant stepped forward and stood beside the kneeling man.

"Add more sugar for him!" ordered Semyon Yakovlevitch after the tea had already been poured. They added more sugar. "More, more for him!" he insisted. More was added a third time, and then a fourth. The merchant obediently drank the syrupy tea.

"Heavens!" people whispered, crossing themselves. The kneeling man sighed deeply again, the sound heavy and loud.

"Father! Semyon Yakovlevitch!" came the sharp, pleading voice of the poor widow. She had been pushed back to the wall by our group. "I've been waiting for your grace for an hour now! Look upon me in my suffering."

"Ask her," Semyon Yakovlevitch said, nodding at the verger, who walked to the partition.

"Have you done what Semyon Yakovlevitch told you to do last time?" the verger asked in a calm, soft voice.

"I tried, Father Semyon Yakovlevitch! How could I manage it with them?" the widow wailed. "They're monsters. They've lodged complaints against me in court! They even threaten to take it to the senate. That's how they treat their own mother!"

"Give her!" Semyon Yakovlevitch said, pointing to a large sugar loaf on the table.

A boy rushed over, grabbed the sugar loaf, and handed it to the widow.

"Oh, Father, your mercy is great! But what am I to do with so much sugar?" the widow cried, overwhelmed.

"More, more," said Semyon Yakovlevitch generously.

Another sugar loaf was brought to her, then a third, and finally a fourth. She was now surrounded by sugar on all sides. The monk from the monastery sighed deeply. All of that sugar could have gone to the monastery, as it usually did.

"What am I to do with all this?" the widow repeated, looking helpless. "It's enough to make someone sick! Is it some kind of prophecy, Father?"

"It must be a prophecy," someone murmured from the crowd.

"Give her another pound!" Semyon Yakovlevitch added.

There was one sugar loaf left on the table, but he ordered a single pound to be given to her instead. The boy handed it over.

"Lord have mercy!" the crowd gasped, crossing themselves. "It must be a sign."

"Take this as a lesson to sweeten your heart with kindness and mercy," said the fat monk, taking on the role of interpreter, his voice self-important. "Then you won't need to file complaints against your children, the flesh of your flesh. That's what this means."

"What are you saying, Father?" the widow suddenly snapped, her face red with anger. "Those villains dragged me into the fire with a rope around me when the Verhishins' house burned down! They locked a dead cat in my chest! They'll stop at nothing!"

"Away with her! Away with her!" Semyon Yakovlevitch suddenly cried, waving his hands.

The verger and the boy jumped up, grabbed the widow by the arm, and began escorting her out. She didn't resist but stared longingly at the sugar loaves as the boy dragged them after her.

"One to be taken back. Take it away," Semyon Yakovlevitch ordered.

A servant hurried after the woman, and a short while later, they returned with one of the sugar loaves, which had been taken back. The widow still carried off three.

"Semyon Yakovlevitch," someone called from the door. "I dreamed of a bird, a jackdaw. It flew out of the water and into the fire. What does it mean?"

"Frost," Semyon Yakovlevitch replied.

"Semyon Yakovlevitch, why don't you answer me?" the elegant lady in our group spoke up again. "I've been so interested in you for a long time now."

"Ask him!" Semyon Yakovlevitch said, ignoring her. He pointed instead at the kneeling man.

The monk walked calmly to the kneeling figure. "What have you done? Were you given some command to follow?"

"I was told not to fight... not to let my hands take control," the man said hoarsely.

"Have you obeyed?" asked the monk.

"I cannot. My own strength gets the better of me."

"Away with him! With a broom, with a broom!" Semyon Yakovlevitch shouted, waving his hands again.

The man scrambled to his feet and rushed out of the room without waiting for punishment.

"He left a gold coin where he knelt," said the monk, picking up the half-imperial from the floor.

"For him," said the saint, pointing to the wealthy merchant. The merchant hesitated but did not dare refuse the coin and pocketed it.

"Gold to gold," the monk muttered to himself.

"And give him tea with sugar," Semyon Yakovlevitch added, nodding toward Mavriky Nikolaevitch.

The servant poured out the tea but handed it to the wrong man—the dandy with the pince-nez.

"No, the tall one, the tall one!" Semyon Yakovlevitch corrected.

Mavriky Nikolaevitch stepped forward, accepted the tea, gave a short military bow, and began drinking it. For some reason, our entire group burst into laughter.

"Mavriky Nikolaevitch," Liza suddenly called out to him. "That kneeling man has gone now. You kneel down in his place."

Mavriky Nikolaevitch looked at her, stunned.

"I'm begging you! You'll do me a huge favor," she continued, her voice excited, rapid, and commanding. "Listen, Mavriky Nikolaevitch! You must kneel down. I must see you kneel down. If you refuse, don't come near me again. I insist! I insist!"

I don't know what she meant by it, but she insisted on it relentlessly, as if she were in some kind of fit. Mavriky Nikolaevitch, as we'll see later, believed these strange outbursts—more frequent lately—came from a deep, blind hatred toward him. It wasn't out of spite; in fact, she respected, loved, and admired him, and he knew that. But there was something inside her, a kind of unconscious anger, which sometimes took hold of her, and she couldn't control it.

Without saying a word, Mavriky Nikolaevitch handed his cup to an old woman nearby, opened the partition door, and, without being invited, walked into Semyon Yakovlevitch's private area. There, in front of everyone, he knelt down in the middle of the room. I think his kind, sensitive heart had been shocked by Liza's cruel, mocking behavior in front of so many people. Maybe he thought that if he humbled himself like that, she would feel ashamed of what she had done. Of course, no one but him would think of using such a strange and risky method to try to reason with her.

He stayed there on his knees, tall and stiff, awkward and ridiculous, yet strangely solemn. No one in our group laughed. The unexpectedness of his action cast a heavy silence over us. Everyone turned to look at Liza.

"Anoint, anoint!" muttered Semyon Yakovlevitch.

Liza suddenly turned pale. She gasped and ran through the partition. A chaotic, emotional scene followed. She grabbed Mavriky Nikolaevitch by the arms and started tugging at him with all her strength.

"Get up! Get up!" she screamed like someone out of her mind. "Get up this instant! How dare you?"

Mavriky Nikolaevitch stood up without a word. She clung to his arms and stared into his face, her eyes full of fear.

"Milovzors! Milovzors!" Semyon Yakovlevitch said again.

Finally, she dragged Mavriky Nikolaevitch back to the other part of the room. There was some commotion among our group. One of the ladies, trying to break the tension, loudly and cheerfully called out to the saint again, smiling as she spoke.

"Well, Semyon Yakovlevitch, won't you say something for me this time? I've been counting on you so much."

"Out with the ——, out with the ——," Semyon Yakovlevitch suddenly spat out, using a shockingly vulgar word. His tone was so harsh and clear that it startled everyone.

The women in our group screamed and rushed toward the door in a panic. The men, on the other hand, burst into loud, uncontrolled laughter. And that was how our visit to Semyon Yakovlevitch came to an end.

However, something puzzling happened as we were leaving. It was this strange event that made me describe the visit in such detail.

As everyone crowded out, Liza—supported by Mavriky Nikolaevitch—bumped into Nikolay Vsyevolodovitch in the doorway. Since the incident on Sunday morning when she fainted, the two of them had not exchanged a single word, though they had seen each other several times. I saw them come face-to-face in the doorway. I thought they both stopped for a moment and gave each other a strange look, though I could have been mistaken in the crush of people.

But others insist—quite seriously—that Liza raised her hand quickly, as if to slap Nikolay Vsyevolodovitch, and he only avoided it by stepping back just in time. Perhaps she didn't like the way he looked at her, or maybe he had smiled at her in a way that seemed inappropriate, especially after what had just happened with Mavriky Nikolaevitch.

I didn't see it clearly myself, but everyone else said they did, though in

362

such a crowd, I don't know how they all could have. Still, I didn't believe it at the time. I do remember, however, that Nikolay Vsyevolodovitch looked rather pale on the way home.

Chapter 5.3

Almost at the same time, and certainly on the same day, the long-anticipated meeting finally took place between Stepan Trofimovitch and Varvara Petrovna. She had been planning this discussion for some time, sending word to her former friend that it was necessary, yet inexplicably delaying it until now. The meeting occurred at Skvoreshniki, Varvara Petrovna's country estate, which she had visited that morning in a state of restless energy. The previous evening, it had been firmly decided that the fête would be held at the marshal's house, but her quick and restless mind had already conceived another idea. No one could stop her from hosting her own separate celebration at Skvoreshniki afterward, gathering the town's elite once again under her roof. Then, all of society could compare the two events for themselves—whose house was more elegant, whose décor was superior, and which hostess had shown better taste in entertaining her guests. This challenge to social prestige seemed to invigorate her spirit.

Altogether, Varvara Petrovna seemed almost unrecognizable that day. She appeared entirely transformed, as though the usually aloof and unapproachable "noble lady"—as Stepan Trofimovitch had always called her—had vanished. In her place stood a lively, animated woman, almost resembling a frivolous, fashion-conscious member of society. It seemed unlike her, and yet, perhaps, this change only touched the surface; deeper down, her old nature remained unchanged.

Upon her arrival at the estate, she immediately set about examining the empty house, accompanied by her trusted old butler, Alexey Yegorytch, and a certain Fomushka, an experienced decorator who had seen much of life. Together, they began discussing every detail of the upcoming event with great seriousness. Which pieces of furniture should be brought from the townhouse? What paintings or decorations would fit best in each room? Where should the new curtains go? How could the conservatory be arranged to maximize the effect of the flowers? Where should the refreshment rooms be located—one or two of them? The planning was meticulous and, to all appearances, invigorating for her.

Then, in the midst of all this activity, an unexpected whim struck her: she sent for Stepan Trofimovitch.

He had been anticipating this summons for days, knowing full well that the meeting was inevitable. As soon as he received the note, he prepared himself, silently crossing himself before stepping into the carriage. To him, this was not just a simple conversation—it was a defining moment, a turning point in his fate. When he arrived at Skvoreshniki, he found Varvara Petrovna seated in the grand drawing room on a small sofa tucked into a recessed corner. A little marble table stood before her, and she sat hunched over it with a pencil and paper, making careful notes.

Fomushka, holding a yardstick, was busy measuring the height of the galleries and windows, reading out the numbers, while Varvara Petrovna jotted them down in the margins of her paper. Without glancing up, she acknowledged Stepan Trofimovitch's arrival with a curt nod and motioned for him to sit beside her. He stammered some sort of formal greeting, but she did not pause in her work. She hurriedly stretched out her hand to him, more out of habit than warmth, and continued writing.

"I sat there waiting for five minutes, trying to control my heart," Stepan Trofimovitch told me later. "The woman sitting before me was not the same woman I had known for twenty years. A sudden, unshakable certainty that everything was over gave me a surprising inner strength. Even she seemed startled by my composure in that final hour."

At last, Varvara Petrovna put her pencil down with a sudden motion and turned to face him.

"Stepan Trofimovitch, we need to talk business," she said quickly, as though impatient to get it over with. "I'm sure you've prepared some grand speech, full of clever phrases and dramatic flourishes, but let's skip all that, shall we? Let's get straight to the point."

Her tone was sharp and determined, leaving no room for hesitation.

Whatever would follow, it was clear she was taking control of the conversation from the start.

"Now, be quiet—don't interrupt me. You'll have your turn to speak, though I don't see what you could possibly say to me," she continued, almost breathlessly. "Here's the situation: the twelve hundred roubles of your pension—those are yours. I see it as a sacred obligation to pay you that sum for as long as you live. Or better yet, let's call it what it really is—a contract. That would make it much clearer and far more practical, wouldn't it? If you want, we'll put it in writing. Arrangements have already been made in case of my death. But in addition to that, you are living off me. Right now, I provide you with lodging, servants, and food. If we were to calculate the cost of that, it would amount to another fifteen hundred roubles a year. So, let's simplify it. I'll increase your allowance by three hundred more, making it three thousand roubles a year in total. Does that seem fair? It's more than generous. If there's ever an extreme need, I might add something extra.

"So, take your money, send back my servants, and live wherever you like—in Petersburg, Moscow, abroad, or even here, if you must. Anywhere but with me. Do you understand?"

Stepan Trofimovitch remained silent for a moment, his sorrowful gaze fixed on her face. Then, speaking slowly and clearly, he replied, "Not so long ago, those same lips issued very different orders to me—just as imperiously, just as suddenly. I submitted then ... and I danced your tune like a little Cossack hopping over his own grave. Oui, la comparaison peut être permise—yes, I can use that comparison. It was like a Cossack from the Don leaping at his own tomb. And now..."

"Stop, Stepan Trofimovitch! You are being absurdly long-winded again!" she interrupted, almost laughing. "Danced? You didn't dance anything. You came to see me dressed up in new clothes, with fresh linen, gloves, and your hair slicked down with pomade. You were hoping for marriage—you know you were. It was written all over your face, and, believe me, it wasn't a flattering expression. I didn't say anything at the time out of delicacy, but you wanted it. Oh, you wanted it badly, despite the dreadful things you wrote about me and your 'betrothed.' But now

365

everything has changed. And what nonsense about a Cossack and a grave? I don't understand the comparison. On the contrary—you should live. Live as long as you can! I'd be delighted."

"In an almshouse?" he asked bitterly.

"In an almshouse? People don't go into almshouses with three thousand roubles a year," Varvara Petrovna laughed, shaking her head as though the very idea amused her. "Ah yes, I remember now," she added, a touch of mockery in her voice. "Pyotr Stepanovitch joked once about an almshouse—though, I must say, there's something to consider in that. There's a special one for respectable people, you know. Colonels live there, even a general tried to get in once, or so I've heard. With your money, you'd be perfectly comfortable. You'd have peace, quiet, your own room, and servants to wait on you. You could sit all day reading or even start a card game if you wanted. Imagine it—your very own intellectual retreat."

"Passons," Stepan Trofimovitch interrupted quietly, almost sighing the word as if he couldn't bear to hear more.

"Passons?" Varvara Petrovna raised her eyebrows slightly, the corner of her mouth twitching with irritation. "Very well, then, passons. But that's all there is to say, Stepan Trofimovitch. You've been informed of my decision: we will live apart from now on. Entirely apart."

"And that's it?" he asked after a pause, his voice hollow and strained. "That's all that remains after twenty years? Just this farewell?"

"You are so fond of exclaiming things, Stepan Trofimovitch," she replied impatiently. "It's completely out of fashion, don't you know? These days, people speak plainly, directly. Enough of your dramatic outbursts! You keep harping on about our twenty years, as though they were something sacred. Twenty years of what, exactly? Mutual vanity and nothing more! Every letter you wrote to me was written with an eye on posterity, not for me. You're not a friend, Stepan Trofimovitch, you're a stylist—there's a difference. And friendship, well, that's just a grand-sounding word. In reality, it's just an exchange of sentimental nonsense."

He looked at her with a kind of stunned sadness. "Good heavens, how many of these phrases you've collected! They're not your own words,

Varvara Petrovna. You've learned them by heart, absorbed them from someone else. And now look at you—they've put their uniform on you too! You, who once stood so proudly alone, have joined their ranks. You're basking in it now, aren't you? Rejoicing in their approval. Chère, chère, what a miserable price you've paid for this mess of pottage they've offered you!"

"I'm no parrot repeating someone else's phrases," she retorted sharply, the anger in her voice rising. "You can be sure of that! I've stored up plenty of thoughts and words of my own. And let me ask you this—what have you ever done for me in these twenty years? Nothing! You couldn't even bring me the books I asked for! Oh, you ordered them, yes, but they would have stayed untouched, uncut, if not for the binder's knife. You were jealous even of my education! You refused to guide me, and all you ever gave me to read was Kapfig—always Kapfig and nothing else. You thought yourself superior, didn't you? Meanwhile, the whole world was laughing at you behind your back. I never thought of you as anything more than a literary critic. That's what you are, and that's all you've ever been."

"Not that, not that," he muttered faintly, almost to himself. "It wasn't like that at all. We were afraid then, afraid of persecution…"

"Nonsense! It was exactly like that," she cut him off. "There was no persecution in Petersburg, not at that time. And don't you remember, in February, when the emancipation news came? You ran to me in a panic, practically trembling, demanding I give you a signed statement. You wanted me to declare that the young people visiting the house were coming to see me, not you. You wanted me to write down that you were just a tutor living in my home, waiting for your salary. Do you deny it? Do you not remember that pathetic display? Oh yes, Stepan Trofimovitch, you've truly distinguished yourself all your life."

"That was only a moment of weakness," he said softly, his voice filled with sorrow. "It was a moment when we were alone, and no one else could see. But is that enough to erase everything? To break it all off over something so petty, so meaningless? After all these years, is there nothing left between us? Nothing at all?"

"You're insufferable," she replied coldly. "You're always calculating, always weighing everything, trying to leave me in your debt. You want me to owe you something, don't you? You want me to feel guilty! And don't forget how you acted when you came back from abroad. You looked down on me, wouldn't let me get a word in. And then, when I returned and shared my thoughts about the Madonna—how it moved me, how beautiful it was—you wouldn't even listen. You just smiled condescendingly, like I was a fool incapable of understanding the same feelings you experienced."

"It wasn't like that," he murmured faintly, shaking his head. "It couldn't have been like that. I've forgotten… j'ai oublié."

"No, it was exactly like that," she insisted firmly. "And let me tell you something else—you have nothing to be proud of. All your ideas, your so-called brilliance—it's all meaningless. You cling to that nonsense about the Madonna, but no one cares anymore. Do you know that? No one spends time thinking about it now. It's only the hopelessly old-fashioned, the relics of a bygone era, who waste their energy on such things. That's the truth, Stepan Trofimovitch. It's already been established."

"Established?" he echoed, his voice heavy with irony.

"Yes, established," she repeated sharply. "You laugh, but I'm serious. People today value things that are useful. This jug here—this jug has value because you can pour water into it. This pencil—it's useful because you can write with it. But the Madonna? That woman's face? It's pointless. Show me a real apple and a painted one side by side, and tell me which one you'd choose. The real one, obviously! That's what we understand now. That's what the dawn of free thought has brought us."

"Oh, indeed," Stepan Trofimovitch whispered bitterly.

"And you used to lecture me about charity, didn't you?" she continued relentlessly. "But charity is an insult—it's immoral, a false virtue. It corrupts both the giver and the receiver. Charity doesn't solve poverty; it makes it worse. Lazy fathers and beggars gather around like gamblers hoping to win, while the pitiful pennies thrown at them achieve nothing. It should be banned by law! And in the future, in the new regime, there will be no poor at all."

"What an eruption of borrowed phrases," he said, shaking his head slowly, his voice quiet but full of sadness. "So it's come to this—the new regime. Poor, wretched woman. God help you."

"Yes, it has come to this, Stepan Trofimovitch," Varvara Petrovna replied coldly, her words measured but full of restrained energy. "You've kept all these so-called 'new ideas' hidden from me for so long— deliberately hidden—while the rest of the world moved ahead. And you didn't do it for any noble reason, no; you did it out of jealousy, pure and simple. You wanted to maintain power over me, to keep me in the dark so you could feel superior. And now even that woman—Yulia—has left me far behind. She's ahead of me by a hundred miles, and whose fault is that? Yours. But don't worry, my eyes are open now, Stepan Trofimovitch. I've defended you for as long as I could, with all the strength I had, but there isn't a soul left who doesn't blame you."

"Enough!" Stepan Trofimovitch suddenly rose from his seat, as though unable to endure it any longer. His face, pale and sorrowful, seemed to sag under the weight of her words. "Enough! What more can I wish for you now, except repentance?"

"Sit down," she commanded, ignoring his attempt to end the conversation. "Sit for a moment longer, Stepan Trofimovitch. I have one more question to ask you, and I expect an answer. You've heard about the invitation for the literary matinée, haven't you? That was arranged through me, by the way. Now, tell me—what are you planning to read there?"

He sighed deeply before answering, as though even the question itself exhausted him. "Why, I will read about the very Queen of Queens. I will speak of the ideal of humanity itself, the Sistine Madonna—she whom you have reduced, in your enlightened view, to something inferior to a jug or a pencil."

Varvara Petrovna looked at him in mournful disbelief, her face softening, though only for an instant. "So you're not choosing something historical?" she asked. "That's what I was hoping for, something entertaining—something to keep the audience awake. But this... this Madonna obsession of yours? They'll never listen to it. You'll put everyone to sleep, I promise you. I'm telling you this for your own good, Stepan Trofimovitch. You'd do much better to pick something short and entertaining—something from Spanish history, perhaps. A lively anecdote of court life, full of intrigue and poisonings, something with wit and charm. Pad it out with your clever little phrases, and everyone will applaud. That's what they want. Karmazinov himself says it would be strange if you couldn't find something worthwhile in Spanish history."

"Karmazinov?" Stepan Trofimovitch's voice was thick with contempt as he spoke the name. "Karmazinov, that dried-up, spiteful fool? That empty shell of a man who's written himself out and now seeks to give me advice? Is he now to dictate what I speak about?"

"Karmazinov is a man of almost imperial intellect," Varvara Petrovna shot back with rising indignation. "You forget yourself. Your language is too free, Stepan Trofimovitch."

"Your Karmazinov is nothing more than an embittered old woman," he said, shaking his head. "His time has passed, and his words carry no weight. And you—you—how long have you been enslaved by all of them, by these new thinkers and their hollow phrases? Oh, my God..."

"I don't care for Karmazinov either," she interrupted sharply, "not for his arrogance or his airs. But I do justice to his intellect, and you should do the same. At least he understands what people want to hear. I have defended you, defended your name, defended your choices—but why do you insist on being absurd? Why must you make yourself ridiculous and tedious? Why can't you face them with dignity, as the representative of your generation? Imagine it—walk out onto the platform with grace, with a little self-awareness. Smile at them, tell them two or three stories, something witty and lighthearted. Show them you understand that your time has passed, that you belong to an older age—but do it with charm. Let them see you for what you really are—a man of the past who is still witty, still good-natured, still capable of appreciating the foolishness of these modern ideas that you once followed. For me, Stepan Trofimovitch, I beg you. Do this as a favor to me."

"Chère, enough," he said softly, his voice low but resolute. "Don't ask me. I cannot. I will speak of the Madonna. I will speak of beauty, of ideals that this generation has forgotten. I will raise a storm, and that storm will either crush them all or destroy me alone."

"It will be you alone, Stepan Trofimovitch," she replied with quiet certainty.

"Then so be it," he said, his voice trembling with emotion. "Such is my fate. I will speak of the contemptible slave—the stinking, depraved flunkey—who will be the first to climb a ladder, scissors in hand, and slash to pieces the divine image of the great ideal. They will do it in the name of equality, envy, and… digestion. Let my curse thunder down upon them, and then—then…"

"And then the madhouse?" she interrupted cruelly.

"Perhaps," he admitted with a faint smile. "But either way, whether I am crushed or victorious, that very evening I will pack my bag—my beggar's bag. I will leave behind all my possessions, all your gifts, all your pensions and promises of charity. I will take nothing, and I will leave. I will walk away on foot, and live as a tutor in some merchant's house, or I will die of hunger somewhere in a ditch. I have said it. Alea jacta est." He rose again, trembling.

"I have been convinced for years," Varvara Petrovna said as she stood too, her eyes blazing, "that your one goal in life is to bring shame on me and my house with your wild accusations! A merchant's tutor? Dying in a ditch? This is all childish nonsense, Stepan Trofimovitch. It's pure spite. Nothing more."

"You've always despised me," he said, his voice full of sadness. "But I will end as a knight faithful to his lady. Your good opinion—your respect—has always meant more to me than anything. From now on, I will take nothing. I will worship you, disinterestedly, from afar."

"How ridiculous," she snapped, though her voice wavered.

"You have never respected me," he went on. "Yes, I've been weak, I've been a burden to you. I have sponged off you, and I won't deny it. I've spoken their language, the language of nihilism, but never—never—

has that been the guiding purpose of my life. I always believed there was something higher between us, something greater than all this. And now I will set off—too late, yes—but I will go. The mist of autumn lies heavy over the fields; the hoarfrost of age covers the path ahead of me, and the wind howls of the grave drawing near. But still, forward I will go, forward toward the end."

He paused, as though struggling with a flood of emotion. Then, suddenly, tears welled up in his eyes. "Farewell, my dreams. Farewell, twenty years. Alea jacta est."

His face was wet with tears as he reached for his hat.

"I don't understand Latin," she said stiffly, though she looked away, as if to hide her own feelings. Perhaps for a moment, just a moment, she felt the urge to cry too. But her pride, her indignation, and her temper won out in the end.

"I know one thing for certain," she continued, "all this is nothing but childish foolishness. You'll never carry out your threats. You'll go nowhere. You won't teach any merchants, and you won't starve in a ditch. You'll stay here. You'll end your days on my hands, taking your pension and entertaining your impossible friends every Tuesday. Good-bye, Stepan Trofimovitch."

"Alea jacta est," he repeated softly. With a deep, almost theatrical bow, he turned and left, his steps unsteady, his heart heavy with emotion.

Chapter 6
Pyotr Stepanovitch Is Busy

Chapter 6.1

The date for the celebration was officially set, and Von Lembke grew more and more troubled. He was filled with strange and dark fears, which made Yulia Mihailovna genuinely worried. In truth, things weren't going very well. The mild-mannered governor had let the province fall into some disarray. At the time, there was a threat of cholera; serious outbreaks of cattle disease had appeared in several areas; fires were frequent in towns and villages that summer; and foolish rumors of arson were spreading among the peasants. Cases of robbery were twice as common as usual. But all of this would have been seen as relatively normal if there hadn't been deeper and more troubling reasons for Andrey Antonovitch's unease. Until recently, he had been in good spirits.

What worried Yulia Mihailovna most was that he was becoming quieter and, strangely enough, more secretive each day. Yet it was hard to imagine what he could possibly have to hide. It's true that he rarely argued with her and usually followed her lead without question. For example, she persuaded him to issue two or three risky and barely legal regulations to strengthen his authority as governor. There were even a few questionable cases where wrongdoers were excused for the sake of maintaining control. Some people who should have been sent to prison or even Siberia were, because of her insistence, rewarded with promotions. Complaints and investigations were deliberately ignored. All of this came to light later. Not only did Lembke sign off on everything, but he also didn't seem to care about the extent of his wife's involvement in his work. On the other hand, he occasionally became stubborn over the smallest matters, which surprised Yulia Mihailovna. It was as if he needed these moments of defiance to make up for his usual submission. Unfortunately, Yulia Mihailovna, for all her insight, couldn't understand this sense of pride in his character. Sadly, she didn't give it much thought, and this led to many misunderstandings.

There are certain things that I shouldn't write about, and in fact, I'm not in a position to do so. It's not my place to discuss mistakes in administration, and I prefer to leave out the bureaucratic aspects altogether. In this account, I have a different goal. Besides, much of it will be revealed by the Commission of Inquiry that's just been appointed for our province; it's only a matter of time. However, some explanations can't be avoided.

But let's return to Yulia Mihailovna. The poor woman (I truly feel sorry for her) could have achieved everything she dreamed of—fame and recognition—without resorting to the dramatic and impulsive actions she chose from the start. Whether it was due to an over-the-top love for the dramatic or the disappointments she had faced earlier in life, she suddenly felt, with her newfound position, that she was one of the chosen few—almost divinely appointed, with a kind of holy flame guiding her. And that flame was the root of her troubles. It wasn't like a hairstyle that could suit anyone. But convincing a woman otherwise is nearly impossible; in fact, anyone who fuels such illusions in her will always be met with success. And people eagerly encouraged Yulia Mihailovna in her delusions. She quickly became a pawn in the hands of opposing influences while firmly believing in her own originality. Many clever individuals took advantage of her simplicity during her brief time in power in the province. And what chaos resulted from her supposed independence! She was equally enchanted by the aristocratic lifestyle, large estates, and the increased power of the governor as she was by democratic ideals, progressive reforms, discipline, and scattered socialist ideas. She admired the refined manners of aristocratic salons but also the casual, almost rowdy behavior of the young people around her. She dreamed of spreading happiness and uniting everyone in admiration of herself. She even had favorites. Pyotr Stepanovitch, for instance, often flattered her shamelessly, which she enjoyed. But her attachment to him was driven by another, even stranger reason—one that truly defined her character. She actually hoped he would reveal a grand conspiracy against the government. As hard as it is to believe, this was true. For some reason, she was convinced that a nihilist plot was secretly brewing in the province. Pyotr Stepanovitch, with his silence at times and vague hints at others, only reinforced this bizarre idea. She imagined he was connected to every revolutionary group in Russia while being completely devoted to her. She dreamed of uncovering the conspiracy, earning the government's gratitude, launching a brilliant career, influencing the youth with kindness, and steering them away from extremes. All of these hopes coexisted in her wild imagination. She believed she had "saved" Pyotr Stepanovitch and won him over (why she thought this is unclear) and that she would save others too. She wouldn't let anyone fall; she'd save them all. She would write fair reports, act with the highest sense of justice, and perhaps future generations and Russian liberals would praise her name. Yet, she would still uncover the conspiracy. Every possible benefit rolled into one.

Still, Andrey Antonovitch needed to be in a better mood before the festival. He had to be reassured and cheered up. To that end, she sent Pyotr Stepanovitch to him, hoping he would lift his spirits somehow, maybe by sharing some firsthand information. She trusted entirely in his skill.

It had been a while since Pyotr Stepanovitch visited Mr. von Lembke's office. He arrived just as Lembke was in an especially stubborn and irritable mood.

Chapter 6.2

A series of unfortunate events had emerged, creating a situation that Mr. von Lembke found completely beyond his ability to handle. In the same district where Pyotr Stepanovitch had been enjoying himself at a festival, a young sub-lieutenant was summoned for a reprimand by his commanding officer. This dressing-down occurred in front of the entire company. The sub-lieutenant, a quiet and brooding young man recently arrived from Petersburg, had a dignified presence despite being short, stout, and rosy-faced. However, he took the criticism poorly. Suddenly, with an ear-piercing scream that startled everyone, he charged at his superior officer like a wild animal, head down, and bit him savagely on the shoulder. It took considerable effort to pull him off. Clearly, the young man had lost his sanity—or so it seemed. Reports later revealed that he had been behaving in bizarre ways for some time. For instance, he had thrown two religious icons belonging to his landlady out of his apartment, smashing one of them with an axe. In his own room, he had set up three stands resembling lecterns, each holding books by Vogt, Moleschott, and Büchner, and before these stands, he would burn church wax candles in some kind of ritual.

From the number of books found in his room, it was clear that he was well-read. Some speculated that if he had been wealthy, he might have embarked on a whimsical journey, perhaps sailing to the Marquesas Islands, much like the cadet Herzen humorously mentioned in his writings. When he was arrested, the authorities discovered bundles of the most radical manifestoes stuffed in his pockets and scattered throughout his lodgings.

These manifestoes, however, were not entirely unusual and, to my mind, not worth much concern. We had seen similar ones before, and they were not even new. As it turned out, they were the same as those distributed in the neighboring X province. Liputin, who had visited that area and the adjacent province six weeks earlier, claimed to have seen identical leaflets there. Yet what most troubled Andrey Antonovitch was a report from the overseer of Shpigulin's factory. Around the same time, the overseer brought two or three packets of identical leaflets to the police, claiming they had been dropped in the factory overnight. Interestingly, the bundles had not been opened, and none of the workers had read them. While this incident seemed minor on the surface, it planted a seed of deep concern in Andrey Antonovitch's mind. The situation now appeared more tangled and unsettling.

This particular factory was already embroiled in what later became the notorious "Shpigulin Scandal," a case that made waves even in the Petersburg and Moscow papers. About three weeks earlier, a worker at the factory had fallen ill and died of Asiatic cholera, with several others soon contracting the disease. The town was gripped by panic, as the cholera outbreak was edging closer, having already struck the neighboring province. Although sanitary measures had been taken to address the looming threat, the Shpigulin factory—a large establishment owned by wealthy and well-connected millionaires—had somehow been overlooked. Public outcry erupted, with accusations that the factory and its workers' quarters were filthy and likely a breeding ground for the disease. Some claimed that an outbreak there was inevitable even without the presence of cholera in the region.

Immediate action was ordered, and Andrey Antonovitch firmly insisted on the factory being cleaned within three weeks. The factory was indeed sanitized, but the Shpigulin brothers responded in an unexpected and questionable manner. One brother, who lived in Petersburg, remained conspicuously absent, while the other left for Moscow as soon as the cleaning orders were issued. Meanwhile, their overseer began dismissing workers en masse, exploiting the opportunity to underpay them scandalously. The workers, though not initially riled up, began murmuring amongst themselves and foolishly sought help from the police. Their complaints were mild and orderly, but it was during this time that the overseer brought the suspicious bundles of manifestoes to Andrey Antonovitch.

When Pyotr Stepanovitch entered Lembke's study unannounced, he did so with the casual air of a close friend or even a family member. He also carried a message from Yulia Mihailovna. However, his arrival clearly displeased Lembke, who frowned deeply and remained standing by the table, without offering him a greeting. Moments before, Lembke had been pacing the room in a heated discussion with his secretary, Blum, a gruff and clumsy German whom he had brought from Petersburg despite Yulia Mihailovna's strong objections. Upon Pyotr Stepanovitch's entrance, Blum stepped toward the door but lingered, seemingly hesitant to leave. Pyotr Stepanovitch even thought he caught a meaningful exchange of glances between Blum and Lembke.

"Aha, caught you in your lair at last, you secretive ruler of the town!" Pyotr Stepanovitch exclaimed with a mischievous laugh, placing his hand over the stack of manifestoes on the table. "Adding more to your collection, I see?"

Lembke flushed a deep red, his face twitching with irritation. "Stop it—stop it this instant!" he shouted, visibly trembling with anger. "And don't you dare... sir..."

"What's gotten into you? Are you actually upset?" Pyotr Stepanovitch responded, feigning innocence.

"Allow me to inform you, sir, that I will no longer tolerate your familiarities. Kindly remember that—"

"Well, I'll be damned! He's serious!" Pyotr Stepanovitch interrupted.

"Quiet, quiet!" Lembke roared, stamping his foot on the carpet. "And don't you dare—"

What might have happened next is anyone's guess. Unfortunately, neither Pyotr Stepanovitch nor even Yulia Mihailovna herself was aware of one critical detail. The unfortunate Lembke had become so unsettled in recent days that he had begun to harbor secret suspicions of his wife's relationship with Pyotr Stepanovitch. In his moments of solitude, especially at night, he endured many unpleasant and distressing thoughts.

"Well," Pyotr Stepanovitch said with a touch of offended dignity, "I thought that if a man spends two nights in a row reading his novel to me and asks for my opinion, he's setting aside official formalities, at least for the moment. Yulia Mihailovna treats me as a friend, but with you, there's just no figuring you out." With that, he set down a large manuscript, wrapped in blue paper, on the table. "Here's your novel, by the way."

Lembke's face changed; despite his attempts to appear indifferent, a rush of relief and joy was evident. "Where did you find it?" he asked cautiously.

"Funny story! I must have tossed it carelessly onto a chest of drawers before going out. It rolled underneath, and it wasn't found until they cleaned the floor the day before yesterday. You certainly gave me a task with this!"

Lembke, still flustered, took the manuscript, locked it in his oak bookcase, and took the opportunity to motion discreetly for Blum to leave. Blum exited with a long, dejected look.

"I've had nothing but trouble lately," Lembke muttered, sitting down at the table and frowning. "Say what you came to say, but in the future, don't barge in so rudely. It's—"

"My manners are always consistent."

"I know, I know," Lembke sighed, his frustration ebbing slightly. "And I understand you don't mean any harm, but sometimes it's… well, when one has pressing matters…"

Pyotr Stepanovitch immediately lounged on the sofa, pulling his legs up beneath him as if entirely at ease.

Chapter 6.3

"What sort of worries? Surely not over these insignificant trifles?" Pyotr Stepanovitch gestured toward the manifesto on the table. "I can bring you as many of these as you'd like. I became quite familiar with them during my time in the X province."

"You mean when you were staying there?" asked Von Lembke, his brow furrowed with curiosity.

"Of course, it wasn't during my absence," Pyotr Stepanovitch replied dryly. "I distinctly remember there was a hatchet printed at the top of it. Allow me." He reached for the manifesto on the table and pointed to the design. "Yes, there it is—the hatchet. It's exactly the same one."

"Indeed, there's a hatchet. You see, a hatchet," Von Lembke repeated, his tone stiff and uneasy.

"Well then, is it the hatchet that's troubling you?"

"No, it's not the hatchet… and I am not troubled, exactly. But this situation—it's not as simple as it looks. It's… complicated."

"Complicated because it came from the factory? Ha! You know, at this rate, the workers there will soon start writing their own manifestoes."

"What do you mean by that?" Von Lembke demanded, narrowing his eyes. His voice took on a more severe tone as he stared at Pyotr Stepanovitch, who seemed entirely unfazed.

"Exactly what I said. Take a good look at them! You're far too soft, Andrey Antonovitch. You write novels when what's needed is firm action—the kind that gets results."

"And what, pray tell, do you mean by firm action? What sort of advice are you trying to give me?" Von Lembke asked sharply. "The factory has already been cleaned. I gave the order, and it's been carried out."

"And the workers are in rebellion now. They need to be dealt with firmly, every last one of them. A good flogging would end it all in no time."

"In rebellion? Nonsense!" Von Lembke retorted, his voice rising slightly. "I gave the order, and they followed it. The factory has been cleaned, as I said."

"Ah, you're too soft, Andrey Antonovitch," Pyotr Stepanovitch replied with a smirk.

"In the first place, I'm not as soft as you think," Von Lembke said

379

defensively, his tone growing more agitated. "And in the second place…"
He trailed off, irritated by the young man's audacity but also intrigued
enough to continue the conversation, hoping it might lead to something
useful.

Before he could finish, Pyotr Stepanovitch interrupted, seizing
another document lying under a paperweight on the table. His eyes lit up
with recognition. "Ha! An old friend, I see!" he exclaimed, holding up the
paper. "This one looks familiar too—printed abroad, isn't it? And written
in verse! Oh, come on, I know this one by heart. It's titled 'A Noble
Personality.' Let's have a look. Yes, that's it, 'A Noble Personality.' I came
across this charming piece while I was abroad. Where on earth did you
dig it up?"

"You've seen this abroad?" Von Lembke asked eagerly, leaning
forward.

"I should think so. It was about four or five months ago, if I recall
correctly."

"You certainly seem to have seen a great deal while you were abroad,"
Von Lembke remarked, attempting a subtle yet probing tone.

Without acknowledging the comment, Pyotr Stepanovitch unfolded
the document and began reading aloud, his voice carrying a theatrical edge:

"A Noble Personality

He was not of rank exalted,
He was not of noble birth,
He was bred among the people
In the breast of Mother Earth.
But the malice of the nobles
And the Tsar's revengeful wrath
Drove him forth to grief and torture
On the martyr's chosen path.
He set out to teach the people
Freedom, love, equality,
To exhort them to resistance;

But to flee the penalty
Of the prison, whip and gallows,
To a foreign land he went.
While the people waited hoping
From Smolensk to far Tashkent,
Waited eager for his coming
To rebel against their fate,
To arise and crush the Tsardom
And the nobles' vicious hate,
To share all the wealth in common,
And the antiquated thrall
Of the church, the home and marriage
To abolish once for all."*

Pyotr Stepanovitch finished the poem and looked up with a sly smile. "I assume you got this from that officer?"

"Why, do you know that officer as well?" Von Lembke asked, surprised.

"Know him? I spent two lively days with him back then. He was bound to lose his mind."

"Or perhaps he didn't lose his mind after all," Von Lembke suggested hesitantly.

"You mean because he started biting people? Is that your reasoning?" Pyotr Stepanovitch replied with a laugh.

"But wait," Von Lembke interjected, "if you saw these verses abroad and now they've appeared here, at that officer's—"

"What's confusing you?" Pyotr Stepanovitch interrupted again, his tone suddenly adopting an air of exaggerated dignity. "Are you trying to examine me, Andrey Antonovitch? Let me remind you, I've already given all the necessary explanations regarding my activities abroad. These explanations were deemed satisfactory, or else I wouldn't be gracing this town with my presence. As far as I'm concerned, that chapter is closed. I owe no further account of myself, not because I'm unwilling, but because I acted as I had to. Those who wrote to Yulia Mihailovna about me knew

381

exactly what they were talking about—they called me an honest man. And that's the end of it. But enough of this. I didn't come here to rehash old stories. I came about something important—something that matters to me."

"Important, you say?" Von Lembke murmured, his curiosity piqued despite himself. "Very well, I'm listening. But I must admit, Pyotr Stepanovitch, you have a way of surprising me."

Von Lembke, clearly uneasy, fidgeted slightly in his chair, his agitation visible. Pyotr Stepanovitch, meanwhile, crossed his legs casually, reclining as though entirely at home. His confident demeanor was impossible to ignore.

"In Petersburg," Pyotr Stepanovitch began with a deliberate tone, "I spoke openly on most subjects, but there were certain matters—this, for instance," he tapped his finger pointedly on the paper containing A Noble Personality, "that I chose to remain silent about. First, because they were not worth discussing. Second, because I only ever answered direct questions. I'm not the type to offer unsolicited commentary on sensitive matters. That, you see, is the distinction between a scoundrel who seeks opportunities to exploit and an honest man forced into difficult circumstances. But, well, let's set that aside. Now..." He leaned forward slightly, his tone growing more urgent. "Now that these fools have brought this out into the open—now that it's landed in your hands—and knowing that a man like you, with your sharp eyes and keen sense, will inevitably uncover the whole story, I've come to ask something of you. And these fools—they just keep at it, pushing things further. So, here I am, trying to do something humane, even if it feels futile."

He paused, his agitation plain, and then suddenly exclaimed with raw emotion, "Yes, that's it—I've come to beg you to save someone! A man who's just as much a fool as the rest, probably mad. But I'm asking this of you for the sake of his youth, his hardships, his misfortunes. In the name of your humanity, I implore you. Surely, you're not only humane in the novels you dream up!"

The sarcasm in his voice was sharp, and he finished with an impatient wave of his hand. Despite this brashness, his plea had a kind of awkward sincerity, even a desperate honesty. It painted him as a straightforward individual, someone who was clumsy and ill-suited to the art of persuasion, and perhaps too sensitive for his own good. His manner suggested a man burdened by excessive emotion, and, as Von Lembke quickly surmised with a subtle shift in his expression, a man of limited intelligence.

For some time now, Lembke had suspected as much. It had crossed his mind more than once—particularly during moments of frustration in his private study, where he'd quietly cursed this man's inexplicable influence over Yulia Mihailovna. The very idea had gnawed at him.

"Who exactly are you interceding for, and what does all of this mean?" Von Lembke inquired with a calm but authoritative tone, carefully masking his rising curiosity.

"Damn it! Is it my fault that I trust you? Can you blame me for seeing you as an honorable man, a sensible man?" Pyotr Stepanovitch's voice cracked slightly as he spoke, his usual composure slipping. "You're capable of understanding me, aren't you? Of seeing through all of this madness? Damn it…" His voice trailed off, revealing his inner turmoil.

Gathering himself, he pressed on. "Look, you must understand—by speaking his name, I'm betraying him. That's right, betraying him! And yet, what choice do I have? I trust you, don't I? But trust comes at a price, and here I am, handing him over. Am I not betraying him?"

"But how am I to guess anything if you refuse to speak plainly?" Von Lembke countered, his voice edged with impatience. "You must tell me more clearly what this is all about."

"That's just it!" Pyotr Stepanovitch threw up his hands in frustration. "You always cut the ground out from under people's feet with your damned logic. Fine, fine—here it is. The 'noble personality,' the 'student' mentioned here, is Shatov. There, I've said it."

"Shatov? What do you mean it's Shatov?" Von Lembke asked, leaning forward, his interest now fully piqued.

"Shatov is the 'student' mentioned in the manifesto. He lives here. He's a former serf—the same one who gave that infamous slap."

"I know who Shatov is," Von Lembke said slowly, narrowing his eyes. "But tell me, what exactly is he being accused of? And, more importantly, what is it that you are asking of me?"

"I'm asking you to save him!" Pyotr Stepanovitch cried, his composure breaking completely. "Do you understand? I knew him eight years ago—once, I might even have called him a friend. But that's beside the point; I'm not here to recount the details of my personal history to you. That's irrelevant. What matters is that this isn't some grand conspiracy. At best, it involves three men, maybe a few others scattered abroad—a dozen, if that. It's nothing, nothing! What I'm asking is for you to show humanity and reason. To see this for what it is—a foolish dream of a man who's been driven mad by endless misfortunes, not some grand, treasonous plot against the state!"

His words spilled out in a rush, his breathing heavy by the time he finished.

"Hmm, I see," Von Lembke said slowly, his tone measured and deliberate. "So he's the one responsible for the manifestoes with the axe symbol?"

"Perhaps," Pyotr Stepanovitch admitted, throwing up his hands again. "But listen, if it's only him, how do you explain the distribution of those same leaflets in other districts and even in the X province? And where did they come from in the first place?"

"I've already told you—I don't know," Pyotr Stepanovitch said with rising exasperation. "I have no idea! Damn it, can't you understand what 'nothing' means? That officer you mentioned, maybe someone else here, and yes, maybe Shatov—fine, I'll grant that—but beyond that, who knows? The point is, I've come to intercede for Shatov. That's what matters. You see, this poem—A Noble Personality—it's his work. He wrote it himself. And yes, I know for a fact that it was through him that it was published abroad. But as for the manifestoes? I swear, I know nothing about them."

"If the poem is his, it stands to reason the manifestoes might be as well," Von Lembke replied thoughtfully. "But what evidence do you have to accuse him of this?"

With a visible expression of annoyance, Pyotr Stepanovitch reached into his pocket, pulled out a worn notebook, and removed a single piece of paper. "Here are the facts!" he exclaimed, slapping it onto the table.

Von Lembke unfolded the note carefully. It was dated six months prior and had been sent from this very town to an address abroad. The message was short, just two lines:

"I can't print 'A Noble Personality' here, and in fact, I can do nothing; print it abroad.

Iv. Shatov."

Lembke's gaze flicked back to Pyotr Stepanovitch, his expression difficult to read. In that moment, his face took on a sheep-like quality that had been noted by others before.

"You see?" Pyotr Stepanovitch said with a strained voice, gesturing at the paper. "It's clear as day! He wrote that poem here, but he couldn't get it printed locally—he needed it done abroad. Isn't it obvious?"

"That much is clear," Lembke conceded, a note of irony creeping into his voice. "But to whom was this letter sent? That's not so obvious."

"Kirillov, of course!" Pyotr Stepanovitch shot back, his frustration boiling over. "The letter was written to Kirillov abroad. Surely you must have known that already! Or are you just toying with me? You knew about this poem and everything else all along, didn't you? Why else would it be sitting on your table now? How did it even get there? And if you did know, why put me through this torment?"

Mopping his forehead with a handkerchief, he stared at Lembke with a mix of irritation and desperation. Lembke, for his part, remained composed, responding with deliberate vagueness.

"Perhaps I know something," he replied. "But tell me—who is this Kirillov?"

"An engineer who recently arrived in town," Pyotr Stepanovitch began, speaking with a mixture of irritation and amusement. "He was Stavrogin's second in that duel—a complete maniac, absolutely deranged. Your sub-lieutenant might be suffering from a passing bout of delirium,

385

but Kirillov? Kirillov is a certified madman, through and through, and that I can guarantee. If only the government truly understood what kind of people these so-called conspirators are, they wouldn't even have the heart to arrest them. Every last one of them belongs in an asylum, not a prison. I saw plenty of them during my time in Switzerland, especially at the congresses they organize."

"Congress meetings," Lembke repeated, leaning forward slightly. "And from there, they coordinate the movement here, correct?"

"Coordinate? Ha!" Pyotr Stepanovitch let out a bitter laugh. "What coordination are you talking about? It's run by three and a half men—three and a half! The very thought of it makes one sick. And what kind of movement is it, anyway? Manifestoes, scattered propaganda, and empty rhetoric! And who are their recruits? Sub-lieutenants in the midst of brain fever and two or three immature students who barely know what they're doing! Tell me this, Andrey Antonovitch—you're a sensible man, after all—why don't people of consequence join their ranks? Why is it always students and half-baked boys barely out of adolescence? And not even many of those! I'd wager there are thousands of investigators, spies, and informants tracking them down, but how many real conspirators have they actually uncovered? Seven? Seven! And even that feels like a stretch. Honestly, the whole thing is enough to turn your stomach."

As Pyotr Stepanovitch spoke, Lembke listened attentively but with a reserved expression, one that seemed to say, "You can't nourish sensible minds with fairy tales."

"Excuse me," Lembke interjected finally, his voice calm but probing. "You claimed earlier that the letter was sent abroad, yet it lacks an address. How, then, do you know it was directed to Kirillov and sent overseas? And furthermore, how are you so certain it was written by Shatov?"

"Simple," Pyotr Stepanovitch replied, with an air of exasperated certainty. "Fetch any sample of Shatov's handwriting and compare it. Surely, you have something of his in your office—a signature, a report, anything. As for it being addressed to Kirillov, that's an easy one. Kirillov himself showed it to me at the time."

"Then you were personally involved..." Lembke began, trailing off with deliberate ambiguity.

"Of course, I was," Pyotr Stepanovitch snapped. "They showed me plenty of things while I was abroad. And this poem," he gestured toward A Noble Personality, "do you know what they claim? They say Herzen wrote it as a tribute to Shatov back when they met overseas, a kind of praise or recommendation, as if to say, 'Here is a remarkable young man, worthy of recognition.' Damn it all! And now Shatov circulates it among the young people, letting them believe, 'This is how Herzen saw me—this was his opinion of me.'"

Lembke's face lit up with sudden understanding. "Ha! So that's it!" he exclaimed, clearly feeling as though he had unraveled part of the mystery. "I was wondering about the purpose of the poem. I can understand the use of the manifesto, but the poem—it seemed strange to me. What's the point of it?"

"Of course, you'd see it," Pyotr Stepanovitch said, with an almost mocking grin. "I don't know why I've even been wasting my breath explaining this to you. But listen—spare Shatov for me. Let the others go to hell. Even Kirillov, who, by the way, is hiding now. He's locked up in Filipov's house—yes, the same house where Shatov lives. They don't like me much because I've 'turned around,' so to speak, but that's beside the point. I'm telling you this because I trust you. Promise me Shatov's safety, and I'll hand them all over to you on a silver platter. I can be useful to you, Andrey Antonovitch, and you know it! We're talking about a pitiful handful of men here—nine or ten at most. I've been keeping an eye on them myself, out of personal interest. We already know three: Shatov, Kirillov, and that sub-lieutenant. As for the rest, I'm observing them closely—don't worry, I've got sharp eyes."

He paused for effect, then continued with a flourish, "It's the same story as in the X province—two students, a schoolboy, two twenty-year-old noblemen, a teacher, and some drunken half-pay major in his sixties. That's all they could muster! A pitiful lot. I tell you, even the authorities were surprised at how little they found. But I need time—six days. I've calculated everything, and six days is what I need. No more, no less. If you leave them undisturbed for six days, I'll deliver results. But if you make a move before then, they'll scatter like frightened birds, and we'll be left empty-handed. Spare me Shatov—that's all I ask. And don't involve Yulia Mihailovna in this—above all, not her. This has to remain between us. Can I trust you to keep this a secret?"

"A secret?" Lembke repeated, his eyes widening. "Are you telling me you haven't spoken a word of this to Yulia Mihailovna?"

"To her? God forbid!" Pyotr Stepanovitch exclaimed, shaking his head vehemently. "Andrey Antonovitch, you must understand—I value her friendship and respect her deeply. Truly, I do. But I'm no fool. I know better than to confide in her about matters like this. I don't argue with her—arguing with her is a dangerous game, as I'm sure you're well aware. I might've dropped a vague hint here or there because she likes to feel involved, but to mention names or specifics to her? Never! Why do you think I'm coming to you? Because you're a man of experience, someone serious, with old-fashioned principles and a wealth of service behind you. You've seen life. You must know how to handle delicate situations like this from your years in Petersburg. But if I were to tell her? She'd stir up a storm, and you know it as well as I do. She'd turn it into some grand spectacle just to astonish Petersburg."

"Yes, she does have a certain… passion for drama," Lembke murmured, half to himself. Though he was somewhat pleased by the compliment, he couldn't help but bristle at Pyotr Stepanovitch's casual way of speaking about Yulia Mihailovna. It bordered on disrespect.

"Exactly—drama!" Pyotr Stepanovitch agreed quickly, sensing an opportunity to press further. "She's a remarkable woman, no doubt, perhaps even a genius in her own way. But six days of silence? She couldn't manage six hours without stirring up trouble. Trust me, Andrey Antonovitch, tying a woman down for six days is an impossible task! You know I have experience in these matters. You know I wouldn't ask for six days if I didn't have a reason. I'm asking you to trust me on this."

Lembke hesitated, his face betraying his inner conflict. "I've heard…" he began slowly, "that when you returned from abroad, you expressed some kind of… repentance, as it were, in the proper circles?"

"Well, that's as it may be," Pyotr Stepanovitch replied evasively, his tone sharp but guarded.

"I don't want to pry," Lembke continued cautiously, "but it has seemed to me that you've spoken in quite a different tone before—about the Christian faith, about social institutions, and even about the government…"

"Of course, I've said a lot of things. I'm still saying them! But the difference is how those ideas are applied. Those fools don't understand that. What good does it do anyone to bite a superior officer's shoulder? You agreed with me yourself, Andrey Antonovitch, though at the time you said it was premature."

"I didn't mean it in that sense," Lembke muttered, his brow furrowed in irritation and mild confusion.

"You weigh every word you say, don't you? Ha ha! A careful man through and through!" Pyotr Stepanovitch observed suddenly, his tone light and almost playful. "But listen, old friend, I had to get to know you— that's why I've been speaking to you in my own way. That's how I work. You're not the first person I've approached like this. Perhaps I needed to get a sense of your character."

"My character? And why would my character matter to you?" Lembke asked stiffly, his expression both wary and curious.

"Who knows what it might mean to me?" Pyotr Stepanovitch laughed, his tone light but with a glimmer of something sharper beneath it. "You see, my dear and most respected Andrey Antonovitch, you're a shrewd man, but let's not get ahead of ourselves. It's not as if I'm here to spy on you—far from it. Nobody's tasked me with investigating you, and I haven't volunteered for such a job, either. Think about it: I didn't have to tell you those two names just now. I could have taken them straight to headquarters—after all, that's where I explained myself upon returning from abroad. But I didn't. If I were acting in my own interests, if I had something to gain, wouldn't it have made more sense for me to curry favor directly with them? Instead, I've come to you. And why? For Shatov's sake. Out of sheer humanity, because of our old friendship. I'm

389

not trying to profit here. But you, my dear sir—when you pick up your pen to write to headquarters, you might put in a kind word for me, just to note my diligence. I wouldn't object to that—he he!" He ended his speech with a grin that was both playful and self-satisfied.

Lembke looked at him with a mix of skepticism and reluctant warmth. The flattery had clearly hit its mark, and Pyotr Stepanovitch knew it. "Well, I must say, I'm glad the situation has been clarified," Lembke admitted as he rose from his chair. "I accept your assistance and will not forget to acknowledge it. You can rest assured I will report on your diligence… appropriately."

"Six days," Pyotr Stepanovitch reminded him earnestly as he, too, got to his feet. "The key thing is six days. I need those six days without any disturbances. Don't stir the nest too early, or you'll ruin everything. I'm relying on your wisdom and experience for that."

"Agreed," Lembke replied, nodding.

"Of course, I wouldn't presume to tie your hands," Pyotr Stepanovitch added quickly, with a cheerful wave of his hand. "You can keep watch however you see fit—of course, that's your job. But please, don't scare the birds too soon. You've got bloodhounds and trackers of your own, no doubt—ha ha!" he blurted out with the easy carelessness of youth.

"Not as many as you might think," Lembke replied, smiling faintly. "Young men often imagine a great deal going on behind the scenes, when really there is very little."

"Still," Pyotr Stepanovitch said slyly, "you must admit you've thought about it. By the way, one little thing—since we're being honest. If Kirillov was Stavrogin's second in that duel, then what about Stavrogin? Are they not closely connected?"

"What are you suggesting?" Lembke asked sharply, narrowing his eyes.

"I mean, if they're such close friends…" Lembke trailed off, leaving his meaning unsaid but perfectly clear.

"Oh no, no, no!" Pyotr Stepanovitch burst out, almost gleefully.

"You're quite mistaken there! Quite the opposite, in fact. I must say, I'm surprised. I thought someone with your connections would have better information than that. Stavrogin? It's not what you think. Quite the contrary. Avis au lecteur, as they say—'let the reader beware!'"

"Is that really so?" Lembke muttered, clearly suspicious but also intrigued. "I must admit, Yulia Mihailovna heard otherwise. Word from Petersburg suggested that Stavrogin might be acting on some kind of... instructions."

"I don't know a thing about it. Nothing at all," Pyotr Stepanovitch said abruptly, his tone sharp and final. "Not a word. Adieu. Avis au lecteur!" He turned toward the door with such determination that Lembke, startled, hurried to stop him.

"Wait, Pyotr Stepanovitch, wait!" Lembke cried. "One small matter— I promise it won't take a moment." He opened a drawer and pulled out an envelope. "Here, take a look at this. I'm showing it to you as proof of my complete trust in you. I want your opinion."

He handed the envelope to Pyotr Stepanovitch, who took it with obvious irritation. Inside was a letter, strange and anonymous, which Lembke explained had mysteriously appeared in the porter's room the day before. Pyotr Stepanovitch unfolded the paper and, with barely concealed disgust, read the following:

"Your Excellency,—For such you are by rank. Herewith I make known that there is an attempt to be made on the life of personages of general's rank and on the Fatherland. For it's working up straight for that. I myself have been disseminating unceasingly for a number of years. There's infidelity too. There's a rebellion being got up and there are some thousands of manifestoes, and for every one of them there will be a hundred running with their tongues out, unless they've been taken away beforehand by the police. For they've been promised a mighty lot of benefits, and the simple people are foolish, and there's vodka too. The people will attack one after another, taking them to be guilty, and, fearing both sides, I repent of what I had no share in, my circumstances being what they are. If you want information to save the Fatherland, and also the Church and the ikons, I am the only one that can do it. But only on condition that I get a pardon from the Secret Police by telegram at once, me alone, but the rest may answer for it. Put a candle every evening at seven o'clock in the porter's window for a signal. Seeing it, I shall believe and come to kiss the merciful hand from Petersburg. But on condition there's a pension for me, for else how am I to live? You won't regret it for it will mean a star for you. You must go secretly or they'll wring your neck. Your Excellency's desperate servant falls at your feet.

Repentant free-thinker incognito."

Pyotr Stepanovitch tossed the letter back onto the table, his lip curling in disdain. "And what do you think of this?" he asked, almost rudely.

"I think it's a prank—an anonymous skit meant as a joke," Lembke replied with visible annoyance.

"Most likely it is," Pyotr Stepanovitch said with a dismissive wave of his hand. "You're not so easy to fool."

"The sheer stupidity of it gives it away," Lembke added.

"Have you received letters like this before?" Pyotr Stepanovitch inquired sharply.

"Once or twice," Lembke admitted.

"Oh, of course they wouldn't be signed," Pyotr Stepanovitch sneered. "Different styles, different handwritings, I assume?"

"Yes," Lembke nodded. "And the content was equally absurd—though far more distasteful."

"Well, there's your answer. If you've seen them before, this is just more of the same," Pyotr Stepanovitch concluded flatly, as if he could barely tolerate another moment of the conversation.

"Especially because it's so stupid," Lembke said, his voice carrying a hint of exasperation. "I mean, these people are supposed to be educated, aren't they? Someone educated wouldn't write something so clumsy and idiotic."

"Of course, of course," Pyotr Stepanovitch replied with a faint smile, but his tone hinted at impatience.

"But what if," Lembke continued, lowering his voice slightly as if the idea embarrassed him, "this is someone who genuinely wants to turn informer? Someone who's too frightened or confused to approach things in a proper way?"

"It's not very likely," Pyotr Stepanovitch snapped, his tone sharp and dismissive. "Just look at the content of this nonsense—asking for a telegram from the Secret Police, and even a pension! It's absurd. This whole letter screams hoax."

"Yes, yes," Lembke said quickly, as though retreating from his own suggestion. His face flushed slightly, and his tone grew subdued. "You're probably right."

"I tell you what," Pyotr Stepanovitch said suddenly, leaning forward and tapping the letter with his finger for emphasis. "Why don't you let me take this off your hands? I'll look into it myself. It won't distract me from the other matters, and I can find out who's behind it soon enough. Before long, we'll have our answer."

"Take it," Lembke agreed after a brief pause, though his hesitation was obvious. He reached out reluctantly, sliding the envelope across the table toward Pyotr Stepanovitch.

"Have you shown this to anyone else?" Pyotr Stepanovitch asked casually, though there was a sharp undertone in his voice.

"Is it likely?" Lembke exclaimed, shaking his head. "Of course not. I've kept it entirely to myself."

"Not even to Yulia Mihailovna?" Pyotr Stepanovitch pressed, raising an eyebrow.

"Oh, Heaven forbid!" Lembke cried out in alarm, the very thought of it making him flustered. "No, absolutely not! And for God's sake, don't you dare show it to her either! She'd be beside herself, and—" He hesitated for a moment, clearly troubled. "She'd be furious with me. You have no idea how dreadfully angry she can get."

"She'd tear into you, no doubt about that," Pyotr Stepanovitch said with a sly grin. "She'd probably say it was your fault, that you somehow invited this kind of nonsense by being careless. Women's logic—always so sharp and fair, isn't it?"

"Exactly," Lembke muttered with a weak sigh. His discomfort was palpable, and he shifted in his chair. "I can't imagine the scene that would follow. Best she doesn't hear about it at all."

"Don't worry," Pyotr Stepanovitch said breezily, folding the letter and tucking it away. "I'll keep it strictly between us. I'd say give me a couple of days—three at most—and I'll likely bring you the writer of this ridiculous note. We'll have it all sorted out soon enough."

He stood up as he spoke, adjusting his coat as though preparing to leave. "Above all, don't forget our compact," he added with a pointed look, his voice light but carrying an undercurrent of seriousness.

"Of course," Lembke murmured, nodding slowly. He remained seated, his eyes following Pyotr Stepanovitch as he moved toward the door.

Chapter 6.4

Though Pyotr Stepanovitch was by no means a fool, Fedka the convict had remarked perceptively about him: "He'd invent a man out of thin air and then live with him as though he were real." This observation wasn't far from the truth. Pyotr Stepanovitch left his meeting with Lembke feeling triumphant, fully convinced that he had successfully calmed the man's nerves for at least six days. This window of time was critical for his own plans. Yet, his confidence rested on a flawed assumption—he had created in his mind an image of Andrey Antonovitch as a harmless simpleton, an image he clung to without question.

In reality, like many deeply suspicious people, Andrey Antonovitch had a contradictory nature. Once he felt he was on solid ground, he became excessively trusting, even joyful, in his relief. The new developments, despite their challenges and complications, initially struck him as somewhat positive. At the very least, they seemed to dispel his earlier fears and doubts. Moreover, he was utterly exhausted—mentally and physically. The strain of the past few days had left him drained, and his spirit longed desperately for rest. But this respite was short-lived. The scars left by his years in Petersburg, where intrigue and conspiracy were ever-present, remained deeply embedded in him. His curiosity about the "younger generation," their manifestoes, and their secret activities had once led him to collect subversive materials, but he had never truly understood any of it. Now, he felt like a man lost in a dense and unfamiliar forest. Something about Pyotr Stepanovitch's words struck him as grotesque, incongruous, and out of place, though he couldn't put his finger on exactly what. "With this 'younger generation,' anything seems possible," he thought to himself. "The devil only knows what's going on among them."

As if to compound his unease, Blum appeared, poking his head through the door. Blum had been lingering nearby throughout Pyotr Stepanovitch's visit, biding his time. Blum was an interesting figure in Lembke's life, though not in a flattering way. A distant relative of Andrey Antonovitch, their familial connection was an awkward secret that had always been carefully hidden. I must beg the reader's indulgence for dwelling briefly on this otherwise insignificant individual, but his peculiarities warrant some attention.

Blum was one of those peculiar Germans often referred to as "unfortunate." Such people weren't lacking in intelligence or competence, but for some inexplicable reason, they were perpetually plagued by ill fortune. This type of "unfortunate German" was not a myth; they genuinely existed and were even found in Russia. Blum was an almost textbook example. Despite his precision and effort, nothing ever seemed to go right for him. If he were appointed to a position, the department would be restructured or abolished soon after. If a new superior officer arrived, Blum would inevitably fall out of favor. Once, he had even been mistakenly rounded up during a police raid. He was meticulous and hardworking, yet his gloomy and overly serious demeanor often worked against him.

Blum was tall, with red hair, a perpetually hunched posture, and an air of perpetual melancholy. Despite his misfortunes, he was stubborn—an obstinacy that always surfaced at precisely the wrong moments. Andrey Antonovitch had a soft spot for him, a peculiar sympathy that persisted through the years. As Lembke advanced in his career, he ensured Blum always had a subordinate position under him. Blum, in turn, and his long-suffering wife and children, regarded Lembke with reverent devotion. This loyalty, however, wasn't shared by anyone else. Yulia Mihailovna, for instance, had detested Blum from the moment she first encountered him.

Her disdain for Blum had led to the first real quarrel of her marriage. It had been a bitter moment, occurring during the early days of their honeymoon. Yulia Mihailovna, much to her horror, discovered not only Blum's existence but also the humiliating secret of his family connection to her husband. Lembke had pleaded with her, his hands clasped in supplication, recounting the story of his childhood friendship with Blum and their shared hardships. Yulia Mihailovna, however, felt irreparably disgraced and had resorted to fainting in protest. But Lembke, unyielding in his loyalty, had refused to part with Blum. His stubbornness ultimately wore her down, and she was forced to accept the arrangement. However, they agreed to conceal the relationship even more thoroughly than before, to the extent of changing Blum's name so it no longer reflected their shared patronymic. Despite this compromise, her disdain never abated.

Blum was acutely aware of his precarious position and led a solitary, frugal life. He had few acquaintances in the town, apart from the local German chemist. He spent most of his time alone, rarely calling on anyone. He had long known of Lembke's literary ambitions and peculiar indulgence in writing novels. Often, Blum was summoned for private readings of these works, where he would sit stiffly for hours on end, straining to stay awake and muster an encouraging smile. At home, he would groan to his equally lanky and miserable wife about their benefactor's unfortunate obsession with Russian literature.

Now, standing in the doorway, Blum's appearance filled Lembke with a renewed sense of anguish. He was desperate to avoid any continuation of the conversation that had been interrupted by Pyotr Stepanovitch.

"I beg you to leave me alone, Blum," Lembke said hastily, his voice tinged with agitation.

Blum, however, remained resolute. "This matter can be arranged delicately and discreetly, without any unnecessary attention. You have the full authority to act," he insisted, his posture stooped as he stepped closer to Lembke.

"Blum, your devotion to me is so overwhelming that it terrifies me," Lembke replied, attempting to inject some levity into the moment. But his voice betrayed genuine unease.

"You always say such witty things," Blum retorted with a faint trace of reproach. "Then you sleep peacefully, satisfied with your own words, but in the end, it's this very wit that damages you."

"Blum," Lembke said, raising his hand as though to ward him off, "I've just realized—it's all a mistake, a complete mistake."

"A mistake? Surely not based on the flattery of that deceitful young man? He has charmed you with his praise of your literary talent," Blum said obstinately.

"You understand nothing about it, Blum," Lembke shot back, his irritation mounting. "Your plan is absurd. We'll find nothing, and it will only cause an uproar—laughter, even! And then there's Yulia Mihailovna…"

"We will certainly find everything we need," Blum interrupted firmly, placing his hand on his chest as though making an oath. "If we conduct a search early in the morning, following all the legal formalities, I am confident we will uncover the evidence. Young men like Lyamshin and Telyatnikov, who visited there regularly, have assured me we will find it. Everyone in town knows Mr. Verhovensky harbors forbidden books— Herzen's works, Ryleyev's writings, and more. I even have a rough catalog prepared."

Blum's confidence only deepened Lembke's unease as he stared at his obstinate subordinate. The weight of conflicting advice and looming complications pressed heavily on his already exhausted mind.

"Oh heavens! Everyone has these books nowadays; you're far too simple, my poor Blum," Andrey Antonovitch exclaimed with a mix of exasperation and fatigue.

Blum, however, was undeterred and pressed on as if he hadn't heard.

"And there are plenty of manifestoes too," he added stubbornly, his voice low but resolute. "If we search properly, we'll undoubtedly find evidence of those manifestoes here as well. That young Verhovensky—I feel very suspicious of him."

"But you're confusing the father with the son," Von Lembke interrupted impatiently, rubbing his temples. "They're not on good terms at all! Don't you know the son openly mocks and laughs at his father? It's no secret."

"That's nothing but a mask," Blum replied obstinately, with a gleam in his eye that betrayed his refusal to back down. His voice rose slightly, his certainty hardening with each word.

"Blum, you're determined to torment me!" Lembke groaned, throwing up his hands. "Think for a moment! The elder Verhovensky is a well-known figure here, a public person! He's been a professor, for God's sake. People respect him, or at least they know who he is. If we make a move against him, there'll be an uproar—gossip, mockery, and scandal all over the town. We'll make fools of ourselves, and it'll be a complete mess! Do you know how the papers in Petersburg love a scandal like this? And besides, think of how Yulia Mihailovna will react. She'll be furious, and you know what that means!"

But Blum was now immune to Lembke's arguments. His stooped posture seemed to straighten slightly as he pressed forward, his words carrying the momentum of an argument rehearsed many times in his mind. "A professor! Only a lecturer, and a minor one at that. His rank was insignificant when he retired! He's never been distinguished by any notable marks of service or merit." Blum struck his chest with a clenched fist, a gesture meant to emphasize his righteous determination. "He was dismissed from his post on suspicion of being involved in seditious plots against the government. His record is far from spotless. He's been under secret police surveillance before—years ago—and I'd wager he still is! You know as well as I do that once the government begins to suspect someone, those suspicions rarely vanish. In light of the recent disturbances and the evidence we're uncovering now, you are obligated—obligated, Andrey Antonovitch—to act. Your duty demands it! You're letting the true culprit slip through your fingers, and with it, a perfect chance for recognition and distinction."

"Yulia Mihailovna!" Lembke suddenly gasped, paling as he heard the faint but unmistakable sound of his wife's voice coming from the adjoining room. He straightened, panic flickering in his eyes. "Get away, Blum!" he whispered sharply, his voice hoarse with desperation. "Leave, now! Do whatever you want later—just go! Oh, my God, go!"

Blum started at the sudden shift in tone but refused to surrender so easily. He stepped forward again, pressing both hands fervently against his chest, as if his physical posture could drive home his insistence. "Allow me, allow me to finish," he muttered stubbornly, his voice still low and reverent but increasingly desperate.

"Get away, I said!" Lembke hissed through gritted teeth, leaning toward him with an expression of near hysteria. "Do what you want later! But now, for God's sake, go!"

At that moment, the heavy curtain to the adjoining room rustled and lifted. Yulia Mihailovna stepped into the room with her usual commanding air, her gaze sweeping across the scene with a mixture of icy disdain and regal offense. She stopped in her tracks at the sight of Blum, her expression hardening instantly. Her sharp, imperious glance seemed to say that Blum's very presence in her home was a personal affront, an insult she would neither forgive nor overlook.

Blum, for his part, froze momentarily under her gaze before bowing deeply, almost absurdly, as if attempting to shrink himself out of existence. His bow was so exaggerated that his stooped frame seemed to double over entirely, and he began moving backward toward the door on tiptoe, his arms held awkwardly away from his sides in a gesture of awkward, almost comical reverence. His red hair glowed under the light, making him look even more conspicuous.

Yulia Mihailovna watched him leave without a word, though her scornful silence said more than any reprimand could. The moment he disappeared through the door, she turned her steely gaze back to Andrey Antonovitch.

Blum, however, seemed to take Lembke's last frantic outburst—"Do what you like later!"—as permission, or perhaps even encouragement, to proceed with his plan. Whether he genuinely believed he had been authorized, or whether his persistence had simply overtaken his better judgment, is unclear. What is certain is that this conversation marked the beginning of a surprising and rather ridiculous event that would soon capture the entire town's attention. It would not only amuse many people and stir up gossip, but also enrage Yulia Mihailovna to the point of fury. And as for Andrey Antonovitch? When the moment of reckoning arrived, he would find himself so thoroughly bewildered and reduced to indecision that his reputation—such as it was—would be utterly compromised.

Chapter 6.5

It was a particularly busy day for Pyotr Stepanovitch. After leaving Von Lembke, he hurried toward Bogoyavlensky Street to attend to pressing matters. However, as he passed down Bykovy Street, he caught sight of the house where the celebrated writer Karmazinov was staying. Without any apparent reason, he stopped abruptly, grinned to himself, and decided to go inside. He had not mentioned any plans to visit, so he was mildly intrigued when the servant informed him that he was expected.

In truth, Karmazinov had been expecting him, not only that day but for the past two days as well. Three days earlier, Karmazinov had handed over the manuscript of his latest work, Merci, which he planned to read aloud at Yulia Mihailovna's literary matinée during the upcoming fête. This gesture was ostensibly one of courtesy, but Pyotr Stepanovitch had seen through it. Karmazinov had convinced himself that allowing the young man a preview of his masterpiece was a generous act, a subtle form of flattery for Pyotr Stepanovitch's ego. But Pyotr Stepanovitch had long suspected the truth: this vainglorious, self-absorbed writer, who carried himself with the aloofness of a statesman, was actually trying to ingratiate himself with him. Karmazinov believed Pyotr Stepanovitch to be deeply embedded in the secret revolutionary movement sweeping across Russia, if not one of its principal leaders. In his vanity, the writer had come to view him as an essential contact, someone with influence over the younger generation.

Karmazinov's state of mind amused Pyotr Stepanovitch, who had no illusions about the man's pretensions. Despite this, he had deliberately avoided clarifying his role in the revolutionary activities, finding it useful to maintain the ambiguity.

Karmazinov was staying in his sister's house, a grand residence owned by her husband, a kammerherr with a nearby estate. Both his sister and brother-in-law revered the great writer and were deeply regretful that they happened to be in Moscow during his visit. Consequently, the task of hosting him fell to an old lady, a poor relation of the family who managed the household. This elderly woman treated Karmazinov with an almost religious devotion, tiptoeing around the house to avoid disturbing him. She sent regular updates to Moscow about his well-being, his meals, and even his minor ailments, once dispatching a telegram to announce that after a dinner at the mayor's, he had needed a dose of medicine. Though Karmazinov was courteous to her, his manner was dry and distant. Their conversations were limited to practical matters, which suited her just fine, as she was too intimidated to linger in his presence.

When Pyotr Stepanovitch entered the house, he found Karmazinov in the middle of his habitual late-morning meal: a single cutlet and half a glass of red wine. This was a routine scene for Pyotr Stepanovitch, who had visited him before and always found him engaged in this ritual. As usual, the writer continued eating without offering his guest anything. After the cutlet, a small cup of coffee was brought in by a footman impeccably dressed in a swallowtail coat, noiseless boots, and gloves.

"Ah, there you are!" Karmazinov exclaimed, rising from the sofa with an air of delight and wiping his mouth delicately with a napkin. He approached Pyotr Stepanovitch with an exaggerated warmth typical of illustrious Russians. As was his custom, he offered his cheek for a kiss but made no effort to return the gesture. Pyotr Stepanovitch, familiar with this peculiar ritual, mirrored the gesture, ensuring their cheeks merely brushed. Karmazinov pretended not to notice and motioned for Pyotr Stepanovitch to sit in an armchair opposite him. Pyotr Stepanovitch lounged comfortably in the chair, stretching out as though entirely at home.

"You don't want some lunch, do you?" Karmazinov asked, breaking his usual habit of neglecting to offer hospitality. His tone, however, suggested he expected a polite refusal.

"Yes, I would like some lunch," Pyotr Stepanovitch responded immediately, to his host's evident surprise. A shadow of irritation flickered across Karmazinov's face, but he quickly masked it. With a slight grimace, he rang for the servant and, unable to entirely suppress his annoyance, gave the order for a second lunch with a touch of scorn in his voice.

"What will you have? A cutlet? Coffee?" Karmazinov asked, his tone cool but outwardly polite.

"I'll take both, and have him bring more wine too. I'm quite hungry," Pyotr Stepanovitch replied nonchalantly, while taking the opportunity to scrutinize his host's appearance. Karmazinov was wearing a short, wadded indoor jacket with pearl buttons that barely concealed his rounded stomach and broad hips. A checkered woolen plaid draped over his knees and fell to the floor, though the room was comfortably warm.

"Are you feeling unwell?" Pyotr Stepanovitch asked, his gaze lingering on the plaid.

"No, not unwell," Karmazinov replied in his thin, high-pitched voice, each word articulated with a soft lisp. "But in this climate, one must take precautions."

"I see," Pyotr Stepanovitch replied, smirking faintly.

"I've been expecting you since yesterday," Karmazinov said, steering the conversation back to his own concerns.

"Why? I never said I'd come," Pyotr Stepanovitch replied bluntly.

"No, but you have my manuscript. Have you… read it?" Karmazinov asked eagerly, leaning forward.

"Manuscript? Which one?" Pyotr Stepanovitch asked with feigned confusion.

Karmazinov's face fell, and his voice took on a tone of mild panic. "But you've brought it with you, haven't you? Surely you haven't lost it?"

"Ah, you mean that Bonjour piece…"

"Merci," Karmazinov corrected sharply.

"Yes, Merci," Pyotr Stepanovitch said indifferently. "I haven't had a chance to read it. Honestly, I forgot about it. It's probably on my table somewhere."

Karmazinov paled. "No, I must send for it at once. It could be stolen, or worse, lost entirely!" he exclaimed, his voice rising in alarm.

"Who would want it?" Pyotr Stepanovitch replied, smirking. "Besides, you've got copies everywhere—at notaries, in Petersburg, in Moscow, and even in a bank, from what I hear."

"Moscow could burn again, and my manuscript with it!" Karmazinov cried, waving his hand dramatically. "No, I must send for it immediately."

"Wait—here it is!" Pyotr Stepanovitch exclaimed, pulling a crumpled roll of papers from the back pocket of his coat. "It's a bit wrinkled. It's been sitting in my pocket with my handkerchief since you gave it to me."

Karmazinov snatched the manuscript from his hands, his face a mixture of relief and indignation. He carefully smoothed out the pages, counted them to ensure none were missing, and placed the manuscript on a side table, arranging it so that it remained within his sight. Only then did he allow himself to exhale and relax, his composure gradually returning.

"You don't seem to read very much, do you?" Karmazinov hissed suddenly, unable to restrain himself, his thin lips curling into a faint sneer.

"No, not very much," Pyotr Stepanovitch replied indifferently, as he exhaled a thin stream of cigarette smoke and leaned back lazily in his chair.

"And nothing at all in the way of Russian literature?" Karmazinov pressed, his tone sharpening as though personally offended.

"Russian literature?" Pyotr Stepanovitch furrowed his brow, as if racking his brain. "Let me see… I think I read something once—On the Way or Away! or maybe At the Parting of the Ways… something like that. I can't quite recall. It was about five years ago, and I haven't had time since then."

A silence followed. Karmazinov's face twitched with irritation. His carefully maintained composure, his aristocratic air of superiority, was starting to crack.

"When I first arrived here, I assured everyone that you were a very intelligent young man," Karmazinov said at last, with an edge of bitterness. "And now, it seems, everyone in town is completely wild about you."

"Thank you," Pyotr Stepanovitch replied serenely, as if the compliment had been delivered without any sarcasm.

The servant entered, carrying Pyotr Stepanovitch's lunch. Karmazinov watched with barely concealed disgust as his guest fell upon the cutlet with what seemed to be genuine hunger. He devoured it quickly, tossed back the wine, and finished his coffee without ceremony, all while Karmazinov observed him from the corner of his eye.

"This boor," thought Karmazinov, swallowing his indignation, "this uncultured boor probably caught the barb in my words, understood perfectly what I was getting at, and is simply lying—pretending ignorance, perhaps to irritate me. Or worse—what if he truly hasn't read my manuscript? What if he really is as stupid as he appears? Could he be? But then again… perhaps he's some kind of idiot savant, a 'genius among the rabble,' as it were? The devil take him!"

He stood up abruptly, unable to sit still any longer, and began pacing back and forth across the room. It was his habit after meals—a necessary exercise, as he explained to his hosts, for the sake of his digestion. As he turned at each end of the room, his right leg gave an almost imperceptible, jaunty twitch, as if to punctuate each step.

"Are you leaving here soon?" Pyotr Stepanovitch asked lazily, still lounging in the armchair as he lit another cigarette.

"I only came to settle matters with my estate—I'm in the hands of my bailiff at the moment," Karmazinov replied loftily, his tone more affable now, though it still carried a note of self-importance.

"You left, I believe, because they were predicting an epidemic after the war?" Pyotr Stepanovitch remarked with a faint smirk.

"N-no, not entirely for that reason," Karmazinov replied with measured politeness, drawing out his words. He spoke softly, in his gentlemanly lisp, but the venom beneath the surface was unmistakable. "I've made up my mind to live as long as I can." He laughed faintly, though there was no real mirth in it. "You know, there's something peculiar about our Russian nobility—it wears itself out remarkably quickly, from every point of view. Physically, morally, intellectually—it all seems to deteriorate too soon. But as for me, I intend to 'wear out' as late as possible. That's why I'm going abroad for good. The climate is better there, the houses are of stone, the infrastructure stronger. Europe will last my time, I think. What do you say?"

"How should I know?" Pyotr Stepanovitch replied, blowing out a cloud of smoke.

"H'm." Karmazinov paused briefly, eyeing his guest with faint contempt. "But if—if—this Babylon of theirs does fall one day, and great will be the fall thereof—about which, by the way, I completely agree with you—I do think it will still last my time. Meanwhile, there is nothing to fall here in Russia. What would fall here? There aren't even stones left to collapse; everything will simply crumble into dust, dirt, mud. Holy Russia has less resistance in her than anything else on earth. The Russian peasantry? Perhaps they're still held together by their so-called 'Russian God.' But from what I hear, the Russian God has been losing credibility ever since the emancipation. It dealt Him a terrible blow. Now we have railways, now we have you... No, I don't believe in the Russian God anymore."

"And how about the European one?" Pyotr Stepanovitch asked, grinning wickedly.

"I don't believe in Him either," Karmazinov replied bluntly, without a flicker of hesitation. "But the trouble is, I've been slandered. To the youth of Russia, I mean. They think I'm some sort of enemy to their ideas when, in fact, I've always sympathized with every new movement. I've seen the manifestoes circulating here. Everyone looks at them with unease because of their blunt, almost brutal language—but at the same time, everyone senses their power. They frighten people because they tell the truth openly. And what is Russia today if not a country rolling downhill with nothing to hold onto? Everyone knows it."

He paused mid-step and turned sharply, his voice gaining momentum as his irritation bled into something like conviction. "That's why wealthy Russians all flock abroad—it's not cowardice, it's instinct. The rats leave the ship when it's sinking, after all. And Russia is sinking. Holy Russia is a country of wood, of poverty, and of danger—a nation where the upper classes are nothing but ambitious beggars while the vast majority rot in their miserable little huts. Offer them any escape, any path out, and they'll take it eagerly. The government still tries to resist, but it's swinging blindly in the dark, striking its own people more often than not. Everything is doomed here, waiting for its inevitable collapse. I tell you, Russia has no future as she is. I've already become a German, and I take pride in that."

"You mentioned the manifestoes," Pyotr Stepanovitch cut in suddenly. "What do you think of them, exactly? Tell me everything."

Karmazinov's face brightened slightly; his vanity was piqued. "The manifestoes?" he repeated. "Their power lies in their boldness. They speak the truth, harshly, unsparingly. They unmask all the lies we tell ourselves and reveal that there is nothing—nothing—in this country to lean upon. They scream aloud while the rest of us cower in silence. That's what gives them their strength. And it's a uniquely Russian phenomenon. No one in Europe has the audacity yet to face the truth so boldly. Europe is a place of stone; there, things are still solid. Here, everything crumbles into dust at a touch."

He paused dramatically, his thin lips curling into a faint smile. "I must admit," he continued, "I rather admire the idea of abolishing honour altogether. Honour is useless to a Russian—it has always been a superfluous burden, something he's carried throughout history for no good reason. The right to dishonour—that's what will appeal to the Russian soul. It's bold, unflinching, and fearless. The rest of Europe wouldn't understand such a thing, but here? It's perfect."

Karmazinov stopped pacing and turned to face Pyotr Stepanovitch directly. "As for me, I still cling to the concept of honour, I suppose, but only out of habit. You see, I belong to the older generation. I'm too timid to change. So, I hold onto the old forms... because, after all, one must live out the rest of one's days somehow, don't you think?"

He suddenly stopped mid-thought, struck by a realization.

"I'm the one doing all the talking," he mused. "Meanwhile, he just sits there in silence, watching me, analyzing me. He's waiting for me to ask the question—pushing me to it with his stillness. And I will ask it. I'll walk straight into his game."

At that very moment, Pyotr Stepanovitch broke the silence. "Yulia Mihailovna has been up to her tricks again," he said casually. "She asked me, in a roundabout way, to discover what surprise you've been planning for the ball tomorrow. Some kind of secret, I hear."

Karmazinov straightened up slightly, his posture stiffening with self-importance. His face took on an air of mock seriousness, though it was clear he was savoring the moment. "Yes, there will indeed be a surprise," he said with deliberate slowness, drawing out the suspense. "I assure you, I shall astonish... quite a few people."

"What kind of surprise?" Pyotr Stepanovitch pressed mildly, though it was clear he didn't really care.

Karmazinov shook his head with theatrical gravity. "Ah, but that is my secret," he said, his voice filled with an almost childish glee. "I wouldn't dream of telling you."

Pyotr Stepanovitch didn't press further. He simply nodded and shifted the conversation in a different direction, as if the secret held no importance to him whatsoever.

"There's a young man in town by the name of Shatov," Karmazinov remarked suddenly. "Curious, isn't it? I haven't even met him yet."

"A decent fellow," replied Pyotr Stepanovitch, his tone light. "Why do you ask?"

"Oh, no particular reason," Karmazinov said, waving his hand as though dismissing the subject. "He talks about something or other. Isn't he the one who slapped Stavrogin in the face?"

"Yes, that's the one," Pyotr Stepanovitch confirmed with a faint smile.

"And what's your opinion of Stavrogin?" Karmazinov asked, his tone growing sharper, though he tried to maintain an air of detachment.

"I don't really know what to make of him," Pyotr Stepanovitch answered nonchalantly. "He's such a… flirt."

Karmazinov's lips twisted into a bitter smile. He detested Stavrogin, primarily because Stavrogin ignored him—a slight Karmazinov could neither forgive nor forget. "That flirt," he said with a dry chuckle, "will be the first to hang if your manifestoes ever see the light of day."

"Perhaps even sooner," Pyotr Stepanovitch replied unexpectedly, his voice turning cold.

"Quite right too," Karmazinov said gravely, his chuckle fading into an expression of solemn agreement.

"You've said that before, you know," Pyotr Stepanovitch continued, his eyes narrowing. "And, interestingly enough, I repeated it to him."

"What?" Karmazinov exclaimed, his chuckle returning, though now tinged with nervousness. "You actually repeated it? How deliciously bold!"

"He told me," Pyotr Stepanovitch said with a faint smirk, "that if he were to hang, it would be worth it just to see you flogged first. And not as a mere formality, but flogged properly—thoroughly—just as they flog peasants."

Karmazinov froze for a moment, caught off guard. His face darkened, but he quickly masked his discomfort with a strained laugh. Pyotr Stepanovitch, sensing his host's unease, took his hat and rose to leave.

Karmazinov stood too, stretching out both hands in an exaggerated gesture of farewell. "And tell me," he said suddenly, his voice softening into a honeyed, almost pleading tone, "if everything you and your… associates are planning were to come to pass, how soon do you think it might happen?"

"How could I possibly know?" Pyotr Stepanovitch answered gruffly, brushing off the question. But their eyes locked, and an unspoken understanding seemed to pass between them.

"At a guess?" Karmazinov pressed, his voice growing even sweeter.

"Roughly, perhaps?"

Pyotr Stepanovitch hesitated for a moment, his gaze hardening. "You'll have plenty of time," he muttered roughly. "Time to sell your estate. Time to clear out."

Their eyes met again, this time with an intensity that bordered on hostility. The air between them felt thick with unspoken tension.

A long silence followed. Then, with sudden clarity and precision, Pyotr Stepanovitch added, "It will begin early next May. By October, it will all be over."

Karmazinov's lips parted slightly in surprise, and a flicker of unease passed across his face. Then, recovering himself, he pressed Pyotr Stepanovitch's hands in both of his and said in a voice saturated with affected sincerity, "Thank you. Thank you most sincerely."

Pyotr Stepanovitch said nothing. He pulled his hands away, turned abruptly, and walked out of the house without another word. As he stepped into the street, his lips curled into a sardonic grin.

"You'll have time to jump ship, you rat," he thought to himself, his amusement growing with every step. "So, the 'imperial intellect' wanted the day and the hour spelled out for him, did he? And then had the gall to thank me so earnestly for the favor! Ha! Well, one thing is clear: he's no fool. He's a coward, but he's not stupid. And cowards like him—they don't tattle. They know how to survive."

Still grinning, Pyotr Stepanovitch quickened his pace, heading straight for Filipov's house in Bogoyavlensky Street.

Chapter 6.6

Pyotr Stepanovitch went first to Kirillov's house. He found him, as usual, alone and at the moment doing some exercises. Kirillov was standing with his legs apart, waving his arms above his head in a strange way. On the floor, there was a ball. The tea on the table had gone cold, left there since breakfast. Pyotr Stepanovitch stood for a moment in the doorway.

"You seem to care a lot about staying healthy," he said in a loud, cheerful voice as he stepped into the room. "That's a nice ball, though. Wow, it really bounces! Is it part of your workout too?"

Kirillov put on his coat.

"Yes, it's for my health too," he said dryly. "Sit down."

"I'm only staying a minute, but sure, I'll sit," said Pyotr Stepanovitch, taking a seat. "Health is important, but I'm here to remind you about our arrangement. The time we talked about is getting close … in a way," he added awkwardly.

"What arrangement?" Kirillov asked.

"What? How can you even ask?" Pyotr Stepanovitch seemed both surprised and a little shaken.

"It's not an arrangement or an obligation. I never promised anything. That's your mistake," Kirillov said firmly.

"Wait, what are you saying?" Pyotr Stepanovitch stood up suddenly.

"I'm saying I do what I want," Kirillov replied.

"What do you mean by that?" Pyotr Stepanovitch asked sharply.

"The same as I've always meant."

"What am I supposed to make of this? Does this mean you're still thinking the same way?"

"Yes. But there's no arrangement, never was, and I didn't promise anything. I'm free to do whatever I choose, and I still am."

Kirillov's tone was short and dismissive as he spoke.

"Fine, fine. Be as free as you want as long as you don't change your mind," Pyotr Stepanovitch said as he sat back down, looking satisfied. "You're upset over a single word. You've gotten really touchy lately, which is why I've been staying away. Still, I knew you'd stick to your word."

"I don't like you, but you can count on me," Kirillov replied coldly. "Though I don't see it as loyalty or disloyalty."

"But listen," Pyotr Stepanovitch said, startled again, "we really need to go over this carefully so nothing gets messed up. This is serious, and you keep catching me off guard. Can I talk to you about it?"

"Speak," Kirillov snapped, turning his gaze away.

"You decided a long time ago to take your life … I mean, you had the idea in your head. Is that the right way to put it? Am I wrong about that?"

"I still have the same idea."

"Good. Just to be clear, no one has pressured you into this."

"Of course not; what nonsense you're saying."

"I admit I might not be saying it well. Forcing someone into it would obviously be ridiculous. Let me continue. You were part of the group before it was reorganized and mentioned it to one of the members."

"I didn't confess it; I just mentioned it."

"Exactly. Confessing something like that would be absurd. What a thing to confess! You simply said it. Perfect."

"No, it's not perfect, because you're being annoying. I don't owe you an explanation, and you wouldn't understand my reasons anyway. I want to end my life because that's my belief, because I don't want to fear death, and because … well, you don't need to know why. What do you want? Do you want some tea? It's cold. I can get you a fresh glass."

Pyotr Stepanovitch had already picked up the teapot and was searching for an empty glass. Kirillov walked over to the cupboard and brought back a clean one.

"I just ate lunch at Karmazinov's," Pyotr said, "then I listened to him ramble and got all sweaty again running over here. I'm terribly thirsty."

"Drink. Cold tea is fine."

Kirillov sat back down and fixed his eyes on the far corner of the room.

"The idea came up in the group," he continued in the same tone, "that I could be useful if I killed myself. The plan was that, if you caused some kind of trouble here and they started looking for the culprit, I could shoot myself and leave a note claiming responsibility. That way, you'd avoid

411

suspicion for a while."

"For at least a few days; even one day is valuable."

"Fine. So they asked me if I'd wait. I said I would until they picked the date, since it doesn't matter to me."

"Yes, but remember you agreed not to write your final note without me, and in Russia, you'd be at my disposal—well, only for that purpose. Of course, in every other matter, you're free," Pyotr added with an almost friendly tone.

"I didn't bind myself; I agreed because it makes no difference to me."

"Fine, fine. I don't mean to offend your pride, but …"

"It's not about pride."

"Still, remember that a hundred and twenty thalers were collected for your trip, so you've taken money."

"Not true." Kirillov's temper flared. "The money wasn't given on that condition. Nobody takes money for something like this."

"People do sometimes."

"That's a lie. I sent the money from Petersburg, and when I was there, I gave you a hundred and twenty thalers myself—I put it straight into your hand. That money was sent on, unless you kept it for yourself."

"All right, all right. I'm not arguing. It was sent. All that matters is you're still thinking the same way."

"Exactly the same. When you come and tell me it's time, I'll do it. Will it be soon?"

"Not too many days from now. But remember, we'll write the note together that same night."

"The same day, if you want. You're saying I need to take responsibility for the manifestos?"

"And one other thing."

"I'm not going to take responsibility for everything."

412

"What won't you take responsibility for?" Pyotr asked again.

"For anything I don't want to. That's all there is to it. I don't want to talk about it anymore."

Pyotr Stepanovitch held himself back and changed the subject.

"Let's talk about something else," he began. "Will you join us this evening? It's Virginsky's name day, and that's our excuse for meeting."

"I don't feel like it."

"Do me a favor. Please come. You need to. We need to make an impression with both our numbers and our presence. You have a face … well, let's just say you have a face that makes an impact."

"You think so?" Kirillov laughed. "Fine, I'll come, but not because of my face. What time is it?"

"Oh, it's quite early, around half-past six. You can go in, sit down, and not talk to anyone, no matter how many people are there. Just don't forget to bring a pencil and paper with you."

"What's that for?"

"It doesn't matter to you, but it's something I'm asking you to do. All you have to do is sit there quietly, don't speak to anyone, listen, and sometimes pretend to jot something down. You can even doodle if you want."

"What nonsense! Why?"

"Because it doesn't matter to you! You keep saying everything is the same to you."

"No, tell me why."

"Well, I told some of the group here that the inspector from the society might show up tonight. They'll think you're him. Since you've already been here three weeks, it'll surprise them even more."

"Tricks and theatrics. You don't even have an inspector in Moscow."

"Maybe not—who cares! What difference does it make to you? It's no trouble for you. After all, you're part of the society."

"Fine. Tell them I'm the inspector. I'll sit there quietly and not say a word, but I won't use the pencil and paper."

"But why not?"

"Because I don't want to."

Pyotr Stepanovitch turned pale with anger, but he managed to control himself. He stood up and grabbed his hat.

"Is that man still staying with you?" he asked suddenly, lowering his voice.

"Yes."

"Good. I'll take him away soon. Don't worry."

"I'm not worried. He only stays here at night. The old woman's in the hospital, and her daughter-in-law passed away. I've been alone for two days. I showed him the spot in the fence where he can take a board out to slip through without anyone noticing."

"I'll get him out of here soon."

"He says he has plenty of places to stay the night."

"That's nonsense. They're looking for him, but he's safe here. Do you talk to him much?"

"Yes, at night. He complains about you a lot. I've been reading him passages from the 'Apocalypse' at night, and we drink tea. He listens closely, very closely, the whole night."

"Damn it, you're going to turn him into a Christian!"

"He's already a Christian. Don't worry, he'll do the murder. Who do you need killed?"

"No, I don't want him for that. I need him for something else.... Does Shatov know about Fedka?"

"I don't talk to Shatov, and I don't see him."

"Is he mad at you?"

"No, we're not mad at each other. We just avoid one another. We spent too much time together in America."

"I'm going to see him now."

"As you wish."

"Stavrogin and I might stop by your place afterward, around ten."

"Alright."

"I need to talk to him about something important.... By the way, could you give me your ball? You don't need it anymore. I could use it for my exercises too. I'll pay you if you want."

"Take it. No need to pay."

Pyotr Stepanovitch picked up the ball and tucked it into the back pocket of his coat.

"But I won't help you with anything against Stavrogin," Kirillov muttered as he saw him out. Pyotr glanced back at him in surprise but said nothing.

Kirillov's parting words puzzled Pyotr Stepanovitch. He didn't have time to figure out what they meant just yet. As he climbed the stairs to Shatov's apartment, he forced himself to let go of his irritation and put on a friendly expression. Shatov was at home and feeling unwell, lying on his bed fully dressed.

"What bad luck!" Pyotr Stepanovitch exclaimed as he stepped into the room. "Are you really sick?"

The friendly look on his face disappeared, replaced by a sharp, spiteful glint in his eyes.

"Not at all," Shatov said quickly, standing up nervously. "I'm not sick … just a bit of a headache."

He seemed uneasy, clearly startled by the sudden appearance of such a visitor.

"You can't afford to be sick for the matter I came about," Pyotr Stepanovitch said, speaking quickly and firmly. "Mind if I sit down?" (He sat without waiting for a reply.) "And you can sit back on the bed. That's better. Tonight, there's a gathering of our group at Virginsky's under the excuse of celebrating his birthday. Don't worry—it won't have any political undertone; we've made sure of that. I'll be coming with Nikolay Stavrogin. Normally, I wouldn't drag you there, knowing how you feel these days—mainly to spare you the discomfort, not because we doubt your loyalty. But as things stand, you'll have to attend. You'll meet the people who'll help finalize how you'll leave the group and to whom you'll hand over everything in your possession. We'll do it discreetly; I'll pull you aside into a quiet corner. There will be plenty of people there, so no one needs to know. I've already done my part arguing on your behalf. They've finally agreed—on the condition that you hand over the printing press and all the papers. After that, you're free to go wherever you want."

Shatov listened, frowning with clear annoyance. The nervousness he'd shown moments before was completely gone.

"I don't recognize any obligation to explain myself to anyone," he said firmly. "No one has the authority to 'set me free.'"

"That's not entirely true. You were entrusted with a lot. You didn't have the right to just walk away without clarification. And you didn't make things clear when you left, which left them in an uncertain position."

"I made my position perfectly clear in a letter as soon as I arrived here," Shatov replied.

"No, it wasn't clear," Pyotr Stepanovitch said calmly. "I sent you 'A Noble Personality' to print, intending for the copies to be kept here until needed, along with the two manifestos. You returned everything with a vague letter that explained nothing."

"I refused to print them, and I made that clear."

"No, you didn't. You wrote that you couldn't do it, but you didn't say why. Saying 'I can't' isn't the same as saying 'I won't.' It could be interpreted as you being unable due to circumstances. That's how they saw it and assumed you still intended to stay involved. They might have trusted you with more later, which could have exposed them. Now, some of them believe you intended to deceive them so you could betray them when you had the chance. I've defended you as best as I could, even showing your short note to back up your case. But I have to admit, after rereading it, those two lines were vague and inconclusive."

"So you kept that note so carefully, did you?"

"Yes, I still have it, but that doesn't mean much."

"Well, I don't care, damn it!" Shatov burst out angrily. "Let your idiots think I betrayed them if they want—what difference does it make to me? I'd like to see what you think you can do about it!"

"Your name would go on their list, and when the revolution succeeds, you'd be hanged."

"That's if you ever manage to take control of Russia, right?"

"Laugh all you want. But I'll say it again: I defended you. Still, I strongly suggest you show up tonight. Why let your pride ruin things? Wouldn't it be better to part on good terms? In any case, you'll need to hand over the printing press, the old type, and the papers. That's what we need to discuss."

"I'll come," Shatov muttered, looking down thoughtfully.

Pyotr Stepanovitch gave him a sidelong glance from where he was sitting.

"Will Stavrogin be there?" Shatov suddenly asked, lifting his head.

"He'll definitely be there."

"Ha ha!"

They both fell silent for a moment. Shatov smirked, his expression filled with irritation and disdain.

"And that pathetic 'Noble Personality' piece of yours, the one I refused to print here. Did it get printed somewhere else?" he asked.

"Yes."

"To trick the schoolboys into thinking Herzen himself wrote it for your album?"

"Yes, Herzen himself."

They sat in silence again for three long minutes. Finally, Shatov stood up from the bed.

"Get out of my room. I don't want to sit here with you."

"I'm leaving," Pyotr Stepanovitch replied quickly, standing up without hesitation. "Just one thing: Kirillov is all alone in the lodge now, right? No servants with him?"

"Yes, he's completely alone. Now go—I can't stand being in the same room as you."

"Well, you're a cheerful one these days!" Pyotr Stepanovitch thought to himself as he stepped outside onto the street. "And you'll be just as delightful tonight, which is perfect for me. Absolutely perfect! It's like the Russian God Himself is lending me a hand."

Chapter 6.7

He had probably spent the day running various errands, seemingly with success, judging by the self-satisfied expression on his face when he arrived at Stavrogin's at six o'clock that evening. However, he wasn't admitted right away. Stavrogin had locked himself in his study with Mavriky Nikolaevitch. This news immediately made Pyotr Stepanovitch uneasy. He sat down near the study door, waiting for the visitor to leave. He could hear voices but couldn't make out the words. The meeting didn't last long; soon there was the sound of an extremely loud and abrupt voice, then the door opened, and Mavriky Nikolaevitch came out, his face very pale. He didn't notice Pyotr Stepanovitch as he passed quickly by. Pyotr immediately entered the study.

It's impossible to skip over the details of the brief but significant meeting that had just taken place between the two "rivals"—a meeting that seemed almost inconceivable under the circumstances, yet it had happened.

Here's how it unfolded. Nikolay Vsyevolodovitch had been napping on the couch in his study after lunch when Alexey Yegorytch announced an unexpected visitor. Hearing the name, Stavrogin jumped up, unable to believe it. But soon, a smile appeared on his face—a proud and

418

triumphant smile mixed with disbelief. As Mavriky Nikolaevitch entered, he seemed startled by Stavrogin's expression and hesitated in the middle of the room, unsure whether to step further in or leave. Stavrogin quickly changed his expression to one of calm surprise and took a step forward. The visitor didn't take the hand he offered but awkwardly moved a chair and sat down without waiting for Stavrogin to do the same. Stavrogin took his seat on the sofa, sitting at an angle to face Mavriky Nikolaevitch, and waited silently.

"If you can, marry Lizaveta Nikolaevna," Mavriky Nikolaevitch finally said, breaking the silence. What was curious was that his tone gave no clue whether it was a plea, advice, surrender, or command.

Stavrogin didn't respond right away. The visitor seemed to have said everything he had come to say and stared at him, waiting for an answer.

"If I'm not mistaken (and I'm certain of it), Lizaveta Nikolaevna is already engaged to you," Stavrogin finally said.

"She is promised and betrothed," Mavriky Nikolaevitch replied firmly.

"Have you two quarreled? Excuse me for asking, Mavriky Nikolaevitch."

"No, she 'loves and respects me.' Those are her words, and they mean more to me than anything."

"There's no doubt about that."

"But let me tell you this: even if she were standing in the church, ready to be married, and you called her, she would leave me—and everyone else—and go to you."

"From the wedding?"

"Yes, even after the wedding."

"Are you sure you're not mistaken?"

"No. Beneath her constant, sincere, and passionate hatred for you, there's a spark of love—intense, endless love mixed with madness. On the other hand, behind the love she feels for me, which is also sincere, there's hatred—the deepest hatred. I've never seen emotions shift so dramatically before."

"But I'm curious: how can you come here and offer Lizaveta Nikolaevna's hand in marriage? Do you even have the right to do that? Did she give you permission?"

Mavriky Nikolaevitch frowned and looked down for a moment.

"You're just throwing words at me," he said suddenly. "Words of revenge and triumph. Is this really the time for such petty games? Haven't you had enough satisfaction? Do I really need to humiliate myself further by spelling it all out? Fine, if you insist on my humiliation, I'll spell it out. No, I have no right. No, she hasn't authorized me. Lizaveta Nikolaevna knows nothing about this. Her fiancé has finally lost his mind and is only fit for an asylum. And to top it off, he's come here to tell you all this himself. You're the only man in the world who can make her happy, while I'm the one who will make her miserable. You're chasing her, but for some reason, you refuse to marry her. If this is all because of some lovers' quarrel from abroad, then I'll be the sacrifice to end it. She's too unhappy, and I can't bear it. My words aren't an endorsement or a demand, so your pride remains intact. If you want to take my place at the altar, you can do it without my blessing, and there's no reason for me to be here making this mad proposal—especially since our marriage is now completely impossible after what I'm doing here. I can't lead her to the altar feeling like such a miserable wretch. Coming here to offer her to you, perhaps her worst enemy, is so degrading to me that I'll never recover from it."

"Will you shoot yourself on our wedding day?"

"No, much later. Why ruin her wedding dress with my blood? Maybe I won't shoot myself at all—either now or later."

"I suppose that's meant to comfort me?"

"You? What difference would one more death make to you?" He turned pale, and his eyes glinted sharply. They sat in silence for a moment.

"Excuse me for the questions I've asked," Stavrogin began again. "Some of them were inappropriate, but one of them, I believe, I have every right to ask. Tell me, what facts have convinced you of my feelings for Lizaveta Nikolaevna? I mean, what gave you the certainty to come here and make such a proposal?"

"What?" Mavriky Nikolaevitch was visibly startled. "Haven't you been trying to win her? Aren't you still pursuing her and wanting to win her?"

"In general, I don't discuss my feelings for one woman or another with a third party. It's a principle of mine. But to make up for it, I'll tell you the truth about everything else: I am married, and it's impossible for me to marry anyone or even to try 'winning' anyone."

Mavriky Nikolaevitch was so stunned that he leaned back in his chair and stared at Stavrogin's face for a long moment.

"I never even considered that possibility," he muttered. "You said that morning you weren't married … and I believed you."

He turned pale, then suddenly slammed his fist on the table with all his strength.

"If, after admitting this, you don't leave Lizaveta Nikolaevna alone—if you make her unhappy—I swear I'll kill you with my stick like a dog in the gutter!"

He stood abruptly and stormed out of the room. Pyotr Stepanovitch, who rushed in soon after, found Stavrogin in an unexpectedly lighthearted mood.

"Ah, it's you!" Stavrogin exclaimed with loud laughter, his amusement seemingly triggered by Pyotr Stepanovitch's eager and curious entrance. "Were you listening at the door? Wait, what brings you here? Did I promise you something? Ah, yes! To meet 'our fellows.' Let's go. I couldn't be more delighted. It's the perfect idea."

He grabbed his hat, and they left the house together immediately.

"Are you laughing because you're looking forward to seeing 'our fellows'?" Pyotr Stepanovitch asked cheerfully as he darted around Stavrogin, trying to keep up. Sometimes he walked alongside Stavrogin on the narrow pavement; at other times, he ended up stepping into the mud on the road. Stavrogin strode down the center of the sidewalk, oblivious to the lack of space he left for anyone else.

"I'm not laughing at all," Stavrogin replied loudly and cheerfully. "On the contrary, I'm convinced you've gathered the most serious people around."

"'Surly dullards,' as you once called them."

"Sometimes nothing is more amusing than a surly dullard."

"Ah, you mean Mavriky Nikolaevitch? I'm sure he came to give up his fiancée to you, didn't he? I indirectly encouraged him to do it, believe it or not. And if he doesn't willingly give her up, we'll take her anyway, won't we?"

Pyotr Stepanovitch was fully aware he was taking a risk with his bold remarks, but his excitement made him reckless. Stavrogin only laughed in response.

"You still think you can help me?" Stavrogin asked.

"If you call on me. But you know there's one way that works best."

"Do I know your way?"

"No, it's still a secret for now. But remember, secrets come with a price."

"I know exactly what it costs," Stavrogin muttered to himself, then fell silent.

"What it costs? What did you say?" Pyotr Stepanovitch asked, startled.

"I said, 'Damn you and your secret!' You'd better tell me who will be there. I know we're going to a name-day party, but who else is coming?"

"Oh, all sorts! Even Kirillov."

"All members of the circles?"

"Not quite! There isn't a single circle fully formed yet."

"Then how did you manage to distribute so many manifestoes?"

"At the party, only four are actual members. The rest are on probation, spying on each other with suspicious enthusiasm and reporting back to me. They're reliable enough. It's raw material we need to organize before we move forward. You wrote the rules yourself, so you already understand."

"Are things going badly? Is something holding you back?"

"Going badly? On the contrary, everything's going perfectly. You'll find this amusing: one thing that works incredibly well is giving people titles. Titles have a tremendous effect. I've invented ranks and duties—secretaries, spies, treasurers, presidents, registrars, assistants—and they love it. It's been a great success. Another powerful tool is sentimentality. Socialism among us often spreads through pure sentiment. But then there are the troublemakers, like the overly eager lieutenants who complicate things, or the outright scoundrels who are useful but take up too much of my time. And, of course, the most important force of all: their shame at having their own opinions. That's the glue holding everything together. None of them dare think for themselves anymore—they see originality as something shameful."

"If that's the case, why put in so much effort?"

"Why? If people are just sitting there, open-mouthed and waiting for direction, how could you resist leading them? Don't tell me you doubt the possibility of success. You believe in it—you just lack the will. It's with people like this that success is entirely possible. I could make them walk through fire if I simply convinced them they weren't progressive enough. Some call me deceptive for exaggerating about the central committee and its 'innumerable branches.' Even you once criticized me for it. But where's the deception? You and I are the central committee, and we'll create as many branches as we like."

"And it's always the same sort of rabble!"

"Raw material. Even they can serve a purpose."

"And you're still counting on me?"

"You're the leader, the head. I'll just be your assistant, your secretary. We'll board our little ship, you know—the oars made of maple, the sails of silk, and steering the helm, a lovely maiden, Lizaveta Nikolaevna ... wait, how does it go in the ballad?"

"You're stuck," Stavrogin laughed. "No, let me give you my version. You sit there tallying up your so-called forces in the circles. All those titles and sentimentality are a decent glue to hold them together, but there's something much stronger. Get four members of the circle to kill a fifth under the pretense that he's a traitor, and you'll bind them with the blood they've spilled as if tying a knot. They'll be your slaves, too scared to rebel or question you. Ha ha ha!"

"You … you'll pay for those words," Pyotr Stepanovitch thought to himself, "and sooner than you think—tonight, in fact. You've gone too far."

This, or something close to it, must have been his reflection as they neared Virginsky's house.

"You've probably introduced me as some kind of foreign member, an inspector tied to the Internationale?" Stavrogin asked suddenly.

"No, not an inspector. You're not going to be an inspector. Your role is as one of the original foreign members who knows the most important secrets. That's how I've presented you. You're planning to speak, right?"

"Why would you think that?"

"Now you have to speak."

Stavrogin stopped abruptly in the middle of the street, not far from a streetlamp, looking at him in astonishment. Pyotr Stepanovitch met his gaze calmly, almost defiantly. Stavrogin cursed under his breath and kept walking.

"Are you going to speak?" he suddenly asked Pyotr Stepanovitch.

"No, I'll be listening to you."

"Damn you—you're actually giving me an idea!"

"What idea?" Pyotr Stepanovitch asked quickly.

"Maybe I will speak. And afterward, I'll beat you—and not lightly, either."

"By the way, I told Karmazinov this morning that you said he deserves a good thrashing—not a symbolic one, but one that actually hurts, like how peasants are flogged."

"But I never said that! Ha ha!"

"It doesn't matter. Se non è vero ..."

"Well, thanks for that. I'm truly grateful."

"And another thing. Do you know what Karmazinov says? He claims the essence of our beliefs is the rejection of honor, and that if you openly advocate for a right to be dishonorable, you can win over a Russian more easily than with anything else."

"An excellent observation! Brilliant words!" Stavrogin exclaimed. "He's absolutely right! The right to dishonor—why, they'd all rush to join us for that, not one would stay behind! By the way, Verhovensky, you're not secretly working for the higher police, are you?"

"Anyone who seriously wonders about that doesn't say it out loud."

"I understand, but it's just the two of us here."

"No, for now, I'm not working for the higher police. That's enough. We're here. Compose yourself, Stavrogin. I always adjust my face before going in. A gloomy look is all you need—it's simple enough."

Chapter 7

A Meeting

Chapter 7.1

Virginsky lived in his own house—or rather, his wife's—in Muravyin Street. It was a single-story wooden house with no lodgers. About fifteen guests had gathered there that evening under the pretext of celebrating Virginsky's name-day. However, the gathering was nothing like a typical provincial name-day party. From the start of their marriage, Virginsky and his wife had agreed that inviting friends for such occasions was pointless and "nothing worth celebrating." Over time, they had successfully isolated themselves from society.

Although Virginsky was intelligent and not particularly poor, people considered him eccentric, preferring solitude, and "standoffish" in conversation. His wife, Madame Virginsky, was a midwife by profession, which placed her on the lowest rung of the social ladder—even below a priest's wife, despite her husband's status as an officer. However, she showed no humility fitting her position. After a scandalous and unapologetic affair with Captain Lebyadkin—a man with a terrible reputation—even the town's more tolerant women shunned her with obvious disdain. Yet Madame Virginsky seemed to accept this treatment as if it were exactly what she wanted.

Ironically, these same women turned to Arina Prohorovna (Madame Virginsky) for help when they were expecting a child, choosing her over the town's three other midwives. Even families from nearby villages sought her out, trusting her skill and success, especially in complicated cases. Eventually, she catered only to wealthy clients and became greedy for money. Feeling her power, she grew increasingly indifferent to anyone's feelings. In fact, she often scared nervous patients by showing blatant disregard for good manners and mocking "everything sacred" at the most inappropriate moments. For instance, the town doctor, Rozanov—who was also a midwife—claimed that during one labor, Arina Prohorovna made a shocking and irreverent remark when the patient cried out to God. Her comment startled the patient so much that it sped up the delivery.

Despite being a nihilist, Madame Virginsky wasn't above taking advantage of social traditions when it suited her. She never missed a baby's christening, always wearing a green silk dress with a train and styling her hair in curls and ringlets for the occasion—though she was usually unkempt. During the ceremony, she adopted a rude and insolent attitude, embarrassing the clergy. Yet afterward, she would serve champagne to the guests (the real reason she attended), ensuring no one could take a glass without making a donation to her "porridge bowl."

That evening, the guests at Virginsky's house—mostly men—had a casual but unusual air. There was no supper and no cards. In the middle of the large drawing room, which was papered with old, faded blue wallpaper, two tables had been pushed together and covered with a large but slightly stained tablecloth. Two samovars boiled on the tables, and a large tray with twenty-five glasses and a basket of sliced French bread sat at one end, resembling the setup of a school dining hall.

The tea was served by Arina Prohorovna's sister, a thirty-year-old unmarried woman with flaxen hair and no eyebrows. She was a quiet but hostile figure who shared her sister's radical views and intimidated even Virginsky at home. Only three women were present: the hostess herself, her eyebrowless sister, and Virginsky's younger sister, who had just arrived from Petersburg.

Arina Prohorovna, a striking and full-figured woman of twenty-seven, sat looking confidently at the guests with bold, fearless eyes. She wore a plain green wool dress and seemed eager to show she wasn't intimidated by anyone. Virginsky's sister, a cheerful student and a fellow nihilist, was rosy-cheeked, short, plump, and round like a little ball. She sat next to Arina Prohorovna, still in her traveling clothes, holding a roll of paper and scanning the room impatiently.

Virginsky himself, feeling unwell that evening, sat in an armchair near the tea table. All the guests were seated as well, their orderly arrangement suggesting the atmosphere of a formal meeting. It was clear that everyone was waiting for something, filling the time with loud but meaningless chatter.

When Stavrogin and Verhovensky arrived, the room fell silent at once.

But before continuing, I must provide a few explanations to clarify the situation.

I believe that everyone who had gathered there came with the pleasant expectation of hearing something particularly interesting and likely had some notice of it beforehand. They represented the most radical and progressive group in our old town, carefully selected by Virginsky for this "meeting." It's worth noting that a few of them, though not many, had never visited him before. Most of the guests, however, had no clear idea why they had been invited.

At that time, nearly everyone believed Pyotr Stepanovitch was a fully authorized representative from abroad. This notion had taken root quickly and flattered those in attendance. Among the citizens gathered that evening under the guise of celebrating a name-day, there were a few who had been approached with specific proposals. Pyotr Verhovensky had managed to form a "quintet" in our town, similar to the ones he had already organized in Moscow and, as later became evident, in our province among the officers. It was rumored he had another in X province.

This local quintet of the chosen few was sitting at the main table, skillfully blending in so that no one could tell who they were. Now that it's no longer a secret, their identities can be revealed: first, Liputin; then Virginsky himself; next, Shigalov, a man with strikingly long ears and the brother of Madame Virginsky; Lyamshin; and finally, a peculiar individual named Tolkatchenko. The latter was around forty years old and was known for his vast knowledge of the lower classes, especially thieves and robbers. He frequented taverns under the guise of studying the people, though that wasn't his only reason for going. He took pride in his shabby clothes, tarred boots, cunning winks, and his ability to sprinkle his speech with peasant phrases.

Lyamshin had brought Tolkatchenko to Stepan Trofimovitch's gatherings once or twice, though he hadn't made much of an impression. Tolkatchenko would show up in town from time to time, mostly when he was out of work. His usual employment was on the railway.

Every member of this quintet believed with great enthusiasm that their group was just one of hundreds or even thousands of similar groups spread across Russia, all connected to a vast and secret central authority, which, in turn, was tied to the revolutionary movement across Europe. Yet, even at that time, disagreements were already beginning to arise among them.

Although they had eagerly awaited Pyotr Verhovensky's arrival—first anticipated through rumors brought by Tolkatchenko and later by Shigalov—and had expected extraordinary results from his leadership, things soured quickly. They had responded to his summons without hesitation, but once the quintet was formed, many felt insulted, likely because they had agreed to join so readily. Their motivation wasn't entirely dishonorable; they feared being accused later of lacking courage if they had refused. Still, they believed Verhovensky should have recognized their boldness and rewarded them with valuable information.

Instead, Verhovensky gave them only the essentials, treated them with strictness, and appeared indifferent. This left them irritated, and Shigalov, in particular, had already begun urging the others to demand an explanation from him—though, of course, not at Virginsky's house, where so many outsiders were present.

I suspect that the members of this first quintet also suspected that some of Virginsky's other guests might belong to additional groups Verhovensky had established in town. This led everyone to be wary of each other, adopting various poses and attitudes, which gave the gathering a peculiar and almost mysterious atmosphere.

However, some people in attendance were clearly not part of any such schemes. For example, a major in the service, a relative of Virginsky, was an entirely innocent guest. He hadn't even been invited but had shown up on his own for the name-day celebration, making it impossible to turn him away. Virginsky wasn't particularly worried about him, as the major was "incapable of betrayal." Despite his lack of intelligence, he had always been drawn to gatherings of extreme Radicals—not because he agreed with their ideas, but because he enjoyed listening to them.

Interestingly, the major had even been involved in suspicious activities in the past. In his youth, bundles of manifestoes and copies of The Bell had passed through his hands. Though he had been too frightened to open them, he considered it dishonorable to refuse to distribute them. Even today, there are people like him in Russia.

The rest of the guests were a mix of personalities, each embodying unique traits and dispositions. Some were people whose sense of self-worth had been deeply wounded, leaving them bitter and resentful. Others were filled with the passionate idealism of youth, eager to act but often lacking direction. Among them were two or three teachers. One of these was a lame man in his mid-forties, a high school instructor known for his sharp tongue and unusually inflated sense of self-importance. His vanity was striking, and his malicious remarks often set him apart.

There were also a couple of military officers in attendance. One of them, a very young artillery officer who had only recently graduated from a military academy, stood out for his quiet demeanor. He seemed shy and had not yet made friends with anyone in the group. Throughout the evening, he carried a pencil and a notebook, jotting things down as he listened. While everyone noticed his actions, they pretended not to see, as though it were a matter of unspoken agreement.

Also present was an idle divinity student, a stout young man with an air of casual confidence. He had once helped Lyamshin play a cruel prank by slipping inappropriate photographs into the pack of an elderly woman who sold gospels. This student carried himself with a steady, sarcastic smile and a sense of smug superiority, as though he was firmly convinced of his own moral and intellectual excellence.

Another attendee was the mayor's son, a pale, unhealthy-looking young man who had been mentioned earlier in the story of the lieutenant's wife. He seemed entirely drained of energy, sitting silently for the entire evening, his expression detached and uninterested.

One of the most curious figures was a disheveled schoolboy, no older than eighteen, who carried himself with the serious air of someone who believed his dignity had been offended. He was clearly uncomfortable with his youth, as though he saw it as a hindrance. Despite his age, he had already managed to become the leader of an independent group of conspirators formed within the upper grades of the local gymnasium. When this revelation came to light later, it surprised everyone who had been at the gathering.

Shatov, who also attended, sat quietly at the farthest corner of the table. His chair was pushed back slightly, as if to signal that he wasn't part of the gathering but was there strictly on his own terms. He kept his gaze fixed on the ground, refusing tea and bread. Throughout the evening, he held his cap tightly in his hand, as if to show he could leave at any moment. His demeanor was not that of a guest but of someone attending to urgent business, ready to rise and go as soon as his purpose was fulfilled.

Not far from him sat Kirillov. He, too, was silent, but unlike Shatov, his eyes were wide open and fixed intently on each speaker. His gaze was lifeless yet penetrating, and he listened to every word without betraying the slightest hint of emotion or surprise. Those who hadn't met him before couldn't help but glance at him with a mix of curiosity and unease, as though trying to decode his enigmatic presence.

As for Madame Virginsky, it's uncertain how much she knew about the secret quintet. Perhaps her husband had confided everything to her; perhaps not. The girl student, however, was entirely uninvolved in the proceedings. She had her own mission: she planned to stay in town for only a couple of days before traveling from one university city to another, spreading awareness of student suffering and inspiring protests. She carried with her hundreds of copies of a lithographed pamphlet, rumored to be her own creation, which she intended to distribute during her journey.

Interestingly, an intense dislike sprang up almost immediately between the girl student and the young schoolboy. Though they had never met before, they seemed to loathe each other on sight. The schoolboy's hatred for her was nearly murderous, and she appeared to feel the same toward him.

The girl student's uncle, the major, had only just met her again that day after a gap of ten years. Their reunion had not gone smoothly. By the time Stavrogin and Verhovensky arrived, the girl's cheeks were flushed a deep red, as bright as cranberries. She had just finished arguing with her uncle over his views on women's rights, a subject that had clearly stirred strong emotions on both sides.

Chapter 7.2

With a deliberate air of indifference, Verhovensky slouched in the chair at the head of the table, barely acknowledging anyone as he entered. His demeanor was haughty, his expression disdainful, as if the gathering was beneath him. Stavrogin, by contrast, bowed politely, though it was clear that everyone had been waiting for their arrival. Yet, as though by prior agreement, the assembled group barely reacted to them, maintaining an air of studied nonchalance. The hostess, however, wasted no time in addressing Stavrogin directly as soon as he sat down.

"Stavrogin, will you have tea?" she asked sternly.

"Yes, please," he replied simply.

"Tea for Stavrogin," she instructed her sister, who was stationed at the samovar. "And you?" she asked, turning to Verhovensky.

"Of course," he said with exaggerated disdain. "What kind of question is that to ask a guest? And make sure to give me cream this time. You always serve such terrible tea, and this at a name-day party, no less!"

"What, you still believe in celebrating name-days?" the girl student suddenly interjected with a sharp laugh. "We were just talking about how outdated that is."

"That's an old argument," muttered the schoolboy from the other end of the table.

"What's outdated?" the girl shot back, leaning forward in her chair with sudden energy. "Ignoring conventions—even the so-called harmless ones—is far from outdated. On the contrary, it's still a fresh and revolutionary act in a world that clings to them so stubbornly. And besides, there are no truly harmless conventions," she added with fervor.

"I only meant," the schoolboy began in a loud, flustered voice, "that while conventions are, of course, outdated and should be eradicated, wasting time on trivial things like name-days is pointless. It's time we focused on sharpening our minds with more useful topics—"

"You're dragging it out so much that no one can follow what you're saying," the girl interrupted impatiently, her voice rising.

"I think everyone has a right to express their opinion just as much as anyone else," the schoolboy retorted heatedly, his words stumbling over each other in frustration. "If I want to share my opinion, I will—"

"No one is denying your right to speak," the hostess cut in sharply. "But you're rambling so much that no one can understand you."

"Well, if I couldn't express my thought clearly, it's not because I didn't have one—it's because I was overthinking it!" the schoolboy muttered, clearly flustered, his voice trembling with a mix of anger and humiliation.

"If you can't talk properly, you'd be better off keeping quiet," the girl snapped.

The schoolboy shot up from his chair, his face crimson with embarrassment and fury. "I only meant to say," he shouted, barely able to contain himself, "that you're just trying to show off because Mr. Stavrogin walked in—that's all!"

"That's a vile and baseless accusation," the girl shot back, her tone icy with indignation. "It only shows how shallow your thinking is. I'd appreciate it if you didn't address me again."

"Stavrogin," the hostess interjected suddenly, trying to steer the conversation in a different direction, "we were discussing the rights of the family before you arrived. This officer here"—she nodded toward the major—"brought up the topic. Of course, I won't bore you with old arguments, but here's the real question: how did the rights and duties of the family come to exist in the superstitious form we see today? What's your opinion?"

"What do you mean by 'come to exist'?" Stavrogin asked, raising an eyebrow.

"For instance, it's well known that belief in God originated from fear of thunder and lightning," the girl student interjected again, her eyes wide with excitement as she stared at Stavrogin. "Primitive humans, terrified by these natural phenomena, created the idea of a god to explain them. But how did the superstition of the family arise? How did the family itself come into being?"

"That's not quite the same thing," Madame Virginsky murmured, trying to temper her enthusiasm.

"I think answering that question wouldn't be entirely appropriate," Stavrogin replied calmly.

"Why not?" the girl pressed, leaning forward. But before Stavrogin could respond, a low chuckle rippled through the group of teachers, quickly picked up by Lyamshin and the schoolboy at the other end of the table. Even the major let out a gruff laugh.

"You should write vaudevilles," Madame Virginsky remarked dryly to Stavrogin.

"That's hardly a credit to you, whoever you are," the girl snapped, her voice full of righteous indignation.

"And don't get too full of yourself," the major boomed, his tone half-joking but laced with condescension. "You're a young lady, and you ought to act with more modesty instead of bouncing around like you're sitting on a needle."

"Keep your insults to yourself!" the girl retorted sharply. "And don't address me so familiarly with your crude comparisons. I don't know you, and I don't acknowledge any relationship between us."

"But I'm your uncle!" the major protested, his voice rising in frustration. "I used to carry you around when you were just a baby!"

"I don't care whose babies you carried!" the girl shot back, her voice trembling with anger. "I never asked you to carry me. If you did, it must have been for your own amusement. And let me make this clear—you will not address me so familiarly again, unless it's as a fellow citizen. I forbid it. Once and for all."

"There, they're all like that!" the major exclaimed, slamming his fist on the table as he directed his words toward Stavrogin, who sat across from him. His voice was loud and forceful, as if demanding attention from everyone in the room. "But let me tell you, Stavrogin, I'm a man who appreciates liberalism and modern ideas. I genuinely enjoy listening to intelligent conversation—masculine conversation, though, I must warn you. But to sit here and listen to these women—these endless, chattering windmills—is unbearable! It makes my whole body ache. And don't you dare jump up again!" he bellowed at the girl student, who had begun to rise from her chair in protest. "It's my turn to speak now—I've been insulted, and I will have my say!"

"You never have anything worthwhile to say," Madame Virginsky interjected indignantly, glaring at the major. "And all you do is stop others from speaking."

"I'll still say my piece!" the major shot back hotly, refusing to back down. He turned to Stavrogin with a dramatic flourish. "I'm counting on you, Mr. Stavrogin. You're a new face, a fresh voice. I don't have the honor of knowing you, but I hope you'll bring some sense into this chaos. Without men, these women are doomed to collapse like flies. That's what

434

I believe! All this nonsense about the woman question—it's nothing but a lack of originality. I'll tell you, the entire concept of the woman question was invented by men—fools who didn't realize they were hurting themselves in the process. Thank God I've never married! Women lack variety; they can't even create anything on their own—they need men to do it for them!"

He gestured dramatically toward the girl student. "Take her, for example. I carried her in my arms when she was a child, danced the mazurka with her when she was ten years old. Now she returns, and naturally, I rush to embrace her. And what does she do? By the second word, she tells me there's no God! Couldn't she have waited a bit? She was in such a hurry to prove her cleverness. Clever people may not believe in God—that's fine, it's their intelligence—but what do you know about God, I asked her? Some student taught her this nonsense. If that same student had told her to light a lamp before the icons, she would have done that too!"

"You're a liar and a spiteful person," the girl retorted coldly, her voice filled with disdain. She leaned back in her chair with an air of superiority, as though addressing someone beneath her. "I explained to you very clearly just now why your argument doesn't hold up. According to the Catechism, if you honor your parents, you'll live a long life and gain wealth. That's in the Ten Commandments. If your God thinks it necessary to offer rewards for love and respect, then your God is immoral. That's what I told you. And it wasn't the second word I said to you—it was because you asserted your rights over me. If you're too stupid to understand, that's not my fault. Your generation is defined by your resentment and pettiness."

"You're a goose!" the major snapped back.

"And you're a fool!"

"At least I'm not resorting to insults!"

"Excuse me, Kapiton Maximitch," Liputin piped up from the other end of the table, his tone sly. "Didn't you tell me once yourself that you don't believe in God?"

"So what if I did?" the major replied defensively. "That's a different matter entirely. I might not believe completely, but I don't go around saying God should be shot! When I was in the hussars, I thought a lot about God. Sure, people think hussars do nothing but drink and party—and yes, I did drink—but would you believe I used to get out of bed at night, stand in my socks, and cross myself in front of the icons? I prayed to God to give me faith because I couldn't stop worrying about whether He existed. It troubled me so much! Of course, by morning, I'd be back to my amusements, and my faith would seem to disappear again. I've noticed faith always feels weaker in daylight."

"Haven't you got any cards?" Verhovensky interrupted with an exaggerated yawn, turning to Madame Virginsky as though dismissing the entire conversation.

"I sympathize with that question," the girl student interjected passionately, her cheeks flushed with indignation at the major's words. "I sympathize entirely!"

"We're wasting valuable time listening to nonsense," the hostess snapped, her frustration now directed at her husband.

The girl student straightened herself, trying to regain composure. "I intended to make a statement about the suffering of students and their protests, but with time being wasted on such immoral conversation—"

"There's no such thing as moral or immoral," the schoolboy interrupted abruptly, unable to hold back any longer.

"I knew that long before you were even taught it, Mr. Schoolboy," the girl replied coolly.

"And I'll say," the schoolboy shot back angrily, "that you're just a child from Petersburg who thinks she can enlighten all of us. But we already know the commandment to 'honor thy father and mother,' and we also know how immoral it is—Byelinsky told us that ages ago!"

"Are we ever going to move on from this?" Madame Virginsky said firmly, turning to her husband. As the hostess, she was clearly embarrassed by the direction of the conversation, especially since she noticed signs of amusement and even disbelief among some of the newer guests.

"Gentlemen," Virginsky suddenly raised his voice, attempting to regain control, "if anyone has something relevant to say or a statement to make, I urge you to do so now without wasting any more time."

"I'd like to ask a question," the lame teacher said smoothly. He had been sitting quietly, observing the room, and chose this moment to speak. "Are we gathered here as part of an official meeting, or are we simply a casual group of visitors? I ask purely for the sake of clarity and order."

His pointed question caused a ripple of reaction among the guests. They exchanged uncertain glances, each expecting someone else to respond. Then, as if by an unspoken signal, all eyes turned toward Verhovensky and Stavrogin.

"I suggest we vote on whether this is a meeting or not," Madame Virginsky proposed, breaking the silence.

"I agree entirely," Liputin chimed in quickly. "Though the question itself is a bit ambiguous."

"I agree as well," came another voice.

"And so do I," echoed several voices from around the room. The agreement seemed to ripple through the gathering as more joined in. "I also think it would bring some order to our proceedings," Virginsky affirmed, trying to project authority and calm.

"Then let's move to a vote," his wife declared, taking charge. "Lyamshin, sit at the piano. You can cast your vote from there when the voting begins."

"Again?" Lyamshin protested, rolling his eyes. "I've played enough for you already."

"I'm asking you very specifically, as a favor to the cause," Arina Prohorovna pressed, her tone firm and unyielding. "Surely you care enough to contribute something useful?"

"But honestly, Arina Prohorovna, no one's eavesdropping. That's just your imagination! The windows are too high, and even if someone did hear, they wouldn't understand a thing."

"We don't even understand it ourselves," someone muttered under their breath, eliciting a smothered laugh.

"I'm telling you, one must always be cautious!" Arina Prohorovna snapped, choosing to ignore the comment. "I mean in case there are spies lurking about," she explained, directing her words toward Verhovensky. "Let them hear music and think it's just a harmless name-day party."

"Fine, fine!" Lyamshin exclaimed in exasperation. He stomped over to the piano and began hammering out a waltz, banging on the keys at random, his frustration evident in every note.

"I propose that those who want this to be considered an official meeting should raise their right hands," Madame Virginsky announced, determined to restore some semblance of order.

What followed was chaos. Some people raised their hands immediately, others hesitated, and a few put their hands up only to lower them again and then raise them once more.

"Ugh! I don't understand what's going on at all!" an officer shouted from his seat, throwing up his arms in frustration.

"Neither do I!" another chimed in, looking equally confused.

"Oh, it's simple enough," a third voice called out. "If you're in favor, you raise your hand."

"But what exactly does 'in favor' mean?" someone else asked.

"It means we're agreeing to treat this as a meeting," came the response.

"No, it means the opposite—it's not a meeting," countered another voice.

"I voted for it to be a meeting," the schoolboy piped up, addressing Madame Virginsky directly.

"Then why didn't you raise your hand?" she demanded, her tone sharp and accusing.

"I was watching you," the schoolboy admitted sheepishly. "You didn't raise your hand, so I didn't raise mine."

"How ridiculous! I didn't raise my hand because I was the one proposing the vote," Madame Virginsky snapped. "Let's try this again, gentlemen. Now I propose the opposite. Those who want this to be a meeting, do nothing. Those who don't, raise their right hands."

"Wait, what?" the schoolboy stammered. "Do nothing if you want it to be a meeting? Or raise your hand if you don't? I'm lost!"

"Are you deliberately trying to confuse everyone?" Madame Virginsky shouted angrily.

"No, no!" he protested. "But I need to know exactly what we're voting on."

"Those who don't want it to be a meeting should raise their hands," someone clarified.

"Yes, but what if you do want it to be a meeting? Should you hold your hand up or not?" an officer asked, his face a mask of confusion.

"Clearly, we're not accustomed to constitutional methods yet!" the major quipped, his tone dripping with sarcasm.

"Mr. Lyamshin, would you kindly stop banging on the piano so loudly?" the lame teacher interjected, his voice calm but insistent. "No one can hear anything over that noise."

"Fine! Fine! But really, Arina Prohorovna, no one is paying attention to the music!" Lyamshin exclaimed, leaping to his feet. "I won't play anymore! I came here as a guest, not as a drummer!"

"Gentlemen," Virginsky interjected, raising his voice above the clamor, "let's settle this once and for all. Simply answer verbally: are we a meeting or not?"

"We are! We are!" came voices from all directions.

"Well, then, there's no need for further voting," Virginsky declared, relieved to have reached some kind of conclusion. "Is everyone satisfied? Or does anyone still object?"

"No objections! We all agree!"

"Very well. But what exactly does 'meeting' mean?" someone called out hesitantly, their voice cutting through the momentary silence.

No one answered.

"In that case, we need to elect a chairman," several voices proposed almost simultaneously.

"Our host! Our host!" the suggestion echoed around the room.

"Gentlemen," Virginsky began solemnly, now officially the chairman, "I propose that we return to the original purpose of this gathering. If anyone has something important to say, or a statement to make relevant to the subject, let them do so now without further delay."

The room fell into an expectant silence. All eyes turned toward Verhovensky and Stavrogin, waiting for them to speak.

"Verhovensky, have you nothing to say?" Madame Virginsky asked directly, her voice breaking the quiet.

"Nothing at all," Verhovensky replied with a yawn, stretching lazily in his chair. "But I wouldn't mind a glass of brandy."

"And you, Stavrogin?" she pressed. "Do you have anything to say?"

"Thank you, I don't drink," he answered curtly.

"I'm not offering you brandy; I'm asking if you wish to speak," she clarified, her irritation evident.

"To speak? About what? No, I have nothing to say," Stavrogin replied, his tone as indifferent as Verhovensky's.

"Well, someone will bring you your brandy," she said to Verhovensky with a dismissive wave.

The girl student suddenly stood up, her movements quick and determined. She had risen from her seat several times before, but now she seemed resolute.

"I have come to make a statement," she began, her voice loud and clear, "about the suffering of impoverished students and the ways we can inspire them to protest—"

But she stopped abruptly. At the other end of the table, someone else had stood up, drawing all eyes toward him.

It was Shigalov, the man with the long ears. He rose slowly, his movements deliberate, and placed a thick notebook filled with tiny, cramped handwriting on the table in front of him. His expression was dark and brooding, his gaze heavy with purpose. He remained standing in silence.

Many in the room stared at the notebook with a mixture of unease and curiosity, unsure of what was coming. However, Liputin, Virginsky, and the lame teacher exchanged glances of approval, their faces lighting up with anticipation.

"I request permission to address the meeting," Shigalov announced, his tone sullen but resolute as he stood, clutching his thick notebook.

"You have permission," Virginsky replied, nodding to signal his approval.

Shigalov sat back down slowly, pausing for half a minute to gather his thoughts. When he finally began, his voice was solemn, as though he were delivering a lecture to a room of attentive students.

"Gentlemen!" he declared, with an air of gravity that seemed almost theatrical.

Before he could continue, the sister who had been busy pouring tea earlier returned with a bottle of brandy. She placed it before Verhovensky with an air of contempt, along with a wineglass she had brought without a tray. Her disdain was evident in her curt movements and expression, as though she resented being sent on such an errand.

The interruption forced Shigalov to pause again. He sat in silence, his face composed but his annoyance barely concealed.

"Never mind, go on. I'm not listening," Verhovensky called out nonchalantly, pouring himself a glass of brandy with casual indifference.

Shigalov drew a deep breath and began again. "Gentlemen, asking for your attention and, as you will soon see, soliciting your assistance in a matter of great importance, I must first make a few preliminary remarks."

"Arina Prohorovna, do you have a pair of scissors?" Verhovensky suddenly asked, cutting across Shigalov's speech without hesitation.

"What do you need scissors for?" she asked, wide-eyed with surprise.

"I've been meaning to cut my nails for three days now," Verhovensky replied casually, holding up his hands to inspect his long, grimy nails with an expression of complete composure.

Arina Prohorovna flushed red with embarrassment, while her sister, Miss Virginsky, seemed oddly amused.

"I think I saw a pair on the windowsill just now," she said, rising eagerly. She fetched the scissors and handed them to Verhovensky, who didn't even glance at her. He took them and immediately began trimming his nails, seemingly oblivious to the room around him.

Arina Prohorovna, realizing this display was meant to project some form of "realism," felt ashamed of her earlier reaction and quickly masked her emotions. The room fell into a tense silence as people exchanged uneasy glances. The lame teacher shot Verhovensky a look filled with both resentment and envy.

Unperturbed, Shigalov pressed on. "Having dedicated myself to the study of the social structure that must inevitably replace the current system, I have come to a startling conclusion. All the creators of social systems, from ancient times to the present day, have been nothing more than dreamers, peddlers of fairy tales, and fools who have contradicted themselves. They understood neither natural science nor the peculiar creature known as man. Plato, Rousseau, Fourier—all of them, along with their columns of aluminum, are fit only for sparrows, not human society."

He tapped his notebook emphatically before continuing. "Now that we are preparing to take action, it is essential to create a new model for social organization. To avoid any ambiguity, I propose my own system of world organization. The details are here," he said, gesturing toward the notebook.

"I intended to present my ideas as concisely as possible," Shigalov added, "but I now realize that explaining them thoroughly would require at least ten evenings—one for each chapter of my book."

This remark prompted a ripple of laughter through the room, mostly from the younger and less invested guests. Shigalov paused, his expression unshaken by the mocking response.

"I must also point out," he continued, raising his voice slightly, "that my system is not yet complete."

More laughter followed, louder this time, though Madame Virginsky, Liputin, and the lame teacher exchanged looks of irritation.

"I admit," Shigalov said, undeterred, "that I am puzzled by my own findings. My conclusions directly contradict the fundamental premise from which I began. Starting with the principle of unlimited freedom, I have arrived at the necessity of unlimited despotism. And yet," he added firmly, "there is no alternative. My solution is the only viable one."

The laughter grew louder still, but it came mainly from those unfamiliar with Shigalov's eccentricity. The faces of Madame Virginsky and a few others reflected both annoyance and frustration.

"If your system is inconsistent and has driven even you to despair, what could we possibly do with it?" an officer asked cautiously, his tone skeptical.

"You are correct, Mr. Officer," Shigalov snapped, turning to him sharply. "Particularly in your choice of the word despair. Yes, I am in despair. But even so, my system is irreplaceable. Nothing can take its place, and there is no alternative solution to the social problem. That is why I am urging all of you to listen to my book, chapter by chapter, over the course of ten evenings. Only after that will you be in a position to judge its worth."

He paused, looking around the room. "If this group refuses to listen, then let us dissolve right now. Let the men return to government service and the women to their kitchens. But remember this: if you reject my solution, you will inevitably return to it later. It is the only way forward."

The room stirred uneasily. Voices whispered questions: "Is he mad? What does he mean?"

"So the crux of the matter lies in Shigalov's despair," Lyamshin remarked with a smirk. "The essential question is whether his despair should concern us or not."

"Shigalov's personal despair has no bearing on the larger cause," the schoolboy declared, crossing his arms with an air of authority.

"I propose we vote on two things," an officer suggested cheerfully. "First, whether Shigalov's despair affects the common cause, and second, whether his system is worth listening to at all."

The suggestion drew murmurs of agreement, though the tension in the room remained palpable as all eyes returned to Shigalov, who sat with an air of wounded dignity, waiting for the room to make its decision.

"That's not entirely correct," the lame teacher finally chimed in, his voice calm but carrying a subtle undertone that was difficult to interpret. He often spoke with a faint, mocking smile that left others unsure whether he was serious or simply poking fun. "Gentlemen, Mr. Shigalov is overly modest about his own ideas. I am familiar with his book, and I must say, it presents a highly detailed and thought-provoking solution to the social problem. His final proposition is quite striking. He suggests dividing humanity into two unequal groups. One-tenth of the population will enjoy absolute liberty and unlimited power over the remaining nine-tenths. The majority, in turn, will surrender all individuality, forming a submissive and obedient collective—a sort of human herd. Through this boundless submission, they will eventually achieve something akin to primeval innocence, a return to an earthly paradise reminiscent of the Garden of Eden."

He paused for effect, then added, "Of course, they'll still have to work, and the process of transforming generations to reach this state is no simple matter. The methods Mr. Shigalov outlines to strip nine-tenths of their freedom and individuality are both remarkable and deeply grounded in nature. His logic, while controversial, is undeniably rigorous. One might not agree with all his conclusions, but it's impossible to deny the depth of his intelligence or the breadth of his research. It's unfortunate that we cannot dedicate the ten evenings he requests to fully explore these ideas. I suspect they would prove to be as fascinating as they are unsettling."

"Are you serious?" Madame Virginsky broke in, her voice tinged with unease. She looked at the lame teacher with a mixture of disbelief and disapproval. "You're defending a plan that enslaves nine-tenths of

444

humanity just because its creator doesn't know what else to do with them? I've suspected him of dangerous ideas for a long time."

"And you say that about your own brother?" the lame teacher responded with a touch of irony.

"Relationship? Are you trying to make a joke at my expense?" she shot back, her voice sharpening.

"And besides," the girl student interjected fiercely, "forcing the majority to labor for a small elite and treating them as gods is disgusting and degrading!"

"What I propose isn't degrading—it's paradise, an earthly paradise," Shigalov replied with authority. "There can be no other paradise on this earth."

"For my part," Lyamshin said with a mischievous grin, "if I didn't know what to do with nine-tenths of humanity, I'd blow them all into the air. Then I'd leave just a small, educated elite to live happily ever after, guided by scientific principles."

"No one but a clown would say something so absurd!" the girl exclaimed, her cheeks flushed with anger.

"He is a clown," Madame Virginsky whispered to her in a low voice, "but he's a useful one."

"And yet," Shigalov said, turning to Lyamshin with surprising intensity, "there's something profound in what you've just said, even if you meant it as a joke. Perhaps your solution is the simplest and most effective. However, since it's unlikely to be feasible, we must settle for an earthly paradise instead—call it what you will."

"This is utter nonsense," Verhovensky muttered under his breath. He didn't bother to look up from his nails, which he continued trimming with complete indifference.

"Why do you call it nonsense?" the lame teacher asked sharply, as though he had been waiting for Verhovensky to speak so he could pounce on his words. "What's so nonsensical about it? Yes, Mr. Shigalov's ideas may seem extreme, but they stem from his passionate concern for humanity. And don't forget, many great thinkers have proposed equally despotic and seemingly fantastical measures. Fourier, Cabet, and even Proudhon advocated ideas that were far more impractical than Mr. Shigalov's. Compared to them, Shigalov is surprisingly sober in his proposals. When you read his book, it's hard not to find yourself agreeing with at least some of his points. His vision of an earthly paradise is, in many ways, closer to reality than any other we've seen—or at least to the kind of paradise humanity has been longing for since its fall from grace."

"I knew this would turn into something ridiculous," Verhovensky muttered again, his tone as nonchalant as before.

"Allow me to continue," the lame teacher said, his voice growing more animated. "Discussions and debates about the future organization of society are not only relevant but practically necessary for any thinking person today. Herzen, for instance, devoted his entire life to pondering such questions. And Byelinsky—let me assure you—would spend entire evenings with his friends debating the details of how society might function in the future, down to the smallest, most domestic arrangements."

His enthusiasm was evident now, his earlier mocking tone replaced by genuine fervor. The room grew quieter as people began to sense the weight of his words, even if they didn't entirely agree.

"Some people seem to go mad over these ideas," the major interjected suddenly, his voice cutting through the growing tension in the room.

"We're more likely to achieve something by actually discussing these matters," Liputin hissed, his tone sharp and laced with contempt, "rather than sitting in silence and posing as all-knowing dictators." It was clear that he had been waiting for an opening to launch his attack.

"I wasn't referring to Shigalov's theories when I said it was nonsense," Verhovensky muttered lazily, barely lifting his eyes. "You see, gentlemen," he continued with a slight drawl, "in my view, all these books—Fourier, Cabet, and the rest of them, including Shigalov's grand ideas—are nothing more than aesthetic diversions, novels of sorts. You could write a hundred thousand of them. They are intellectual entertainment, nothing more. And, honestly, I get it. Living in a small, sleepy town like this, you must be terribly bored. So naturally, you turn to ink and paper for amusement."

"Excuse me," the lame teacher cut in, shifting in his chair, his voice rising slightly as he took offense. "We may be provincials, and perhaps you pity us for that, but I'd like to remind you that nothing truly new or revolutionary has happened in the world to warrant our regret for missing it. What's being suggested to us, often in clandestine pamphlets distributed from abroad, is that we should form secret groups dedicated solely to universal destruction. They tell us the world is beyond repair, that no amount of tinkering can fix it. So, they propose we cut off a hundred million heads, lighten the load, and leap across the abyss to some imagined future. A fine idea, I suppose, but no more practical than Shigalov's theories, which you so condescendingly dismissed just now."

"Perhaps," Verhovensky replied nonchalantly, "but I didn't come here to debate." He leaned forward to adjust the candle, seemingly unaware of the weight of his words or the ripple of unease they caused.

"It's a pity," the lame teacher responded sharply, "a great pity, in fact, that you didn't come to debate. And it's even more unfortunate that you seem more concerned with your personal grooming than with the conversation at hand."

"What does my grooming have to do with you?" Verhovensky retorted, his voice as indifferent as ever.

"It's just as impractical to cut off a hundred million heads as it is to transform the world through propaganda," Liputin interjected again, emboldened now. "In fact, I'd argue that such a massacre would be even more difficult, especially in Russia."

"Yet it's Russia they're pinning their hopes on," an officer remarked dryly.

"Yes," the lame teacher added, his tone dripping with irony. "We've all heard about the mysterious finger pointing to our beloved homeland as the ideal place to carry out this grand task. But consider this: with propaganda, I might achieve something tangible. I could engage in spirited discussions, gain some recognition for my service to society, maybe even earn a nod of approval from the government. But with the quick method—lopping off a hundred million heads—what's in it for me? If anything, I'd risk losing my tongue for even suggesting it."

"Yours certainly would be the first to go," Verhovensky observed with a faint smirk.

"Exactly!" the lame teacher exclaimed, leaning forward. "And let's not forget—this isn't something that could be accomplished overnight. Even under the best circumstances, it would take decades—thirty, maybe fifty years. And, gentlemen, we are not dealing with sheep. People won't line up quietly for slaughter. Wouldn't it be wiser, then, to pack up, move to some peaceful island far beyond the chaos, and live out the rest of one's days in tranquility? Believe me," he added, tapping the table for emphasis, "all this talk of mass destruction will do nothing but encourage emigration—nothing more!"

He leaned back in his chair, clearly triumphant. A few people exchanged smiles, while others nodded in agreement. Liputin smirked slyly, and Virginsky listened with a somewhat dejected expression. The rest of the room watched the exchange intently, particularly the officers and the women, who seemed both amused and uneasy. It was clear to everyone that the advocate of the "hundred million heads" theory had been cornered, and they waited eagerly to see how Verhovensky would respond.

"That was an interesting point," Verhovensky said at last, his tone bored and dismissive. "Emigration is a valid idea. But let me tell you, my friend, if so many people are still coming forward, ready to fight for the common cause despite all the obvious drawbacks you've pointed out, it's because this movement is no longer just politics. It's a new religion, replacing the old one. That's why more and more people are willing to join the fight. But as for you, I'd suggest emigration. Go to Dresden, not some distant island. For one thing, Dresden has never been struck by an epidemic, and I assume a cultured man like you fears death. Second, it's close to the Russian border, so you can still receive your income from your beloved Fatherland. And third, it boasts treasures of art, which should appeal to someone with your aesthetic sensibilities. After all, you were a literature teacher, weren't you? And finally, it has a miniature

Switzerland for your poetic inspiration. It's a perfect little haven!"

There was a stir in the room, especially among the officers. A hum of voices began to rise, as if everyone wanted to speak at once. But before the room could erupt into chaos, the lame teacher took the bait and rose irritably.

"No, I'm not giving up the common cause!" he declared emphatically. "You must understand that—"

"What's this?" Verhovensky interrupted suddenly, his voice louder and sharper than before. He set down the scissors and fixed his gaze on the lame teacher. "Would you join the quintet if I proposed it to you?"

The question hung in the air, freezing the room. Everyone seemed startled by Verhovensky's bluntness. He had revealed too much, speaking openly of the quintet—a term that had until now been shrouded in mystery.

"Every honest man feels obliged to do his part for the common cause," the lame teacher stammered, trying to find a way out. "But—"

"No, no!" Verhovensky cut him off, his tone harsh and commanding. "This is not a matter for hesitation. I demand a direct answer. Gentlemen, I understand that by coming here and calling you together, I owe you an explanation." This unexpected admission drew murmurs from the room. "But before I provide one, I need to know where you stand. Let's not waste time with endless debates and dithering, as people have done for decades. I ask you now: which do you prefer? The slow, academic approach of composing socialistic romances and planning humanity's future a thousand years from now? Or a swifter, more decisive path that unties our hands and allows humanity to build its society in freedom and action, rather than on paper? People talk about 'a hundred million heads'—maybe that's just a metaphor. But even if it's not, why fear it? With the slow approach, despotism will devour not a hundred but five hundred million heads over the next century. And let me remind you, an incurable patient will not recover no matter how many prescriptions you write. Delay will only make things worse, corrupting society until it collapses entirely."

He paused, scanning the room with a fiery intensity. "So tell me: do you prefer to crawl at a snail's pace through the swamp or to power through it at full steam?"

"I'm all for full steam ahead!" the schoolboy shouted, his face lighting up with excitement.

"Same here!" Lyamshin chimed in eagerly.

"There's no question about it," murmured one officer, followed quickly by another and then several more voices.

It was clear that Verhovensky's assertiveness had struck a chord. Even the skeptical major, after a moment of hesitation, nodded and said, "Well, I prefer a more humane approach, but if everyone else is on board, I'll go along with the majority."

Verhovensky turned back to the lame teacher with a faint smile. "And you? Even you seem ready to join."

"I wouldn't say that exactly," the lame teacher replied, flushing slightly. "But if I do agree, it's only to avoid causing division—"

"That's always the way with you," Verhovensky interrupted with a scornful laugh. "You'll argue for months just to hear yourself talk, but in the end, you always follow the herd. So, gentlemen, is it true? Are you all ready?"

"Ready for what?" someone muttered, the question hanging in the air like an unspoken challenge. It was vague but undeniably captivating, stirring a quiet tension in the room.

"Of course, we're ready!" came a smattering of voices. But even as they spoke, the guests glanced around uneasily, gauging each other's reactions, their earlier certainty faltering.

"But afterward, won't some of you regret agreeing so quickly?" Verhovensky asked with a sly smile, his words laced with mockery. "That's usually how it goes with you."

The unease in the room grew, manifesting in nervous fidgeting and half-formed murmurs. The lame teacher could no longer contain himself. He pushed back in his chair and leaned forward, his voice sharp with irritation. "Allow me to point out that answering such a question is inherently conditional. Even if we've given an answer, it's only fair to note that the way you posed the question—"

"In what way?" Verhovensky interrupted, feigning confusion.

"In a way that no proper question should be asked!" the lame man retorted, his voice rising.

"Ah, then teach me the proper way," Verhovensky said, his tone dripping with mock innocence. "But I knew it—you'd be the first to take offense."

"You've forced an answer about our readiness for immediate action," the lame teacher continued, undeterred. "But what gives you the authority to ask such a question? By what right do you demand this from us?"

"You should have thought to ask that before you answered," Verhovensky countered, his tone turning sharp. "Why agree only to backtrack later? You commit and then retreat—how typical!"

"But the nature of your question," the lame man insisted, "leads me to believe that you have no authority, no legitimate standing. You're asking purely out of personal curiosity."

"What?" Verhovensky exclaimed, his voice suddenly louder, his demeanor shifting to one of feigned alarm. "What do you mean by that?"

"I mean," the lame man replied, his irritation boiling over, "that matters of initiation, or whatever this is supposed to be, are conducted privately, not in the presence of twenty strangers! This is absurd!" His frustration spilled out unchecked, his words cutting through the murmurs of the group.

Verhovensky turned slowly, addressing the room with an exaggerated expression of alarm. "Gentlemen, I must declare that this has gone too far. Our conversation is verging on dangerous nonsense. Let me make it clear: I have initiated no one into anything. No one can say otherwise. We were merely exchanging ideas, discussing opinions. Isn't that right?" He paused, scanning the room as if seeking validation. "But still, this concerns me deeply. Are you suggesting it isn't safe to speak even of innocent matters here? Must we fear informers? Could there truly be an informer among us?"

The murmurs in the room grew into a chaotic hum of voices, as excitement and suspicion rippled through the group.

"If that's the case," Verhovensky continued, raising his voice to cut through the noise, "then I'm more compromised than anyone here. So, I'll ask you all a single question—a simple one, entirely voluntary. Answer only if you wish." He paused dramatically, the tension thick in the air.

"What question?" several voices called out at once.

"A question to determine whether we remain together or part ways here and now. If anyone among us knew of a planned political murder, would they, considering all the consequences, inform the authorities or stay silent and await events? That's all. Your answer will decide whether we go forward together or scatter forever. Let me start with you," he said, turning to the lame teacher.

"Why start with me?" the lame man asked, bristling.

"Because you were the first to challenge me. And don't try to wriggle out of it. Be straightforward—it's up to you."

"Excuse me, but your question is outright insulting," the lame man protested, his anger rising.

"No, be more precise. Would you inform or not?" Verhovensky pressed.

"I've never been an agent of the Secret Police," the lame man replied, his voice shaking slightly, his body writhing in discomfort.

"Stop evading. Just give us a clear answer," Verhovensky demanded, his tone hardening.

The lame man glared at him, his face flushed with fury. For a moment, he seemed ready to explode. Finally, he shouted, "No! Of course not!"

"And no one else would either!" several voices echoed.

"Let me ask you now, Major," Verhovensky continued, pivoting to another guest. "Would you inform or not? I'm asking you specifically for a reason."

"I wouldn't inform," the major said curtly.

"But if it were an ordinary crime—say, a robbery or murder—you'd report it, wouldn't you?" Verhovensky pressed further.

"Of course. But that's different. That's personal. A political betrayal is another matter entirely. And let me repeat—I've never been an agent of the Secret Police."

"And none of us here have!" several voices chimed in indignantly. "This question is unnecessary."

At that moment, the girl student's voice cut through the crowd. "What's that man getting up for?" she asked, pointing across the room.

All eyes turned to Shatov, who was rising from his chair. He held his cap tightly in his hand, his face pale and tense. He seemed to struggle with something unsaid, staring directly at Verhovensky before finally turning toward the door.

"Shatov, this won't improve your position," Verhovensky called after him, his voice tinged with something unspoken, almost threatening.

"But it will improve yours, spy and scoundrel that you are!" Shatov shouted back from the doorway before storming out.

The room erupted in chaos, voices overlapping in a cacophony of accusations and questions. "Who is he?" "Why was he here?" "Will he inform?" "How did he even get invited?"

"If he were an informer, he wouldn't have left like that," someone remarked thoughtfully. "He'd have played along instead of storming out."

"And now Stavrogin is getting up too!" the girl student exclaimed, her voice rising with urgency. "He hasn't answered the question either!"

All eyes turned to Stavrogin, who had risen calmly from his seat. At the same moment, Kirillov stood as well, his expression unreadable.

"Mr. Stavrogin," Madame Virginsky said sharply, her voice cutting through the din, "everyone else has answered the question. Are you leaving without giving an answer?"

"I see no reason to answer your question," Stavrogin muttered, his voice low but firm.

"But we've all compromised ourselves, and you won't!" several voices shouted indignantly.

"That's your business, not mine," Stavrogin replied with a cold laugh, though his eyes flashed with suppressed emotion.

"What do you mean, 'your business'?" voices clamored angrily. Chairs scraped against the floor as more people stood up, their frustration spilling over.

"Allow me to point out," the lame man interjected, trying to regain control of the situation, "that Mr. Verhovensky hasn't answered the question either. He's only asked it."

The remark hit like a lightning bolt, silencing the room. Everyone turned to Verhovensky, their faces a mixture of curiosity and accusation.

Stavrogin chuckled at the lame man's observation, a sharp, mocking laugh that echoed in the tense silence. Without another word, he walked out, followed closely by Kirillov. Verhovensky, visibly rattled, rushed after them into the hallway.

"What are you doing?" he demanded, grabbing Stavrogin's arm in desperation. "I need to see you—immediately. Meet me at Kirillov's. It's crucial!"

"It's not crucial for me," Stavrogin replied curtly, pulling his arm free.

"It is for you, Stavrogin," Kirillov interjected, his voice calm but firm. "And I'll prove it to you there."

Without another word, the three men disappeared into the night, leaving the rest of the group in disarray, their earlier confidence shaken to its core.

Chapter 8
Ivan The Tsarevitch

They were gone. Pyotr Stepanovitch hesitated for a moment at the doorway, glancing back toward the chaotic meeting he had left behind. It was clear that the group was in disarray, but instead of returning to restore order, he seemed to decide it wasn't worth the trouble. With a muttered curse, he turned and rushed into the night, his mind set on catching up with Stavrogin and Kirillov.

As he darted through the muddy streets, a shortcut came to mind—one that would take him directly to Filipov's house. The path was treacherous, thick with mud that sucked at his boots, but he pushed on, his urgency driving him forward. His gamble paid off; just as he reached the gate of the house, Stavrogin and Kirillov appeared, stepping through it.

"Here already?" Kirillov noted, his voice flat but with a hint of approval. "Good. Come in."

"You told us you lived alone," Stavrogin remarked as they passed a boiling samovar in the narrow hallway.

"You'll see who I live with soon enough," Kirillov muttered cryptically. "Go on in."

The three of them entered the dimly lit room, and without a word, Verhovensky reached into his pocket and pulled out the anonymous letter he had taken from Lembke. He handed it directly to Stavrogin and gestured for him to sit. Stavrogin took a seat and read the letter silently, his face impassive.

"Well?" he said after a pause, his tone betraying neither interest nor concern.

"That scoundrel will do exactly what he threatens," Verhovensky replied, leaning forward. "He's dangerous, and you know it. He could go to Lembke as early as tomorrow. We have to act."

"Let him go," Stavrogin said, his tone casual, almost dismissive.

"Let him go? When we could stop him?" Verhovensky's voice rose, his frustration seeping through.

"You misunderstand me," Stavrogin replied coolly. "He isn't under

455

my control. Besides, he doesn't pose a threat to me. He's your problem."

"He's a threat to you too," Verhovensky retorted sharply. "And even if he weren't, there are others who won't spare you if this gets out. Surely you see that. Listen, Stavrogin, stop playing word games. You can deal with this easily. It's just money. Surely you don't begrudge spending a little money?"

"Money? What are you talking about?"

"Fifteen hundred, maybe two thousand. That's all it would take. Give me the money today, or tomorrow at the latest, and I'll take care of it. I'll send him to Petersburg. That's exactly what he wants. If you prefer, he can even take Marya Timofyevna with him."

Stavrogin raised an eyebrow, watching Verhovensky with a mix of curiosity and contempt. The man seemed distracted, almost frantic, his words tumbling out without thought.

"I have no reason to send Marya Timofyevna away," Stavrogin said calmly.

"Perhaps you don't even want to," Verhovensky shot back with a sardonic smile.

"Perhaps I don't," Stavrogin agreed, his expression unchanging.

"Enough of this!" Verhovensky snapped, his voice rising. "Will there be money or not?"

Stavrogin leaned back, scrutinizing Verhovensky with a piercing gaze. "There won't be money," he said finally.

Verhovensky's face twisted in frustration. "You're hiding something," he accused. "You know something or you've already done something. What are you up to, Stavrogin?"

His mouth twitched, and suddenly he let out a strange, unprovoked laugh. It was brief and unsettling, breaking the tension in an unexpected way.

"You've had money from your family," Stavrogin said calmly, ignoring the outburst. "Didn't my mother send you six or eight thousand

456

for Stepan Trofimovitch? Use that to pay your fifteen hundred. I've already given enough. I'm done footing the bill for others."

"So now it's a joke to you?" Verhovensky sneered.

Stavrogin rose from his chair. Instinctively, Verhovensky sprang to his feet, moving to block the door. It was an impulsive act, and Stavrogin paused, his eyes narrowing as he studied him.

"I won't let you harm Shatov," Stavrogin said, his voice low but firm.

Verhovensky froze, visibly startled. Their eyes met, and for a moment, the room felt unbearably still.

"I told you why you want Shatov's blood," Stavrogin continued, his voice cutting through the silence. "It's the glue you need for your schemes. You want his murder to bind your little groups together, to make them complicit, to make them loyal. That's why you provoked him earlier, drove him away. You knew he wouldn't lie to you, that he wouldn't promise to stay silent. But what do you want from me? Why won't you leave me alone? Ever since we met abroad, you've been circling me, pushing me. And now you're asking me to pay so you can have Lebyadkin murdered—and maybe my wife too. Is that your plan? To trap me in your web with this crime? What do you want from me, Verhovensky? Am I your pawn? Your talisman? Let me go!"

"Has Fedka been to you?" Verhovensky asked breathlessly.

"Yes," Stavrogin replied. "He named the same price—fifteen hundred. But here, let him tell you himself." He gestured toward the doorway, where a shadowy figure emerged.

It was Fedka, dressed in a worn sheepskin coat. He stood at the threshold, grinning broadly, his white teeth gleaming in the dim light. His dark, restless eyes flicked around the room, trying to gauge the situation. He looked to Kirillov for direction but hesitated to step further inside.

"I suppose you brought him here to witness our deal," Stavrogin said coldly. "Or maybe to see the money in hand. Is that it?"

Without waiting for an answer, Stavrogin strode past Fedka and out the door. Verhovensky, nearly frantic, chased after him.

"Stop!" he cried, grabbing Stavrogin's arm at the gate. Stavrogin wrenched his arm free, his patience finally snapping. Gripping Verhovensky by the hair, he flung him to the ground with all his strength and stormed off into the night.

But Verhovensky was relentless. Scrambling to his feet, he ran after Stavrogin, catching up within thirty paces.

"Let's make peace!" he pleaded, his voice trembling. "We can work this out. Just tell me what you want. I'll give it to you—anything you ask!"

"Get away from me," Stavrogin snarled, not even turning to look at him.

"I'll give you Shatov!" Verhovensky cried desperately. "You want him? Take him!"

Stavrogin stopped abruptly and turned to face him. "So it's true—you meant to kill him?"

"What's Shatov to you?" Verhovensky gasped, his voice breaking. "Why do you care? Let's settle this, Stavrogin. Whatever it takes—let's settle it!"

Stavrogin stared at him, bewildered. Verhovensky's face was unrecognizable, his usual composure shattered. His eyes were wild, his voice raw with desperation.

"What's wrong with you?" Stavrogin demanded. "Why are you like this? Is there something I don't know? Am I that important to you?"

"We're starting a revolution," Verhovensky muttered feverishly. "A real revolution. Everything will be uprooted. Karmazinov was right—there's nothing left to hold onto. But with ten groups like mine across Russia, I'll be untouchable."

"And these groups of fools—these clowns—are your grand plan?" Stavrogin said, his voice dripping with disdain.

"Don't underestimate them," Verhovensky shot back. "You don't believe in them because you're afraid. But we'll succeed. And you—you're part of it whether you like it or not."

"Take Shigalov," Stavrogin said coldly. "And leave me alone."

They walked on in silence, but Stavrogin could feel Verhovensky's madness bubbling beneath the surface, a storm waiting to break.

Pyotr Stepanovitch continued speaking with feverish energy, his words tumbling over one another as though he could not restrain the torrent. "Do you know what Shigalov's manuscript is really about?" he asked, his tone somewhere between fascination and disdain. "It's not just about a system; it's about control. Spying, informing, slandering, even murdering—he's got it all worked out. Every member of society is to spy on the others, inform against them, and live as a slave. Not just a slave, but an equal one, bound in the same chains as everyone else. In his world, individuality is crushed. There's no room for greatness, no room for intellect, no room for freedom. And yet, somehow, this is supposed to be equality."

Stavrogin quickened his pace, clearly uneasy. "If this lunatic is drunk, how did he manage it?" he thought. "Was it the brandy? Or is this his natural state?"

"Think about it!" Verhovensky continued, his voice rising. "He wants to reduce everyone to the lowest common denominator. No more intellects, no more science, no more culture. Why? Because the great intellects always seize power—they can't help it. They rise above the herd and become despots. Shigalov's solution is simple: cut them down, root them out, extinguish them before they even have a chance to flourish. Cicero? Tongue cut out. Copernicus? Eyes gouged. Shakespeare? Stoned to death by the mob. That's Shigalovism—slavery dressed up as equality!"

Verhovensky laughed abruptly, a sharp, mirthless sound that grated on Stavrogin's nerves. "Equality through despotism," he said. "That's the only way it's ever been achieved. The herd demands it, craves it, even. They need their chains. It's their nature."

Stavrogin muttered something under his breath and picked up his pace, clearly eager to put distance between himself and this maddening tirade. But Verhovensky followed, undeterred.

"Listen, Stavrogin," he went on, his voice now almost pleading.

"Destroying culture is not an absurd idea; it's necessary. Science? We've had enough. The thirst for knowledge is an aristocratic trait, tied to property, tied to love, tied to family. We'll stamp out those desires. We'll make drunkenness, slander, and corruption tools of the state. Genius? We'll crush it in the cradle. Ambition? Stifled before it breathes. The world will be a flat, even plain, and everyone will be equal. Absolute submission! Absolute conformity! And then, once every thirty years, we'll give them a 'shock.' Let them tear each other apart for a bit, just to stave off boredom."

"Boredom?" Stavrogin repeated, incredulously.

"Yes, boredom! It's an aristocratic disease, Stavrogin. The herd won't have it, not under Shigalov's rule. They won't have desires. Desires lead to suffering, and suffering is for us, the directors. They'll be content, and we'll bear the burden of ambition for them."

"You seem to exclude yourself from this grand plan," Stavrogin said, his voice cold.

"Of course," Verhovensky replied without hesitation. "And you too, Stavrogin. You and I—we're above it. We'll direct it. Don't you see? The Internationale will unite with the Pope, and together we'll rule. Imagine it—millions flocking to us, craving order, discipline, salvation. The Pope barefoot, leading the masses, and beneath him, Shigalovism. It's genius!"

"Enough!" Stavrogin snapped, his patience wearing thin. "You're drunk or mad—or both."

"Drunk? Mad? Perhaps. But Stavrogin, you're beautiful," Verhovensky said suddenly, his voice softening. There was a strange reverence in his tone now, an almost worshipful quality. "Do you know that? You're beautiful in a way that terrifies people. You're pure, untainted, and yet everyone hates you. They fear you because you treat them as equals, and that's the most terrifying thing of all. You are the man we need—the man I need. Without you, I am nothing. With you, I am invincible."

He seized Stavrogin's hand and kissed it fervently. Stavrogin jerked it away, a shudder running through him.

"Madman!" Stavrogin hissed, his voice trembling with disgust.

"Maybe I am," Verhovensky replied, his tone suddenly desperate. "But I've thought of the first step, Stavrogin. The first step! Shigalov couldn't have imagined it. It's bold, it's brilliant, and it starts with you. Without you, I'm just an idea in a bottle. With you, I'm Columbus discovering America!"

Stavrogin stopped and turned to face him. Verhovensky's eyes were wild, his face flushed with a manic intensity.

"First, we'll shake the world," Verhovensky said, clutching at Stavrogin's sleeve like a drowning man. "We'll reach the peasants, infiltrate the schools, the courts, the churches. We already have so many on our side—teachers who mock God in front of children, lawyers who defend murderers as if it's their duty, juries who acquit every criminal. They don't even know they're working for us, but they are. The docile, the vain, the bitter—they're all ours."

"And what about the rest?" Stavrogin asked, his voice flat. "What happens to them?"

"We corrupt them," Verhovensky said, his tone darkening. "We feed their vices, drown them in vodka, strip them of self-respect. Two generations of monstrous, abject vice—that's all it will take. After that, they'll be ready. Ready for what we have planned. Ready for Shigalov's paradise."

"And what about you?" Stavrogin asked. "Do you even believe this madness?"

"I don't need to believe it," Verhovensky replied, laughing bitterly. "I'm a scoundrel, not a philanthropist. This isn't about belief; it's about power. And with you, Stavrogin, we'll have it all."

Stavrogin shook his head and began walking again, faster this time, desperate to escape the man's voice. But Verhovensky followed, relentless, his words growing more incoherent but no less fervent. Stavrogin could feel the weight of the man's obsession bearing down on him, a feverish intensity that refused to let him go.

"Well, Verhovensky, this is the first time I've truly heard you speak your mind," Stavrogin said, his voice edged with a mix of curiosity and incredulity. "And I must say, I'm amazed. So you're not a socialist after all? What are you, then? Some kind of ambitious politician?"

"A scoundrel! A scoundrel, that's what I am!" Pyotr Stepanovitch burst out, his tone a mixture of mockery and fervor. "You're wondering what drives me, aren't you? I'll tell you, Stavrogin. I've been leading up to it all along. It wasn't for nothing that I kissed your hand just now. Mark my words, the people need to believe in something, believe that we know exactly what we're doing, while those on the other side flounder and self-destruct, hitting their own followers instead of their enemies. But we—we'll proclaim destruction! It's irresistible, Stavrogin. The idea itself is a force, a magnet that draws men to it."

He paused, his eyes alight with a kind of manic enthusiasm. "We'll set fires, start legends, create myths that will burn brighter than anything the world has ever seen. Even the most wretched of groups can serve our cause. Out of those very groups, I'll pull men so devoted, so zealous, they'll shoot without hesitation and thank me for the privilege. Just wait—there will be chaos, upheaval, a darkness so absolute it will swallow Russia whole. The old gods will fall, the earth will tremble, and then—then we will bring forth someone new. Someone to fill the void."

"And who would that be?" Stavrogin asked, his voice low, almost weary.

"Ivan the Tsarevitch," Verhovensky said, his voice dropping into a reverent whisper.

"Ivan the what?" Stavrogin's expression hardened with suspicion. "A pretender? Is that what you're aiming for?"

"Yes, yes! Ivan the Tsarevitch!" Verhovensky's voice quivered with excitement. "And you—yes, you—will be that figure, Stavrogin. You'll be the one who is 'in hiding.' Do you know the power of that phrase? 'He is in hiding.' It's magic, pure magic. The people will cling to it, feed on it, believe in it as if it's a lifeline. They'll wait for you, speak of you, create legends about you. And when you appear—ah, when you appear, the world will change. That's the lever we need to lift the earth."

Stavrogin studied him, his eyes narrowing. "You've truly been counting on me for this?" he asked, his tone sharp with disbelief. "So this is your grand plan at last?"

"Why do you laugh?" Verhovensky demanded, his voice breaking with something close to desperation. "Don't mock me, Stavrogin. I'm like a child now, vulnerable to every shadow of doubt in your eyes. Listen! No one will see you—not fully, at least. You'll remain hidden, a mystery. Perhaps I'll show you to one in a hundred thousand, just enough to fan the flames of the legend. 'We've seen him,' they'll say. 'He exists. He is coming.' And they'll wait, Stavrogin. They'll wait for their savior, their deliverer, their new truth."

"Madness," Stavrogin muttered, shaking his head. "Complete madness."

"Why? Why don't you want this?" Verhovensky's voice rose, trembling with a mixture of anger and pleading. "Are you afraid? Is that it? That's why I've chosen you, because you're afraid of nothing. You laugh, you sneer, but you don't truly care. And that's why you're perfect. Don't you see? I'm like Columbus without America, Stavrogin. I've discovered the idea, but I need you to make it real."

They reached the steps of the house, and Verhovensky grabbed Stavrogin's arm, leaning close to whisper. "Listen. I'll settle everything for you. Marya Timofyevna will be taken care of tomorrow, no payment needed. And I'll bring you Liza—yes, Liza herself. Tomorrow. Would you like that?"

Stavrogin stared at him, a faint smile of disbelief on his lips. "Is he truly insane?" he thought. The front door creaked open, spilling dim light into the night.

"Stavrogin—is America ours?" Verhovensky asked, his voice trembling as he clutched at Stavrogin's hand.

"For what purpose?" Stavrogin replied coldly, his tone sharp and cutting.

"You don't care, do you?" Verhovensky burst out, his composure fracturing into fury. "You miserable, self-indulgent, perverted aristocrat! You're lying! You do care—you care more than anyone else! You think you're above it all, but I know you. I created you! Abroad, watching you, it all came to me. If it weren't for you, none of this would exist!"

Without another word, Stavrogin turned and ascended the steps, leaving Verhovensky behind. But even as he entered the house, he heard the frantic cry behind him: "Stavrogin! I give you a day—two days—three at most. After that, you'll have to answer!"

Chapter 9
A Raid at Stepan Trofimovitch's

Meanwhile, an event occurred that both astonished me and completely unhinged Stepan Trofimovitch. Early in the morning, around eight o'clock, Nastasya burst into my house, her face pale and her words tumbling out in a frantic rush. "Master's been raided!" she exclaimed, wringing her hands. At first, I couldn't make any sense of what she was saying. She kept repeating that officials had come to his house, seized his papers, and that a soldier had tied everything into a bundle and carted it away in a wheelbarrow. It sounded absurd, almost fantastical, but her distress was genuine. Without hesitation, I hurried to Stepan Trofimovitch's home.

When I arrived, I found him in a most peculiar state—distressed, agitated, yet oddly triumphant at the same time. His room was in disarray; the samovar on the table was boiling away, though the tea poured into the glass beside it remained untouched. He was pacing around the room in his red knitted jacket, peering into corners and muttering to himself. When he saw me, he immediately stopped, grabbed his coat and waistcoat from a chair, and hastily put them on, as if embarrassed to be caught in his casual attire. This was unusual; he had never bothered about such things with me before. Grasping my hand warmly, he exclaimed, "Enfin un ami! Cher, I've sent for you alone—no one else must know of this."

His tone was conspiratorial, and his face bore an uneasy mixture of relief and paranoia. "We must instruct Nastasya to lock the doors and admit no one—except them, of course. Vous comprenez?" His voice dropped to a whisper as though he feared someone might overhear.

I tried to calm him and urged him to explain what had happened. His words came out in a torrent, disjointed and full of dramatic parentheses, but gradually I pieced together the story. That morning, at seven o'clock, an official from the provincial government had shown up at his door, demanding to see his books and manuscripts.

"Pardon, I've forgotten his name. He's not from here, I'm sure of that. I think he came with Lembke—a heavy, Germanic face, something blunt and stupid in his expression. Rosenthal? No, wait, it was Blum!"

"Blum?" I repeated.

"Yes, yes! Vous le connaissez? Quelque chose d'hébété et très content dans la figure, yet très sévère et sérieux—very much the type of a police lackey. I recognized it at once. Ah, the life of a gentleman teaches one to spot such people instinctively! I was still in bed when he arrived. Can you imagine? He asked to see my papers—used that exact phrase! Of course, I understood everything immediately. Voilà vingt ans que je m'y prépare. Twenty years, my friend, I have been ready for this!"

He launched into a description of how he had handed over the keys to his drawers and cabinets with what he insisted was calm dignity. He gave Blum everything—letters, manuscripts, even a few copies of his poem and a bound edition of Herzen's works.

"Nastasya claims they wheeled it all away in a barrow, covered with an apron. Yes, an apron! Picture it!" he cried, his voice tinged with hysterical laughter.

The entire scene sounded so implausible that I pressed him for more details. Had Blum come alone? By what authority had he acted? How had he dared to conduct such an outrageous search without formal charges?

"He was alone, bien seul," Stepan Trofimovitch replied, "though I think someone else was in the hall. Yes, there was a guard, I remember now. You must ask Nastasya; she saw everything. But he said very little— it was I who did all the talking. I gave him my entire life's story, from that point of view, of course! J'étais surexcité, but calm—calm and dignified. Perhaps I shed a tear or two, but only from moral indignation. It was all so … so theatrical."

He paused, then added with sudden alarm, "You must understand, my dear friend, this is no ordinary matter. I suspect a telegram from Petersburg was sent. Yes, that must be it!"

"A telegram? About you?" I exclaimed in disbelief. "Because of Herzen's works and your poem? Surely you don't believe they'd arrest you over that?"

"You don't understand!" he cried, waving his hands dramatically. "These are dangerous times, and I am a man of ideas. Do you think they don't know what I represent?"

He rambled on, describing how he had begged Blum to keep the matter quiet to avoid public scandal. "We parted en amis," he assured me, though his expression betrayed doubt. "He even agreed that no charges would follow—unless, of course, they find something. But they won't, because, voyez-vous, I am beyond reproach."

Despite my attempts to reason with him, his paranoia was palpable. He had hidden thirty-five roubles in the lining of his waistcoat, convinced they wouldn't search there, and left a few coins on the table "to maintain appearances." He insisted that Nastasya light a lamp before the ikon, something he had never done before, reasoning that such a display of piety would leave a favorable impression on any potential intruders.

Finally, I persuaded him to lie down and rest. As I placed a vinegar-soaked towel on his forehead, he muttered, "Chaque moment ... they may come and take one, and phew!—a man disappears."

"Who would come? Who would take you?" I asked, trying to mask my exasperation.

He glanced towards the door, then whispered, "The wheels of power are always turning. One must be prepared for everything."

His delusions, though absurd, were tinged with a tragic sincerity that left me feeling both pity and exasperation. I could only sit by him, trying to make sense of what had really happened, while he lay there, lost in his chaotic thoughts.

I was truly upset and found myself raising my voice at him. He made a sour grimace, his expression showing not so much annoyance at my exclamation as mortification at the very idea that there might be no grounds for his imagined arrest.

"In these times, who can tell what one might be arrested for?" he muttered cryptically, almost to himself, as if the thought carried a deep, personal weight.

A ridiculous idea sprang into my mind, so absurd that I nearly hesitated to voice it. But curiosity got the better of me.

"Stepan Trofimovitch," I began earnestly, leaning towards him, "tell me the truth—as a friend, as someone who would never betray your confidence: are you, by any chance, part of some secret society?"

To my astonishment, he hesitated, his expression flickering between confusion and something resembling guilt. It was as though even he wasn't entirely certain of the answer to my question.

"That depends," he said cautiously. "Voyez-vous, when one devotes oneself wholly to progress, to the ideals of a brighter future... who can truly say? One may believe oneself unattached, yet discover that one has, in some mysterious way, become part of something larger."

"What? That's impossible! Surely it's a matter of yes or no," I said, incredulous. "One either belongs or doesn't."

"It dates back to Petersburg," he admitted, avoiding my gaze. "When she and I were dreaming of founding a magazine together... that's where it all began. She disappeared, and they seemed to forget about us. But now—now, they've remembered!"

He suddenly grabbed my hand, gripping it tightly as tears welled up in his eyes. "Cher, cher, you know me, don't you?" His voice cracked with emotion. "They'll come for us, throw us into a cart, and drag us off to Siberia. Or worse, they'll lock us in some dreadful dungeon and forget we ever existed!"

To my utter dismay, he broke into uncontrollable sobs. His face crumpled, and he buried it in his red silk handkerchief, his shoulders shaking with convulsive weeping. He cried like a frightened child expecting punishment, his tears flowing freely for a full five minutes. It was both heartbreaking and unsettling to witness this man, once revered as a prophet and a pillar of intellect in our circles, reduced to such a state of helpless despair. The contrast was staggering: here was someone we had admired for his lofty ideals and unwavering dignity, now trembling and weeping over an imagined threat. I couldn't help feeling both pity and discomfort.

Eventually, his sobs subsided, and he rose from the sofa, pacing the room once again. His movements were restless, his eyes darting to the window and the door as if expecting an ambush at any moment. Though I tried my best to reassure him, my words seemed to bounce off him without effect. Still, I could see that my presence brought him some measure of comfort. He clung to our conversation, even as it wandered erratically between topics. It was clear that he needed me there, that he was terrified of being left alone in his current state. So I stayed, and we spent more than two hours together.

At one point, he mentioned that Blum had taken two manifestos during the search.

"Manifestos?" I repeated, startled. "Surely you're not saying you—"

"Oh, there were ten in total," he said irritably, cutting me off. "But I had already gotten rid of eight. Blum only found two."

His mood swung wildly again. He flushed with indignation, his tone shifting from proud defiance to something more plaintive and self-pitying. "Vous me mettez avec ces gens-là? Do you think me capable of working with those scoundrels, those cowards, those anonymous slanderers—my own son, Pyotr Stepanovitch, among them? Avec ces esprits forts de lâcheté? Mon Dieu!"

His outburst startled me, and I tried to calm him. "Surely they haven't mixed you up with such people. It's nonsense—it can't be so."

"Savez-vous," he muttered suddenly, his voice dropping to a conspiratorial whisper, "at moments, I feel I might create a scandal there—wherever they take me. Yes, I might! Oh, don't leave me alone. Don't go! My career is finished, I feel it. It's all over. Do you realize, I might lose control and bite someone, like that lieutenant we once heard about!"

He gave me a strange look, a mixture of fear and a strange desire to frighten me. His agitation grew as time passed without the dreaded police cart appearing. He was like a coiled spring, his anxiety transforming into anger. When Nastasya accidentally knocked over a clothes-horse in the passage, the clatter sent him into a panic. He froze in terror, his face turning pale. But when the cause of the noise was revealed, he exploded at her, yelling and stamping his feet until she retreated to the kitchen.

A moment later, he collapsed onto the sofa beside me, his face a picture of despair. "Cher," he whispered, "it's not Siberia I fear. I swear it's not!" His voice broke, and tears glistened in his eyes once more. "I am not afraid of punishment. Je vous jure. It's something else, something worse..."

"What are you talking about?" I asked gently. "What could be worse?"

He leaned in close, as if revealing a terrible secret. "Disgrace," he whispered. "I am afraid of disgrace."

I tried to reassure him, to convince him that nothing he had done could lead to such a result. "This will all be cleared up today," I insisted. "You'll see. It will turn out in your favor."

But he shook his head, unconvinced. "You think they'll pardon me?" he asked, his voice trembling.

"Pardon you? For what? You've done nothing wrong!"

"Qu'en savez-vous?" he retorted bitterly. "They'll dig up everything, every mistake I've ever made, and if they find nothing... it will be worse. Far worse."

"Worse? How could it be worse?"

"They'll flog me," he said at last, his voice barely audible. The words sent a chill through me.

"Flog you? Where? Who would do such a thing?" I cried, horrified.

"Where? Why, there... wherever such things are done," he murmured cryptically, his face contorted with anguish.

"Ah, cher," he whispered so close to my ear that I could feel his breath, "the floor beneath you suddenly gives way—you find yourself dangling halfway through. Everyone knows such things happen."

"Old wives' tales!" I exclaimed, realizing what he meant. "Legends passed down and exaggerated. Surely you haven't believed in them all this time?" I laughed, hoping to dispel his fear.

"Tales they may be, but legends don't arise from nothing. Flogged men don't live to tell their stories. And I've imagined it, you know—ten thousand times over."

"But why you?" I pressed, trying to reach his rational side. "You've done nothing. Why should they come for you?"

"That," he said, his voice low and foreboding, "is precisely why. They'll discover I've done nothing, and for that, they'll flog me."

"And you're convinced they'll take you to Petersburg for this?" I asked, struggling to keep the disbelief out of my voice.

"My friend, I've already told you—I regret nothing now. My career is over, finie. From the moment she said goodbye at Skvoreshniki, my life lost all meaning. But disgrace … disgrace … what will she think if she hears of it?"

His face flushed deeply as he spoke, and his eyes darted to mine, filled with desperation. I felt the weight of his shame and lowered my own gaze to the floor.

"She won't find out," I said firmly, hoping to reassure him. "Nothing will happen to you. Honestly, I feel as though I'm speaking to someone entirely new this morning, Stepan Trofimovitch. You've surprised me in ways I didn't think possible."

"My friend, this isn't fear," he insisted, his voice trembling with emotion. "Even if they pardon me, even if nothing happens—still, I'm ruined. She will suspect me, toujours. Me—the poet, the thinker, the man she revered for twenty-two years!"

"It won't even occur to her," I replied, trying to calm him.

"Oh, but it will," he whispered with such certainty that it sent a chill through me. "We spoke of it, you know. Back in Petersburg, during Lent, before we left. We were both afraid then. Elle me soupçonnera toute sa vie. And how will I ever convince her otherwise? It will sound implausible. In this dreary little town, who would believe me? C'est invraisemblable. And women—ah, women! She will grieve, yes, like a true friend. But secretly, she will be pleased. I will have handed her a weapon against me— a weapon she can use for the rest of my life. Oh, it's all over! Twenty years of perfect happiness with her ... and now this!"

He covered his face with his hands, overwhelmed by the weight of his own thoughts.

"Stepan Trofimovitch," I said gently after a moment, "perhaps you should inform Varvara Petrovna about all this. She may be able to help."

"God forbid!" he cried, leaping from his seat as though struck by lightning. "Never! Not after the things that were said at our parting in Skvoreshniki. Never!"

His eyes flashed with a mixture of anger and despair, and I realized how deeply the events of that morning had shaken him. For over an hour, we sat together, both waiting for some resolution or development. His agitation seemed to grow with each passing minute, yet he lay down at one point, closing his eyes for what I thought was a brief rest. I even began to believe he had fallen asleep. But after about twenty minutes, he suddenly sprang to his feet with startling energy.

Ripping the towel from his head, he hurried to the mirror. With trembling hands, he adjusted his cravat and called out in a booming voice to Nastasya, ordering her to bring his overcoat, new hat, and walking stick.

"I can bear this no longer," he declared, his voice breaking with emotion. "No longer! I am going myself."

"Going where?" I asked, alarmed as I jumped to my feet.

"To Lembke. My friend, I must. It's my duty as a man and a citizen! I am not some useless, insignificant chip of wood. I have rights—rights that I have neglected for far too long. But no longer. I will demand to know the truth. He received a telegram, didn't he? He must explain himself. Let him arrest me if he dares!"

His voice rose to a near-shriek as he stamped his foot.

"I agree with you," I said, keeping my tone as calm as I could despite my growing concern. "It's better to act than to remain here in this state. But look at yourself—your appearance, your manner! You can't present yourself to Lembke like this. Il faut être digne et calme. You must be dignified and calm. Otherwise, you might—heaven forbid—lose control entirely."

"I am walking straight into the lion's jaws," he retorted dramatically. "I am ready to face whatever comes."

"Then I'll go with you," I offered.

"I expected nothing less," he said, his voice softening for a moment. "You are a true friend. But you must stop at the house, only the house. You should not compromise yourself further by being seen as my accomplice. No, no, croyez-moi, I will remain calm. I feel it—I am elevated to the heights of all that is sacred at this moment."

"I might even go into the house with you," I suggested, "on a pretext. I received a message yesterday from their ridiculous committee through Vysotsky. They invited me to serve as one of the stewards for tomorrow's fête. One of the six young men who help with the trays and escort the guests to their seats. I was going to refuse, but perhaps I could use this as an excuse to speak with Yulia Mihailovna."

He nodded absentmindedly, though I doubted he fully understood what I was saying. As we stood in the doorway preparing to leave, he turned to the small lamp burning before the ikon.

"My friend," he murmured, stretching out his hand toward it, "I have never truly believed in this. But … so be it. Let it be as it will."

He crossed himself, an act so out of character that it startled me, and then motioned for us to leave. As we stepped out into the fresh morning air, I thought the walk might do him good, perhaps even calm his nerves enough for us to turn back. But as we made our way down the road, an unexpected encounter added to his agitation and solidified his resolve to press on—a moment that revealed a surprising spirit and determination I hadn't thought possible in my poor, dear friend.

Chapter 10
Filibusters. A Fatal Morning

Chapter 10.1

The incident that occurred as we made our way to Lembke's house was nothing short of astonishing, both in its absurdity and the sheer intensity with which it unfolded. But before I delve into it, let me provide some necessary background. Just about an hour before Stepan Trofimovitch and I stepped out onto the street, a group of over seventy workers from Shpigulins' factory had marched through the town. Their silent procession, conducted with a deliberate sense of order, had caught the attention of many onlookers. Whispers and speculations followed them as they made their way toward the governor's residence.

It was later said that these seventy workers were representatives, selected from the nine hundred employed at the factory, to present their grievances directly to the governor. Their complaint centered on the factory manager, who had exploited and cheated them when closing the factory and dismissing them en masse. The manager's actions, as subsequent investigations revealed, were nothing short of brazen fraud. However, some skeptics argued that the group wasn't representative at all but consisted solely of the most aggrieved workers, those whose situations were the most desperate. The idea of a general strike or organized mutiny was dismissed by some as baseless hysteria, while others vehemently insisted that this was no mere labor dispute but an orchestrated uprising incited by revolutionary propaganda.

The truth, as it often does, lay somewhere in between. While it's possible that figures like Pyotr Stepanovitch, Liputin, and even Fedka had tried to stir unrest among the workers, evidence suggested that their success was limited. These men were far too disconnected from the realities of the workers' lives to inspire genuine allegiance. The factory hands, for the most part, were focused on immediate survival rather than abstract revolutionary ideals. Indeed, many of them likely wouldn't have understood the convoluted rhetoric of the manifestoes even if they had read them. Yet, the desperation of their plight—combined with the ineffectiveness of the local authorities—had driven them to act. The idea of appealing directly to "the general himself" was not born of rebellion but rather of the deeply ingrained Russian tradition of seeking justice from a higher authority. It was as though they were appealing to a feudal lord, not an appointed official.

By the time the workers reached the open square before the governor's house, they had already drawn a significant crowd of curious onlookers. The workers arranged themselves in neat rows, caps in hand, and waited patiently for the governor to appear. For a full thirty minutes, they stood silently, gazing at the imposing front door. Their decision to remove their caps—an almost instinctive gesture of respect—added a strange solemnity to the scene.

Meanwhile, the local police, having noticed the gathering, scrambled to react. At first, individual officers approached the crowd, barking orders for them to disperse. When this proved ineffective, reinforcements were called, and soon a sizable contingent surrounded the square. Yet, the workers remained resolute, responding simply and repeatedly: "We are here to see the general himself." The police, caught between their duty and their inability to act without clear orders, fell into nervous discussions among themselves. The head of the police, hesitant to provoke further unrest, decided to await the governor's return.

Rumors began to fly almost immediately, painting a far more dramatic picture of events than the reality. It was said that soldiers armed with bayonets had been summoned, that barrels of water had been brought to drench the crowd, and that artillery units were en route. In truth, none of this happened. The barrels of water, it seems, were inspired by a sarcastic outburst from Ilya Ilyitch, the chief of police, who had exclaimed, "Not one of them will leave here dry if they don't disperse!" This hyperbolic remark was soon exaggerated into tales of firefighters soaking the crowd with hoses.

When the governor, Von Lembke, finally arrived, the situation took a stranger turn. It's worth noting that Von Lembke had a penchant for theatrical entrances. Known for his habit of racing through the streets in a carriage with a bright yellow back, pulled by a team of frantic, head-tossing horses, he would often rise to his full height, gripping a specially installed strap, and extend his arm like a statue surveying the world. On this occasion, his arrival was somewhat less dramatic but no less fraught. Stepping out of his carriage, he surveyed the scene with a mixture of confusion and exasperation. It's reported that he muttered a colorful curse under his breath—likely to maintain his reputation for toughness.

What remains unclear, however, is why the governor and his officials immediately interpreted the peaceful gathering as a dangerous rebellion. Some speculate that Ilya Ilyitch, eager to protect the factory manager (a close associate of his), deliberately exaggerated the threat posed by the workers. Others suggest that Von Lembke, eager to prove his worth to his superiors in Petersburg, leapt at the chance to frame the situation as a political crisis. His recent, cryptic conversations with Ilya Ilyitch hinted at his preoccupation with Socialist conspiracies, and it seems he was almost eager for an opportunity to validate his fears.

Regardless of the motivations behind their decisions, the authorities soon escalated matters. They ordered the crowd to disperse under the threat of force, but the workers remained steadfast. Their simple insistence on speaking to the governor—unwavering and devoid of malice—was misinterpreted as defiance. Meanwhile, rumors of revolution spread like wildfire, fueled by speculation and fear.

As Stepan Trofimovitch and I made our way through the town, the growing tension was palpable. People whispered in doorways, peered cautiously from windows, and exchanged hurried rumors in the streets. By the time we reached the square, the atmosphere was electric, charged with a mix of fear, curiosity, and the inexplicable energy that accompanies the anticipation of chaos. It was against this surreal backdrop that our own peculiar adventure unfolded, throwing us directly into the swirling maelstrom of events that seemed to have taken hold of the entire town.

I am firmly convinced that poor Andrey Antonovitch, despite his flaws, would never have wished for rebellion, even if it promised to elevate his career. He was, at his core, a conscientious and dutiful man, one who had lived an unassuming and innocent life until the upheaval of his marriage. Could it truly be his fault that fate had replaced a simple, modest allowance of government firewood and the companionship of an equally modest Minnchen with the complications of a lofty position and the domineering presence of a princess aged forty? His innocence, his adherence to duty, and the fragile balance of his mental state were tragically ill-equipped to withstand such a transformation.

It is a matter of near certainty, based on both private observation and certain confessions made later by Yulia Mihailovna herself, that the mental decline which ultimately led Andrey Antonovitch to a sanatorium in Switzerland began on that very morning. However, it's just as likely that the first inklings of this distress appeared the night before, though less obviously. Yulia Mihailovna, not in triumph but with a tinge of remorse— though true, thorough remorse seems to elude most women—later shared with me, reluctantly, that in the early hours of the previous night, past two in the morning, her husband had come into her room unannounced. Waking her abruptly, he insisted on presenting an "ultimatum," demanding her immediate attention.

Yulia, disheveled and indignant, had no choice but to rise, curl-papers and all, and listen to his ramblings from her seat on the couch. As she endured his incoherent declarations, she realized for the first time just how strained her husband's nerves had become. She was horrified, though not softened. Instead, she concealed her alarm beneath an iron mask of sarcasm and indifference. Like many wives in her position, she had her own peculiar methods for managing her husband. Her weapon of choice was the icy silence of contempt—an unbroken wall of indifference that could last for hours, days, or even three nights if necessary. It was a strategy she had wielded before, always driving him to near-madness. For a sensitive man like Andrey Antonovitch, it was a torment beyond bearing.

Perhaps she intended to punish him for his bungled actions of the past few days or for his wounded pride as governor, feeling eclipsed by her social influence. Perhaps her irritation stemmed from his inability to grasp her grand political strategies or from his irrational jealousy of Pyotr Stepanovitch. Whatever her reasons, she chose not to relent, even though it was the dead of night and her husband was clearly unraveling before her eyes.

Pacing the length of her boudoir, Andrey Antonovitch poured out his frustrations, his voice breaking as he aired every grievance that had festered within him. His words tumbled out in a chaotic rush, devoid of coherence, but laden with the bitterness of long-held resentment.

"I've become a laughingstock!" he cried, waving his arms wildly. "They're leading me by the nose! Curse the expression—I know you're smirking—but it's the truth! No, madam, this is no time for your laughter and womanly arts. We are not in some frilly boudoir, but as two beings trapped in a balloon, forced to speak only the truth!"

His metaphors grew more absurd as he went on, but the essence of his despair was unmistakable. "It is you, madam, who have ruined everything. I accepted this position only for your sake, for the sake of your ambition! And yet, what have you done? You have created two centers of power—mine as governor, and yours here, in this very boudoir! I cannot tolerate it. I will not tolerate it! In government, as in marriage, there must be one center, one authority, one axis around which everything revolves. Two centers are an impossibility!"

He accused her of undermining his abilities, forcing him into a humiliating position where he constantly had to prove his worth—not only to her but to everyone in their circle. "Our marriage," he declared, stamping his feet on the carpet with such force that Yulia Mihailovna rose from her seat in startled dignity, "has been nothing but a relentless contest where you prove I am a nonentity, a fool, and even a villain, while I degrade myself trying to prove I am none of those things! Isn't this demeaning for both of us?"

The more he spoke, the more agitated he became, transitioning from bitterness to outright pathos. Tears streamed down his face as he sobbed openly, thumping his chest and accusing her of orchestrating his downfall. He railed against her admiration for the young radicals and intellectuals in her social circle and railed against her infidelity—not in the romantic sense, but in loyalty to him as her husband and the governor.

Then, in a moment of desperation, he made the fatal mistake of revealing his jealousy of Pyotr Stepanovitch. Realizing he had overstepped, his sorrow turned to rage. "I will not stand by and let these irresponsible infidels mock God under my roof!" he shouted. "I will send them all packing—every last one of them. Tomorrow, I will break up their foolish fête, dismiss every governess in the province, and send them off with a Cossack escort if necessary!"

As his tirade escalated, he accused her of inciting the factory workers against him, claiming that her "rascals" were stirring rebellion. He babbled incoherently about knowing the names of four conspirators and lamented that he was losing his mind. "Hopelessly! Hopelessly!" he cried out in despair.

Yulia Mihailovna stood silently through it all, her face betraying no emotion. She offered no rebuttal, no sympathy, no sign of softening. Her implacable demeanor only fueled his fury, pushing him to the brink of collapse. When he finally subsided, spent and trembling, he collapsed into a chair, muttering incoherent threats and accusations.

That night marked a turning point, not only in their marriage but in the trajectory of Andrey Antonovitch's fragile mind. It was as though the last threads of his composure had unraveled entirely, leaving him adrift in a sea of humiliation, resentment, and despair.

At this point, Yulia Mihailovna suddenly broke her protracted silence. Her tone was icy and commanding, and her words came with a sharp finality that sent ripples of tension through the room. She declared that she had been aware for some time of the supposed criminal schemes and considered them nothing more than foolishness. She dismissed her husband's concerns as overblown, insisting that he had taken everything far too seriously. As for the "troublemakers," she claimed not only to know the four individuals he mentioned but all of them, though this was a blatant lie. She added, with pointed confidence, that she had no intention of losing her composure over such trivial matters. Instead, she planned to use her superior intellect to guide the situation to a harmonious resolution. Her strategy? To encourage the younger generation, confront them with the evidence of their exposed plans, and redirect their energy toward more rational and noble pursuits.

The effect of her words on Andrey Antonovitch was electric. At first, he stood frozen, staring at her as though she had struck him. The implications of her statement hit him like a wave: Pyotr Stepanovitch had duped him once again, played him for a fool, and done so right under his nose. Worse, his wife—his supposed partner—had been privy to far more information than he, the governor, had been. The realization that Pyotr Stepanovitch might even be the instigator of these conspiracies sent him spiraling into a frenzy.

"You senseless, malignant woman!" he bellowed, his voice trembling with rage and humiliation. The outburst shattered the tense air in the room like a thunderclap. "Let me tell you, I'll arrest your worthless lover this very instant! I'll have him clapped in irons and thrown into the fortress! Or—" He paused, his face twisting in torment, "I'll jump out of this window before your very eyes!"

Yulia Mihailovna, far from being cowed by his vehemence, turned green with fury. But instead of responding in kind, she did something far more devastating—she laughed. It was not a chuckle, nor even a sarcastic giggle, but a full-throated, ringing peal of laughter that echoed through the room. It was the sort of theatrical laughter one might hear from a Parisian actress, calculated to humiliate and belittle.

Andrey Antonovitch recoiled as if struck. He staggered toward the window, his arms flailing in a mix of despair and anger. But as he reached it, he stopped suddenly, rooted to the spot. Folding his arms tightly across his chest, his face as pale as a corpse, he turned to gaze at his wife. His eyes were hollow, his expression a blend of pleading and menace. "Do you know, Yulia," he said in a trembling, gasping voice, "do you know that even I am capable of something?"

His words, however, were met with renewed laughter. This time it was even louder, more cutting. She laughed as though mocking not only his threat but the very idea of him taking decisive action. It was a moment too cruel to endure. His clenched teeth, the groan that escaped his lips, and the fist he raised—these were the gestures of a man pushed to the brink. Yet, even in his desperation, he did not strike her. Instead, he turned abruptly, storming from the room like a man fleeing his own humiliation.

Once in his own quarters, he collapsed onto his bed, still fully dressed, and pulled the sheet over his head as though trying to vanish from the world. For two hours, he lay there, not moving, not thinking—just existing in a void of despair. His body shivered uncontrollably with feverish tremors, and his mind flickered with random, irrelevant memories. He thought of an old clock that had hung in his Petersburg apartment fifteen years ago, its minute hand missing. He remembered a cheerful clerk, Millebois, with whom he had once caught a sparrow in Alexandrovsky Park, laughing loudly enough to draw attention from passersby. These fragmented memories seemed to mock the man he had once been—a man of dignity, intelligence, and purpose.

At some point, he must have drifted into a restless sleep. When he awoke at ten o'clock, his first thought was of the previous night's humiliations. He leapt from the bed, slapped his forehead in frustration, and paced the room like a man possessed. Breakfast was refused, messengers were ignored, and urgent reminders of his gubernatorial duties were brushed aside. He could think of only one thing: Yulia Mihailovna.

Driven by an overwhelming need to see her, to be near her, and perhaps to win her forgiveness, he ordered his carriage. He imagined her smiling at him, forgiving him with a kind word or gesture. "Drive faster!" he barked at the coachman as they sped toward Skvoreshniki, where he had learned Yulia Mihailovna had gone with a group to plan the upcoming fête.

But as they neared the estate, something changed. The rush of desperate resolve seemed to ebb. He instructed the coachman to turn back toward town, only to stop again moments later. He got out of the carriage and wandered into a barren field, staring aimlessly at the dying wildflowers battered by the autumn wind. The coachman, puzzled and uneasy, watched his master pick a few wilted blooms, as though their forlorn state mirrored his own inner turmoil.

It was in this strange tableau that the police superintendent,

Flibusterov, found him. The officer, known for his zealous approach and frequent inebriation, arrived breathlessly, blurting out with alarming urgency, "There's a riot in the town!"

Andrey Antonovitch turned to him with a stern expression, as though he had been standing in that field for hours, contemplating profound truths. "Filibusters?" he muttered thoughtfully, as though the word itself carried some hidden meaning.

This surreal moment, laden with absurdity and tragedy, would mark the beginning of the end for the once-respected governor.

The events that unfolded were extraordinary in their absurdity, though they retained a certain ominous weight, as though something irrevocable were taking place. When the police superintendent Flibusterov blurted out, "The Shpigulin men are making a riot," it was as though a spark had been struck in the dry tinder of Andrey Antonovitch's disordered mind. The mention of the "Shpigulin men" seemed to trigger a cascade of chaotic thoughts in his head. He repeated the words aloud, "The Shpigulin men!" as though trying to extract meaning from them. His finger pressed against his temple, and his gaze seemed to look inward, grappling with fragmented memories or an elusive realization. Without another word, he walked toward the carriage with an unsettling calm, seated himself, and ordered the coachman to drive back to town.

As they approached the open square in front of his house, where the crowd of factory workers had gathered, his demeanor changed. The sight that greeted him—a disciplined line of workers facing the house, encircled by a cordon of hesitant police officers, with the chief of police standing by ineffectually—acted as a trigger. The air of expectation, the collective gaze of the crowd, and the implicit demand for authority weighed on him. Something inside him snapped. All at once, his face drained of color, and he stepped out of the carriage with trembling urgency.

"Caps off!" he whispered hoarsely. His voice was barely audible, yet it carried a sharp edge. Then, to the astonishment of everyone present, he raised his voice to an unnatural pitch and shrieked, "On your knees!" It was as though he were commanding the entire scene to bow before him, demanding submission not only from the crowd but from the circumstances themselves.

The effect was surreal. The workers, who had stood silently awaiting justice, were stunned. A few crossed themselves instinctively, as if caught in a religious procession rather than a protest. Three or four men even hesitated, half bending their knees, unsure whether to comply. But the group as a whole, like a single organism, instinctively moved a few steps forward, and their murmur of voices swelled into a wave of incoherent speech. Words like "hired," "term," "manager," and "Your Excellency" floated indistinctly in the air, blending into a formless cacophony.

To Andrey Antonovitch, it was as though the world itself were unraveling. The flowers he had absentmindedly picked earlier still hung limply in his hands, their yellow petals fluttering in the breeze. In his mind, the orderly ranks of workers were no less threatening than an armed rebellion, and the faces in the crowd seemed to merge with the specter of Pyotr Stepanovitch. That face, grinning and taunting, loomed in his imagination as the source of this chaos, an embodiment of the betrayal and mockery that had haunted him since the day before.

"Rods!" he bellowed suddenly, his voice breaking. The single word cut through the air, freezing everyone in place. A heavy silence fell, broken only by the rustling of the wind.

The inexplicable command seemed to galvanize the chief of police, who had evidently prepared for such an eventuality. Within moments, rods were produced and distributed among a few officers. Though only two or three men were flogged in total—a fact that has been widely distorted in subsequent rumors—the sheer spectacle of it was enough to ignite a storm of gossip that would later transform the incident into a legend of brutality. Tales circulated of dozens of workers being whipped, of women and elderly passersby being caught in the fray, and even of an old woman named Avdotya Petrovna Tarapygin, who, it was said, had been flogged for merely expressing her outrage. This latter tale, which even inspired a subscription fund for her benefit, was later debunked as pure invention. No such woman ever existed, though the story persisted for years.

Amid the confusion, I lost sight of Stepan Trofimovitch. We had entered the square together, but my momentary pause to question a bystander had given him the opportunity to slip away. My heart sank as I realized he must have wandered into the very heart of the commotion. Driven by an unshakable sense of dread, I pushed my way toward the center, where I found him standing, not with fear but with a strange, dignified resolve. His face was pale, but his expression was serene, almost imperious. He stood tall, gripping his stick like a scepter, and surveying the scene as though he were an offended patriarch confronting a wayward congregation.

"Cher," he said to me, his voice trembling with emotion but steady in its authority, "if they deal so unceremoniously with people here, in an open square, what horrors might we expect if men like that—" and here he pointed an accusing finger at Flibusterov—"act on their own authority?"

The gesture was too bold to be ignored. Flibusterov, already red-faced and agitated, turned sharply at the accusation. "What man? What authority?" he snarled, stepping forward with fists clenched. "And who are you, eh? Who are you?" His voice rose to a hysterical pitch, and for a moment, it seemed inevitable that he would seize Stepan Trofimovitch by the collar.

At that critical moment, Governor Lembke turned his head, his gaze falling on the confrontation. His eyes lingered on Stepan Trofimovitch with a mixture of curiosity and vague recognition. Then, with an impatient flick of his hand, he signaled Flibusterov to stand down. The officer, though visibly bristling with anger, obeyed. It was enough of an opening for me to seize Stepan Trofimovitch by the arm and pull him away.

"We must go home," I whispered urgently. "Thanks to Lembke, we've avoided disaster."

But Stepan Trofimovitch resisted at first. "Go, my friend," he said solemnly. "I alone am to blame for exposing you to this. Your life still holds promise, while mine—mon heure est sonnée."

Nevertheless, I managed to steer him toward the governor's residence, where we were admitted to the waiting room after a brief explanation. We sat apart in tense silence, he lost in somber thought, his head bowed and his fingers lightly drumming on his cane. I, meanwhile, watched him with growing apprehension, sensing that the events of the morning had stirred something deep and irrevocable within him.

Chapter 10.2

Lembke entered abruptly, walking quickly and accompanied by the chief of police. His movements were brisk, almost mechanical, and his gaze seemed preoccupied. He glanced at us briefly but without recognition, as if we were indistinguishable from the furnishings of the room, and appeared intent on heading directly to his study. But before he could reach the door, Stepan Trofimovitch stepped forward, planting himself firmly in Lembke's path. His tall, distinctive figure and composed demeanor seemed to command attention, and Lembke, startled, came to an abrupt halt.

"Who is this?" Lembke asked, his tone perplexed and impatient, as though he were addressing the chief of police without turning to him. His eyes, however, were fixed on Stepan Trofimovitch with a blank stare that betrayed both confusion and irritation.

"Retired college assessor, Stepan Trofimovitch Verhovensky, your Excellency," announced Stepan Trofimovitch, bowing with measured dignity. His voice was clear, and his manner carried a subtle but unmistakable authority.

Lembke continued to gaze at him, still seemingly unable to piece together who he was or why he was there. "What is it?" he said curtly, tilting his head slightly as if to offer his ear, but his tone was filled with disdainful impatience, the sort of dismissiveness often reserved for those presumed to be bearing trivial grievances.

"I was visited today, your Excellency," Stepan Trofimovitch began with deliberate formality, "and my house was subjected to a search by an official acting in your name. Therefore, I have come to seek an explanation—"

"Name? Name?" Lembke interrupted, his voice sharp and clipped, as though the question itself might clarify the matter. He appeared to be grasping at an idea that remained just out of reach.

"Stepan Trofimovitch Verhovensky," repeated Stepan Trofimovitch, his tone now touched with a shade of majestic reproach, as though offended by the interruption.

Lembke's face changed as some faint recognition flickered in his mind. "Ah! It's ... that hotbed ... You've shown yourself, sir, in such a light... Are you a professor? A professor?"

"I once had the honor of giving lectures to the young men of the X university," Stepan Trofimovitch replied, his voice calm yet firm.

"The young men!" Lembke exclaimed, his tone rising in sudden agitation. He appeared startled, as though the phrase had conjured a cascade of alarming associations. Yet it seemed clear from his expression that he still comprehended very little of what was happening or of who exactly stood before him.

"That, sir, I won't allow!" he suddenly cried, his voice trembling with anger that seemed to come from nowhere. "I won't allow young men! It's all these manifestoes, this assault on society—a piratical attack, filibustering.... What is your request?"

Stepan Trofimovitch, unperturbed, responded with measured dignity, "On the contrary, it was your wife, your Excellency, who requested that I deliver a reading at her fête tomorrow. I have not come to make a request but to ask for an explanation—"

"At the fête? There'll be no fête! I won't allow your fête! A lecture? A lecture?" Lembke's voice grew shrill as he practically shouted the last word, his face contorted with sudden fury.

"I should appreciate it if your Excellency would address me with greater politeness," Stepan Trofimovitch said, his voice edged with quiet authority. "I am not a boy to be shouted at or stamped at."

Lembke's face turned crimson, and his voice trembled with restrained fury as he shot back, "Perhaps you understand whom you are speaking to?"

"Perfectly, your Excellency," Stepan Trofimovitch replied, bowing slightly, his demeanor unyieldingly composed.

"I am protecting society, while you—while you destroy it!" Lembke retorted, his voice trembling with indignation. "You were a tutor in the house of Madame Stavrogin, weren't you?"

"Yes, I served as tutor in Madame Stavrogin's household," Stepan Trofimovitch affirmed, each word carefully enunciated.

"And for twenty years, you have been the hotbed of all that has accumulated—the fruits of it all!" Lembke continued, his words growing increasingly incoherent as his anger took control. "You were in the square just now, weren't you? Look out, sir—your way of thinking is known to me! I cannot allow your lectures; I will not have them!"

He made to move past, but Stepan Trofimovitch held his ground. "Your Excellency," he said, his voice as steady as before, "you are mistaken. It was your wife who invited me, not to deliver a lecture but to give a literary reading. However, I decline to do so now. What I seek is an explanation of why an official search was conducted in my home today, during which my private books, papers, and letters were taken and paraded through the town in a barrow."

Lembke, startled into something like clarity, froze and stared at Stepan Trofimovitch. "Who searched you?" he asked abruptly, his voice taut.

"This official here," Stepan Trofimovitch replied, gesturing toward the doorway, where the figure of Blum had just appeared. Blum stepped forward, his face betraying neither regret nor defensiveness but simply a kind of blank acknowledgment of his involvement.

"Vous ne faites que des bêtises!" Lembke snapped at Blum with sudden exasperation, as though all his fury now had a single target. His face flushed deeply, and he seemed to come back to himself in a rush of embarrassed realization. "Excuse me," he muttered, his voice lower now, almost faltering. "All this ... all this must have been a mistake, a misunderstanding, nothing but a misunderstanding."

Stepan Trofimovitch's lips curled faintly in a wry smile. "Your Excellency," he began, his tone heavy with meaning, "once, in my youth,

I witnessed an incident in which a man mistakenly struck another in the face in the lobby of a theater. Upon realizing his error, he declared, 'Excuse me, it was a misunderstanding.' But when the injured party protested, he retorted angrily, 'Why, I said it was a misunderstanding! What are you crying out about?'"

Lembke attempted a feeble smile, but his face was crumpling. "You don't understand," he said, his voice breaking. "Can't you see how unhappy I am myself?" His words were almost a sob, and his hands fluttered toward his face as though he might hide behind them.

For a moment, Stepan Trofimovitch stared at him, his stern expression softening. Finally, he inclined his head and spoke with measured gravitas. "Your Excellency, trouble yourself no further with my grievances. I ask only that my books and letters be returned to me."

At that precise moment, the doors opened with a burst of sound and movement as Yulia Mihailovna swept in, surrounded by her entourage, bringing with her an air of chaotic authority. But what followed deserves the most careful and detailed recounting.

Chapter 10.3

The entire company, which had filled three carriages, crowded into the waiting room in a noisy, almost theatrical procession. The group had a separate entrance that led directly to Yulia Mihailovna's apartments, but this time they all chose to pass through the public waiting area, as if deliberately seeking to make a spectacle. It was impossible not to feel that Stepan Trofimovitch's presence there, along with the fresh gossip about the Shpigulin affair, had played some role in this calculated deviation. The news of his ordeal had reached Yulia Mihailovna's ears during her journey back to town, courtesy of Lyamshin, who, in his usual meddlesome manner, had galloped ahead on a wretched Cossack nag to intercept the returning cavalcade with his "breaking news."

Yulia Mihailovna, no stranger to dramatic flair, was momentarily disconcerted by the report. However, if there was any hint of unease, it quickly evaporated. The political dimension of the Shpigulin incident, after all, hardly troubled her. Pyotr Stepanovitch had repeatedly assured her that the "Shpigulin ruffians" deserved nothing less than a sound flogging, and her trust in his counsel had grown almost unshakable in recent weeks. Still, her annoyance at her husband's potential mishandling of the situation simmered beneath her composed exterior. "He will answer for this," she must have thought with a mixture of frustration and resolve.

Curiously, Pyotr Stepanovitch himself was absent, as though intentionally avoiding the scene. No one had seen him all day, adding another layer of intrigue to an already convoluted series of events. Meanwhile, Varvara Petrovna had also returned to town, riding in the same carriage as Yulia Mihailovna, ostensibly to attend the final meeting of the committee organizing the next day's fête. Yet, her presence seemed unusually charged; there was no doubt that Lyamshin's revelations about Stepan Trofimovitch had sparked her interest, if not outright agitation.

The atmosphere in the waiting room grew electric as Yulia Mihailovna entered, radiating confidence. Without so much as glancing at her husband, she made a beeline for Stepan Trofimovitch. Her face lit up with an enchanting smile as she extended her exquisitely gloved hand to him. Her greeting was a cascade of flattering phrases, delivered with such warmth and spontaneity that it seemed as though her sole purpose that morning was to honor him with her charm. There was not a single reference to the morning's humiliating search of his home, nor a word or glance directed at Lembke, who stood awkwardly to the side, his presence reduced to insignificance. In one deft move, she claimed Stepan Trofimovitch entirely, ushering him into her drawing room with an air of proprietorship, as though his interview with Lembke was an inconsequential prelude.

This calculated slight toward her husband was a grave misstep, one that was compounded by the presence of Karmazinov. He had joined the outing at Yulia Mihailovna's invitation, using the opportunity to pay a formal visit to Varvara Petrovna, who, to her eternal shame, had been utterly delighted by his condescension. As soon as Karmazinov spotted Stepan Trofimovitch, he exclaimed dramatically from the doorway, "What years! What ages! At last ... my excellent ami!" With exaggerated exuberance, he surged forward, interrupting Yulia Mihailovna, and extended his cheek as though expecting an embrace. Stepan Trofimovitch, flustered and caught off guard, felt compelled to comply.

"Cher," he confided to me that evening, his voice trembling with anger and humiliation, "at that moment, I wondered who among us was more contemptible—he, degrading me with his theatrical embrace, or I, despising him utterly yet still stooping to kiss that repugnant face. Ah, foo!"

"Come now, tell me everything," Karmazinov lisped in his affected manner, squeezing Stepan Trofimovitch's shoulder in a mockery of camaraderie. "Tell me about your life, all of it. We must catch up, must we not?"

Stepan Trofimovitch, his composure partially restored, attempted a more measured reply. "Remember, cher M. Karmazinov, the last time we met was at the Granovsky dinner in Moscow, twenty-four years ago—"

"Ce cher homme," Karmazinov interrupted with shrill familiarity, cutting him off and gesturing as though to dismiss the intervening decades with a wave of his hand. "Quickly now, let's hear it all! Take us to your drawing room, Yulia Mihailovna, where he can recount everything at leisure."

That evening, Stepan Trofimovitch could hardly contain his indignation as he recounted the scene to me. "We were never friends, even in our youth," he fumed. "I had begun to detest him the moment we first crossed paths, just as he detested me. And yet there I was, reduced to playing his foil!"

The drawing room filled rapidly. Among the crowd were Varvara Petrovna, whose forced indifference could not conceal her simmering emotions; Liza, radiantly light-hearted and careless; and Mavriky Nikolaevitch, who hovered near her with his usual quiet vigilance. Scattered throughout were the usual assortment of young ladies and men, whose affected wit and vulgar antics masqueraded as sophistication. A few new faces stood out: an overly obsequious visiting Pole, a boisterous German doctor who laughed uproariously at his own jokes, and a young princeling from Petersburg, whose high collar and mechanical demeanor gave him the air of a marionette. Yulia Mihailovna's anxious attentiveness toward this last guest revealed her hope that he would find her salon suitably impressive.

Seated on the sofa in a carefully composed pose, Stepan Trofimovitch began to speak, his tone suddenly taking on a dainty lisp that mimicked Karmazinov's. "Cher M. Karmazinov," he began, "the life of a man of our convictions, even over the span of twenty-five years, is bound to appear monotonous…"

His words were interrupted by the German doctor's explosive guffaw, as though he had just heard the wittiest remark in the world. Stepan Trofimovitch paused, gazing at him with a look of studied incredulity, but the doctor remained impervious, laughing heartily. The princeling turned to observe the commotion, raising his pince-nez with the detached curiosity of an entomologist studying an insect.

Thus began an afternoon as absurd as it was illuminating—a kaleidoscope of egos, pretensions, and unspoken rivalries, each more grotesque than the last.

"… Is bound to seem monotonous," Stepan Trofimovitch repeated deliberately, stretching each syllable as though savoring the weight of his own words. He maintained an air of serene detachment, as if the audience's reactions, however varied, were of no consequence to him. "And so my life has been throughout this quarter of a century. Et comme on trouve partout plus de moines que de raison, and, as I am entirely in agreement with this sentiment, it has naturally followed that during this long interval I…"

He trailed off with an almost languid gesture, leaving the sentence open-ended. Yulia Mihailovna, clearly enraptured by his demeanor, leaned toward Varvara Petrovna and murmured, "C'est charmant, les moines," with a conspiratorial smile. The soft trill of her French accent, though deliberate, was meant to underscore her refinement.

Varvara Petrovna, whose pride had been simmering since the beginning of the gathering, returned the comment with a look of satisfaction, her gaze lingering on Stepan Trofimovitch as though he were her personal creation—a statue brought to life by her patronage. Yet the moment of triumph was short-lived, as Karmazinov, ever sensitive to being upstaged, swiftly interjected with his shrill, condescending tone.

"As for myself, I have long ceased to be troubled by such quaint philosophical musings," he began, lifting his chin as though surveying a distant horizon. "For the past seven years, I've been settled at Karlsruhe. Last year, when the town council proposed the installation of a new water-pipe, I confess I found myself far more deeply moved by the deliberations over that practical matter than by all the so-called reforms currently plaguing my precious Fatherland."

His delivery was so self-satisfied that a ripple of polite laughter ran through the room. Stepan Trofimovitch inclined his head in a gesture of exaggerated empathy and remarked, "I can't help sympathizing, though it goes against the grain." The significance of his words was marked by the slight lowering of his voice, as though he were imparting some profound wisdom.

Yulia Mihailovna, sensing the moment ripen for intellectual profundity, was quick to seize it. "Ah, the conversation is becoming substantial!" she whispered to herself, her triumphant smile growing.

"A drain-pipe, did you say?" the German doctor suddenly inquired in a booming voice, his thick accent distorting the words.

"A water-pipe, doctor," Karmazinov corrected icily. "A water-pipe. And, I must add, I even had the honor of assisting them in drafting the plans."

The doctor erupted into a hearty guffaw, his laughter startling in its volume and abruptness. His unrestrained amusement infected several others in the room, though it was apparent they were laughing at him rather than with him. Blissfully unaware, the doctor grinned broadly, basking in the unintended attention.

"You must forgive me, Karmazinov," Yulia Mihailovna interjected, her voice full of faux-gravity, "but I find it hard to believe your professed indifference to your homeland. Karlsruhe may have its charms, but no Russian writer has ever captured the modern spirit, its conflicts, and its ideals as thoroughly as you. Your portrayal of contemporary types and your exploration of the pressing issues of our time are unparalleled. You put your finger precisely on the pulse of the modern man of action. We cannot accept that you care more about water-pipes than your Fatherland."

"Perhaps, perhaps," Karmazinov replied, feigning modesty as he waved his hand dismissively. "I merely portrayed, in my Pogozhev, all the failings of the Slavophils, and in my Nikodimov, all the failings of the Westerners. But I assure you, it was done only to pass the tedious hours and to appease the incessant demands of my fellow-countrymen."

"I would hardly say you captured all the failings," Lyamshin muttered under his breath, but loud enough to elicit a smirk from those nearby.

"Oh, no doubt," Yulia Mihailovna continued, unfazed, "and tomorrow we shall have the pleasure of hearing one of your latest and, sadly, last literary pieces—Merci. It's a graceful farewell to your public, in which you declare your decision to lay down your pen forever, regardless of any pleas from angels or society to continue. A most noble gesture, a testament to your loyalty to true Russian thought."

She practically glowed with admiration, her eyes sparkling with excitement at her own eloquence.

"Yes," Karmazinov drawled, his tone growing softer and more melancholic, "I shall say my Merci, my farewell, and then depart. And there, in Karlsruhe, I shall close my eyes." His voice quivered ever so slightly as though on the verge of tears.

This maudlin display might have been poignant had it not been so overblown. Stepan Trofimovitch, seated on the sofa in his picturesque pose, allowed himself a faint, ironic smile. It was unclear whether he was amused or simply weary of the spectacle unfolding before him. Meanwhile, the German doctor, oblivious to the subtleties of the exchange, let out another resounding guffaw, startling the young princeling, who adjusted his pince-nez with an air of detached curiosity.

Like many of our celebrated writers (and indeed we seem to have an inexhaustible supply of them), Stepan Trofimovitch could not entirely resist the allure of praise. He appeared to soften and lose some of his usual sharpness of wit under its influence—a trait not uncommon even among the most penetrating minds. In fact, it is said that one of our more illustrious "Shakespeares" once admitted in private that "we great men can't help it," and seemed genuinely oblivious to the self-indulgence of such a statement.

"There in Karlsruhe, I shall close my eyes," Stepan Trofimovitch repeated, his voice heavy with theatrical melancholy. "When we have fulfilled our duty, there is nothing left for great men like us but to hasten to close our eyes, seeking neither reward nor recognition. That will be my fate as well."

"Do give me the address of your tomb in Karlsruhe," the German doctor interjected with boisterous laughter. His humor was coarse but infectious, drawing scattered chuckles from others in the room.

"They ship corpses by rail these days," remarked one of the less consequential young men present, his tone laced with casual cynicism.

This comment sent Lyamshin into convulsions of laughter, practically shrieking with delight, though his antics earned a sharp frown from Yulia Mihailovna. The room, now charged with an odd mixture of jest and discomfort, suddenly fell silent as Nikolay Stavrogin walked in, commanding attention without effort.

"Why, I was told that you were locked up?" Stavrogin said plainly, addressing Stepan Trofimovitch in front of everyone, his voice carrying an edge of curiosity.

"No, on the contrary, it was a case of unlocking," Stepan Trofimovitch replied with a faint, sardonic smile, the corners of his mouth twitching in amusement at his own cleverness.

But before the room could fully settle into the rhythm of this exchange, Yulia Mihailovna intervened, her tone bright with determination. "I trust this unfortunate morning's annoyance, of which I knew nothing, will not deter you, dear Stepan Trofimovitch, from gracing us with your much-anticipated reading at tomorrow's literary matinée," she said, her voice rich with the practiced warmth of a consummate hostess.

"I… I am not certain…" he began hesitantly, his earlier theatricality fading into genuine uncertainty.

"I am truly most unlucky," Yulia Mihailovna pressed on, turning to Varvara Petrovna with a glimmer of playful reproach. "Just imagine, I had so eagerly anticipated making the acquaintance of one of Russia's most remarkable and independent minds, and now he talks of abandoning us!"

"Your compliment is delivered so audibly that I ought to pretend not to hear it," Stepan Trofimovitch replied, his voice tinged with mock humility. "But I cannot believe that my insignificant presence could be so indispensable to your fête tomorrow. Still, I…"

"You'll spoil him completely!" Pyotr Stepanovitch burst into the room, cutting him off abruptly. "He's already unbearable! This morning he's been searched, arrested, manhandled by the police—and now, look at him! Sitting here basking in the governor's drawing-room as if it were his rightful throne. Every bone in his body must be aching with joy! He's probably planning to denounce the Socialists now, just to prolong the excitement."

"Impossible, Pyotr Stepanovitch! Socialism is far too grand a concept to be misunderstood by Stepan Trofimovitch," Yulia Mihailovna countered with fervor, rising to the challenge.

"Socialism may be grand," Stepan Trofimovitch murmured, lifting himself gracefully from his chair, "but its advocates are not always great men. And on that note—let us change the subject, my dear son."

At that moment, a shift in the atmosphere occurred. Von Lembke, who had been standing near the door, went almost unnoticed by the gathering until now. He had taken his position quietly, wearing a somber expression, as though grappling with internal discord. His presence, though understated, seemed to thrum with a restless energy. Upon hearing Stepan Trofimovitch's passing remark about Socialists, he suddenly moved forward with unexpected vigor.

"Enough!" he declared, his voice cutting through the room. He strode up to Stepan Trofimovitch and seized his hand in both of his, gripping it tightly with a force that seemed almost desperate. "Enough!" he repeated, his tone growing more impassioned. "The filibusters of our day have been unmasked. Not another word. Measures have been taken."

His voice carried enough authority to silence the gathering, but the room was charged with a sense of unease. The intensity of his proclamation seemed disproportionate, and his sudden movement startled several people nearby. I noticed Yulia Mihailovna pale visibly, though she maintained her composure.

Then, as if to add to the surreal absurdity of the moment, Von Lembke turned abruptly toward the door, took two brisk steps, and promptly stumbled over a rug. He lurched forward, narrowly avoiding a fall, and then stood there, frozen, staring at the offending rug as though it were a personal affront. Finally, he barked, "Change it!" before exiting the room with a swift, jerky motion.

Yulia Mihailovna darted after him, her composure slipping just slightly as she disappeared through the doorway. Her abrupt exit left the room in chaos. An uneasy murmur rose as people exchanged glances, whispering hurried speculations. Lyamshin, standing in the corner, made a theatrical gesture by placing two fingers above his forehead, as though mimicking horns—a not-so-subtle insinuation of madness.

Hints of "domestic difficulties" began circulating in hushed tones. Yet, despite the tension, no one seemed ready to leave. There was an unspoken sense that the drama was far from over. Five minutes later, Yulia Mihailovna returned, her expression composed once more, though her color had not entirely returned.

"Andrey Antonovitch is rather agitated," she announced lightly, "but it's nothing of consequence. He has been prone to such excitement since childhood. A pleasant day tomorrow will surely cheer him." Her voice was steady, but her attempt to dismiss the episode rang hollow.

Turning to Stepan Trofimovitch, she added with a bright smile, "We must now focus on the upcoming meeting. Let us proceed, gentlemen."

With that, the non-committee members began to shuffle towards the exit, though the sense of unease lingered. Yet, even with this incident, the day's trials were not yet fully concluded.

When Nikolay Stavrogin entered the room, I immediately noticed a peculiar reaction from Liza. Her eyes darted to him with an intensity that seemed almost involuntary, and once fixed on him, they refused to look away. She gazed at him for so long and so intently that others began to notice as well. Mavriky Nikolaevitch, standing behind her, leaned forward as though intending to whisper something to her, but after a moment's hesitation, he straightened abruptly, his expression guilty and uneasy as his eyes darted around the room. Stavrogin himself appeared unusually pale, and there was something in his demeanor—a distant, almost disoriented air—that drew attention. After asking his curt question of Stepan Trofimovitch, he seemed to forget the entire exchange, as though it had never happened.

What struck me most was how utterly oblivious he appeared to Liza. It wasn't the deliberate avoidance of someone trying to hide their thoughts but the genuine inattention of someone whose mind was elsewhere entirely. And then, just as Yulia Mihailovna was inviting the group to begin the meeting, Liza's voice suddenly rang out, clear and musical, yet trembling with an unmistakable edge. She spoke loudly, addressing Stavrogin directly.

"Nikolay Vsyevolodovitch," she said, her tone both challenging and desperate, "a captain who claims to be related to you, the brother of your wife—a man by the name of Lebyadkin—has been writing me impertinent letters. He complains about you and offers to share certain 'secrets' about you. If he is indeed your relation, kindly tell him to stop harassing me and spare me this unpleasantness."

The room seemed to hold its breath. Everyone present understood the gravity of her words; the accusation was as pointed as it was public. Yet there was also an air of recklessness in her tone, as though she had flung these words out without fully considering their consequences, like someone leaping off a precipice with no thought of what lay below.

But it was Stavrogin's response that truly stunned us all. He did not flinch or show even the faintest sign of surprise. His expression remained calm, composed, and utterly unperturbed. He listened with a quiet, almost unnerving attentiveness. When he spoke, it was with a simplicity and

496

directness that only deepened the shock.

"Yes," he said, his voice steady and deliberate, "I have the misfortune to be connected with that man. I have been married to his sister for nearly five years. You can be assured that I will deliver your message to him immediately. I will personally see to it that he ceases to trouble you."

His words landed like a thunderclap in the room. Varvara Petrovna, seated nearby, reacted as though physically struck. She rose abruptly, her right hand lifting in a defensive gesture, her face frozen in an expression of utter horror. Stavrogin turned his gaze from her to Liza, then to the rest of the room. For a moment, his eyes swept over the stunned faces surrounding him, and then he smiled—a faint, contemptuous smile that conveyed a disdain so profound it was almost regal. Without another word, he turned and walked deliberately out of the room.

Liza's reaction was no less dramatic. The moment he turned to leave, she sprang to her feet, and for an instant, it seemed as though she might rush after him. Her body leaned forward, her intention almost palpable, but she stopped herself. Containing her emotion with visible effort, she walked out of the room in silence, without so much as a glance at anyone. Mavriky Nikolaevitch, true to form, immediately followed her, his steps hurried and anxious.

The room exploded into a cacophony of murmurs and whispers the moment the door closed behind them. Speculation flew wildly, each more outlandish than the last. That evening, the entire town buzzed with gossip and conjecture, the revelations and ensuing drama overshadowing every other topic of conversation.

Varvara Petrovna, it was said, returned to her town house and locked herself away, refusing to see anyone. Nikolay Stavrogin, meanwhile, left directly for Skvoreshniki, bypassing his mother entirely. Stepan Trofimovitch, on hearing the news, was beside himself with despair. He sent me that very night to Varvara Petrovna to implore her to see him, but she refused me entry.

"Such a marriage! Such a disgrace! Such a calamity for the family!" he wailed when I returned, his voice trembling with emotion. He paced the room in agitation, tears streaming down his face. But even amidst his sorrow, he found time to rail against Karmazinov, pouring out his frustration with a venom that seemed to energize him. In the midst of this emotional storm, he also threw himself into preparations for his upcoming reading at the fête. With the intensity only an artist can muster, he rehearsed before the mirror, revising his phrases and inserting witticisms from a notebook he had kept over the years.

"My friend," he said to me that evening, his voice laden with dramatic conviction, "I do this for a great idea. For twenty-five years, I have stood still, a statue collecting dust. But now—now I am in motion. Where I am going, I do not yet know, but at last, I have begun to move."

PART 3

Chapter 1
The Fête—First Part

Chapter 1.1

The fête proceeded as planned, despite the tumultuous events of the previous "Shpigulin" day. It seemed as though even the gravest catastrophe could not have deterred its happening, so deeply did Yulia Mihailovna attach her ambitions and self-worth to its success. Her obliviousness to the true state of public sentiment was astonishing. To the last moment, she clung to the belief that she was adored by her followers and that her leadership was appreciated. Little did she know that a storm of resentment was brewing, an implacable irritation simmering beneath the surface of the town.

It wasn't mere excitement for a scandal, though the promise of a dramatic spectacle certainly delighted many; this was something deeper, a collective cynicism that bordered on malice. Discontent had permeated every stratum of society. Among the women of the town, feelings were particularly intense. In a rare show of unity, women from all social circles shared an unrelenting disdain for Yulia Mihailovna. Ironically, she remained completely unaware of this hostility, still believing herself to be the center of adoration.

Amidst this discontent, the town had seen the rise of dubious figures, individuals of little standing who thrived on the upheaval. They were not the ideological "advanced thinkers" with a clear, if misguided, purpose. These were opportunists and troublemakers, riding the wave of uncertainty for their own chaotic amusement. In any period of transition, such riff-raff emerges—people without vision or ideas, yet full of restlessness and discontent. The peculiar tragedy of these moments is how easily these mischief-makers fall under the sway of slightly more organized groups with genuine agendas, though even those groups often lack true coherence or competence.

In our town's case, the confusion and tension of the time created a fertile ground for such disorder. It was later claimed that the Internationale was behind it all, with Pyotr Stepanovitch acting as their agent and using Yulia Mihailovna as a puppet to organize and manipulate an eclectic crowd of malcontents. Whether true or not, this theory became a convenient explanation for the irrational behavior that had gripped so many. Even the more sober minds in the community, looking back, were astonished at how easily they had been drawn into the chaos.

What exactly defined this moment of transition remains unclear. What was this change we were supposedly undergoing? Nobody could quite say, except perhaps for a few of the outsiders who had arrived to stir the pot. And yet, in this uncertain atmosphere, the usual boundaries and hierarchies crumbled. People who had previously been silent suddenly gained a voice, while those who had long commanded respect found themselves marginalized or ignored. The absurdity of the situation was evident everywhere: homegrown radicals spouting second-rate revolutionary ideas, self-styled intellectuals with no real insight, and even a handful of poets in peasant garb affecting a "rustic" authenticity that was as unconvincing as it was pretentious.

The fête itself had become a focal point of this strange upheaval. What had started as a charitable event had grown into a spectacle of rumors and expectations. Talk of lavish entertainments, princely guests, and theatrical literary performances swirled through the town. There were whispers of a quadrille performed in costume, each dancer representing a different philosophical or literary idea. Even the famously reclusive Karmazinov was rumored to be reading his latest farewell piece, Merci, dressed in an outfit meant to parody the governesses for whom the ball ostensibly raised funds.

With such promises, who could resist attending? Subscriptions poured in from every corner of society, even from those who had initially sworn off the event in protest. The irresistible pull of spectacle and the need to be seen among one's peers overrode all reservations. As the day approached, the anticipation reached fever pitch. No one could predict what would happen, but everyone was certain that it would be unforgettable.

Chapter 1.2

The programme for the fête was divided into two parts: the literary matinée, which would run from midday until four o'clock, and a grand ball that would commence at ten in the evening and last through the night. However, even the carefully laid programme concealed seeds of potential chaos. From the very outset, a rumor began to circulate among the townsfolk about a grand luncheon, said to be included in the festivities immediately after the literary matinée or possibly even during an interval. This luncheon, naturally, would be free and accompanied by champagne. The substantial ticket price of three roubles lent credibility to the rumor.

"Surely, no one would pay so much for nothing," the townspeople reasoned. "The fête is an all-day affair; people will need food. It stands to reason." This logic gained traction, and the notion of a luncheon became a fixture in the public's imagination.

Unfortunately, Yulia Mihailovna herself unintentionally fueled these expectations through her early enthusiasm. In the first flush of excitement over her grand project, she had spoken about it freely to anyone willing to listen. She had even submitted a paragraph to a Petersburg newspaper outlining her ambitious plans, including elaborate toasts and speeches that would define the fête. The toasts, in particular, captivated her imagination. She envisioned herself proposing them, drafting and redrafting the wording in her head, hoping they would clarify her lofty ideals. She dreamed these speeches would catch the attention of the higher powers in the capital and spark admiration and imitation across the provinces.

But toasts required champagne, and champagne could not be consumed on an empty stomach—thus, a luncheon seemed indispensable. However, as the planning progressed and a committee was established, the reality of the budget became glaringly apparent. If they indulged in the imagined banquet, there would be little money left for the governesses, the ostensible beneficiaries of the event.

Two starkly different paths emerged: a lavish banquet with toasts and a meager ninety roubles for the governesses, or a more modest fête focused on maximizing the funds raised. The committee, seeking a middle ground, devised a compromise: a respectable fête without champagne or extravagance, but one that would generate a substantial sum, far exceeding ninety roubles. Despite the practicality of this solution, Yulia Mihailovna's pride could not tolerate such a mundane approach. To her, a diluted version of her original vision felt like a personal defeat.

In a fit of frustration and determination, she proposed a bold alternative: abandoning all compromise and raising a truly monumental sum that would surpass anything seen in neighboring provinces. "The public must understand," she proclaimed during an impassioned committee meeting, "that the pursuit of an ideal for the betterment of humanity is infinitely more noble than fleeting indulgences. The fête itself should stand as a proclamation of this great idea! Let us cast aside these corporeal pleasures and content ourselves with a simple, frugal gathering—perhaps even dispense with the ball altogether!" Her vehemence made it clear she had developed a sudden disdain for the entire concept of the ball.

Eventually, she was talked down from her extremism. In an effort to reconcile her grand ideals with the practicalities of the fête, the committee introduced several new, creative features. The "literary quadrille" was conceived, along with other artistic amusements meant to distract from the lack of fine dining. It was at this point that Karmazinov finally relented and agreed to read his Merci at the matinée, a gesture calculated to uplift the intellectual tone of the event and eradicate any lingering associations with food or drink.

The ball, however, retained its prominence, albeit in a refined and restrained form. To provide a modest concession to practicality, it was decided that tea with lemon and biscuits would be served at the beginning of the ball, followed later by orgeat and lemonade, and eventually even ices. For those with a more insatiable appetite, a small buffet was proposed, to be overseen by Prohorovitch, the club's esteemed head cook. Under the watchful eye of the committee, the buffet would operate on a fixed-price basis, with refreshments available for purchase. A notice would clearly state that these were not included in the fête's ticket price.

However, on the morning of the fête, a decision was made to forego even this modest concession. The committee feared the buffet might disrupt the matinée, despite being situated five rooms away from the White Hall where Karmazinov was to deliver his reading. Thus, the fate of the buffet was sealed, further heightening the tension between the committee's lofty ideals and the townspeople's simple expectations.

As the day of the fête dawned, the stage was set for a spectacle that seemed poised to unravel under the weight of its own contradictions.

The significance the committee, even its most practical members, placed on Karmazinov's reading was extraordinary. For those with artistic and poetic leanings, such as the marshal's wife, it was nothing short of a historic event. She went so far as to inform Karmazinov that, immediately after his reading of Merci, she would commission a marble plaque to be mounted on the wall of the White Hall. This plaque, she explained, would bear an inscription in gold letters commemorating the day, stating that here, in this very place, the great writer of Russia and Europe had read Merci, marking his formal farewell to the Russian public. The inscription would also note that this august audience was comprised of the leading citizens of their town. According to her, this tribute would be ready for all to read during the ball, which was scheduled to begin just five hours after the reading.

Karmazinov himself attached no less importance to the occasion. It was he, in fact, who insisted that there be no buffet or refreshments of any kind during the matinée while he was reading. Some committee members protested, arguing that such a restriction was contrary to local traditions and the comfort of the audience, but Karmazinov remained adamant. To him, such distractions were unthinkable. The audience must focus entirely on the lofty literary moment he was bestowing upon them.

Meanwhile, the townspeople clung to their expectations of a sumptuous banquet, a feast reminiscent of Belshazzar's, complete with an array of refreshments provided by the committee. These expectations persisted up until the very last moment. The young ladies, in particular, had been dreaming of tables laden with sweets, preserves, and perhaps even delicacies beyond their imaginations. Such dreams were encouraged by the general knowledge that the fête had garnered significant financial support. Subscriptions had reached an impressive sum, tickets were in high demand, and people were traveling from neighboring districts just to attend.

Additionally, there were whispers of generous contributions outside the ticket sales. For instance, it was widely known that Varvara Petrovna had paid an extravagant three hundred roubles for her ticket. Moreover, she had contributed nearly all the flowers from her conservatory to adorn the White Hall. The marshal's wife, a prominent committee member, had offered her residence for the event and provided the lighting. The local club supplied the music, attendants, and even Prohorovitch, their head cook, for the entire day. Lesser contributions were also made, with various townspeople chipping in to support the cause.

The high level of financial support was so impressive that the committee briefly entertained the idea of reducing the ticket price from three roubles to two. They were initially concerned that three roubles might be too steep for young women and their families to afford. As a compromise, they proposed a family ticket: a family would pay for one daughter, while any additional daughters, even if there were a dozen, would be admitted free of charge. But these worries proved unfounded.

To everyone's surprise, it was the young ladies who turned out in droves. Even the poorest clerks managed to bring their daughters, as if the allure of the event had become an unmissable social milestone. In many cases, it seemed that the presence of young women was the primary reason for attendance. One insignificant little secretary arrived with not just one or two, but all seven of his daughters, along with his wife and even a niece. Remarkably, each one of them held a ticket, fully paid at the original price of three roubles—a small fortune for such a large family.

It became evident that the fête had transcended its original purpose. It was no longer merely a fundraiser or a literary occasion but had grown into a grand social phenomenon. People from all walks of life were drawn to it, each bringing their own hopes, expectations, and ambitions, and it seemed that for many, the act of attending was as important as the event itself.

The fête, divided into two distinct parts—a literary matinée followed by an evening ball—created an upheaval in the town, the scale of which was unprecedented. It required extraordinary preparation, not just in terms of logistics but also personal expenditures. Each lady needed not one but two costumes for the occasion: an elegant morning dress for the matinée and a grand ball gown for the evening. This double requirement turned the town into a whirlwind of activity. Many middle-class families pawned their valuables to afford suitable attire. Even essentials like family linen, sheets, and mattresses were surrendered to the ever-growing number of Jewish pawnbrokers who had settled in the town over the past few years. Some officials took salary advances, while certain landowners sold livestock they could scarcely spare—all for the sake of presenting their wives and daughters as grand as marchionesses.

The magnificence of the dresses was unprecedented, exceeding anything ever seen in the region. For weeks beforehand, the town buzzed with rumors and amusing anecdotes about the preparations. These stories, often delivered with sharp wit, invariably made their way to Yulia Mihailovna's court, where they were gleefully shared and recorded, even sketched as caricatures in her personal album. Unfortunately, this contributed to a growing hostility towards her. Families who became the butt of these jokes seethed with indignation, fueling the town's simmering resentment. By the time of the fête, this animosity had crystallized into a collective hatred, one that only awaited a spark to ignite it into open contempt. It was clear that any mishap during the event, no matter how trivial, would provoke an eruption of discontent.

The festivities began precisely at midday, with the orchestra striking its opening notes. As one of the appointed stewards—marked by the distinctive rosette on my shoulder—I witnessed the chaotic start firsthand. The crowd at the entrance swelled rapidly, creating a crush of bodies. This was unusual for our orderly town, where people rarely jostled each other. The scene was compounded by the arrival of carriages, which soon blocked the street entirely.

The root of the problem, as I later understood, lay in the inclusion of unsavory elements. Certain individuals, including Lyamshin and Liputin, had smuggled in members of the town's lower classes without tickets. Some of these gate-crashers were locals, while others had traveled from surrounding districts, lured by rumors of lavish refreshments. Their first question upon entering the hall was, "Where's the buffet?" When they discovered none existed, their anger boiled over. Many cursed openly, displaying a crudeness that was shocking even for them. A few were already drunk, while others stood dumbfounded at the grandeur of the White Hall, their coarse faces reflecting awe and disbelief.

The hall itself was indeed a sight to behold. Though the building was old and somewhat dilapidated, its vast size, gilded ceiling, and rows of mirrors gave it an air of faded splendor. Marble statues, albeit nondescript ones, adorned the space, while the walls were draped with rich red and white fabric. A high platform had been erected for the literary readings, and rows of chairs were arranged in neat aisles, reminiscent of a theatre.

Despite the initial awe, disorder soon reigned. Some rabble began shouting nonsensical demands: "We didn't come for a reading! We paid for entertainment!" Their brazen insolence suggested they had been incited beforehand. A particularly memorable incident involved a drunken, pockmarked captain who demanded to know the buffet's location. He confronted a princeling steward, an automaton-like figure with a stiff collar and a waxen expression. The princeling, though taciturn, acted decisively: he summoned a police sergeant, who promptly dragged the captain out despite his drunken protests.

Meanwhile, the respectable public began to trickle in, filing into their seats in three long lines. Their demeanor was subdued, even uneasy. Many of the ladies appeared frightened, their smiles strained, while the men bore an air of suppressed frustration. At last, the music stopped, and the audience settled into an expectant silence. Yet the atmosphere was palpably tense. People began blowing their noses and glancing about, their unease growing as the minutes passed. The absence of the Lembkes was particularly conspicuous.

The hall, however, glowed with opulence. Silks, velvets, and diamonds shimmered under the light, while the air was heavy with perfume. Men wore their full decorations, and several older gentlemen were resplendent in uniform. The anticipation was broken when the marshal's wife entered, accompanied by Liza. Liza was a vision of beauty that morning, her charm amplified by an exquisite gown and artfully arranged curls. Her radiant smile and sparkling eyes captivated the room, and whispers of admiration followed her every step. Yet, behind her apparent joy, there was something enigmatic in her expression.

At the time, I could not reconcile her radiance with the events of the previous day. Why did she seem so elated, almost triumphant? It was only later that I understood the depth of the emotions she had concealed, emotions that would soon play a dramatic role in the unfolding of that fateful day. For now, however, she moved through the room like a queen, the cynosure of all eyes, while the undercurrent of unease continued to ripple through the crowd.

The Lembkes' delayed appearance caused growing unease in the hall. Whispers turned to murmurs, and the polite patience of the better-class audience began to wear thin. Even among the distinguished attendees, there was an undercurrent of frustration. Some openly speculated whether the fête would happen at all, spinning absurd rumors that Lembke might be gravely unwell or that the event was a poorly executed sham. The lower ranks of the audience, meanwhile, started clapping sporadically, mimicking the impatient applause of a restless theatre crowd. The tension in the room grew almost palpable.

Yulia Mihailovna, as I later learned, had been waiting until the very last moment for Pyotr Stepanovitch, whose absence left her unmoored. Though she would never admit it, she relied on him to guide her through such moments of uncertainty. The previous day's committee meeting had already thrown her into disarray when Pyotr Stepanovitch refused to wear the steward's rosette, an emblem she had counted on him to don. His refusal hurt her deeply, even bringing her to tears. Yet what truly unnerved her was his complete disappearance on the day of the matinée. His absence was not just conspicuous; it was disruptive. By the time the Lembkes finally entered, the audience's collective mood had begun to sour.

When they did appear, at last, arm in arm, they dispelled many of the wild conjectures. Andrey Antonovitch appeared perfectly well, his countenance composed. Observant onlookers noted the absence of any visible signs of illness or disarray. Indeed, some of the town's higher officials, who had been critical of him the day before, now praised his conduct in the recent crisis, even rationalizing his earlier outburst in the square. "It's what should have been done from the start," they murmured approvingly, though they conceded he might have handled it with more composure. Still, they chalked it up to his being new to his position.

Yulia Mihailovna, on the other hand, drew immediate attention for her radiant demeanor. She seemed to glow with an aura of triumph, her face exuding the confidence of a woman who believed herself to have secured a grand success. What the audience could not know—and what I later pieced together—was that she and her husband had reconciled late the previous night. After their private, hours-long conversation, Andrey Antonovitch had emerged contrite and devoted, even kneeling at her feet in a display of remorse. Yulia Mihailovna, for her part, forgave him graciously, sealing the reconciliation with a tender gesture that spoke volumes about her ability to command and forgive in equal measure. This personal victory fueled her spirited appearance at the matinée.

As they walked to their seats at the front of the hall, bowing and smiling in acknowledgment of greetings from every direction, the Lembkes appeared, to all outward appearances, to be the picture of composure and harmony. The marshal's wife rose from her seat to meet them halfway, reinforcing the sense of ceremony. But this carefully maintained dignity was shattered almost immediately.

The orchestra, without any cue or apparent reason, struck up a flourish. It was not the grand, triumphal march appropriate to such an occasion but a short, almost absurd flourish more suited to a provincial club's dinner toast. The effect was jarring. People exchanged confused glances, unsure whether to applaud or laugh. To make matters worse, scattered cries of "Hurrah!" erupted from the back rows and the gallery. Though faint and half-hearted, the cheers dragged on long enough to deepen the awkwardness. It was a calculated act of mischief, and I later learned that it was orchestrated by Lyamshin, who had, in his capacity as a steward, prearranged the musical interruption.

Yulia Mihailovna flushed crimson. Her eyes darted around the room, flashing with indignation and embarrassment. Andrey Antonovitch, meanwhile, froze beside his chair. He turned toward the source of the cheers with a stern, almost regal air, scanning the audience as though daring anyone to continue. The moment stretched unbearably long. When he finally sat down, his face bore an unsettling expression—a strange, resigned smile that seemed to echo the one he had worn the morning before in his wife's drawing room. It was the look of a man determined to endure whatever indignity might befall him for the sake of his wife's ambitions.

Sensing the need to shift the attention, Yulia Mihailovna urgently beckoned me over. Leaning close, she whispered for me to find Karmazinov and implore him to begin his reading without delay. I hurried off to carry out her instructions, but as I made my way toward him, another, far more humiliating incident unfolded, one that would set the tone for the rest of this ill-fated day.

The startling turn of events began when Captain Lebyadkin, clad in a dress coat and white tie, unexpectedly appeared on the platform. His bulky figure loomed against the sparse setting—a small table with a glass of water on a silver salver and a single chair—stopping the murmurs of the audience in their tracks. For a moment, I thought I must be imagining things. His face, flushed and bloated from intoxication, broke into a vacant, foolish grin at the sudden recognition from the crowd.

A voice from the audience shouted, "Lebyadkin! You?"

At this, the captain seemed to collect himself—or rather, resign himself to his awkward predicament. He rubbed his forehead with a massive hand, shook his head vigorously, and took two tentative steps forward. Then, as if unable to contain himself, he burst into a series of prolonged, gurgling guffaws, his entire body shaking as his eyes screwed shut in mirth. The absurdity of the spectacle rippled through the audience, sparking laughter from some and uneasy frowns from others. A smattering of applause erupted in pockets of the hall, while many in the serious section of the audience exchanged grim and disapproving looks.

The farce lasted only a moment before Liputin, donning the steward's rosette of authority, hurried onto the platform. Flanked by two servants, he seized the situation with calculated efficiency. Approaching Lebyadkin, he whispered something in his ear, all while maintaining an expression that mixed disapproval and restrained amusement. The captain scowled, muttered something unintelligible, and waved a meaty hand dismissively. With the servants holding him firmly by the arms, he lumbered off the platform, his bulk casting shadows as he disappeared into the wings.

But the drama was far from over. Liputin returned almost immediately, stepping onto the stage with the faintly malicious smile that was his hallmark—a mixture of vinegar and sugar, as though he relished the chaos but sought to appear above it. He held a folded sheet of paper in his hand, moving with hurried, nervous steps toward the edge of the platform.

"Ladies and gentlemen," he began, his voice ringing out with a politeness that barely concealed his glee, "a small misunderstanding has arisen, which, I assure you, has been swiftly resolved." He paused to savor the moment, his sugary tone grating against the tension in the hall. "But I've taken the liberty, at the earnest and most respectful request of a local poet, to offer something... unplanned. This poet, deeply touched by the humane and noble purpose of today's event—to aid the poor but well-educated governesses of our province—wishes to share a brief piece in honor of the occasion."

There was a murmur of interest, though it was tinged with skepticism. Liputin, emboldened, continued with faux humility.

"This is not, I must clarify, an official item on the program. The poem arrived just half an hour ago. But upon reading it, we—" he gestured vaguely, as though supported by some invisible committee—"felt that its remarkable combination of naïveté, gaiety, and, dare I say, truthfulness, makes it an ideal addition to today's celebration."

A voice boomed from the back of the hall, "Read it!" Others joined in, and the calls became louder. Liputin bowed slightly, as though seeking their consent.

"With your permission, then, I will read it," he said, feigning reluctance. But there was no mistaking his excitement. Unfolding the paper with deliberate care, he began in a loud, theatrical voice:

"To the local governesses of the Fatherland from the poet at the fête:

Governesses all, good morrow,

Triumph on this festive day.

Retrograde or vowed George-Sander—

Never mind, just frisk away!"

The first lines drew scattered laughter, but the reaction quickly soured as the crowd recognized the verses. "That's Lebyadkin's! Lebyadkin's!" several voices cried out. Some laughed nervously, others clapped half-heartedly, but most sat frozen in stunned silence.

Liputin pressed on undeterred: "Teaching French to wet-nosed children,

You are glad enough to think

You can catch a worn-out sexton—

Even he is worth a wink!"

There was an audible gasp. A few drunken voices shouted "Hurrah!" from the back, but the audience's discomfort deepened. Liputin's smile wavered, but he plowed through to the end of the mocking verses:

"But henceforth, since through our feasting

Capital has flowed from all,

And we send you forth to conquest

Dancing, dowried from this hall—

Retrograde or vowed George-Sander,

Never mind, rejoice you may,

You're a governess with a dowry,

Spit on all and frisk away!"

The scandal was unmistakable. The offensive nature of the poem, coupled with Liputin's smug delivery, made it impossible to dismiss as a mere lapse in judgment. It was clear that Liputin had orchestrated this insult deliberately, perhaps with the intent of inciting chaos. Even the rabble in the audience, who had initially cheered, fell silent as the weight of the verses sank in.

The reaction among the more respectable members of the audience was one of horror and indignation. A distinguished elderly gentleman rose abruptly, helping his equally appalled wife to her feet. They left the hall without a word, their departure casting a long shadow over the gathering. Whispers of anger and shock swept through the room, and for a moment, it seemed the entire event might collapse into an irreparable scandal.

But at that critical moment, Karmazinov himself appeared on the platform, dressed immaculately in a formal coat and carrying a manuscript in his hand. His sudden arrival, with all the calculated grandeur of a seasoned performer, arrested the growing uproar. Yulia Mihailovna turned toward him with a look of desperate gratitude, as though a savior had materialized to rescue her fête from ruin.

I, however, had no time to witness what followed. My attention was fixed on Liputin, who slipped off the stage, his smug expression now replaced by one of uncertainty. I resolved to confront him at once, to understand just how far this farce was intended to go—and what more chaos might yet lie in store.

"You planned that deliberately!" I exclaimed, grabbing Liputin by the arm, my voice sharp with indignation.

"I assure you, I didn't," he replied hastily, his tone shifting to one of feigned remorse. His attempt to look contrite was undermined by his habitual sneer. "The verses were just brought to me—I thought they'd be an amusing pleasantry…"

"You didn't think that for a moment," I interrupted, incredulous. "You know perfectly well it's not amusing in the least. That ridiculous drivel can't possibly strike even you as a pleasantry!"

"Yes, it does," he said, defiantly, though his eyes betrayed his growing irritation.

"You're lying," I pressed, my anger mounting. "It wasn't just brought to you. You helped Lebyadkin compose it—yesterday, most likely. You wanted a scandal. The last verse reeks of your handiwork, and the part about the sexton could only be yours. Why was Lebyadkin dressed up in a formal suit? You must have planned for him to read it himself if he hadn't been too drunk."

Liputin's expression shifted as he looked at me, his eyes cold and calculating. A faint smirk played on his lips.

"What does it matter to you?" he asked with unsettling composure, his tone almost indifferent.

"What does it matter?" I repeated incredulously. "You're wearing the steward's badge! This whole thing is a deliberate attempt to sabotage the event. Where's Pyotr Stepanovitch?"

"I don't know. Somewhere around here, I suppose. Why are you asking?"

"Because this reeks of a plot," I retorted. "It's clear now—you're working to ruin Yulia Mihailovna's fête with this farce."

Liputin tilted his head slightly, his grin widening. "And why is that your concern?" he said mockingly, shrugging as he turned away.

His dismissive tone and the sheer audacity of his words left me stunned. The truth hit me like a wave—I had been right to suspect foul play all along. Every doubt, every lingering hope that I had misunderstood, vanished in an instant. Liputin's complicity and his complete indifference to the harm he was causing confirmed the worst.

What could I do? My first thought was to seek out Stepan Trofimovitch for advice, but I caught sight of him near the mirror, utterly engrossed in trying on smiles. He held a small sheet of notes and muttered to himself as he rehearsed. He was up next, scheduled to follow Karmazinov, and his nerves were clearly frayed. It was futile to expect any coherent discussion from him now.

Should I run to Yulia Mihailovna? The idea flashed through my mind, but I quickly dismissed it. She was too entrenched in her illusions—her belief that she was surrounded by a devoted following blinded her to the truth. She wouldn't believe me, dismissing my concerns as overblown or fantastical. Besides, what could she even do to salvage the situation? No, it was too early for her to receive such a lesson; she needed the stark reality to crash down on her.

A new thought surfaced: What if I simply walked away? The temptation was strong. I could take off my steward's badge and leave before things spiraled further. I even caught myself thinking, I'll leave when it begins. That phrase stuck with me: when it begins. Deep down, I knew chaos was inevitable.

Reluctantly, I turned my attention back to the unfolding events. Glancing behind the scenes, I noticed an unusual number of people milling about—some were clearly outsiders, including several women. The space behind the curtain was narrow and cramped, serving as a makeshift greenroom for the readers awaiting their turns. Among the chaotic activity, my attention was drawn to the reader scheduled to follow Stepan Trofimovitch.

This man, whose name I never quite learned, had an enigmatic air that made him stand out. I later discovered he was some sort of professor who had left an educational institution under a cloud of controversy after a student uprising. He had only arrived in town days earlier, apparently on someone's recommendation, and Yulia Mihailovna had taken him into her circle with unwarranted reverence. Yet his presence was unsettling.

I recalled the single evening he had spent in her company, listening in silence with an ambiguous smirk while the others joked and conversed freely. His aloofness had left an unpleasant impression on everyone present. He seemed constantly on the verge of taking offense, his haughtiness barely concealed beneath an outward meekness. Now, as I observed him pacing the cramped space behind the curtain, his peculiar behavior made me uneasy.

He walked in rigid, deliberate strides, muttering to himself, his eyes fixed on the ground. His expression alternated between sullen concentration and a strange, rapacious smile. Unlike Stepan Trofimovitch, who rehearsed smiles before the mirror, this man clenched his fists at regular intervals. Every so often, he would raise one hand high above his head and then bring it crashing down, as though crushing some unseen adversary. The gesture was so forceful and repeated so frequently that it seemed like a reflex.

The sight made my skin crawl. Whatever was brewing in his mind was not something I wanted to delve into. The tension in the air was palpable, and I knew I couldn't stay behind the scenes any longer. Determined to see how the next act unfolded, I left in search of a seat to listen to Karmazinov. For better or worse, the real performance was about to begin.

Chapter 1.3

There was a palpable sense in the hall that something was amiss once again. To begin, let me clarify that I hold the deepest respect for genius. However, it is baffling why some of our great minds, in the twilight of their illustrious careers, often behave as though they were mischievous schoolboys. Yes, Karmazinov entered the stage with the grace and dignity of five court chamberlains combined, but how could he seriously expect our audience to sit attentively for an entire hour, listening to a single paper?

I have observed that no matter how profound or celebrated a genius may be, holding the attention of a frivolous audience at a literary matinée for longer than twenty minutes is a feat rarely achieved. True, Karmazinov's entrance was met with respect—some of the most austere men in the room displayed genuine interest, and the ladies even managed a flutter of enthusiasm. The applause, however, was brief, uncertain, and far from unanimous. For a moment, the back rows behaved themselves. But this decorum began to falter almost as soon as Karmazinov started speaking.

It was not outright rebellion; rather, the issue arose from a misunderstanding. Karmazinov's voice, shrill and almost feminine, with a distinctly aristocratic lisp, grated on the nerves of the audience. It had barely filled the air with a few carefully enunciated phrases when someone in the back laughed out loud—a coarse, unrestrained guffaw. Most likely, this came from some uneducated, irreverent fool who had no understanding of social propriety.

The interruption was met with sharp reprimands of "Shh!" from all sides, and the offender quickly silenced. Yet the damage was done. Karmazinov's affected tone and his opening remarks about how he had initially refused to read at all—remarks made with an air of indulgent condescension—did not help matters. He declared that certain lines in his work were so sacred and intimate that they could scarcely be read aloud. "Such things," he intoned, "should not be exposed to public scrutiny." One could almost hear the collective thought of the audience: Then why read them at all?

Still, these theatrical flourishes might have been forgiven had he chosen to read a short tale—a vignette in his usual elaborate and occasionally witty style. But no, what followed was far from a story. It was an oration, sprawling and incoherent, the very embodiment of self-indulgence. The audience, even the intellectuals present, struggled to follow its meandering logic. For the first half of the reading, they strained to decipher its meaning; by the second half, they listened out of sheer politeness, though many were visibly restless.

The subject matter? It defied comprehension. Ostensibly, it was a series of personal impressions and reminiscences, but the content was so obscure and pretentious that even the sharpest minds were left perplexed.

Love, or rather the genius's love, was a central theme. But it was not ordinary love—far from it. The great man described his first kiss in such terms that it bordered on the ludicrous. The juxtaposition of this poetic exaltation with his short and rather stout figure was impossible to ignore and drew awkward chuckles from the audience.

What made it worse was the absurd specificity of his imagery. The kiss was set beneath a tree in Germany, which had to be described as orange in hue—an inexplicable detail that seemed to mock the audience's imagination. A framework of gorse surrounded the scene, and the sky radiated a shade of purple that no mortal had ever observed. The great genius, however, described it as though it were the most natural and obvious phenomenon, his tone dripping with superiority.

The narrative veered into outright absurdity. Pompey and Cassius appeared on the eve of battle. A wood nymph squeaked in the bushes, while Gluck played an obscure piece on the violin—its full title provided, though none could recognize it without consulting a musical encyclopedia. A fog rolled in, but not an ordinary one. No, this fog resembled "a million pillows," more tangible than vaporous. And just as abruptly, the scene shifted to the frozen Volga, where the genius found himself crossing during a thaw, falling through the ice into the frigid waters below.

One might have expected him to drown, but no—this plunge served only to inspire yet another overwrought image. As he sank, gasping for breath, he glimpsed a fragment of ice no larger than a pea. Its crystalline purity, likened to a frozen tear, reflected the iridescent skies of Germany, transporting him back to the memory of another tear, shed under an emerald tree. There, a lover's philosophical exchange had ended in eternal separation.

From there, the narrative spiraled further. She departed for the sea coast; he descended into caves beneath the Suharev Tower in Moscow. For three years, he wandered the earth's bowels until he stumbled upon a hermit praying before a flickering lamp. But the hermit's sigh was not what captivated him—no, it was a faint echo of her sigh, thirty-seven years earlier, in Germany, beneath that improbable agate tree.

By the time Ancus Marcius appeared above the rooftops of Rome, wearing a laurel wreath and heralded by the strains of Chopin, half the audience had succumbed to either confusion or sheer exhaustion. And still, the genius droned on, utterly oblivious to the growing unrest in the hall.

The tension was unbearable. Some stifled yawns, others exchanged glances of disbelief, and a few bold souls shifted audibly in their chairs. What began as reverence for Karmazinov's stature as a writer had now morphed into an endurance test. The audience seemed poised on the edge of collective rebellion. It was only a matter of time before something snapped.

Perhaps my attempt at recounting the chaos doesn't quite capture the absurdity of the moment or the nuances of the scene, but this much is certain: the entire atmosphere was laced with an air of strained tension and disarray. The tone of Karmazinov's pretentious oration, with its jests cloaked in intellectual superiority, was not just tiresome but insulting. It epitomized the peculiar vice of certain great Russian intellects—a tendency to jest about the gravest matters with a smirking air of condescension.

To the great Russian genius, even the monumental achievements of European philosophers, scientists, and inventors are trivial, mere toys for his wit. These great figures, toiling under the burden of their labor, are reduced to the status of cooks in the kitchen of his intellect. He mocks them, and, with equal fervor, jeers at the inadequacies of Russia itself. Yet, when it comes to himself, there is no humility. No, the great genius positions himself above all, crafting clever epigrams by stitching together ideas and their antitheses with practiced ease.

Crime exists; crime doesn't exist. Justice is real; justice is an illusion. Darwinism, atheism, the Moscow bells—he scoffs at them all. And yet, he no longer believes in any of these symbols, mocking even laurels as meaningless. His tone flits between a Byronic sneer, Heine's sharp wit, and the brooding affectations of Petchorin. The result is a whirlwind of contradictions delivered at full speed—yet it's a whirlwind that no one truly wants to endure for an hour.

Naturally, it couldn't end without some measure of conflict, and sadly, it was Karmazinov himself who invited it. For a good while, as he droned on with his lisping, theatrical delivery, the audience endured with increasing discomfort. Feet shuffled, noses were blown, coughs echoed intermittently—all subtle signals that the crowd's patience was wearing thin. But Karmazinov, lost in his lofty rhetoric, remained oblivious.

Then, the inevitable happened. A solitary voice in the back, weary and exasperated, broke through the restraint:

"Good Lord, what nonsense!"

The words echoed loudly and seemed involuntary—a cry of pure frustration rather than deliberate dissent. Yet the damage was done. Karmazinov stopped mid-sentence, his aristocratic features frozen in surprise. With a sarcastic smile, he addressed the room:

"I'm afraid I've been boring you dreadfully, gentlemen?"

Here lay his critical error. By acknowledging the interruption, he opened the floodgates. Had he maintained his composure and ignored the outburst, the crowd would have likely settled back into uneasy decorum. Instead, his question practically invited the rabble to respond. And respond they did.

"You never did see Ancus Marcius—that's all brag!" came an irritated retort from another corner.

"Exactly! No such things as ghosts these days. Look it up in a scientific book," someone else chimed in with exasperation.

Karmazinov, genuinely taken aback, tried to salvage his dignity. "Gentlemen, there was nothing I expected less than such objections," he began, his tone both puzzled and defensive. Clearly, his years in Karlsruhe had distanced him from the sensibilities of his compatriots.

A young lady's voice rang out sharply: "Nowadays, it's absurd to say the world stands on three fishes! You can't have gone down to the hermit's cave, Karmazinov. Who even talks about hermits anymore?"

The great man faltered visibly. "What surprises me most is that you take it all so seriously. However... however, you are perfectly right. No one has greater respect for truth and realism than I do..." His tone wavered, teetering between wounded pride and desperate self-justification. His expression seemed to plead: I am not your enemy; I am one of you! Just praise me, I beg you. Praise me more—I thrive on it.

But the crowd was not inclined to oblige. His audience, long fatigued and irritated, grew restless. Whispers spread through the hall, accompanied by the occasional disrespectful laugh.

Finally, Karmazinov, now thoroughly mortified, admitted defeat. "Gentlemen," he declared with a theatrical flourish, "I see my poor poem is entirely out of place here. Indeed, I fear I am out of place here myself."

This might have been a dignified exit had it ended there. But alas, a drunken voice in the audience shouted, "You threw at the crow and hit

519

the cow!"

The insult hung in the air, provoking both laughter and astonishment. Instead of ignoring it, Karmazinov seized upon the remark, his voice rising to a shrill pitch. "A cow, you say?" he exclaimed indignantly. "As for crows and cows, gentlemen, I shall refrain from comparisons, out of respect for my audience. But I must say…"

He paused dramatically, as though searching for a retort that would crush his detractors. But whatever he intended to say next was lost amidst the rising clamor of whispers, chuckles, and scattered jeers. His authority was shattered, his performance a failure, and the hall descended further into chaos.

The hall was still echoing with a cacophony of scattered applause, jeers, and frustrated murmurs when Stepan Trofimovitch was ushered onto the platform. Karmazinov's departure had left the audience in a peculiar state of restlessness—part amusement, part annoyance, and part hunger-driven dissatisfaction. The disorder was tangible, as though the room itself was teetering on the edge of chaos.

As Stepan Trofimovitch appeared, there was a momentary lull. His striking, almost theatrical appearance seemed to draw the audience's fragmented attention for a moment. Dressed impeccably, with a slightly nervous but dignified expression, he clutched his manuscript tightly. His face was pale, but he managed a faint, habitual smile as he glanced over the crowd. For an instant, there was a spark of hope that this "distinguished professor" might redeem the event.

Alas, the murmurs resumed almost immediately. In the back rows, disgruntled voices muttered complaints:

"Another reader? How long is this going on?"

"Didn't they say there'd be a buffet?"

"Who is this one, anyway?"

Stepan Trofimovitch stepped to the front of the platform and, clearing his throat delicately, began his address. His opening lines were laden with the lofty, archaic phrasing for which he was known—a style that, though respected in certain circles, was entirely unsuited to the agitated and impatient mood of the audience.

"Ladies and gentlemen," he began, his voice quivering slightly, "it is with a sense of profound humility that I stand before you, conscious of the solemnity of this occasion and the lofty purpose that has brought us together..."

But before he could finish his sentence, a loud voice interrupted from the back:

"Get to the point!"

Laughter broke out in several corners of the hall, though it was quickly shushed by the more decorous attendees. Stepan Trofimovitch hesitated, his nervousness momentarily visible, but he soldiered on:

"I have prepared a modest essay, a meditation, if you will, on the eternal harmony of man and the cosmos..."

"Is there food in the cosmos?" another voice shouted, provoking more laughter.

Someone clapped sarcastically. Others joined in with exaggerated enthusiasm, and the applause quickly devolved into mockery. It was evident that Stepan Trofimovitch's poetic musings were falling on deaf ears. Yet, to his credit, he continued reading, his voice growing steadier and more impassioned as he delved into the core of his essay.

The essay itself was a curious mix of philosophical reflections and personal anecdotes, sprinkled with literary allusions. At another time, in a smaller, more respectful gathering, it might have been well received. But here, with an audience growing more restive by the moment, his words seemed only to fan the flames of discontent.

"Didn't he say 'harmony'? What harmony? There's no harmony here!"

"Bravo! Harmony and no buffet!"

Stepan Trofimovitch raised his voice, striving to rise above the interruptions:

"Indeed, harmony is the ultimate aspiration of the human soul, transcending the material, the transient…"

"Speaking of transient, how long is this going to last?" someone jeered loudly, to the delight of the back rows.

In the front, Yulia Mihailovna and the marshal's wife exchanged uneasy glances. Even they could no longer ignore the disruptive undercurrent that was steadily growing. The marshal's wife leaned over and whispered something, clearly urging Yulia to take action. But Yulia, though visibly flustered, hesitated—perhaps hoping against hope that Stepan Trofimovitch could salvage the situation.

He pressed on, oblivious to the storm brewing around him, or perhaps determined to ignore it. His voice grew more impassioned, his gestures more dramatic, as he reached the crescendo of his essay:

"And so, my friends, let us not forget that it is only through the unity of spirit and the eternal striving toward truth that mankind…"

"Unity of spirit won't fill my stomach!"

This final outburst, met with uproarious laughter, was the breaking point. Stepan Trofimovitch faltered, his words trailing off as his composure finally cracked. He stood there, clutching his manuscript, his face a mixture of bewilderment, hurt, and indignation.

At this moment, a loud crash from the back of the hall drew everyone's attention. A chair had toppled over as a particularly rowdy guest attempted to climb onto it for a better view. The ensuing commotion was enough to completely derail what little semblance of order remained.

Yulia Mihailovna, seeing that the situation was spiraling out of control, rose from her seat and clapped her hands sharply. "Ladies and gentlemen," she called out in a commanding voice, "I must insist on decorum! This behavior is disgraceful and entirely unworthy of our gathering!"

Her words managed to subdue the crowd momentarily, but the damage was done. Stepan Trofimovitch, visibly shaken, bowed stiffly and stepped back from the platform. As he disappeared behind the curtain, the audience erupted into a cacophony of applause, laughter, and scattered jeers.

Behind the scenes, he sank into a chair, his head in his hands. "Cher ami," he murmured to me later, "I am a relic of a bygone age. Harmony, unity of spirit—these are meaningless words to them. I should have known... I should have known..."

There was no consolation I could offer. The fête, which had begun as a grand vision of unity and culture, was unraveling before our eyes. And the worst, I feared, was yet to come.

Chapter 1.4

I ran backstage in a last-ditch effort to dissuade him. Seeing Stepan Trofimovitch poised to step onto the platform, I seized his arm and said hurriedly, almost imploringly, "For heaven's sake, don't go through with it! The atmosphere is poisonous, the audience is hostile, and this will end badly. Say you're unwell, anything—let me accompany you home."

He stopped abruptly, drew himself up, and fixed me with a gaze so haughty, so distant, that I felt as though I had committed an unpardonable offense merely by speaking. Then, with an icy calm and a deliberate tone that cut through the noise backstage, he said:

"And do you imagine, sir, that I am capable of such cowardice?"

I recoiled. His expression carried a mixture of wounded pride and disdainful defiance. Without another word, he adjusted his coat and ascended the steps to the platform.

I stood frozen, the weight of inevitability pressing down on me. My earlier conviction solidified into dread: this would not end well. As I turned, I caught sight of the professor who was scheduled to speak next. He was pacing back and forth with unnerving intensity, clenching and unclenching his fists in an almost ritualistic manner. Every few steps, he would stop, raise his fist above his head as though crushing an imaginary opponent, and then resume his muttering. His triumphant smirk made my unease grow.

On an impulse I could not explain, I approached him. "If I may offer

523

a suggestion," I said, trying to keep my voice steady, "lectures at events like this rarely hold an audience for more than twenty minutes. Even the most celebrated figures struggle to sustain attention beyond that point."

He halted mid-step, glaring at me as though I had insulted his very existence. His contempt was palpable. "Do not trouble yourself," he said with quiet venom before turning and continuing his ritual, as if I had not spoken.

I sighed and turned toward the hall. Stepan Trofimovitch had already begun speaking. His voice rang out, clear but trembling with the strain of suppressed emotion. The room, still restless from the previous debacle, began to quiet down. Heads turned toward the platform, curiosity momentarily overcoming the lingering irritation.

"Ladies and gentlemen," he began, his tone measured, "this morning, I came across one of the illegal manifestoes that have been circulating among us recently. As I read it, I asked myself yet again, 'What is the source of its power? What is its secret?'"

The hall went silent. It was as though a collective breath had been held. Even those who moments ago had been exchanging sneers or complaints now leaned forward, intrigued despite themselves. His opening had struck a nerve.

Behind me, Liputin and Lyamshin emerged from the wings, their expressions sharp with interest. From across the room, I caught Yulia Mihailovna's frantic gesturing. She waved at me urgently, mouthing the words: "Stop him! Stop him, no matter what!"

How could I? He was already fully immersed, his voice rising as he spoke with growing fervor.

"Ladies and gentlemen," he continued, "I have solved the riddle. The secret of these manifestoes lies in one quality and one quality alone: their sheer, unadulterated stupidity."

A ripple of shock ran through the audience, followed by murmurs and gasps. Stepan Trofimovitch's eyes burned with a fierce light, and his voice grew stronger. He seemed to feed on the tension in the room.

"Yes," he declared, "stupidity! If this stupidity were intentional—if it were feigned or calculated—it might be worthy of respect, a stroke of cunning genius even. But no, there is no pretense. It is stupidity in its purest, most elemental form. C'est la bêtise dans son essence la plus pure, une sorte de simple chimique. Its very simplicity is its weapon. Because it is so utterly devoid of nuance, so stripped of depth, people cannot believe it. They search for hidden meanings, for mysteries between the lines, and in doing so, they grant it a power it does not deserve."

A wave of agitation passed through the hall. Some faces registered alarm; others, fascination. But in the back rows, the stirrings of discontent began to bubble to the surface.

"'It cannot be so stupid,' they say to themselves," Stepan Trofimovitch went on, his voice tinged with irony. "And thus, they lend weight to the very nonsense they ought to dismiss outright. Oh, never has stupidity been rewarded so richly!"

He paused dramatically, his expression triumphant. "For, let us admit it—stupidity has served humanity almost as much as genius."

The uproar began. A murmur of dissent swelled into audible protests. Someone from the back row shouted mockingly, "Epigram of 1840!"—a jibe at the outdated tone of his rhetoric. Laughter, jeers, and shouts erupted sporadically.

Yulia Mihailovna, her composure cracking, leaned forward and hissed sharply to her companions, "He's ruining everything!"

On the stage, Stepan Trofimovitch stood firm, his face pale but resolute. He had gambled everything on his words, and now the hall teetered on the brink of chaos. As more voices joined the fray, the sound became a chaotic symphony of indignation, derision, and faint applause.

I sank into my seat, powerless to intervene, watching as the moment unraveled before me. Stepan Trofimovitch, who had sought a triumphant moment of redemption, had instead thrown himself into the lion's den—and the lions were hungry.

"Ladies and gentlemen, hurrah! I propose a toast to stupidity!" Stepan Trofimovitch exclaimed, raising his voice to defy the swelling chaos of the audience. His words, delivered with a strange mixture of fervor and desperation, seemed to electrify the room, provoking a fresh wave of shouts and laughter. His face was pale but flushed with a feverish determination, and his trembling hand clutched the edge of the table for support.

Seeing the situation rapidly spiraling out of control, I hurried to the platform, using the excuse of pouring him a glass of water. "Stepan Trofimovitch," I whispered urgently, "for heaven's sake, stop this. Yulia Mihailovna begs you to leave the stage. Please!"

He turned on me with a wild expression, his voice cutting across the hall. "No, leave me alone, idle young man!" he cried at the top of his voice, gesturing dramatically for me to step aside. "This is my moment! I must speak!"

There was nothing more I could do. I retreated, helpless, as he turned back to the audience, raising both hands in a theatrical gesture of reconciliation. "Messieurs," he called out, his voice ringing with a quivering resolve, "why this uproar? Why these cries of indignation? I come bearing an olive branch! I bring you the last word—yes, the last word in this debate. And that word is reconciliation!"

"Down with him!" came a shout from the back.

"Let him speak! Let him finish!" countered another voice.

The hall was divided, with voices clashing and the mood growing increasingly volatile. The young district schoolteacher, emboldened by his earlier outburst, seemed particularly agitated, standing in his place and gesturing emphatically.

Stepan Trofimovitch, undeterred, pressed on. "Messieurs, I declare, with all the solemnity of an old man at the twilight of his life, that the spirit of life breathes within us still! There is strength, a living strength, in the young generation, in you! What we see is not a decay, but merely a shift—a change of aim, a replacing of one ideal, one beauty, with another! The question is not one of vitality, but of preference: which is more beautiful—Shakespeare or boots? Raphael or petroleum?"

The room erupted.

"Agent provocateur!" someone snarled.

"Betrayal!" growled another voice.

"He's mocking us!" a third shouted.

Stepan Trofimovitch raised his voice to a near shriek, his words barely intelligible over the din. "But I maintain, I insist, that Shakespeare and Raphael are more precious than the emancipation of the serfs! More precious than Nationalism, more precious than Socialism, more precious than the chemistry you worship, more precious than your young generation itself, more precious than bread even—because they are the fruit of humanity, its highest fruit! Without them, without beauty, life is impossible. Yes, impossible! Science, your precious science, would crumble without beauty to inspire it. It would sink into drudgery and servitude. Without beauty, you wouldn't even invent a nail!"

He paused, his chest heaving, and then, as if overcome by his own fervor, he slammed his fist onto the table with all his might. "I will not yield an inch!" he bellowed.

The hall had reached a fever pitch. Some in the front rows stared at him, stunned, while others looked ready to burst into laughter. Meanwhile, the back rows were in complete disorder. People were shouting, laughing, and rising from their seats. A few bold individuals pushed their way toward the platform as though intending to confront him directly.

"Sit down! Stop this nonsense!" someone bellowed.

Others shouted back, "Let him speak! He's right!"

It all happened far more quickly than I can describe. The air was thick with tension, the noise deafening, and the movement chaotic. I could see that the disorder was spreading like wildfire, consuming the room. Some faces were furious, others amused, and still others bewildered by the sheer absurdity of it all.

Amid the cacophony, Stepan Trofimovitch stood rigid, clutching the edge of the table as though bracing himself against a storm. His face bore an expression of mingled defiance and despair, and for a moment, I wondered if he truly believed in the words he had spoken—or if he was simply carried away by the spectacle he had created.

"It's all very well for you, pampered creatures, with everything provided for you!" bellowed the same divinity student, standing near the platform and grinning as if savoring the moment. His words, sharp and mocking, were directed squarely at Stepan Trofimovitch, who caught sight of him and, with a sudden burst of energy, darted to the very edge of the stage.

"Haven't I just declared," Stepan Trofimovitch cried, his voice trembling with passion, "that the enthusiasm of the young generation is as pure and bright as ever? Haven't I said that their ruin lies only in being misled by false forms of beauty? Isn't that enough for you? And when I, a father crushed and insulted, proclaim this with tears, do you not see— oh, shallow and ungrateful hearts—that I rise to the utmost heights of fairness and impartiality? Why, why can't you be reconciled?"

His voice broke, and he dissolved into hysterical sobs, wiping the tears from his face with trembling fingers. His whole body heaved with the effort of his emotions, and he seemed entirely oblivious to the world around him. The sight was too much for the audience, and a wave of panic swept through the hall. People began to rise from their seats; some stared in open-mouthed astonishment, while others made for the exits in a flurry of agitation.

Even Yulia Mihailovna, usually composed and authoritative, sprang to her feet, clutching her husband's arm. She pulled him up beside her, her face stricken with disbelief. The entire scene was utterly beyond comprehension, a surreal spectacle unfolding in real time.

"Stepan Trofimovitch!" the divinity student roared again, this time with a gleeful and almost venomous tone. "Tell me something. There's Fedka the convict, wandering about the town right now, escaped from prison. He's a robber, a murderer—and recently he committed yet another crime. But let me ask you this: if you hadn't sold him as a recruit fifteen years ago to cover a gambling debt—or, more simply put, if you hadn't lost him at cards—do you think he would have ended up in prison? Do you think he'd be cutting men's throats now in his struggle for survival? Tell me, Mr. Æsthete, what do you say to that?"

The hall erupted into chaos. Applause broke out—not from the majority, but from a loud and rowdy fifth of the audience. Their clapping and cheers were furious, almost as if in defiance of the rest. Meanwhile, the more respectable members of the crowd were appalled. Many ladies screamed; some of the young girls began to cry, begging to be taken home. The exits became clogged as people surged toward them, creating a bottleneck of confusion and tension.

Lembke, who had been standing stiffly by his chair, now looked around wildly, his face pale and stricken. He seemed utterly incapable of making sense of the pandemonium. Beside him, Yulia Mihailovna appeared dazed, her usually commanding demeanor shattered for the first time. She looked helpless, as if her carefully orchestrated event was slipping irretrievably out of her control.

As for Stepan Trofimovitch, he stood motionless on the platform, visibly stunned by the student's words. For a moment, it seemed as though he might crumble entirely under the weight of the accusation. But then, in a sudden and dramatic gesture, he flung his arms upward as if invoking some higher power, and cried out in a voice that echoed through the hall:

"I shake the dust from my feet, and I curse you! Yes, I curse you all! This is the end—the end!"

And with that, he turned abruptly and fled behind the scenes, waving his hands wildly as though casting off some unbearable burden. His exit left the hall in an uproar, with the more volatile members of the crowd shouting, "He's insulted us! Verhovensky! Verhovensky!" A few even surged toward the platform, as if intending to pursue him.

But before they could act, another shock descended upon the already chaotic scene. The third reader—the peculiar man with the clenched fists who had been pacing behind the curtain—suddenly burst onto the platform. His appearance was nothing short of alarming. His broad smile and wild, triumphant eyes radiated a manic energy. It was clear he had been eagerly awaiting this moment of disorder.

"Ladies and gentlemen!" he shouted, his shrill and piercing voice cutting through the noise. "Ladies and gentlemen, please, listen to me!"

The audience fell silent for a moment, caught off guard by his sheer audacity. People turned to one another, whispering, "Who is this? What does he want?"

The man stepped boldly to the very edge of the platform, surveying the crowd with an air of boundless self-assurance. "Twenty years ago," he began, "on the eve of war with half of Europe, Russia was hailed as an ideal country by officials of every rank. Our literature bowed to the censorship, our universities taught nothing but military drill, and our soldiers were trained like dancers. Peasants paid taxes with their backs under the lash of serfdom, and patriotism meant squeezing bribes from the living and the dead alike!"

His words were delivered with such passion and vehemence that the audience was momentarily stunned into silence. But as he continued, his tone growing more scathing and dramatic, the murmurs of confusion and disapproval began to rise again. The chaos that had momentarily abated threatened to engulf the hall once more.

He raised his fist high above his head, his face alight with an ecstatic and menacing fervor, and then brought it down with all his strength, as though smashing an invisible adversary into dust. The gesture seemed to electrify the room. A frenzied roar erupted from the audience, shaking the hall to its very rafters. Applause, wild and unrestrained, echoed from almost half the crowd, their enthusiasm bursting forth like a tidal wave. It was a moment of catharsis for many—a public shaming of Russia, brazen and unfiltered, laid bare for all to witness. Who among them could resist cheering?

"This is it! Finally, the real deal! None of your pretentious aesthetics!" someone shouted, barely audible over the uproar.

"Yes, this is it! Hurrah!" cried another voice.

The orator, his energy unfaltering, continued his tirade with manic fervor:

"Twenty years have passed! Universities have been built and multiplied! The era of military drills has faded into legend; officers are short by the thousands. The railways, like ravenous beasts, have devoured the nation's capital and sprawled across Russia in a tangle, so chaotic that perhaps, in another fifteen years, one might even get somewhere! Fires in the towns, once capricious, now occur like clockwork, in due season, as though ordained. Judgments in the courts flow with the wisdom of Solomon, while the jury take bribes not from greed but from sheer desperation in their 'struggle for existence'! The serfs are free—oh, yes, free indeed—to flog one another instead of enduring the lash of the landowners. Seas of vodka drown the nation to keep the budget afloat, and across from the ancient and now meaningless St. Sophia of Novgorod rises a colossal bronze globe—a grotesque monument to a thousand years of chaos and confusion! Europe scowls at us, uneasy once more.... And after fifteen years of reforms, reforms upon reforms, what do we find? Never has Russia..."

The rest of his words were swallowed in a deafening cacophony. Cheers, clapping, and shouts erupted anew. People leapt to their feet, their excitement knowing no bounds. Some of the more excitable audience members were hollering incomprehensibly; even a few women joined the shouting, while others clapped their hands fervently. "Enough! Nothing can top that!" someone screamed in exhilaration. It seemed as though the crowd had lost all sense of decorum. A few voices slurred their cheers—perhaps drunkenly—but the overwhelming tide of enthusiasm swept even them along.

The orator stood at the edge of the platform, scanning the chaos he had incited with something akin to rapture. His face glowed with triumph as his eyes darted from one ecstatic face to another, seeming to drink in the spectacle of his own making. It was as if he thrived on their disorder, reveling in their adulation.

In the midst of this pandemonium, I noticed Lembke in the crowd. He appeared to be in an indescribable state, gesturing wildly and pointing something out to a nearby official. His movements were frantic, almost incoherent, while his face was a mask of agitation. Nearby, Yulia Mihailovna, pale and visibly shaken, leaned toward the prince, speaking rapidly and gesturing with urgency. Whatever she said seemed to heighten his alarm.

At that moment, a group of six men—officials, judging by their demeanor—charged onto the platform. They seized the orator, grabbing him roughly by the arms and attempting to drag him away. The orator resisted with surprising strength, his voice still ringing out above the chaos. Somehow, impossibly, he wrenched himself free. Darting back to the edge of the platform, he managed to shout once more, his fist raised in the air:

"But never has Russia sunk…"

Before he could finish, they seized him again. This time, a second group of fifteen men stormed the stage—not by crossing it in an orderly fashion but by tearing down the flimsy screen at its side. They rushed behind the scenes, seemingly determined to rescue him. The noise and confusion doubled as they collided with the first group, their scuffle hidden from the audience but audible in the shouts and crashing sounds that emanated from backstage.

And then, as though the madness had not reached its peak, I caught sight of a new figure mounting the stage. It was the plump and rosy-faced girl student, Virginsky's sister. She carried her familiar roll of paper under her arm, her expression resolute, and she was flanked by a small entourage of two or three women and an equal number of men. To my utter astonishment, beside her stood her mortal enemy, the fiery schoolboy who had earlier been her antagonist. Together they advanced to the center of the platform.

"Ladies and gentlemen!" she declared loudly, her voice piercing through the din. "I have come to draw attention to the plight of poor students and to rouse them to a general protest—"

I heard no more. My instincts took over, and I fled. Slipping through the chaos, I shoved my steward's badge deep into my pocket and took refuge in the back passages of the building. The sounds of the uproar faded behind me as I made my way into the street. My only thought was to reach Stepan Trofimovitch's house, as if his presence might restore some semblance of sanity to this surreal and spiraling disaster.

Chapter 2
The End of The Fete

Chapter 2.1

He refused to see me. From behind his locked door, his voice—calm yet resolute—declared:

"My friend, I have completed everything that was required of me. What more can anyone demand?"

I persisted, knocking harder, pleading through the barrier of wood.

"You've completed nothing," I exclaimed. "You've only made a chaotic situation worse. Stepan Trofimovitch, for God's sake, no epigrams now! Open the door. We must act quickly; they might come here to insult you—or worse!"

I allowed my frustration to overtake me. The events of the day, the escalating chaos, and my genuine concern for him gave me a sense of entitlement to be both stern and unyielding. I feared he was brooding over some new folly, but to my astonishment, his response revealed an unexpected firmness.

"Do not be the first to insult me, then," he retorted. "I thank you for the past, but I repeat—I am finished with all men, both good and bad. I am writing to Darya Pavlovna, whom I have inexcusably neglected till now. You may deliver this letter to her tomorrow if you wish. Beyond that—merci."

"Stepan Trofimovitch," I implored, my tone harsher than I intended, "this situation is far more serious than you seem to realize. Do you think your performance has crushed anyone? You've crushed no one—only shattered yourself like a fragile, empty bottle."

Yes, I was coarse. I recall those words with shame. He, however, remained unperturbed.

"You have no reason to write to Darya Pavlovna," I added hastily. "And what will you do with yourself without me? You have no sense of practical life—none at all. I know you're plotting something again, aren't you? You'll only make another mess!"

I heard him rise. He approached the door, and his voice, low and deliberate, carried through the keyhole with unexpected gravitas.

"My dear boy, you have been among them such a short time, yet you have already absorbed their coarse tone and manner. Dieu vous pardonne, mon ami, et Dieu vous garde. Yet, I have always believed you capable of delicate feeling, and I trust you will outgrow this phase—après le temps, as we Russians so often must. As for my so-called impracticality, let me remind you of an observation I recently shared: in this country, countless people do little else but denounce others for impracticality with all the persistence of summer flies, attacking everyone but themselves. Cher ami, I am agitated, so I beg you not to distress me further."

There was a pause, as though he were gathering his words with great care. Then he continued, his tone adopting a more reflective and ironic edge.

"Once again, merci for everything. Let us part now, as Karmazinov bade farewell to his audience—with as much mutual generosity as we can muster. Though Karmazinov's plea to be forgotten was merely a pose, I lack such conceit. I place my hopes in the youth of your inexperienced heart. Surely, you will not long remember a futile old man such as myself. Live more, my friend, as Nastasya, the housemaid, advised me on my last name day. Ces pauvres gens, they sometimes speak with a charming, almost philosophical simplicity."

I stood silent, clutching at the sliver of the doorframe, as though my grip could somehow convey the urgency he would not hear. He went on, his tone softening yet maintaining its ironic detachment.

"I do not wish you much happiness—it will only bore you. Nor do I wish you much suffering. But, following the philosophy of the peasant, I say simply this: live more, and strive not to grow too weary of life. This, at least, I add from myself. Now, good-bye, and good-bye for good. Do not stand at my door—I will not open it."

He moved away from the door, his footsteps fading into the stillness beyond it. I called his name once more, but there was no reply.

For all his declarations of "excitement," his voice had been measured, deliberate, and strangely composed, as though he were performing for an unseen audience. It was evident that he was slightly vexed with me, his tone carrying subtle hints of wounded pride. Perhaps he was avenging himself for the coarse candor I had shown him the day before, or for the indignity of shedding public tears in the morning—a triumphal moment turned faintly comic, a fact that would have stung his sensitive pride.

He valued his dignity above all else, even with his closest friends. But his ironic detachment and calculated formality, rather than comforting me, gave me false confidence. I told myself that such a man, so concerned with appearances, could not be on the verge of anything tragic. He was far too steady, too composed.

How catastrophically I misjudged him. I had left out too much in my reasoning, had overlooked too many subtleties. And so I left, chastising myself but reassured—for the moment.

In anticipation of later events, I will quote the opening lines of the letter that Stepan Trofimovitch wrote to Darya Pavlovna—a letter she indeed received the very next day:

"Mon enfant, my hand trembles as I write, but I have finished with everything. You were absent from my last struggle; you chose not to attend the matinée, and you were right to stay away. But you will hear, no doubt, that in this Russia of ours, so impoverished in men of genuine character, one man found the courage to stand and proclaim the truth— proclaim it boldly, in the face of deadly threats hurled at him from every side. He dared to tell the fools that they are fools. Ah, ce sont des pauvres petits vauriens et rien de plus, des petits—fools—voilà le mot! The die is cast. I am leaving this town forever, and I do not know where I shall go. Every person I loved has turned away from me.

"But you—you are pure, you are naïve, you are unspoiled. You, whose gentle soul was nearly bound to mine by the capricious and imperious will of another heart; you, who perhaps looked at me with contempt on the eve of our thwarted union when I shed those pitiful tears; you, who, in any case, can only see me as a ridiculous and comical figure—for you, mon enfant, for you is this last cry of my heart. For you alone I write this, my final duty. I cannot vanish from your life forever leaving you to think of me as an ungrateful fool, a coarse and selfish egoist. Yet, I fear that this is how a cruel and implacable heart—one whom, alas, I cannot forget—speaks of me to you every day...."

And so the letter rambled on for four large, densely filled pages.

When I reflect on that letter now, I can see how perfectly it encapsulated the man's essence: his vanity, his wounded pride, his capacity for self-pity mingled with genuine pathos, and, above all, his need to stage even his departures and failures as if they were dramatic acts in some grand personal narrative. Yet, at the time, I had neither the patience nor the composure to analyze it.

After his resolute refusal to open the door and his dismissive declarations, I had shouted at him through the door with a burst of frustrated defiance:

"You'll send Nastasya running after me three times today, begging me to come back—but I won't come! Do you hear me? I won't come!"

With that, I pounded on the door three times with my fist, as though each knock might penetrate his barricaded retreat. But when no answer came, I finally surrendered, turned away, and left him to his solitude. I didn't look back as I ran off, this time heading straight for Yulia Mihailovna. It seemed the only course left to me at that moment, though deep down, I already suspected it would lead to nothing but fresh chaos.

Chapter 2.2

I was witness to a deeply distressing scene, a revolting spectacle in which a woman was blatantly deceived, right before my eyes, and I found myself utterly powerless to intervene. What could I have said to her? By then, I had already reconsidered my position, realizing that I had no concrete evidence to act upon—nothing but a vague unease, a collection of instincts and forebodings that amounted to little more than suspicion.

When I arrived, I found her in a state of near hysteria, her face streaked with tears and her hands trembling as she clutched a glass of water. Compresses soaked in eau-de-Cologne were pressed to her forehead as if to steady her. Before her stood Pyotr Stepanovitch, talking incessantly, and the prince, whose silence seemed as though it had been locked and bolted. With choking sobs and words that quavered, Yulia Mihailovna reproached Pyotr Stepanovitch for his perceived desertion. What struck me immediately was her belief that his absence was the sole cause of the morning's disaster—the entire ignominy of the matinée, all its public humiliation, rested squarely, in her mind, on his shoulders.

In Pyotr Stepanovitch, I noted an unusual shift: he seemed slightly anxious, almost serious—traits entirely foreign to his usual demeanor. Ordinarily, even when angry (and he was often angry), he had a mocking, almost gleeful quality, always laughing, even at his own vexation. But now, his tone was coarse, sharp, and tinged with impatience. He claimed that he had been unwell, that he had fallen ill while visiting Gaganov's lodgings early that morning. The poor woman, desperate for reassurance, seemed ready—almost eager—to believe him once again.

The main topic of their discussion, which I found myself dragged into, was whether or not the ball—the second and supposedly grander half of the fête—should proceed as planned. Yulia Mihailovna insisted that she could not bring herself to appear at the ball after the morning's insults and mortifications. Yet it was clear, even to me, that beneath her declarations was an unspoken desire: she wanted to be persuaded otherwise, and not by anyone, but specifically by Pyotr Stepanovitch. He had become her oracle, the center of her schemes and dreams of influence, and I could see that if he abandoned her, she would collapse entirely, perhaps even take to her bed in defeat.

But Pyotr Stepanovitch had no intention of abandoning her; on the contrary, he was determined that the ball should go on and that she must make an appearance. He pressed her relentlessly, brushing aside her protests with a mix of irritation and urgency.

"Come now, what's there to cry about?" he said brusquely. "Do you need to have a scene, to vent your anger on someone? Well, vent it on me if you like—but make it quick, because time is passing, and you need to make up your mind. We bungled the matinée, but we can salvage everything with the ball. Isn't that right, Prince?"

He turned pointedly to the prince, who had initially expressed opposition to the ball—or, more precisely, to Yulia Mihailovna attending it. But Pyotr Stepanovitch's repeated references to his opinion, laced with subtle manipulations, gradually wore him down. The prince began to grunt vague affirmations, his earlier resistance eroded.

I was shocked not only by the forcefulness of Pyotr Stepanovitch's tone but by its outright rudeness. It was appalling, and yet I could not intervene. Later, I heard despicable rumors about some supposed liaison between Pyotr Stepanovitch and Yulia Mihailovna, rumors I reject with the utmost indignation. Such a relationship was not only impossible but absurd. His control over her was rooted not in intimacy but in flattery—gross, calculated flattery—and his skill in exploiting her ambitions. He had fueled her dreams of social and political influence, feeding her plans and making himself indispensable. Now, she relied on him as though he were the air she breathed.

When she noticed me, her tear-streaked face lit with a flash of angry determination.

"Ask him!" she cried, her voice quaking with emotion. "He was there beside me the whole time, just as the prince was. Tell me, isn't it obvious that this was a prearranged plot? A vile, deliberate scheme to discredit Andrey Antonovitch and me as much as possible? Oh, they had a plan! It's a party, a faction!"

"You exaggerate as always," Pyotr Stepanovitch interjected with a sneer. "You've always got some romantic notion stuck in your head. But since he's here, let's hear his opinion." He pretended, with a theatrical pause, to have forgotten my name.

"My opinion," I began sharply, determined not to falter, "is the same as Yulia Mihailovna's. The plot is clear—only too clear. I've brought these ribbons for you, Yulia Mihailovna. As for the ball, whether it proceeds or not is not for me to decide; I'm no longer involved. My duties as a steward are over, and I must excuse myself. Forgive me, but I cannot act against common sense or my own convictions."

I placed the ribbons on the table and turned away, unable to bear any more of the scene. I felt a deep and growing unease—not just about the situation but about my inability to change its course.

"You hear! You hear!" she exclaimed, clasping her hands together as if to ward off some invisible threat. Her voice trembled with indignation, her eyes wide with disbelief.

"I hear perfectly well," Pyotr Stepanovitch responded with a deliberate calmness that bordered on derision. Turning to me with a sharp look, he added, "And let me tell you this: all of you are acting like you've collectively lost your wits. To my thinking, absolutely nothing extraordinary has occurred. Nothing has happened here today that hasn't happened before or couldn't have been anticipated in this town. A plot, you say? Nonsense! This was nothing more than a poorly executed debacle, a disgracefully stupid one at that. But a plot? Against Yulia Mihailovna?" He laughed dryly, shaking his head. "Against a woman who has pampered them, shielded them, and indulged their juvenile antics? It's absurd."

He pressed on, ignoring her attempts to interrupt. "What have I been telling you for the last month? What have I been hammering into your head incessantly? What did I warn you about? What was the point of all this, bringing these people together, these individuals who could never and would never unite under any circumstances? What did you think you were achieving by involving yourself with this riffraff? What was the purpose, the aim? To unite society?" He let out a derisive snort. "But good heavens, could you ever expect such people to unite? It's a farce."

"When did you warn me?" Yulia Mihailovna cried out, her voice cracking under the weight of her emotions. "You didn't warn me—you approved of it! You encouraged it! You insisted on it! I can't believe what I'm hearing from you now. You even brought these strange people to see me yourself!"

"On the contrary," he countered, his tone growing sharper. "I never approved, never supported it. Yes, I brought some of them, but only after you'd already opened the floodgates and let them pour in by the dozens. And only later, mind you, to fill in gaps in your so-called 'literary quadrille.' It was a circus, and we couldn't proceed without a few clowns. But don't think for a moment that I didn't see this coming. I'll bet you anything that at least a dozen more riffraff slipped in today without tickets."

"Not a doubt of it," I interjected reluctantly, sensing the escalating tension.

"There, you see?" Pyotr Stepanovitch exclaimed triumphantly. "Even he agrees. Just think about the tone that's prevailed in this wretched town lately—the audacity, the impudence, the constant scandals. Who has been encouraging it? Who's been shielding them with her authority, enabling their antics? Who has been turning the smallest fish into puffed-up little sharks? And those caricatures in your album—family secrets mocked openly! Wasn't it you who patted those poets and satirists on the back, wasn't it you who let Lyamshin kiss your hand as if he were some sort of courtier? Didn't you laugh along when a divinity student insulted a state councillor in your presence, ruining his daughter's dress with his filthy tarred boots? And now you're surprised the public has turned against you?"

She gasped, her face pale with a mixture of rage and hurt. "It was you—you caused all of this! You pushed me into it! Oh, my goodness!"

"No," he said firmly, his voice rising. "I warned you—repeatedly. We even quarreled about it. Do you hear me? We quarreled!"

"You're lying!" she screamed, her composure breaking entirely. "You're lying to my face!"

"Of course it's easy for you to say that," he replied coldly, his tone laced with disdain. "You need someone to blame, a scapegoat to unload your fury on. Well, go ahead, vent it on me. I told you, I'm ready to be your sacrificial lamb."

He turned to me abruptly. "And you," he continued, "what do you think? Let's dissect this step by step. I maintain that aside from Liputin's idiocy, there was no premeditated plot. None! Do you honestly think what Liputin did was part of some grand conspiracy? I'll tell you what happened: he thought it would be clever, a cheap laugh, nothing more. He probably believed he was entertaining everyone, Yulia Mihailovna included."

"You can't be serious!" she burst out, her voice trembling with indignation. "You're calling that garbage clever? Those verses—so crude, so tactless, so utterly contemptible—were intentional! You must be saying this on purpose, just to taunt me. I'm starting to think you're in on it, part of the plot yourself!"

Her words rang out, heavy with accusation, as the tension in the room reached an unbearable pitch.

"Of course, I was behind the scenes. I was in hiding. I set it all in motion. But, let me clarify one thing—if I were truly part of a conspiracy, as you claim, it certainly wouldn't have ended with Liputin's little fiasco. Do you mean to suggest that I even coordinated with my father to stage such a scene on purpose? Come now, think about it. Whose fault is it that my father was allowed to take the platform and read? Who made the decision? And, who was it that tried to stop you just yesterday from letting him do it, warning you about the potential consequences?"

Yulia Mihailovna looked both indignant and bewildered. "Oh, but hier il avait tant d'esprit! Yesterday, I was counting on him! He has such manners, such style. I thought he and Karmazinov would elevate the occasion. Only think of it!"

"Yes, only think of it," Pyotr Stepanovitch retorted with biting sarcasm. "And yet, despite his supposed esprit, he has made an utter mess of everything. If I'd known just how bad it would turn out, I would never have persuaded you yesterday to keep the goat out of the kitchen garden, as they say. You must admit, I tried to dissuade you. I foresaw it might go wrong—though not quite to this extent. But these nervous old men are unpredictable; they can't be counted on like others. He probably didn't know himself what he'd end up saying until the words were already out of his mouth."

He smirked briefly before continuing. "But you can still salvage the situation. To quell the outrage, send two doctors to him tomorrow, by administrative order, with all the ceremonial trappings. Have them inquire into his mental health and, if necessary, take him to a hospital for observation. Apply cold compresses, wrap him in officialdom. People will laugh, yes, but it'll defuse the tension. I'll even make light of it at the ball tonight, as his son. Let the audience see there was nothing malicious in it."

"As for Karmazinov," he continued, "well, he's a separate matter entirely. The man dragged out his article for an entire hour, drowning everyone in his own self-conceit. If anyone was in a plot to sabotage your fête, it was certainly him. He must have thought, 'I'll make a fool of myself too, just to bring Yulia Mihailovna down a notch.'"

"Quelle honte! Karmazinov was unbearable!" she exclaimed, her hands trembling with frustration. "I burned with shame for his audience. I could hardly bear to look at them!"

"You shouldn't have burned with shame—you should've cooked him instead!" Pyotr Stepanovitch snapped, his tone sharp. "The audience was right to react as they did. Who was responsible for Karmazinov, though? Not me. Did I bring him to you? Was I one of his admirers? Let him hang himself, I say. But the third maniac, the political firebrand—now that's a different story altogether. That disaster wasn't solely my doing; it was everyone's blunder."

Yulia Mihailovna visibly paled at the mention of the third speaker. "Oh, don't speak of him! It was dreadful, dreadful! That was entirely my fault."

"Of course it was, but I don't hold it against you," Pyotr Stepanovitch replied, his tone oddly conciliatory. "These candid souls—they're impossible to predict or control. Even in Petersburg, they cause trouble. He came highly recommended, didn't he? Glowing terms, no less! But now you have a duty: you must appear at the ball tonight. It's imperative. You need to make it clear to the public that you had nothing to do with his ravings, that he was a madman, and that you, too, were deceived. You must denounce him with indignation, as a victim of his madness. Because that's all he is—a madman. Not someone you would ever align yourself with."

"But they're saying—" she began hesitantly, her voice breaking.

"They're saying what?" Pyotr Stepanovitch interrupted.

"They're saying something about a senator. I've heard whispers, rumors," she admitted, her face flushing deeply.

"Ah, the senator rumor," he said, nodding with exaggerated understanding. "Yes, it's all over town. They believe a senator has been appointed to replace you and Andrey Antonovitch, that you're being superseded by orders from Petersburg. Absurd, of course, but that's what people are saying."

"Who started such nonsense?" she demanded, her voice rising.

"Who can say where it began?" he shrugged. "But it's being repeated everywhere. Even yesterday, I heard it from several people, and they were dead serious about it. It's all the more reason for you to go to the ball tonight, to show these fools how utterly ridiculous their ideas are."

"I suppose you're right," she murmured, though her hesitation was palpable. "But what if no one comes? What if people stay away out of spite? I can't bear the thought of facing another humiliation."

"No one will come? Really, Yulia Mihailovna, have you lost all perspective? Think of the dresses, the new gowns, the expense. Do you think the women in this town will pass up the chance to parade in their finery? The very idea is absurd!"

"But the marshal's wife—she won't come. I know she won't."

"And what has she to be angry about?" Pyotr Stepanovitch shot back. "What, exactly, has happened that is so unforgivable? The failure of the matinée? That was the fault of rowdy troublemakers, nothing more. If anything, the respectable members of society—your patresfamilias— should have done more to maintain order. Instead, they sulked and stayed silent. But this is precisely why society must learn to protect itself. The police can't be everywhere at once."

His words hung in the air, and for a moment, no one spoke. Finally, with visible reluctance, Yulia Mihailovna nodded. "Very well," she said softly. "I'll go to the ball."

"Ah, that is the simple truth! They sit quietly, sulking, and simply gaze about them, as though waiting for someone else to act," Pyotr

Stepanovitch declared with a hint of mockery in his tone.

"And if it's the truth," he continued with more fervor, "you should say it aloud—proudly, sternly—to those respectable citizens, those venerable mothers of families. Let them see that you are not defeated. You, Yulia Mihailovna, have the gift for such moments, when your head is clear. Gather them around you and speak with the authority and confidence they expect. Let them know what you stand for. Imagine a strong paragraph about your stance appearing in The Voice or the Financial News. Just wait—I'll handle that for you myself, make sure the narrative is favorable. But there's still so much to manage—buffet arrangements, the prince's involvement, and, of course, Andrey Antonovitch. You must appear arm-in-arm with him. Speaking of which, how is Andrey Antonovitch?"

At this sudden mention, Yulia Mihailovna's face flushed with emotion. She clasped a handkerchief to her eyes, and her voice trembled with a mixture of indignation and pain. "Oh, how unjustly, how cruelly, how untruthfully you've always judged that angelic man!"

Pyotr Stepanovitch appeared momentarily taken aback. "Good heavens! I? What have I ever said against him? I've always—"

"Never!" she interrupted passionately. "Never have you done him justice! You've always misunderstood him."

"There's no understanding a woman," he muttered under his breath, a sardonic smile curling his lips.

"He is the most sincere, the most delicate, the most angelic of men! The kindest-hearted man alive!" she exclaimed, her voice breaking.

"Well, really, as for kind-heartedness ... I've always acknowledged that about him," Pyotr Stepanovitch responded, though his tone betrayed his irritation.

"Never! Never! But let us drop the subject," she said abruptly, clearly struggling to compose herself. "I am too clumsy in defending him. Besides, this morning that insufferable little Jesuit, the marshal's wife, dropped her own sly, sarcastic hints about yesterday's events. Can you imagine?"

"Oh, she's moved on from yesterday already," Pyotr Stepanovitch said dismissively. "She's consumed with today's drama. Why are you so upset at her absence from the ball tonight? Naturally, she won't come after her involvement in such a scandal. Maybe it wasn't entirely her fault, but her reputation … well, her hands are stained."

"What do you mean? Her hands are stained?" Yulia Mihailovna asked, perplexed.

"I can't vouch for its truth," he replied, his voice suddenly lowering, as though confiding a grave secret, "but the town is buzzing with rumors. They say she was the one who facilitated the meeting."

"Facilitated? Facilitated what? Who?" she demanded, her bewilderment deepening.

"Come now," Pyotr Stepanovitch said with feigned surprise. "You mean to tell me you don't know? Phew! Well, it's quite the romantic tragedy. They say that Lizaveta Nikolaevna, in broad daylight, got out of the marshal's wife's carriage, climbed straight into another carriage waiting nearby, and drove off—to Skvoreshniki—with Stavrogin."

"What? How? When?" came the collective outcry, disbelief etched on every face.

Pyotr Stepanovitch seemed to relish the astonishment around him. "Hardly an hour ago," he replied casually. "I was passing by and happened to witness it myself—quite by chance, of course."

The room fell into stunned silence. Yulia Mihailovna's face turned ashen. "Explain yourself. How did it happen?" she demanded.

He gave a theatrical shrug. "It's all very simple. When the marshal's wife was driving Liza and Mavriky Nikolaevitch back from the matinée to visit Praskovya Ivanovna, they passed a carriage waiting a short distance away from the front door. Liza jumped out, ran straight to it, got in, and the carriage sped off toward Skvoreshniki. She even called out to Mavriky Nikolaevitch, 'Spare me,' before disappearing."

"And Stavrogin?" someone asked, almost breathlessly.

Pyotr Stepanovitch spread his hands. "I didn't see him. Maybe he wasn't in the carriage—perhaps just the old butler, Alexey Yegorytch. But where else would she go if not to him?"

"And Mavriky Nikolaevitch?" Yulia Mihailovna pressed, her voice trembling.

"Did nothing. He didn't pursue her, didn't even try to stop her. In fact, he restrained the marshal's wife when she started screaming, 'She's going to Stavrogin!'"

The revelation struck like a thunderclap. At that moment, I couldn't contain my fury. "It's your doing!" I shouted, pointing an accusatory finger at Pyotr Stepanovitch. "You schemed with Stavrogin! You orchestrated it all! You helped her into that carriage. You're behind everything!"

Pyotr Stepanovitch turned toward me with an expression of mock innocence. "Oh, come now," he said with exaggerated patience. "Why would I—"

"You're her enemy, Yulia Mihailovna!" I cried, cutting him off. "You'll ruin her, just as you ruin everything you touch. Mark my words— beware of him!"

I ran out of the house in a state of uncontrollable agitation, my mind a blur of anger and confusion. Even now, I cannot fully comprehend what drove me to speak so sharply to Pyotr Stepanovitch, nor how I managed to articulate my accusations with such precision. Yet, in hindsight, my suspicions proved remarkably accurate; events had unfolded almost exactly as I had implied. What stood out most was the peculiar, almost calculated manner in which he revealed the news. He had not come in announcing it with the shock and significance it warranted but acted as though we already knew—an impossibility, given the short time since the incident. Furthermore, had we known, we could not have kept silent until he broached the topic. His insinuation that the town was already "ringing with gossip" about the marshal's wife was equally implausible within such a brief span. Most damning of all, he had twice smirked in a crude, self-satisfied way, as if amused by how thoroughly he believed he had deceived us.

But I had no energy left to spare for him or his connivance. The raw fact of the catastrophe consumed me, cutting deeply into my emotions. It pained me to my core, and I found myself trembling with a mixture of despair and helplessness. Tears may have come; I cannot recall for certain. At that moment, I felt utterly lost. My first instinct was to go to Stepan Trofimovitch. Surely, he would understand the gravity of what had happened and help make sense of it. But, to my exasperation, he refused to open his door yet again. Nastasya whispered with reverence that he had gone to bed, but I did not believe her. It seemed impossible for him to remain indifferent at such a time.

Desperation drove me next to Liza's house. There, I was able to speak briefly with the servants, who confirmed the truth of her elopement but knew little more. The household was in turmoil. Their mistress, Praskovya Ivanovna, had been overtaken by fainting fits, and Mavriky Nikolaevitch remained by her side. Though tempted, I refrained from asking to see him. Instead, I inquired indirectly about Pyotr Stepanovitch. The servants told me he had been in and out of the house frequently, sometimes twice a day, over the past week. They seemed subdued and unusually respectful when speaking of Liza, whom they clearly held in great affection.

The certainty that Liza's reputation was irreparably ruined weighed heavily on me. I could not fathom her actions, especially in light of the previous day's tumultuous encounter with Stavrogin. It seemed incomprehensible that she would act so recklessly. I felt no desire to parade around town gathering gossip from acquaintances, many of whom were likely reveling in the scandal. Such behavior struck me as both degrading and disrespectful to Liza's dignity. Yet, inexplicably, I found myself drawn to Darya Pavlovna's house.

No one admitted me there, as the household had been closed to visitors since the previous morning. What I intended to say to her or why I felt compelled to go remains a mystery even now. Thwarted, I redirected my steps to her brother Shatov's lodgings. He listened to my frantic account with visible irritation, his face set in a sullen scowl. His preoccupation was evident, and he responded to me only with apparent effort, saying little and pacing his small room with loud, deliberate steps. Finally, as I was leaving, he called out sharply, "Go to Liputin's—you'll hear everything there."

Though I considered his suggestion briefly, I ultimately decided against visiting Liputin. The thought of dealing with his smirking cynicism repelled me. Instead, I wandered aimlessly, only to find myself turning back toward Shatov's house once more. Without entering, I pushed open his door slightly and, with no explanation, suggested curtly, "Why don't you visit Marya Timofyevna today?" His response was a string of curses hurled in my direction as I withdrew.

Later, I learned that he had, indeed, gone to see Marya Timofyevna that evening. He found her in good health and high spirits, while Lebyadkin lay passed out drunk on a sofa in the adjoining room. This was at about nine o'clock, and Shatov himself shared the details with me the following day when we crossed paths briefly on the street.

By ten o'clock that night, unable to resist my curiosity, I resolved to attend the ball—not as a steward (for I had left my rosette at Yulia Mihailovna's) but as a silent observer. I was driven by an insatiable desire to gauge the town's reaction to the day's events and to see Yulia Mihailovna herself, even if only from a distance. Guilt gnawed at me for having left her so abruptly earlier that afternoon, and I wanted to understand the full scope of the fallout from the disastrous matinée.

Chapter 2.3

The events of that night, laden with grotesque incidents and culminating in a dreadful dénouement in the early morning, still linger in my memory as an oppressive nightmare. It remains, for me, the most agonizing chapter of this chronicle. I arrived late to the ball, only to discover it was already unraveling, its fate sealed before I could witness much of it. When I reached the entrance of the marshal's house at eleven o'clock, the same White Hall that had hosted the disastrous matinée earlier in the day had been transformed into the main ballroom, hastily prepared to host what was intended to be a grand event. Yet, the expectations for this gathering had already crumbled into something unrecognizable.

From the start, the ball's failure was apparent. Not a single family of the higher social circles was in attendance. Even the more prominent subordinate officials were conspicuously absent—a glaring statement in itself. Pyotr Stepanovitch's earlier assurances about the success of the event now seemed woefully detached from reality, his duplicity evident. The women and girls he had insisted would flock to the ball were almost entirely missing. Of those who did attend, their numbers were meager— so much so that for every four men, there was scarcely one woman. And as for the women who were present, they were far from the kind of attendees Yulia Mihailovna had envisioned.

Among them were a handful of regimental wives of questionable demeanor, three local doctors' wives accompanied by their daughters, a few impoverished ladies from the countryside, and the secretary with his seven daughters and a niece—an unfortunate spectacle I had already observed at the matinée. Rounding out this gathering were the wives of small tradesmen and low-ranking clerks, as well as other obscure and insignificant figures. Not even a substantial portion of the town's tradespeople had bothered to attend.

The male attendees, though more numerous, created an unsettling impression. There were, to be fair, some respectable officers present with their wives, along with docile, unassuming fathers of families like the aforementioned secretary. But beyond this small contingent of innocuous attendees, the remaining crowd appeared dubious at best. Many seemed out of place, a ragtag assortment of "free-and-easy" types. Among them were individuals whom Pyotr Stepanovitch and I had earlier suspected of entering the matinée without tickets. Their presence now at the ball seemed both deliberate and troubling.

A peculiar detail I noticed was how this questionable element appeared to converge almost immediately in the refreshment bar upon their arrival. It was as though they had prearranged this as their meeting point. This bar had been set up in a large room at the far end of the suite of interconnected chambers. There, Prohoritch presided over an array of tempting drinks and delicacies provided by the club's kitchen. Yet the people occupying this space were far from the refined guests one might expect. Several men wore tattered coats, their entire appearance more suited to a tavern than a ballroom. They were visibly unfit for such an event, with many seemingly hauled from places of debauchery and hastily sobered up just enough to attend. Their sobriety, however, was clearly temporary. I could only speculate on where they had been found and what purpose their presence served, for they were strangers to our town.

It was well known that Yulia Mihailovna had envisioned the ball as a democratic affair, one that welcomed "even working people and shopmen" if they were willing to pay for a ticket. In her committee meetings, she had spoken with brave rhetoric about inclusivity, confident that the impoverished working people of our town, who could scarcely afford such luxuries, would never actually take advantage of this offer. But the sinister-looking attendees who now filled the refreshment bar did not seem to belong to this category. Who had admitted them, and with what motive? These questions gnawed at me.

Adding to my unease, I noticed significant changes among the stewards. Lyamshin and Liputin, who had been stripped of their steward's rosettes after their disgraceful conduct at the matinée, were still present at the ball, but no longer in official capacities. However, to my astonishment, their places had been filled by even more questionable figures. The divinity student who had created a scandal at the matinée with his outburst against Stepan Trofimovitch now wore a steward's rosette. Even more shockingly, Pyotr Stepanovitch himself had taken on a steward's role, striding about with an air of authority.

This development sent a chill down my spine. The replacement of stewards with such figures boded ill for the evening's proceedings. I couldn't help but sense that something ominous was brewing, and under these circumstances, the ball seemed poised for yet another catastrophe. The very presence of Pyotr Stepanovitch, with his duplicitous demeanor and capacity for manipulation, cast a shadow over the entire event. I braced myself for what was to come.

I tried to catch snippets of the conversations around me, though doing so was far from a pleasant task. The ideas being exchanged were so wild, so ludicrous, that they left me stunned. In one cluster of people, it was gravely asserted that Yulia Mihailovna herself had orchestrated Liza's elopement with Stavrogin and had been handsomely paid for her complicity. They even specified the sum she had supposedly received. It was alleged that the entire fête had been planned with this scheme in mind, which explained why half the town had boycotted the ball. They further claimed that this betrayal was the cause of Lembke's disordered state of mind, and, as some whispered with sinister glee, "his wife now had him completely under her thumb." Laughter accompanied these accusations—hoarse, raucous, and laden with malice.

The criticisms of the ball were equally ruthless. Voices rose to ridicule Yulia Mihailovna without hesitation or restraint, dissecting every misstep and perceived humiliation. The entire atmosphere of the refreshment bar, where much of this slander was taking place, was chaotic, drunk with disorder, and riddled with frenzied chatter. Conversations overlapped incoherently, making it nearly impossible to piece together any cohesive narrative. Yet amidst this uproar, there were pockets of calm. A few simple-hearted individuals were genuinely enjoying themselves, finding some measure of solace in the conviviality of the refreshment bar. Some military wives and their husbands, unperturbed by the rumors and scandals, made merry at the small tables, sipping tea and chatting as though nothing were amiss. Their laughter rang out incongruously, creating a bizarre juxtaposition to the growing tension that filled the hall.

Despite this, the stark reality was undeniable: sooner or later, this unruly mass of guests would pour into the ballroom. The thought of what might happen then was dreadful.

Meanwhile, in the White Hall, the prince had managed to organize three scant quadrilles, providing a temporary facade of normalcy. A handful of young ladies twirled to the music while their parents watched from the sidelines, relieved that their daughters were at least getting some enjoyment from the evening. Yet even among these onlookers, many were already calculating how to make a discreet exit before the chaos that everyone anticipated inevitably erupted. The pervasive certainty that "trouble would begin" loomed like a thundercloud over the ball.

As for Yulia Mihailovna, her state of mind was impossible to describe. I refrained from approaching her directly, though I moved close enough to observe her. She did not respond to my polite bow upon entering; in fact, I am certain she didn't even see me. Her face was rigid, marked by an expression of profound distress, her eyes restless and agitated, betraying a mix of contempt and pride. Yet she maintained her composure with visible effort. For whom was she enduring this torment? For what purpose? She should have left immediately—should have taken her husband and abandoned this debacle altogether. Yet she stayed.

It was evident from her countenance that her illusions had been shattered. She was fully aware of the hopelessness of her situation and had abandoned any remaining expectations. Remarkably, she did not even summon Pyotr Stepanovitch, who seemed to be actively avoiding her. I caught sight of him in the refreshment bar, where he was strikingly animated and lively, as though reveling in the unfolding chaos.

Yulia Mihailovna, however, refused to leave Andrey Antonovitch's side, clinging to him almost desperately. Yet, it was painfully clear that even she could no longer deny the truth about his condition. That morning, she would have fiercely rejected any suggestion that his mental state was deteriorating, but now her eyes were being opened to this reality as well.

From the moment I entered, I could see that Lembke looked worse than he had earlier in the day. He seemed adrift, as though lost in a fog of detachment, barely aware of his surroundings. Occasionally, he would glance around with an unexpected air of sternness—twice, he directed this severe gaze at me. At one point, he even began to speak, his voice loud and deliberate, but the words trailed off into silence. The incomplete statement threw a modest old clerk standing nearby into visible panic.

What struck me most was the peculiar behavior of the more subdued attendees. Even those who usually deferred to authority were now avoiding Yulia Mihailovna entirely. Yet, at the same time, they cast strange, almost unnerving glances at her husband—bold, unabashed stares that were entirely out of character for their typically submissive demeanor. The contrast was startling and deeply unsettling.

"Yes, that struck me too," Yulia Mihailovna later confessed to me, "and in that moment, I began to understand what was truly happening with Andrey Antonovitch."

Yes, Yulia Mihailovna bore the blame yet again! It seemed likely that after my departure, in a desperate attempt to salvage the evening, she had conferred with Pyotr Stepanovitch, agreeing not only that the ball should proceed but also that she must attend it herself. It must have taken every ounce of her willpower, along with a liberal use of her persuasive charms, to coax Andrey Antonovitch from his study, where he sat utterly crushed by the events of the matinée. Her success in bringing him to the ball only underscored her misery now—yet she refused to leave. Was it her pride keeping her tethered to the scene of humiliation, or had she simply lost her head entirely?

Despite her characteristic hauteur, she made efforts to engage with the few ladies present, attempting polite conversations interwoven with strained smiles and humility. But these overtures were met with cold monosyllables—barely concealed distrust and avoidance. The gulf between her and the others was insurmountable.

Among the attendees, the sole figure of undoubted importance was the distinguished general, whom I have mentioned before—the one who had, just after Stavrogin's duel with Gaganov, so symbolically opened the door to public dissatisfaction. He strolled through the rooms with measured dignity, pausing to observe the proceedings and making an effort to appear more a curious onlooker than a participant. Eventually, he positioned himself firmly at Yulia Mihailovna's side, evidently with the intention of offering her consolation and support. He spoke incessantly, clearly striving to distract and steady her.

The general, though well-meaning and kind-hearted, was so advanced in age and so disconnected from the passions of the moment that even his compassion must have stung her pride. To find herself in a situation where this venerable but gossipy man not only pitied her but seemed to feel that his presence was a favor—it was almost unbearable. Yet, he stayed resolutely at her side, chattering amiably in an effort to fill the oppressive silence surrounding her.

"They say a town needs seven righteous men to keep it afloat," he began, "though I can't vouch for the number. I do wonder how many of those proverbial righteous are present here tonight. Even their presence doesn't make me feel entirely at ease. Vous me pardonnez, charmante dame, but I am speaking allegorically. I ventured into the refreshment room, and I'm glad I made it out unscathed. Our dear Prohoritch is nowhere to be seen, and I suspect his bar will be left in ruins by morning. But I digress. I'm staying only to see the much-discussed 'literary quadrille,' and then I shall retire. I advise you to do the same, my dear lady. Early to bed and all that."

He prattled on, veering into musings about the town's young women. "I came to observe the roses of our community," he continued. "There's one officer's wife—charming, distinctly charming—and the girls are fresh too, though there's a certain irregularity about Russian beauty. Lovely for two or three years at most, then they bloom out of shape entirely. Such a pity, really, though it gives rise to the woman's movement, if I understand it rightly."

Despite his best intentions, the general's ramblings only underscored the absurdity of the evening. His complaints about the cancan dancers and the skirmishes in the refreshment bar highlighted the mounting chaos. His casual remarks about the absence of Varvara Petrovna's promised flowers and his vague allusions to Liza's rumored elopement added to the discomfort. And yet, even he, at his advanced age, remained out of a strange sense of duty—or perhaps sheer curiosity.

Finally, after much anticipation, the infamous "literary quadrille" began. This had been a hot topic of conversation for weeks, a point of wild speculation and enormous curiosity. Yet the heightened expectations only set the stage for the inevitable letdown.

The side doors of the White Hall swung open, and masked figures stepped into view. A surge of onlookers flooded into the hall, eager to witness this bizarre spectacle. The masked participants took their places for the dance as the crowd pressed closer, murmuring in anticipation. I managed to maneuver my way to a spot directly behind Yulia Mihailovna, Von Lembke, and the general.

At that moment, Pyotr Stepanovitch appeared as if from nowhere. He sidled up to Yulia Mihailovna with the demeanor of a schoolboy caught in mischief. Whispering in a tone dripping with mock contrition, he confessed, "I've been in the refreshment room all this time, observing."

The sight of him sent a flush of anger to her cheeks. Her voice, trembling with suppressed fury, broke through the murmurs of the crowd. "You might at least stop trying to deceive me now, you insolent man!"

Her words, though not shouted, carried enough force to be overheard by others nearby. Pyotr Stepanovitch, unfazed, danced away with a self-satisfied smirk, leaving her seething. It was clear that his aim had been not only to provoke her but to revel in her growing humiliation.

And the ball, with all its absurdity and disgrace, pressed on toward its inevitable collapse.

It is almost impossible to convey the full absurdity, the pitiful banality, and the overwhelming dullness of this so-called "literary quadrille." It was a grotesque attempt at allegory that failed so miserably it became almost painful to witness. The entire performance was so utterly out of place in our provincial society that one could scarcely imagine a more glaring misstep. And yet, it was said to have originated from none other than Karmazinov himself. While Liputin, aided by the lame schoolteacher who had attended the infamous meeting at Virginsky's, handled the arrangements, the concept was reportedly Karmazinov's brainchild. In fact, it was rumored that he had intended to participate in the quadrille personally, dressed in some special and prominently symbolic guise.

The "literary quadrille" featured six pairs of masked dancers, none of whom wore true costumes. Their attire was indistinguishable from that of the rest of the attendees, save for minor, almost laughable embellishments. For example, one short, elderly gentleman wore a grey, artificial beard tied on over his regular dress coat. This beard was his sole "disguise." He shuffled on the spot with tiny, rapid steps, maintaining a stolid and humorless expression as he emitted husky bass sounds, which were evidently meant to parody one of the prominent newspapers of the time.

Opposite this bearded figure danced two tall, awkward men, each with a large letter pinned to their coats—X and Z. Their significance was never explained, leaving the audience baffled as to what they symbolized. Another character, meant to represent "Honest Russian Thought," was portrayed by a middle-aged man in spectacles, a dress coat, and gloves, his wrists adorned with real iron fetters. Tucked under his arm was a portfolio said to contain documents from some legal "case," while a letter peeking from his pocket ostensibly testified to his honesty. This, of course, was all narrated by the stewards since the audience could not read the actual letter.

"Honest Russian Thought" held a raised glass in his right hand as though perpetually on the verge of proposing a toast. On either side of him tripped crop-haired young women, intended to embody Nihilist ideals. Facing him was another elderly man in formal attire, wielding a heavy cudgel meant to represent a formidable provincial periodical. Despite his threatening pose, the cudgel-wielding figure seemed unnerved by the unyielding gaze of "Honest Russian Thought" and frequently averted his eyes, as if writhing under the stings of his conscience. His awkward movements during the pas de deux were meant to signify his inner torment, but the effect was merely farcical.

The entire performance was a series of similarly ridiculous vignettes, all executed with such crude symbolism and ham-handed mockery that it became unbearable to watch. At first, the audience was silent, staring at the bizarre spectacle with a mix of confusion and growing anger. But as the performance dragged on, the silence gave way to a murmur, then to outright grumbling.

"What is this supposed to mean?" someone muttered, emerging from the refreshment bar and joining one of the small groups forming around the room.

"It's nonsense," another replied dismissively.

"They're mocking something literary," someone ventured, "a critique of The Voice maybe?"

"And why should I care?" came the retort, dripping with disdain.

In another cluster of onlookers, the irritation was more direct.

"Idiots!"

"No, it's not them who are idiots—it's us."

"Speak for yourself! I'm no idiot."

"Fine, then neither am I."

Elsewhere, voices grew louder and more belligerent.

"Someone should give them a good thrashing and send them packing!"

"Pull down the hall while we're at it!" another jeered.

One particularly cynical voice cut through the chaos: "I wonder the Lembkes aren't ashamed to sit through this!"

"Why should they be ashamed? Are you?"

"Yes, I am ashamed! And he's the governor, for heaven's sake."

"And you're a pig," someone shot back, to general laughter.

The atmosphere grew increasingly hostile. The performance, instead of entertaining, had succeeded only in stirring resentment, confusion, and scorn among the crowd. As the quadrille limped toward its conclusion, the crowd's anger seemed poised to erupt, leaving an air of uneasy anticipation hanging over the hall. It was evident that this grotesque farce had pushed the gathering one step closer to chaos.

The scene at the ball had descended into utter chaos, a mix of absurdity, rage, and blind panic. The tension had been mounting all evening, and now it was reaching a boiling point.

As the quadrille stumbled to its disastrous end, Yulia Mihailovna stood visibly distressed, trying in vain to maintain composure. Her attempt to deflect the taunt of a particularly vulgar and ill-mannered woman—a lady of questionable reputation and garish attire—was an early sign of her unraveling. The woman had made a pointed comment, loud enough for Yulia to hear, about the "commonplace" nature of the ball, a barb aimed at mocking its failure. When Yulia retorted sharply, the woman was all too eager to escalate the confrontation, but the general intervened, whispering to Yulia in a tone that mixed concern and insistence, urging her to leave while she still could.

But Yulia Mihailovna stayed. Pride, humiliation, or sheer bewilderment—who could say what held her there? And yet, staying was her undoing.

Meanwhile, Andrey Antonovitch, her husband, sat in a state that fluctuated between confusion and fury. As the ridiculous spectacle of the quadrille unfolded, he stared at the dancers, his face etched with a mix of incredulity and anger. The turning point came when Lyamshin, portraying the editor of the menacing non-Petersburg periodical, decided to cap the performance by walking on his head in the final figure of the dance. This ludicrous stunt—meant to symbolize the inversion of logic and common sense—achieved nothing but uproarious laughter from the crowd. The allegory, as clumsy and nonsensical as the rest of the performance, went unnoticed; the laughter was for the absurd sight of a man in a swallow-tail coat performing acrobatics.

For Yulia, this was the final straw. "They concealed that from me," she would later lament in tearful indignation, repeating the phrase like a mantra. But for Andrey Antonovitch, this moment marked a complete breakdown. Rising from his seat, trembling with rage, he pointed furiously at Lyamshin and shouted, "Rascal! Take hold of the scoundrel, turn him over … turn his legs … his head … make his head up … up!"

The command, bizarre and nonsensical, only fueled the laughter. Lyamshin leapt to his feet, grinning stupidly, while the crowd erupted into even greater hilarity. Lembke's fury intensified. "Turn out all the scoundrels who are laughing!" he bellowed, his voice cracking with desperation.

The crowd's mood shifted. The laughter turned bitter, the mockery more pointed. Shouts came from all corners of the room. "You can't treat the public like that!" someone yelled. "You're a fool yourself!" shouted another. And then, from the back of the hall, a chilling cry: "Filibusters!"

The word seemed to strike a nerve. Lembke stopped, his expression blanking into a vacant smile as if some terrible realization had dawned upon him. His wife, now pale and trembling, tried to lead him away. "Gentlemen, excuse Andrey Antonovitch," she pleaded, her voice quavering. "He is unwell … forgive him … forgive him, gentlemen." Her words had an almost theatrical quality, but they only added to the growing chaos.

A wave of unease swept through the room. People began to leave in a rush, and then came the next shock. A piercing shriek echoed from one of the fleeing guests: "Ach, the same thing again!" It was a cry of pure hysteria, and it marked the start of a full-blown stampede. Guests pushed and jostled their way to the exits as confusion and fear overtook the crowd.

And then, like a bombshell, the cry of "Fire!" rang out. Someone shouted it from the stairwell, or perhaps it originated in the hall itself—it was impossible to say in the bedlam. "Fire! The riverside quarter is on fire!"

Panic erupted. Guests rushed to the windows, pulling back curtains and tearing down blinds to see for themselves. The scene outside confirmed their worst fears: flames were rising from multiple spots along the riverside. Though the fire was still in its early stages, its spread was swift and deliberate.

"Arson!" someone screamed. "The Shpigulin men!" echoed another voice.

The accusations flew wildly. "I had a presentiment! I knew there'd be arson!" a man exclaimed, his face pale with terror. "It's them—the Shpigulin men! Who else could it be?"

The frenzy escalated as paranoia gripped the crowd. "We were lured here on purpose!" someone cried. "It's all a trap to burn the town!"

The ball, already a disaster of comedic proportions, had turned into a scene of chaos and horror. The guests—those who weren't rushing out in panic—stood paralyzed, staring at the flames that consumed the riverside district. A tragic irony hung in the air: the fête, meant to unite and uplift the town, had instead left it in ruins, both socially and now literally.

The last and most startling cry came from a distraught woman, a housewife whose home was being consumed by the flames. It was an involuntary, piercing shriek that encapsulated the terror and chaos of the moment. Her cry seemed to electrify the crowd, sending everyone rushing towards the doors in a mad scramble. The vestibule turned into a scene of utter pandemonium as people fought to retrieve their belongings—cloaks, shawls, pelisses—all in disarray. Women shrieked, young ladies sobbed hysterically, and the air was thick with fear and confusion.

In the chaos, some guests left without their wraps, unable to locate them amid the frenzied tumult. This small detail soon spiraled into a local legend, embroidered over time with wild exaggerations, and remained a favorite topic of gossip in the town for years to come. Meanwhile, Lembke and Yulia Mihailovna found themselves caught in the press of the panicked crowd. The governor, already on the brink of a complete breakdown, suddenly erupted with a fresh wave of paranoia and fury.

"Stop, everyone! Don't let anyone out!" he bellowed, his voice cracking with desperation as he stretched his arms out to block the exit.

"Every single person must be searched immediately!" he ordered, his voice trembling with authority that was rapidly losing its grip.

A storm of angry shouts, curses, and protests answered him. The crowd, already on edge, turned hostile. Some tried to push past him, while others hurled insults in his direction. The scene teetered on the brink of violence.

"Andrey Antonovitch! Andrey Antonovitch!" Yulia Mihailovna cried out in despair, her voice breaking as she tried to steady her husband.

But Lembke's madness only deepened. His gaze shifted wildly, and his trembling finger pointed directly at her. "Arrest her first!" he screamed, his words landing like a thunderclap. "Search her! The ball was planned to coincide with the fire!"

Gasps of shock rippled through the crowd. Yulia Mihailovna's face turned pale, and with a strangled cry, she collapsed in a faint. This time, there was no doubt—it was a genuine swoon.

The prince, the general, and I rushed to her side, along with a few sympathetic women from the crowd. Together, we managed to carry her out of the suffocating chaos and into her carriage. She remained unconscious until we reached her home. When she finally came to, her first incoherent words were about her husband. The collapse of all her aspirations and illusions had left her clinging desperately to the one thing still central in her mind—Andrey Antonovitch.

A doctor was summoned immediately. I stayed by her side for an hour, as did the prince, though our presence seemed to do little to soothe her anguish. The general, overwhelmed with compassion despite having been visibly shaken himself, expressed a desire to stay the entire night "at the bedside of the unfortunate lady." Yet within minutes of declaring his noble intentions, he fell fast asleep in an armchair in the drawing room, where we left him.

Meanwhile, the chief of police, who had hastened from the ball to the fire, managed to extract Lembke from the hall and attempted to persuade him to return home and rest. However, Lembke stubbornly refused. He was adamant about going to the fire, and for reasons that remain unclear, the chief of police ultimately complied. Lembke was bundled into a droshky and taken to the scene. Along the way, he gesticulated wildly and issued nonsensical orders that the chief later described as "impossible to obey owing to their unusualness." An official report subsequently stated that his Excellency had been in a state of delirium, brought on by the sudden shock of the evening's events.

As for the ball itself, it devolved into complete anarchy. A group of unruly men—joined by a few equally disorderly women—remained in the hall after most of the guests had fled. With no police present, they took control, refusing to let the orchestra leave and even assaulting the musicians who attempted to escape. By morning, they had completely dismantled Prohoritch's refreshments stall, consumed vast quantities of alcohol, and engaged in wild, unrestrained dancing, including an obscene rendition of the Kamarinsky. The hall was left in a deplorable state, with velvet sofas ruined and the floors sullied beyond repair.

Only as dawn broke did this drunken mob stagger to the site of the fire, where they contributed nothing but further disorder. Those who had passed out were dragged into the street like refuse, their inert bodies dumped on the curb.

Thus ended the ill-fated fête, an event intended to support the governesses of our province but which instead became a night of humiliation, chaos, and devastation that no one in the town would soon forget.

Chapter 2.4

The fire sent shockwaves through the riverside district, and the panic was palpable. The most alarming aspect was the clear evidence of arson, which left the residents shaken and in disbelief. Almost immediately, cries rang out accusing the Shpigulin men of the crime. The suspicion, however, was not entirely misplaced. It was later confirmed that three Shpigulin men had indeed participated in setting the fires, though they were the only workers implicated. The rest of the factory hands were exonerated both officially and by public consensus. Alongside these three culprits, Fedka the convict was strongly suspected of involvement, though concrete details about his role remain elusive. These confirmed elements, however, barely scratch the surface of the chaos and conjectures surrounding the arson.

The fire's spread was terrifyingly swift, driven by a strong wind and fueled by the wooden structures that made up much of the riverside neighborhood. The fact that the flames had been set in three separate locations suggested an orchestrated effort. While two of these spots turned into raging infernos, the third was extinguished almost immediately—though how remains unclear. Despite the valiant efforts of the fire brigade and the zealous help of the townspeople, the fire wreaked significant damage before the wind mercifully died down near morning. The Petersburg and Moscow papers grossly exaggerated the scale of the calamity, though it was still devastating. Approximately a quarter of the riverside district was consumed, leaving dozens homeless and livelihoods destroyed.

When I arrived at the scene an hour after fleeing the ball, the flames were at their peak. A whole street running parallel to the river was ablaze, casting an eerie light that made it as bright as day. The chaos in the adjoining lanes was indescribable. Residents, fearing the worst, were frantically hauling their belongings out of their homes. Feather beds, trunks, and makeshift bundles of clothing were piled haphazardly under windows, with families sitting in stunned silence atop their salvaged goods. Only the children, jolted awake by the commotion, wailed inconsolably. Women keened softly, their voices rising in mournful song, while the men worked feverishly, chopping down fences and even entire huts to create firebreaks. Sparks rained down in every direction, carried by the relentless wind, and people rushed to stamp them out wherever they landed.

Yet, amidst this desperate struggle, there were also onlookers—bystanders captivated by the grim spectacle of the conflagration. Some assisted in fighting the fire, while others simply stared, drawn by the terrible beauty of the scene. Fires at night have an almost primal allure, evoking a mix of fear and exhilaration. Stepan Trofimovitch once remarked to me, after witnessing a similar blaze, "I really don't know whether one can look at a fire without a certain pleasure." Indeed, the sight seemed to stir a latent sense of destruction within even the most mild-mannered of observers—a troubling yet undeniable truth about human nature.

Following the crowd, I managed to reach the epicenter of the disaster, where I finally located Lembke. The scene I encountered was both surreal and deeply unsettling. He stood on the remnants of a charred fence, his hat gone, his face pale, and his eyes ablaze with manic intensity. His position was precarious: thirty paces to his left loomed the skeletal remains of a two-story house, its windows gaping like hollow eyes and its roof collapsed. Flames licked at the charred beams, casting flickering shadows. Nearby, a lodge at the far end of the courtyard was now fully ablaze, while firemen worked frantically to contain the flames. On Lembke's right, efforts were underway to save a larger wooden building, which had caught fire multiple times and seemed destined to be lost.

In the midst of this chaos, Lembke stood shouting and gesticulating wildly, issuing nonsensical orders that no one heeded. It was clear that the people around him had given up trying to reason with him. The crowd, which included gentlemen, laborers, and even the cathedral priest, watched him with a mix of curiosity and unease, but none intervened. His ravings were incoherent yet alarming: "It's all incendiarism! It's nihilism! If anything is burning, it's nihilism!" His words sent a chill through me, even though his descent into madness was not unexpected. The sight of such unbridled insanity, however, is always a shock when confronted directly.

A policeman approached him cautiously, clearly under orders from the chief of police to ensure Lembke's safety and, if possible, persuade him to leave. "Your Excellency," he said with careful deference, "perhaps it would be best to seek the repose of home? It's dangerous for your Excellency to remain here."

But Lembke, oblivious to reason, waved him off with a wild gesture and continued his tirade. The task of escorting him away was clearly beyond the policeman's ability, and Lembke remained rooted to his spot, a tragic figure amidst the flames and chaos.

The fire raged on, a symbol of the disorder and destruction that seemed to have engulfed not just the riverside district, but the entire town. And Lembke, with his bare head and frenzied cries, seemed not only a man undone by the night's calamities but also a harbinger of worse things to come.

"They will wipe away the tears of those whose homes have been destroyed, but they will set the entire town ablaze in the process!" Lembke shouted, his voice a blend of hysteria and fervent authority. His gaze darted wildly as he gestured to the crowd. "It's all the work of four scoundrels—four and a half! Arrest the wretch! He infiltrates families, defiling their honor. They used the governesses as a shield to burn down the houses! It's vile, vile!" His voice cracked, and then, as though seized by a sudden realization, he yelled again. "Aie, what's he doing up there?"

His outburst was directed at a fireman who had climbed to the roof of the burning lodge, precariously perched where the flames were licking dangerously close. The roof beneath him was almost gone, and the smoke wreathed around him in an ominous cloud.

"Pull him down! Pull him down!" Lembke shrieked, waving his arms as if he himself would climb the ladder to drag the man down. "He will fall, or he will catch fire! Put him out! Put him out! What is he doing there?"

"Your Excellency," someone from the crowd ventured timidly, "he's putting out the fire."

"Not likely!" Lembke snapped back. "The fire isn't in the roof; it's in the minds of men! Pull him down—let it all burn itself out! That would be much better, much better!" His voice lowered for a moment, only to rise again as his head whipped around. "Who is crying now? Aie, who is crying? An old woman? Yes, an old woman shouting! Why have they forgotten her?"

Indeed, an old woman's cries were echoing from the ground floor of the burning lodge. She was a frail, hunched figure of about eighty, a distant relation of the shopkeeper who owned the house. She had not been forgotten, as Lembke assumed, but had instead returned to the house on her own, driven by a desperate and irrational determination to save her feather bed. The room she sought was still untouched by flames when she entered, but by the time she reached it, smoke had filled the space, and fire had begun to creep up the walls. Choking and wheezing, she struggled futilely to shove the heavy feather bed through a broken windowpane, all the while letting out a string of hoarse, terrified cries.

Lembke, as if propelled by some impulsive heroism, ran to her aid. To the amazement of the crowd, the governor himself rushed up to the window and grabbed one corner of the cumbersome bed, tugging at it with all his strength. For a brief moment, he seemed almost noble in his frantic attempt to help, but fate intervened cruelly. A charred board, dislodged from the collapsing roof, struck him on the neck as it fell. Though it was not a fatal blow, it was enough to knock him off his feet. He collapsed to the ground, unconscious.

With the governor felled, the chaos only grew more profound. As dawn broke, a gloomy, rain-soaked sky greeted the town. The wind, which had driven the fire to such destructive heights, had finally subsided, and a fine drizzle began to fall, aiding the firemen in their desperate battle. By this time, I had made my way to another part of the district, far from where Lembke had fallen, and I began to overhear snippets of strange and troubling conversations among the gathering crowds.

A peculiar fact had come to light that sent whispers rippling through the townsfolk. On the outskirts of the district, beyond the kitchen gardens and far from any other buildings, stood a small wooden house recently constructed. Situated at least fifty paces from its nearest neighbor, it was so isolated that it could not possibly have caught fire from the main blaze, nor could it have spread flames to other structures even in the strongest winds. Yet, inexplicably, it had been among the very first buildings to ignite.

What made this discovery all the more chilling was that the fire at this house had been deliberately set. A pile of faggots had been heaped against one wall and then ignited. Miraculously, the house itself was not entirely consumed. Its owner, who lived nearby, had noticed the flames early and, with the help of neighbors, managed to douse the fire before it could engulf the building. But when they entered the house, a horrific scene awaited them. The captain who lived there, his sister, and their elderly servant had all been brutally murdered during the night. The chief of police, who had left Lembke to his own erratic devices, had rushed to the scene to begin an investigation.

The fire had been terrifying, but the revelation of murder in its midst cast a darker, more sinister shadow over the night. The town, already reeling from chaos and destruction, now grappled with the chilling reality that some among them had used the cover of flames to commit a gruesome and calculated crime. This was no random disaster—it was a night in which human malice had outstripped even the destructive power of nature.

By morning, the tragic events at the small wooden house had become the talk of the entire town. An immense crowd, composed of people from all classes, even including those riverside dwellers who had been displaced by the fire, had gathered at the barren plot of land where the house stood. The area was so congested with onlookers that it was difficult to make one's way through. Whispers and fragmented accounts of the gruesome discovery passed from person to person, each tale growing more vivid as it traveled.

I was told almost immediately upon arriving that the captain had been found lying fully dressed on a bench, his throat slashed. He must have been dead drunk at the time, they said, as he had not put up any resistance and likely felt nothing. The brutal nature of his death was underscored by the detail that he had "bled like a bull." His sister, Marya Timofeyevna, had met a far more violent end. She was found lying in the doorway, her body covered in stab wounds. From the way she was positioned, it seemed likely that she had woken during the attack and struggled fiercely against her assailant. Meanwhile, their elderly servant had suffered a blow to the head so forceful that her skull was fractured.

The narrative pieced together by the crowd suggested that the captain had been boasting earlier about having a significant amount of money— around two hundred roubles. According to the owner of the house, the captain had paid him a visit the morning before and, in a drunken display of bravado, shown him the wad of cash. When the bodies were found, the captain's worn green pocketbook lay empty on the floor, its contents missing. Curiously, Marya Timofeyevna's belongings, including her locked box, had been left untouched, as had the silver setting of the ikon. The murderer had clearly been in a hurry and focused solely on taking the money. It was apparent that the thief had knowledge of the household and its circumstances, as he had gone straight to the captain's stash without bothering with other valuables. The stack of burning faggots piled against the wall was another grim indicator: had the house burned to the ground as intended, the charred corpses would have left little trace of the manner of their deaths, making investigation all but impossible.

One revelation added a new layer to the story. The house had been rented specifically for the Lebyadkins by none other than Nikolay Vsyevolodovitch Stavrogin, the son of Varvara Petrovna. It was said that Stavrogin himself had arranged the lease, going to great lengths to convince the reluctant owner to part with the property, as the latter had intended to turn it into a tavern. Stavrogin had offered a generous rent and paid six months in advance, which ultimately swayed the owner.

"The fire wasn't an accident," I overheard someone say in the crowd.

Despite such comments, most people remained silent. Their faces were set in grim expressions, though not everyone seemed overtly outraged. There was a heavy atmosphere of speculation and whispered gossip. People murmured about Stavrogin, suggesting that the murdered Marya Timofeyevna was his wife and alleging that her death might have been orchestrated to clear the way for him to marry another woman— specifically, a young lady from one of the most distinguished families in town, Madame Drozdov's daughter. Rumor had it that Stavrogin had "dishonorably" abducted the young woman only the day before, and a formal complaint against him was already being prepared to be sent to Petersburg.

Skvoreshniki, Stavrogin's estate, was less than two miles away, and for a brief moment, I debated whether I should go there and inform them of the swirling accusations and the precarious position Stavrogin was now in. However, as I observed the crowd more closely, I saw no evidence of deliberate incitement. There was no clear leader stoking the flames of unrest. That said, among the onlookers were a few familiar faces from the rowdy group I had noticed in the refreshment room the night before.

One man in particular stood out to me. He was thin and unusually tall, with an emaciated face and thick, curly hair blackened as though by soot. Later, I learned he was a cabinetmaker. Unlike the rest of the crowd, which exuded a kind of subdued passivity, he seemed electrified, his entire demeanor charged with agitation. He moved restlessly among the people, raising his voice to speak, though his words were fragmented and barely coherent. "What do you say, lads?" he shouted, his arms gesturing wildly. "Are things to go on like this?" His tone was accusatory, almost challenging, but it was difficult to discern whether he was trying to provoke action or simply giving voice to the collective unease.

The scene was surreal—an unsettling mix of sorrow, anger, and morbid fascination. As the crowd murmured, gossiped, and speculated, it was clear that the events of the night had left an indelible mark on everyone present, and the repercussions were only beginning to unfold.

Chapter 3
A Romance Ended

Chapter 3.1

From the large ballroom of Skvoreshniki, the remnants of the fire were still visible in the fading glow on the horizon. The room, which had recently witnessed the tense meeting between Varvara Petrovna and

Stepan Trofimovitch, now seemed charged with another kind of tension. It was just past five in the morning, and the faint light of daybreak filtered through the windows, though the lingering gloom made it seem as though night refused to yield its grasp. Liza stood at the farthest window on the right, her figure silhouetted against the glass as she stared intently at the dim horizon. The red-orange hue of the dying flames reflected faintly in her eyes, which were dark with thought and emotion.

She was still wearing the elegant light-green dress she had chosen for the matinée the day before. The lace details that had once looked fresh and delicate now appeared crumpled, as if hastily thrown on. Some of the hooks at the front were undone, and when she suddenly noticed this, a flush of embarrassment swept over her pale cheeks. She hurriedly fastened them, then picked up a red shawl that had been left on a nearby chair and wrapped it loosely around her shoulders. Strands of her thick, dark hair had come loose and rested against her neck, peeking out from beneath the shawl. Her face, though undeniably beautiful, bore the unmistakable signs of weariness and strain, yet her eyes burned with an intense, almost defiant light under her frowning brows.

As she pressed her forehead against the cold windowpane, lost in thought, the door behind her opened quietly. Nikolay Vsyevolodovitch stepped inside, his composed demeanor barely masking the undercurrent of unease beneath his calm exterior.

"I've sent a messenger on horseback," he began, his voice steady but subdued. "We'll have news in ten minutes. For now, the servants say it's part of the riverside quarter that's been burnt—on the right side of the bridge near the quay. The fire started around eleven last night but seems to be dying out now."

He remained standing a few steps away, not approaching the window. Liza didn't turn to face him but spoke irritably, her eyes still fixed on the view outside.

"It ought to be light by now, according to the calendar. And yet look—it's still nearly night."

"The calendar isn't always reliable," he replied with a faint smile, though his tone carried a hint of self-consciousness. After a brief pause, he added, "It's dull to live by the calendar, Liza."

The second sentence seemed to disappoint even him, and he fell silent, as though regretting the remark. Liza gave a faint, sardonic smile but finally turned from the window and sat in a low chair, her movements sharp and deliberate.

"You're right about one thing: I do live by the calendar," she said, her voice tinged with bitterness. "Every step I take, every decision I make—it's all carefully regulated. Does that shock you?"

Nikolay hesitated, then moved to sit beside her, reaching out gently to take her hand. His touch was soft, almost hesitant, as though afraid of being rebuffed.

"Why this tone, Liza?" he asked quietly. "What do you mean by saying we don't have long to be together? Where is all this coming from?"

"You're counting my cryptic phrases now, are you?" she replied with a forced laugh. "Do you remember what I said when I arrived yesterday? I told you I was already dead. You either didn't hear me, or you chose not to notice."

"I don't remember you saying that," he admitted, frowning. "Why would you call yourself dead? You must live, Liza. You must."

"'You must live,'" she echoed mockingly. "Is that all you have to say? You're quite out of words today, Nikolay. But no matter—I've lived my hour, and that's enough."

A shadow passed over his face as she continued, her tone strangely light yet piercing.

"Do you recall Christopher Ivanovitch?" she asked suddenly, tilting her head as though searching his expression.

"No, I don't," he answered, his brow furrowed in confusion.

"Christopher Ivanovitch from Lausanne," she said, with a faint, joyless smile. "He bored you to death, remember? He'd open the door and say, 'I've come for one minute,' only to stay the entire day. Well, don't worry—I won't overstay like Christopher Ivanovitch. I'll be gone before you know it."

Her words seemed to cut through him, and he leaned forward, his voice thick with emotion.

"Liza, please—this language, this affectation—it hurts to hear it. Surely it hurts you, too. Why are you speaking like this? What's the point of it?"

His voice grew more fervent as he gazed at her, his eyes shining with an intensity she couldn't ignore.

"Liza, I swear to you—I love you now more than I did yesterday when you came to me."

"Yesterday, today," she said softly, almost to herself, as though weighing the meaning of his words. "Why bring time into it at all? What do these comparisons matter?"

"You won't leave me," he continued desperately, almost as though willing the words to be true. "We'll leave together. Today. Won't we, Liza? Won't we?"

For a moment, her expression softened, and she seemed to waver. But then she looked away, her gaze returning to the faint, flickering glow on the horizon. Her silence was more eloquent than any response she could have given.

"Aie, don't squeeze my hand so tightly! Why must we even talk of going somewhere together today? To 'rise again' somewhere, perhaps? No, we've had enough experiments, don't you think? They're too slow for me, too heavy, too lofty—I'm not built for that sort of thing. If we were to go anywhere, I'd choose Moscow. Yes, Moscow, to pay visits, throw parties, and entertain the way people do. That's my ideal, you know. Even back in Switzerland, I never pretended to be anything else in front of you, did I? But since Moscow isn't an option, since you're married and all, what's the point of dreaming?"

"Liza! What happened yesterday?"

"What happened is done. Over."

"That's impossible! That's too cruel!"

571

"And if it is cruel? Then you must bear it—like any other cruelty."

"You're punishing me for yesterday's whim," he muttered, a bitter smile twisting his lips. Liza flushed with anger at his words.

"What a vile thing to say!" she shot back.

"Then why," he began, his voice trembling, "did you grant me such… such happiness? Do I at least have the right to know why?"

"No," she said sharply. "You must get through this without clinging to your so-called 'rights.' Don't try to deepen the meanness of your accusations by adding foolishness to them. You're really not doing well today. But since you bring it up, you're not afraid of public opinion, are you? Or worried that someone might hold you accountable for this 'great happiness,' as you call it? If that's what's bothering you, for God's sake, don't be. There's no blame to attach to you at all. You're free to walk boldly and triumphantly among the whole world. When I opened your door yesterday, you didn't even know who was about to come in. It was purely my whim, my choice, and nothing more!"

"Liza, your words, your laughter… they've chilled me to the core, filled me with horror for the past hour. That so-called 'happiness'—you may scorn it, but to me, it's worth everything. Everything! How can you take yourself from me now? I swear to you, I loved you less yesterday. Don't you see what you've done? This hope, this one small glimmer, has cost me my life."

"Your life? Or someone else's?" she asked sharply.

He shot up from his seat, his face ashen.

"What does that mean?" he demanded, his voice taut, his eyes fixed intently on her.

"Exactly what I said: your life or mine? Or perhaps you've lost all capacity for understanding?" she replied, her voice rising with anger. "Why did you jump up like that? Why are you staring at me with such a look? You're frightening me. What are you so terrified of, Nikolay? I've seen it for some time now—that fear in your eyes. And it's here now, this very moment. My God, you're pale as death!"

"If you know something, Liza, I swear to you, I don't know... I wasn't talking about that when I said I'd paid for it with life."

"I don't understand you," she said falteringly, her voice apprehensive.

For a long moment, he said nothing. Then a slow, brooding smile spread across his face. Without a word, he sat back down, bent forward, and covered his face with his hands.

"A bad dream," he murmured. "Delirium. That's all. We've been talking about two entirely different things."

"I have no idea what you were talking about," she said, her voice hard. "But tell me this—did you know yesterday, when I came to you, that I would leave you today? Did you know, or didn't you? Don't lie to me."

"I knew," he said softly.

"Well, then, what more do you want? You knew, and yet you took that moment for yourself. Aren't we even now?"

"Tell me the truth, all of it," he pleaded, his voice raw with pain. "When you opened my door yesterday, did you already know that it was only for one hour?"

She turned her gaze on him, her eyes filled with scorn and hatred.

"You really are the most astonishing man. Even the cleverest of people can ask the most ridiculous questions. Why are you so unsettled? Is it your pride, perhaps? Is it so unbearable that a woman should leave you first, instead of you leaving her? Do you know, Nikolay Vsyevolodovitch, the more I've been with you, the more I've realized how generous you try to be toward me. And that, more than anything, is what I cannot stand."

He rose abruptly from his chair and paced across the room, his steps agitated and uneven.

"Very well, perhaps it was inevitable that things would end like this," he said, his voice tense. "But how—how could it all have unfolded this way?"

"Why are you asking?" Liza retorted, her tone sharp and impatient.

573

"You know perfectly well how it happened. You understand it better than anyone else in the world, and—more than that—you expected it. You counted on it happening exactly this way. I'm just a foolish young woman, one whose heart has been shaped by opera and romantic nonsense. That's how it all began—that's your solution right there."

"No," he said softly, shaking his head as though trying to shake off the truth of her words.

"There's no need to protect your pride," she continued, her voice growing more bitter. "I'm telling you the unvarnished truth. It began with one overwhelming moment—one I couldn't withstand. The day before yesterday, when I 'insulted' you in front of everyone, and you responded so chivalrously, I went home and understood everything. I guessed right away why you were running from me. It wasn't out of disdain, which, as a proper 'fashionable young lady,' I feared more than anything. No, it was because you're married. You were running from me for my own sake, to protect me from my madness. You see, I appreciate your noble intentions. Truly, I do."

She leaned back in her chair, her lips twisting into a bitter smile. "And then, as if on cue, Pyotr Stepanovitch popped up and explained it all to me. He laid it out as if it were a fable: you, dominated by some 'great idea,' one so monumental that neither he nor I could ever compare. But at the same time, I was a stumbling block in your grand path. He even had the gall to include himself in the narrative, insisting that the three of us should collaborate. He spoke about boats and maple-wood oars, pulling metaphors from some Russian folk song. I called him a poet, and, of course, he believed it—he swallowed the compliment whole."

She paused, laughing bitterly. "But none of that mattered. I'd already known, long before he came along, that I wasn't strong enough for anything lasting. So, I made up my mind on the spot. And that's it—that's the whole story. Let's not waste time on further explanations; we might just end up quarreling. Don't trouble yourself about anyone else; I'll take all the blame. I am, after all, a horrid and capricious creature. I was captivated by an operatic illusion, a fleeting moment. I'm just a young lady, after all... but, you know," her voice faltered slightly, "I really did believe you were madly in love with me."

Her gaze dropped to her lap as she finished, "Don't despise this foolish woman, and don't laugh at the tear that just escaped. I cry too easily, especially when I pity myself. But enough—enough. Neither of us is good for anything, Nikolay. You're no better than I am. Let's console ourselves with that thought—it might soothe our wounded vanity."

"Dreams and delirium," Stavrogin exclaimed, throwing up his hands in frustration. He resumed pacing, his movements more frantic now. "Liza, poor child, what have you done to yourself?"

"I've burnt myself on a candle—nothing more," she said coolly. "Surely you're not about to cry as well? Show some self-restraint—at least for appearance's sake."

"Why?" he asked suddenly, stopping in his tracks. His eyes searched hers desperately. "Why did you come to me?"

Her laugh was sharp and mocking. "Don't you see how absurd you're making yourself look by asking that? Can't you grasp how ludicrous it is?"

"Why have you ruined yourself like this?" he cried, his voice breaking. "So needlessly, so stupidly! And now—what are we supposed to do?"

"And this is Stavrogin speaking," she said, her voice dripping with disdain. "Stavrogin, the so-called 'vampire,' as one of your enamored admirers here likes to call you! Listen to me. I told you yesterday: I poured all of my life into one single hour, and I am at peace now. Do the same—take your own hour, your moment, and make it yours. Though, unlike me, you'll have many more to come."

"As many as you? No," he said firmly. "Not one more than you. I swear it."

He continued pacing, oblivious to the brief flash of hope that lit her eyes. But as quickly as it appeared, it was gone, extinguished by his next words.

"If you only knew what it costs me to be unable to speak honestly right now," he muttered. "If I could just—"

"Stop!" she interrupted, her voice trembling with something close to fear. "Don't. Don't tell me anything. I don't want your secrets. God save me from them."

He stopped mid-step, watching her uneasily.

"I've had this feeling for a long time," she went on, her voice cold and measured, "ever since Switzerland. I've suspected you're carrying something monstrous, something vile—maybe even blood on your hands. But at the same time, something that would make you utterly laughable. Don't tell me if it's true; I'll laugh at you. I'll mock you for the rest of your life."

She suddenly rose from her chair, her movements sharp and abrupt. "You're turning pale again? I'm going, I'm going. Don't worry. I won't stay to laugh at you."

"Liza," he whispered hoarsely, reaching out a hand. "Torture me, punish me—do whatever you want. You have every right. I ruined you knowing full well I didn't love you. Yes, I took that moment for myself. It was my last hope, and I couldn't resist. When you came to me yesterday, alone, of your own accord... for one fleeting second, I believed. Maybe I still believe, even now."

"How noble of you to be so candid," she said mockingly. "Let me repay that honesty with some of my own. I won't be your nurse, Nikolay. You need one, yes—desperately. But not me."

Their exchange was interrupted by the creak of a door opening slightly at the far end of the room. A head peeked in and quickly disappeared.

"Alexey Yegorytch, is that you?" Stavrogin called out.

"No, it's just me," Pyotr Stepanovitch said, stepping halfway into the room. "Good morning, Lizaveta Nikolaevna. I thought I'd find you both here. Nikolay Vsyevolodovitch, I must speak with you. Just a moment—absolutely essential."

Stavrogin hesitated, then turned back to Liza. "If you hear anything, Liza, anything at all, know this: it's my fault. All of it."

She stared at him in confusion and dread, but he had already gone.

Chapter 3.2

The adjoining room from which Pyotr Stepanovitch had briefly appeared was an expansive, oval-shaped vestibule. Alexey Yegorytch had been sitting there earlier, but Pyotr Stepanovitch had sent him away before returning to Stavrogin. As the door clicked shut behind them, Stavrogin stood motionless, bracing himself for whatever revelation was about to unfold. Pyotr Stepanovitch's gaze was piercing, scanning Stavrogin's face with a rapid intensity, as though he were trying to plumb the depths of his very soul.

"Well?" Stavrogin asked finally, his voice low but tense.

"If you already know," Pyotr Stepanovitch began hurriedly, his words spilling out like a runaway train, "then let me assure you right now: none of us bear any legal blame. Above all, you have nothing to fear—nothing at all. It's just an incredible chain of circumstances... a freakish coincidence! Legally, you're in the clear. That's why I rushed here—to make sure you understood that."

"Have they been burned? Murdered?" Stavrogin asked sharply, his composure faltering.

"Murdered, yes—but not burned. And that's where the real problem lies," Pyotr Stepanovitch answered, speaking faster now, his words punctuated by nervous glances. "But I swear on my honor, it wasn't my doing! Not in the slightest, no matter what you might suspect. Do you want the whole truth? Fine. I'll tell you: yes, the thought crossed my mind—briefly. I mean, you even teased me about it once, remember? But it was never serious! You didn't mean it seriously, and neither did I. I couldn't bring myself to it, not for anything in the world—not for a hundred roubles. And honestly, what would I have gained from it? Nothing! Nothing at all..."

His voice grew more frantic, the words tumbling out in an almost mechanical rhythm. "Listen to me. The day before yesterday, in the evening—not yesterday after the matinée, but the day before—I gave that drunken fool Lebyadkin two hundred and thirty roubles. My own money, mind you! Not a single rouble of yours was involved, and you know it! I

577

handed it over on the condition that he and his sister would leave town first thing in the morning. I even entrusted Liputin with seeing them off—getting them onto the train, ensuring they were gone."

Pyotr Stepanovitch paused briefly, his tone shifting into one of feigned indignation. "Was it a mistake to use your name when I gave him the money? Maybe, maybe not. But I thought it might help move things along. And then—then everything unraveled."

He stepped closer to Stavrogin and, either in nervous habit or calculated gesture, grabbed the lapel of his coat. Stavrogin reacted immediately, swatting his hand away with a swift, violent motion.

"Don't touch me," Stavrogin said coldly.

Unfazed, Pyotr Stepanovitch shrugged and carried on. "Fine, fine. No need to break my arm. Let me finish explaining. That scoundrel Liputin pulled his little schoolboy pranks instead of doing what I told him. He kept Lebyadkin hidden away until the matinée, then paraded him onto the stage—dressed in a formal coat, drunk out of his mind, and reciting verses that Liputin himself helped him compose! The scene was a disaster. Afterward, Lebyadkin staggered home, more dead than alive, and Liputin stole most of the money, leaving him with just some small change."

Pyotr Stepanovitch leaned in conspiratorially. "But here's the worst part: apparently, earlier that morning, Lebyadkin had already been flaunting the money, boasting about it in the wrong places. That's when Fedka the convict must have gotten wind of it. And you remember Kirillov's house, don't you? That little 'hint' you dropped—it was all Fedka needed. He saw his opportunity."

Stavrogin's face darkened. "What are you trying to say?"

"I'm saying Fedka took matters into his own hands. That's the truth of it. He murdered them both—and the servant too, for good measure. Then he tried to burn the house down to cover his tracks, but the fire didn't spread as he'd hoped. And guess what? He didn't even find the money! He thought he'd score a thousand roubles, but instead, he left empty-handed."

Pyotr Stepanovitch threw his hands up in mock exasperation. "Can you believe it? A complete fiasco! And that fire—don't even get me started. It wasn't part of any plan. It's just reckless stupidity! I've long considered the idea of using a fire strategically—it suits the people's taste for chaos—but I was saving it for the right moment. And now, out of nowhere, they take it upon themselves to act without orders. Such insubordination! It's unacceptable."

"Are they saying I had something to do with it?" Stavrogin asked suddenly, his voice edged with both fear and anger.

"Not yet," Pyotr Stepanovitch replied cautiously, "but rumors spread fast. People are already muttering about your involvement, especially with that absurd story about wanting your wife dead. But legally, you have nothing to worry about. There's no evidence—just unfortunate coincidences."

"And the bodies?" Stavrogin pressed. "Weren't they burned?"

"No," Pyotr Stepanovitch admitted reluctantly. "The fire didn't consume them. They were found—murdered, yes, but not burned. That's what complicates things."

Stavrogin turned away, his face pale and his hands trembling. The room seemed to close in around him as Pyotr Stepanovitch's rapid, rattling voice filled the silence.

Pyotr Stepanovitch's words tumbled out in a flurry, his tone almost jovial but with an undertone of nervous energy. "Not at all! That ruffian couldn't manage anything properly to save his life. But I must say, I'm glad you're so calm about all this. After all, you're not to blame—not in the slightest, not even in thought—but you must admit, this turn of events does solve all your difficulties quite neatly. You're suddenly free— widowed, in fact—and now you can marry a charming girl with a substantial fortune. She's already yours in spirit, isn't she? Just think about it—what an unexpected boon from crude, simple coincidence!"

"Are you threatening me, you fool?" Stavrogin interrupted sharply, his voice like a blade.

"Threaten you?" Pyotr Stepanovitch's expression shifted to mock affront, though his grin betrayed satisfaction. "Come now, why such a tone? Calling me a fool when I've rushed here to help you? You should be grateful, yet you lash out. Do I look like the sort of man who threatens? I've no need to threaten anyone—especially not you. What could I gain from that? I want your cooperation freely, not from fear. You're the sun, the light; it's me who's trembling before you, not the other way around. Do you think I'm Mavriky Nikolaevitch?"

He laughed suddenly, and Stavrogin's brows furrowed.

"And speaking of Mavriky Nikolaevitch—what a sight! As I was racing here, I saw him leaning against the farthest corner of your garden fence, drenched to the bone. He must have been sitting there all night! In this rain, can you imagine? What madness! I didn't stop, of course, but he saw me. Didn't you know he was there? No? Well, I'm glad I told you. A man in his position, with his pride and temperament, and perhaps armed with a revolver—it's a dangerous mix. He's sitting out there, soaking wet, and you can only wonder why."

"Waiting for Lizaveta Nikolaevna," Stavrogin murmured.

"Well! Why would she go out to him in this weather? Rain like this— what a fool!" Pyotr Stepanovitch snorted. "Surely she wouldn't."

"She's going to him now," Stavrogin said quietly but firmly.

That statement made Pyotr Stepanovitch's face light up with mock surprise, though his eyes betrayed an eager calculation. "What? Truly? So that's how it is! But her position is completely different now. What does she need Mavriky Nikolaevitch for, after everything? You're free— unshackled by fate—and can marry her tomorrow. She doesn't know that yet, of course, but leave it to me; I'll smooth everything out. Where is she? Let's put her mind at ease."

"Put her mind at ease?" Stavrogin echoed, his tone icy.

"Of course! We can make everything right. Let's go to her."

"And do you honestly think she won't guess what those dead bodies mean?" Stavrogin's expression twisted into something unreadable as he stared at Pyotr Stepanovitch.

"Why would she?" Pyotr Stepanovitch replied with unshaken

confidence, his grin widening like that of a man who considered himself cleverer than everyone else. "Legally, there's no reason for her to suspect a thing. And women—ah, women! You don't understand them, Stavrogin. They have an uncanny talent for ignoring inconvenient truths when it suits them. Even if she did guess, she'd step over those dead bodies without so much as a glance. Why wouldn't she? It's in her best interest to marry you now, especially after... well, after her little scandal. She's compromised herself, after all. Oh, she'll marry you, all right, and keep those dead bodies tucked away in her memory to throw back at you during some marital quarrel years down the line. Every woman does that."

Stavrogin remained silent for a moment before speaking with slow deliberation. "If you've come here in a racing droshky, take her to Mavriky Nikolaevitch yourself. She just told me she can't bear the sight of me and is leaving. She won't take my carriage."

Pyotr Stepanovitch stared at him, genuinely perplexed for a brief second before breaking into a laugh that bordered on disbelief. "Leaving? You can't be serious. How did that happen?"

"She realized sometime during the night that I don't love her. Something she's known all along."

"And you don't love her?" Pyotr Stepanovitch's tone carried mock astonishment. "Then why, my dear Stavrogin, did you let her stay last night instead of being honest with her, like an honorable man? You could have told her plainly. Instead, you've humiliated both of us. You've made me look a fool in her eyes, too."

Stavrogin chuckled abruptly, the sound sharp and humorless. "I'm laughing at my monkey."

"Oh, so you've caught on!" Pyotr Stepanovitch said with exaggerated delight. "Yes, I was putting on an act! Just for your amusement, naturally. But admit it—you've had a complete fiasco, haven't you? I can tell from your face. Let me guess—you sat up all night in that dreary drawing room, discussing lofty ideals. Wasting precious time! What folly! But never mind, I expected as much. Yesterday, I brought her to you simply to cheer you up, to show you that life with me around would never be dull. If she's leaving now, well, perhaps I overestimated your capacity to entertain yourself."

Pyotr Stepanovitch shifted on his feet, his tone oscillating between feigned nonchalance and barely contained fury. "Fine then, leave it all to me. I can manage to marry her off to Mavriky Nikolaevitch easily enough, though don't imagine I put him out there by the fence. That's entirely his doing. Frankly, I'm a bit afraid of him myself now. You keep mentioning my droshky, but I merely passed by as quickly as I could. What if he has a revolver? It's fortunate I brought mine." He pulled a small revolver from his pocket, flashed it briefly, then tucked it away again. "I thought it wise, considering how far I had to come. But no matter, I'll sort everything out for you in no time. Her tender heart is undoubtedly aching for Mavriky at this very moment—or at least it ought to be. Honestly, I feel a little sorry for her. If I take her to him, the first thing she'll do is start talking about you, praising you to the skies while throwing poor Mavriky under the bus. You know how women are! There you go again—laughing! Well, I'm glad you're in such high spirits now. Come on, let's get moving. I'll deal with Mavriky first, and as for those ... well, the ones who've been murdered ... maybe we should keep quiet about that for now. She'll find out eventually."

"What exactly will she find out?" Stavrogin asked, his tone suddenly sharp. "Who's been murdered? And what were you just saying about Mavriky Nikolaevitch?"

Before Pyotr Stepanovitch could respond, the door opened abruptly, and Liza stood in the frame, her face pale and strained. "What did you just say about Mavriky Nikolaevitch? Has he been murdered?"

Pyotr Stepanovitch froze for an instant but quickly composed himself. "Ah, you were eavesdropping? No, no, Mavriky Nikolaevitch is alive and well. You'll find him just outside, by the garden fence. It seems he's been sitting there all night in the rain. He's soaked to the bone in his greatcoat. I saw him as I drove past."

"That's not true," she insisted, her voice trembling. "You said 'murdered.' Who's been murdered?"

Pyotr Stepanovitch hesitated, but Stavrogin spoke firmly. "The ones who've been murdered are my wife, her brother Lebyadkin, and their servant."

Liza flinched as if struck, her face growing even paler. "Murdered?" she whispered.

"It's a brutal and senseless crime, Lizaveta Nikolaevna," Pyotr Stepanovitch interjected quickly, his words spilling out in a hurried, almost rehearsed fashion. "A straightforward case of robbery under the cover of the fire. Fedka the convict is the culprit—it's all his doing. And that fool Lebyadkin is to blame for flaunting his money around. It's tragic, of course, but Stavrogin had nothing to do with it. I rushed here the moment I heard the news. It was a thunderbolt for both of us. Isn't that right, Nikolay Vsyevolodovitch? We were just discussing whether or not to tell you."

Liza turned to Stavrogin, her voice breaking. "Nikolay Vsyevolodovitch, is any of this true?"

"No," he replied, his voice steady. "It's not true."

"Not true?" Pyotr Stepanovitch exclaimed, his face a mask of feigned indignation. "What do you mean by that?"

Liza clutched at the doorframe for support. "I'll go mad!" she cried. "Tell me the truth! Are you guilty or not? Tell me, as you would before God. I swear I'll believe you. I'll follow you to the ends of the earth if you tell me the truth."

Pyotr Stepanovitch threw up his hands dramatically. "Do you see how you're tormenting her?" he shouted at Stavrogin. "You're mad! Lizaveta Nikolaevna, I swear to you, he's innocent. Completely and utterly innocent. He's as shattered by this as anyone. He was with you all night— he didn't leave your side for a moment. How can you suspect him?"

Stavrogin remained silent for a long moment before speaking in a low, strained voice. "I didn't kill them. I was against it. But I knew they would be killed, and I didn't stop it. Leave me, Liza."

Liza's hands flew to her face as she stifled a sob, then she turned and fled from the room. Pyotr Stepanovitch made a move to follow her but hesitated and instead stormed back into the room, his face twisted with rage.

"So that's your decision?" he hissed, his voice trembling with anger. "That's the path you're taking? Are you planning to betray us all now? Inform on us and retreat to some monastery to absolve yourself? Or maybe just disappear entirely? But let me tell you, I won't let you get away with it!"

Stavrogin stood motionless in the center of the room, staring vacantly ahead. Slowly, he reached up to clutch a lock of his hair, a faint, humorless smile playing on his lips. Pyotr Stepanovitch grabbed his sleeve roughly, shaking him. "Is it all over for you? Is this the end? What are you planning? Do you think I'll just let you go and ruin everything? Do you really think I'll let you escape unscathed?"

Stavrogin turned to him at last, his expression one of weary indifference. "Run after her," he said abruptly. "Order the carriage. Don't let her go near ... near the bodies. Take her home. Make sure no one sees her. Do you understand?"

"She's with Mavriky Nikolaevitch by now," Pyotr Stepanovitch sneered. "Do you think he'll let her into your carriage? Forget it. There are more pressing matters to deal with."

He reached for his revolver again, but Stavrogin didn't flinch. "Go ahead," he said softly, almost wearily. "Shoot me if you like."

Pyotr Stepanovitch's hand dropped, and he let out a frustrated snarl. "Damn it! What a ridiculous mess of sentiment! You deserve a bullet for this—she ought to spit in your face, not weep for you. You're a broken wreck of a man!"

Stavrogin gave him a faint smile, one of both mockery and resignation. "And if you weren't such a clown, I might have even let you."

"Clown or not," Pyotr Stepanovitch growled, "I'm the only one keeping you afloat. Don't forget that."

Stavrogin turned away, his voice cold and distant. "Leave me alone. Come back tomorrow. Maybe then I'll have an answer for you."

Without another word, he walked out, leaving Pyotr Stepanovitch fuming in his wake.

Chapter 3.3

Pyotr Stepanovitch hurried after Lizaveta Nikolaevna, who had only managed to take a few steps from the house before being stopped. She had been detained by Alexey Yegorytch, who trailed behind her respectfully, his thin frame bent slightly forward. The old man, in his tailcoat and without a hat, looked distressed, almost tearful, as he pleaded with her to wait for a carriage.

"Go on, Alexey Yegorytch," Pyotr Stepanovitch interjected brusquely, pushing him aside with a dismissive wave. "Your master needs tea, and there's no one to prepare it for him."

The old man hesitated, but with a bowed head, he retreated. Pyotr Stepanovitch took Liza's arm gently but firmly. She didn't resist, though it was clear she was still in shock, her eyes glassy and her movements unsteady. She seemed barely aware of her surroundings.

"You're going the wrong way," he said hurriedly, his words tumbling out as though he were trying to suppress his own nervousness. "We shouldn't go by the garden. It's not only the wrong direction, but walking is impossible in this weather. It's over two miles, and you're not dressed for it. Just wait here for a moment. I came in a droshky—it's right in the yard. I'll have it ready in no time, and I'll take you home without anyone seeing you."

"How kind you are," Liza murmured, her voice faint and detached, though there was a flicker of irony in her tone.

"Oh, it's nothing. Anyone in my position would do the same," he replied with forced cheerfulness.

She glanced at him then, as though truly seeing him for the first time, and a look of vague surprise crossed her face. "Good heavens! I thought it was still the old man."

"Listen," he continued quickly, ignoring her remark. "I'm glad you're taking this so … well, so calmly. It's all such a ridiculous mess, but since it's come to this, why don't I call for the droshky right away? It'll only take a moment. Let's go back to the porch and wait there while I have it brought around."

"I want to see … where are those murdered people?" she asked suddenly, her voice trembling but resolute.

Pyotr Stepanovitch hesitated, visibly uneasy. "Ah, no, no, no!" he exclaimed hastily. "That's precisely what I was hoping to avoid. There's no reason for you to see them—it won't do you any good."

"I know where they are. I know that house," she said with quiet determination.

"What of it? Even if you know, what difference does it make? It's raining, and there's a thick fog. You're not in a state to—" He stopped mid-sentence, muttering to himself. "Ah, what a mess this 'sacred duty' of mine has become."

"Where is Mavriky Nikolaevitch?" she interrupted, her face suddenly alert. "You said something about him. Where is he?"

Pyotr Stepanovitch sighed. "If you must know, he's just over there. If we go a bit farther, I can show you. But if you're set on seeing him, I'll take you closer. Still, I'd rather avoid a meeting myself, if you don't mind."

Her expression shifted, as though she were caught between disbelief and dawning realization. "He's waiting for me," she whispered. Then, more loudly, as though the words were a revelation, "Good God! He's waiting for me."

"There, you see?" Pyotr Stepanovitch said quickly, seizing on her hesitation. "If you go to him, I'll step back—I won't interfere. But remember, Liza, none of this is my business. I'm just here because I happened to be around, and I want to help. Let me remind you, though, if your 'fairy boat' has turned out to be a rotting old wreck, fit only for kindling—"

"Ah, that's perfect!" she interrupted with a sudden, bitter laugh. "Rotten and sinking. Beautifully put."

"Lovely, isn't it?" he said, his tone dry, though his eyes narrowed slightly. "But you're crying, Liza. Tears don't suit you. You need spirit— you need to rise above it, like a man. Isn't that what's expected of everyone these days? Equal strength, equal resolve…"

"Stop, stop!" she cut him off, her laughter turning into a fit of hysterics. "You're too much. It's … it's perfect!"

Pyotr Stepanovitch paused, visibly irritated. "Look, Lizaveta Nikolaevna, I'm only trying to do what's best for you. If you don't want to see him, fine. But there he is, right where I said he'd be. Can you see him? He's sitting by the fence, drenched through, waiting for you. He doesn't see us yet, so if you'd rather not—"

"Don't let him see me!" she cried suddenly, her voice rising to a near shriek. "Don't let him see! Take me away—away from here, anywhere! To the woods, to the fields—just away!"

And with that, she turned abruptly and began running back the way she had come, her steps faltering but driven by a desperate urgency. Pyotr Stepanovitch hesitated only for a moment before rushing after her again, muttering under his breath.

Pyotr Stepanovitch, panting slightly, chased after Lizaveta Nikolaevna as she ran ahead, her movements frantic and disoriented. "Lizaveta Nikolaevna, this is ridiculous cowardice!" he called out, his voice rising in urgency. "Why won't you let him see you? Why run from him? You should face him—face him with pride! What is there to hide? If it's some absurd notion of modesty or guilt, that's such an antiquated prejudice! So outdated! But where are you even going? Where on earth do you think you're running?"

Liza showed no sign of hearing him, her only answer the sound of her hurried footsteps against the damp ground. Her dress, crumpled and mud-streaked, clung to her as she stumbled forward.

"Where are you going?" Pyotr Stepanovitch continued to shout, now fifty paces behind her. "You're heading straight for the fields! Wait—there, you've fallen!"

He skidded to a halt as Liza tripped over an uneven mound of earth and fell heavily to the ground. Before he could rush to her side, a terrible cry shattered the damp, heavy air. It came from Mavriky Nikolaevitch, who had been waiting by the garden fence and had seen everything. He was already sprinting across the field toward Liza. Realizing the situation had shifted beyond his control, Pyotr Stepanovitch hesitated for a moment, then turned sharply and retreated toward Stavrogin's gate, muttering to himself as he hastily made his way to his waiting droshky.

Mavriky Nikolaevitch reached Liza just as she was pulling herself unsteadily to her feet. He bent over her, gripping her hands in both of his, his face pale with alarm and streaked with tears. The sight of her—the woman he adored—running desperately across the fields in such a state, her dress soiled and torn, and her hair disheveled, overwhelmed him completely. He couldn't speak, his emotions choking his voice. Silently, he shrugged off his heavy greatcoat and, with trembling hands, draped it over her shoulders.

Liza, stunned by his presence, looked up at him. Then, to his utter astonishment, she bent her head and pressed her lips to his hand.

"Liza," he managed to say, his voice trembling. "I—I'm no good for anything, but don't push me away. Don't send me away from you!"

"Oh, no!" she exclaimed with sudden fervor, her voice breaking. "Don't leave me! Take me away from here—please, take me away, now!"

Grasping his hand tightly, she began pulling him with her, her steps hurried and uneven. "Mavriky Nikolaevitch," she murmured after a moment, her voice suddenly timid, "I've been putting on a brave face all this time, but now ... now I'm so afraid. I'm afraid of death. I feel it—I'm going to die soon, very soon, and I ... I'm terrified."

Mavriky Nikolaevitch looked around in desperation, as though searching for someone—anyone—to help. "If only there were a cart, or someone to stop and help us! You're soaked to the bone, Liza, and you'll make yourself ill."

"It's all right," she said, attempting to reassure him, though her voice was shaky. "It's better now that you're here. Hold my hand and lead me, please. Where are we going? Home? No, not home—I need to see them first. The ones who were murdered. They're saying his wife was killed, and he says he's to blame. I have to see for myself, Mavriky Nikolaevitch. I have to know if it's true. Please, make haste."

Her words became a torrent, spilling out in feverish desperation. "It's because of them, isn't it? That's why he's so cold to me now. Since last night ... everything has changed. Oh, my dear one," she cried, gripping his arm tightly. "Don't forgive me in my shame! Why would you forgive me? Strike me, punish me—kill me here, like a dog in this field!"

"No one is your judge now," Mavriky Nikolaevitch replied firmly, his voice steady despite the turmoil in his heart. "God will forgive you, and I ... I am the last person who could judge you."

The two walked on, hand in hand, their pace quickening as though compelled by some shared madness. They were moving directly toward the glow of the fire on the horizon. The rain, fine and cold, continued to drizzle, wrapping the landscape in a gray mist that blurred every shape and line into a dull, smoky haze. Though daylight had broken, the world seemed trapped in a perpetual twilight, dim and lifeless.

Suddenly, through the fog, a strange figure appeared, trudging toward them. Liza stopped abruptly, staring in disbelief. At first, the figure seemed impossibly out of place in this grim tableau, but as it came closer, her expression changed to one of astonished recognition.

"Stepan Trofimovitch?" she gasped, her voice filled with a mixture of surprise and incredulity.

Indeed, it was Stepan Trofimovitch. His appearance was as absurd as it was pitiable. He was dressed in what he must have imagined to be proper "traveling attire"—a wide-brimmed hat, a heavy greatcoat cinched with a shiny patent-leather belt, and a pair of brand-new high boots that seemed designed more for show than practicality. In one hand, he carried an open umbrella; in the other, a small, tightly packed bag. A knitted scarf was wrapped snugly around his neck, and a walking stick completed the peculiar ensemble.

"Lise!" he called out, his voice trembling with emotion as he approached. "Ma chère! You too ... out in this dreadful fog? And this

589

fire … oh, Lise, we are all so wretched. But we must forgive. Forgive everyone and be free—forever free! We must pardon, pardon, pardon!"

"But why are you kneeling down?" Liza asked, her voice tinged with confusion and pity as she watched him drop to the wet ground before her.

"Because, in parting with the world, I wish to bid farewell to everything beautiful in my past through you!" cried Stepan Trofimovitch with fervent emotion, tears streaming down his pale, aged face. He knelt at Liza's feet, clasping her hands with trembling reverence and pressing them to his tear-streaked eyes. "I kneel to all that was luminous, noble, and tender in my life. I kiss it, bless it, and thank it. Now I am severed—one half of me left behind as the foolish dreamer who once aspired to touch the heavens, and the other half, this broken, aging man standing on the edge of oblivion. Twenty-two years of dreams, and now... here I am. A relic, a tutor for some merchant's children, if indeed such a merchant exists!"

Suddenly, his tearful monologue was interrupted as he noticed the sodden hem of Liza's dress. "But you are soaked, my poor child! Absolutely drenched! And out here in this desolation, in such a state? You are weeping too! Mon Dieu, you are as wretched as I am. But—where have you come from?" He stumbled over his words, his voice laced with unease as his confused gaze darted between Liza and Mavriky Nikolaevitch, whose presence seemed to heighten his bewilderment. "Mais savez-vous l'heure qu'il est?" he exclaimed in dismay.

"Stepan Trofimovitch, have you heard about the murders? Is it true? Is it true what they say about the people who were killed?" Liza's voice cut through his confusion, sharp and desperate.

He froze, his expression transforming into one of grim resignation. "Those people... I saw the crimson glow of their misdeeds burning in the sky all night. It was inevitable—it was their destiny to end like this." His voice grew fervent as his eyes took on a wild gleam. "I am running from the madness, from the delirium that grips our time. I am fleeing to seek Russia—true Russia! But tell me, does it even exist? Existe-t-elle, la Russie?"

Abruptly, his tone shifted to a strange note of cheerfulness as he recognized Mavriky Nikolaevitch. "Ah! Captain, my dear captain, here you are! I always knew I would meet you in some momentous adventure! But, oh, take my umbrella at least! Why must you both walk in this weather? I shall soon hire a carriage, you see. I set out on foot to escape unnoticed—Nastasya would have woken the entire street if she'd known I was leaving. Incognito was the only way. And yet, Liza, chère, I heard you speak of someone murdered? But... oh, mon Dieu, you are ill!"

"Come on, come on!" Liza cried suddenly, almost hysterically, as she seized Mavriky Nikolaevitch's arm and began pulling him forward. Then, just as abruptly, she stopped, turning back to Stepan Trofimovitch with a strange mixture of pity and irritation. "Wait, wait. Let me sign you with the cross. Perhaps you should be put under someone's care, but instead, I'll make the sign of the cross over you. Pray for 'poor' Liza, just a little—don't trouble yourself too much over it. And Mavriky Nikolaevitch, give him back his ridiculous umbrella. Yes, that's right. Now, let us go!"

They moved on, leaving Stepan Trofimovitch standing forlorn in the rain. When Liza and Mavriky Nikolaevitch reached the notorious house, the scene was one of chaos. A massive crowd had gathered, many murmuring about Stavrogin and speculating on his supposed involvement in the murders. The more volatile among them, including a wild-eyed cabinet-maker, were loudly airing their outrage. Yet most of the crowd remained eerily silent, their collective mood an unsettling mix of apprehension and grim fascination.

As Liza pushed her way through the throng, her pale, feverish face and erratic movements drew immediate attention. She seemed oblivious to the stares, to the muttering voices rising around her like an ominous tide. "It's Stavrogin's woman!" someone bellowed. Another voice snarled, "Not content with murder, she comes to gloat over the corpses!"

Before anyone could intervene, an arm shot out from the crowd and struck her viciously on the head. Liza crumpled to the ground. Mavriky Nikolaevitch let out a guttural roar of fury and threw himself into the fray, blindly striking at the man nearest him. But chaos reigned; the cabinet-maker lunged at Mavriky Nikolaevitch, seizing him in a brutal grip, and the crowd erupted into a storm of shouts and blows. Liza managed to rise, only to be struck down again by another cruel hand.

Suddenly, the madness seemed to part like a tide. A small clearing opened in the midst of the mob, and there, in its center, lay Liza's motionless figure. Mavriky Nikolaevitch, blood streaming down his face, stood over her, his screams of anguish piercing the damp air as he wept and wrung his hands in despair.

The crowd began to thin as shock replaced violence. Someone shouted for help, and a group of men stepped forward to carry Liza away. She was still breathing, though barely. In the chaos, the cabinet-maker and three other men were seized by the authorities. The others vehemently denied involvement, claiming to have been mistaken for the guilty parties. To this day, the truth of their complicity remains unclear, though the cabinet-maker's erratic behavior and contradictory statements pointed to his guilt.

I, too, was called to testify at the inquest, and I maintained that the tragedy had been the result of drunken, thoughtless men, acting in the heat of the moment without full awareness of their actions. And though my heart remains heavy with the memory of that terrible scene, I believe that explanation to this day.

Chapter 4
The Last Resolution

Chapter 4.1

That morning, many people saw Pyotr Stepanovitch, and everyone who saw him noticed how unusually excited he was. Around two o'clock, he went to visit Gaganov, who had just arrived from the countryside the day before. Gaganov's house was full of people, all heatedly discussing the events from the previous day. Pyotr Stepanovitch talked more than anyone else and managed to hold their attention. Although he was generally seen as "a chatty student with a few screws loose," he now spoke about Yulia Mihailovna, a topic that captured everyone's interest in the charged atmosphere.

Claiming to have been close to Yulia Mihailovna recently, Pyotr Stepanovitch revealed surprising details about her. Along the way, he carelessly repeated some of her remarks about people everyone in the town knew, wounding their pride in the process. He spoke in a wandering and clumsy way, as though he were an honest man reluctantly trying to untangle a huge mess of misunderstandings. He came across as so naive that he didn't seem to know where to start or when to stop. At one point, he let slip that Yulia Mihailovna knew everything about Stavrogin's secrets and had been the mastermind behind the entire plot. He also claimed she had tricked him, too. Pyotr Stepanovitch confessed he had been in love with the unfortunate Liza but was so deceived that he'd almost taken her to Stavrogin himself in the carriage. "Yes, yes, go ahead and laugh, gentlemen," he said. "But if I'd known how things would turn out—if only I'd known!"

When people asked him about Stavrogin, he confidently said the disaster involving the Lebyadkins was pure chance. He explained it was entirely Lebyadkin's own fault for flaunting his money, and his explanation was quite convincing. One of the listeners pointed out that Pyotr Stepanovitch was being hypocritical. They said he had practically lived at Yulia Mihailovna's house—eating, drinking, and even sleeping there—and now he was the first to criticize her. They argued that this wasn't as noble as he seemed to think. But Pyotr Stepanovitch defended himself immediately.

"I didn't eat and drink there because I was desperate for money," he said. "It's not my fault I was invited. Let me decide for myself how grateful I should be for that."

Overall, most people sided with him. They thought, "Sure, he's a bit ridiculous, and maybe not all that serious, but he isn't responsible for Yulia Mihailovna's foolish behavior. If anything, it seems he tried to stop her."

Around two o'clock, word spread that Stavrogin, the man everyone was so curious about, had left for Petersburg on the midday train. This news caused quite a stir, and many people frowned when they heard it.

Pyotr Stepanovitch, however, was so shocked that people later said he turned pale and exclaimed in an odd tone, "How could they let him leave?" He quickly left Gaganov's house after that but was seen visiting two or three other houses later on.

Towards evening, he managed to get in to see Yulia Mihailovna, though it took great effort because she had firmly refused to see him. I only learned about this from her three weeks later, just before she left for Petersburg. She didn't share many details but admitted with a shiver that "he had shocked her beyond belief that day." I suspect all he did was frighten her by threatening to accuse her of being an accomplice if she "said anything." He needed to intimidate her because of his plans at the time, which she knew nothing about. It was only five days later that she began to understand why he had been so unsure of her silence and so nervous about her possibly having another outburst of anger.

Sometime between seven and eight in the evening, when it was already dark, all five members of the group gathered at Ensign Erkel's small, crooked house on the edge of town. Pyotr Stepanovitch had arranged the meeting himself, but he arrived disgracefully late, keeping everyone waiting for over an hour. Ensign Erkel was the young officer who had sat quietly at Virginsky's all evening, holding a pencil and notebook. He hadn't been in town long and lived by himself with two elderly sisters in a quiet side street. Since he was leaving town soon, his house seemed like the safest place for a meeting, as it was unlikely to draw attention. Erkel was a peculiar boy known for being incredibly quiet. He could sit for nights on end in the middle of lively conversation without saying a word, though he would listen closely, watching the speakers with his innocent, childlike eyes.

He had a very handsome face, and there was even a hint of intelligence in his expression. He wasn't officially part of the group; people assumed he had some special role that was purely practical. However, it's now clear he had no such role and likely didn't understand his own position in the group. The truth was he idolized Pyotr Stepanovitch, whom he had only recently met. If Erkel had encountered someone truly evil, someone who convinced him to join a gang of bandits for a romantic or socialist cause and then ordered him to rob and kill the first person he saw as a test of loyalty, he would probably have done it without hesitation.

Erkel also had a sickly mother to whom he sent half of his meager salary. Imagine how that poor woman must have kissed his little blond head, how she must have worried and prayed for him! I'm including these details because I can't help but feel deeply sorry for him.

"Our group" was on edge. The events of the previous night had shaken them deeply, and I think they were starting to panic. The chaos they had eagerly and methodically joined had spiraled out of control in ways they hadn't imagined. The fire during the night, the murder of the Lebyadkins, and the mob's vicious treatment of Liza were all shocking developments that weren't part of their plan. They angrily accused their leader of being controlling and dishonest. While waiting for Pyotr Stepanovitch to arrive, they became so worked up that they decided to demand a clear explanation from him. If he dodged their questions again, as he had before, they were ready to dissolve the group and form a new secret society based on "spreading ideas" with democratic principles and equality. Liputin, Shigalov, and the expert on peasant issues all supported the idea. Lyamshin stayed quiet but looked like he agreed. Virginsky hesitated, saying they should hear Pyotr Stepanovitch out first. In the end, they agreed to listen to him, but his lateness only added to their frustration. Erkel, as usual, remained silent, simply bringing tea in glasses on a tray from his landladies' kitchen. He didn't bring the samovar or let the servant enter the room.

Pyotr Stepanovitch finally arrived at half-past eight. Striding quickly to the round table near the sofa where everyone was seated, he kept his cap in his hand and refused the tea. His expression was angry, stern, and dismissive. He must have noticed right away from their faces that they were upset and rebellious.

"Before I even start talking, you've got something to say. Spit it out," he demanded.

Liputin spoke on behalf of the group, his voice shaking with resentment. He declared, "If things keep going like this, we might as well shoot ourselves." He quickly added that they weren't afraid of dying; in fact, they were perfectly willing to do so, but only if it served the greater cause. This got murmurs of agreement from the others. He insisted that Pyotr Stepanovitch needed to be more transparent with them so they could always understand the plan in advance. "Otherwise, where is this going?" he asked. His words stirred more agreement and grumbles from the group. He went on, saying this kind of behavior was both humiliating and dangerous. "We're not saying this because we're scared, but if one person takes action while the rest of us are left in the dark, mistakes will be made, and everything will fall apart." The others shouted, "Yes, exactly!" in agreement.

"Damn it, what do you all want?" Pyotr Stepanovitch snapped.

"What does the greater cause have to do with Mr. Stavrogin's petty schemes?" Liputin shouted, his anger boiling over. "Maybe he's connected to some mysterious 'central group,' if that group even exists, but that's not our concern. Meanwhile, a murder has been committed. The police are on alert, and if they follow the trail, they might find out where it leads."

"If Stavrogin and you get caught, we'll all get caught," added the peasant expert.

"And it won't do anything to help the cause," Virginsky said gloomily.

"What nonsense! The murder was random. Fedka did it to steal money," Pyotr Stepanovitch said dismissively.

"Hmph! Quite a coincidence, though," Liputin muttered, squirming.

"And if you want the truth, it's your fault," Pyotr Stepanovitch said sharply.

"Our fault?" Liputin shot back.

"Yes. First of all, Liputin, you were involved in the scheme yourself. Second, you were given clear orders to get Lebyadkin out of town and even given money to do it. What did you do instead? If you'd followed through, none of this would have happened."

"But weren't you the one who suggested it might be a good idea to get him to read his poems?"

"A suggestion isn't the same as an order. The order was to get him out of town."

"Order? That's a strange word to use. Actually, your instructions were to delay sending him away."

"You misunderstood and acted foolishly and stubbornly. The murder was Fedka's doing, and he acted alone for the purpose of robbery. You listened to rumors and got scared. Stavrogin isn't an idiot, and the proof is that he left town at noon, right after meeting with the vice-governor. If there had been anything to implicate him, they wouldn't have let him travel to Petersburg in broad daylight."

"We're not accusing Mr. Stavrogin of committing the murder himself," Liputin said spitefully and bluntly. "Maybe he didn't know anything about it, just like I didn't. And you know perfectly well I was unaware, even though I've been dragged into this mess like a piece of meat in a stew."

"Who are you accusing, then?" Pyotr Stepanovitch asked darkly, staring at him.

"Those who benefit from burning down towns."

"You're only making things worse by trying to squirm out of it. Anyway, won't you read this and pass it around? It's just something I thought you'd find interesting."

He pulled an anonymous letter from his pocket, written by Lebyadkin to Lembke, and handed it to Liputin. Liputin read it, looking surprised, then passed it on to the next person. The letter quickly made its way around the group.

"Is that really Lebyadkin's handwriting?" Shigalov asked.

"It is," Liputin and Tolkatchenko, the peasant expert, confirmed.

"I'm only sharing it because I thought it might interest you, especially since you're so sentimental about Lebyadkin," Pyotr Stepanovitch said, taking the letter back. "So, as it turns out, a random Fedka happened to get rid of a dangerous man for us. That's how chance works sometimes. Quite educational, isn't it?"

The group exchanged quick, uneasy glances.

"And now, gentlemen, it's my turn to ask some questions," Pyotr Stepanovitch said, straightening up with a serious expression. "Tell me, what gave you the right to set the town on fire without approval?"

"What? Us? We started the fire? That's a baseless accusation!" they cried out.

"I understand you went too far," Pyotr Stepanovitch said stubbornly. "But this isn't about petty gossip involving Yulia Mihailovna. I gathered you here to make you understand the enormity of the danger you've foolishly created—danger that threatens much more than just yourselves."

"Excuse me," Virginsky, who had been silent until now, said indignantly. "Actually, we were just about to point out how unfair and despotic it was of you to take such a drastic and strange step without consulting the group first."

"So, you deny it? But I insist it was you who set the fire. You and no one else. Gentlemen, don't lie! I have solid proof. Your recklessness has put the entire cause in danger. You're just one link in a vast chain, and your job is to follow orders from the center without question. Yet three of you incited the Shpigulin workers to set the town on fire, even though you had no authorization to do so. And now, the fire has happened."

"Which three? Who are you accusing?"

"The night before last, at three in the morning, you, Tolkatchenko, were provoking Fomka Zavyalov at the 'Forget-me-not' tavern."

"Me? That's ridiculous!" Tolkatchenko shouted, jumping up. "I barely said a word to him, and what I did say wasn't meant seriously. I only spoke because he'd been beaten earlier that day. I stopped right away when I realized he was too drunk. If you hadn't brought it up, I wouldn't have even remembered it. A few words couldn't have started a fire."

"You're like someone surprised that a tiny spark can blow up an entire powder magazine," Pyotr Stepanovitch replied.

"I whispered it to him in a corner. How could you possibly have heard about it?"

Tolkatchenko suddenly paused to think.

"I was sitting there under the table. Don't trouble yourselves, gentlemen; I know every step you take. Are you smiling sarcastically, Mr. Liputin? But I know, for example, that three days ago, at midnight, in your bedroom, you pinched your wife so hard she was bruised black and blue as you were getting into bed."

Liputin's jaw dropped, and his face turned pale. (It was later discovered that Tolkatchenko had learned about Liputin's actions from Agafya, Liputin's servant, whom he had been paying from the beginning to spy on him. This only came to light later.)

"May I make a point?" Shigalov asked, standing up.

"Go ahead."

Shigalov sat back down, taking a moment to collect himself.

"From what I understand—and it's impossible not to understand—you have, on more than one occasion, eloquently but too theoretically described a vision of Russia covered by an endless network of knots. Each of these centers of activity, constantly growing and recruiting, is supposed to systematically discredit local authorities, create confusion in the villages, spread cynicism and scandal, and promote complete disbelief in everything while making people eager for something new. Then, through fires—which you called a distinctly national method—the goal is to push the country, if necessary, into desperation. Are those your words, which I have tried to recall as accurately as possible? Is that the plan you outlined to us as the official representative of the central committee, a committee that remains completely unknown to us and seems almost mythical?"

"That's accurate, but you're unbearably tedious," Pyotr Stepanovitch replied.

"Everyone has the right to express themselves in their own way. You told us the network of knots across Russia now numbers in the hundreds and suggested that if everyone does their job correctly, all of Russia could, at the right moment and on a single signal…"

"Oh, for God's sake, I've had enough of this!" Pyotr Stepanovitch groaned, squirming in his chair.

"Fine, I'll be brief. Let me end by asking this: we've witnessed the unrest, the people's dissatisfaction, the breakdown of local administration, and finally, we've seen the town set on fire with our own eyes. What exactly do you take issue with? Isn't this your plan? What could you possibly blame us for?"

"For acting on your own!" Pyotr Stepanovitch shouted angrily. "While I'm here, you shouldn't have dared to act without my approval. That's enough! We're on the brink of betrayal, and by tonight or tomorrow, you might be arrested. There—you wanted to know? I have reliable information."

Everyone stared at him in shock.

"You're not just going to be arrested as the instigators of the fire but as the quintet. The traitor knows all the details about the entire network. Do you see what a disaster you've caused?"

"Stavrogin, no doubt!" Liputin shouted.

"What... why Stavrogin?" Pyotr Stepanovitch seemed genuinely startled for a moment. "Nonsense!" he exclaimed, quickly regaining his composure. "It's Shatov! You all know by now that Shatov was once part of the society. Let me tell you, after keeping an eye on him through people he doesn't suspect, I've discovered, to my shock, that he knows everything—about the network, the organization, everything. To avoid being accused of his former involvement, he'll turn us in. He's been holding back so far, and I've given him the benefit of the doubt, but your fire has pushed him over the edge. He's shaken and won't hesitate any longer. By tomorrow, we'll be arrested as arsonists and political criminals."

"Is that true? How does Shatov know?" The group's reaction was one of total chaos.

"It's absolutely true. I can't reveal how I found out or who told me, but I can tell you this much: I know a way to influence Shatov through someone he doesn't suspect. This will delay him from turning us in, but only for twenty-four hours—no longer." The group fell silent.

"We really need to get rid of him," Tolkatchenko blurted out.

"It should have been done a long time ago," Lyamshin added darkly, slamming his fist on the table.

"But how are we supposed to do it?" Liputin muttered. Pyotr Stepanovitch immediately took charge of the discussion and laid out his plan. The plan was to lure Shatov to a secluded location the following evening under the pretense of handing over the secret printing press he'd been hiding. The press was supposedly buried in that spot. Once there, they would "deal with him." Pyotr Stepanovitch explained every necessary detail, which will be left out here, and went on to elaborate on Shatov's current uncertain relationship with the central society—a matter the reader is already familiar with.

"That's all fine," Liputin said hesitantly, "but since it's another risky move like the last one, it's going to draw too much attention."

"Of course," Pyotr Stepanovitch agreed, "but I've already planned how to avoid suspicion."

He then explained in detail about Kirillov, his intention to take his own life, and his agreement to wait for their signal and leave a letter behind, taking responsibility for whatever they asked him to confess to— all of which the reader already knows.

"His decision to take his own life—a philosophical, or as I'd call it, insane choice—has been discovered there," Pyotr Stepanovitch explained. "Nothing escapes notice there, not even the tiniest detail; everything is used for the cause. Seeing how useful his decision could be, and confirming that he was serious about it, they gave him the means to come to Russia. For some reason, he insisted on dying here. They gave him a task, which he completed, and made him promise—something you already know—that he wouldn't end his life until they told him to. He agreed to everything. Keep in mind that he's part of the organization in a unique way and is eager to be of service. That's all I can tell you for now. Tomorrow, after the matter with Shatov, I'll dictate a note for him to leave behind, saying he's responsible for Shatov's death. It will seem believable—they were friends, traveled to America together, then had a falling out. It will all be explained in the note. And perhaps, depending on how things go, we could dictate something else for Kirillov to include—

maybe something about the manifestos or even the fire. I'll think about it. Don't worry, he has no scruples; he'll sign whatever we give him."

The group hesitated. The story sounded far-fetched, though they had all heard bits and pieces about Kirillov before. Liputin seemed to know the most.

"What if he changes his mind and refuses?" Shigalov asked. "He's crazy, after all; he's not someone you can rely on."

"Don't worry, gentlemen; he won't refuse," Pyotr Stepanovitch snapped. "I'm obligated by our agreement to warn him the day before, so it has to be today. I'll invite Liputin to come with me now to confirm everything. When he returns, he can tell you if I was telling the truth. If necessary, you'll know today." He suddenly stopped, his tone sharp with irritation, as if he felt he was wasting his time trying to convince them. "But do as you like. If you choose not to go through with it, the union is dissolved—entirely because of your insubordination and betrayal. In that case, we're all independent from this moment forward. But remember, if that happens, aside from the trouble Shatov's betrayal will bring, you'll also face another issue. You were warned about this when the union was formed. As for me, I'm not particularly worried about you, gentlemen. Don't think I'm too tied up in this with you. But that's beside the point."

"Yes, we'll do it," Liputin said decisively.

"There's no other way out," muttered Tolkatchenko. "As long as Liputin confirms what you're saying about Kirillov, then…"

"I'm against it," Virginsky said suddenly, standing up. "With all my heart and soul, I protest against this murderous decision."

"But?" Pyotr Stepanovitch asked, staring at him.

"But what?"

"You said 'but.' I'm waiting."

"I don't think I did," Virginsky said nervously. "I only meant that if you decide to do it, then…"

"Then?"

Virginsky didn't answer.

"I believe it's acceptable to disregard danger to your own life," Erkel said suddenly, speaking up for the first time, "but if it could harm the cause, then I believe it's wrong to ignore such danger..." He trailed off, blushing. The others, absorbed in their own thoughts, stared at him in surprise—it was shocking to see him speak up.

"I'm for the cause," Virginsky said abruptly.

Everyone stood up. It was decided they would communicate again the next day at noon to finalize the details, but they wouldn't meet in person. The location of the hidden printing press was revealed, and each person was assigned a task. Liputin and Pyotr Stepanovitch immediately set out together to see Kirillov.

Chapter 4.2

All their comrades were convinced that Shatov was going to betray them, yet at the same time, they couldn't shake the feeling that Pyotr Stepanovitch was manipulating them like pieces on a chessboard. They resented him deeply for it but also knew there was no escaping what was to come. Regardless of their feelings, they understood they would all show up at the designated spot the next day, where Shatov's fate would inevitably be sealed. The group felt trapped, as if they were helpless flies ensnared in a massive spider's web. Their frustration burned like fire, but beneath their anger was a terror that gripped them and refused to let go.

Pyotr Stepanovitch's approach only worsened their feelings. He could have handled them with more care, softened the edges of the truth, and even framed the situation as a grand, heroic act, something noble and fitting for the likes of ancient Rome. Instead, he chose to lay everything bare in the harshest terms, appealing not to their ideals or principles but to their primal fear of survival. It was insulting, almost degrading. True, they were all aware that nature was governed by the relentless struggle for existence, that survival often came at the expense of others—but even so, they couldn't help but feel they deserved a little more respect.

Yet Pyotr Stepanovitch had no time for embellishments or lofty comparisons to Roman grandeur. His mind was in disarray, his plans unraveling. Stavrogin's abrupt departure had shaken him to his core. Despite his earlier claim that Stavrogin had met with the vice-governor, this was a fabrication. The truth that tormented him was that Stavrogin had left town without speaking to anyone—not even his own mother. It baffled Pyotr Stepanovitch that Stavrogin had been allowed to leave without interference, and this bafflement gnawed at him. (Later, even the authorities would face questions about how such a thing was allowed to happen.) Pyotr Stepanovitch had spent the entire day making inquiries, desperately trying to uncover what had happened, but he had learned nothing. He was more distraught than he had ever been. How could he simply let Stavrogin go like this? How could he let him slip away?

This turmoil left Pyotr Stepanovitch in no mood to deal delicately with the quintet. In his eyes, they were both an inconvenience and a necessity. He had already decided that he needed to pursue Stavrogin immediately, but Shatov still had to be dealt with first. Furthermore, the quintet needed to be bound together more tightly than ever in case of emergencies. "A pity to waste them—they might still be useful," he likely reasoned.

As for Shatov, Pyotr Stepanovitch was utterly convinced that his betrayal was imminent. Everything he had told the others about Shatov was a lie. He had no concrete evidence, no document to support his claims. Yet he believed, as firmly as one believes that two plus two equals four, that Shatov would turn against them. The events surrounding the deaths of Liza and Marya Timofyevna seemed to him like more than enough to push Shatov into action. Perhaps Pyotr Stepanovitch had some grounds for this belief—perhaps not. It's also true that he harbored a deep personal hatred for Shatov, born from an old quarrel. Pyotr Stepanovitch was not the sort to forgive an insult, and it's hard to deny that his grudge played a significant role in his decisions.

In our town, the streets are narrow, with small brick sidewalks in some places and raised wooden planks in others. Pyotr Stepanovitch strode down the middle of the pavement, taking up the entire space, completely ignoring Liputin. Liputin had no choice but to either trail a step behind him or splash through the muddy road if he wanted to keep up. As Pyotr

Stepanovitch walked, he suddenly recalled a recent memory: not long ago, he himself had trudged through the mud to keep pace with Stavrogin, who had walked just as he was walking now, dominating the entire sidewalk. The memory stung, and rage swelled within him.

Liputin, meanwhile, was seething with his own anger. He felt humiliated. It was one thing for Pyotr Stepanovitch to treat the others with contempt, but him? Liputin, who was more involved than any of them, who knew more and had contributed more than anyone else, even if indirectly? Oh, Liputin was well aware that Pyotr Stepanovitch still held enough power to ruin him if things went badly. But this didn't lessen his hatred. He despised Pyotr Stepanovitch, not merely because of the threat he posed but because of his arrogant, domineering manner. Now, as he faced the grim reality of the task before them, Liputin's fury burned brighter than anyone else's. He hated the very thought of what they were about to do, yet he also hated Pyotr Stepanovitch for forcing them into this position.

And still, despite his anger, Liputin knew that the next day he would be the first to arrive at the scene, obedient as a slave, and he would bring the others with him. If he could somehow have murdered Pyotr Stepanovitch that very night—without destroying himself in the process—he would have done it without hesitation.

Lost in his frustration and disgust, Liputin trudged behind Pyotr Stepanovitch, who barely acknowledged his presence, save for the occasional rough shove with an elbow. It seemed as though Pyotr Stepanovitch had completely forgotten about him, which only added to Liputin's growing resentment. Suddenly, Pyotr Stepanovitch stopped in one of the town's busiest streets and stepped into a restaurant.

"What are you doing?" Liputin snapped, his anger bubbling to the surface. "This is a restaurant!"

"I want a beefsteak," Pyotr Stepanovitch replied nonchalantly.

"You've got to be joking! This place is always full of people."

"So what if it is?"

"But… we're going to be late. It's already ten o'clock."

605

"You can't be too late for what we're doing."

"But I'll be late! They're expecting me back."

"Let them wait. Besides, it would be idiotic of you to rush there now. Thanks to your constant complaining, I haven't had dinner. And let me tell you, the later you show up at Kirillov's, the more likely you are to catch him."

Without another word, Pyotr Stepanovitch walked to a private room in the restaurant. Liputin, fuming, sank into a chair across the room, where he could keep an eye on him. His resentment only deepened as he watched Pyotr Stepanovitch take his time with his meal. Half an hour passed, and then some, but Pyotr Stepanovitch showed no intention of hurrying. He ate with relish, savoring every bite, and even called for a different kind of mustard, then a glass of beer. Not once did he acknowledge Liputin. Instead, he seemed to be lost in thought, his face a mask of concentration. It was clear that Pyotr Stepanovitch could perform two tasks at once—eating with enjoyment and planning his next move.

Liputin's hatred grew to unbearable levels. It became an obsession. He counted every bite of beefsteak that Pyotr Stepanovitch took, despising the way he chewed, the way he smacked his lips, the way he even opened his mouth. Liputin loathed the sight of the steak itself, sizzling on the plate, as though it were a symbol of everything he despised. Soon, his vision began to blur, and a wave of nausea washed over him. Hot and cold chills ran down his spine, making him feel faint.

"You're doing nothing. Read this," Pyotr Stepanovitch said suddenly, tossing a sheet of paper onto the table. Liputin, startled, got up and moved closer to the candlelight. The paper was densely written in poor handwriting, filled with corrections and crossings-out. By the time he had finished reading it, Pyotr Stepanovitch had already paid the bill and was ready to leave.

On the pavement outside, Liputin handed the paper back to him.

"Keep it," Pyotr Stepanovitch said curtly. "I'll explain later. But tell me, what do you think of it?"

Liputin shuddered involuntarily. "In my opinion... such a manifesto is nothing but absurd and ridiculous."

His anger boiled over, and he couldn't stop himself from speaking. "If we distribute something like this, we'll only make ourselves look like fools, completely incompetent fools!"

"Hm. I disagree," Pyotr Stepanovitch replied, walking on with determination.

"Surely you didn't write it?" Liputin pressed, struggling to keep up.

"That's none of your business."

"Well, I think that poem, 'A Noble Personality,' is utter nonsense. Trash, even. It's absurd to suggest Herzen could have written something like that."

"You're wrong. It's a good poem."

Liputin, undeterred, continued, his voice rising. "And another thing! This idea that we should act to bring everything crashing down—it's ludicrous. In Europe, maybe, where there's an actual proletariat, but here? We're amateurs! This is just showing off."

"I thought you were a Fourierist," Pyotr Stepanovitch said dryly.

"Fourier's ideas are entirely different. Completely different."

"Fourier's ideas are nonsense."

"No, they're not!" Liputin nearly shouted. "But this... I can't believe anyone seriously thinks there will be an uprising in May."

Liputin was so worked up that he unbuttoned his coat, the heat of his frustration overwhelming him.

"That's enough," Pyotr Stepanovitch cut him off abruptly. "Now, so I don't forget... You will print this manifesto yourself. Tomorrow, we'll dig up Shatov's hidden printing press, and you'll take charge of it. Your task is to print as many copies as possible, distribute them over the winter, and send them to other places as needed. The funds will be provided."

"No, absolutely not. I refuse to take on such a... No. I decline," Liputin stammered.

"You'll do it," Pyotr Stepanovitch said coldly. "I'm acting under the instructions of the central committee, and you are obligated to obey."

"And I think our so-called central committee abroad has lost all connection with what Russia is really like," Liputin shot back, his voice trembling with defiance. "They've forgotten everything, which is why they come up with such nonsense. Honestly, I think we're the only quintet that exists. There's no network at all!"

"All the more contemptible of you, then," Pyotr Stepanovitch sneered, "to keep chasing after the cause without even believing in it. And look at you now, running after me like a pathetic little dog."

"I'm not running after you," Liputin spat. "We have every right to break away and form a new society."

"Fool!" Pyotr Stepanovitch suddenly roared, his eyes flashing with fury.

For a moment, the two stood facing each other, their hatred palpable. Then Pyotr Stepanovitch turned on his heel and walked away, his stride as confident as ever. Liputin, seething, could do nothing but follow.

As they walked, Liputin felt a sudden urge to turn back. A thought, sharp and insistent, cut through his mind: "Turn around now and go back; if I don't do it now, I never will." For ten steps, he wrestled with the idea, weighing his options, his heart pounding with a strange mix of fear and defiance. The notion seemed so clear and urgent that for a moment, he was almost convinced. Yet, by the eleventh step, another idea—far more reckless and desperate—seized him. It was as though his resolve hardened, not in retreat but in resignation. He did not turn back. He continued forward, his pace faltering yet steady, as if some unseen force compelled him.

They were nearing Filipov's house now, its dim silhouette barely visible against the night sky. Liputin expected they would stop there, but instead, Pyotr Stepanovitch abruptly veered down a narrow, almost hidden side street. To Liputin's surprise, it wasn't even a proper street but more of a neglected path running alongside a sagging fence. The ground sloped steeply here, and a shallow ditch ran alongside them. The path was so uneven that they had to grasp the fence to keep their footing, their boots sliding slightly with every step. Liputin stumbled once, nearly losing his balance, but Pyotr Stepanovitch pressed on without a word, seemingly unaffected by the precarious terrain.

As they reached a darkened corner where the fence bent sharply, Pyotr Stepanovitch stopped abruptly. Without saying anything, he crouched and began working at one of the wooden planks in the fence. Liputin stood behind him, peering through the gloom, trying to make sense of what was happening. After a moment of effort, Pyotr Stepanovitch pried the plank loose, leaving a narrow gap just big enough for a person to squeeze through. Without hesitation, he slipped through the opening, vanishing momentarily into the shadows on the other side.

Liputin hesitated, staring at the gap. He felt a surge of unease—where were they going? What was this secretive detour? His instincts screamed at him to stop, to question, to turn back. But before he could think further, Pyotr Stepanovitch's face reappeared through the gap, his eyes glinting in the dim light. He gestured impatiently. "Come on," he whispered sharply.

Still uncertain, Liputin crouched awkwardly and squeezed through the opening. The wooden planks scraped against his shoulders and back as he wriggled through, his movements clumsy and hesitant. Once he was on the other side, Pyotr Stepanovitch swiftly replaced the plank, fitting it back into place with practiced ease. The fence looked as intact as before, as though no one had passed through.

"This is how Fedka used to get to Kirillov," Pyotr Stepanovitch murmured, almost to himself, as he glanced around to ensure no one was watching.

Liputin's unease deepened. He didn't know why this piece of information unsettled him so much, but it did. The thought of Fedka, the shadowy figure whose name was spoken in half-whispers, only added to the creeping sense of dread that was settling over him like a heavy fog.

"Shatov mustn't know we're here," Pyotr Stepanovitch said suddenly, his voice low and stern. His tone carried a weight that made Liputin's heart skip a beat. There was no room for questions, no invitation for argument. The command was absolute.

Liputin nodded silently, though his mind was spinning. He felt trapped, both by the physical confinement of the narrow path and by the strange, ominous game unfolding around him. Yet, despite his apprehension, he followed Pyotr Stepanovitch, the gap in the fence sealing his retreat as effectively as the thoughts he had abandoned just moments before.

Chapter 4.3

Kirillov was seated on his worn leather sofa, calmly sipping tea as he always did at this hour. The room was dimly lit, with a faint glow from a small lamp on the table. The air carried the faint, familiar scent of tea leaves and wood. When the door opened and his visitors entered, he didn't rise to greet them but instead gave a slight start, his face showing a flicker of anxiety. His sharp, penetrating gaze quickly settled on Pyotr Stepanovitch, and his expression turned wary.

"You're not mistaken," Pyotr Stepanovitch began briskly. "It's exactly what you think I've come about."

"Today?" Kirillov asked, his voice steady but tinged with apprehension.

"No, no, tomorrow... around this time," Pyotr Stepanovitch replied hurriedly, moving to sit at the table without waiting for an invitation. He kept a close eye on Kirillov, noting his unease with growing concern. But after a moment, Kirillov's face regained its usual composure, and the brief moment of tension passed. His expression became as neutral and impassive as ever.

"These people still doubt you," Pyotr Stepanovitch said, glancing at Liputin, who had followed him into the room. "You're not annoyed that I brought Liputin along, are you?"

"Today I'm not annoyed," Kirillov replied evenly. "Tomorrow, I want to be alone."

"But not before I arrive," Pyotr Stepanovitch interjected, "and certainly not while I'm here."

"I'd prefer it not to happen in your presence," Kirillov said simply, his tone unchanging.

"You remember you promised to write and sign everything I dictated," Pyotr Stepanovitch pressed, leaning forward slightly.

"I don't care," Kirillov replied flatly. "And now, will you be staying here long?"

"I need to meet someone and stay about half an hour," Pyotr Stepanovitch said, leaning back in his chair with an air of resolve. "So, no matter what you say, I'll remain that half-hour."

Kirillov said nothing in response, his gaze drifting toward the table. Meanwhile, Liputin had taken a seat under the somber portrait of a bishop that hung on the wall. His thoughts churned with growing unease, and the desperate idea that had been simmering in his mind began to take firmer shape. Despite the tension in the room, Kirillov barely acknowledged Liputin's presence. Liputin, for his part, found his usual derision toward Kirillov's theories replaced by a strange, brooding silence. He had often laughed at the man's ideas in the past, but now he sat grimly, his eyes wandering around the room as if searching for answers.

"I wouldn't mind some tea," Pyotr Stepanovitch said abruptly, shifting in his seat. "I just had some steak and was counting on having tea here."

"Drink it, then," Kirillov replied without much interest. "There's some for you if you want."

"You used to offer it to me yourself," Pyotr Stepanovitch remarked sourly, his tone carrying a hint of reproach.

"That doesn't matter," Kirillov said dismissively. "Liputin can have some too, if he wants."

"No, I… can't," Liputin muttered awkwardly, shaking his head.

"Don't want to or can't?" Pyotr Stepanovitch asked sharply, turning to face him.

"I'm not going to drink tea here," Liputin replied with an air of finality, his words loaded with unspoken meaning.

Pyotr Stepanovitch frowned, irritation flashing across his face. "There's a whiff of mysticism about that answer. Honestly, it's impossible to make sense of you people."

No one replied. The silence stretched for a full minute, thick and oppressive.

"Well, I do know one thing," Pyotr Stepanovitch said suddenly, breaking the quiet. His tone was sharp and decisive. "No superstition or mysticism is going to stop any of us from doing our duty."

"Has Stavrogin left?" Kirillov asked, his voice cutting through the air like a blade.

"Yes, he's gone," Pyotr Stepanovitch replied curtly.

"He's done well," Kirillov said with a note of approval.

Pyotr Stepanovitch's eyes flashed momentarily, but he held back whatever emotion stirred within him. Instead, he said, "I don't care what you think, as long as everyone keeps their word."

"I'll keep my word," Kirillov replied simply.

"I always knew you would," Pyotr Stepanovitch said, his tone shifting to something almost admiring. "You'll do your duty like the independent and progressive man you are."

"You're absurd," Kirillov said bluntly.

"That may be, but I'm glad to amuse you," Pyotr Stepanovitch replied with a smirk. "I'm always happy to bring people a bit of enjoyment."

"You're very eager for me to shoot myself," Kirillov said matter-of-factly. "And you're afraid I might change my mind."

"Well, you see, it was your idea to connect your plan to our work. Relying on that plan, we've already taken action. You can't back out now; you've left us no choice."

"You've no claim over me."

612

"I understand that perfectly," Pyotr Stepanovitch said quickly. "You're entirely free to act as you will. We're not involved at all, so long as your free will aligns with what you've promised."

"And am I supposed to take responsibility for all the vile things you've done?" Kirillov asked, his voice calm but cutting.

The room fell silent again, the unspoken tension crackling like electricity in the air.

"Tell me, Kirillov, are you afraid? If you want to back out, say so now," Pyotr Stepanovitch asked sharply, his voice tinged with impatience.

"I am not afraid," Kirillov replied calmly, his tone firm and unshaken.

"I ask because you've been asking so many questions," Pyotr Stepanovitch retorted, his frustration mounting.

"Are you going soon?" Kirillov asked again, his gaze steady and cold.

"More questions?" Pyotr Stepanovitch snapped, narrowing his eyes.

Kirillov regarded him with quiet contempt, a flicker of disdain passing across his face.

"You see," Pyotr Stepanovitch continued, growing visibly agitated, "you want me to leave, to be alone, to gather your thoughts. But honestly, that's a bad sign—especially for you. You're overthinking it, and I don't think that's a good idea. To me, it only means you're wavering. And to be honest, you're making me uneasy."

Kirillov's lips curled slightly, almost into a sneer. "There's only one thing I hate," he said in a low, measured voice, "and that's having a snake like you near me at such a moment."

"Oh, don't worry about that," Pyotr Stepanovitch said with forced casualness. "When the time comes, I'll leave. I'll stand outside on the steps if it makes you feel better. If dying means fussing over such trivial matters, though, it's not a good sign. I'll step out, and you can imagine I know nothing about it, that I'm beneath your notice—a man infinitely below you."

"No, not infinitely below me," Kirillov corrected. "You've got abilities, but you'll never understand certain things because you're a base creature."

"Delighted to hear it," Pyotr Stepanovitch said, his smile sharp and mocking. "I'm always glad to provide a bit of amusement, even at a time like this."

"You understand nothing," Kirillov said, his tone dismissive.

"Well, I might not understand," Pyotr Stepanovitch replied, trying to feign humility, "but I listen with respect, at least."

"You can't even manage that. Even now, you can't suppress your petty malice, though it's against your own interests to show it. Keep pushing me, and I might decide to put this off for another six months."

Pyotr Stepanovitch glanced at his watch, his irritation barely concealed. "I've never really understood your theory," he said, attempting to regain control of the conversation. "But one thing I do know: you didn't create it for our sake. You would carry it out regardless of us. And I know this too—you haven't mastered the idea; the idea has mastered you. That's why I know you won't delay."

"What? The idea has mastered me?" Kirillov asked, raising an eyebrow.

"Yes," Pyotr Stepanovitch replied confidently.

"And not the other way around? I haven't mastered the idea?" Kirillov's lips twitched with faint amusement. "That's an interesting observation. You have a little sense after all. But you still provoke me, and I find myself oddly proud of that."

"Good, good!" Pyotr Stepanovitch exclaimed, feigning enthusiasm. "Pride is exactly what you need right now."

"Enough," Kirillov said firmly. "You've had your tea. Now leave."

"Damn it, I suppose I have to," Pyotr Stepanovitch grumbled, rising reluctantly. "Though it's still early. Listen, Kirillov. That man—you know who I mean—will I find him at Myasnitchiha's, or has she been lying too?"

"You won't find him there because he's here," Kirillov said bluntly.

"Here? Damn it, where?" Pyotr Stepanovitch demanded, his face flushing with sudden anger.

"Sitting in the kitchen, eating and drinking," Kirillov answered coolly.

"How dare he?" Pyotr Stepanovitch snapped, his voice rising. "It was his duty to wait. What nonsense is this? He has no passport, no money!"

"I don't know about that," Kirillov said, shrugging slightly. "He came to say goodbye. He's dressed and ready to leave. He says you're a scoundrel and doesn't want your money."

"Hah! Afraid of me, is he? Afraid that I'll... But even now I can— if—" Pyotr Stepanovitch's voice trailed off as he processed Kirillov's words. "Where is he? In the kitchen?"

Without another word, Kirillov opened a side door that led into a tiny, dimly lit room. From this room, a short staircase descended directly to the kitchen, where a cook's bed was usually tucked behind a partition. In the corner, beneath a cluster of icons, Fedka sat at a plain wooden table. A nearly empty pint bottle stood before him, along with a plate of bread and some cold beef and potatoes on a chipped earthenware dish. He ate slowly and deliberately, savoring each bite, though he was clearly halfway drunk.

Fedka was dressed in his sheepskin coat, his hat resting on the bench beside him. It was obvious he was prepared for a journey. Behind the partition, a samovar hissed and steamed, but it wasn't for Fedka, despite the fact that he had diligently tended it every night for the past week. He had always made sure it was ready for "Alexey Nilitch, who has the habit of drinking tea at night."

It's hard not to believe that Kirillov himself, who had no cook, had prepared the beef and potatoes that morning with his own hands, especially for Fedka.

"What nonsense is this?" Pyotr Stepanovitch exclaimed as he burst into the room, his voice sharp with anger. He strode in briskly, his movements quick and purposeful, and slammed his fist down hard on the table, making the plates and bottles rattle. "Why didn't you wait where you were told to wait?" he demanded, his tone bristling with impatience and barely contained fury.

Fedka, seated at the table, didn't flinch. Instead, he straightened up and adopted an air of mock dignity. His face, ruddy from drink, twisted into an expression of smug self-assurance.

"Hold on, Pyotr Stepanovitch, hold on a minute," he said with exaggerated deliberation, placing special emphasis on each word. His tone was steeped in insolence, his swaggering manner unmistakable. "Let's get one thing straight: you're here on a polite visit to Mr. Kirillov, Alexey Nilitch, who is a man of culture—someone whose boots you'd be lucky to clean any day of the week. And you… well, you're nothing more than— foo!"

With that, Fedka spat theatrically to one side, his haughty contempt evident in every gesture. His demeanor was calm, but the kind of calm that suggested he was gearing up for an outburst. There was a sharp edge to his composure, a latent threat simmering just beneath the surface. Pyotr Stepanovitch, however, failed to grasp the danger. He was too preoccupied, his thoughts scattered by the events of the day, to notice the storm brewing in Fedka's demeanor.

At the top of the three steps leading into the kitchen, Liputin stood frozen, watching intently from the dimly lit room. His curiosity was piqued, his eyes darting between Pyotr Stepanovitch and Fedka, trying to read the tension unfolding before him.

"Do you or don't you want a proper passport and enough money to get where you've been told to go? Yes or no?" Pyotr Stepanovitch snapped, his impatience flaring once again.

Fedka didn't answer right away. Instead, he leaned back in his chair, folding his arms as if preparing for a speech. "Listen here, Pyotr Stepanovitch," he began, his voice steady but laced with mockery. "You've been lying to me from the very start, and that makes you a regular scoundrel—a filthy, crawling louse of a man, if you want my opinion. You promised me all kinds of riches for doing your dirty work, for spilling innocent blood. You swore it was for Mr. Stavrogin's sake. And what do I get for it? Not a single kopek! Not to mention, it's all over town now that Mr. Stavrogin slapped you in the face—yes, we've heard about that."

Fedka's eyes gleamed with drunken defiance as he leaned forward, jabbing a finger toward Pyotr Stepanovitch. "And now you're here again, threatening me, promising me money without explaining what for. I wouldn't be surprised if you're planning to send me to Petersburg to plot some revenge against Mr. Stavrogin out of your spite. Well, let me tell you, that just proves you're the real murderer here."

His voice rose as he gained momentum, his words spilling out faster now, his anger building. "Do you know what you deserve, Pyotr Stepanovitch? For the sheer depravity of your soul, for turning your back on God Himself, the true Creator, you deserve to be cast out like the idol-worshipping Tatars and Mordvins. Alexey Nilitch here, a philosopher and a man of learning, has explained the true Creator to you time and time again—the creation of the world, the destiny of mankind, the transformation of beasts foretold in the Apocalypse. But you, you've closed your ears and your heart, stubborn as an idolater. Worse still, you've dragged Ensign Erkel down with you, seducing him into your so-called atheism."

"Ah, you drunken fool!" Pyotr Stepanovitch burst out, his face dark with fury. "You strip the holy icons of their jewels and then have the gall to preach to me about God!"

Fedka met his outburst with a sly grin. "Yes, I took the pearls from the icons," he admitted, almost proudly. "But how do you know? Perhaps one of my own tears, shed in the furnace of the Most High, was transformed into a pearl to balance my suffering. Do you know the old tale, Pyotr Stepanovitch? Once, in ancient times, a merchant stole a pearl from the halo of the Mother of God. With tearful prayers, he laid the price of it at her feet before the whole congregation, and the Holy Mother, in her infinite grace, sheltered him under her mantle for all to see. It was a miracle, recorded word for word in the Imperial books. And yet you, Pyotr Stepanovitch, you insult the very throne of God with your wickedness."

Fedka's tone suddenly grew darker, more menacing. "If you weren't my master by nature—if I hadn't cradled you in my arms when you were but a boy—I'd deal with you here and now. I wouldn't move from this spot until I'd finished you off!"

His words hung in the air, heavy with threat and venom. Pyotr Stepanovitch, momentarily taken aback, glared at him, his anger warring with a flicker of unease. Liputin, still watching from the shadows, remained silent, his presence almost forgotten amidst the rising tension in the room. The air felt charged, as though something explosive was about to unfold.

Pyotr Stepanovitch exploded into a violent rage, his face contorting with fury. His voice, sharp and cutting, filled the room.

"Have you seen Stavrogin today?" he demanded, his eyes blazing.

"Don't you dare question me!" Fedka barked back, leaning forward with a look of defiance. "Mr. Stavrogin is amazed at you, utterly amazed. He's had no part in this—not in thought, not in instruction, and certainly not in giving you money. You've overstepped your bounds with me, Pyotr Stepanovitch."

"You'll get your money," Pyotr Stepanovitch snapped, trying to reassert control. "And when you get to Petersburg, you'll receive another two thousand rubles in one lump sum, and there will be more after that."

Fedka let out a sharp, mocking laugh, his contempt evident. "You're lying through your teeth, my fine gentleman. And it's laughable to see how easily you're fooled. Don't you see? Mr. Stavrogin is far above you—he stands at the very top of the ladder, looking down while you bark at him from below like a silly little puppy. He probably thinks it would be too much of an honor to spit on you."

"You scoundrel!" Pyotr Stepanovitch shouted, his rage reaching its peak. "Do you know what I could do to you? I won't let you take another step from here. I'll hand you straight over to the police!"

Before Pyotr Stepanovitch could react, Fedka sprang to his feet, his drunken swagger vanishing in an instant. His eyes flashed with fury, his body taut with anger. Pyotr Stepanovitch, caught off guard, fumbled for his revolver, yanking it out in a panic. But before he could even raise it, Fedka moved with lightning speed, swinging around and delivering a powerful slap across Pyotr Stepanovitch's face.

The sharp sound of the blow echoed through the room, followed immediately by another, and then another. Each slap landed with brutal force, each one directed squarely at Pyotr Stepanovitch's cheek. He stumbled under the onslaught, his eyes wide and unfocused, as if the world had tilted on its axis. He muttered something incoherent, his voice barely a whisper, before collapsing to the ground with a heavy thud, sprawling full length on the floor.

"There you go, take him!" Fedka shouted triumphantly, his voice filled with mockery and disdain. Without wasting a second, he grabbed his cap and the small bag that had been stashed under the bench. With a jaunty air, he strode out of the kitchen, his boots echoing against the wooden floor, and disappeared into the night.

Pyotr Stepanovitch lay motionless, gasping for breath. His face was pale and slack, his body unnaturally still. Liputin, who had been peering nervously into the kitchen from the adjoining room, stared in horror. For a brief, heart-stopping moment, he thought that Pyotr Stepanovitch had been killed. Then Kirillov burst into the room, his usual composure shattered.

"Water!" Kirillov shouted, his voice urgent as he grabbed an iron dipper from a bucket. He quickly ladled water and poured it over Pyotr Stepanovitch's head, the cold splash breaking the silence of the room. Slowly, Pyotr Stepanovitch began to stir. He groaned softly, raising his head as though it weighed a hundred pounds. Finally, he sat up, blinking dazedly as he tried to gather his bearings.

"How are you feeling?" Kirillov asked, his tone neutral but edged with curiosity.

Pyotr Stepanovitch stared at him blankly for a moment, his expression unreadable. Then his eyes shifted, and he caught sight of Liputin, who was still standing frozen in the doorway. A hateful smile curled across Pyotr Stepanovitch's lips, and he suddenly rose to his feet, scooping up the revolver that had fallen from his hand.

"If you take it into your head to run away tomorrow like that wretch Stavrogin," he spat, turning furiously toward Kirillov, "I'll hang you... like a fly… or crush you… even if you're at the other end of the world! Do you understand me?"

His hand shook as he raised the revolver, pointing it directly at Kirillov's head. For a tense, electrifying moment, the room seemed to hold its breath. Then, as if coming to his senses, Pyotr Stepanovitch lowered the gun abruptly. He shoved it into his pocket, his expression hardening. Without another word, he turned on his heel and stormed out of the house, his steps heavy with fury.

Liputin hesitated only for a moment before rushing after him. The two men clambered through the same narrow gap in the fence and began walking quickly along the sloping path. Pyotr Stepanovitch moved with such speed that Liputin struggled to keep up, his heart racing from the adrenaline of the scene they had just left behind.

At the first street crossing, Pyotr Stepanovitch stopped abruptly and turned to face Liputin. His expression was sharp and challenging.

"Well?" he barked, his voice cutting through the stillness.

Liputin, still trembling from what he had witnessed, found himself unable to think clearly. His words came out in a stammer. "I think… I think that…"

"What did you see Fedka drinking in the kitchen?" Pyotr Stepanovitch interrupted suddenly, his tone oddly calm.

"What he was drinking?" Liputin repeated, confused. "He was drinking vodka."

"Good," Pyotr Stepanovitch replied, his lips curling into a cold smile. "Then let me tell you this—it's the last time in his life he'll drink vodka. Remember that, and think about it carefully."

Without waiting for a response, he added harshly, "And now, get lost. You're not needed until tomorrow. But don't do anything stupid!"

With that, he turned and strode off down the street, leaving Liputin standing there in stunned silence. After a moment, Liputin turned and rushed home at full speed, his thoughts a chaotic jumble as the night swallowed him.

Chapter 4.4

Liputin had long kept a passport prepared under a false name, hidden away like a secret talisman against some distant and undefined calamity. The very idea seemed almost absurd. Here was a meticulous man, known for his sharp business acumen, his domineering grip on his household, and his status as a petty official, not to mention his eccentric devotion to Fourierist ideals. Yet, despite his calculated prudence, Liputin had indulged in the fantastic project of acquiring a false passport—just in case. He had no clear vision of what that "case" might entail, but the possibility of some vague, looming catastrophe had always lingered at the edges of his mind, unformed and formless.

Now, however, that hazy "if" suddenly took shape, arriving in a manner he could never have predicted. The reckless idea that had seized him after overhearing Pyotr Stepanovitch mutter "fool" on the pavement crystallized into a desperate plan: he would abandon everything, leave at dawn, and flee abroad. It was madness, and yet, if one were to study the biographies of Russian exiles, one would find that many had fled under similarly irrational circumstances. In such moments, it was not reason that dictated their actions but the overpowering grip of phantoms—vivid, half-formed fears that compelled them to act without reflection or justification.

Upon reaching home, Liputin locked himself in his room. He immediately dragged out his traveling bag and began to pack with feverish intensity, his hands trembling as he worked. His thoughts raced, but his primary concern was money. How much could he gather? How much could he salvage from the ruin he felt was inevitable? He thought of it not as securing funds but as "rescuing" them, as though he were saving something precious from the clutches of disaster. The sense of urgency gnawed at him; he felt as though he couldn't afford to linger another hour. By daylight, he was determined to be far away, already on the high road leading to safety.

His plans were haphazard and incomplete. He had no idea which train station he would use. In his mind, he vaguely resolved to avoid the one closest to town, opting instead for a second or third station further afield.

If necessary, he would walk miles to reach it. His hands darted from one item to another, stuffing his bag with a whirl of disjointed thoughts. Then, suddenly, he stopped. His hands froze, his breath caught in his throat, and he slumped onto the sofa with a deep, guttural groan.

As he lay there, a terrible realization began to settle over him. He could escape—his passport was ready, and there was nothing physically stopping him—but he found himself paralyzed by indecision. Should he flee before Shatov's death or after? The question hung in his mind like a lead weight, and he could not answer it. He felt as though he were no longer a man of will but a lifeless, inert object, moved not by his own choices but by an external, inescapable force. The decision was no longer his to make. Whether he stayed or fled, the outcome felt predetermined, signed, and sealed by some awful, unseen hand. The realization left him trembling with fear and loathing, not only of his circumstances but of himself.

For the rest of the night, Liputin remained in this state of torment. Alternating between groans of despair and stretches of numb terror, he endured the hours locked in his room, lying motionless on the sofa. By eleven o'clock the next morning, his anguish reached its peak, and the shock he had been dreading finally arrived. When he unlocked his door and stepped out to speak with his household, they greeted him with startling news: at daybreak, the runaway convict and infamous brigand Fedka had been found murdered. His body was discovered five miles from town, near a turning off the high road. The entire town was already buzzing with the story.

Liputin's mind reeled. He rushed out of the house, desperate for more information. From his inquiries, he learned that Fedka had been killed by a blow to the head, his skull crushed in, and that he had apparently been robbed. The police, he was told, had already identified a prime suspect: Fomka, one of the Shpigulin workers. Fomka, they said, had been Fedka's accomplice in the murder of the Lebyadkins and the arson of their home. It appeared the two had quarreled on the road over a large sum of money stolen from Lebyadkin, which Fedka was rumored to have hidden.

Still shaken, Liputin hurried to Pyotr Stepanovitch's lodgings. He managed to slip in through the back door and confirm, to his surprise, that Pyotr Stepanovitch had returned home the previous night around one o'clock and had slept soundly until eight in the morning. There was nothing outwardly suspicious about his behavior. The rational part of Liputin's mind told him that Fedka's death was not extraordinary. Such men often met violent ends. But the eerie coincidence of Pyotr Stepanovitch's chilling remark—"it's the last time Fedka will drink vodka"—with the brutal timing of Fedka's death was impossible to ignore. It felt like a stone had been dropped on him, crushing him under its weight.

When Liputin returned home, he made no effort to continue packing. Instead, he shoved his half-filled traveling bag under the bed without a word. By the evening, when the appointed hour arrived to meet Shatov, Liputin was the first to appear at the designated spot. His passport remained in his pocket, but the desperate resolve to flee had drained away, leaving only a hollow shell of the man who had feverishly planned his escape the night before.

Chapter 5
A Wanderer

Chapter 5.1

The tragedy involving Liza and the death of Marya Timofyevna had a profound and devastating impact on Shatov. As I mentioned before, I passed him that morning and found him visibly shaken, as though he were not himself. Among other things, he told me that the evening before, around nine o'clock—three hours before the fire started—he had visited Marya Timofyevna. Later that morning, he went to see the bodies but, as far as I know, did not provide any statements or evidence about the events. However, as the day went on, his inner turmoil grew into a raging storm. By dusk, I am almost certain he reached a point where he felt an overwhelming urge to get up, go out, and reveal everything he knew. What "everything" meant, only Shatov himself could say.

Of course, even if he had gone through with it, his actions would likely have accomplished nothing. He would have only incriminated himself. He had no solid evidence to convict those responsible for the crimes—only vague suspicions that, to him, felt like absolute certainty. Yet he was prepared to ruin his own life if it meant exposing and "crushing the scoundrels," as he put it. Pyotr Stepanovitch had guessed fairly accurately that Shatov might act on this impulse, and he knew he was taking a significant risk by delaying the execution of his latest grim plan until the next day. Still, Pyotr Stepanovitch's usual overconfidence in his ability to manipulate people and his deep contempt for Shatov left him unbothered. He had long despised Shatov, whom he considered weak and pathetic—a "whining idiot," as he had once called him during their time abroad. Pyotr Stepanovitch was certain that he could control Shatov, watch him closely all day, and stop him at the first sign of trouble.

Yet what temporarily saved the perpetrators from Shatov's potential actions was something entirely unforeseen.

Around eight o'clock that evening, while the quintet was meeting at Erkel's house, filled with indignation and impatience over Pyotr Stepanovitch's absence, Shatov was lying in the dark on his bed. He had a headache and felt chilled, as if he might be coming down with something. His mind was tormented with uncertainty, anger, and a sense of helplessness. He kept making decisions and then doubting them, cursing himself for his indecisiveness, and feeling that none of it would make any difference. Slowly, he drifted off into a restless sleep, his thoughts still swirling. In his brief slumber, he had a strange and unsettling nightmare.

In his dream, he was tied to his bed with ropes, unable to move. Somewhere nearby, he heard a loud banging that seemed to shake the entire house. The pounding came from everywhere—on the fence, at the gate, at his door, and even at Kirillov's lodge. Along with the noise, a voice echoed faintly, growing louder, one that sounded familiar and tugged painfully at his heart. It called out to him in desperation, pleading and piteous. The dream's intensity jolted him awake, and he sat up in bed, his chest heaving.

To his shock, the banging at the gate was not just part of the dream—it was real. Though not as violent as it had seemed in his sleep, the persistent knocking continued, breaking the stillness of the night. The voice he had heard so vividly in his dream still called out, though it no longer sounded pleading. Instead, it was now sharp and impatient, alternating with another, calmer voice that sounded more ordinary. Alarmed, Shatov jumped out of bed, hurried to the window, opened the casement, and stuck his head out into the night air.

"Who's there?" Shatov called out, his voice trembling with fear, as if he were frozen in place.

"If you're Shatov," came a harsh and determined voice from below, "just tell me plainly and honestly—are you going to let me in or not?"

It was true; he recognized the voice immediately.

"Marie!... Is that you?"

"Yes, yes, it's me, Marya Shatov, and I can't keep the driver waiting a minute longer," she replied sharply.

"Just a second... I'll get a candle," Shatov said faintly, almost choking on his words. He rushed to find matches, but as often happens in moments like this, they seemed to have disappeared. In his frantic search, he knocked the candlestick and candle to the floor. Hearing her impatient voice calling from below again, he gave up, abandoning the search, and dashed down the steep stairs to open the gate.

"Hold this bag while I deal with this idiot," Marya Shatov said as she thrust a small, lightweight canvas handbag into his hands. The bag was cheaply made, covered with brass studs, and clearly from Dresden. Without waiting for a response, she turned to the driver, her voice sharp with irritation.

"Let me tell you, you're charging far too much! If you've been driving me around for an extra hour through these awful streets, that's on you, not me. You clearly didn't know where this stupid street or this idiotic house was. Take your thirty kopecks and accept that you're not getting a kopeck more."

"Lady, you told me Voznesensky Street yourself, and this is Bogoyavlensky Street! Voznesensky is much further away. You've driven the poor horse into a sweat."

"Voznesensky, Bogoyavlensky—aren't you supposed to know these ridiculous names better than I do? You live here! Besides, I told you right from the start I needed Filipov's house, and you said you knew where it was. If you want to complain, take me to court tomorrow. But for now, I insist that you leave me alone."

"Here, take another five kopecks," Shatov said hastily, pulling a coin from his pocket and handing it to the driver in an attempt to calm the situation.

"Please don't you dare do that!" Marya flared up, glaring at him, but the driver had already pocketed the extra money and driven off without another word.

Shatov, still holding her hand, gently but firmly guided her through the gate, finally bringing an end to the tense exchange.

"Hurry, Marie, hurry … it doesn't matter, and … you're soaked through. Be careful, we're going up here—sorry there's no light. The stairs are steep; hold on tight, hold on tight! Well, this is my room. I'm sorry there's no light … one moment!"

He grabbed the candlestick, but it took him a long time to find the matches. Madame Shatov stood still in the middle of the room, silent and motionless, waiting.

"Thank God, here they are at last!" he exclaimed in relief as he lit the candle, filling the room with a dim, flickering glow. Marya Shatov took a quick look around the room, her expression growing sour.

"They said you lived poorly, but I didn't think it would be this bad," she said with obvious disgust, moving toward the bed.

"Oh, I'm so tired," she said as she sank down onto the hard mattress, her voice heavy with exhaustion. "Put the bag down and sit in the chair, if you want. Or don't—it's up to you. But you're in the way just standing there. I've come to stay with you for a while, at least until I can find work. I don't know this place at all, and I don't have any money. But if I'm going to be a burden, please, just say so now. That's the honest thing to do. I could sell something tomorrow and get a room at a hotel, but you'll have to take me there yourself … Oh, I'm so tired."

Shatov was trembling from head to toe.

"You can't, Marie! You mustn't go to a hotel! A hotel? Why? What for? What for?" he stammered, clasping his hands as if begging her.

"Well, if I can manage without a hotel … but I need to make things clear," she said firmly, straightening her back. "Shatov, remember we lived as husband and wife in Geneva for a little over two weeks. It's been three years since we parted, and there wasn't any big fight or anything. But don't think for a second that I've come back to rekindle any of that foolishness from the past. I've come here to find work, and the reason I came to this town is because it doesn't matter to me where I go. And let me make one thing absolutely clear—I'm not here to apologize for anything. Don't think something that ridiculous."

"Oh, Marie! There's no need for this—none at all," Shatov mumbled vaguely, overwhelmed by her directness.

"If that's the case, and if you're decent enough to understand what I'm saying, then I'll add this: the only reason I've come straight to you and am standing in your room now is because I always believed you weren't like the rest of those … scoundrels!"

Her eyes flared with anger. It was clear she had suffered greatly at the hands of such "scoundrels."

"And don't think I was mocking you when I said you were good. I meant it, plainly and honestly. I can't stand fancy words or empty flattery. But all of this doesn't matter. I just hope you've got enough sense not to bother me with anything silly. That's all. I'm exhausted."

She gave him a long, weary look. Shatov stood at the other end of the small room, about five paces away, watching her nervously. His face lit up with a mix of joy and disbelief. This rugged, rough-edged man, who usually bristled with pride and quick temper, was suddenly soft and glowing with quiet happiness. A wave of unexpected emotion surged through him.

Three years of separation and a broken marriage had done nothing to dull his feelings. Perhaps every single day of those years, he had thought about her, dreamed of her—the one person who had once told him, "I love you." Knowing Shatov, it was certain he had never allowed himself to imagine such words coming from any woman. He was painfully modest, harshly critical of himself, and deeply ashamed of his appearance and character. He saw himself as an ugly, awkward creature, something fit only for a sideshow. His pride, though fierce, was rooted in a belief in honesty and a relentless devotion to his ideals.

But this woman, Marya Shatov, had once loved him for a short, beautiful time—he had never doubted that. To him, she was someone far above him, even though he clearly understood her flaws. She was someone he could forgive for anything, absolutely anything. In fact, he believed all blame lay with him alone. And now, she was here, standing in his room, in his presence once more. It felt impossible, like a dream.

The situation was overwhelming—a strange blend of terror and joy. Shatov could barely process what was happening, perhaps because he didn't want to or was too afraid to. But when she looked at him with that tired, tormented gaze, something inside him shifted. He realized, with a pang of sorrow, that the woman he loved was in pain. She had suffered, perhaps deeply. His heart ached as he studied her face, looking for clues.

The youthful energy that once defined her was long gone. Her face, though still beautiful to him, was pale and worn, the vibrancy of youth replaced by signs of strain and hardship. She was still striking, with her strong build, dark brown hair, and large, fever-bright eyes. To him, she was as beautiful as ever. But the cheerful, carefree spirit he remembered had been replaced by a bitter irritability and a hardened cynicism. It was as though she carried a heavy weight she had not yet grown used to.

Most of all, Shatov could see that she was unwell. That realization pierced him deeply. Despite his awe of her, despite his belief that she was far above him, he suddenly found the courage to step forward. He crossed the room and, trembling with emotion, gently took her hands in his.

"Marie... you must be so tired. For God's sake, please don't be upset... Would you agree to have some tea, maybe? Tea is so refreshing, isn't it? Please say yes!"

"Why even ask?" she replied sharply. "Of course I'll have some tea.

You're still such a child. If you can get it, bring it. This place is so cramped, and it's freezing!"

"I'll bring logs for the fire right away! Logs… I've got logs." Shatov was rushing about, clearly flustered. "Logs… but first, I'll get the tea. Yes, tea! I'll get it right away," he added with sudden determination, snatching up his cap.

"Where are you going? You don't even have tea in the house, do you?"

"There will be tea, there will be everything—just wait! I… I…" He grabbed his revolver from the shelf. "I'll sell this revolver right now—or pawn it—anything!"

"Don't be ridiculous!" she snapped. "And what a waste of time that would be! Just take my money if you have nothing. I've got eighty kopecks here—that's all I've got. This is like some kind of madhouse."

"I don't want your money! I don't need it!" he cried, almost offended. "I'll be back right away, in just a minute. I can manage without selling the revolver!"

With that, he rushed out of the house and straight to Kirillov's. This must have been two hours before Pyotr Stepanovitch and Liputin visited Kirillov. Despite living in the same yard, Shatov and Kirillov rarely interacted. When they did cross paths, they didn't even nod or exchange words, a result of their long and complicated history of "lying side by side" during their time in America.

"Kirillov! You always have tea. Do you have tea and a samovar?" Shatov blurted out as he entered Kirillov's room.

Kirillov, who had been pacing the room as he often did late at night, stopped and looked at his visitor with mild curiosity but no surprise.

"I have tea, sugar, and a samovar," Kirillov replied. "But there's no need for the samovar right now. The tea's already hot. Sit down and drink it."

"Kirillov… we lived side by side in America… My wife has come back to me… I need tea… and I'll need the samovar."

"If your wife is here, then you'll need the samovar," Kirillov said calmly. "Take it later. I have two. For now, take the teapot on the table. It's hot, boiling hot. Take everything—sugar, bread, all of it. There's some veal, too. And here's a rouble."

"Thank you, my friend! I'll pay you back tomorrow!" Shatov said with emotion. "Oh, Kirillov!"

"Is it the same wife from Switzerland? That's good. And you rushing in like this—that's good too," Kirillov remarked.

"Kirillov," Shatov said, holding the teapot under one arm and balancing the bread and sugar in both hands, "if only you could rid yourself of those dreadful ideas—your atheistic ravings—what a man you could be, Kirillov!"

"You must love your wife very much after Switzerland. That's good— you love her after Switzerland. Come back for tea anytime. Come all night if you want. I don't sleep. I'll have a samovar ready. Take the rouble. Go to your wife. I'll stay here and think about you and her."

Shatov hurried back, and Marya was visibly pleased by how quickly he returned. She eagerly reached for the tea but drank only half a cup, nibbling on a small piece of bread. She refused the veal with clear disgust and irritation, pushing it aside as though the very sight of it annoyed her.

"You're not well, Marie. All of this is a sign that you're sick," Shatov said softly, almost timidly, as he stood nearby, ready to help her.

"Of course I'm sick. Sit down, please. Where did you get the tea if you didn't have any?"

Shatov quickly explained how he had gone to Kirillov for it. She seemed vaguely aware of who Kirillov was.

"I know about him. He's insane, isn't he? That's enough, say no more. There are plenty of fools out there. So, you've been in America? I heard about it. You wrote me."

"Yes, I… I wrote to you in Paris."

"Enough. Let's talk about something else. Are you still a Slavophile in your beliefs?"

"I... I wouldn't say exactly... Since I couldn't be a true Russian, I became a Slavophile," he replied with a wry, almost painful smile, as if realizing the awkwardness of his joke even as he said it.

"What do you mean, you're not Russian?"

"I'm not."

"That's ridiculous. Sit down, please. Why are you pacing like that? Do you think I'm delirious? Maybe I will be. You said there were only two of you in this house?"

"Yes... just the two of us now..."

"And both of you so clever. But what's downstairs? You mentioned downstairs."

"No, nothing."

"What do you mean, nothing? I want to know."

"I just meant that now it's only the two of us here in the yard. But the Lebyadkins used to live downstairs..."

"You mean that woman who was murdered last night?" she asked suddenly, sitting up slightly. "I heard about it. I heard about it as soon as I got here. There was a fire too, wasn't there?"

"Yes, Marie, yes. And maybe right now I'm doing something terrible by forgiving the ones who did it..." He suddenly stood up and began pacing around the room, throwing his arms in the air as if overcome by emotion.

But Marie didn't fully grasp what he was saying. She seemed to only half-hear his answers, asking questions without really listening to the responses.

"Such awful things happen here! It's disgusting. All men are scoundrels. But sit down, I'm begging you. You're driving me crazy!" She sank back against the pillow, her voice weak with exhaustion.

"Marie, I won't... Should you lie down, Marie?" he asked gently.

She didn't reply. Instead, she closed her eyes, her pale face looking almost lifeless. Within moments, she drifted into a deep sleep.

Shatov stood nearby, watching her closely. He adjusted the candle, snuffing it to make the light dimmer. His gaze lingered uneasily on her face, which now seemed peaceful in sleep. He pressed his hands together tightly and walked on tiptoe out of the room and into the hallway.

At the top of the stairs, he stopped in a corner and turned to face the wall. He stood there silently, unmoving, for ten minutes. It seemed as though he could have stayed there even longer, lost in thought or overwhelmed by the moment. But then, he suddenly heard soft, cautious footsteps coming from below.

Someone was climbing the stairs.

Shatov's heart sank as he realized he had forgotten to fasten the gate.

"Who's there?" Shatov asked in a whisper, his voice tense.

The unknown visitor continued climbing the stairs slowly, saying nothing. When he reached the top, he stopped. It was too dark to see his face. Suddenly, Shatov heard a cautious question:

"Ivan Shatov?"

Shatov confirmed who he was but immediately held out his hand to stop the visitor from coming any closer. The man took his hand, and Shatov shuddered, feeling as if he'd just touched something slimy and dreadful.

"Stay here," he whispered quickly. "Don't go in. I can't receive you right now. My wife has just returned. I'll fetch a candle."

When he returned with the candle, Shatov saw a young officer standing before him. He didn't know the man's name but recognized his face.

"Erkel," the officer introduced himself. "You've seen me before at Virginsky's."

"I remember," Shatov said, his voice rising in sudden agitation as he stepped closer to him. "You were the one writing something down. Listen!" His whisper turned frantic. "You gave me a signal just now when

632

you shook my hand. But you should know I despise these signals! I don't acknowledge them. I reject them! I could throw you down these stairs right now—do you understand that?"

"I don't know what you're so angry about," the visitor replied calmly, almost innocently. "I'm just here to deliver a message, nothing more. I didn't want to waste any time. You have a printing press that doesn't belong to you, and you need to account for it. I've been sent to ask you to hand it over tomorrow at seven in the evening to Liputin. I was also instructed to tell you that nothing more will be demanded of you."

"Nothing else?"

"Absolutely nothing. Your request has been granted, and you've been removed from our list. I was told to make that very clear."

"Who told you to say that?"

"The same people who gave me the signal."

"Did you come from abroad?"

"I… I don't think that matters to you."

"Oh, for heaven's sake! Why didn't you come earlier if you were told to deliver this message?"

"I followed certain instructions, and I wasn't alone."

"I get it; you weren't alone. Fine. But why didn't Liputin come himself?"

"I'll come to pick you up tomorrow at exactly six in the evening, and we'll walk there together. Only the three of us will be there."

"Will Verhovensky be there?"

"No, he won't. Verhovensky is leaving town at eleven tomorrow morning."

"Just as I thought!" Shatov hissed furiously, slamming his fist against his hip. "The coward is running away!"

He fell into deep, agitated thought. Erkel stood silently, watching him with a calm and patient expression.

"But how are you planning to take it? You can't just pick it up and carry it in your hands."

"There won't be any need for that. You'll just show us where it's buried. We already know the general area but not the exact spot. Have you shown it to anyone else yet?"

Shatov stared at him.

"You... a foolish boy like you, caught in this mess like a helpless sheep? That's exactly what they want—young blood! Go on, then. Oh, that scoundrel fooled all of you and now he's run off."

Erkel continued to look at him calmly, not appearing to grasp the weight of Shatov's words.

"Verhovensky has run away!" Shatov growled through clenched teeth.

"But he hasn't left yet," Erkel replied softly. "He's still here. He doesn't leave until tomorrow morning. I even asked him to be present as a witness for this, but he refused. He said he was in too much of a hurry."

Shatov glanced at the young man again, this time with a tinge of pity, but almost immediately waved it away in despair, as if deciding, "They're not worth pitying."

"Fine, I'll come," he said abruptly. "Now get out of here. Go."

"I'll be here at six sharp tomorrow," Erkel said, bowing politely before walking down the stairs.

"Little fool!" Shatov couldn't help shouting after him.

"What did you say?" Erkel called back from the bottom of the stairs.

"Nothing. Just go."

"I thought you said something."

"Forget it," Shatov muttered, turning away.

Chapter 5.2

Erkel was a "fool," but only in the sense that he lacked higher reasoning and the ability to think critically. He was not short on practical sense or even cunning, however. Fanatically and almost childishly devoted to "the cause," or more precisely to Pyotr Verhovensky, Erkel carried out instructions with unquestioning loyalty. At the meeting of the quintet, when responsibilities for the next day were divided, Pyotr Stepanovitch had assigned him the role of messenger. Erkel even managed to pull Verhovensky aside for a private ten-minute conversation, eager to understand every detail of his task.

Erkel's nature craved action and a sense of purpose. He wasn't one to reflect deeply or question anything; instead, he longed to follow someone else's lead, believing that doing so served "the greater good." For Erkel, serving a cause was inseparable from serving the person who represented it. Despite his sensitive and kind-hearted demeanor, Erkel was perhaps the coldest of Shatov's would-be killers. He bore no personal grudge against Shatov but would have stood by at his murder without blinking. He had been instructed, for example, to observe Shatov's surroundings carefully while delivering his message. When Shatov, caught up in the moment, mentioned that his wife had returned, Erkel's instinctive cunning kept him from showing any curiosity. Still, the thought flashed through his mind that her return was a critical detail for the success of their plans.

Indeed, her return played a crucial role in shaping the events to come. It distracted Shatov, pulling him out of his usual routine and leaving him less cautious than he would normally have been. With his mind consumed by thoughts of his wife, Shatov was unlikely to focus on his own danger. On the contrary, he quickly latched onto the idea that Verhovensky was fleeing the next day, as it fit perfectly with his suspicions.

After leaving Erkel, Shatov returned to the room, sat down in a corner, rested his elbows on his knees, and buried his face in his hands. His mind churned with bitter thoughts, one after another.

But he couldn't stay seated for long. Every so often, he would lift his head and tiptoe over to look at his wife as she slept. "Dear God! She'll have a fever by tomorrow morning—maybe it's already started! She must have caught cold. She's not used to this horrible weather. And then traveling in a third-class carriage, in that storm and rain, wearing such a thin little coat, no proper wrap at all.... And now to leave her like this, to abandon her when she's so helpless!"

He glanced over at her small, battered bag. "Her bag—look at it! Such a tiny thing, so light, so crumpled, it probably weighs less than ten pounds. Poor thing, she's so worn out. What has she been through? She's too proud to complain, but I can see it's all been too much for her. And she's so irritable—yes, very irritable. But that's only because she's sick. Even an angel would be irritable when they're ill."

His gaze softened as it lingered on her face. "Her forehead—it's so dry, it must be burning up. The dark circles under her eyes... but still, the shape of her face, that beautiful oval, it hasn't changed. And her hair, so rich, so..."

His thoughts trailed off, consumed by a mix of anguish and tenderness.

He quickly turned his eyes away and walked to the corner of the room, as if frightened by the thought of seeing her as anything other than a helpless, worn-out person who needed care. "How could I let myself think of hopes? Oh, how low, how selfish people can be!" he thought. He sank back into his corner, covered his face with his hands, and drifted into dreams and memories again—yet those same hopes crept back into his mind.

"I'm so tired, so tired," he remembered her saying, her voice weak and broken. "My God! She has only eighty kopecks. She held out her little purse, such an old, tiny thing. She came here to find work—what does she know about finding work? What do they know about Russia? They're like naive children, chasing after dreams they made up themselves. And now she's upset, poor thing, because Russia isn't what she imagined. The poor, innocent soul!... And it really is cold in here."

He remembered her complaining about the cold and how he'd

promised to heat the stove. "There are logs here—I can get them without waking her. Yes, I can do it quietly. But what about the veal? When she wakes up, she might be hungry.... Well, that can wait. Kirillov doesn't sleep at night; I could ask him for something. But she's sleeping so soundly, and she must be cold—she has to be cold!"

He walked over to look at her again. Her dress had shifted slightly, and her right leg was uncovered up to the knee. Startled, he turned away quickly, almost in alarm. Taking off his warm overcoat, he carefully draped it over her, leaving himself in his thin, worn jacket. He tried not to look as he did it.

Much of the night passed like this: tending to the fire, walking quietly on tiptoe, gazing at her sleeping form, retreating to his corner to think, and then looking at her again. Two or three hours went by in this manner. During that time, Verhovensky and Liputin had been to Kirillov's. At last, he began to doze off in his corner, exhausted.

Then he heard her groan softly. She stirred, waking up, and called his name. Shatov sprang to his feet as though he'd been caught doing something wrong.

"Marie, I must have fallen asleep.... Oh, what a fool I am, Marie!"

She sat up, looking around the room with confusion, as if she didn't recognize where she was. Then, all at once, she leapt to her feet, her face flushed with anger and indignation.

"I've taken your bed!" she exclaimed. "I was so tired, I fell asleep without thinking. How could you let me? How dare you not wake me? How could you let me do this? Do you think I came here to be a burden to you?"

"How could I wake you, Marie?" Shatov asked softly.

"You should have! You had to! This is your only bed, and I've taken it. You've put me in a position I never intended to be in. Do you think I came here to live off your charity? No! Get in your bed at once—I'll sleep in the corner on some chairs."

"Marie, there aren't enough chairs, and there's nothing to put on them to make them comfortable."

"Then oil the floor. Or you sleep on the floor, and I'll stay on the bed. But I'm not staying here—I'll lie on the floor right now, right this moment!"

She stood up and tried to take a step, but a sudden, sharp pain stopped her in her tracks. With a loud groan, she fell back onto the bed, her strength completely gone. Shatov rushed to her side, but Marie buried her face in the pillow, gripping his hand tightly with all her might. Her grip was so strong it hurt, and it lasted for nearly a minute.

"Marie, my dear, there's a doctor here—Frenzel. He's a friend of mine. I could go get him right now," Shatov offered anxiously.

"Don't be ridiculous," she muttered.

"What do you mean ridiculous? Marie, tell me where it hurts. Maybe we could try some warm compresses… maybe on your stomach? I can do that myself, without a doctor. Or maybe mustard poultices would help?"

She raised her head and looked at him with a mix of confusion and disbelief. "What is this?" she asked strangely.

"What do you mean, Marie?" Shatov asked, baffled. "What are you asking about? My God, I don't understand. I'm sorry—I'm completely lost."

"Forget it," she said with a bitter smile. "It's none of your business to understand. Besides, it would just be absurd." She paused, then continued in a strained voice, "Talk to me about something. Walk around the room and talk. Don't stand there staring at me. I've asked you a hundred times not to do that!"

Shatov began pacing the room, staring at the floor and doing his best not to glance at her.

"There's—don't be upset, Marie, please—there's some veal here, and tea not far away. You barely ate anything before," he said nervously.

She waved her hand dismissively, her face showing irritation. Shatov immediately regretted mentioning it and bit his tongue in frustration.

"Listen," he began again, "I've been thinking about starting a bookbinding business here. It would be based on cooperative principles. Since you're here now, what do you think? Do you think it could work?"

Marie scoffed. "People don't even read books here, let alone bind them. There aren't even any books around."

"Who do you mean by 'they'?" he asked.

"The locals—the readers, the townsfolk," she replied sharply.

"Well, you could explain that more clearly. Who are 'they,' anyway? You sound like you don't even know grammar," she snapped.

"It's just the way people speak," Shatov muttered defensively.

"Oh, spare me your language lessons," she said dismissively. "Why wouldn't the local readers want to bind their books?"

"Because reading and binding books are two completely different stages of progress," Shatov explained. "There's a big gap between them. First, people get used to reading. That takes ages, of course, and during that time, they don't take care of their books. They toss them around like they're nothing. Binding books shows respect for them. It means they see books as valuable. That stage hasn't arrived in Russia yet. In Europe, though, they've been binding books for a long time."

"That's a pedantic explanation," she remarked, her voice dripping with disdain. "But at least it's not stupid. It reminds me of you three years ago. You used to have clever ideas sometimes back then."

"Marie, Marie," Shatov said, turning to her with deep emotion. "If only you knew how much has happened in these three years! I heard later that you despised me for changing my beliefs. But look at the people I broke away from! They're enemies of true life, old-fashioned Liberals who are afraid of real independence. They're flunkeys of thought, enemies of individuality and freedom. All they stand for is decay, mediocrity, and shallow, envious equality—equality without dignity. It's the kind of equality you'd find in flunkeys or in the French Revolution of '93. And the worst part is, they're crawling with scoundrels, so many scoundrels!"

"Yes, there are plenty of scoundrels," she said suddenly, her voice strained. She lay motionless, her head tilted back on the pillow, staring at the ceiling with exhausted yet burning eyes. Her face was pale, her lips dry and feverish.

"You see it, Marie. You see it," Shatov exclaimed passionately.

She tried to shake her head, but another spasm of pain overtook her. She turned her face into the pillow again and gripped Shatov's hand tightly, her nails digging into his skin. He winced but didn't pull away.

"Marie, Marie! This could be serious!" Shatov cried in panic.

"Be quiet!" she shouted, turning her face upward again. "I won't have it—I won't! Don't you dare look at me with that pity in your eyes! Walk around the room! Say something—talk!"

Shatov started muttering incoherently, pacing like a man distraught.

"What do you do here?" she interrupted impatiently.

"I work in a merchant's office," Shatov answered hesitantly. "I could make decent money here if I wanted to, Marie."

"Good for you," she replied flatly.

"Oh, Marie, don't take it that way! I didn't mean anything by it," he stammered.

"And what else do you do? What are you preaching now? You can't survive without preaching—that's just who you are!"

"I'm preaching about God, Marie," he said earnestly.

"About a God you don't even believe in yourself. I never understood that," she replied coldly.

"Let's leave that for now, Marie; we can talk about it later."

"What kind of person was this Marya Timofyevna?"

"We'll talk about that later too, Marie."

"Don't you dare speak to me like that! Is it true that her death might have been caused by… the cruelty of those people?"

"Without a doubt," Shatov muttered grimly.

Marie suddenly lifted her head and cried out in pain, her voice trembling with emotion.

"Don't you dare bring that up to me again—don't you dare! Never, never again!"

She collapsed back onto the bed, writhing in the same convulsive agony as before. It was the third time, but this time her groans turned into screams.

"Oh, you impossible man! You unbearable man!" she cried, thrashing about as she pushed Shatov away when he leaned over her.

"Marie, I'll do whatever you want! I'll walk around, I'll talk—anything!"

"Surely you can see—it's starting!"

"What's starting, Marie?"

"How would I know? Do you think I understand?... Oh, curse everything! Curse it all from the very beginning!"

"Marie, please, if you'd just tell me what's happening—what's starting—or else I... How can I know if you don't tell me?"

"You're useless! Just a talker full of theories. Oh, curse everything on earth!"

"Marie, Marie!" Shatov cried, now genuinely afraid she might be losing her mind.

"Can't you see I'm in labor!" she screamed, sitting up and glaring at him with such raw anger and desperation that it twisted her face. "I curse this child before he's even born!"

"Marie!" Shatov gasped, the realization hitting him all at once. "Marie... but why didn't you tell me before?"

He pulled himself together instantly, grabbing his cap with newfound determination.

"How could I tell you when I walked in here? Do you think I'd have come if I'd known? They told me it wouldn't happen for another ten days! Where are you going? Where are you going? You mustn't!"

"I'm going to find a midwife! I'll sell the revolver if I have to—we need money right away."

"Don't you dare! Don't you dare fetch a midwife! Bring a peasant woman, some old woman—there are plenty around. I've got eighty kopecks in my purse. Peasant women have babies without midwives. And if I die, then so much the better!"

"You'll have both—a midwife and an old woman. But how can I leave you here alone, Marie?"

He hesitated, torn, but then realized it was better to leave her alone now than to leave her without help later. Ignoring her groans and angry protests, he rushed out of the room, flying down the stairs as quickly as he could.

Chapter 5.3

Shatov's first stop was Kirillov's house. By then, it was already past one in the morning. Kirillov was standing in the middle of his room when Shatov burst in.

"Kirillov, my wife is in labor!" Shatov blurted out.

"What do you mean?" Kirillov asked, looking puzzled.

"She's having a baby! She's in pain!"

"Are you sure?"

"Of course, I'm sure! She's suffering terribly! I need a woman—any old woman—immediately. Can you help me find one? You used to know plenty of women like that."

"I'm sorry," Kirillov said thoughtfully, "but I'm no good when it comes to childbirth. That is to say, I'm not capable of helping with it… or, well, I don't even know how to say it properly."

"You mean you can't deliver a baby yourself? That's fine—that's not what I'm asking. I just need an old woman, a nurse, or a servant. Someone who knows what to do!"

"I can find you an old woman, but it might take a little time. If you

642

want, I could come instead."

"No, that's impossible! I'm heading to Madame Virginsky, the midwife, right now."

"She's a horrible woman," Kirillov commented.

"Yes, I know, Kirillov, but she's the best we've got. Still, the whole situation is awful—there's no reverence, no joy, only contempt and abuse, even in the face of such a miracle as a new life being born. And Marie... she's already cursing it all!"

"If you'd like, I—"

"No, no! But while I'm gone—and I'll bring Madame Virginsky, no matter what—can you go to the bottom of my staircase and quietly listen? Just in case something dreadful happens. Don't go inside; you might frighten her. Only go in if it's absolutely necessary."

"I understand," Kirillov said, handing Shatov a rouble. "Here, take this. I was going to use it to buy a chicken tomorrow, but I don't need it now. Hurry—run as fast as you can. The samovar's on all night if you need tea."

Kirillov didn't know about the current plot against Shatov, nor did he realize how much danger Shatov was in. He was vaguely aware that Shatov had conflicts with "those people," but his own involvement with them had always been minor and distant. Over time, Kirillov had stopped participating in their plans entirely, devoting himself instead to quiet contemplation. Even though Pyotr Stepanovitch had suggested during the meeting that Liputin accompany him to ensure Kirillov would take responsibility for the "Shatov matter," Pyotr had avoided mentioning Shatov during their visit. Perhaps he thought Kirillov was unreliable or believed it was better to bring it up after everything was over, when it wouldn't matter to Kirillov anymore. Liputin noticed this omission but was too rattled to protest.

Shatov, meanwhile, was running like a madman toward Virginsky's house, cursing the distance and feeling like the journey would never end.

When he finally arrived, he had to knock and shout for a long time.

Everyone in the house was fast asleep, but Shatov was relentless, even pounding on the shutters with all his strength. A dog in the yard began barking furiously, and soon other dogs in the neighborhood joined in, creating a deafening chorus.

At last, a voice came from the window. It was Virginsky, his tone gentle and unbothered, showing no irritation at the "outrage" of being woken so late. "Who's there, and what do you want?" he asked.

The shutter creaked open slightly, and the window was cracked ajar.

"Who's there? What scoundrel is making that racket?" screeched a woman's voice, sharp and full of indignation. It was the old maid, a relative of Virginsky's, and she seemed ready to defend her home from the perceived "outrage."

"It's Shatov! My wife has returned, and she's in labor!" he called out urgently.

"Well, leave her alone and get out of here," the old maid retorted coldly.

"I've come for Arina Prohorovna, and I won't leave without her!"

"She can't go running around for everyone. Night visits are a special service. Go to Maksheyev's instead, and stop making such a racket," she snapped, her irritation rising.

Shatov could hear Virginsky trying to calm her down, but the old maid shoved him away and kept ranting.

"I'm not leaving!" Shatov shouted, determined.

"Wait a moment, wait a moment," Virginsky finally managed to interrupt, his voice pleading as he overpowered her protests. "Shatov, I beg you, give me five minutes. I'll wake Arina Prohorovna. Just stop knocking and shouting… Oh, how terrible this all is!"

After what felt like an eternity, five long minutes later, Arina Prohorovna appeared at the window.

"Your wife has come?" she asked. Her tone was surprisingly calm—not angry, but still firm and direct, as was her habit.

"Yes, my wife. She's in labor," Shatov replied quickly.

"Marya Ignatyevna?"

"Yes, Marya Ignatyevna. Who else would it be?"

There was a pause. Shatov waited, straining to hear the murmured voices whispering inside the house.

"How long has she been here?" Arina Prohorovna asked again.

"She arrived this evening at eight. Please hurry."

The whispering resumed, as though they were discussing something important.

"Are you sure you're not mistaken? Did she send you for me herself?"

"No, she didn't send me. She asked for a peasant woman instead, so she wouldn't burden me with expenses. But don't worry—I'll pay you."

"All right, I'll come, payment or not. I always respected Marya Ignatyevna for her independence of spirit, though she might not remember me. Do you have the basic supplies ready?"

"I have nothing yet, but I'll get everything we need."

"There's something noble in people like her," Shatov thought as he hurried to Lyamshin's house. "Their convictions and their actions are two entirely different things. Maybe I've judged them too harshly. We're all guilty, all of us… If only everyone could see it that way."

At Lyamshin's, Shatov didn't have to knock long. To his surprise, Lyamshin opened the window almost immediately, leaping out of bed barefoot and in his nightclothes, despite the chill. This was especially remarkable given his usual hypochondria and constant anxiety about his health.

But tonight was different. Lyamshin had been on edge all evening, unable to sleep after the tense meeting of the quintet. His nerves were frayed, haunted by the fear of unexpected visitors. The possibility of Shatov betraying them gnawed at him relentlessly. So when the loud, insistent knocking at his window came, it seemed to confirm his worst fears.

Shatov's sudden appearance terrified Lyamshin so much that he immediately slammed the window shut and jumped back into bed. Shatov, however, began banging on the frame and yelling furiously.

"How dare you make this kind of racket in the middle of the night?" Lyamshin shouted, his voice shaking with fear. After two minutes of hesitation, he finally reopened the window, realizing Shatov was alone.

"Here's your revolver back! Take it and give me fifteen roubles," Shatov demanded, his voice sharp.

"Are you drunk? What's wrong with you? This is absurd! I'll catch a cold like this. Wait, let me throw on my rug," Lyamshin replied, trying to gather himself.

"Fifteen roubles, right now! If you don't give it to me, I'll keep knocking and yelling until morning! I'll smash your window!" Shatov threatened.

"And I'll yell for the police! You'll end up in the lock-up," Lyamshin countered, though he sounded far from confident.

"And you think I can't yell for the police too? Let's see who has more to fear from them—you or me?" Shatov shot back, his voice dripping with scorn.

"You're hinting at something despicable… I know what you mean! Stop, stop! Don't start knocking again!" Lyamshin begged, his panic mounting. "Honestly, who has money at this hour? What do you need it for? Are you drunk?"

"My wife has come back. I'll knock ten roubles off the price—I haven't even fired it once. Just take the revolver. Take it, now!" Shatov insisted.

Lyamshin hesitated, then reached out mechanically to grab the revolver through the window. For a moment, he seemed to consider something, and then, trembling, he leaned his head out.

"You're lying. Your wife hasn't come back. This is just an excuse for you to run away," he accused.

"You idiot! Run away? Where would I even go? It's Pyotr

Verhovensky who should be running, not me. I just came from the midwife, Madame Virginsky, and she agreed to come right away. Ask her yourself if you don't believe me! My wife is in pain, and I need the money!"

Lyamshin's crafty mind raced through possibilities, each idea flashing like fireworks. The situation suddenly seemed less threatening but still left him too anxious to think clearly.

"But... you aren't living with your wife," Lyamshin muttered, confused.

"I'll break your skull for that!" Shatov snapped, his patience wearing thin.

"Oh, I see, I understand now. Forgive me, I was caught off guard," Lyamshin stammered, flustered. "Wait—did you say Arina Prohorovna agreed to come? I thought you said she wasn't coming. See? You're lying every step of the way!"

"She's probably with my wife already! Don't waste my time. You're just making things harder," Shatov barked.

"That's a lie! I'm no fool! But excuse me... I really can't..." Lyamshin trailed off, beginning to shut the window again. Shatov let out such a yell that he stopped and leaned out once more.

"This is just harassment! What do you even want? Spell it out clearly! And think—it's the middle of the night!" Lyamshin shouted, his voice cracking.

"Fifteen roubles, you blockhead!" Shatov roared.

"But what if I don't want the revolver back? You can't force me! You bought it, and that's that. Besides, who has that kind of money in the middle of the night?"

"You always have money, you miser! I'm even giving you a discount, but everyone knows you're a stingy coward."

"Come back the day after tomorrow at noon, and I'll give you the full amount. Will that work? Come on, just leave me alone for now," Lyamshin pleaded.

Shatov slammed his fists against the window frame again. "Give me ten roubles now, and I'll come for the other five tomorrow morning."

"No, the other five the day after tomorrow. I swear I won't have it tomorrow. Don't bother coming tomorrow," Lyamshin responded desperately.

"Ten roubles, you scoundrel!" Shatov shouted.

"Why so rude? Wait, let me light a candle. You're going to break the window! Who screams like this at night? Here, take it!" Lyamshin reluctantly handed out a five-rouble note.

Shatov snatched it. "Is that it?" he growled.

"On my honor, I can't give more, even if you kill me. I'll have the rest the day after tomorrow. Now leave me alone!" Lyamshin wailed, his panic reaching a fever pitch. He handed out two more notes, each worth a rouble, bringing the total to seven.

"Fine, you bastard! I'll come back tomorrow. But if you don't have the other eight, I'll thrash you!" Shatov warned, turning to leave.

"You won't find me at home, you idiot!" Lyamshin muttered under his breath, already thinking of ways to avoid him.

"Wait, wait!" Lyamshin shouted suddenly, panicked. "Come back! Is it true? Is it really true your wife has returned?"

"Fool!" Shatov yelled over his shoulder, waving him off with disgust before sprinting home as fast as he could.

Chapter 5.4

Anna Prohorovna had no knowledge of the decisions made at the meeting the day before. When Virginsky returned home, worn out and overwhelmed, he couldn't bring himself to share the full extent of what had been resolved. However, he couldn't resist sharing part of it—specifically, what Verhovensky had said about Shatov's supposed plan to betray them. Even then, he added that he wasn't entirely convinced of its truth. This half-revealed information left Anna Prohorovna deeply shaken. So, when Shatov arrived to fetch her, she agreed to go without hesitation, even though she was utterly exhausted from working through the previous night at a delivery.

She had always believed that someone as pitiable as Shatov was fully capable of committing political treachery. However, the sudden arrival of Marya Ignatyevna changed her perspective. Shatov's clear distress, the desperate tone in his voice, and the way he pleaded for her help convinced her that his feelings had undergone a profound shift. She reasoned that a man bent on betrayal for selfish motives would have behaved very differently. Determined to judge the situation with her own eyes, Anna Prohorovna decided to investigate. Virginsky, relieved by her decision, felt as if a massive weight had been lifted off his shoulders. He even began to feel a glimmer of hope. To him, Shatov's demeanor seemed completely incompatible with Verhovensky's accusations.

When Shatov returned home, he found Anna Prohorovna already with Marya. She had arrived just moments before, curtly dismissed Kirillov, who was lingering near the bottom of the stairs, and introduced herself to Marya. The latter didn't recognize her as someone she had once known. Marya was in poor spirits—agitated, irritable, and overcome with hopeless despair—but Anna Prohorovna silenced all of her protests within five minutes.

"Why do you keep insisting that you don't want a professional midwife?" she was saying when Shatov walked in. "That's nonsense. It's just an idea you've latched onto because of your current state of mind. If you rely on some random old peasant woman, you'll only increase the risks. Things could easily go wrong, and in the end, you'd spend more time, money, and effort dealing with the consequences than if you had a proper midwife. What makes you think I'm expensive? You can pay me later. I won't charge you much, and I can guarantee success. You won't die under my care—I've handled much worse cases than yours. If you want, I can arrange for the baby to be sent to a foundling home tomorrow and eventually raised in the countryside. It's really not a big deal. Meanwhile, you can regain your strength, find some meaningful work, and soon enough, you'll be able to repay Shatov for helping you. The costs won't be as much as you're imagining."

"It's not that … it's just that I don't feel I have the right to be a burden…" Marya muttered faintly.

Shatov will hardly spend anything if he can manage to think clearly and stop acting so irrationally," Arina Prohorovna declared bluntly. "He just needs to avoid doing something ridiculous, like running around the town shouting and waking everyone up. If he doesn't calm down, he'll be banging on every doctor's door by morning. I've already said there's no need for a doctor. I'll handle everything. You can hire an old woman to assist you if you like—it won't cost much. Besides, Shatov can do more useful things with his hands and feet, like running errands to the pharmacy, instead of playing the role of a saint. Benevolence has nothing to do with this! Isn't he the one who dragged you into this situation in the first place? Didn't he selfishly persuade you to leave the family where you were working as a governess so he could marry you? We all heard about it. Sure, he ran to fetch me like a madman, yelling so loudly that everyone in the street must have heard, but let's be honest—he's not exactly thinking clearly."

She paused, observing Marie's growing irritation before continuing. "I'm not here to force myself on anyone. I came because I thought it was my duty, based on the principle that we should all help each other. And I made that clear to him before leaving my house. If you think I'm in the way, I'll leave right now. But if I go, don't blame me if you run into trouble that could have been avoided."

She even stood up as if ready to leave. Marie, however, was so overcome with pain, helplessness, and a fearful anticipation of what lay ahead that she couldn't bring herself to let Arina Prohorovna leave. Still, Marie found herself resenting this woman; her words weren't what Marie wanted to hear. Something deeper was troubling her, something that made her despise Arina's tone. But the thought of dying at the hands of an inexperienced peasant midwife outweighed her aversion. However, her anger shifted entirely toward Shatov. She became increasingly demanding and harsh, forbidding him not only to look at her but even to stand facing her.

As her labor pains intensified, so did her outbursts. Her curses and yelling grew louder and more frantic with every moment.

"Let's just send him away," Arina Prohorovna snapped, glancing at Shatov dismissively. "He's just scaring you. Look at him—he's as pale as a ghost! What's he even doing here? He's utterly useless in this situation."

Shatov said nothing, deciding it was best to remain silent.

"I've seen plenty of ridiculous fathers losing their minds in moments like this," Arina continued. "But at least they manage to—"

"Shut up or leave me to die!" Marie screamed. "Don't say another word! I can't stand it anymore!"

"It's impossible not to speak when there are things that need to be done!" Arina retorted sharply. "We need to talk about what's necessary. Tell me, do you have anything prepared?" She turned to Shatov. "Answer me. She can't."

"Tell me what we need," Shatov replied, trying to maintain his composure.

"So, you don't have anything ready." Arina listed the essentials they needed, making it clear she was only asking for what was absolutely necessary. Some of the items Shatov already had.

Marie handed him her key and insisted he look in her bag. But as Shatov's hands trembled, it took him longer than expected to open the unfamiliar lock. Frustrated, Marie erupted in anger. When Arina Prohorovna stepped forward to help, Marie shrieked that no one but Shatov could touch her bag, bursting into tears as she insisted on this point.

Shatov realized he would have to fetch some items from Kirillov's place. As soon as he turned to leave, Marie began screaming for him to come back. He hurriedly returned, explaining that he'd only be gone a minute to get something essential and would return immediately.

"Honestly, you're impossible to please," Arina said with a laugh. "One minute you want him to stand in the corner, not even daring to look at you. The next, you're in tears because he's leaving the room for just a second. At this rate, he might start imagining things. Come now, stop

651

crying. I was only joking."

"He wouldn't dare imagine anything!" Marie shot back, her voice trembling with anger.

"Fine, fine," Arina said, trying to placate her. "If he didn't love you so much, like some kind of loyal sheep, he wouldn't have been running all over town, shouting his head off and waking every dog in the neighborhood. By the way, he even managed to break my window frame!"

Chapter 5.5

He found Kirillov pacing back and forth in his room, so deep in thought that he seemed to have completely forgotten about the arrival of Shatov's wife. When Shatov spoke, Kirillov appeared to hear him but didn't understand at first.

"Oh, yes!" Kirillov said suddenly, as if pulling himself out of some consuming idea for just a moment. "Yes… an old woman. A wife or an old woman? Wait… a wife and an old woman, is that it? I remember now. I went, and the old woman will come, just not right now. Take the pillow. Anything else? Yes… Hold on, do you ever have moments of eternal harmony, Shatov?"

"You know, Kirillov, you shouldn't keep staying up all night like this," Shatov said.

Kirillov seemed to shake off his daze. Strangely, he spoke more clearly than usual, as though he had thought through his response long ago, perhaps even written it down.

"There are these moments," Kirillov began, "maybe five or six seconds at a time, when you suddenly feel like you've reached perfect harmony. It's not of this world—not in a heavenly way, but in the sense that a person in their earthly body can't endure it. You'd have to be physically transformed or else die. It's so clear, unmistakable. It's like you understand all of nature at once and can say, 'Yes, this is right.' You know how God, when He created the world, said after each day, 'It is good'? It's like that.

"It's not about being overwhelmed with emotion. It's just pure joy. There's no need to forgive anyone because there's nothing left to forgive. It's not even love—no, it's something higher than love. What's frightening is how clear it is, and how overwhelmingly joyful. If it lasted longer than five seconds, your soul wouldn't survive it; you'd perish. In those five seconds, I feel like I've lived a whole lifetime, and I'd trade my entire life just to have those moments again. They're worth it. To endure it for even ten seconds, I think a person would have to be changed entirely. That's why I think humans should stop having children—what's the point of children, or even evolution, when the ultimate goal has already been reached? It's written in the Gospel that in the resurrection, there will be no childbearing, and men will be like the angels of God. That's a clue. By the way, is your wife having a child?"

"Kirillov, does this happen to you often?" Shatov asked.

"Once every three days, or maybe once a week," Kirillov replied.

"Are you sure you're not having fits?" Shatov asked, concerned.

"No," Kirillov answered.

"Well, you might. Be careful, Kirillov. I've heard that's how seizures begin. An epileptic once described exactly the same sensation you just described, word for word. He even mentioned five seconds, saying it was impossible to endure any more than that. Remember the story of Mahomet and the pitcher of water? Not a single drop spilled while he circled Paradise on his horse. That sounds exactly like your eternal harmony. Mahomet was epileptic, Kirillov. You need to be cautious—it could be epilepsy."

"It won't have the chance," Kirillov said softly, smiling.

Chapter 5.6

The night dragged on. Shatov was sent running back and forth, scolded, and called back again. Marie was overcome with a desperate fear of dying. She screamed that she wanted to live, insisting, "I must, I must!" Her cries grew frantic as she repeated, "I don't want to, I don't want to!" Without Arina Prohorovna, things would have fallen apart entirely. Gradually,

Arina Prohorovna gained complete control over Marie, who began following her every word and command like an obedient child. Arina ruled with strictness, not kindness, but she was exceptionally skilled at her work.

As the night gave way to dawn, a cold, damp light began to creep into the room. Arina Prohorovna suddenly imagined that Shatov had gone out to the stairs to pray, and she started laughing. Marie joined in with spiteful, bitter laughter, as though it gave her some kind of release. Finally, they managed to send Shatov away entirely.

Morning broke, gray and chill. Shatov stood in a corner, pressing his face against the wall just as he had done the night before when Erkel had arrived. He trembled like a leaf, terrified to let his thoughts run wild, yet unable to stop his mind from darting from one thought to another, like in a restless dream.

His mind wandered into daydreams that snapped off abruptly, like a thread breaking. The sounds from the room changed; the groans turned into horrific, primal cries, wild and unendurable. Shatov tried to block his ears, but he couldn't. He sank to his knees, whispering, "Marie, Marie," over and over again without realizing it.

Suddenly, a new sound cut through everything—a small, sharp cry, weak and discordant but unmistakable. Shatov froze and then leapt to his feet, startled by the unfamiliar sound. It was the cry of a baby. Crossing himself instinctively, he rushed into the room.

Inside, Arina Prohorovna was holding a tiny, red, wrinkled creature in her hands. It flailed its little arms and legs helplessly, screaming as though declaring its right to exist, fragile yet full of life. Marie lay there, motionless, as if she had fainted, but after a moment, her eyes opened. She looked at Shatov with an expression he had never seen before—a look that was entirely new, strange, and indescribable.

"Is it a boy? Is it a boy?" Marie asked weakly, her voice barely above a whisper.

"It's a boy," Arina Prohorovna replied loudly as she wrapped the baby in a cloth.

When she had wrapped the baby up and was about to lay him between the pillows on the bed, she handed him to Shatov for a moment. Marie gestured to Shatov discreetly, as if she didn't want Arina Prohorovna to notice. He understood immediately and brought the baby over to show her.

"He's so... beautiful," she whispered softly, smiling faintly.

"What a funny little face he has!" Arina Prohorovna said with a cheerful laugh, clearly amused, glancing at Shatov's expression.

"You can laugh, Arina Prohorovna, but... this is such a joy," Shatov stammered, his face glowing with a kind of foolish happiness. Marie's quiet remark about the child had completely enchanted him.

"What's so joyful about it?" Arina Prohorovna replied, amused but good-natured as she moved around, tidying up and working tirelessly.

"It's the mystery of a new life, something incredible and unexplainable. It's such a shame you can't understand that, Arina Prohorovna," Shatov said in a dazed and ecstatic tone. His words poured out as if they weren't entirely under his control, something inside him breaking loose.

"There were two of us, and now there's a third—a whole new person, a new soul. It's not something man could ever make. It's like a new thought, a new kind of love. It's... it's almost terrifying, but it's the greatest thing in the world."

"Oh, what nonsense you're spouting!" Arina Prohorovna said with a hearty laugh. "It's just biology, nothing mysterious about it. If you think like that, every fly would be a miracle! But let me tell you something: people who aren't needed shouldn't be born at all. First, we need to change the world so there's no such thing as unnecessary people, and only then should we think about bringing new lives into it. As it is now, we'll just end up taking this one to the orphanage in a couple of days... which is exactly how it should be."

"I will never let him be sent to an orphanage," Shatov declared firmly, staring at the floor.

"So, are you going to adopt him, call him your own?"

"He is my son," Shatov replied resolutely.

"Well, of course, legally he's a Shatov. But don't act like some grand humanitarian. Men love their big words. All right, all right, no need to get worked up." She glanced at her work, finally satisfied. "Now, my friends, it's time for me to leave. Everything has gone well, so I need to check on my other patients who've been waiting for me for hours. I'll come back later this morning and again tonight if needed. But in the meantime, Shatov, you should stay here with her. Even if you're no expert, you might still be useful. I doubt Marya Ignatyevna will send you away." She laughed and added, "Don't worry, I'm just teasing."

At the gate, where Shatov accompanied her, she leaned in and said quietly, "You've given me something to laugh about for the rest of my life. I won't even charge you for this. I'll be laughing about you in my sleep! I've never seen anything funnier than you last night."

She left, quite pleased with herself. Shatov's behavior and words had made it obvious to her: he was taking fatherhood seriously and looked like a fool for it. She rushed home, eager to share the story with Virginsky, even though it would've been quicker to visit another patient.

"Marie, she told you not to fall asleep for a little while, but I can see how hard it is for you," Shatov said timidly. "I'll sit by the window and keep an eye on things, all right?"

He sat down quietly behind the sofa, out of her sight. But within moments, she called him back, asking irritably for help with her pillow. He clumsily adjusted it, and she frowned at the wall.

"That's not right, that's not right... What clumsy hands!"

He tried again, more carefully this time.

"Bend closer to me," she said suddenly, her voice tense and wild.

Startled, he leaned down as she asked.

"Closer... no, not like that... closer," she insisted. Then, with a sudden, impulsive movement, she wrapped her arm around his neck and pressed a warm, damp kiss to his forehead.

"Marie!" he exclaimed, overwhelmed.

Her lips trembled, and it seemed like she was struggling with herself. But then she straightened up slightly, her eyes flashing as she declared, "Nikolay Stavrogin is a scoundrel!"

She collapsed back onto the pillow, sobbing uncontrollably, while gripping Shatov's hand tightly.

From that moment on, she wouldn't let him leave her side. She insisted he sit by her pillow, smiling at him with a newfound joy. She couldn't talk much, but her eyes followed him, filled with a blissful softness. It was as though she had suddenly become a carefree girl again, as if everything had changed.

Shatov wept openly, like a child, then rambled about everything and anything—wild, inspired thoughts about their future, about life, about God, and about how good people truly were. Marie seemed entranced, listening as she gently ruffled his hair with her weak hand, smoothing it down and gazing at him with admiration. He spoke of Kirillov, of starting "a new life," of faith and hope. She brought out the baby again to look at him with awe and wonder.

"Marie," he said, holding the baby close, "all the old madness and shame is behind us now, isn't it? Let's work hard and start fresh—the three of us together. Yes, yes! Oh, Marie, what should we name him?"

"What should we name him?" she repeated, looking startled. Suddenly her face was clouded with deep sorrow.

She clasped her hands together, gave Shatov a look full of reproach, then buried her face in the pillow.

"Marie, what's wrong?" he asked anxiously, his voice filled with concern.

"How could you ask that? Oh, how could you... You ungrateful man!"

"Marie, please forgive me... I didn't mean anything by it. I just wanted to know what name you'd like to give him."

"Ivan, Ivan," she said, lifting her flushed, tear-streaked face. "How could you even think we'd call him something else? That awful name!"

"Marie, calm down. You're so upset—oh, you're in such a nervous state!"

"There you go, blaming my nerves again. I bet if I had suggested that other terrible name, you wouldn't even have noticed! You would've just gone along with it. Men are so heartless and selfish, all of you!"

Of course, a few minutes later, they were reconciled. Shatov gently convinced her to rest. She fell asleep, still clutching his hand as if afraid he might leave. Occasionally, she would wake, glance at him to make sure he was still there, and drift off again.

Kirillov sent an old woman "to give her congratulations," along with hot tea, some freshly cooked cutlets, broth, and white bread for Marya Ignatyevna. She eagerly sipped the broth. The old woman unwrapped the baby and carefully re-swaddled him. Marie insisted that Shatov eat a cutlet as well.

Time slipped by. Exhausted, Shatov dozed off in his chair, his head resting against Marie's pillow. That was how Arina Prohorovna found them when she returned as promised. She woke them with cheerful banter, asked Marie a few important questions, checked the baby, and once again told Shatov not to leave her side. Then, with a mix of humor and condescension, she teased the "happy couple" before leaving, as pleased as she had been earlier.

When Shatov woke, it was already dark. He quickly lit a candle and went to fetch the old woman. But as he started down the stairs, he heard soft, deliberate footsteps approaching. It was Erkel.

"Don't come in," Shatov whispered, grabbing Erkel's hand and pulling him toward the gate. "Wait here; I'll be right back. I completely forgot about you—oh, how it all came rushing back!"

He was in such a hurry that he didn't even stop by Kirillov's but instead called for the old woman directly. Marie was upset and indignant that he would even consider leaving her alone.

"But this is the last thing I have to do," he told her joyfully. "After this, it'll be a fresh start, and we'll never, ever think about those terrible old days again!"

He managed to calm her down, promising to return by nine o'clock. He kissed her warmly, kissed the baby, and hurried down to join Erkel.

Together, they set off for Stavrogin's park at Skvoreshniki. In a secluded spot at the edge of the park where it met the pine woods, Shatov had buried a printing press eighteen months earlier. The location was wild and hidden, far from the Stavrogins' house and about two or three miles from Filipov's place.

"Are we walking the whole way? I'll get a cab," Shatov said.

"I ask you not to do that," Erkel replied firmly.

They insisted on it. A cab driver could become a witness.

"Well, whatever! I don't care, as long as it's done with."

They walked quickly.

"Erkel, you're just a kid," Shatov suddenly said. "Have you ever been truly happy?"

"You seem pretty happy right now," Erkel replied, looking at him curiously.

Chapter 6
A Busy Night

Chapter 6.1

During the day, Virginsky spent two hours visiting the members of the quintet to inform them that Shatov was unlikely to betray them because his wife had returned and given birth to a child. He argued that no one who understood human nature would believe Shatov posed a threat at such a moment. However, he was disappointed to find no one at home except Erkel and Lyamshin.

Erkel listened quietly, looking Virginsky in the eyes, and when asked directly whether he would come at six o'clock, he smiled brightly and said, "Of course I will."

Lyamshin, on the other hand, was in bed, apparently seriously ill, with his head buried under a quilt. When Virginsky entered, Lyamshin seemed alarmed and waved him off from beneath the covers, begging to be left alone. He still listened to Virginsky's explanation about Shatov, though, and appeared particularly struck when told that no one else had been at home. Lyamshin, who had already heard about Fedka's death from Liputin, shared the news hurriedly and incoherently with Virginsky, leaving the latter equally surprised. But when asked whether he would attend the meeting or not, Lyamshin waved his hands again, insisting it wasn't his concern and that he didn't know anything about it.

Virginsky returned home feeling dejected and deeply worried. It weighed heavily on him that he couldn't share the situation with his family—he was used to telling his wife everything. However, his feverish mind hatched a new idea, a plan to mediate and find a solution. This gave him some relief and even a sense of hope. Impatiently, he awaited the appointed hour and set off for the meeting place earlier than necessary.

The meeting spot was a gloomy area at the far end of a large park. Later, I visited the place myself to see it. On that chilly autumn evening, it must have looked especially eerie. The area was on the edge of an old Crown-owned forest, where tall, ancient pines loomed as dark, shadowy figures in the night. It was so dark that they could barely see each other a few steps away. Fortunately, Pyotr Stepanovitch, Liputin, and eventually Erkel brought lanterns.

At some point in the past, a crude stone grotto had been built there for no clear reason. The table and benches inside had long since decayed. About two hundred paces to the right lay the bank of the park's third pond. These three ponds stretched for nearly a mile from the house to the park's edge. It was unlikely that any noise—shouts or even gunshots—would reach the inhabitants of Stavrogin's empty house. With Nikolay Vsyevolodovitch having left the day before and Alexey Yegorytch absent, only a handful of people remained in the house, most of them unwell. Even if cries for help did reach them, it was safe to assume they would stir up fear rather than action. No one would likely leave the warmth of their stove to investigate.

By twenty past six, nearly everyone except Erkel, who had been sent to fetch Shatov, had arrived at the meeting place. Pyotr Stepanovitch was punctual this time, arriving with Tolkatchenko. Tolkatchenko looked anxious, his earlier bravado and false confidence gone. He stayed close to Pyotr Stepanovitch, almost clinging to him, and repeatedly whispered nervously in his ear. Pyotr Stepanovitch, however, barely responded, brushing him off irritably.

Shigalov and Virginsky had arrived earlier and stood apart, maintaining a heavy and deliberate silence. Pyotr Stepanovitch raised his lantern to examine them closely, his scrutiny sharp and almost mocking. A thought flashed through his mind: They're planning to say something.

"Isn't Lyamshin here?" he asked Virginsky. "Who said he was sick?"

"I'm here," Lyamshin answered, stepping out from behind a tree. He was wrapped in a warm coat and covered with a thick rug, making it hard to see his face even by lantern light.

"So, Liputin's the only one missing?" Pyotr Stepanovitch asked.

Liputin also emerged from the grotto without saying a word. Pyotr Stepanovitch lifted the lantern again.

"Why were you hiding in there? Why didn't you come out?"

"I imagine we still have the freedom to act as we choose," Liputin muttered, though he seemed uncertain about what he was trying to say.

"Gentlemen," Pyotr Stepanovitch began, raising his voice for the first time above a whisper, which startled the group, "I think we all understand there's no need to repeat everything. We discussed it thoroughly yesterday, openly and directly. But from the looks on your faces, it seems someone has something to say. If so, I urge you to speak quickly. Time is short, and Erkel could bring him any minute now…"

"He'll definitely bring him," Tolkatchenko added, though it wasn't clear why he spoke up.

"If I'm not mistaken, the printing press will be handed over first?" Liputin asked, though it sounded like he wasn't sure why he asked.

"Of course. Why should we lose it?" Pyotr Stepanovitch replied, holding the lantern closer to his face. "But as we all agreed yesterday, it's not necessary to retrieve it right away. He only needs to show you where it's buried; we can dig it up later ourselves. I know it's about ten paces from a corner of this grotto. Damn it, Liputin, how could you forget? We decided you would meet him alone first, and then we'd all come out. It's odd that you're even asking—or did you not mean what you said?"

Liputin remained silent, his expression gloomy. The group stood quietly as the wind rustled the tops of the pine trees.

"I trust, gentlemen, that everyone here will do their duty," Pyotr Stepanovitch said sharply, growing impatient.

"I heard Shatov's wife has returned and had a child," Virginsky said suddenly, his voice trembling with emotion. He gestured wildly, barely able to get his words out. "Knowing how people are, it's clear he won't inform on us now. He's happy. I went around this morning to tell everyone, but no one was home. So maybe there's no need to do anything now…"

He stopped, catching his breath.

"If you suddenly found happiness, Mr. Virginsky," Pyotr Stepanovitch said, stepping closer to him, "would you abandon—not just giving information, because that's not the point—but any risky action you saw as a duty, even if it cost you your happiness?"

"No, I wouldn't! I wouldn't give it up for anything!" Virginsky replied, his voice filled with fervor, his body trembling.

"You'd rather lose your happiness than betray your principles?"

"Yes, absolutely… no, I mean… I'd rather be miserable than be a scoundrel!"

"Well then, let me tell you this: Shatov views betraying us as a moral duty. It's his strongest belief, and he's willing to risk his own safety for it. Even if he's pardoned for informing, he'll regret it later and go straight to the police. Mark my words. And honestly, I don't see what happiness there is in having his wife come back after three years to give birth to Stavrogin's child."

"But no one's actually seen Shatov's letter," Shigalov interrupted firmly.

"I've seen it," Pyotr Stepanovitch snapped. "It exists, and this whole conversation is a waste of time."

"I protest!" Virginsky suddenly burst out, his emotions boiling over. "I strongly protest! Here's what I suggest. When he arrives, we should all confront him and ask him directly. If he admits it, we should try to make him change his mind. If he gives us his word of honor, we let him go. But it must be done openly, after a fair trial. We can't ambush him like this!"

"Relying on his word of honor to protect the cause is the height of stupidity! Damn it, how ridiculous this has all become, gentlemen! And what a sorry role you've chosen to play at such a critical moment!"

"I protest! I protest!" Virginsky insisted loudly.

"Stop yelling, at least. We won't hear the signal. Shatov, gentlemen... (Damn it, how stupid this is!) I've already told you, Shatov is a Slavophil, which means he's part of one of the most idiotic groups of people out there. But forget that—it's irrelevant! You're distracting me... Shatov is a bitter man, gentlemen, and since he's been involved with the group in some way, whether willingly or not, I held out hope, even to the last minute, that he might be useful to the cause—useful as an embittered man. I spared him. I kept him in reserve, despite very clear instructions to the contrary. I've given him a hundred times more leniency than he deserved! But now he's betrayed us. And you know what? I don't care anymore! Try running away now, any of you! None of you has the right to abandon this task! Hug him if you want, but you can't risk the cause on his word of honor! That's behaving like pigs—or worse, spies working for the government!"

"Who here is a government spy?" Liputin muttered under his breath.

"Maybe you are. Shut up, Liputin; you always talk just to hear yourself. Listen, gentlemen: anyone who panics at the critical moment and shirks their duty is a spy. That's just how it is. There are always fools who, at the last second, will panic and cry, 'Oh, forgive me, and I'll tell you everything!' But let me remind you, betrayal won't save you now. Even if the punishment is lessened, you'll still face Siberia. And beyond that, the people we're up against won't let you escape their vengeance, and their methods are far more brutal than the government's!"

Pyotr Stepanovitch was visibly angry, his words spilling out faster than he likely intended. With deliberate steps, Shigalov moved closer to him. His tone, calm and measured as always, betrayed no emotion.

"Since last night, I've given this matter serious thought," Shigalov began, speaking with his usual precision. "Upon reflection, I've concluded that this proposed murder is not only a waste of valuable time—time that could be better spent on more appropriate efforts—but also represents a dangerous departure from the methods that should guide us. History has shown that such deviations, driven by shallow political thinkers rather than true socialists, have consistently set back the progress of our cause. I came here tonight solely to express my opposition to this plan for everyone's benefit. After that, I intend to leave before this so-called 'dangerous moment' you keep referring to. My departure isn't motivated by fear of danger or sympathy for Shatov—I have no inclination to kiss him, after all—but purely because this entire scheme is against my principles. As for any concerns that I might betray you or be working for the government, you can rest assured I will not."

With that, Shigalov turned and began walking away.

"Damn it, he'll run into them and warn Shatov!" Pyotr Stepanovitch shouted, pulling out his revolver. The group heard the click of the trigger.

"You can be certain," Shigalov said, pausing to look back, "that if I meet Shatov, I may nod to him, but I won't warn him."

"Do you realize, Mr. Fourier, that this decision could cost you dearly?" Pyotr Stepanovitch growled.

"Let me remind you, I am not Fourier. If you confuse me with that sentimental theorist, you clearly haven't understood my manuscript, even though it's been in your hands. And as for your threats, pulling out your pistol right now is a foolish move—it goes entirely against your interests. You can shoot me tomorrow, or the next day if you like, but it won't help you. You might kill me, but sooner or later, you'll still come around to my system. Goodbye."

At that moment, a whistle sounded in the park, about two hundred paces away, near the pond. Liputin immediately responded with a whistle, as had been planned the night before. Because he had lost some teeth and doubted his ability to whistle properly, he had bought a small clay whistle at the market that morning for a few pennies. Erkel had already told Shatov about the whistle signal on the way, so Shatov wasn't alarmed when he heard it.

"Don't worry, I'll avoid them, and they won't even notice me," Shigalov whispered confidently. Without any hurry, he calmly walked away into the darkness of the park.

Every detail of this horrifying event is now known. Liputin met Erkel and Shatov at the entrance to the grotto. Shatov did not greet Liputin or shake his hand. Instead, he immediately spoke in a loud, hurried voice:

"Well, where's the spade? Don't you have another lantern? Don't worry, there's no one here, and even if we fired a cannon, they wouldn't hear it at Skvoreshniki. This is the spot—right here." He stomped his foot about ten paces from the end of the grotto, pointing toward the woods.

At that moment, Tolkatchenko leaped out from behind a tree and grabbed Shatov from behind, while Erkel seized his arms. Liputin attacked from the front. Together, they forced Shatov to the ground. Pyotr Stepanovitch rushed forward, holding a revolver. It's said that Shatov managed to turn his head and recognize him before three lanterns lit up the grim scene. Shatov let out a short, desperate scream, but they quickly silenced him. Pyotr Stepanovitch pressed the revolver firmly against Shatov's forehead and pulled the trigger. The gunshot wasn't loud, and nothing was heard at Skvoreshniki. Shigalov, standing only three paces away, later testified that he heard the scream and the shot but didn't stop or turn around.

Death was almost instant. Pyotr Stepanovitch remained composed, though it's doubtful he was completely calm. Squatting on his heels, he searched Shatov's pockets with steady hands. He found no money— Shatov's purse had been left under Marya Ignatyevna's pillow. He discovered a few scraps of paper: a note from his office, the title of a book, and an old restaurant receipt from abroad that had inexplicably been in his pocket for two years. Pyotr Stepanovitch pocketed these items and, noticing the others staring at the body in silence, began angrily shouting at them to hurry up and get to work.

Tolkatchenko and Erkel snapped out of their stupor and rushed to the grotto, where they had prepared two heavy stones earlier that morning. Each stone weighed about twenty pounds and was tied with cords. The plan was to sink the body in the nearest pond. They tied one stone to Shatov's feet and the other to his head. Pyotr Stepanovitch worked on fastening the cords while Tolkatchenko and Erkel assisted by holding the stones and passing them over. Erkel took the lead, and while Pyotr Stepanovitch cursed and tied the cord around Shatov's feet—a slow task—Tolkatchenko awkwardly held the other stone at arm's length, bending forward as if ready to hand it over immediately. It never occurred to him to set it down while he waited.

Finally, the stones were secured. Pyotr Stepanovitch stood up to examine the faces of his companions, and then something utterly unexpected happened.

As I mentioned before, everyone except maybe Tolkatchenko and Erkel stood still, doing nothing. Virginsky had rushed at Shatov with the others but hadn't touched him or helped hold him down. Lyamshin only came closer after the shot was fired. For the next ten minutes, while Pyotr Stepanovitch dealt with the body, none of them seemed fully aware of what was happening. They stood around, more amazed than alarmed. Liputin was closest to the corpse, with Virginsky behind him, peering over his shoulder with a strange, detached curiosity, even standing on tiptoe to see better. Lyamshin stayed behind Virginsky, peeking out occasionally but quickly retreating again.

When the stones were tied to the body and Pyotr Stepanovitch stood up, Virginsky suddenly began trembling, clasped his hands, and shouted bitterly at the top of his voice, "This isn't right, it's all wrong, it's not right at all!" He might have said more, but Lyamshin didn't let him. Suddenly, Lyamshin grabbed him from behind and squeezed him tightly while letting out a strange, inhuman shriek. In moments of extreme emotion, like terror, a person's voice can change, sounding nothing like themselves, and this can be horrifying. Lyamshin's scream was more like an animal's than a human's. He clung to Virginsky, shaking uncontrollably, stomping his feet as if he were drumming on the ground.

Virginsky was terrified and screamed back furiously, a side of him no one expected. He scratched and hit Lyamshin, trying to break free. Finally, Erkel stepped in to pull Lyamshin away. But when Virginsky managed to jump ten paces back, Lyamshin turned his wild focus on Pyotr Stepanovitch. Still shrieking, he stumbled over the corpse and threw himself at him, gripping him tightly. Pyotr Stepanovitch shouted and swore, punching Lyamshin in the head. He finally broke free, pulled out his revolver, and shoved it into Lyamshin's open mouth. Even then, Lyamshin kept screaming until Erkel, acting quickly, stuffed a silk handkerchief into his mouth. The screaming stopped. Meanwhile, Tolkatchenko tied Lyamshin's hands with leftover rope.

"This is bizarre," Pyotr Stepanovitch muttered, staring at Lyamshin like he was trying to figure him out. "I didn't expect this from him."

Erkel stayed with Lyamshin while the others hurried to dispose of the body, worried the noise might have been overheard. Tolkatchenko and Pyotr Stepanovitch lifted the body by the head, while Liputin and Virginsky carried the feet. The stones made it incredibly heavy, and the pond was over two hundred paces away. Tolkatchenko, the strongest of them, suggested they walk in step, but no one responded, and they stumbled along clumsily. Pyotr Stepanovitch carried the head on his shoulder, supporting the stone with his free hand. At one point, frustrated by Tolkatchenko's lack of help with the stone, he shouted angrily at him.

When they finally reached the pond, Virginsky, exhausted and stooping under the weight, cried out again in a loud, despairing voice, "This isn't right! It's all wrong!"

The spot they chose was at the far end of the third pond, the most secluded and overgrown part of the park. They set down the lantern and swung the body into the water. A dull splash echoed as the corpse sank immediately under the weight of the stones. They all peered into the water, trying to catch a glimpse, but the body was gone. Ripples spread across the pond's surface before fading into stillness. It was done.

Virginsky left with Erkel, but not before Erkel handed over Lyamshin to Tolkatchenko. Erkel reported to Pyotr Stepanovitch that Lyamshin had calmed down, was regretful, and claimed to remember nothing of his outburst. Pyotr Stepanovitch then left alone, taking the longer route around the pond and through the park. To his surprise, Liputin caught up with him halfway.

"Pyotr Stepanovitch! Lyamshin is going to talk!" Liputin blurted out.

"No, he won't. Once he calms down, he'll realize he'd be the first to go to Siberia if he said anything. None of you will talk. Even you won't."

"What about you?"

"Don't worry about me. If anyone tries to betray us, I'll take care of them before they can. You all know that. But no one will turn traitor. Did you run a mile just to tell me this?"

"Pyotr Stepanovitch, we might never meet again!"

"What makes you think that?"

"Just answer one thing for me."

"What is it? Though I'd rather you leave me alone."

"Are we the only group like this, or are there others like us everywhere? This is important—please, I need to know."

"You're more dangerous than Lyamshin," Pyotr Stepanovitch replied. "But fine. What's your real question?"

"You're a fool! I would've thought it didn't matter to you anymore whether this is the only group or just one of many."

"So it is the only one! I knew it, I always knew!" Liputin cried out. "I was sure of it all along." Without waiting for a reply, he turned and disappeared into the darkness.

Pyotr Stepanovitch stood for a moment, thinking.

"No, none of them will betray us," he decided firmly. "But the group must stay together and follow orders, or else… What a pathetic bunch they are, though!"

Chapter 6.2

After returning home, he carefully packed his trunk without rushing. There was an early morning train leaving the town at six o'clock, a special express that only ran once a week as a trial. Although Pyotr Stepanovitch had told the quintet members that he was only going away briefly, his real plans, as later became clear, were very different. Once he finished packing, he settled his account with the landlady—having already given her notice of his departure—and took a cab to Erkel's place near the station. Around one o'clock in the morning, he walked to Kirillov's house, using the hidden path by Fedka's usual route.

Pyotr Stepanovitch was visibly unsettled. Besides the major issues already weighing on him—particularly his failure to get any news about Stavrogin—it seemed likely he had received a warning of imminent danger, possibly from Petersburg. Although details from this time are clouded by rumors and speculation, it is reasonable to assume that Pyotr Stepanovitch had other dealings elsewhere, perhaps even other revolutionary cells or associates in places like Moscow or Petersburg. It was also clear that he maintained curious and complex relationships with them. Three days after he left town, an order for his arrest arrived from Petersburg, likely connected to events elsewhere or in our town. This order only heightened the panic that gripped the local authorities and townsfolk after the shocking discovery of Shatov's murder—a grim culmination of the senseless acts that had plagued the area. Yet the order came too late. Pyotr Stepanovitch was already in Petersburg under an alias, and once he learned of the developments, he quickly fled abroad. But this is jumping ahead.

When he entered Kirillov's home, he looked irritable and confrontational. Beyond the task at hand, he seemed eager to vent a personal grudge against Kirillov. Meanwhile, Kirillov, who appeared to have been waiting for him with tense anticipation, was seated on the sofa. His face was pale, and his dark eyes were fixed and heavy.

"I thought you weren't coming," Kirillov said in a flat, tired tone, not getting up to greet him.

Pyotr Stepanovitch stood in front of him, studying his face before speaking.

"So, everything's ready, and you're not backing out. Bravo!" he said with an arrogant smile. "Though, if I was late, you shouldn't complain—I gave you three extra hours as a gift."

"I don't need your extra hours as a gift, and you can't give me anything... you fool!" Kirillov snapped.

"What?" Pyotr Stepanovitch was taken aback but quickly regained his composure. "What a temper! You're acting like a savage," he said with the same condescending tone. "At a time like this, you need to stay calm. Think of yourself as Columbus and me as a mouse, and don't let anything I say offend you. I gave you this advice yesterday."

"I don't want to see you as a mouse," Kirillov replied coldly.

"What's this, a compliment? But the tea is cold—that's a sign that everything's in chaos. Bah! But look, there's something on a plate in the window." He walked over. "Oh, boiled chicken and rice! But why haven't you eaten it yet? So you're in such a state of mind that even chicken..."

"I've eaten already, and it's none of your business. Shut up!"

"Of course, of course. It's no big deal—though, honestly, it is for me right now. Believe it or not, I barely had any dinner. So if that chicken isn't needed anymore... eh?"

"Eat it if you can."

"Thanks. And then I'll have some tea."

He quickly settled himself at the other end of the sofa and started devouring the chicken with surprising greed. All the while, he kept a sharp eye on Kirillov, who stared at him with a mix of anger and disgust, as though unable to look away.

"By the way," Pyotr Stepanovitch said suddenly, still chewing, "what about our business? We're not backing out, are we? What's going on with that document?"

"I decided last night that it doesn't matter to me. I'll write it. About the manifestoes?"

"Yes, the manifestoes too. But I'll dictate it. Of course, it doesn't matter to you. Why would you care about what's in the letter at a time like this?"

"That's not your concern."

"Of course, it's not. It only needs to be a few lines—something about you and Shatov distributing the manifestoes with the help of Fedka, who stayed at your place. That last part, about Fedka and your lodgings, is really important—the most important part, actually. You see, I'm being completely open with you."

"Shatov? Why bring up Shatov? I won't mention him for anything."

"What difference does it make to you? It won't hurt him now."

"His wife came back. She woke up and sent someone to ask me where he is."

"She sent someone to ask you?" Pyotr Stepanovitch looked uneasy. "Huh… that's unfortunate. She might send someone again. No one can know I'm here."

"She won't find out. She's gone back to sleep, and there's a midwife with her—Arina Virginsky."

"So that's how it is. She won't overhear us, will she? Maybe you should lock the front door."

"She won't hear anything. And if Shatov shows up, I'll hide you in another room."

"Shatov won't come. And you need to write that you had a falling out with him because he turned traitor and informed the police. Say it happened this evening… and that it led to his death."

"He's dead!" Kirillov jumped up from the sofa.

"He died at seven this evening—or rather, yesterday evening. It's one o'clock now."

"You killed him! I knew this would happen—I saw it coming yesterday!"

"Of course you did! With this revolver right here." Pyotr Stepanovitch pulled out his revolver as if to show it off but didn't put it away, keeping it ready in his hand. "You're a strange man, Kirillov. You knew just as well as I did that the idiot was going to meet this end. What was there to foresee? I've made it perfectly clear all along. Shatov was planning to betray us—I had my eye on him, and it couldn't be allowed. You were supposed to be keeping an eye on him too. You told me that yourself three weeks ago."

"Shut up! You did this because he spit in your face in Geneva!"

"For that, yes, and for other reasons—for many other reasons; but not out of spite. Why are you jumping up? Why that look? Oh, so that's how it is?"

He leapt up, holding his revolver in front of him. Kirillov had grabbed the revolver from the window, where it had been loaded and ready since morning. Pyotr Stepanovitch stood his ground, pointing his weapon at Kirillov. The latter gave an angry laugh.

"Admit it, you coward—you brought your revolver because you thought I might shoot you. But I won't shoot you... although..."

He turned the revolver toward Pyotr Stepanovitch again, almost rehearsing the action, as though enjoying the thought of pulling the trigger. Pyotr Stepanovitch stayed put, waiting without firing, even at the risk of being shot first—it wouldn't have been surprising from "the lunatic." But at last, Kirillov lowered his hand, trembling, gasping for breath, unable to speak.

"You've had your fun, and that's enough," Pyotr Stepanovitch said, lowering his weapon. "I knew it was all just playacting. Still, you took a risk, let me tell you—I could have fired."

He sat down on the sofa, pretending to be calm, and poured himself some tea, though his hand shook slightly. Kirillov placed his revolver on the table and began pacing the room.

"I won't write that I killed Shatov. I won't write anything now. You won't get your document."

"I won't?"

"No, you won't."

"What stupidity and cowardice!" Pyotr Stepanovitch's face turned pale with rage. "I expected this, though. You haven't surprised me. Fine, have it your way. If I could force you, I would. You're still a scoundrel, though." He was losing control, his voice rising. "You begged us for money, made all sorts of promises... But I won't leave here empty-handed. I'll at least see you blow your brains out first!"

"I want you to leave. Right now," Kirillov said firmly, standing before him.

"No, I can't do that." Pyotr Stepanovitch picked up his revolver again. "You might change your mind out of spite or fear and betray us tomorrow to get more money. They'd pay you for that, wouldn't they? Damn it, men like you will do anything! Don't worry, though—I've planned for that. I'll put a bullet in your head myself, just like I did to Shatov, if you don't do it yourself. Damn you!"

"You're that desperate to see my blood, are you?"

"It's not about spite. I couldn't care less. I'm doing it to protect the cause. You see how unreliable people are. You can see that for yourself. I don't even understand why you're so obsessed with this idea of killing yourself. It wasn't my idea—it came from you. You talked about it to the committee abroad long before you said anything to me. Nobody forced you to say it. Nobody knew who you were. You volunteered it yourself, out of some kind of sentimental foolishness. And now, our plans—plans you agreed to—depend on it. You put yourself in this position. You know too much. If you're foolish enough to go to the police tomorrow, it'll be disastrous for us. You know that, don't you? Yes, you've tied yourself to this. You gave your word, and you took money. You can't deny that."

Pyotr Stepanovitch was visibly agitated, but Kirillov had stopped paying attention to him. He paced back and forth in the room, deep in thought.

"I feel sorry for Shatov," Kirillov said suddenly, stopping in front of Pyotr Stepanovitch.

"Why? I feel sorry too, if that's all you mean. Do you think—"

"Shut up, you scoundrel!" Kirillov roared, making a sudden, unmistakably threatening movement. "I'll kill you."

"Calm down, calm down! I lied, I admit it. I'm not sorry at all. There, is that better? Let's not make a scene," Pyotr Stepanovitch said, raising his hands defensively and stepping back.

Kirillov let it go and resumed pacing the room.

"I won't delay any longer. I want to kill myself now. Everyone is a scoundrel."

"Well, that's one way to look at it. Sure, everyone's a scoundrel, and life is unbearable for any decent man…"

"Idiot! I'm just as much a scoundrel as you, as everyone else. I'm no decent man. There's never been a decent man anywhere."

"Well, he's finally figured it out! How could someone as smart as you not see until now that all people are the same? There aren't better or worse people—just some who are dumber than others. If everyone's a scoundrel (which is nonsense, by the way), then no one would stand out as not being one."

"Oh? So you're being serious?" Kirillov asked, staring at him with mild surprise. "You're speaking passionately, like you really believe it… Can it be that even people like you have convictions?"

"Kirillov, I've never understood why you want to kill yourself. All I know is that it comes from some deep conviction—a very strong one. But if you feel like explaining it, I'm listening… Just don't forget the time."

"What time is it?" Kirillov asked.

"Two o'clock," Pyotr Stepanovitch replied, glancing at his watch while lighting a cigarette.

"Maybe we can come to an understanding after all," Pyotr Stepanovitch thought to himself.

"I have nothing to say to you," Kirillov muttered.

"I remember something about God being part of this," Pyotr Stepanovitch said. "You explained it to me once—twice, actually. If you stop yourself, you become God. Is that it?"

"Yes. I become God."

Pyotr Stepanovitch didn't even crack a smile; he waited in silence. Kirillov looked at him sharply.

"You're a political manipulator and a liar. You're trying to pull me into some philosophical discussion, stir up my emotions, and calm me down. Then, when I've made peace with you, you'll ask me for a note saying I killed Shatov."

Pyotr Stepanovitch responded with almost disarming honesty.

"Well, even if I am a scoundrel, what difference does it make to you now, Kirillov? Why are we even arguing? You're one kind of person, and I'm another—so what? We're both just…"

"Scoundrels," Kirillov interrupted.

"Yes, scoundrels, if you like. But you know those are just words."

"My whole life, I didn't want it to be just words. I've lived because I wanted more than that. Even now, every single day, I don't want it to just be words."

"Well, everyone looks for where they'll be most comfortable. That's all anyone wants—comfort. That's been said for centuries."

"Comfort, you say?"

"Oh, let's not argue about words."

"No, you were right—comfort. God is necessary, so He must exist."

"Well, that settles it, then."

"But I know He doesn't, and He can't."

"That's probably true."

"Don't you see? A person who holds both those ideas can't keep living."

"You mean he has to shoot himself?"

"Yes. Don't you understand that someone might shoot himself for that alone? Can't you imagine one person out of millions who wouldn't stand for it and just refuses to?"

"All I see is that you're hesitating. That's a bad sign."

"Stavrogin is driven by an idea too," Kirillov said gloomily as he paced the room, ignoring the previous remark.

"What's that?" Pyotr Stepanovitch's ears perked up. "What idea? Did he tell you something?"

"No, I figured it out. If Stavrogin has faith, he doesn't believe in his faith. If he doesn't have faith, he doesn't believe in that either."

"Well, Stavrogin's got worse things going on in his head," Pyotr Stepanovitch muttered irritably, watching Kirillov carefully and noticing how pale he had become.

"Damn it, he's not going to shoot himself," he thought. "I suspected it—it's just some crazy idea stuck in his head. What a bunch of useless people."

"You're the last person I'll see. I don't want to part on bad terms with you," Kirillov suddenly said.

Pyotr Stepanovitch hesitated. "What's he up to now?" he wondered.

"I assure you, Kirillov, I have no personal grudge against you. I've always…"

"You're a scoundrel and a fraud. But I'm no better than you. The only difference is, I'll shoot myself, and you'll stay alive."

"You're saying I'm so low that I'd want to keep living?"

He couldn't decide whether it was a good idea to continue this conversation or not. He chose to let the moment guide him. Still, Kirillov's constant tone of superiority grated on him, especially now when he seemed like a man halfway out of this world.

"You almost sound like you're bragging about killing yourself."

"I've always been amazed that people keep living," Kirillov said, ignoring him again.

"Huh, that's one way to think about it, but..."

"You're just pretending to agree to make me slip up. Be quiet—you don't understand anything. If there's no God, then I am God."

"I never got that part—why are you God?"

"If God exists, everything is His will, and I can't escape it. If He doesn't, then it's all my will, and I have to show it."

"Your will? But why do you have to?"

Because all will belongs to me now. Can it be that no one on this planet, after rejecting God and believing only in their own will, dares to prove it on the most crucial point? It's like a beggar inheriting a fortune but being too scared to touch the gold, feeling too weak to claim it. I want to show my will. Maybe I'm the only one, but I'll do it."

"Then go ahead."

"I have to shoot myself because the ultimate act of my will is to take my own life with my own hands."

"But you wouldn't be the first to commit suicide; many people do that."

"Yes, but they all have reasons. To do it for no reason at all—purely to prove my will—that's something only I will do."

"He's not going to do it," Pyotr Stepanovitch thought again.

"You know," he said irritably, "if I were you, I'd kill someone else to show my will instead of killing myself. You could actually be useful. I'll even tell you who, if you're not afraid. Then you wouldn't have to do it today. We could work something out."

"To kill someone would be the lowest form of self-will, and that shows exactly what you are. I'm not like you. I want the highest form, and I'll kill myself."

"He's arrived at this on his own," Pyotr Stepanovitch muttered with bitterness.

"I must prove my disbelief," Kirillov said, pacing the room. "I have no greater idea than my disbelief in God. The entire history of mankind supports me. Humanity has done nothing but invent God to keep themselves from killing themselves; that's the whole story of history up until now. I will be the first in human history to reject God completely. Let everyone know it."

"He's not going to do it," Pyotr Stepanovitch thought nervously.

"Who do you want to know?" he asked, trying to push him. "It's just you and me here. Do you mean Liputin?"

"Everyone will know. They'll all know. There's nothing hidden that won't be revealed. He said that."

Kirillov pointed passionately at the image of the Savior, before which a small lamp was burning. Pyotr Stepanovitch completely lost his temper.

"So you still believe in Him, and you've lit the lamp—just to be safe, I suppose?"

Kirillov didn't respond.

"You know, I think you believe in Him more deeply than any priest."

"Believe in who? In Him? Listen." Kirillov stopped walking and stared ahead with an intense, almost trance-like expression. "Listen to this great idea: once, there was a day on earth, and on that day, three crosses stood in the center of the world. On one of them, a man had such faith that he told another, 'Today you'll be with me in Paradise.' The day ended; both of them died and vanished. But there was no Paradise, no resurrection. His promise didn't come true.

"Listen to me. That man was the greatest to ever live. He was the meaning of life itself. Without Him, this entire planet and everything on it is pure madness. There was no one like Him before, and there hasn't been since—not even close. And that's the miracle, that there will never be another like Him. But if even He, the miracle, wasn't spared by the laws of nature, if those laws allowed Him to live a lie and die for it, then

678

the entire planet is built on lies and mockery. The very foundation of everything becomes a farce, a devil's joke. So tell me—what's the point of living? Answer me, if you're truly human."

"That's a different question," Pyotr Stepanovitch replied calmly. "It seems to me you're mixing two separate ideas, and that's always risky. But let me ask—what if you really are God? What if the lies ended, and you realized that all the deception comes from belief in that old God?"

"Ah, so you've finally understood!" Kirillov cried out, his face lighting up with an almost feverish joy. "So it is possible to understand—even for someone like you! Do you see now that salvation lies in proving this idea to everyone? But who will prove it? I will! I don't understand how an atheist can know there's no God and not immediately kill himself. To understand there's no God and not also realize that you yourself are God is ridiculous. If you understand this, you become sovereign. Then, you don't need to kill yourself—you live in absolute glory. But someone has to be the first to prove it, to show the way. That's why I must kill myself. I'll begin, and I'll prove it. Right now, I'm a reluctant god, and that makes me miserable because I have to assert my will.

"Everyone is unhappy because they're too afraid to express their will. Humanity has always been poor and miserable because people have only dared to assert their will in trivial things, like children. I'm deeply unhappy because I'm terrified. Fear is humanity's curse. But I will break through. I will believe that I don't believe. I'll start, I'll finish, I'll open the door, and I'll save others. That's the only thing that will save humanity and rebuild the next generation physically. Because as people are now, they can't survive without the God they used to believe in—I'm convinced of that.

"For three years, I've been searching for the defining quality of my godhood, and I've found it. My godhood is self-will. That's how I'll prove my ultimate independence and my new, terrifying freedom. And it is terrifying. I'm killing myself to show my independence and to claim this terrifying freedom."

Kirillov's face had turned unnaturally pale, and his eyes carried a heavy, haunted look. He seemed delirious, as if on the edge of collapse. Pyotr Stepanovitch watched him closely, convinced he might fall to the floor at any moment.

Kirillov suddenly shouted, "Give me the pen!" His voice was frenzied, almost desperate. "Dictate! I'll sign anything. I'll even sign that I killed Shatov. Go on, dictate while I feel like it. I don't care what the proud slaves think! You'll see soon enough that all secrets will be revealed, and you will be destroyed. I believe it—I believe it!"

Pyotr Stepanovitch jumped up immediately, grabbing the inkstand and paper. His hands trembled with urgency as he seized the moment. "I, Alexey Kirillov, declare..." he began to dictate.

"Wait! I won't!" Kirillov interrupted, trembling violently, his entire body shaking as though gripped by fever. His mind was consumed with the strange idea of writing this declaration, as though it offered some fleeting escape from his inner torment. "To whom am I even declaring this? I need to know to whom!"

"To no one—or to everyone! Whoever reads it. Why limit it? Write it for the whole world!"

"The whole world! Yes, that's it! But no repentance—I don't want repentance! And it's not for the police!"

"Of course not. Damn the police!" Pyotr Stepanovitch cried out, his voice bordering on hysteria. "Write it if you're serious!"

"Wait! I want to start it with a drawing of a face sticking out its tongue."

"Don't be ridiculous," Pyotr Stepanovitch snapped. "You can express all that without a drawing—use the tone!"

"The tone? Yes, you're right—the tone. Dictate it. Let's get the tone right."

"I, Alexey Kirillov," Pyotr Stepanovitch dictated forcefully, leaning over Kirillov's shoulder as the latter wrote with shaking hands. "I, Alexey Kirillov, declare that today, the —th of October, at around eight o'clock in the evening, I killed the student Shatov in the park for betraying us and giving information about the manifestoes and Fedka, who has been hiding with us for the last ten days at Filipov's house. I am taking my own life today with my revolver, not out of repentance or fear, but because I decided long ago, while I was abroad, to end my life."

"Is that it?" Kirillov asked, his voice filled with disbelief and irritation.

"Not another word!" Pyotr Stepanovitch exclaimed, waving his hand and trying to snatch the paper.

"Wait," Kirillov said firmly, placing his hand over the document. "That's nonsense! I want to say who helped me. Why just Fedka? And what about the fire? I want everything included! And the tone—it must be abusive too. Abusive!"

"That's enough, Kirillov! I promise you, it's enough!" Pyotr Stepanovitch begged, his voice almost pleading, his anxiety palpable as he feared Kirillov might destroy the paper. "They'll believe it more if it's vague and cryptic, just hints. You only need to give them a glimpse of the truth, enough to leave them guessing. They'll create their own story, one more convincing than anything we could write. And they'll believe their version more than ours! This is perfect as it is—absolutely perfect! Just give it to me!"

And he kept trying to grab the paper. Kirillov stared at him with wide eyes, as though he was trying to think, but he seemed too far gone to understand anything now.

"Damn it," Pyotr Stepanovitch snapped suddenly, his tone impatient. "He hasn't signed it! Why are you just staring? Sign it!"

"I want to insult them," Kirillov muttered. But he picked up the pen and signed. "I want to insult them," he repeated.

"Write 'Vive la république,' that'll be enough," Pyotr Stepanovitch suggested.

"Brilliant!" Kirillov almost shouted with excitement. "'Vive la république démocratique sociale et universelle ou la mort!' No, no, wait— that's not it. 'Liberté, égalité, fraternité ou la mort.' Yes, that's better, much better." He eagerly wrote it beneath his signature.

"That's enough," Pyotr Stepanovitch said again.

"Wait, just a little more. I'll sign it again in French. 'De Kirillov, gentilhomme russe et citoyen du monde.' Ha ha!" Kirillov burst into laughter. "No, no, hold on—I've got something even better. Eureka! 'Gentilhomme, séminariste russe et citoyen du monde civilisé!' That's perfect!" He jumped up from the sofa, then suddenly, with a swift motion, grabbed the revolver from the window, ran into the next room, and shut the door behind him.

Pyotr Stepanovitch paused for a moment, staring at the door and thinking.

"If he does it right away, maybe he'll follow through. But if he starts overthinking it, he won't."

He sat down with the paper, examining it once more. The wording still satisfied him.

"What's needed right now? Just something to throw them off and keep them occupied for a while. The park? There's no actual park in town—they'll figure out it's Skvoreshniki on their own. But it'll take time for them to get there, then even more time to search. By the time they find the body, the story will be confirmed, and they'll assume it's all true— even about Fedka. And Fedka explains the fire and the Lebyadkins. Everything connects. They'll think it was all planned here, at Filipov's, while they missed all the signs. It'll mess with their heads completely! They won't even think about the quintet—just Shatov, Kirillov, Fedka, and Lebyadkin, and why they killed each other. That'll be the puzzle for them." He glanced up suddenly, annoyed. "Damn it, I don't hear the shot!"

Though he had been reading the paper and feeling satisfied, he had been listening carefully the whole time. Now, his irritation boiled over. He checked his watch—it was getting late. Ten minutes had passed since Kirillov went into the other room.

Grabbing the candle, Pyotr Stepanovitch moved toward the door. Just as he reached it, he realized the candle was almost burned out and wouldn't last another twenty minutes. There wasn't another one in the room. He grabbed the handle and listened closely. Not a single sound came from inside.

He suddenly flung the door open and raised the candle high. Something inside roared and lunged at him. Slamming the door shut with all his strength, he pressed his weight against it. Then everything went silent again, unnervingly still, as though nothing had happened.

He stood for a long time, unsure of what to do, holding the candle in his hand. He had only caught a quick glimpse when he opened the door, but he had seen Kirillov's face at the far end of the room by the window and the wild rage with which he had rushed toward him. Pyotr Stepanovitch shivered, quickly set the candle on the table, readied his revolver, and tiptoed to the farthest corner of the room. He positioned himself so that if Kirillov opened the door and lunged toward the table with a weapon, he would have enough time to aim and fire first.

Pyotr Stepanovitch had completely lost faith in the suicide happening. "He was standing in the middle of the room, thinking," he thought anxiously. "And the room was dark and eerie too. He roared and charged at me. There are two possibilities: either I interrupted him just as he was about to pull the trigger, or he was plotting how to kill me. Yes, that must be it—he was planning it. He knows I won't leave without killing him if he backs out of doing it himself, so he has to kill me first to stop me. And again, there's silence. I'm genuinely frightened. He could fling the door open at any moment. The worst part is he believes in God, just like a priest. He'll never shoot himself! There are so many people like this nowadays, these so-called free thinkers. A worthless bunch! Oh, damn it, the candle—it'll burn out in less than fifteen minutes for sure. I have to put an end to this somehow. I have to act. With the document here, no one will suspect me of killing him. I could stage it to look like he shot himself—place an empty revolver in his hand and make it seem convincing. Damn it! But how do I kill him? If I open the door, he'll rush out again and try to shoot me first. Damn it all, he's bound to miss!"

He was consumed by indecision, trembling at the thought of having to act. At last, he grabbed the candle and approached the door again, revolver raised and ready. He placed his left hand, holding the candle, on the door handle. But he fumbled, and the handle rattled and creaked. "He'll shoot now," flashed through Pyotr Stepanovitch's mind. With his foot, he kicked the door open forcefully, holding the candle high and the revolver aimed. But no sound or cry came from within. The room was empty.

He froze in place. The room had no other exit, no way out. He raised the candle higher, scanning the room carefully. It was empty. He called Kirillov's name softly, then louder. No response.

"Could he have escaped through the window?" He noticed one of the windows was open. "Impossible. He couldn't have climbed out through the window." Pyotr Stepanovitch crossed the room to check. "No, it's not possible." Suddenly, he turned around sharply and felt a jolt of fear.

Against the wall to the right of the door stood a cupboard. In the corner between the cupboard and the wall stood Kirillov. He was completely still, standing straight with his arms rigidly at his sides. His head was tilted back and pressed tightly against the wall, as if he were trying to blend into the corner and make himself invisible. It looked as though he was hiding, but something about his stance made it hard to believe. From where Pyotr Stepanovitch stood, he could only see part of Kirillov's figure. He hesitated, unable to make himself move to the side for a full view. His heart pounded, and rage overtook him. Shouting and stamping his feet, he charged toward the eerie corner.

When he finally reached Kirillov, he stopped abruptly, frozen in horror. What shocked him most was that, despite his yelling and rushing toward him, Kirillov didn't move a muscle. He stood completely still, as if he were made of stone or wax. His face was unnaturally pale, and his black eyes stared blankly into the distance. Pyotr Stepanovitch lowered the candle and raised it again, examining him from every angle. Suddenly, he realized that although Kirillov was staring straight ahead, he might be watching him out of the corner of his eye. An idea struck Pyotr Stepanovitch—to hold the candle close to Kirillov's face, even scorch him, to see how he would react. But just as he thought this, it seemed as though Kirillov's chin twitched, and a mocking smile flickered on his lips, as if he had guessed Pyotr Stepanovitch's thoughts. Shuddering, Pyotr Stepanovitch reached out and grabbed Kirillov's shoulder.

What happened next was so shocking and brief that Pyotr Stepanovitch could never fully recall it. The moment he touched Kirillov, the man suddenly bent down and knocked the candle out of Pyotr Stepanovitch's hand with his head. The candlestick clattered to the ground, and the candle went out. At the same time, Pyotr Stepanovitch felt a sharp, excruciating pain in the little finger of his left hand. He cried out and, in a frenzy, struck Kirillov three times on the head with the revolver. Kirillov had bent forward and was biting his finger. Finally, Pyotr Stepanovitch yanked his hand free and bolted toward the exit, groping his way in the dark. From behind, he could hear Kirillov shouting repeatedly, "Directly, directly, directly!"—ten times in all. But he kept running and had nearly reached the porch when he heard a loud gunshot. He froze in the dark entryway, standing there for five minutes, trying to decide what to do. At last, he turned back toward the house.

He needed to find the candle. Feeling around the floor near the cupboard, he located the candlestick, but lighting the candle was another problem. A memory surfaced: the previous day, when he had run into the kitchen to confront Fedka, he had noticed a large red box of matches on a shelf in the corner. He felt his way to the door leading to the kitchen, crossed the hallway, and went down the steps. Sure enough, on the same shelf, he found the box of matches. Grabbing it, he hurried back upstairs without striking a match. Only when he reached the spot where he had hit Kirillov and been bitten did he remember his injured finger. The pain flared up unbearably. Clenching his teeth, he managed to light the candle, place it back in the candlestick, and look around.

Near the open window, with his feet pointing toward the corner, lay Kirillov's lifeless body. The gunshot wound was to the right temple, and the bullet had exited through the top of his skull, shattering it. Blood and brain matter were splattered around the area. The revolver was still in his hand, lying on the floor. Death must have been instantaneous. After carefully surveying the scene, Pyotr Stepanovitch got up and tiptoed out of the room. He left the candle burning on the table in the outer room, reasoning that it wasn't likely to cause a fire. Pausing briefly, he glanced at the document on the table, smiled faintly, and then left the house, still walking on tiptoe for some reason. Once outside, he slipped back through Fedka's hidden passage, taking care to replace the posts behind him.

Chapter 6.3

Precisely at ten minutes to six, Pyotr Stepanovitch and Erkel were pacing back and forth along the railway platform beside a rather lengthy train, shrouded in the bustle of passengers preparing to board. The platform was alive with the sounds of footsteps, murmured conversations, and the occasional call from a conductor, blending into the crisp morning air. Pyotr Stepanovitch was leaving, and Erkel had come to see him off. The luggage had already been stowed, and Pyotr Stepanovitch's bag was placed securely in his chosen seat within a second-class carriage. The first bell had rung, signaling the approaching departure of the train, leaving them both aware that time was running out before the second bell would call for the final boarding.

Pyotr Stepanovitch moved with an air of composure, scanning the platform openly and observing the passengers as they made their way into the train. His gaze was direct and deliberate, as though he were studying each face and movement for hidden intent. Yet, among the crowd, he encountered no one of particular significance to him. Twice, he exchanged brief nods of acknowledgment: once with a merchant he vaguely recognized and again with a young village priest who was likely heading to a parish a couple of stations away. Erkel, meanwhile, seemed burdened by unspoken concerns. He glanced at Pyotr Stepanovitch repeatedly, his unease growing more palpable, but hesitated to voice what was on his mind. It was clear he had something important to say, though he may not have fully grasped what it was himself. The tension between the desire to speak and the hesitation to interrupt Pyotr Stepanovitch's calculated calm hung heavily in the air.

"You're looking at everyone so openly," Erkel finally ventured, his tone cautious, almost as though he were offering a subtle warning.

"Why shouldn't I?" Pyotr Stepanovitch replied without hesitation, brushing off the remark with a calmness that felt almost dismissive. "Now isn't the time to keep my head down. It's too soon for that. Don't trouble yourself." A hint of irritation crept into his voice, though he tried to conceal it. "The only thing I'm worried about is that devil Liputin. If he happens to sniff me out and come running here, that could be a nuisance."

"Pyotr Stepanovitch, they're not to be trusted," Erkel said firmly, his voice growing steadier as he braced himself to deliver this warning.

"Liputin?" Pyotr Stepanovitch asked, narrowing his eyes.

"Not just Liputin. None of them, Pyotr Stepanovitch," Erkel clarified with quiet conviction.

"Nonsense!" Pyotr Stepanovitch retorted sharply. "After what happened yesterday, they're all locked in. None of them would dare turn traitor now. No one throws themselves into certain destruction unless they've completely lost their wits."

"But, Pyotr Stepanovitch," Erkel insisted, his tone resolute, "they might lose their wits."

This thought had evidently crossed Pyotr Stepanovitch's mind as well, and hearing Erkel say it aloud only heightened his annoyance. He shot a glare at Erkel, who, despite his inner apprehension, held his ground.

"Don't tell me you're getting cold feet too, Erkel," Pyotr Stepanovitch snapped, his voice sharp but tinged with a faint note of disbelief. "You're the one I count on more than any of them. I've seen what they're all worth now, and you're the only one with a level head. Listen to me. Tell them everything I've told you today. They're your responsibility now. Go to each of them this morning—don't waste any time. When they've calmed down a bit, maybe tomorrow or the day after, get them together and read them my written instructions. By then, the panic will have made them pliable as wax, believe me. Fear has a way of doing that." He paused, softening his tone just slightly. "But you—whatever happens—don't lose heart."

"Ah, Pyotr Stepanovitch," Erkel said with a sigh, his voice low but heavy with meaning. "It would be better if you weren't leaving."

"I'm only going for a few days," Pyotr Stepanovitch replied briskly. "I'll be back before you know it."

Erkel hesitated, then pressed on cautiously but with determination. "Pyotr Stepanovitch, what if you're going to Petersburg?" His words hung in the air for a moment, charged with both concern and understanding. "Of course, I know you're doing what's necessary for the cause."

Pyotr Stepanovitch gave him a brief, appraising look. "I expected no less from you, Erkel. If you've guessed that I'm heading to Petersburg, then you can also understand why I couldn't tell the others yesterday. You saw what a state they were in—it would've only made things worse. But you, Erkel, you understand. You know I'm going for the cause, for critical work, not for personal safety as Liputin might think."

Erkel nodded but remained visibly uneasy. Pyotr Stepanovitch turned his gaze back to the train, his thoughts already leaping ahead to the tasks awaiting him, but he offered Erkel a fleeting, almost imperceptible smile of reassurance. The second bell rang, jolting them both into action.

At ten minutes to six, the railway platform was alive with the usual clamor and bustle of passengers boarding a rather lengthy train. Pyotr Stepanovitch paced along the platform with Erkel at his side, their conversation overshadowed by the faint whistles of the station and the clanging of baggage carts. Pyotr Stepanovitch was preparing to leave, and Erkel had come to see him off, carrying an air of unease that he struggled to hide. The luggage had already been stowed, and Pyotr Stepanovitch's bag rested neatly on the seat he had secured in the second-class carriage. The first bell had already rung, a signal that their time together was running short.

Erkel looked at Pyotr Stepanovitch hesitantly, his thoughts clearly weighed down by a concern he couldn't quite put into words. He studied his companion's face as they walked, noting the confident composure with which Pyotr Stepanovitch watched the other passengers. He scanned the crowd openly, his gaze pausing briefly here and there, as though evaluating each figure that passed. Twice he nodded in acknowledgment—once to a merchant he vaguely recognized and another time to a young village priest heading to his parish a few stations away. But his air of calm did little to soothe Erkel, who felt an increasing urge to speak yet couldn't summon the right words.

"Pyotr Stepanovitch, what if you were going abroad?" Erkel finally asked, his voice quivering with uncertainty. "I'd understand. I would, really. I'd understand that you need to protect yourself because you are everything, and we … we are nothing. I'd understand, Pyotr Stepanovitch."

Pyotr Stepanovitch turned toward him with a faint smile, touched more by the earnestness in Erkel's voice than by his words. "Thank you, Erkel," he replied smoothly. Then, wincing slightly, he withdrew his hand as Erkel inadvertently pressed against his bandaged finger. "Ah, careful—you've hit my bad finger. No matter." He flexed his hand briefly before continuing. "But let me reassure you again. I'm only going to Petersburg to sniff around, so to speak. I might be there no more than twenty-four hours before heading straight back. And when I return, I'll stay at Gaganov's country place for appearances' sake. Believe me, if there's any real danger, I'll be the first to face it. If I do end up staying longer in Petersburg, I'll inform you immediately—exactly as we've arranged—and you'll pass the message along to the others."

The second bell rang, signaling that only five minutes remained before the train's departure. The sound seemed to deepen Erkel's unease, but Pyotr Stepanovitch pressed on.

"I don't want the group here to fall apart," he said firmly. "Don't worry about me. I have plenty of fallback centers, but it's always good to maintain as many as we can. Still, I'm confident in leaving you here, even if you're practically alone with those idiots. They won't turn traitor—they won't have the courage. Fear will keep them in line."

Erkel's brow furrowed as he hesitated, his concern growing heavier with each passing moment. "Pyotr Stepanovitch, they aren't as reliable as you think. They might lose their nerve."

"Are you losing yours too, Erkel?" Pyotr Stepanovitch snapped, though his tone softened almost immediately. "I rely on you more than any of them. You've seen what they're worth. You'll be fine. Pass on my instructions to them today, and when they've recovered from yesterday's panic—by tomorrow or the day after—get them together and read my written orders. They'll be malleable then, trust me."

Erkel opened his mouth to reply, but before he could, Pyotr Stepanovitch's attention was caught by a cheerful voice calling out to him. A young man, dressed in travel clothes and exuding an easy confidence, approached them with a bright smile.

"Ah, you're traveling today too?" Pyotr Stepanovitch called out in an entirely different tone, one of cheerful camaraderie. "I didn't know you were taking the express. Off to see your mother?"

The young man, a distant relative of Yulia Mihailovna's and the son of a wealthy landowner, chuckled and shook his head. "No, I'm headed farther—to R——. Eight hours on the train. And you—off to Petersburg?"

"What makes you think that?" Pyotr Stepanovitch replied, laughing even more openly.

The young man wagged his finger playfully. "You're always up to something."

"Well, you've guessed right," Pyotr Stepanovitch whispered conspiratorially. "I'm carrying letters for Yulia Mihailovna and calling on a few important people. Tedious business, honestly."

Their exchange continued, light and animated, as the young man invited Pyotr Stepanovitch to join a card game in the first-class carriage. With a quick glance at Erkel and a hasty goodbye, Pyotr Stepanovitch moved his belongings to the first class, leaving Erkel standing alone on the platform.

The third bell rang, and Pyotr Stepanovitch, seated by the window, extended his hand briefly. "Well, Erkel. I'll see you soon. Don't worry—it's all in your hands now."

Erkel nodded but felt a pang of sadness as Pyotr Stepanovitch turned away quickly to speak with his companions. Left alone, Erkel began the walk back home, a sense of unease gnawing at him. It wasn't fear for the group's safety or even for Pyotr Stepanovitch's departure. It was something deeper, a sting he couldn't quite name—the way Pyotr Stepanovitch had turned away so abruptly, without so much as a heartfelt farewell.

Chapter 7
Stepan Trofimovitch's Last Wandering

Chapter 7.1

It seems certain that as the date for Stepan Trofimovitch's ill-conceived venture approached, he was overwhelmed with a profound sense of fear. The night before his departure must have been particularly torturous, filled with terror and uncertainty. Nastasya later mentioned that he had gone to bed late and managed to fall asleep. But such details mean little; after all, it is said that even men sentenced to execution can sleep soundly the night before their death. Though he set out during daylight—when the morning light might provide a semblance of courage to a nervous man—there is little doubt that the idea of being utterly alone on the open road must have filled him with dread.

The sheer desperation of his emotions likely dulled the initial shock of the solitude he experienced as soon as he left the warm and familiar corner where he had spent the past twenty years. Yet, no amount of forethought could mitigate the horror of being utterly alone. And still, even with the full knowledge of the trials awaiting him, he would have chosen to step onto the high road. Something proud and defiant about the undertaking drew him forward despite his fears. He could have remained under Varvara Petrovna's care, accepting her provisions and continuing his existence as a dependent. But he chose instead to leave of his own volition, holding high the banner of what he likely believed was a noble cause. To him, the act of leaving symbolized more than rebellion; it was a declaration of principle—a decision to walk into the unknown for the sake of an idea, even if that idea ultimately led him to ruin.

Another question arises: why did he choose to flee on foot rather than simply hire a carriage or buy tickets for a train? At first, I attributed it to his romanticized and impulsive mindset. For someone like him, prone to theatrical gestures, the idea of trudging along a rain-soaked road, umbrella in hand, likely appealed to his dramatic sensibilities more than a practical journey by carriage. A pilgrimage, with all its inherent symbolism, was far more in character than taking the straightforward route of purchasing posting tickets. But upon reflection, the reasoning might have been simpler. He likely feared that hiring horses or purchasing tickets might alert Varvara Petrovna, who would undoubtedly have intervened to stop him. And if she had done so, he would have given in immediately, abandoning his so-called great idea entirely.

Then there was the torment of deciding on a destination. To buy a ticket, he would have needed to know where he was going, and the mere thought of choosing a specific town must have seemed unbearable. The moment he named a destination, the absurdity of his plan would have become undeniable to him. What would he do in that town? Whom would he seek? The thought of ce marchand—this mysterious merchant he imagined finding—filled him with both dread and fascination. He was terrified of meeting this merchant yet equally horrified at the thought of not finding him. The open road, endless and undefined, offered the illusion of purpose without the weight of specifics. There, on the high road, he could simply keep walking without thinking of where he was headed. The road stretched endlessly before him, like life itself, full of possibilities but devoid of certainty. In contrast, posting tickets felt like an admission of defeat—an end to all dreams and ideas.

After his unexpected encounter with Liza, which left him even more disoriented, he resumed his aimless journey, lost in a haze of forgetfulness. The high road lay about half a mile from Skvoreshniki, and it was some time before he realized he had reached it. His mind, unable to bear the burden of logical thought, retreated into a kind of numbness. A fine drizzle fell intermittently, but he took no notice of the rain. He didn't even seem to realize when he adjusted his bag over his shoulder, finding it more comfortable to carry that way. He must have walked nearly a mile before he stopped abruptly and looked around.

The old road stretched ahead like a dark ribbon marked with deep wheel ruts, bordered on both sides by rows of willows. To the right, barren fields extended as far as the eye could see, their harvest long since gathered. To the left, dense bushes grew, and beyond them stood a small copse. In the far distance, the faint line of a railway cut across the horizon, and a thin wisp of smoke marked the passage of a train. The silence was complete; even the train made no sound as it moved.

Stepan Trofimovitch hesitated, a flicker of timidity crossing his face, but the feeling passed quickly. He sighed deeply, as though resigning himself to his situation, and lowered his bag beside a willow tree. Wrapping himself tightly in his rug to ward off the chill, he sat down, opened his umbrella against the drizzle, and settled into stillness. He sat there for some time, gripping the umbrella handle firmly, his lips moving occasionally as if in conversation with himself. His thoughts came in rapid succession, feverish and disjointed, as if his mind were conjuring images faster than he could make sense of them.

The open road stretched before him, endless and indifferent, while Stepan Trofimovitch sat beneath the willows, caught between despair and the faintest glimmer of pride in his so-called journey.

"Lise, Lise," Stepan Trofimovitch thought to himself, his mind wandering as he trudged along the road. "And with her, ce Maurice... Strange people, indeed. But what was that peculiar fire they spoke of, and who were those murdered? Something dreadful, no doubt. I suppose Nastasya hasn't found out yet and must still be waiting for me with my coffee." His thoughts spiraled into disarray. "Cards? Did I truly lose men at cards? H'm! Such things happened in Russia during the times of serfdom, so-called... My God, yes—Fedka!"

Suddenly, a jolt of terror ran through him, and he stopped in his tracks, looking around nervously. "What if that Fedka is hiding somewhere behind these bushes? They say he has a whole gang of robbers prowling this highway. Oh, mercy, what will I do?" His imagination ran wild. "I'll tell him everything—the entire truth. I'll confess that it was my fault and that I've suffered for it for ten long years, far more than he ever did as a soldier. Yes, I'll even give him my purse. But... h'm, I've only got forty roubles in total. He'll take the money and kill me all the same."

He closed his umbrella abruptly, as if by doing so he might conceal himself better, and placed it on the ground beside him. Far off in the distance, a cart emerged on the high road, approaching slowly from the direction of the town. Relief swept over him at the sight. "Grace à Dieu, it's only a cart, coming along at a walking pace. That can't be dangerous. These miserable little horses they breed here... I always said they were a disgrace. But wait, what's that behind the cart? I think there's a woman sitting in it. A peasant and a woman—cela commence à être rassurant.

The woman is behind, and the man is at the front—c'est très rassurant. And there's a cow tied to the back of the cart, by the horns—c'est rassurant au plus haut degré."

As the cart drew closer, he studied it intently. It was a sturdy peasant cart, and a woman sat on a tightly packed sack in the back while a man sat at the front, his legs dangling toward the road. The red cow ambled behind, secured by the horns to the cart. The man and the woman stared at Stepan Trofimovitch in open curiosity as they passed, and he gazed back at them with equal wonder. But once the cart had traveled about twenty paces beyond him, a sudden impulse struck, and he hurried to catch up with it. He felt safer walking near the cart's presence, as though it shielded him from some imagined threat. Yet even as he walked alongside it, his mind drifted back into a fog of disconnected thoughts and fleeting fancies.

Unbeknownst to him, the two peasants found him utterly fascinating. To them, this strange figure on the high road was an enigma—a gentleman perhaps, or some kind of wanderer unlike anyone they'd ever encountered. Finally, the woman, unable to contain her curiosity, spoke up. "What sort may you be, pray, if it's not too bold to ask?"

Her voice broke his reverie. He turned to her with a mournful expression, as if he'd been woken from a dream. "You... you are addressing me?" he stammered.

"A merchant, for sure," the peasant man interjected confidently. He was a tall, broad-shouldered fellow of about forty, with a reddish beard and an intelligent, thoughtful expression.

"No, not exactly a merchant," Stepan Trofimovitch replied vaguely. "Moi, c'est autre chose." He evaded the question, stepping back a little from the cart to put some distance between himself and their curiosity. He found himself walking alongside the cow instead.

"Hearing words like that, he must be a gentleman," the man concluded. He tugged gently at the reins as if this resolved the matter.

"That's what made us wonder," the woman added with a smile. "You seem to be out for a walk, perhaps?"

"You... you ask me that?" he muttered, feeling both irritated and embarrassed.

"Sometimes foreigners come by train from other parts," she continued, glancing at his boots. "Your boots don't look like they're from hereabouts."

"They're army boots," the man said confidently, his tone suggesting he was an expert in such matters.

"No, I am not precisely in the army," Stepan Trofimovitch replied, feeling increasingly uncomfortable. "What an inquisitive woman," he thought with growing vexation. "And the way they stare at me! But why do I feel guilty in front of them? I've done them no harm."

The woman leaned toward the man, whispering something. After a moment, she called out to Stepan Trofimovitch again. "If it's no trouble, we'd give you a lift if you'd like."

Her offer jolted him from his thoughts. "Yes, yes, my friends, I accept with pleasure, for I am very tired. But... but how do I get in?"

He paused, marveling at his own lack of foresight. "How extraordinary," he thought. "I've been walking beside this cart all this time and never once thought to ask for a ride. This 'real life' has such an odd and original quality about it."

But the peasant man hadn't stopped the cart just yet. "Where are you headed?" he asked, his tone cautious.

Stepan Trofimovitch hesitated, not immediately understanding the question. "Hatovo, I suppose?"

"Hatovo? No, not to Hatovo exactly... I don't know Hatov, though I've heard the name," he replied hastily, misunderstanding.

"The village of Hatovo—it's about seven miles from here," the man clarified.

"A village? C'est charmant! To be sure, I've heard of it..." Stepan Trofimovitch trailed off, realizing he was still walking beside the cart rather than riding in it. Suddenly, inspiration struck.

"You might think I am..." He paused dramatically, then declared, "I've got a passport. I am a professor—or rather, if you like, a head teacher. Yes, a head teacher. Oui, c'est comme ça qu'on peut traduire. I should be very grateful for a lift and, as thanks, I'll buy you... I'll buy you a quart of vodka."

"It'll cost you half a rouble," the man replied bluntly. "The road's bad."

"Or it wouldn't be fair to ourselves," the woman added with a nod.

"Half a rouble? Very well, half a rouble," Stepan Trofimovitch agreed, though his mind was already spinning with the calculation. "C'est encore mieux. I have forty roubles in total, but..."

His voice trailed off as he prepared to climb into the cart, feeling a mix of relief and apprehension about this curious turn of events.

The peasant finally brought the horse to a halt, and with a bit of maneuvering and effort from all sides, Stepan Trofimovitch was helped into the cart. He found himself seated awkwardly on the sack beside the woman. His thoughts, which had been racing chaotically, continued to swirl as he tried to settle into this new situation. Every now and then, he became dimly aware of his scattered state of mind and how disconnected his thoughts had become. This realization brought him fleeting moments of discomfort, as if he were wrestling with an inner humiliation.

"How... how is it you've got a cow tied to the cart?" he asked suddenly, as though the thought had only just occurred to him.

The woman chuckled. "Why do you ask, sir? Haven't you seen a cow before?"

"We bought it in town," the peasant added. "Our cattle all died off last spring, the plague got them. Nearly every beast around here has died. It's heartbreaking—there's hardly any left."

He lashed the horse lightly, trying to pull it out of a rut.

"Yes, yes, I see... that happens sometimes. Among us in Russia, well..." Stepan Trofimovitch trailed off mid-thought, his words dissolving into a murmur.

"If you're a teacher, what business do you have in Hatovo? Or are you heading farther?" the woman asked curiously.

"I... I'm not going farther exactly... C'est-à-dire, I'm going to a merchant's," he answered vaguely.

"To Spasov, I suppose?" the peasant chimed in.

"Yes, yes, to Spasov... but that doesn't matter," Stepan Trofimovitch replied hastily, his tone growing slightly impatient.

"If you're heading to Spasov on foot, it'll take you a week in those boots," the woman teased, laughing.

"Perhaps, perhaps... it doesn't matter, mes amis, it doesn't matter," he said abruptly, waving off her comment with a dismissive gesture.

He silently observed how inquisitive they were, particularly the woman. Yet, he couldn't help but notice that her speech was somewhat refined for a peasant. "Their language has changed a little since February 19," he thought, referring to the Emancipation of the Serfs. "And yet, what's it to them where I'm going? I'll pay them for the ride, so why do they care?"

"If you're going to Spasov, you'd best take the steamer," the peasant continued, seemingly unfazed by Stepan Trofimovitch's curt responses.

"That's true," the woman agreed enthusiastically. "If you travel along the riverbank, it's twenty-five miles shorter."

"Thirty-five," the man corrected her confidently.

"You'll just catch the steamer at Ustyevo around two o'clock tomorrow," the woman concluded with a sense of finality.

Stepan Trofimovitch, however, fell silent, refusing to engage further. His companions, too, sank into their own quiet. Occasionally, the peasant tugged at the reins to urge the horse onward. The woman whispered brief remarks to him now and then, but for the most part, the journey continued in relative stillness. Eventually, Stepan Trofimovitch dozed off, lulled by the cart's slow and rhythmic movement.

He was startled awake when the woman nudged him gently, laughing as she spoke. "You've had a good nap, sir."

"What? Where am I? Oh... yes. Well... it doesn't matter," he muttered groggily, sighing as he clambered out of the cart.

The scene before him was unfamiliar. They had arrived in a rather sizable village, and he found himself at the doorstep of a modest cottage with three small windows. He looked around mournfully, feeling a strange sense of detachment, as if the world around him were oddly distant.

"And the half-rouble—I nearly forgot!" he exclaimed suddenly, turning to the peasant with hurried movements, as though reluctant to part from his unlikely companions.

"Let's settle it inside. Come on in," the peasant invited warmly.

"It's warm and comfortable inside," the woman added reassuringly.

Stepan Trofimovitch hesitated for a moment, then climbed the rickety wooden steps. "How has it come to this?" he murmured under his breath, filled with apprehension. But he entered the cottage anyway, as though carried forward by some unseen force.

The interior was light and clean, a typical peasant's home with two rooms and three windows. It wasn't quite an inn, but clearly a place where travelers often stopped to rest. Stepan Trofimovitch wandered to a corner without a word, sat down, and fell into deep thought. He seemed oblivious to his surroundings, even forgetting to greet anyone.

Gradually, a pleasant warmth seeped into his body. After hours spent traveling in the damp, the coziness of the cottage was a balm to his chilled and weary frame. A slight shiver ran down his spine—a familiar sensation for someone of his nervous temperament when moving from cold to warmth. Yet, even this was oddly comforting.

The enticing aroma of hot pancakes reached him, tickling his nostrils. The woman of the house was busy at the stove, flipping them onto a large plate. Stepan Trofimovitch leaned forward, a childlike smile spreading across his face.

"What's that? Pancakes?" he asked, his voice filled with an innocent curiosity. "Mais… c'est charmant."

"Would you like some, sir?" the woman offered politely, turning to him with a kind smile.

"I would indeed! I should like that very much. And... could I ask you for some tea as well?" he replied, his spirits lifting slightly.

"Of course! I'll get the samovar ready right away," the woman said cheerfully.

Soon, a plate piled high with pancakes was placed before him. They were peasant-style pancakes, thin and golden, made from a mix of wheat flour and dripping with fresh, hot butter. He tasted one and immediately sighed with delight.

"How rich, how delicious! And... if one might have un doigt d'eau de vie," he added wistfully.

"You mean a drop of vodka?" the woman guessed, her tone lighthearted.

"Yes, exactly! Just a little, un tout petit rien," he said with a faint laugh, feeling, for the first time in hours, a flicker of warmth in his weary soul.

"Five farthings' worth, is it?" Stepan Trofimovitch asked again, his tone tinged with an almost childlike wonder.

"Yes, five farthings, just a little," he murmured with a blissful smile, nodding as though to affirm the decision.

When a peasant is asked to perform a task, he will typically approach it with a measured calmness, perhaps even a touch of solemnity, as if every duty is a small but meaningful part of the day's rhythm. But the moment vodka enters the equation, something changes. That same peasant will spring to action with an eager enthusiasm, a burst of energy that suggests he takes equal delight in the task as the one who will drink the vodka. It is as though the prospect of your enjoyment brings him an indirect satisfaction, a sense of participation in the celebration, however minor it might be.

Within mere minutes, the peasant returned from the nearby tavern, setting down a bottle and a greenish, slightly clouded wineglass on the table before Stepan Trofimovitch.

"All this for me?" Stepan Trofimovitch asked, his eyes widening in genuine astonishment as he took in the sight of the glass and bottle. "I've had vodka before, but I never realized you could get so much for five farthings!"

He poured the wineglass full, then stood up with a certain gravity, as if embarking on a ceremonial act. Holding the glass carefully, he crossed the room to the corner where the black-browed peasant woman—his fellow traveler, who had both shared the sack with him and pestered him with her many questions—was sitting. The woman looked startled, glancing up at him with wide eyes. At first, she began to decline his offer with polite gestures, but after a moment of obligatory resistance, she stood up and accepted. Taking the glass in hand, she drank it in three deliberate sips, her face tightening with every swallow as though she were enduring some great trial. When she finished, she handed the glass back to him with a slight bow, her expression marked by a mixture of gratitude and discomfort.

Stepan Trofimovitch returned the bow with equal formality, his posture straight and his movements deliberate. He walked back to the table with an air of pride, as though he had just completed a grand gesture worthy of admiration.

The entire episode had been entirely unplanned, a sudden impulse that took him by surprise as much as anyone else. Only seconds before, he had no intention of offering her a drink. Yet now, with the act completed, a deep sense of satisfaction welled up in him.

"I have always known how to connect with peasants, perfectly, absolutely perfectly," he thought to himself, pouring what remained of the vodka into his glass. "And I've always told them so."

Although less than a full glass remained, it warmed him from within as he drank, soothing his nerves and even creating a slight buzz that momentarily lifted his spirits.

"Je suis malade tout à fait, mais ce n'est pas trop mauvais d'être malade," he mused aloud, half to himself.

"Would you care to make a purchase?" came a soft and feminine voice nearby.

Startled, he raised his head and found himself looking at a woman—

a lady, in fact. Her modest demeanor and simple attire—a dark gown and a gray shawl draped over her shoulders—did not conceal a certain refinement. She appeared to be slightly over thirty, with an air of calm kindness in her expression that immediately put him at ease.

She had just returned to the cottage, where her belongings—a small pack made of American leather and a portfolio—lay on a nearby bench. These items had caught his eye earlier when he first entered. Now, from her pack, she withdrew two finely bound books, each adorned with a cross on the cover, and offered them to him.

"Et... mais je crois que c'est l'Evangile... with the greatest pleasure," Stepan Trofimovitch exclaimed, taking the books gently in his hands. "Ah, now I see. Vous êtes ce qu'on appelle a gospel-woman. I've read about this before. Half a rouble, is it?"

"Thirty-five kopecks," she replied with a warm smile.

"With the greatest pleasure," he repeated, his voice earnest. "I have nothing against the Gospel, and I've been meaning to reread it for some time."

A thought crossed his mind: it had been decades since he last read the Gospel in earnest. At most, he had skimmed a few passages seven years ago while reading Renan's Vie de Jésus. The realization was both humbling and oddly stirring.

Reaching into his pocket, he retrieved four ten-rouble notes—the entirety of his remaining funds. Handing one to the woman of the house, who quickly offered to fetch change, he suddenly became aware of a subtle shift in the room. Glancing around, he noticed that several people had gathered, their quiet conversations punctuated by the occasional glance in his direction. They were clearly talking about him.

The cart driver, now back from the town with his cow, was animatedly discussing the recent fire. He spoke of arson and pointed fingers at the Shpigulin men.

"How strange," Stepan Trofimovitch thought. "He talked about everything on the way here but never mentioned a fire. Why would he leave that out?"

"Master, Stepan Trofimovitch, sir, is that really you?" a voice exclaimed, interrupting his musings.

Looking up, he saw a middle-aged man with no beard, dressed in an overcoat with a wide, old-fashioned collar. His face bore the unmistakable marks of a former house-serf.

"Excuse me," Stepan Trofimovitch muttered, taken aback. "I... I don't quite recall you."

"You don't remember me? I'm Anisim, Anisim Ivanov. I served the late Mr. Gaganov and saw you many times at the late Avdotya Sergyevna's, when you visited with Varvara Petrovna. I even brought you books from her—twice, I think—and once a box of Petersburg sweets."

"Ah, yes, Anisim," Stepan Trofimovitch said, smiling faintly as recognition dawned. "Of course, I remember now. Do you live here?"

"I live near Spasov, close to the V—— Monastery, in the service of Marta Sergyevna, Avdotya Sergyevna's sister," Anisim began, with a polite but familiar air. "Perhaps your honour remembers her? She's the one who broke her leg falling out of her carriage on the way to a ball. Now she lives near the monastery, and I've been in her service ever since. And as your honour can see, I am now on my way to town to visit my kinsfolk."

"Yes, yes, quite so, quite so," Stepan Trofimovitch muttered distractedly, trying to piece together the fragments of memory stirred by this sudden reappearance from his past.

"I can't tell you how glad I was to see you, sir. You used to be so kind to me," Anisim continued with a broad smile. "But, if I may ask, where are you heading, sir? And all by yourself, too? I don't believe I've ever known you to take a journey alone."

The question struck Stepan Trofimovitch like a blow. His composure wavered, and his face grew tense.

"I... yes... well..." he stammered. "I am... I am going to Spasov."

"Ah, to Spasov! Il me semble que tout le monde va à Spassof," he added nervously, trying to lighten the moment with a weak smile.

"You don't mean you're going to see Fyodor Matveyevitch, do you?

If so, they'll be delighted to see you! He always spoke so highly of you in the old days and often mentions you even now."

"Yes, yes, to Fyodor Matveyevitch's," Stepan Trofimovitch confirmed hurriedly, though in truth, he had no idea where he was going.

"To be sure, to be sure. The peasants here are talking, you know— they say they met you walking along the high road. It set them wondering; they're a foolish lot."

"I... I..." Stepan Trofimovitch faltered, beads of perspiration appearing on his forehead. "Yes, well, you know, Anisim, I made a wager... you see... like an Englishman, that I would go on foot, and so I..."

He trailed off, his voice trembling under the strain of maintaining the facade.

"To be sure, to be sure," Anisim replied, though his tone carried a trace of skepticism. His gaze lingered on Stepan Trofimovitch with merciless curiosity, his interest in the peculiar situation only deepening.

Stepan Trofimovitch felt the walls closing in. Overcome with discomfort, he was on the verge of fleeing the cottage entirely when the arrival of the samovar provided an unexpected reprieve. At the same moment, the gospel-woman, who had stepped out for a time, returned. Grasping at the opportunity to redirect the conversation, he turned to her with an air of exaggerated politeness.

"Would you care for some tea?" he offered, his voice strained but eager.

Anisim, sensing the dismissal, shrugged and wandered toward the passage, leaving Stepan Trofimovitch to grapple with his swirling thoughts and the unsettling murmurs that seemed to ripple through the room.

The peasants had indeed begun to whisper among themselves, their curiosity about the peculiar traveler growing with each passing moment. "Who is he, really?" they murmured. "He's wandering the high road like a lost soul, calling himself a teacher but dressed like a foreigner. He doesn't seem to have much sense, yet he carries money with him! What sort of man is this?"

The seeds of suspicion began to take root, and the notion of informing the authorities gained traction. The lingering unease about recent events in the town—the fire, the unrest—only fueled their doubts.

But Anisim, with his knack for storytelling and a flair for smoothing over doubts, quickly dispelled their concerns. Standing in the passage, he regaled the gathering with tales of Stepan Trofimovitch's distinguished past.

"He's not just any teacher," Anisim explained with a knowing air. "He's a man of great learning, a true scholar! Why, he's a landowner from this very district and has been living for over twenty years with Madame Stavrogin, the widow of a general. Everyone in town knows him, and he's held in the highest regard. At the club of the nobility, he'd lose fifty, even a hundred roubles in a single evening, and think nothing of it. And his rank! A councillor, no less—practically a lieutenant-colonel, which is just a step away from being a full colonel. As for his money, he has more than he knows what to do with, thanks to Madame Stavrogin!"

Back inside the cottage, Stepan Trofimovitch began to recover from the ordeal. His gaze wandered to the gospel-woman, who sat sipping tea from a saucer while nibbling thoughtfully on a piece of sugar.

"Mais c'est une dame et très comme il faut," he mused, noting her refined yet unassuming manner. There was a quiet dignity about her, an air of independence softened by an undercurrent of gentleness.

With some coaxing, he learned that her name was Sofya Matveyevna Ulitin. She was a widow, like her sister, who lived in K——. Her late husband, a sub-lieutenant who had risen through the ranks, had died heroically at Sevastopol.

"But you're still so young," he remarked with genuine surprise. "Vous n'avez pas trente ans."

"I'm thirty-four," she replied with a modest smile.

"What, you understand French?" he exclaimed, his curiosity piqued.

"A little," she admitted. "I spent four years in a gentleman's household, working as a governess, and picked it up from the children."

As she spoke, she shared more of her story: how she had been widowed at eighteen, had served as a nurse in Sevastopol, and had eventually turned to traveling and selling the gospel.

"Mais, mon Dieu," he interrupted, his voice trembling with indignation. "Wasn't it you who had that dreadful adventure in our town? Ces vauriens, ces malheureux!"

Her cheeks flushed, confirming his suspicions. Painful memories stirred within him, and for a brief moment, he seemed lost in his thoughts.

"Bah, she's gone again," he muttered, snapping back to the present and realizing that Sofya Matveyevna had quietly stepped out. "She's always busy about something... and yet here I am, sinking into my own egoism."

He raised his eyes again and found himself staring at Anisim, but this time the scene had shifted to something far more ominous. The entire cottage was now filled with peasants, a gathering that had clearly been summoned by Anisim himself. Among them were the owner of the house, the peasant with the cow, two other men who turned out to be cab drivers, and a small, half-drunk man, clean-shaven but dressed like a peasant. This last figure seemed to be a ruined townsman who had fallen into poverty through drink, and he was the loudest and most talkative of the group. It was clear they were all discussing him, Stepan Trofimovitch, their voices overlapping in an animated debate.

The peasant with the cow was loudly insisting that going around by the lake would add a full thirty-five miles to the journey and that taking the steamer was the only sensible option. The half-drunk man and the owner of the house argued heatedly against this, each attempting to prove their superior understanding of the matter.

"Of course, it's true that it's shorter for his honour to take the steamer across the lake," admitted the man of the house with a grudging nod. "But with the way things are now, who knows if the steamer is even running? It's late in the season!"

"It'll go! I'm telling you, it's still running for another week!" shouted Anisim, his voice rising above the others, his eagerness to assist Stepan Trofimovitch palpable.

"But it's not reliable now!" retorted the half-drunk man. "It might stop for three whole days at Ustyevo and not move at all. What will his honour do then?"

"No, no, it'll be there tomorrow at two o'clock sharp! You'll be at Spasov by evening, without a doubt," Anisim declared, his face flushed with enthusiasm, determined to prove himself helpful.

"Mais qu'est-ce qu'il a cet homme," thought Stepan Trofimovitch anxiously, his mind racing. He trembled as he tried to anticipate what might come next, his growing terror making it hard to focus.

The cab drivers pushed their way forward, adding their voices to the commotion. They began haggling over the cost of driving him to Ustyevo, insisting on three roubles. The others in the room backed them up, saying that was the standard fare, the going rate they had charged all summer.

"But ... it's nice here too.... And I don't want ..." Stepan Trofimovitch stammered weakly, trying to resist the relentless tide of decisions being made for him.

"Nice it is, sir, you are right there," one of the cab drivers chimed in, misunderstanding his protest. "Spasov's wonderfully pleasant this time of year, and Fyodor Matveyevitch will be overjoyed to see you."

"Mon Dieu, mes amis," Stepan Trofimovitch muttered, glancing around helplessly. "All this is such a surprise to me."

Just then, Sofya Matveyevna re-entered the cottage, her expression heavy with disappointment. She sat down on the bench and sighed.

"I can't get to Spasov," she said quietly to the woman of the house, her voice tinged with frustration.

"What's that? You're bound for Spasov too?" Stepan Trofimovitch exclaimed, sitting up straight and looking at her with sudden interest.

She explained that she had been promised a ride to Spasov by a lady who had told her to wait at Hatovo. But the lady had failed to show up, leaving her stranded and unsure of what to do next.

"What am I to do now?" she repeated, more to herself than to anyone else.

"Mais, ma chère et nouvelle amie!" Stepan Trofimovitch cried, seizing the opportunity with newfound energy. "I can take you just as well as this lady! We can go together to the village where I've already hired horses. And tomorrow—yes, tomorrow—we'll head on to Spasov together!"

"You're going to Spasov too?" she asked, surprised but clearly heartened by the offer.

"Mais que faire? And I am enchanted by the prospect! I shall take you with the greatest pleasure. You see, I've already made arrangements. Which of you did I hire?" He turned suddenly to the peasants, his enthusiasm now uncontainable. For reasons even he couldn't fully understand, the idea of going to Spasov now seemed irresistible.

Within fifteen minutes, they were seated together in a covered trap. Stepan Trofimovitch appeared unusually lively, his spirits lifted by the company and the prospect of the journey ahead. Sofya Matveyevna, with her pack carefully placed beside her, smiled gratefully, though her expression retained a trace of melancholy.

Anisim, ever the busybody, hovered around the trap, fussing with the arrangements and offering words of encouragement.

"A good journey to you, sir," he said, bowing slightly. "It's been a treat to see you again."

"Goodbye, my friend, goodbye," Stepan Trofimovitch replied, leaning out of the trap to shake his hand. "And thank you."

"You'll see Fyodor Matveyevitch, sir?" Anisim added eagerly.

"Yes, yes, my friend, I will. But now, goodbye!"

As the trap began to move, Stepan Trofimovitch settled back into his seat, a strange mixture of relief and anticipation washing over him. He glanced at Sofya Matveyevna, who was gazing out at the road ahead, and allowed himself a small, contented smile. For the first time in days, he felt as though he were heading toward something, rather than fleeing from everything.

Chapter 7.2

"You see, my friend... may I call myself your friend, n'est-ce pas?" Stepan Trofimovitch began hurriedly, his words tumbling over one another as soon as the trap started moving. "You see, I... J'aime le peuple, c'est indispensable, mais il me semble que je ne m'avais jamais vu de près. Stasie... cela va sans dire qu'elle est aussi du peuple, but the real people, the true ones on the open road, seem to care for nothing. And yet... where exactly am I going? Let bygones be bygones, though. I fancy I'm rambling, speaking at random—but that's only because I'm flustered. Yes, flustered."

"You don't seem well," Sofya Matveyevna said, watching him intently, her expression a mix of concern and respect.

"No, no, I just need to wrap myself up more thoroughly. The wind is fresh—very fresh, in fact. But let's not dwell on that." He shook his head, as if trying to dispel his discomfort. "That's not what I wanted to say. Chère et incomparable amie, I find myself almost happy at this moment, and it's entirely because of you. But you see, happiness isn't always good for me; it makes me rush to forgive all my enemies in an instant."

"But isn't that a good thing, sir?" she asked, her tone gentle.

"Not always, chère innocente," he replied, a faint smile playing on his lips. "L'Evangile... voyez-vous, désormais nous prêcherons ensemble. I will gladly help you sell your beautiful little books. Yes, perhaps that is an idea—quelque chose de très nouveau dans ce genre. The peasants are religious, that's a given, but they don't yet know the gospel as they should. I will explain it to them, correct its misunderstandings with verbal clarity... all while walking the open road. I've always been of service, always, and I'll prove it again."

He paused, his voice softening as his thoughts seemed to drift. "We'll forgive, yes, we'll forgive everyone, always and entirely. We'll hope for forgiveness ourselves, too. After all, we've all wronged one another. All of us are guilty."

"That's a wise thing to say, I think," Sofya Matveyevna murmured, nodding.

"Yes, yes... I feel I'm speaking well, very well indeed. But what was it I meant to say? I keep losing the thread. My thoughts wander. Will you allow me to remain by your side for now? There's something in your eyes, something... calming. And I must say, I'm surprised by your demeanor. You're simple-hearted, yet refined. You call me 'sir,' and you turn your cup upside down on your saucer like someone from another world... but there's a charm to it, truly. And I can see it in your features."

He leaned closer, his voice dropping to an almost conspiratorial whisper. "Oh, don't blush, and don't be afraid of me. Chère et incomparable, pour moi une femme c'est tout. A woman is everything to me. I can't live without one. But only by her side, you understand—only beside her. Never more than that."

He paused again, pressing a hand to his temple as if to steady his spinning thoughts. "I'm rambling terribly. Awfully muddled. I can't even remember what I wanted to say. But there's an idea here—a lofty one. Yes, a lofty idea in the open road itself! That's it! I've remembered now, though it kept slipping away from me. And yet... why have they taken us farther along this road? It was nice where we were before. Here, it's too cold. Cela devient trop froid."

Suddenly, he fumbled in his coat and pulled out a wad of notes. "A propos, j'ai en tout quarante roubles. Voilà cet argent. Take it—take it, please! I can't be trusted with it. I'll lose it or someone will take it from me..."

His voice faltered, and he slumped slightly against the side of the trap. "I feel... dizzy. Yes, dizzy. My head is spinning. But how kind you are—what's this you're wrapping around me?"

"You're unwell," she said softly, pulling a rug over his shoulders. "You've caught a fever, I think. Rest now."

"Oh, how kind you are!" he murmured, his voice fading. "Let's not speak of the money anymore. It pains me... You're so kind..."

His words trailed off, and he fell abruptly into a fitful, feverish sleep.

The road ahead was rough, and the carriage jolted relentlessly, but every so often, he stirred. Each time, he would lift his head from the small pillow Sofya Matveyevna had slipped beneath it, grasp her hand tightly, and ask, "Are you still here?" as though afraid she might vanish.

At one point, he whispered hoarsely, "I dreamed of... terrible jaws, gaping wide, full of sharp teeth. It was... unpleasant. Very unpleasant."

Sofya Matveyevna shivered at his words, her worry growing as the miles passed. She kept watch over him, murmuring soft reassurances whenever he woke, and tried to keep him warm against the chill creeping through the air.

At last, they reached their destination—a large cottage with a frontage of four windows and additional rooms extending into the yard. The driver pulled up, and Stepan Trofimovitch, still groggy, stumbled out of the trap. Despite his obvious exhaustion, he immediately straightened and hurried into the cottage, his demeanor shifting to one of sudden importance. He walked directly to the largest room and began speaking to the landlady, a stern-looking woman with dark hair and a slight moustache.

"I need this entire room to myself," he announced, his words hurried and slightly slurred. "Shut the door—no one else must come in. We have important matters to discuss. Yes, chère amie, much to discuss. I'll pay, of course, I'll pay," he added with an impatient wave toward the woman.

The landlady, though grim-faced, nodded her agreement and left them to their privacy.

As soon as the landlady had left, Stepan Trofimovitch sank onto the sofa with a sigh of relief and beckoned Sofya Matveyevna to sit beside him. Though the room contained several armchairs, they were so worn and uninviting that neither gave them a second glance. The room itself was peculiar—a large space partitioned in one corner to include a bed, its walls papered with faded yellow sheets that were peeling in places. Crude lithographs of mythological figures hung at odd angles, their colors long since dulled. Opposite the door, a row of painted icons and brass relics lined the wall, glinting dimly in the fading light. The overall effect was a discordant mix of rustic peasant simplicity and an awkward attempt at urban refinement. Outside, the vast expanse of the lake shimmered faintly, its edge barely seventy feet from the cottage. Yet Stepan Trofimovitch seemed oblivious to it all.

"At last, we are alone! No one shall disturb us now!" he exclaimed with fervor. "I want to tell you everything—everything from the beginning!"

Sofya Matveyevna, however, hesitated, her face clouded with unease. "Are you aware, Stepan Trofimovitch..." she began, but stopped herself, glancing nervously at the closed door, as though fearing an eavesdropper.

"Comment, vous savez déjà mon nom?" he interjected, delighted by her familiarity.

"I heard it this morning," she admitted. "When you were speaking with Anisim Ivanovitch. But please allow me to tell you something..."

Lowering her voice, she whispered hurriedly about the village they were in, painting a bleak picture. It was, she explained, a place notorious for exploiting stranded travelers. Though most of the villagers made their living as fishermen, their primary income came from overcharging summer visitors. The village, tucked away off the main road, only drew travelers because of the steamer that occasionally stopped there. When the weather was poor, the steamer sometimes skipped its stop, leaving travelers stranded for days. During such times, every cottage would be full, and the villagers would seize the opportunity to charge exorbitant prices for even the most basic accommodations. Their host, she added, was particularly proud and avaricious, boasting of owning a net that had cost him a thousand roubles—a fortune in those parts.

Stepan Trofimovitch listened, his expression growing more pained with each word. Several times he raised his hand as if to halt her, but she pressed on, determined to share all she knew. She recounted how she had once been stranded in this very village for two days with a refined lady from the town. The experience had been so dreadful that she shuddered to think of it.

"And now, Stepan Trofimovitch," she continued, "you've requested this entire room for yourself. I only want to warn you... There are already travelers in the other room—an elderly man, a young man, and a lady with children. By tomorrow, this entire house will be packed, especially since the steamer hasn't arrived for two days. They'll charge you a fortune—for this room, for dinner, for pushing out the other travelers. It will be more than what's charged in the capital..."

He waved his hand, as though to dismiss her concerns. "Assez, mon enfant," he interrupted, his voice tinged with hysteria. "We have money— nous avons notre argent—et après, le bon Dieu. Why do you fill me with such alarm for the future? It's unbecoming of you, with your lofty ideas. Assez, assez, je vous en prie!"

Without waiting for her response, he launched into his story, speaking so hurriedly that his words tumbled over one another. His narrative flowed on without pause, meandering through his childhood, his two marriages, his time in Berlin, and the philosophical dilemmas that had shaped his life. The soup arrived, then the fowl, and finally the samovar— but still, he talked.

He spoke with such a fevered intensity that Sofya Matveyevna feared he would exhaust himself entirely. His words were scattered, his thoughts darting in every direction. Occasionally, his account veered into near incoherence, as he tried to explain how no one had ever truly understood him, not even Varvara Petrovna. "Men of genius are wasted in Russia," he lamented, his voice trembling with emotion.

Sofya Matveyevna, poor woman, was overwhelmed. Much of what he said was incomprehensible to her, and his sudden shifts in tone only added to her confusion. He alternated between lofty intellectual musings and biting sarcasms about the nihilists and the modern age, which left her utterly bewildered. She tried to laugh at his witticisms but only managed a strained smile that made her look more frightened than amused.

When he began to recount the romantic entanglements of his life, she finally found some measure of relief, though even this was short-lived. He described Varvara Petrovna as a radiant brunette who had captivated the courts of Petersburg and Europe, while her husband had perished heroically at Sevastopol, sacrificing himself out of love for her. This tale, heavily embellished and bordering on the absurd, was delivered with such conviction that even Stepan Trofimovitch seemed to believe it himself.

"Don't be shocked, ma chère," he implored, reaching for Sofya Matveyevna's hand. "It was a love so profound, so subtle, that we never spoke of it—not even to each other."

The convoluted story unfolded further, involving a blonde lady, unspoken rivalries, and two decades of silent pining. By the time he concluded with a melodramatic declaration about the passion that had consumed his youth, Sofya Matveyevna was utterly lost.

"Oh, what a passion it was!" he exclaimed, clutching his chest. "To see her walk by, ashamed of her own beauty... or perhaps, ashamed of her size." He faltered, realizing his blunder, but recovered quickly. "And now, here I am, casting off the feverish dreams of vingt ans. I have found my purpose—on the open road!"

Sofya Matveyevna, round-eyed and bewildered, could only murmur a faint, "Indeed, sir," before falling silent. Her evident distress did little to deter him, and he continued speaking, his voice rising and falling like the cadence of a sermon.

Then, in what could only be described as a feverish delirium, Stepan Trofimovitch began speaking to Sofya Matveyevna with an intensity that bordered on reverence. He waxed poetic about the profound significance of their meeting, describing it as "a chance encounter imbued with eternal fate." The earnestness of his tone, however, only heightened Sofya Matveyevna's discomfort. She grew more flustered by the moment, and when he suddenly moved as though to kneel before her in a grand, almost theatrical gesture, she was so overwhelmed that tears sprang to her eyes.

"It's getting late," she stammered. The dimming light of dusk cast long shadows across the room. They had been shut inside for hours now, and she could feel the weight of the stares and murmurs from beyond the closed door. "No, no, I must go to the other room. People will begin to think... It's better if I leave."

She tried to move toward the door, but he clasped her hand in desperation, begging her to stay. When she finally managed to tear herself away, he reluctantly let her go, promising—rather weakly—that he would retire to bed immediately. As they parted, he pressed a trembling hand to his forehead and confessed that his head was throbbing with pain.

Sofya Matveyevna, who had left her belongings in the outer room intending to stay the night with the family of the house, spent the remainder of the evening in restless unease. She did not sleep.

In the deep hours of the night, the malady that had plagued Stepan Trofimovitch so many times before returned in full force. It was the familiar "summer cholera" that seemed to manifest whenever he experienced great emotional strain. The attacks were both frightening and exhausting. Sofya Matveyevna, compelled by compassion, spent the entire night tending to him.

Her ministrations required her to move in and out of the cottage frequently, passing through the landlady's room where other travelers were also trying to sleep. The grumbling began quietly at first—a sigh here, a muttered curse there—but as dawn approached, the irritation of those she disturbed boiled over into outright complaints. By the time she set about preparing the samovar to brew tea for her patient, the landlady and the travelers had begun openly swearing.

Meanwhile, Stepan Trofimovitch lay half-conscious, his mind drifting in and out of a foggy awareness. He caught glimpses of the samovar being set, of hands lifting a steaming cup to his lips, and of warm compresses being placed against his chest. These fragmented sensations blended into the hazy recognition that Sofya Matveyevna was there—always there. Her presence was an unbroken thread of comfort amidst the chaos of his ailment. She lifted him from the bed, settled him back down, adjusted his blankets, and soothed him as best she could.

By three in the morning, the worst of the attack had passed. He woke briefly, sitting up on the edge of the bed and dangling his legs over the side. Without warning, he sank to the floor and prostrated himself at Sofya Matveyevna's feet.

This gesture was entirely unlike his earlier, theatrical attempt to kneel before her. It was raw, desperate, and uncalculated. He pressed his lips to the hem of her dress, overcome by an emotion so intense that it seemed to render him incapable of speech.

"Please, sir, get up," she begged, trying to help him back into bed. Her voice trembled with embarrassment and concern. "I'm not worth this. Please…"

"You are my savior," he whispered, his voice breaking. "Vous êtes noble comme une marquise! But I… I am a wretch. My whole life has been a lie."

"Calm yourself," she implored, her hands shaking as she grasped his arms.

"No, you must know," he cried, pulling away slightly to look up at her. His face was pale and glistening with perspiration. "Everything I said last evening—it was all lies. Lies to glorify myself, to make myself seem grand and important. I was vain and foolish… oh, I am a wretch!"

The outpouring of self-recrimination marked the beginning of yet another attack—this time of hysterical remorse. His mind raced wildly, alighting on fragmented memories and unresolved guilt. He spoke of Lise, lamenting their meeting the previous morning. "There was something so awful in her eyes," he murmured, clutching at Sofya Matveyevna's sleeve. "There must have been a disaster… something terrible, and I didn't ask. I didn't find out! I thought only of myself. What's the matter with her? Do you know what's the matter with her?"

Then, his remorse took on a new and fervent direction. He vowed that he would never change and that he would go back to Varvara Petrovna. "We will go together," he declared, his voice trembling with conviction. "We'll stand at the steps of her carriage each morning, just to catch a glimpse of her. I will wish her to smite me on the other cheek! Oh, the joy of wishing it! Only now, at this moment, do I understand what it means to turn the other cheek. I never understood before."

For Sofya Matveyevna, the two days that followed were among the most harrowing of her life. Stepan Trofimovitch's condition worsened to the point where he was unable to board the steamer, which arrived promptly at two in the afternoon. She found herself unable to leave him behind, despite her own plans to continue on to Spasov.

Remarkably, Stepan Trofimovitch seemed delighted when he learned that the steamer had departed without them. "Well, that's a good thing," he muttered weakly from his bed. "That's capital. I've been afraid all this time that we might go. But here… it's nice here. Better than anywhere else. And you—you won't leave me? Oh, you haven't left me."

In truth, "here" was far from nice. The discomforts and tensions of their lodgings mounted, but Stepan Trofimovitch remained blissfully detached from these realities. His mind floated somewhere between fevered dreams and the strange fantasies he now wove about their future. He thought only of how they would travel together, selling the gospel books and expounding upon their meanings to the peasants they met along the way.

At his insistence, Sofya Matveyevna began reading aloud from the gospel. When she reached the Sermon on the Mount, he interrupted her after the first line.

"You read beautifully," he said, his voice filled with admiration. "I see now—I wasn't mistaken about you."

Despite his evident weakness, his enthusiasm seemed boundless. At intervals, he confessed to Sofya Matveyevna with trembling fervor. "I've told lies my entire life," he admitted. "Even when I spoke the truth, it was always for my own sake, never for the truth itself. I knew this before, but only now do I truly see it."

When she timidly suggested calling for a doctor, he recoiled in alarm. "What for? Est-ce que je suis si malade? What do we need outsiders for? No, no, we'll be together. Only together."

And so the hours stretched on, his feverish thoughts drifting like mist over the surface of his mind, while Sofya Matveyevna remained steadfast at his side.

"Oh, je m'en souviens, oui, l'Apocalypse. Lisez, lisez," Stepan Trofimovitch urged Sofya Matveyevna with growing excitement. "I am trying our future fortunes by the book. I want to know what has turned up. Read on from there."

"'And unto the angel of the church of the Laodiceans write: These

716

things saith the Amen, the faithful and true witness, the beginning of the creation of God;

"'I know thy works, that thou art neither cold nor hot; I would thou wert cold or hot.

"'So then because thou art lukewarm, and neither cold nor hot, I will spue thee out of my mouth.

"'Because thou sayest, I am rich and increased with goods, and have need of nothing: and thou knowest not that thou art wretched, and miserable, and poor, and blind, and naked.'"

As she read, his pale face seemed to ignite with an inner flame. His eyes, usually veiled in thought, now shone with a strange clarity. "That too... and that's in your book too!" he exclaimed suddenly, lifting his head from the pillow. His voice, frail yet fervent, filled the small room. "I never knew that grand passage! You hear, better be cold, better be cold than lukewarm, than only lukewarm. Oh, I'll prove it! Only don't leave me, don't leave me alone! We'll prove it, we'll prove it!"

"I won't leave you, Stepan Trofimovitch. I'll never leave you!" Sofya Matveyevna replied with quiet resolve, taking his trembling hand in both of hers and pressing it to her chest. Her eyes brimmed with tears, and her voice carried the sincerity of someone who would endure anything for the sake of another. Later, she would recall the moment with deep emotion, saying simply, "I felt very sorry for him at that moment."

But his moment of fervor was fleeting. A shadow of panic passed over his face at her next suggestion. "But, Stepan Trofimovitch," she began hesitantly, "what are we to do though? Oughtn't we to let some of your friends know, or perhaps your relations?"

At once, he was seized with visible terror. He gripped her hands tightly, shaking his head with a kind of desperation. "No one!" he cried, his voice breaking. "No one, no one! We'll be alone, by ourselves, alone, nous partirons ensemble."

Meanwhile, trouble was brewing elsewhere in the house. The villagers, increasingly uneasy, had begun to grumble audibly. The man of the house, emboldened by his suspicions, insisted on seeing Stepan Trofimovitch's

717

papers. Though weak and exhausted, Stepan Trofimovitch managed a faint, derisive smile as he pointed toward his little bag. Sofya Matveyevna rummaged through it and produced a faded certificate—a relic from his days at the university, which had served as a kind of makeshift passport throughout his life. The man was not appeased. He muttered darkly that the house was not a hospital and that, should the sick man die there, "there'd be no end of trouble." The villagers' complaints grew louder, and their tone more menacing. Sofya Matveyevna tried to speak of fetching a doctor, but the cost of sending for one from the town was prohibitive. Helpless and distraught, she returned to her patient.

By this point, Stepan Trofimovitch had grown weaker. His body seemed to shrink into the bed, his pale hands trembling as he reached out for her. "Now read me another passage," he whispered hoarsely. "About the pigs."

"The pigs?" Sofya Matveyevna repeated, alarmed by the strange request.

"Yes… about the pigs. Ces cochons," he insisted, his fever-bright eyes fixed on her. "The devils entered into swine, and they all drowned. I need to hear it. I want to remember it word for word. It's important."

Though unsettled, she flipped through the gospel until she found the passage he was referring to. It was in St. Luke, the story of the possessed man and the herd of swine. Her voice quavered slightly as she began to read:

"'And there was there one herd of many swine feeding on the mountain; and they besought him that he would suffer them to enter into them. And he suffered them.

"'Then went the devils out of the man and entered into the swine; and the herd ran violently down a steep place into the lake, and were choked.

"'When they that fed them saw what was done, they fled, and went and told it in the city and in the country.

"'Then they went out to see what was done; and came to Jesus and found the man, out of whom the devils were departed, sitting at the feet of Jesus, clothed, and in his right mind; and they were afraid.'"

As she finished, he stirred and leaned toward her with feverish excitement. "My friend," he said, his voice trembling with intensity, "savez-vous, that extraordinary passage has been a stumbling block to me all my life... dans ce livre. I remembered it even as a child. Now—an idea has occurred to me. Une comparaison."

He paused, as though summoning the strength to continue. "You see," he began slowly, "that is exactly like our Russia. Those devils, those unclean spirits—they are the sores, the foul contagions, the impurities that have infected our beloved Russia for ages. But one day, a great Will shall come, and it will encompass all, just as Jesus healed the lunatic. And when that Will commands, all the devils will pour forth—into swine, into the unworthy, into those of us who are beyond redemption."

His voice grew hoarser, but he pushed on. "And then, we—yes, we, the swine—we will rush headlong, possessed and raving, into the depths of the sea, and we will drown. And it will be good—it will be right— because only then will the sick man, Russia herself, be healed. She will sit at the feet of Jesus, clothed and in her right mind. And all the world will look upon her with wonder."

Exhausted by his own fervor, he fell back against the pillow, his eyes fluttering shut. "Vous comprendrez après," he murmured faintly. "We will understand together."

He slipped into a delirium that lasted through the night and well into the next day. Sofya Matveyevna, though physically and emotionally drained, refused to leave his side. Her quiet strength seemed to hold the fragments of his scattered mind together. It wasn't until the third morning that he regained full consciousness. He opened his eyes, looked at her, and smiled weakly.

"Tiens, un lac!" he exclaimed, noticing the vast expanse of water outside the window for the first time. "Good heavens, I had not seen it before!"

Just then, the rumble of carriage wheels and the sound of voices at the door broke the stillness of the cottage, heralding a new and unexpected turn of events.

Chapter 7.3

It was Varvara Petrovna herself. She arrived with an air of authority that seemed to overwhelm everyone present. Accompanied by Darya Pavlovna, she had traveled in a closed carriage drawn by four stately horses, attended by two footmen. Her sudden appearance in this remote village seemed almost miraculous, but the explanation was simple. Anisim, consumed by his curiosity, had gone to her residence the very day after his return to the town. There, he eagerly recounted to the household staff his encounter with Stepan Trofimovitch—alone, disheveled, and walking through the countryside. He added with relish that peasants had seen the same lonely figure on the high road and that Stepan Trofimovitch had eventually set off for Spasov in the company of a certain Sofya Matveyevna, traveling in a rustic cart.

This news reached Varvara Petrovna, who was already frantic with worry and had been making every effort to track down her fugitive friend. The mention of Sofya Matveyevna seemed to ignite a spark of both outrage and determination. Without hesitation, she ordered her carriage prepared and set off at once for Ustyevo, driven by equal parts concern and indignation.

Her arrival at the cottage was nothing short of dramatic. Her stern, commanding voice filled the small house, intimidating even the previously defiant landlord and his wife. She wasted no time interrogating them and piecing together the details of Stepan Trofimovitch's condition. Initially convinced that he must have already reached Spasov, she was visibly agitated to learn that he was still here—and gravely ill. Without pausing for pleasantries, she swept into the cottage like a force of nature.

"Well, where is he? Ah, that's you!" she barked, her sharp eyes landing on Sofya Matveyevna, who had just emerged from the adjoining room. Her disdain was immediate and palpable. "I can guess from your shameless face that it's you. Go away, you vile hussy! Don't let me find a trace of her in the house! Turn her out immediately, or mark my words, I'll have her locked up again. Yes, again—she's been in prison before, hasn't she? And she can go back there!"

Sofya Matveyevna froze, trembling visibly, while Varvara Petrovna continued her tirade. Turning to the landlord, she added imperiously, "And you, my good man, don't you dare let anyone in while I'm here! I am Madame Stavrogin, and I'll take the whole house. As for you, my dear," she said, addressing Sofya Matveyevna with icy disdain, "you'll have to give me a full account of all this."

The familiar, authoritative tone struck Stepan Trofimovitch like a thunderclap. He began trembling uncontrollably. Varvara Petrovna, wasting no time, stepped behind the screen to confront him. Her sharp, flashing eyes bore into his frightened face as she dragged a chair into place with her foot and sat down with an air of ominous finality.

"Well, how are you getting on, Stepan Trofimovitch? So you've been enjoying yourself?" she asked, her voice dripping with scornful irony.

"Chère," he stammered, his words barely coherent, "I ... I have come to know real life in Russia ... et je prêcherai l'Evangile."

"Shameless, ungrateful man!" she cried, her voice rising to a wail as she clasped her hands in exaggerated despair. "As if you hadn't disgraced me enough, you've now taken up with... oh, you shameless old reprobate!"

"Chère..." he began again, but his voice faltered and broke. His wide eyes, filled with terror, pleaded with her for mercy.

"Who is she?" Varvara Petrovna demanded.

"C'est un ange; c'était plus qu'un ange pour moi," he replied, his voice cracking with desperation. "She stayed all night ... oh, don't shout, don't frighten her, chère, chère..."

His words were cut short as Varvara Petrovna pushed back her chair with a loud scrape and cried out in alarm. "Water, water!" she called urgently. The sight of his pallid, distorted face seemed to jolt her out of her fury. For the first time, she realized the gravity of his condition.

"Darya," she called in a hushed but urgent tone, summoning Darya Pavlovna from the other room. "Send for the doctor immediately. Salzfish, no one else. Let Yegorytch hire horses if he has to and bring another carriage from the town. The doctor must be here by night!"

Darya rushed to obey. Meanwhile, Varvara Petrovna turned back to Stepan Trofimovitch, who continued to gaze at her with wide, frightened eyes. His lips moved soundlessly as if he were trying to speak.

"Wait a bit, Stepan Trofimovitch, wait a bit, my dear," she said soothingly, her tone uncharacteristically gentle. "There, there. Darya will come back, and we'll see to everything. My goodness, where's the landlady? You—woman—come here, quickly!"

In her impatience, she went to fetch the landlady herself. A moment later, she returned, dragging a terrified and trembling Sofya Matveyevna by the hand.

"Here she is," she announced, thrusting the poor woman into the room. "See? I haven't eaten her. You thought I'd eaten her, didn't you?"

Stepan Trofimovitch, overcome with emotion, reached out for Varvara Petrovna's hand. Clutching it tightly, he raised it to his lips and burst into convulsive sobs. "There, calm yourself, calm yourself," she said, her voice wavering between exasperation and concern. "Oh, you bane of my life!"

Turning to Sofya Matveyevna, he murmured weakly, "My dear… please wait outside. I need to speak here…"

Sofya Matveyevna hurried out without a word. As soon as she was gone, Stepan Trofimovitch turned back to Varvara Petrovna.

"Chérie… chérie…" he gasped, his voice barely audible.

"Don't talk now, Stepan Trofimovitch. Wait a little until you've rested," she said firmly, though there was a note of tenderness in her voice. She handed him a glass of water and sat down beside him. He held her hand tightly, refusing to let go, and raised it to his lips again and again, kissing it fervently. She sat stiffly, her teeth clenched, her gaze fixed on a distant corner of the room. For a long while, neither of them spoke. The only sounds were his labored breathing and the faint murmur of voices from the other room.

"Je vous aimais," Stepan Trofimovitch whispered at last, his voice trembling with raw emotion. The words seemed to echo in the room, carrying a weight that made Varvara Petrovna flinch. Never before had she heard such words from him, uttered in such a tone, and for a moment, she froze.

"H'm!" she grunted dismissively, though her posture stiffened.

"Je vous aimais toute ma vie ... vingt ans!" His voice cracked as he poured out his confession.

For a long moment, she said nothing, her face impassive. Then, in a low, almost inaudible voice, she murmured, "And when you were getting yourself up for Dasha, you sprinkled yourself with scent."

Stepan Trofimovitch blinked, stunned into silence.

"You put on a new tie," she continued, her voice sharpening as if each word was meant to cut.

He could only stare at her, his mouth dry, his horror mounting.

"Do you remember the cigar?" she demanded suddenly, her eyes narrowing.

"My friend," he stammered weakly, his breath catching as a cold dread settled over him.

"That cigar by the window in the evening," she pressed on, her voice dropping to a menacing whisper. "The moon was shining ... after the arbour ... at Skvoreshniki. Do you remember, do you remember?"

With a sudden burst of fury, she leapt from her seat, grabbed the corners of his pillow, and shook it violently, his head still resting on it. "Do you remember, you worthless, worthless, ignoble, cowardly, worthless man! Always worthless!" Her whisper had become a hiss, trembling with barely contained rage.

At last, she dropped the pillow and retreated to her chair, burying her face in her hands. For a moment, there was silence, punctuated only by the sound of her heavy breathing.

"Enough," she said abruptly, straightening up. Her tone was clipped and final. "Twenty years have passed, and there's no calling them back. I'm a fool too."

"Je vous aimais," he whispered again, his hands clasped in a gesture of entreaty.

"Why do you keep on with your aimais and aimais? Enough!" she snapped, leaping to her feet. "And if you don't go to sleep at once, I'll—" She broke off, glaring at him. "You need rest; go to sleep, go to sleep at once! Shut your eyes. Ach, mercy on us, perhaps he wants lunch! What do you eat? What does he eat? Ach, mercy on us! Where is that woman? Where is she?"

The room erupted into a flurry of activity as she called for the landlady and issued sharp orders. But Stepan Trofimovitch, his voice weak, interrupted to murmur that he would like to rest for une heure and then have un bouillon, un thé.

His evident exhaustion seemed to calm her for the moment. He leaned back against the pillows, his eyelids fluttering shut. Whether he actually slept or only pretended to, Varvara Petrovna watched him for a while before tiptoeing out of the room.

She moved purposefully into the landlady's quarters, where she promptly evicted the landlady and her husband. Turning to Darya Pavlovna, she ordered brusquely, "Bring me that woman."

Sofya Matveyevna was ushered in, trembling like a leaf. Varvara Petrovna motioned for her to sit down.

"Tell me everything, my good girl," she commanded, her voice low but edged with steel. "Sit down beside me. That's right. Now, speak."

Sofya Matveyevna began hesitantly, "I met Stepan Trofimovitch—"

"Stop! Hold your tongue!" Varvara Petrovna interrupted sharply. "I warn you, if you tell lies or try to hide anything, I'll find out. Now, start again. Well?"

Sofya Matveyevna gulped and began anew, recounting how she had met Stepan Trofimovitch, her books, and how he had treated the peasant woman to vodka.

"Good, good, don't leave out a single detail," Varvara Petrovna urged, leaning forward with a stern intensity that made Sofya Matveyevna's hands tremble in her lap.

As the story unfolded, Sofya Matveyevna described how they had traveled together, Stepan Trofimovitch talking incessantly, recounting his life from the very beginning.

"Tell me about his life," Varvara Petrovna said sharply.

Sofya Matveyevna hesitated, her face crumpling with distress. "I ... I can't tell you much, madam," she stammered. "I could hardly understand it. He spoke so ... so intellectually."

"Nonsense! You must have understood something."

"Well ... he spoke for a long time about a grand lady with black hair," Sofya Matveyevna admitted, flushing deeply. She glanced at Varvara Petrovna's fair hair, realizing with horror how different it was from the lady in Stepan Trofimovitch's story.

"A black-haired lady? Go on," Varvara Petrovna ordered.

"He said she was deeply in love with him her whole life but never dared to tell him because she was ... she was ashamed of being ... well, stout," Sofya Matveyevna stammered, her voice trailing off.

"The fool!" Varvara Petrovna declared, her tone flat but resolute.

Tears welled up in Sofya Matveyevna's eyes. "I don't know how to explain it properly, madam," she said tearfully. "I was so frightened for him. And I couldn't understand much of what he said; he's such a learned gentleman."

"It's not for a goose like you to judge his intellect," Varvara Petrovna snapped. Then, her tone turning sharper, she demanded, "Did he propose to you?"

Sofya Matveyevna froze, her entire body stiffening.

"Did he fall in love with you? Speak! Did he offer you his hand?" Varvara Petrovna thundered.

"Well ... yes, that's how it seemed," Sofya Matveyevna admitted at last, her voice trembling. "But I thought it was because of his illness. I didn't take it seriously."

"What's your name?" Varvara Petrovna asked abruptly.

"Sofya Matveyevna, madam," she replied softly.

"Well, Sofya Matveyevna," Varvara Petrovna said with icy finality, "let me tell you, he is a wretched, worthless little man."

"Good Lord! Do you think I am some kind of wicked woman?" Varvara Petrovna demanded suddenly, her voice trembling with intensity. Her sharp words startled Sofya Matveyevna, who gazed at her wide-eyed, unable to find an answer.

"A wicked woman? A tyrant? Do you think I've ruined his life?" she pressed on, her tone more subdued but no less pressing.

"How can that be, madam, when you're crying yourself?" Sofya Matveyevna ventured timidly, her voice soft but earnest.

Varvara Petrovna blinked, momentarily disarmed. Tears had indeed gathered in her own eyes, though she hadn't realized it. She wiped at them brusquely, regaining her composure.

"Well, sit down," she said firmly, gesturing to a chair. "Sit down, don't be frightened. Look me straight in the face again. Why are you blushing like that?" Her tone softened, though there was still an edge of impatience in it. "Dasha, come here. Look at her. What do you think of her?"

Darya Pavlovna approached hesitantly, casting a quick glance at Sofya Matveyevna.

"Her heart is pure," Varvara Petrovna declared abruptly, surprising both women. Then, to Sofya Matveyevna's utter bewilderment and alarm, she reached out and patted her cheek, an oddly maternal gesture that left her more flustered than before.

"It's just a pity she's a fool," Varvara Petrovna added after a pause, her tone almost reflective. "Too much of a fool for her age. But that's all right, my dear. I'll look after you."

Sofya Matveyevna stammered something about needing to leave, but Varvara Petrovna silenced her with a wave of her hand.

"Hold your tongue," she said curtly. "Don't make excuses. You'll stay nearby for the time being. I'll see to it that a room is arranged for you, and you'll have food and everything else you need—from me. You'll stay until I call for you."

"But, madam, I must—" Sofya Matveyevna tried again, her voice trembling with urgency.

"Nonsense! If I hadn't come, you would have stayed with him all the same, wouldn't you?" Varvara Petrovna interrupted sharply, fixing her with an unyielding gaze.

"I wouldn't have left him for anything," Sofya Matveyevna admitted quietly, her voice resolute despite the tears streaming down her face.

It was late into the night when Doctor Salzfish finally arrived. He was a dignified older man with a wealth of experience, though his recent dismissal from service after a disagreement over a point of honor had left him somewhat embittered. Varvara Petrovna, ever decisive, had already taken him under her wing, appreciating his competence and reliability.

The doctor examined Stepan Trofimovitch carefully, his expression growing graver as the minutes passed. He spoke to Varvara Petrovna in low, measured tones, cautious but clear. "The patient's condition is highly precarious," he informed her. "There are serious complications, and you must prepare yourself for the possibility of … the worst."

For once, Varvara Petrovna, who had grown accustomed over the years to regarding Stepan Trofimovitch's ailments as theatrical exaggerations, turned pale. "Is there really no hope?" she whispered, her voice almost inaudible.

The doctor hesitated. "Hope is never entirely absent," he said gently. "But in this case … it is tenuous."

She did not go to bed that night, instead sitting vigil by his side, her thoughts a tumult of worry and regret. The hours dragged, and morning seemed an eternity away. When Stepan Trofimovitch finally stirred and opened his eyes, she leaned over him with a look of steely determination.

"Stepan Trofimovitch," she said briskly, "one must be prepared for anything. I've sent for a priest. You must do what is right."

His brows furrowed in mild confusion. "Am I really so ill, then?" he murmured.

"Nonsense, nonsense!" she exclaimed, her voice rising with agitation. "This is no time for whims. You've played the fool enough!"

To her surprise, he did not argue. He agreed, almost thoughtfully, and showed no fear of death—an attitude that puzzled her deeply.

The priest arrived and administered confession and the sacrament, which Stepan Trofimovitch received with an unexpected serenity that moved everyone in the room. His sunken face and trembling lips inspired pity in all who saw him, and even the servants were brought to tears.

"Oui, mes amis," he said weakly, "I can only wonder why you take so much trouble for me. I shall most likely get up tomorrow, and then we will set off. Toute cette cérémonie … for which I feel every proper respect, of course … was—"

"Enough, enough," Varvara Petrovna cut in hurriedly, addressing the priest. "Father, please stay with the patient a little longer. When tea has been served, I beg you to speak of religion, to strengthen his faith."

The priest nodded and began to speak gently of the comfort faith could bring in times of trial. Stepan Trofimovitch listened, a faint smile playing on his lips.

"Mon père, je vous remercie, et vous êtes bien bon, mais …" he began, but Varvara Petrovna, leaping from her chair, cut him off.

"No mais, no mais at all!" she exclaimed, her frustration bubbling over. "He is a man who will need to confess again in another hour. That's the sort of man he is!"

Despite her exasperation, Stepan Trofimovitch smiled faintly. "My friends," he said, his voice breaking but his spirit strangely luminous, "God is necessary to me, if only because He is the only being whom one can love eternally."

For the first time, his words seemed to suggest a genuine shift, a stirring within his soul that hinted at transformation. Whether it was the solemnity of the sacrament or the culmination of a lifetime of reflection, his next words left everyone in the room profoundly moved.

"If I have once loved Him and rejoiced in that love," he said, his voice trembling with conviction, "how could He extinguish me and my joy, bringing me to nothingness? If there is a God, then I am immortal. Voilà ma profession de foi."

Varvara Petrovna burst into tears, overcome by an emotion she scarcely understood. "There is a God, Stepan Trofimovitch," she implored him. "I assure you there is! Drop all this foolishness for once in your life!"

He looked at her with an expression that was both tender and tired. "My friend," he said softly, "tomorrow ... tomorrow we will all set out together."

She pressed his hand to her lips, unable to say more. As his strength waned, he turned his gaze toward the door.

"Where is she? Bring her to me," he whispered.

Varvara Petrovna signaled for Sofya Matveyevna, who approached timidly. Stepan Trofimovitch smiled at her with a tenderness that seemed to transcend his frailty.

"Oh, how I wish I could live again!" he exclaimed suddenly, his voice trembling with a surge of energy. "Every moment, every breath ought to be a blessing to man. We must make it so—such is the law of our nature.... If only I could see Petrusha ... and all of them ... Shatov ..." His voice trailed off as exhaustion overcame him.

His voice faded into a faint whisper, overwhelmed by the weight of his thoughts and the ebbing of his strength. Exhaustion claimed him, leaving a haunting silence in its wake. It is worth noting that, at this time, none of those present—neither Varvara Petrovna, nor Darya Pavlovna, nor even Doctor Salzfish—had any inkling of Shatov's grim fate. That dreadful news had not yet reached them.

Stepan Trofimovitch, despite his physical frailty, grew more feverishly animated, his spirit surging beyond the limits of his body. His words, though fragmented by his labored breath, carried an almost unearthly fervor.

"The mere knowledge," he began, his voice trembling with emotion, "that somewhere, there exists something infinitely more just and infinitely happier than I am—that alone fills my soul with an indescribable ecstasy. It glorifies me, even in my insignificance, even in all that I have done or failed to do. This, my friends, is the essence of existence: not personal happiness, but the unwavering faith that there exists a serene and perfect happiness for all humanity, for all creation. Without this belief, man cannot endure."

He paused, gasping for breath, his eyes burning with a fervid light.

"Man must bow before something infinitely great," he continued, his voice cracking under the strain. "Without the Great, without the Infinite, life is nothing but despair, and despair will consume mankind. The Infinite and the Eternal are as vital to us as the very air we breathe or the earth beneath our feet. Friends, hear me! Let us hail the Great Idea—the Eternal, Infinite Idea! Every man, no matter how humble, no matter how foolish, must bow before it. Even Petrusha... oh, how I long to see them all again! They don't realize, they don't see it yet—that same Eternal, Great Idea lives within them all!"

His voice crescendoed to a final burst of energy, as though his very soul were straining to communicate this truth before it was too late. The room had fallen into an awed silence, but this exaltation was too much for his weakening frame.

Doctor Salzfish, arriving suddenly, was horrified at the spectacle. He immediately ordered the room cleared, insisting that the patient must be shielded from all such excitement. The gathered group dispersed reluctantly, leaving Stepan Trofimovitch alone to rest.

Three days later, his life quietly slipped away. By then, he had fallen into a complete unconsciousness from which he never awoke. His end was peaceful, like the soft extinguishing of a candle that had burned to its wick.

After arranging a dignified funeral service, Varvara Petrovna took Stepan Trofimovitch's body to Skvoreshniki. There, he was laid to rest within the grounds of the church. His grave is now marked by a simple yet elegant marble slab, awaiting the addition of an inscription and wrought-iron railing, which are to be completed in the spring.

Varvara Petrovna's absence from town stretched to eight days. During this time, Sofya Matveyevna accompanied her back to Skvoreshniki in the carriage and, to the surprise of many, seemed to settle there permanently. The arrangement began on the morning that Stepan Trofimovitch received the sacrament. Once he slipped into unconsciousness, Varvara Petrovna had firmly requested—though it felt more like a command— that Sofya Matveyevna leave the cottage. She insisted on attending to the ailing man alone, unassisted, until his final breath. However, the moment he passed away, she immediately sent for Sofya Matveyevna to return.

Sofya Matveyevna was deeply unnerved by Varvara Petrovna's next pronouncement. Without preamble, the lady declared her intention for Sofya Matveyevna to remain at Skvoreshniki indefinitely. The younger woman protested, stammering about her need to continue traveling and selling her gospels, but Varvara Petrovna silenced her objections with a brusque wave.

"That's nonsense," she said firmly. "I'll go with you to sell the gospel, if need be. I have no one in the world now."

Doctor Salzfish, who had stayed to oversee the aftermath, gently interjected, "You still have a son, however."

"I have no son," Varvara Petrovna snapped, her voice cutting through the room like a blade. The words hung in the air, heavy with finality—an eerie prophecy of what was to come.

Conclusion

All the crimes and wrongdoings were uncovered with shocking speed—much faster than Pyotr Stepanovitch had ever anticipated. It all began in the early hours of the morning following the murder of Shatov. Marya Ignatyevna woke up before dawn, panicked when she realized her husband wasn't beside her, and became uncontrollably distressed. The woman hired by Anna Prohorovna to stay with her that night tried unsuccessfully to calm her. As soon as daylight broke, the woman rushed to fetch Arina Prohorovna, assuring Marya Ignatyevna that she knew where her husband was and when he would return.

Meanwhile, Arina Prohorovna herself was growing uneasy. Her husband had come home late the previous night in a dreadful state, both physically and emotionally. He threw himself face down on the bed, shaking with sobs, and kept repeating, "It's wrong! It's all so wrong!" In his frantic state, he confessed everything to her—though he didn't tell anyone else in the house. Arina Prohorovna, though deeply unsettled, remained composed. She warned him to cry quietly into his pillow so no one would hear him and advised him to avoid showing any signs of distress the next day.

Despite her outward calm, Arina began preparing for the worst. She hid or destroyed any incriminating documents, including suspicious papers, books, and possibly revolutionary manifestoes. As she reassured herself that neither she nor her family—including her sister, aunt, her sister-in-law the student, or even her somewhat foolish brother—had much to fear, she couldn't shake the lingering anxiety. She was desperate to confirm whether her husband's frantic claim—that Kirillov would sacrifice himself for their shared cause—was true.

By the time Arina reached Marya Ignatyevna's home, it was already too late. Left alone after the hired woman had gone, Marya couldn't bear the uncertainty. Wrapping herself in the first garment she could find—something far too light for the cold, damp weather—she grabbed her baby and rushed out to Kirillov's lodge, hoping he might know something about her husband's whereabouts. What she found there was so horrifying that it defied words. In her terror, she didn't even notice Kirillov's final letter lying plainly on the table. Instead, she fled back to her room, took her baby, and ran into the street, still dressed inappropriately for the cold.

The morning was foggy and wet, and the street she found herself on was deserted. Desperately, she began knocking on doors. At the first house, no one answered. At the second, the delay in answering drove her to leave and try another. At the third house, belonging to a merchant named Titov, her frantic knocking finally brought a response. She screamed incoherently that her husband had been murdered, throwing the entire household into an uproar. The Titovs knew some of Shatov's story, and they were horrified to see her running about in such attire, clutching her barely-covered baby, especially as they understood she had only given birth the day before.

Initially, the Titovs thought she was delirious, particularly since she couldn't clearly explain whether it was Kirillov or her husband who had been murdered. When they didn't believe her, she tried to run to another house, but they forcibly restrained her. She screamed and struggled, but they refused to let her go. Within two hours, news of Kirillov's suicide and the letter he had left behind had spread throughout the entire town. The authorities arrived to question Marya Ignatyevna, but she couldn't provide coherent answers. She hadn't read Kirillov's letter and couldn't explain why she was certain her husband had been murdered. All she could do was scream that if Kirillov had been killed, then her husband must have been too, because they had been together.

By midday, Marya Ignatyevna's condition had worsened, and she sank into unconsciousness. She never regained consciousness and passed away three days later. Tragically, her baby caught cold during their flight and died before she did.

Arina Prohorovna, not finding Marya Ignatyevna at home and realizing something was wrong, started to head back to her own house. At the gate, however, she thought better of it and sent the hired nurse to Kirillov's lodge to inquire whether Marya Ignatyevna was there. The nurse returned in a panic, screaming incoherently. Arina Prohorovna, with characteristic composure, persuaded her to stop shouting and not tell anyone, warning her that she'd "get into trouble" if she did. Then she discreetly slipped away from the yard.

Later that morning, Arina Prohorovna was questioned by the authorities, as she had served as midwife during Marya Ignatyevna's labor. However, she gave them little information. She calmly recounted only what she had personally witnessed at Shatov's house and insisted that she had no knowledge of what had happened afterward. Her demeanor was cool and rational, but she revealed nothing more.

It's easy to imagine the uproar that broke out in the town. Another shocking crime—a new "sensation!" But this time, there was something more. People began to realize that a secret society of murderers, arsonists, and revolutionaries truly did exist. The horrifying death of Liza, the murder of Stavrogin's wife, Stavrogin's own mysterious involvement, the fire, the ball for the governesses, and the questionable behavior in Yulia Mihailovna's social circle—all of it pointed to something sinister. Even Stepan Trofimovitch's sudden disappearance seemed suspicious. Rumors about Nikolay Vsyevolodovitch spread rapidly. By the end of the day, news of Pyotr Stepanovitch's absence had also reached people, but strangely enough, less attention was paid to him than to anyone else.

What everyone talked about most was "the senator." Filipov's house drew a crowd nearly all day. The police, meanwhile, were misled by Kirillov's letter. They believed Kirillov had murdered Shatov before taking his own life. Although the authorities were confused, they weren't entirely fooled. For instance, the word "park," vaguely mentioned in Kirillov's letter, didn't baffle anyone as Pyotr Stepanovitch had hoped. The police immediately rushed to Skvoreshniki—not only because it was the only park nearby, but also because a strange instinct seemed to draw them there. After all, every terrible event of recent days was somehow tied to Skvoreshniki. That's just my theory. (Incidentally, Varvara Petrovna had left town early that morning in search of Stepan Trofimovitch and was unaware of the events unfolding.)

That evening, Shatov's body was found in the pond. The discovery was triggered by the finding of Shatov's cap at the murder scene—a piece of evidence carelessly overlooked by the killers. The state of the body and the subsequent medical examination quickly raised suspicions that Kirillov hadn't acted alone. It became clear that there truly was a secret society, one connected to Shatov, Kirillov, and even the revolutionary manifestoes. The pressing question was: who were Kirillov's accomplices? Oddly enough, no one thought of the quintet members that day. It was discovered that Kirillov had lived like a recluse, in such isolation that even while Fedka hid with him for days during an active manhunt, no one noticed. What puzzled everyone most was how chaotic and disconnected all the events seemed, with no clear link tying them together.

It's hard to say what wild conclusions the frightened townspeople might have reached if the mystery hadn't been unraveled the next day, thanks to Lyamshin.

Lyamshin broke down completely. He behaved exactly as Pyotr Stepanovitch had feared he might in the end. Left in the care of Tolkatchenko and later Erkel, he spent the entire day lying silently on his bed, his face turned toward the wall. He hardly spoke, even when addressed. Because of this, he remained unaware of the chaos in the town. By evening, however, Tolkatchenko—who had been keeping up with all the news—decided to abandon his responsibility. He left town entirely, essentially fleeing. It seemed they were all losing their nerve, just as Erkel had predicted. On that same day, Liputin also disappeared, leaving town before noon. However, his absence wasn't reported to the authorities until the following evening, when the police visited his terrified family. Fearful of the consequences, his relatives had remained silent until then.

As for Lyamshin, once he was left alone (Erkel had gone home early, trusting Tolkatchenko to stay), he panicked and ran out of his house. It didn't take long for him to hear about the unfolding events. Without returning home, he also tried to escape but had no clear destination. The night was dark, and the idea of fleeing was so overwhelming that after wandering through a few streets, he returned home, locked himself inside, and remained there all night. It's believed that he attempted suicide in the early hours but failed. He stayed locked in until midday, when, suddenly, he ran to the authorities.

He arrived in a state of complete hysteria. Reportedly, he crawled on his knees, sobbing and screaming, and kissed the floor, begging forgiveness and declaring himself unworthy to kiss the boots of the officials. The authorities calmed him down and treated him with unexpected kindness. His interrogation lasted about three hours. During this time, Lyamshin confessed to everything. He revealed every detail, answered every question eagerly, and even provided extra information without being asked. His account shed light on the murders of Shatov and Kirillov, the fire, the deaths of the Lebyadkins, and more. But these events were quickly overshadowed by what he revealed about Pyotr Stepanovitch and the secret society.

When asked about the purpose of all these crimes, Lyamshin explained in a frantic rush that the goal was to systematically destabilize society by destroying its foundations. The aim was to confuse everyone, disrupt order, and create chaos. Then, once society was crumbling and desperate for stability, the revolutionaries would step in, rallying support through their secret network of quintets. These groups were already recruiting members and identifying society's weak points for future attacks. He added that the events in their town were just an experimental trial—a model for what the quintets would replicate elsewhere.

Lyamshin claimed this theory as his own idea and emphasized that he hoped the authorities would note his willingness to cooperate. When asked how many quintets existed, he said the network was vast, stretching across all of Russia. Though he provided no concrete proof, his sincerity was evident. He handed over a program for the society, printed abroad, and a rough outline of plans in Pyotr Stepanovitch's handwriting. Interestingly, the phrase about "undermining the foundation" was quoted verbatim from this document, despite Lyamshin claiming it as his own idea.

He also made an unsolicited comment about Yulia Mihailovna, insisting she was innocent and had been manipulated. However, he surprised everyone by exonerating Nikolay Stavrogin from involvement in the society or any collaboration with Pyotr Stepanovitch. According to Lyamshin, Stavrogin had no role in the deaths of the Lebyadkins, which had been orchestrated solely by Pyotr Stepanovitch to entangle Stavrogin in the crime and make him dependent on the group. Instead of gratitude, Stavrogin had responded with outrage and despair. Lyamshin even hinted that Stavrogin might be an important figure, living incognito, possibly on an assignment, and might return in a different capacity. He claimed to have heard this from Pyotr Stepanovitch, who, he said, was secretly Stavrogin's enemy.

Two months later, Lyamshin admitted that he had purposely defended Stavrogin in the hope that Stavrogin would protect him. He imagined that Stavrogin could get his sentence reduced and even help him financially and with letters of introduction when he was sent to Siberia. This confession showed how wildly Lyamshin had overestimated

Stavrogin's influence.

On the same day, the police arrested Virginsky, and in their eagerness, they also detained his entire family. (Arina Prohorovna, along with her sister, aunt, and even the young student, had already been released some time ago. There's also talk that Shigalov will soon be set free since he doesn't seem to be directly connected to the others. But for now, this is just a rumor.) Virginsky immediately confessed his guilt. He was already bedridden with a fever when they arrested him. People say he seemed almost relieved, reportedly admitting, "It's like a weight has been lifted from my heart." According to rumors, he is cooperating fully with the investigation, speaking openly but with dignity. He has not abandoned his "bright hopes" for the future but has expressed regret for the political strategies he was swept into "by the force of circumstances" and now openly criticizes. His actions during the murder are viewed in a somewhat favorable light, and many believe he could receive a lighter sentence as a result. This, at least, is the opinion circulating in the town.

Erkel, however, does not appear to have any hope for mercy. Since his arrest, he has remained stubbornly silent or has distorted facts as much as possible. He has shown no regret, no matter how hard the interrogators try to draw it out of him. Yet even the harshest judge on his case has felt some pity for him. His youth, his apparent helplessness, and the clear evidence that he was merely a misguided pawn in the schemes of a political manipulator have softened their views. What moves people most, though, is the story of his relationship with his mother. It's said that he sent nearly half of his meager salary to her regularly. His mother, now in town, is a frail and sickly woman who seems older than her years. She weeps constantly and even falls to the ground, begging for mercy on her son's behalf. Whatever the outcome, many feel sympathy for Erkel.

Liputin was arrested in Petersburg, where he had been living for two weeks. His behavior during that time is both baffling and shocking. He reportedly had a forged passport, a significant sum of money, and every opportunity to escape abroad. Yet instead of fleeing, he stayed in Petersburg. At first, he searched for Stavrogin and Pyotr Stepanovitch, but then he inexplicably spiraled into drunken debauchery, acting as though he'd completely lost his senses. He was eventually arrested while drunk in a brothel. Strangely, Liputin does not seem to have lost his spirit. Reports suggest he lies during questioning but remains optimistic about his trial, even speaking as though he expects a positive outcome. He is said to be preparing a speech for the courtroom.

Tolkatchenko, who was caught ten days after fleeing the area, has shown much more dignity in comparison. He has been honest during questioning, readily admitting his guilt without attempting to justify himself. He takes full responsibility for his actions, though he has a tendency to speak grandly, especially when discussing revolutionary ideas and the attitudes of the peasants. He, too, is reportedly planning to deliver a speech at the trial. Both he and Liputin appear oddly unafraid, which is puzzling to many.

The case itself is far from resolved. Now, three months after these events, the local community has begun to recover from the shock. People have formed their own opinions, and some have even started to view Pyotr Stepanovitch as a kind of genius—or at least someone with "a touch of genius." At the club, a few individuals speak admiringly of his "organization," as though it were an extraordinary accomplishment. However, such opinions are rare. Most agree that while he was clever, he was hopelessly out of touch with reality—too theoretical, absurdly one-sided, and ultimately shallow. When it comes to his moral character, however, there is complete agreement: everyone condemns him.

I am not sure who to mention next to avoid leaving anyone out. Mavriky Nikolaevitch has left town for good; no one knows where he's gone. Old Madame Drozdov has fallen into senility. I do have one last grim story to share, but I will limit myself to stating the facts.

Upon returning from Ustyevo, Varvara Petrovna stayed at her townhouse. The avalanche of accumulated news hit her all at once, leaving her deeply shaken. She locked herself in her room. It was evening, and everyone else in the house, weary from the day, retired early.

The following morning, a maid, wearing an air of secrecy, handed Darya Pavlovna a note. The maid explained that it had arrived late the previous evening when everyone had already gone to bed, and she hadn't dared to wake her. The note had not come by mail but had been delivered directly into Alexey Yegorytch's hands at Skvoreshniki by an unknown person. Alexey Yegorytch had rushed to deliver it himself before returning to Skvoreshniki.

Darya Pavlovna stared at the envelope with a pounding heart, hesitating to open it. She already knew who had written it—Nikolay Stavrogin. The envelope was addressed, "To Alexey Yegorytch, to be given secretly to Darya Pavlovna."

This is the letter, transcribed exactly as it was written, reflecting the imperfect Russian of an aristocrat who, despite his European education, had never fully mastered the language:

Dear Darya Pavlovna,

At one time, you said you wanted to be my nurse and made me promise to call on you if I ever needed you. I'm leaving in two days and won't be coming back. Will you come with me?

Last year, like Herzen, I became a citizen of the canton of Uri, though no one knows about it. I've already bought a small house there. I still have twelve thousand roubles left. We'll live there forever. I don't want to go anywhere else.

It's a very dull place—a narrow valley surrounded by mountains that hem in both sight and thought. It's a gloomy place, but I chose it because the house was for sale. If you don't like it, I'll sell it and buy another somewhere else.

I'm not well, but I hope the air there will free me of hallucinations. The physical issues, perhaps. As for the moral ones, you know everything—or do you?

I've told you a lot about my life, but not everything. Not even to you. For instance, I feel guilty for my wife's death. I haven't seen you since it happened, which is why I repeat it now. I feel guilty about Lizaveta Nikolaevna too, but you already know that—you practically predicted it.

It's probably better if you don't come. My asking you to is a terrible selfishness. Why should you throw your life away on me? You're dear to me, and when I was miserable, being with you helped. You were the only

739

one I could truly talk to about myself. But that doesn't mean anything. You once called yourself "a nurse" to me—those were your words. Why sacrifice so much for someone like me? Understand this: I lack both pity and respect for you if I'm asking this of you. And yet, I ask. I need your answer soon because I must leave. Otherwise, I'll go alone.

I don't expect anything from Uri. I'm just going. I didn't pick the place because it's gloomy. I have no ties left in Russia. Everything here feels as foreign to me as anywhere else. I dislike living here, but I don't hate it. I can't even hate.

You told me to test myself and "find out who I am." I've done that. While experimenting, I seemed limitless—to myself and others. Before your eyes, I endured your brother's blow. I publicly acknowledged my marriage. Yet I've never known where to direct my strength. I've always felt I could do good and enjoy it—but I've also desired evil and enjoyed that too. Both desires are small and weak, never guiding me. A log can help you cross a river, but not a chip of wood. I say this so you won't think I'm going to Uri with any hopes.

I blame no one. I've indulged in vice and wasted my strength on it. But I never liked it, and I never really wanted it. Recently, I've envied those iconoclasts—not for their beliefs, but for their hopes. But don't worry; I could never join them. I share nothing with them.

Dear friend, you're so kind. Maybe you think you could give me enough love to inspire me, to give me a purpose. Don't count on it. My love is as small as I am. You'll only end up unhappy.

Your brother once said that a man who loses touch with his homeland loses his gods—his purpose. Maybe he's right. All I've ever done is deny things, but not with strength or spirit. Even my negations lack substance. Kirillov was willing to die for his beliefs, but he was mad. I'll never lose my sanity, nor believe in anything that much. I could never even shoot myself.

I should kill myself—brush myself off the earth like an insect. But I won't. I'm afraid of faking one last grand gesture, another lie in a life full of lies. What's the point? I lack even the strength for despair.

Forgive me for going on so long. Ten lines would've been enough to ask if you'd be my nurse. Since leaving Skvoreshniki, I've been staying at the sixth station with the stationmaster, an old acquaintance from my wilder days. No one knows I'm here. Write to him. I've enclosed the address.

Nikolay Stavrogin

Darya Pavlovna immediately showed the letter to Varvara Petrovna, who read it, then asked Dasha to leave so she could read it again in private. Moments later, she called her back.

"Are you going?" she asked hesitantly.

"I am," Dasha replied.

"Then get ready. We'll go together."

Dasha stared at her, puzzled.

"What else is there for me to do here?" Varvara Petrovna said. "It won't be a problem. I'll naturalize in Uri too and live in the valley. Don't worry—I won't get in your way."

They began packing quickly to catch the midday train. But within half an hour, Alexey Yegorytch arrived from Skvoreshniki with surprising news. Nikolay Vsyevolodovitch had returned that morning by the early train. He was now at Skvoreshniki, but "in a state where he didn't answer questions, walked through the house, and locked himself in his wing."

Varvara Petrovna immediately ordered the carriage. She and Dasha left for Skvoreshniki, where they arrived to find Nikolay's wing empty. The servants suggested the loft. Pale and trembling, Varvara climbed the steep ladder. Moments later, Dasha screamed and fainted.

Nikolay Stavrogin was hanging from the rafters. A note on the table read: "No one is to blame. I did this myself." The preparations—soap, nails, and a strong silk cord—showed clear intent.

The doctors confirmed: it was not insanity.

THE END

Thank you for Reading

You've Just Read a Piece of the Greatest Library Ever Rebuilt

Thank you for reading.

This book is one of thousands we're restoring, reimagining, and translating as part of the **Modern Library of Alexandria** — a global movement to preserve and share humanity's most important ideas.

What was once lost to fire and time is now rising again — not just as memory, but as living, breathing knowledge, freely accessible to all.

What You Can Do Next:

- **Keep Reading.**

  Discover more legendary works — in beautiful print, audiobook, or digital form — at LibraryofAlexandria.com.

- **Build Your Own Library.**

  Every title is available as a paperback, hardcover, or collectible boxset — at true printing cost. Craft a personal library worthy of display.

- **Spread the Light.**

  Share this book. Tell others about the movement. Help us translate every timeless work into every language, so no reader is ever left behind.

By finishing this book, you've already taken part in something extraordinary.

Join us at LibraryofAlexandria.com

Together, we're rebuilding the greatest library the world has ever known.

With appreciation,
The Modern Library of Alexandria Team

Visit:

www.libraryofalexandria.com

Or scan the code below:

www.ingramcontent.com/pod-product-compliance
Lightning Source LLC
Chambersburg PA
CBHW010235100426
42812CB00009B/2462